PIERRE MENDES FRANCE

PIERRE MENDES FRANCE

JEAN LACOUTURE

translated by George Holoch

HOLMES & MEIER
New York London

First published in the United States of America 1984 by
Holmes & Meier Publishers, Inc.
30 Irving Place
New York, N.Y. 10003

Great Britain:
Holmes & Meier Publishers, Ltd.
Unit 5   Greenwich Industrial Estate
35 Woolwich Road   Charlton, London SE7

Book Design by Stephanie Barton

Library of Congress Cataloging in Publication Data
Lacouture, Jean.
  Pierre Mendès France.

  Translation of: Pierre Mendès France.
  Bibliography: p.
  Includes index.
    1. Mendès-France, Pierre, 1907–   . 2. France—
Politics and government—1945–1958. 2. France—Politics
and government—1958–   . 4. Statesmen—France—
Biography. 5. Prime ministers—France—Biography.
I. Title.
DC407.M4L3213   1984   944.082′092′4 [B]   —84-10912
ISBN 0-8419-0856-7
ISBN 0-8419-0857-5 (pbk.)

Manufactured in the United States of America

I believe that, although History has a direction, it is, nevertheless, to a certain extent malleable. There are possibilities of fluctuation, acceleration, or delay, favorable circumstances allowing for unexpectedly rapid forms of progress, and unfavorable circumstances that may delay their fruition. If men on whom power has been conferred interpret appropriately the historical reality that they confront, they may help to bring certain things to birth and make the process less difficult and painful. Or, on the contrary, they may put a brake on any particular advance.

Within the confines of a basic historical determinism, which seems to me to be a constraining force in the very long run, men who help to shape public opinion and who are thereafter given positions of responsibility have the capacity to be useful or harmful. In this connection, there is some interest in thinking about the positive or negative influence that any particular man may have had.

—Pierre Mendès France
conversation with Jean Lacouture, 1976

CONTENTS

Prologue: June Night   3

THE SCHOOL OF THE REPUBLIC
1. Roots   19
2. First in His Class   35
3. A Twenty-Five-Year-Old Deputy   57
4. With Blum   80

THE WIND OF FREEDOM
5. The Insult and the Pity   101
6. I Go to War   136
7. Minister of Rigor   155
8. Cassandra and Indochina   175
9. In the Antechamber   193

THE FIRE OF ACTION
10. PMF   211
11. The Geneva Rice Paddy   219
12. Six Days That Reassured the World   231
13. Building Carthage   243
14. The "Mendès System"   257

15. The European Defiance Community   265
16. The Subcontracting of the Economy   283
17. A Rope and Some Knives   289
18. Algeria Is France   304
19. America without Dollars and Europe without Joy   312
20. "Tonight or Never!"   328

THE PASSION TO BE RIGHT

21. Radically Yours, or the Very Young Turks   345
22. Under the Phrygian Cap   352
23. No to De Gaulle   374
24. For a Concrete Socialism   386
25. The Youngest Electorate in France   397
26. Charléty: A Reformist in the Revolution   402
27. The Shocking Behavior of Grenoble   416
28. The Stones of Sisyphus   422
29. Making Reality Rational   436
    Afterword   458
      The Death of Pierre Mendès France
        by President François Mitterand   460
    Notes   468
    Index   480

PIERRE MENDES FRANCE

PROLOGUE: JUNE NIGHT

At a little after three in the afternoon on June 17, 1954, in the aquarium light that bathed the doings of the representatives of the nation in gloomy unreality, Pierre Mendès France,[1] deputy from Eure, chairman of the Finance Committee of the National Assembly, undersecretary of state for the treasury in Léon Blum's second government, former minister under General Charles de Gaulle, stepped to the podium. Four days earlier, after nine years out of power, he had been named by President Coty as head of the fifteenth government of the Fourth Republic. He was forty-seven, but looked younger. Thickset, rather short, wearing his usual dark suit, he ascended the steps with a nearly Roman gravity.

Out of ambition, vocation, abnegation, or pride, he was totally devoted to public service. Everyone who contemplated him at this solemn moment knew that, however banal and repetitious the rite of passage of a parliamentary vote of confidence might be in that place, it was being confronted this time by a different man who would make it into a different kind of test with a different meaning. They were about to accept or reject not merely one more head of government, but a strong will with a new program. What was at stake was a basic political change, a break with the past. Hence, he was greeted with passionate expectation by some and suppressed irritation by others.

He was a born Jacobin and secularist; he had been a model pupil of the public educational system and a brilliant student at the Faculty of Law

3

and the School of Political Science. He had become a "Radical" at sixteen, but was so steeped in the idea of the complex continuity of the state that he had equal admiration for Jaurès, Poincaré, and Caillaux. He had been the youngest lawyer and youngest deputy in France. He had been a secretary of state at thirty-one and a minister at thirty-seven. Everything in this background led toward his exercise of the highest and weightiest responsibilities.

On that June 17, he proposed to take them on in tragic circumstances. In Indochina, six weeks after the fall of the fortress at Dien Bien Phu, the leaders of the decimated expeditionary force were awaiting, even more impatiently than public opinion, the end of the fighting. The man who presented himself before his peers knew very well that he had been offered this austere "opportunity" only so that he might bring about the agonizing peace that he had been calling for from this same platform for four years and for which no one dared to pay the price.

He had regular, strong features, a prominent chin always shadowed by an incipient beard, a high forehead framed by dark hair, coal-black eyebrows shadowing his handsome and melancholy eyes, like charcoal strokes in a portrait by Rouault. The pallor that now spread over his face was not due only to the harsh solemnity of the hour. It was natural to him, like the dry cough, slightly aggravated by emotion, that sometimes interrupted the flow of his speech, obscuring his normally clear and precise voice, a firm, steady, reasonable voice, like the voice, one would imagine, of King Solomon rendering judgment. At the same time, it was an oddly youthful voice which, for the moment, was delivering words designed to restore a little confidence to a dispirited public that no longer dared even hope for a "savior."

Before he could begin to speak, the prognoses were not very favorable. A year earlier, already attempting to gain the premiership by arguing for peace in Indochina (but before Dien Bien Phu), he had lost by only 13 votes: 301 instead of the "constitutional" majority of 314. This time, while the corridors of the Chamber were alive with maneuvers, whispers, "secrets," and attacks on this "appeaser," this "defeatist," this character who could not possibly have genuinely "French" reactions, the same result was predicted. The Gaullists were more favorably disposed toward him, but the Mouvement Républicain Populaire (MRP, a Christian-Democratic party) was less so. And if the Communists voted for him this time, that would frighten off the center and the right. Neither he nor his friends had neglected these considerations. But he also knew that what he was about to say might upset calculations, hesitations, and predictions.

> For several years now, a compromise peace, a peace negotiated with the enemy, has seemed to me demanded by the facts, while that peace in turn

demanded the restoration of fiscal order and the recovery and expansion of our economy. For this war has placed an unbearable burden on our country.

And now a new and terrible threat has appeared: If the Indochina conflict is not settled—and settled very quickly—we must recognize the risk of war, international and perhaps atomic war.

It is because I wanted a better peace that I wanted it earlier, when we held more cards. . . . The safety of the expeditionary force and the maintenance of its strength are imperious duties which will be upheld by both the government and the Parliament. This is why . . . the man who is before you, and whose feelings about the Indochina problem have not varied, calls for the support of a majority made up of men who have never, directly or indirectly, espoused the cause of those who are fighting us, of men who can therefore call upon the confidence of our soldiers and negotiate with the enemy with complete independence. I have studied the question at length and with seriousness. I have consulted the most qualified military and diplomatic experts. I have been confirmed in my conviction that a peaceful resolution is possible.

It is therefore necessary that a cease-fire be arranged promptly. The government I will establish will set, for itself and for our enemies, a deadline of four weeks to achieve this. Today is June 17. I shall appear before you on July 20 to report on the results we have obtained. If no satisfactory solution has been reached by that date, you will be released from the contract binding us, and my government will submit its resignation to the president of the Republic.[2]

The reaction, on the floor of the Assembly and in the visitors' galleries crowded with the public and foreign diplomats, more numerous and attentive than ever, was electrifying. What was meant by what the deputies and the press soon called a "wager," and what André Siegfried for one characterized as an "ultimatum laid down for oneself"?[3]

From the moment Pierre Mendès France had been named by the head of state four days earlier to resolve the crisis, which meant to him to make peace in Indochina, he had incessantly consulted military experts. Without exception, they had stressed the extreme urgency of a solution. Hanoi and the delta of the North were terribly threatened and the entire expeditionary force in danger. It was perhaps a question of weeks. In the course of a discussion with four generals, when he suggested that it was necessary to reach a solution within a month, two of them exclaimed: "A month is too long!" And they put forward General Salan's gloomy predictions and the opinion expressed by Marshal Juin, who favored an immediate evacuation of Hanoi.[4]

The problem was to bring this urgency to bear on the negotiations. The Vietminh knew that time was on their side. Since the disaster at Dien Bien Phu, the expeditionary force had been fighting with its back to the wall. Ho Chi Minh and his allies in Moscow and Peking would not move quickly unless they knew that the figure who had just appeared, who had been calling for negotiations for four years, who appeared to be a man of peace, would be there for only one month. Once he had gone, the opportunity would be lost, with the return to power of a government with a mandate for massive increases in French military capabilities and whose determination could not fail to take the form of a strategic association with the United States, opening the way to an internationalization of the war.

It was thus important to indicate dramatically that France rejected a second Panmunjom, the negotiations on Korea that, two years earlier, had dragged on for months with meager results. It was also important to show the world that a time of peace had just begun, during which France would display all the good faith symbolized by the name of the new premier, and that during that time, unless they wanted to show themselves as a bellicose power, the Vietminh could not possibly unleash a large-scale offensive.

The speaker was thus aiming both to make the enemy understand that the opportunity for peace would not recur and to hold off an attack. Half ultimatum, half "God's truce," it was also a psychological operation through which the premier-designate intended to strike public opinion, to involve the public, and to stimulate its enthusiasm for peace and for the man who proposed to bring it about.

Once the audience had subsided, Pierre Mendès France continued with the offer of a "contract" between himself and the Assembly.

> My government's plan of action will contain three stages:
>
> 1. Before July 20, it will attempt to obtain a settlement of the Indochina conflict;
>
> 2. At that point, at the latest, it will submit to you a coherent and detailed program for economic recovery and will ask for the powers necessary to carry it out;
>
> 3. Finally, and also before the end of the session, it will submit proposals to you which will enable you to make decisions, without further delay, on our European policy.
>
> If, at any one of these successive stages, I have not succeeded in reaching the objective I have set, my government will submit its resignation to the president of the Republic.
>
> The government will be as good as its members. If you name me to establish it, I will call on men capable of serving, men of character, will, and faith. I will establish it without any concern for political balance. I do not even exclude the possibility, so vigorous is my desire to create the broadest possible national unity, of asking for the participation of deputies who, for respectable reasons, have not found themselves able to vote for me on this occasion.

I will accept no demands and no veto. The choice of ministers, by virtue of the Constitution, belongs to the elected premier, and to him alone. I am not disposed to compromise the rights that you will have given me by your vote of confidence.

Ladies and gentlemen, I have sometimes been taxed with pessimism, as though I took some somber pleasure in predicting catastrophes and preaching penitence. The severity of my judgments depended, in reality, only on a profound optimism about the capacities of France and the opportunities that are offered to it. It is because we can restore ourselves by relying on realities that I have denounced illusions.

I have a full awareness of the responsibilities that will weigh upon me in negotiations that will no doubt be difficult and intractable. But I will be supported by my consciousness of the great interests that you will have entrusted to me. And I will also have clearly in mind the sacrifices of our soldiers, the suffering and anguish of families, and the fate of prisoners.

For the man who is before you, it will be a moving honor to have helped to extricate the country from a bloody path; and for you, representatives of the people, it will be the highest honor to have granted to France the inestimable benefits of peace.

This eminently "Mendésian" speech, which affirmed both the spirit of contract and the taste for action, along with a dramatic sense designed to put public opinion on his side, provoked what a Gaullist deputy called at the time an "electric shock." A few MRP deputies spoke of "charlatanism," and a group of independents of a "bizarre" plan. And a spokesman for the extreme right, Jean Legendre, warned against this "government of four Thursdays." But from the galleries crowded with ambassadors to the corridors where Jacques Soustelle (oracle of Gaullism) and Jacques Duclos (who had just returned from Prague) were particularly visible, and audible, the reaction was very powerful.

The MRP, however, refused to be carried along. Georges Bidault had just "come down from the clouds," as he said. He had come from Geneva, where the day before he had been carrying on the Indochina negotiations. With the biting voice of an impassioned prosecutor, he expressed a feeling shared not only by his friends but by all those in the Chamber who were preparing to unite against Mendès France: "The question is whether we are going to acknowledge that, for the last eight years, we have been criminals or traitors!" It would be harder to find a better summary for the spirit of a coalition.

The session resumed, for questions to the "candidate." It is surprising that such a remarkable speech produced such restrained reactions, even on the part of a spokesperson of a party directly challenged, Mme. Poinso-Chapuis, who rather ponderously expressed the strong distrust of the MRP. But then François Billoux, deputy from Bouches-du-Rhône and spokesman of the Communists, mounted the rostrum. Silence fell. The remarks of another former minister of General de Gaulle were worth listening to.

> You have stated that you have given yourself the task of obtaining a cease-fire in Indochina within four weeks. This declaration is a change from the behavior of the Laniel–Bidault government.
>
> It is in consideration of this particular declaration that the Communist group will decide its vote of confidence.
>
> You have said yourself that there is a sacred task to accomplish: to reestablish peace in Indochina, the peace we have constantly called for from the beginning of this unjust war. We are certain that by doing so we acted as clear-sighted patriots, concerned with the cause of the working class, of the people, and of France.
>
> Our action has powerfully contributed to the fact that today, in your person, a premier-designate has said from this rostrum that the first priority is peace in Indochina, for that is the will of the people. By voting for your candidacy, we will give you the means to make peace in Indochina.

Feeling ran so high that a recess, immediately proposed by President Le Troquer (in accordance with Mendès France's wishes) only succeeded in increasing it. The corridors and galleries were at the boiling point. "A wonderful assassination! They've stabbed him in the back! You wouldn't have thought they would dare." For the first time in seven years, since their expulsion from the Ramadier government and the beginning of the cold war, the Communists were voting for a government in which they were not represented. Why?

It was not only a matter of embarrassing a patiently detested public man toward whom the Communist Party had constantly expressed its hostility, from the sabotage of the austerity plan he proposed in 1944 as General de Gaulle's economics minister to his attempt at the premiership in 1953. The person, or even the policies of Mendès France were less in question than the establishment of a new strategy for the PCF (Parti Communiste Français). A few months after the death of Stalin in March 1953 and the rise to power of the Malenkov group, Maurice Thorez and his comrades took the opportunity of a meeting of the Central Committee in Drancy, in October, to rectify the Party's "line." It no longer excluded support of "bourgeois" governments, as long as they were opposed to the Indochina was and the CED (Communauté Européene de Défense).[5]

Thus the Communists had voted in December for Marcel-Edmond Naegelen, Socialist candidate for president, and in January for André Le Troquer, SFIO (Section Française de l'Internationale Ouvrière, the Socialist Party) candidate for the presidency of the Assembly, both of whom were opposed to the CED.[6] Although as far as Europe was concerned Mendès was ambiguous, his position on Indochina was popular.

The vote of the leaders of the PCF against him in June 1953 had provoked protests from the rank and file. Moreover, by supporting his candidacy (he might not reach the necessary 314 votes without them), the PCF would place itself in a useful position of control, at least during the Indochina negotiations.

Pierre Mendès France had asked for a recess until nine o'clock to prepare his responses to other speakers, and particularly to the PCF. He reentered the Chamber at nine-thirty. He was more of an arguer than an orator, a debater rather than a speechmaker, but on this occasion he reached the peak of his oratorical art, if not of his political pertinence.

> I am eager to offer my thanks to M. Billoux for the precious assistance he has offered me from this podium and for the ninety-five extra votes he was so kind to bring to my candidacy.
>
> No doubt M. Billoux, devoting all his time to the preparation of his important speech, has neglected to read the papers in the last few days, and no doubt he is unaware of the decision I have made—and that I confirmed in my speech of candidacy from this podium—to refuse to include in my confidence majority the votes he has so generously offered to me.
>
> A short time ago, I referred to the situation of our soldiers in Indochina. I ask M. Billoux himself: How would our soldiers feel tomorrow if they were to learn that their country, the country for which they are fighting, the country for which they are shedding their blood, was governed by men who had been, if only partially, chosen by a party that has for so many years repudiated them, condemned their fight, and gone so far as to refuse to pay the homage due to "those who have faithfully died for the nation"?
>
> That is not all. Political reasons also govern my decision. Tomorrow we are going to negotiate in Geneva with men who have been our enemies for years. I do not intend to create in their minds the slightest illusion or to lead them to believe that France is now, confronting them, represented by a government that owes its existence to the Communist Party, a party that has so often expressed not only its sympathy for them but also its solidarity with them.
>
> And when in a month I return before you, bearing, I hope, a negotiated agreement, I want all of you to have no doubt about the conditions under which that agreement has been reached and not to suspect for an instant that any political circumstance whatsover might have undermined the independence of the French delegation to Geneva. I have been told that certain colleagues—and, first of all, I understand their scruples—do not want to join their votes to those of the Communist group. Does that mean that, in the future, it would be enough for the Communists to vote in favor of a candidate, for no matter whom, to dissuade a large number of other deputies from doing the same?
>
> My dear colleagues, I would like you to remember a quotation from an old textbook we all used in school: "When the barbarians invaded Athens, they burned all the houses, leaving only Pericles' untouched. In this way,

they sought to provoke the distrust of his compatriots against the citizen they hated the most, the one who had served his country well."

The Communist Party tonight has indulged in a political maneuver. I would ask you this question: Will you allow this maneuver to succeed? Will you refuse approval to a man who has committed himself to finding an honorable peace within a brief space of time and with conditions you would have approved had this maneuver not taken place? Will we be the playthings of the Communist Party? And will the country, reading my speech tomorrow, understand all of this?

You are the ones who must provide the answer.

I repeat, in any case, and to conclude on this point without any ambiguity, that since the constitutional majority is 314 votes, as far as I am concerned it must be made up of deputies whom I called upon in my declaration of candidacy, and I will consider that majority to have been reached only under those conditions.

JACQUES DUCLOS: That's unconstitutional!

Not swayed by this incidentally pertinent argument, Pierre Mendès France concluded with a passage inspired by Blum and in the style of Clemenceau.

A political man can choose only to repeat himself or to contradict himself. I belong to the school of those who repeat themselves. . . . If you were to ask me to sum up my policy in a phrase, I would answer: I will make peace.

This rejection of Communist votes, which was felt as a slap in the face by Duclos and his comrades, was clearly not a declaration of principle. In other circumstances, Mendès France had profited from Communist votes and from transfers of votes in runoff elections, and he would do so in the future. And it goes without saying that for such a punctilious democrat the votes of the working class were at least as valuable as any others. But this was a special situation, and twenty-five years later Mendès France continued to justify himself with passion:

I did not reject "Communist" votes, but the votes of men and of a party who had very publicly proclaimed their unconditional support for and active solidarity with those who were still our enemies, at whose hands our soldiers were still dying, and whom we had to *oppose* in the negotiations. What strength would I have had, confronted with the Vietminh negotiators, with their demands, justifiably increased by their victories, demands that I, as representative of the French people, was obliged to contain and limit to the greatest extent possible, if they knew that my government depended on the support of their friends, if they knew that I was subject to pressure from within my own majority?

I made that cruel decision as a free negotiator, not as a democrat of the left. But it goes without saying that in every other area, particularly in my efforts to rebuild a more just French society, I hoped for Communist help, I remained a representative of the Popular Front, to which I owed my election in 1936 and my brief tenure as undersecretary of the treasury in 1938.

This speech, delivered as night wore on, and which, as *Le Monde* reported the next day, "provoked an ovation the like of which has rarely been heard in the National Assembly," with its evocation of Pericles and the barbarians that was the envy of Herriot, slumped on his bench like a beached whale in a Fellini movie, stirred the deputies, and created an uproar in the corridors.

Jacques Duclos was seized with an uncontrollable rage. The little man exploded in the Salon des Quatre-Colonnes: "He's a coward! The country will see him as a coward who talks and talks and doesn't dare to act."[7] And as the circle around him grew denser and curiosity changed to stupefaction, he continued his diatribe with an (improved) quotation of Napoleon's epigram on Talleyrand:[8] "He's shit without the silk stockings." "And you'll still vote for shit?" "We have no choice."

Elsewhere, reactions were obviously different. "He got to me," sighed an MRP deputy who decided to change his vote. "Excellent, he's gained some ground with us," asserted a Gaullist. But the most curious reversal took place among the "independents and peasants," where the premier-designate did not expect much support. To be sure, Paul Antier, the huge leader of the "peasants," had been his comrade in arms in London. But members of the group had rarely made a war record in London. And Mendès could hardly count on this kind of affinity. Then, what happened?

During the long recess following the passage on the barbarians, from ten until after midnight, the very influential deputy from Puy-de-Dôme, Jacques Bardoux, member of the Institut, pondered his vote. He was the grandfather of Valéry Giscard d'Estaing (who was to play a role in Mendès's government on the staff of Edgar Faure), and also great-uncle of Léone Georges-Picot, press secretary of the premier-designate. He asked his great-niece for a moment's conversation: "Léone, do you have any confidence in this Mendès France?" "But, Uncle Jacques, if I didn't have confidence in him I wouldn't have agreed to do what I'm doing." "Yes, but, I mean, is he a man of honor?" The answer was enough to relieve the careful historian's doubts.

Whether or not this family conversation helped to switch the opinions of a segment of the parliamentary right in favor of Mendès, the fact is that by midnight it was estimated that the candidate was assured of about twenty "moderate" votes. For the Socialists, Guy Mollet grumbled that it was "impossible not to vote for him" (only a deputy named Le Bail refused to support the man the members of the SFIO called "the best of the others"). Robert Buron went to great lengths to extract votes for Mendès from the MRP. By midnight, a decision had been made. In retaliation for his condemnation of their leader and the risks the candidate posed to the construction of military unity in Europe, the friends of Georges Bidault would abstain. But there were a dozen "defections" in favor of Mendès.

As for the Gaullists, they seemed more and more to be confusing Louviers with Colombey. In a few minutes it would be June 18, and there was a stirring sweetness in the symbol. "Here is a man who offers a change," said General Koenig, while Jacques Chaban-Delmas pulled out all the stops for the candidate. And even Montsabert, a particularly obtuse Gascon militarist, having "executed" Mendès a year earlier, rose to the challenge on this occasion to assure his victory.

According to the *Journal officiel,* the session resumed on "Friday, June 18, at five minutes after midnight." Passions ran high, and spectators seemed to be hanging from the galleries. Within a few hours, it would be known whether the government of France was finally entrusted to a "different" man to carry out a "different" policy. Predictions remained very cautious. The moment had come to explain one's vote. It was particularly surprising to hear the sparkling Emmanuel d'Astier de la Vigerie unreservedly joining his aristocratic voice to those of the Communist Party leadership.

> Mister premier-designate, a dozen years ago we fought together against a politics that misused the word *national* and used some of the same techniques you yourself have used from this podium. Neither you nor General de Gaulle thought at the time of rejecting the support you were offered, support that has perhaps brought you to this point tonight.
>
> But . . . we believe that there is no task more urgent than a cease-fire and a political settlement in Indochina. That is what will motivate our votes. What you think of those votes and of our support is of little concern to us. Those votes are not cast for you but for peace.
>
> Perhaps there will be some dupes here tonight, but we will not be among them.

In the name of the SFIO, its president, Charles Lussy, declared:

> In voting for you today, we know that we are responding to the feelings of the country, where your statements have created a good deal of emotion and great hopes, just as the boldness of your first statement won our support.
>
> In voting for you, we are voting for hope. In giving you our support, we intend to vote for a premier of peace.

The MRP could not be content with champing at the bit and taking refuge in abstention. It was obliged to snipe at the candidate whose conduct in power would amount to putting on trial the men who had carried on the Indochina war for eight years. To accomplish this, the "popular republicans" chose a young man who had been waiting in the wings with clenched teeth and the face of a pious seducer, Jean Lecanuet, who had long been chief of staff for the minister in charge of Indochinese affairs and who was therefore directly concerned by what Mendès France had said and would do. It was a remarkable attack.

In your last speech as a candidate, you said of the government that its work should not be halted by the constant fear of falling, and you added: "Parliament no doubt has the right to withdraw its confidence from the government at any moment, but the government must also be able to act at every moment as though it were certain to last for twenty years."

Today you have given yourself four weeks!

We were surprised to hear you say that if you did not achieve peace within four weeks, you would resign and leave to your successor the task of making war. Allow me to say that your politics of choice in this instance has taken on the guise of a politics of shirking responsibility.

On the other hand, we were extremely pleased to hear you say that by continuing the efforts undertaken by the French delegation in Geneva, you thought you could obtain a cease-fire by July 20. This represents a tribute, belated as it may be, to the minister of foreign affairs, whose actions, as you have noted today, have been effective in the service of peace. But if this is the case, what is the reason for this debate and this crisis? Why interrupt or threaten to interrupt the Geneva conference, since you yourself have now said and it is generally recognized that continuation of this diplomatic procedure can genuinely and quickly lead to peace?

Why has the Communist party now assented to the conditions, the means, and the diplomatic framework of negotiations which until now it has systematically condemned?

Perhaps something else is involved, perhaps another intention is hidden beneath the disguise of a passionate search for peace. Are we not witnessing an attempt to call into question the entire foreign policy of France, and particularly its European policy? Perhaps the only explanation is that the Communist Party wants to attempt to show, not only to the French but to the entire world, that it could, if not tonight then no doubt tomorrow—and we have just heard the warning—create an alternative majority, which gives a peculiar meaning, if you will allow me to say so, my dear colleagues, to the alternative solutions that have been the subject of so much discussion today.

Then, from the second row of the Communist benches, there arose a massive bald man with the appearance of a peasant: Waldeck-Rochet, entrusted with the task of dotting the i's, in his heavy-handed way, in the Communist support of Mendès France. He spoke with little delicacy. It was clear that what he had to say would have no effect on the outcome of the debate once Mendès France had established the rules of the game so as to exclude what he might offer or refuse. But he was listened to with all the attention deserved by a man who spoke in the name of five million voters.

Ladies and gentlemen, M. Mendès France thought it necessary to launch an attack against the Communist Party. . . . In order to try to justify the attitude he has adopted toward the Communist group, M. Mendès France has pointed to our opposition to the Indochina war from the very beginning. It's true, we have been struggling against the Indochina war for more than seven years, and we are proud of it.

As Karl Marx said a century ago: "A people that oppresses another cannot be a free people."

PIERRE JULY: What if it oppresses several others?

SEVERAL VOICES FROM THE CENTER AND THE RIGHT: Long live Poland!

This was not enough to disconcert an old hand at political meetings like Waldeck-Rochet.

Whether you like it or not, following that path of political discrimination amounts to deciding that the five million workers who have confidence in the Communist Party should no longer be represented in Parliament. Whether you intend it or not, this is a typically fascist notion, and M. Pierre Mendès France should be the first to recognize that this kind of discrimination bears a strong resemblance to the McCarthyism that led to the murder of the Rosenbergs.

PIERRE MONTEL: Then you're going to vote for a fascist?

The speaker continued unmoved.

Yesterday, to bring down the Laniel-Bidault government, whose policies he thought disastrous and dangerous, our votes had to be counted! . . .

We want to place M. Mendès France in a position to realize his intentions, to match his actions to his words. Our party has decided that it is ready to support any initiative by a government declaring itself in favor of an immediate cease-fire and the establishment of peace.

M. Mendès France's feelings toward us and M. Mendès France's moral character do not count, what counts is the will of the people.

The debate, at least in public, was finished.

PRESIDENT LE TROQUER: In conformity with paragraph 3 of article 48 of the Constitution, I call for a vote, by secret ballot, on the motion of election.[9]

I remind you that the constitutional majority is 314 votes. The balloting is open.

The session was recessed at 1 A.M. Immediately thereafter, in the corridors, the representatives of the right-wing group ARS thought it necessary to make it clear that they would refuse to join the government. Did that mean that the candidate's victory was certain? By one-thirty, Mendès France no longer seemed so sure. But he was already indicating some of the procedures he would follow: "In any case, to form the government, I will not consult organized groups. I will offer positions directly to senators as well as to deputies." But in the bustle back and forth between the ballot box and the Salon des Quatre-Colonnes that had turned the Palais-Bourbon into a stock exchange, the candidate's popularity was constantly on the increase. By one-forty-five, he seemed to have won the game: it was said that there were more than 310 certain votes, not counting the 100 Communists (he would not count among the latter the four "progressives," including his friends Pierre Cot and d'Astier, but he would count André Marty, who had been expelled from the Communist Party two years earlier and was listed as an "independent"). And as success appeared to be certain, the neophyte was heard to ask in a timid voice: "Won't I have to go to the president of the Republic, afterward?" as though he were afraid to wake him at that hour.

Names of cabinet ministers began to circulate—Mitterrand, Berthoin, Chaban, Buron. And already, although they came from such divergent groups, they began to show a kind of ministerial solidarity. They stayed together with a modestly virtuous expression on their faces. And when the bell announcing the close of balloting and the report of the results rang at two o'clock, the candidate's supporters moved briskly back to the Chamber in a climate of victory. Its size was unexpected. It was five after two. The *Journal officiel* described the conclusion of this memorable session:

THE PRESIDENT: The Assembly is in session.
This is the official result of the balloting on the motion of confidence:

Number of votes	466
Constitutional majority	314
In favor	419
Against	47
Abstentions	143

Since the constitutional majority has been reached, M. Mendès France has been named premier.

Accompanied by his wife Lily, whose smiling presence had been noted throughout the long, hard day, Pierre Mendès France left the Palais-Bourbon at two-fifteen for the Elysée Palace where René Coty was waiting. Coty kept him there for nearly an hour, listening with amused surprise to his narrative of the "wild night."

Before leaving the Parliament, Mendès France had had a private talk with his closest friend and adviser, Georges Boris, a member of his staff as chairman of the Finance Committee. Neither of these old *compagnons* of Free France was unmoved by the fact that the vote had taken place on June 18. Together they hastily scribbled a telegram to De Gaulle: "On this anniversary when I am undertaking such heavy responsibilities, I remember the great lessons of patriotism and devotion to the public welfare that your trust allowed me to receive from you."[10]

When Lily and Pierre Mendès France returned to their apartment on the rue du Conseiller-Collignon, where their two sons were waiting for them, it was four o'clock. The face of the new head of government reflected fatigue accentuated by his pallor, and his chin already showed an unsightly stubble.

What he thought at that moment he found written a few hours later in the unusual heading that Hubert Beuve-Méry, editor-in-chief of *Le Monde,* placed over his journalists' articles.

It was useless to hope or plan for anything as long as all kinds of feudal baronies were able to make the interests of their clientele prevail in Parliament over the interests of the nation.

A first step, for which we hardly dared hope, has just been taken. A man who has particularly distinguished himself by refusing to be a minister in governments whose policies on essential points he rejected has just been given the responsibility, in conditions that do him honor, of removing crushing burdens, particularly the heaviest burden of all, the war in Indochina.

The immediate future will show whether this man has the necessary qualities to translate into action the principles he clearly expressed in Parliament and whether, faced with the particular threat of what may be the final collapse of French greatness and power, the political parties will finally agree to stop playing fatal games. Will M. Mendès France have the intelligence and strength to carry out the necessary restoration of French politics and, at the same time, to save democratic institutions?

THE SCHOOL OF THE REPUBLIC

1.
ROOTS

Luis de França landed in Bordeaux in 1684. Fleeing the persecutions of the Portuguese Inquisition, according to a letter, he had planned to go to Rome to throw himself at the feet of Pope Innocent VII. But there is no trace of this journey. He probably came directly from Lisbon, his native city, after a stop at La Rochelle. In any case, he was nothing but a solitary émigré, separated from his family, cut off from one community and rejected by another. He was a man from nowhere if such a creature ever existed, but he was the heir and the progenitor of a vigorous lineage.

> The history of my family is of interest only insofar as it concerns ordinary people. Some of them may have been brilliant. Others had more or less distinguished careers. Many of them had hard lives, and a few were even impoverished. But they never stepped out of the ordinary. This is what gives this history its full meaning.

Pierre Mendès France recalled his family's past with passionate precision and meticulous tenderness. From 1935 on, he continuously amassed enormous documentation about it, annotated and arranged with an archivist's care and preserved in a solid Norman armoire in his house in Louviers. The history of these "ordinary people" sheds much light on conflicts of religion, morals, business, and politics in Western Europe between the fifteenth and twentieth centuries. And it also sheds light on the still more unusual fate of a statesman of our time.

> The genealogical fever came upon me in the mid-1930s, when I obtained documents, memoirs, and family papers that had been kept by my paternal grandfather. It happened that my investigations turned immediately toward Portugal, where genealogy is a great passion—there are ten times more genealogists in the Lisbon phone book than in the Paris book.
>
> When I began this research, I was barely conversant with Talmudic law; it never occurred to me to consider the women, not to mention how much more difficult that would have been. Following the male line, then, I found some Mendes de França in Portugal in the early sixteenth century. A member of a large and influential family, the Mendes of Vasconcellos, a certain Pedro Mendes Ribeiro, who married three times, had as his second wife Isabel de França. The two sons born to this couple, Gaspard and Luis, were called Mendes de França.

The first name is very common in Portugal,[1] as common as Ferreira or Soares. It means "people from Mendo," and it has no Jewish connotation. But converts often assumed a banal Christian name, the better to blend into the crowd. The name França is less common without being extraordinary. Probably derived from French émigrés of the fourteenth century (there were for a time some d'Alençon de França in Lisbon), it was the name of a missionary in the sixteenth century who attempted to convert the king of Ethiopia to the Catholic religion.[2]

The history of Portuguese Judaism, less glorious perhaps than that of Spain but a little less tragically afflicted, goes back, according to some sources, to one of Nebuchadnezzar's lieutenants, according to others, to Pompey. Since the community had begun to settle in Portugal before Christ's crucifixion, one tradition, even in certain Christian circles, maintained that they were therefore exculpated.[3] Around 1789, one of Malesherbes's agents in Bordeaux noted that "the Portuguese[4] are not Talmudists and claim descent from Nebuchadnezzar."[5]

Until the end of the fifteenth century, in any case, the Portuguese state seems to have tolerated, and sometimes respected, this active and loyal community. One of Vasco da Gama's companions, Abraham de Beja, was a Jew, as was General Salomon Ben Yoshua, who led a Portuguese army. But in 1498, the "Catholic sovereigns" Ferdinand and Isabella of Spain inserted into the marriage contract between one of their daughters and King Manoël of Portugal a clause extending to the neighboring country the expulsion of the Jews that had been decreed six years earlier in their kingdom. From that point on, Portuguese Jews could choose only between flight (but where? Spain was hounding them; France had driven them out under Charles VI the Mad. There remained Amsterdam and the Papal States) and conversion. Many resigned themselves to the latter, receiving the name of "new Christians." They were subject to vague suspicions to which the Inquisition gave terrible form a half-century later.

Let us quote Montaigne, whose mother, Antoinette de Louppes (or Lopès), came from precisely this community: "Some of them became Christians, but even today few Portuguese are confident of their faith or their race, although habit and the passage of time are much more persuasive than any other constraint" (a passage added, after some unknown discovery, to the 1588 edition of the *Essais*).

But "habit and the passage of time" were persuasive for only a few of the enlightened, like the Marquis de Pombal, who rebuilt Lisbon after the great earthquake. The following story is told of him. King Joao had decreed that everyone of Jewish origin was to wear a yellow hat. Pombal appeared at court one day carrying three yellow hats under his arm. When the sovereign expressed his surprise, he said: "By order of the king. I don't know anyone who doesn't have a few drops of Jewish blood in his veins." "But why three hats?" "One for me, the second for the Grand Inquisitor, and, in case you might wish to cover your head, the third for Your Majesty."

But Pombal was already a man of the Enlightenment, although, as we shall see, that period was not free from the most virulent kind of anti-Semitism. The obligation to wear yellow hats was only one of the immediate humiliations and threats suffered by Portuguese Jews, whether or not they were disguised as Marranos.[6] Hence, there was a large increase in individual and group Jewish migration beginning around the middle of the sixteenth century. Relying on "liberal" proclamations by Henri II and Henri III, many set out for France.

Nearly a century before Luis de França arrived in Bordeaux, a Gonçalvo de Mendes had landed in Nantes with his wife and children. Henri IV granted him "letters of naturalization" on June 22, 1598.

In documents discovered in Nantes and Rennes, he is sometimes called Mendès Franco, sometimes Mendès Franc. He had come from the little Vila Viçiosa in the Alto Alentejo, a noble city whose duke had protected the Jews and which seems to have been the birthplace of the family. But there is no trace of the Gonçalvo descendants or of their links with Luis de França, whom Mendès France considered the ancestor of the family. Thus, we must return to Luis and his immediate ancestors.

The second son of Pedro Mendes Ribeiro and Isabel de França, Luis Mendes de França, studied at the University of Coïmbra, and was then an *enquiridor,* that is, an employee of the Inquisition. His son Francisco "the Red" (*el rojo*), who never used the family name Mendes, according to the documents I have found, was the first family member to carry on commerce. He was a goldsmith, a profession often, though not always, exercised by Jews. Up to that point, all these people were Christian, purely Christian. You certainly had to be to be employed by the Inquisition, like Luis, Francisco the Red's father. But Francisco, who lived in a quarter of the city inhabited by many Jews, married a Christian, Antonia Freire, whose mother was a Marrano. This was the first appearance of a drop of "impure blood." And Antonia had serious difficulties with the Inquisition.

At this point, we have to turn to the documents found in the armoire in Louviers. Under the title "Santo Oficio, inquisiçao de Lisboa," we find the minutes of Antonia's trial. Brought as a prisoner before the inquisitor Manoël de Magalhaès Menesès, she declared that she "had no connection with the category of convert except through her mother," Dionisia, since she was the "daughter of Gonçalo da Costa, an old Christian, a goldsmith, from Algarve." She was plied with questions about her "joining the faith of Moses," on the Jewish practices attributed to her ("eating neither pork nor rabbit, nor strangled fowl, nor fish without scales," observing "Esther's fast in February," "removing the sciatic nerve from the hindquarters of small livestock," or "sweeping the house backwards, toward the inside"); she was called on to denounce those with whom she was supposed to have done these things. In the face of the terrible tribunal, she denied everything, for months. She maintained that the only accusations came from a group of women of Abrantès with whom she had had a quarrel.

Twenty months after the beginning of the trial, on August 31, 1656, the tribunal of the Holy Office ruled that "the accused prisoner could not be considered to have committed the crime of Judaism," but "because of lingering indications of belief in the Law of Moses, she was to be put to torture, since the doctor and surgeon had determined that she could bear it." Since she nevertheless persisted in her denials, she was led eighteen days later to the torture chamber where, "seated on the little bench, she was stripped of her clothes while the official declared that if, during the torture, an accident happened, she broke a limb or lost one of her senses, the fault would be hers alone for so boldly exposing herself to this danger."

With Antonia insisting that she had nothing to say, "they began to lift her up,[7] while continuing to admonish her to confess. As she refused, the torment continued, and the accused was lifted up to the top of the device, constantly crying out and calling on the Holy Virgin. She was let down and, the judgment having been satisfied, she was sent back to her cell after another admonition. The session lasted for about a quarter of an hour."

Because of the "slight suspicion" that continued to weigh on her faith, Antonia was sentenced to appear at an autodafé celebrated on September 29 in front of the palace, in the presence of the king and the infantes, to "anathematize all forms of heresy," and to pay "50,000 reals for expenses" (a third of all she owned). The only redress available to her husband, Francisco the Red, son of the *enquiridor,* was to address a memorandum to the tribunal asserting that his wife had been the victim of the machinations of a few gossips. According to Pierre Mendès France,

> At the time of Antonia's trial, her third son was twelve. He was named Luis. Not Mendes de França like his grandfather, nor Mendes like his father, but de França. It is easy to imagine how their mother's tragic experience must have disturbed the children. Luis was extremely sensitive and intelligent. His letters show that he was cultivated to some degree, and that he was troubled, haunted by metaphysical questions. He had certainly carried on religious studies. He was a nervous, unstable man, in fragile health. He sold tobacco and fabrics after having been a customs employee. Despite the dangers to which his mother's trial by the Inquisition subjected the family, he frequented Judaizing intellectuals, particularly a certain poet-apothecary named Ferrao.

One day in February 1683, Luis de França was arrested by order of the Inquisition and turned over to the Holy Office. Oddly enough, he declared to the tribunal that his father Francisco Mendes was a "new Christian," that is, a converted Jew (for which there is no other evidence), "he did not know of how many degrees," and that his mother, the tortured Antonia, was "one-half new Christian," that is, with one Jewish parent. On this basis, he claimed to be "one-quarter new Christian." He pointed out that he was married to Lucia Berlinque, an "old Christian," that their two children were baptized, as they were, and finally he declared that he was in prison "because of false testimony by his enemies." (In a letter to the tribunal he explained that he did not lack enemies, since he had once wounded a lieutenant in the hand with a knife, and another time had shot at a man who was threatening him. In short, he had something of a past.)

Luis did not have his mother Antonia's admirable firmness in confronting the inquisitors. He soon revealed the name of Ferrao and two or three others with whom, he said, he had become an adept "of the Law of Moses." The inquisitors insisted. They knew, they said, more about him.

On July 29, 1683, the Holy Office informed him that it had taken "the stern decision to subject him to torture, if he did not finally confess his sins." Two days later, like his mother, he was led to the torture chamber. Then, "with his hand on the Holy Gospels," he went on and on remembering people with whom, fifteen or twenty years before, he had agreed to live "according to the Law of Moses for the salvation of his soul": his aunt Joana, his old friend José da Cruz, his brothers Antonio and Miguel, his sister Dionisia, and several others. He was not tortured. The next day, the tribunal asked him if he remembered his confessions of the day before, now that he was no longer in the torture chamber, "without fear and without the constraint of violence." He retracted nothing.

Luis de França was nevertheless sentenced perpetually to wear a penitential costume, to abjure his "heresy" at an autodafé, and to have his possessions confiscated. By "special grace," the tribunal granted him the right to be "received in the bosom of the holy Church," but it forbade him to leave the territory of Portugal without its express authorization.

But a few weeks later, Luis set sail for France. The connections he had maintained as a former customs agent enabled him to embark clandestinely on a French ship sailing for La Rochelle. And it was on board ship that he wrote a startling letter to the Inquisition in which he denied his confession and retracted his accusations against others, before the tribunal and in the torture chamber.

Luis explained to his judges that, warned of his danger the day before his arrest, he had consulted his brother, his brother-in-law, and a nobleman, the Marquis de Cascaïs, who "knew him well as a good and faithful Christian," and that all of them had advised him to have confidence in the justice of the Inquisition. Relying on this advice, he had refused to flee on the ship of his French friend Godefroy, heading for Genoa, and had decided to submit to ecclesiastical justice.

> But as soon as he was arrested, he asserted, he was afflicted with melancholic vapors, a profound hypochondria, and racked with pain throughout my body, in my spine, my kidneys, my leg joints, with wanderings of the understanding and many visions. I was becoming completely mad. And as my understanding no longer enabled me to weigh the good of my soul, dazed and blinded by the advice of the inquisitor, and having been told that I would be put to the garrote in prison, I accused my soul and the souls of my friends of what had not happened. . . . It was a false confession. . . . One of those who was present asserted that now I had told the truth. Then I stood up and said in a loud voice: "What I have just said is false. I am a faithful son of Holy Mother Church." Then they made so many threats and promises of punishment that I had to restate the falsehood and deny my Jesus Christ. They had hung a bull whip at the door of my dungeon!
>
> Now, I am going to La Rochelle, and from there, to go to Rome, I will have to walk two hundred miles over land, with the great infirmities I have from the Inquisition. . . . May all those against whom I testified and who have been arrested because of me be recognized as good and faithful Christians: I am going to Rome expressly to ask for absolution from His Holiness and to give him a copy of this rectification.
>
> > From the French war supply ship
> > October 27, 1683, The humble captive
> > of Your Excellency who hopes for
> > an answer at Rome.
> >
> > Luis de França

In the trials of the people he had denounced, Pierre Mendès France noted,

> they put forward his accusations, not his retractions. In any event, when he fled, he took neither his wife nor his children with him. Did he really intend to

throw himself at the feet of the Pope? There is no definite evidence. But there is a gap of one year before he is found settled in France. Besides, I am still looking for evidence of his passage through La Rochelle.

One thing is certain: Luis de França, who was thenceforth known as Louis Mendès France, was in Bordeaux in September 1684. It was there that he received from a priest the certificate of Catholicism which is mentioned in the first document attesting to his presence in France, found in the departmental archives of Lot-et-Garonne.

On November 22, 1684, Louis Mendès France, native of the city of Lisbon in Portugal, making profession of the Catholic, apostolic, and Roman religion, as it appears to us by the attestation of September 17 of the vicar of Saint-Heloy (sic) of Bordeaux, certified by the act and seal of Monseigneur the Archbishop of Bordeaux, signed Louis, Archbishop of said city, promising and having taken an oath before M. Daunefort, first consul, to be a good and faithful servant of the king, to acknowledge the law and its magistrates in all matters concerning the public good and the service of the king, under which conditions he has been received as a resident of the instant city to enjoy the privileges of the other residents of the instant city, and has promised to grant and deliver to the arsenal a good musket and a bandolier. (There is a note: paid for the musket and the bandolier, which was placed in the arsenal with the bandolier.)

Why had Louis Mendès France not remained in Bordeaux, the French city which at the time provided the warmest welcome for "Portuguese merchants"? This had been true since the letters patent granted to them in 1550 by Henri II, confirmed by two decrees issued by Henri III in 1574 that vigorously condemned the "calumnies, hateful insolence, threats, and intimidations" against the "Spanish and Portuguese of Bordeaux and Guyenne," to whom he offered his "special protection." Around the "Mont Judaic," the Porte-Dijeaux (or of the Jews), and the rue Bouhaut, there lay the "Jewish quarter," where, except in 1684, no violence had affected the community, which was, it seems, treated more with distrust than with aggression.

It happened that the trial and flight of Luis de França coincided with a collective drama. An expulsion edict issued by the Portuguese sovereign Don Pedro III had provoked a sudden exodus of "new Christians," a substantial number of whom had tried to settle north of the Pyrenees, from Bayonne to Orthez and Bordeaux. This gave rise to an all too frequently observed response of rejection, which was the source of a royal decree of November 20, 1684, expelling from the territory a certain number of "new Christian" families. It should be noted that only poor families were affected. The rich were "forgotten."[8]

Now, it was exactly on November 22 of that year that Luis (or Louis) sought refuge in Agen. As a poor man, he may have been turned away from Bordeaux and sent to a more modest town where immigrants were rare. Or it may have been an application of an established practice of the community of "Portuguese merchants" of Bordeaux and the authorities or the *parlement* of the city, regulating by mutual agreement the flow of newcomers. After being provided with the appropriate certificates and recommendations, they were distributed in various localities, apparently to facilitate their settlement.

> So, there was Louis Mendès France, provided with his certificate of Catholicism, established in Agen, where he dealt in woolens and various fabrics. He visited the seven other Portuguese inhabitants of the town, among them a man named Moustapha. He lived with a woman who was certainly not the one he had left when he fled Lisbon, Lucia Berlinque. I have the signatures of the two women: the first, neat and fine, reveals a certain cultivation; the other signature is that of a provincial illiterate of the time. Was Lucia dead? Was Louis a bigamist? The second wife was named Marie Vivès, or Villa, or Bellix, or Viva. She gave him two children, who were baptized—it was impossible to do otherwise at the time. In any event, the behavior of Louis Mendès France remains murky, equivocal.

Ten years after settling in Agen, Louis Mendès France decided to return to Bordeaux, where he acquired a house whose location is particularly significant. The rue Sainte-Catherine crosses the place Saint-Project. At the time, the street was narrow and twisting and filled with stalls and shops owned by Jews. In the area around the rue Bouhaut it had something of the character of a ghetto. But the front door of Louis's house gave, symbolically, on the Christian quarter. At the time, he frequented Jews as well as Christians; his doctors (he was in ill health as we have seen) were Christians as well as Jews. If he was circumcised, this happened only after his arrival in France. No trace of such an operation has been found in the register of circumcisions at the Bordeaux City Hall.

> In 1695, in the course of one of his frequent fits of rage, he committed suicide. The neighbors heard two shots, thought he had shot his wife, broke down the door, and found him lying dead. At the time, suicide was a crime; thus, there was a trial, the transcript of which is eloquent. Despite the affluence he had achieved, Louis had remained in anguish, a disturbed man whose troubles could only have been aggravated by the procedures of the Inquisition and what he must have reproached himself for as a betrayal. He was subject to frequent fits of rage. When they occurred, according to witnesses who often called him the "mad Spaniard," he sometimes "bit his wife." He had also been violent in Portugal, fighting with knives, quick to shoot his gun.
>
> At the time of his death, was he a Jew or a Christian? He himself must have constantly asked this question. It seems that he was accepted by neither community, as at the time of his flight from Portugal. But his children, baptized though they were, and endowed with rich and noble godparents, chose to declare themselves as Jews around 1720. Louis's wife (or companion) in

Agen, Marie, was probably a Christian, and declared herself to be one. Their children had been given the names Jeanne and Jean. But when Jean, who was born in Agen in 1688, and married the first time in Bordeaux around 1710, remarried in the same city around 1745, it was to a Jewish woman in a Jewish ceremony. And he asserted that his father was named Mardochée and his mother Esther Maïmon—a totally unexpected name that had never been heard of in the region. Following the customs of the time and, I have been told, Talmudic tradition, one would change one's name, either after a conversion or after recovering from an apparently mortal disease. Had this happened to Mardochée's mother? In any event, in the course of the half-century 1695 to 1745, from Louis to Mardochée, the family became Jewish. So that, at the beginning, by following the male line backward, you find a family in Portugal that was unquestionably Christian, but by 1720 or 1725, in Bordeaux, the Jewishness of the Mendès France family was well known and fully lived out, with one exception that we will come to.

In the course of the second half of Louis XV's reign, the condition of the Jewish community had evolved considerably. According to Benjamin Francia, a local scholar from a very influential family with no connection to the Mendès family, it was around 1690 that the new "new Christians" began to display their faith, even though they continued to pay heavily for it. Now called "Portuguese merchants," they had their own cemetery by 1718. In 1735, they had seven synagogues, which were called "oratories." The first rabbi, named Falcon, arrived from Jerusalem around that time. There were, of course, no more forced baptisms. As for marriages, they were celebrated according to Jewish ritual and then registered with the parish priest. During the severe illness of the "well-beloved king" in 1744, public prayers for his health were delivered in Hebrew.

The "Portuguese merchants" of Bordeaux had a striking reputation for cleverness and generosity. As early as 1718, a secret report sent to the regent by a local official named Courson noted that "they carry on their trade with honor" and that "without them, the commerce of Bordeaux and the region would inevitably perish." Indeed, a few years earlier, after riots tinged with anti-Semitism, the fact that the leaders of the community let it be known that they might advise their constituents to follow the example of two families who had decided to emigrate to Amsterdam had been enough to create a veritable panic among the municipal authorities. There was no question of allowing the Gradis, the Pereires, the Rabas, the Peixottos, or the Da Costas to leave.

A consideration of the census figures, however, indicates the surprisingly small size of the Jewish community of Bordeaux, in which the Mendès France family was to play a rather modest role. But its growth is also striking. In 1718, there were 100 families and 400–500 people; in 1752, 327 households and 1,598 individuals; by 1790, the population was greater than 4,500. The community had increased tenfold in two-thirds of a century. And its prestige had also grown. When Abraham Gradis, head of the most illustrious family, fell gravely ill in 1780, the king's two brothers, the Comte de Provence and the Comte d'Artois, who were passing through Bordeaux, went to the synagogue to attend the prayer service for the recovery of his health. It was true that the Gradis family had financed the expedition to America, which had earned for David Gradis the honor of being the first Jew named chevalier de Saint-Louis, an unequaled distinction at the time. Two prominent members of the community were given titles: Nounes Pereire became Baron d'Ambès and Vicomte de la Menande, and Paul Peixotto, Baron de Beauleiu. When the latter was baptized, he chose the King of Spain as his godfather.

The Mendès France family laid claim to no such honors. Jean-Mardochée, who had become Mardochée-Jean, and then simply Mardochée, was a medium-sized merchant. He seems at first to have been associated with a money-changer before becoming involved in the naval supply business with his son Isaac. Tax records indicate that while the most celebrated of his coreligionists, the Pereires and the Peixottos, paid between 120 and 130 livres, he had to pay only 15. Indeed, the Mendès France family was noteworthy during this period chiefly because of the conversion of Mardochée's daughter Rebecca, wife of Isaac Peixotto, to Catholicism.

Although conversions (or reconversions) of Bordeaux Jews to Catholicism were not uncommon at the time, since the end of persecution had brought about a weakening of religious ties that had been revived during the preceding century, they were generally due, according to a contemporary police report, "less to the love of Christian religion than to the love of marriage."[9] But the unique case of Rebecca involved the marriage of a mature woman of thirty-six with two children. "Touched by grace," she said, the new Christian (the term was appropriate in this instance), whose godfather was M. de Vigier, procurator of the *parlement,* withdrew to a convent in 1755 and assumed the name Armande. It was a rather significant incident that indicated once again the cultural and religious ambiguity of a family that was to remain constantly open to new perspectives and challenges and whose Judaism was never at rest or a refuge.

For more than a century, the fortune of the family was tied to that of Bordeaux, to its greatness and its decline. The greatness was associated with the enterprise of the colonization of Santo Domingo, and the decline a consequence of the policy of the continental blockade. In any event, from the end of the Regency to the Empire, Bordeaux and those who had the boldness and the means to contribute to its expansion constantly prospered. While the colony of "Portuguese merchants" tripled in a century, the population of the city itself more than doubled, growing from

45,000 at the end of the seventeenth century to 110,000 at the beginning of the Revolution, not to mention its revenues, whose growth is attested to by the size and beauty of the buildings of the time.

Oddly enough, only one branch of the Mendès France family, whose ancestor was Isaac, followed this rising curve. The other branch, descended from Moïse, Mardochée's other son (to which Pierre Mendès France belonged), for long had a much more modest fate, profiting little from Bordeaux's golden age, but suffering harshly from the city's decline in the nineteenth century. Moïse Mendès France was a discreet money-changer established in the place Sainte-Eulalie. His descendants did not maintain this modest condition. Whether from timidity, bad luck, or lack of business sense at a time when the Jewish condition was tied to commercial activity, the fact remains that the Mendès France family was illustrated almost entirely by the descendants of Isaac. They appear in the West Indies, involved in some strange events.

Mendès France recounted two curious anecdotes about the "colonial" adventures of his ancestors.

> At the time he launched the New Deal, applying more or less consciously the precepts of Keynes, who started from the principle that the unemployed had to be put to work doing anything at all that would give them a job and a salary, even digging holes and filling them in again, Roosevelt had trouble finding an occupation for a certain number of intellectuals who had studied in France. One day, someone pointed out to him that, since the purchase of Louisiana from Bonaparte, no one had bothered to go through those French archives, and that that was perhaps a way of putting these unemployed French-speaking intellectuals to work. That was what he did. So, thanks to Keynes and Roosevelt, the traces of David Mendès France, New Orleans merchant, and my "American" family were rediscovered.
>
> Some years later, right after the war, I decided to pursue the research I had already begun before the outbreak of hostilities, at the Bibliothèque Nationale. I was stunned to realize that the Germans themselves had done the work, had systematically studied the eighteenth-century French press of Santo Domingo. They had even, with a thoroughness that leads one to think that they were not "disinterested" historians but people charged with a specific mission, underlined passages and made notes in the margins. The librarian helping with my research in fact remembered their investigation. What were they looking for? Elsewhere, they had recovered my marriage certificate. Here, they had tracked down not only the traces of the Mendès France family but the whole of the French colonization of Santo Domingo.

Isaac Mendès France was an extraordinary character. After an adventurous youth that led him from Amsterdam to Frankfurt and marriage to Judith Dacosta, daughter of one of the great "Portuguese merchant" families of Bordeaux, with interests in Nantes, he became involved in large-scale enterprises around 1740, sometimes in association with the

Gradis. In particular, he equipped the *Heureuse-Marie*. The name was ironic, because the Seven Years' War and the opportunities it offered to English pirates to seize French-flag ships ruined him. He went bankrupt in 1756. But his powerful father-in-law Dacosta helped him to reach an arrangement with his creditors. And to reestablish himself, after the treaty of 1763, he set out to make his fortune in Santo Domingo, where his older brother David had already established a trading post in Port-au-Prince, as well as one in New Orleans.

He had wandered in the interim and, in Thann in Alsace, had become connected with the Brunswick family, particularly with one of the daughters, named Fayette, whose character was as strong as his own. They seem to have set up house together. They landed in Santo Domingo together, along with Isaac's eldest son Mardochée, and settled in a locality called Le Petit-Goave (which gave its name to a street in Bordeaux). They lived there for twelve years, prosperous and respected. Their holdings, the Trou Canari and the Fonds des Nègres, included as many as 150 slaves. Those slaves, or some of them, were to be the source of many difficulties.[10]

In 1775, Isaac and Fayette set sail for Nantes on the *Marquis-de-Lévy* so that Isaac's eye trouble might be treated in Paris. They were accompanied by three of their "blacks," Pampy, Cezar, and Julienne. Prosperous colonials had the habit of taking some "servants" with them on their trips to France.

Isaac set up house in Paris with his little group toward the end of the year and could finally be treated. But on January 19, 1776, the master of Le Petit-Goave received an astounding summons. The procurator Dejunquières, in the name of "Gabriel Pampy, black from Petit-Goave, and Amynte Julienne, a native of the Congo, on the Guinea coast" (Cezar had in the meantime disappeared), demanded of their master that he emancipate them, relying on a 1315 edict of Louis X, called *le Hutin*, which had abolished slavery in France.

The first petition presented "to the Marble Table to our lords of the admiralty" against "sire Mendès, a Jew," led to an order directing Isaac Mendès France to pay 60 livres to the two slaves who could leave and go "wherever they liked." Isaac struck back and petitioned the admiralty in turn to vacate the proceedings, pleading a royal decree of 1738 which authorized "Americans" to bring their slaves to France for a brief stay. He lost once again. By finding against Mendès France, the magistrates of the Marble Table may have been motivated by the anti-Semitism that was soon to give rise to the discriminatory measures taken against Jews in Santo Domingo by the admiral Comte d'Estaing, governor of the island, or they may have been moved by their wish to demonstrate their power against the royal authority expressed in the 1738 decree. In this "Mendès affair," rather than a somber judicial pogrom, it is probably more accurate to see an indication of the prerevolutionary stirrings of officials, preparing the way for the movement of 1789.

Isaac turns up again in Bordeaux, once again prosperous, respected, and enterprising. In 1779, he was made a *bourgeois* of the city, one of only two "Portuguese" to receive this distinction, apart from those who had been titled, like Gradis, Pereire, and Peixotto. The title *bourgeois* gave one the right to carry a sword and significant fiscal advantages. When he died as a patriarch in 1785, he bequeathed to his legitimate wife Judith three properties, in Floirac, Caudéran, and Libourne. Thereafter, we must return to the other branch of the family to rediscover signs of their enterprising spirit. At sixteen, Moïse-Joseph signed on as a cabin boy aboard the *Vengeur*, in the year III of the Republic. He took part in the unsavory removal, by the soldiers of the Revolution, of the bronze horses of Venice. Then he fell into the hands of the English, was sent to the prison-ships of Corsica, and escaped by boat with a companion. They headed northwest, but the winds drove them off course toward the Italian coast. They landed in the hope of joining Bonaparte's army, whose presence in the vicinity could hardly go unnoticed. They joined it at Arcole. The date is uncertain. Moïse-Joseph's notebook mentions first "two days after the celebrated battle." But this notation has been crossed out, perhaps by him. He was known to everyone as a "hero of Arcole." Moreover, when he reenlisted, he was named *tambour* of the regiment. Anyone might have surrendered to the temptation of making a minor adjustment in history. Captured again by the English, he was not released until 1815. On his service record, the following notation is found: "shoots even on Saturdays." Settled first in Bordeaux, he died in Marseille. There was no more opportune place to be buried and to have inscribed on his tombstone: "Drummed out the charge on the bridge of Arcole."

The Mendès Frances of Bordeaux had already begun to disperse. The policy of the continental blockade had begun to ruin Bordeaux, the principal port of France at the end of the eighteenth century. From then on, one can say that those "Portuguese merchants" who wanted to maintain or develop the prosperity conquered in Bordeaux in the century of the American expedition set out for Paris.

The Parisian Mendès Frances were not without social skills. From 1850 on, we encounter some who succeeded in business, others in music or painting. Almost all of them had two first names, one Jewish, the other Christian or with an ancient flavor: Mardochée-Alexis, David-Maxime, Samuel-Virgile, Moïse-Osiris. Mardochée-Alexis, who had been preceded in Paris by his enterprising nephew Oscar, was associated with the

Pereires in the creation of the "Pereire quarter," which was one of the most remarkable developments in the Paris region in the second half of the nineteenth century.

His niece Léontine, daughter of Jacob-Eugène Mendès France, a famous lover of roses, sang at the Opéra, where her portrait is preserved in the role of Mignon. Born in the United States, she had received second prize in the *opéra-comique* competition at the Conservatory and made her debut at the Opéra in *Faust*. The magazine *L'Entr'acte* greeted her appearance with great praise. Also noted in the arts was René Mendès France, whose paintings have found a steady market for the last forty years. He was one of the moving forces behind the Salon des Surindépendants.

The Bordeaux branch of the family remained more unassuming, more faithful, in short, to the example of the merchant of the place Saint-Projet, the "mad Spaniard," than to the brilliant tribulations of Isaac, the master of Le Petit-Goave. To be sure, David-Cheri (his real name), grandson of Moïse, seemed to be attached to family splendors when he married Abigaïl Barabraham, daughter of a well-known figure in the city, assistant to the mayor of Bordeaux. But, showing little concern for this fortune, he was especially known as an ardent republican under the Empire, and even as a militant of the left.

Thereafter, there are only modest people, beginning with one of David-Cheri's daughters, Corinne, who came close enough to poverty to be forced to sell newspapers in the streets. There was a Rebecca Mendès France who married a Gomez-Vaez, whose name was associated with that of a prosperous bank, later the Banque de l'Aquitaine. But Rebecca's sister Rachel was reduced to poverty.

Pierre Mendès France, Rachel's great-nephew, had the following to say:

> Among these modest Mendès Frances of Bordeaux was my grandfather, Jules-Isaac. Born in 1851, he enlisted for the war of 1870, which he ended as a corporal. A fervent admirer of the Commune, he wrote a poem which called down the curses of the people on Thiers. In fact, he versified often on all kinds of subjects. I've kept his notebooks of poems, songs, epigrams, and wedding toasts, all naive and charming. He even succeeded in making a song out of "a day in the life of a fertilizer salesman," in which he gently mocks his clients, buyers of "guano." I haven't found anything about Jaurès, whom he admired above all. Perhaps he didn't think himself worthy.
>
> For a long time he was a traveling salesman, criss-crossing the provinces from Bordeaux to Limoges and from Rochefort to Nîmes. He finally settled in Paris around 1885, and opened a retail store on the avenue Secretan in the twentieth *arrondissement*. After the death of his first wife, Emilie Strauss, he married Berthe Marchetti, whom I knew well. She was a generous and gay

woman whom he loved dearly. My grandfather loved his wife Berthe so much that when she died he simply let himself waste away. He died on the day of my wedding in 1933. I will never forget the way he told me about Victor Hugo's funeral and the wake around the Arc de Triomphe.

One of his nephews, Jean Mendès France, bastard son of poor Corinne, my father's cousin, was also a very interesting character. Along with his wife, a militant Catholic worker, he was very active in the Bordeaux metal-workers union, especially among the women. In 1917, together, they organized strikes to win better working conditions for women defense workers. In Bordeaux at the time there were no fewer than 2,500 unionized female workers, a number much higher than the national average.

And then we come to Cerf-David Mendès France, my father, born in 1874, place de la Motte in Limoges, where the vagaries of business had brought Jules-Isaac and his family. My father did not carry on the family business. He wanted to create his own textile business, which he set up first on rue de Cléry, then transferred to rue Réaumur, then rue Turbigo, then rue Etienne-Marcel, where the family lived for a long time, and finally rue Léopold-Bellan. He had enlisted in the army at eighteen and then traveled. In 1905, he was in Strasbourg on business. There he met Palmyre Cahn, daughter of a respectable merchant of the city. She was pretty, six years younger than he, and he married her: the first "misalliance" in my Sephardic family which shied away from marriages with Ashkenazim (there had been the episode of Isaac and Fayette, but that was in the distant past). Besides, all that had practically no meaning for a man like my father, who was not very religious and was thoroughly assimilated.

Although I am less familiar with it, as I have told you, my mother's family was also interesting. It was even more modest than the Mendès France family. They were Alsatians, originally from Sarrebourg, and there are records of them in France from before 1750. They were hard-working, opinionated, upstanding, and very patriotic. In their circles, it was thought that the emancipation of the Jews under the Revolution tied them to France with indissoluble bonds. I knew my grandfather, Isidore Cahn, only in my early childhood. He died in 1917, when I was ten, but we had obviously been separated from 1914 on. One of my last memories of visiting my grandparents in Strasbourg is of shouting "Vive la France!" from the family terrace while occupation troops marched by below. I wasn't even seven. My grandfather punished me for it, probably thinking all the while that blood will tell.

He was an extreme nationalist and anti-Prussian. He had always refused to learn and to speak German. His name was Isidore, as I've told you—one of my names too—which is written without an "e" in German. In an advertising campaign he conducted at the time for Cahn shoes, with posters on the streets and inserts in newspapers, he spelled his name Isidore. The authorities were angered and imposed various fines and penalties on him, so he had posters printed and signs painted and put up in the streets on which the final "e" was crossed out in such an obvious way that it was a provocation. He was a rather short, stocky man with a triangular head, his chin accentuated by a short, pointy beard, with slightly slanted, light blue eyes. His early life had been very difficult. In a letter of 1903, he complained about his "hard life." He had developed a great reputation for wisdom. He was often consulted by members of the Jewish community on questions of business ethics or general behavior. I don't know whether he was very pious, but he said he was proud to be a Cohen,[11] and he was very involved in community affairs and debates.

I knew my grandmother, whose maiden name was Henriette Wolff, much better. She was very pious, so fervent in fact that, for a while, some of her piety rubbed off on me. When I was twelve, a year I spent with her, I went through a "mystical" period, which didn't last very long. It was especially because of her that I was bar mitzvahed in Strasbourg. Moreover, she was a very cultivated woman, musical like many Alsatians, with broad interests. I was never able to discover the source of this cultivation, which was rather unusual in her circles. In any event, she made sure that my mother had a thorough education in the *lycée* of Neudorf, which was particularly noted for its teaching of German.

My parents were married in Strasbourg, and their marriage contract was drawn up in German. In 1906, they settled in Paris, where I was born in January 1907. My parents' married life was happy. My father loved my mother dearly, even though he wasn't always faithful to her. My sister Marcelle and I—I'm three years older than she—grew up in an atmosphere of harmony without material needs. The family library was extensive and varied. My father loved above all Hugo, Balzac, the Goncourt brothers, Zola, Anatole France, and Dumas *père* and *fils:* he had their works bound in handsome red leather.

When my mother was widowed in 1957, she decided to give herself some good times. Instead of retreating into her sorrow, like so many widows, my mother, who had lived all her life for others, discovered life, traveled, bought dresses, and even went to a few casinos, taken with a belated and rather timid passion for gambling. It was a touching recompense for a life of austere devotion entirely directed toward her family.

2.
FIRST IN HIS CLASS

Pierre Mendès France was a descendant of these "ordinary people" who traveled the world, confronted the Inquisition, and built a colonial estate: wanderings, suffering, and hope. One would think that these were the ingredients of a sensitive consciousness haunted by the Jewish mystery and the anguish of being chosen. But this would be a serious oversimplification. Pierre Mendès France was indeed an heir to these struggles, the call of open spaces, the sometimes cruel tribulations, but also, and even more, of an education which was quintessentially, from elementary school to his doctorate of law, the secular education of the Radical Republic.

Cerf-David Mendès France was rigorously areligious. The Dreyfus affair had been the great battle of his life; it had mobilized him as much as the First World War, which he began as a noncommissioned officer and ended as a lieutenant in the light artillery under Colonel Alfred Dreyfus,[1] who had impressed him as a fanatical and authoritarian patriot and a stickler for the rules. But he had experienced the affair less as an involved Jew than as an indignant democrat, and a democrat of the left, like his father Jules-Isaac, even though he had never joined a political party or, like his father, written a polemic against the repression of the Communards.

Pierre's mother (he had no idea of the origin of her strange name Palmyre) was clearly more involved with Judaism. According to him, it was in a slightly infantile fashion: "But she was not very observant, except for Yom Kippur. She fasted on that day but didn't make us fast. She never imposed the slightest dietary law on us, or any other law. My father looked on all of this with Voltairean irony." And Pierre's sister Marcelle Grumbach pointed out:

> Our mother was more superstitious than believing. Pierre was not bar mitz-vahed at home but at our grandparents' in Strasbourg. It's worth remember-ing that our paternal grandfather's second wife was a Christian, Berthe, whom we all loved very much. Religious problems did not arise, at least not in our generation.

They may very well not have been practicing Jews, but the question remains of their Jewish consciousness, beyond their basic and obvious solidarity with Jewish martyrs and their opposition to racism, a solidarity that had frequently and courageously been demonstrated. In a 1976 inter-view with the Jewish magazine *L'Arche* about his origins and his connec-tions with Judaism, Pierre Mendès France, who was about to travel to Israel, said:

> I am constantly intrigued and impressed by the Jewish phenomenon. It is not a religious phenomenon, since there are a large number of men who are not believers and are not observant but who nevertheless consider themselves Jews. Nor is it a racial phenomenon, since we know that down through the centuries there have been intermarriages, mixed marriages of all kinds; there were some in my family, and my blood is mixed, as for most families.
>
> It is neither a religious nor a racial phenomenon. Then what precisely is it? I don't know. Some have said—this was Sartre's theory—that there is no fundamental Semitism but that anti-Semitism gives Jews the feeling that they make up a specific community and that, as a consequence, Jewishness is a product of anti-Semitism.
>
> If that is true, one might suppose that over time—it will take many years, generations, I have no illusions about it—the disappearance of anti-Semitism would one day bring about the disappearance of Judaism. I am skeptical about the theory. In any case, I have no definitive, scientific answer to the question you have asked me, and that I ask myself.

And when the interviewer from *L'Arche* objected: "You know very well, Mister Prime Minister, that the theory doesn't stand up to analysis. Even Sartre no longer defends it. The Jewish phenomenon is a positive phenomenon," Mendès France retorted: "When you say, 'You know very well,' you're going beyond what I know. I know that I am a Jew. My children, who are no more religious than I, know that they are Jewish. I feel that anti-Semites think of me as a Jew. Those are the facts."

All of this, of course, does not sum up Mendès France's connection to Judaism. The "facts" do not say everything. And the "facts" themselves, in the course of his life, sometimes spoke in a more strident voice. But it is clear that, after the "mystical crisis" he went through with his grandmother Cahn in Strasbourg, his life had no religious dimension and that whatever awareness he may have had of his Jewishness never interfered with his utmost sympathetic understanding of other communities. Like his ancestor Luis de França on the place Saint-Projet in Bordeaux, his front door faced the Christian quarter. Many of his friends were Jewish, beginning with the most influential one, Georges Boris. He married two Jewish women. But many of the men he most admired or respected, from Jaurès to Herriot, from Pierre Cot to Mauriac, were not Jews.[2] And however attentive he may have been to the fate of the Jewish community in France, however passionately interested he may have been in Arab–Israeli relations, no French statesman ever demonstrated a more serene impartiality in these areas.

In short, he had a secular childhood. He was less the heir of Luis the fugitive or Isaac the adventurer than of a particular educational system that had already shaped his father and made him a particular kind of student and a particular kind of citizen. Paternal authority in the family was very strict. When their mother was not pleased, she threatened the children: "I'll tell your father." He was feared. But he was sensitive and generous, and rather cheerful as well, fond of jokes and with a weakness for women. His son admired and loved him. But he was shaped less by his father, essentially, than by the anonymous teachers of his neighborhood schools.

There was first the elementary school on the rue de la Jussienne. War broke out when Pierre was seven, but students only worked all the harder. His elementary school teacher insisted that he take the entrance exam early for the nearby "special school," the Lycée Turgot, which was then only an upper primary school.[3]

"I took the exam without really knowing what would happen. Competition was rather stiff at the time. I was accepted. Chance would have it that the Lycée Turgot was located in the middle of the neighborhood where I was born." It was a significant accident; the fact that the school was located near his birthplace gave his education an intimate character, closely connected to the emotions of childhood. In his case, it was hard to tell where school began and family ended.

It was there that I decided that I had to continue my studies, and I prepared for the *baccalauréat* on my own, outside school—which was only adequate for that level in scientific subjects—and by taking private tutoring. That was how I came to take the *baccalauréat* as young as fifteen (I needed special dispensation). Later I was praised for being the youngest doctor of law, the youngest deputy, the youngest deputy minister, and so on. In fact, it was at school that I got ahead of my contemporaries. After that, I followed the normal course.

For the second *baccalauréat,* however, I had to go to a *lycée,* Louis-le-Grand. It didn't go very well: I no longer felt guided or encouraged. I was disoriented by the lack of discipline in the school. And the philosophy course troubled me even more. I had a professor named Bernès, who had the reputation of being brilliant. But I didn't "bite." I was a bad student of philosophy. In the end, I took the exam, of course.

This determined student, submissive to his teachers, disconcerted by the absence of discipline and guidance, seems to have been totally devoted to his studies, like a young Spartan in training. His sister Marcelle qualified this picture a little.

Pierre was brilliant, argumentative, provoking, and capable of rebelling. We had a *Fraülein* at home. Pierre was good in German. One day in class, his teacher, M. Potut, translated a sentence. Pierre stood up: "That's wrong!" He was kicked out of class. A few days later, M. Potut admitted his mistake, and they became friends. My brother was devoted to his studies, that's true, but he was also urged on by our father, who was very demanding and unstinting in providing space for work and a comfortable way of life. The apartment we lived in on the rue Etienne-Marcel was spacious and comfortable. Pierre had a studious but happy childhood.

As for racism, both Marcelle and Pierre asserted that it affected them little when they were growing up. In the second and third *arrondissements* there were so many Jewish schoolchildren that any racist provocation was quickly brought under control. It was only later, in the Latin Quarter, and especially at the Faculty of Law, that Mendès France discovered this kind of challenge, to which he responded with high-hearted courage. In his neighborhood, between le Sentier and les Halles, la République and la place des Victoires, he was the son of a textile merchant, which was rather banal. In the Faculty of Law, he was a little less banal.

There was nothing very pressing to distract him from his studies. As for reading, he became enamored of Zola only later in life, although he read some while he was young, but without being really absorbed. He liked Balzac, Anatole France, Daudet, and Dumas *père,* but no more than he liked his history text. He liked music, as his mother did, and practiced a little on the piano. But "tickling the keys for twenty minutes a night" was not enough to reach the level he aspired to, to be able to decipher and interpret the pieces he liked. "If I had been a girl, I think I would have given up a lot for the piano." He spoke of it with a hint of nostalgia, but just a hint.

He had no interest in sports. His mother, brought up in the German style in Alsace, tried to interest him in Swedish gymnastics. He later reproached her for not having insisted. He found it terribly boring, even during his military training for reserve officers' school. It was only later that he discovered skiing and swimming, which gave him much pleasure.

There were, of course, the movies and the theater, where he would go with a few friends in the early 1920s. But, in reality, he never joined up with a group of the kind that draws you in at that age and makes you believe that you, too, like cards, tobacco, Pernod, or prostitutes. He soon became interested in girls and was known as being rather flirtatious. But there was a time for everything, especially for his *baccalauréat* and the other diplomas that he constantly pursued from the time he entered the *lycée*. It was an uncompromising and passionate pursuit.

One thing was clear: he would not succeed his father as head of the family business. However great the respect and affection he felt for the man, and however strong his father's wish to have him as a successor, he made it very clear immediately after the *baccalauréat* that that was out of the question. Cerf Mendès France did not insist; his authority stopped at that point. Pierre's mother, whose influence in the end was greater than that of his father, had no taste for anything but intellectual professions— engineer, doctor, lawyer. She particularly favored the bar, and her wishes prevailed. The young man, who was attracted by the law, didn't dare—or didn't think of it at the time—to turn toward the profession he later regretted not having followed.

> I should have been a teacher. That was what really attracted me. I should have taught history, or economics. That was, I think, my vocation. And when I think about it again today, I think I may have followed the wrong track. I am not sure I was a very good lawyer, or in any case that I was gifted enough to become one. But the profession gave me the opportunity to discover certain social realities, peasant poverty, for example, that motivated my political activity. In that sense, I'm grateful to my mother for having pushed me toward the law.

Thus, he became a student at the Faculty of Law on the rue Saint-Jacques. But he was also a student at the School of Political Science, and he undertook a *licence* in history—which he did not complete, receiving only three of the necessary certificates. He was put off by geography, which was then an integral part of historical studies.

The Faculty of Law was perhaps not the place he would have chosen to work at above all others. But he was very interested by the study of law. The school had prestigious professors, like Gaston Jéze, Achille Mestre, Geouffre de la Pradelle, and especially Juliot de la Morandière, with whom he maintained relations for a long time. Chesnon, a professor of legal history, particularly interested him, as did Joseph Barthélemy, a constitutional expert with a biting wit, who also taught at the School of

Political Sciences. "He was a brilliant teacher. But that didn't keep him from turning out badly." Mendès encountered him again as a right-wing deputy and then discovered, at his expense, that he had become a minister for Pétain, originator of the terrible repressive tribunals of Vichy, the "special sections."

But Mendès France was particularly interested in economics and finance, subjects oddly taught in the same faculty as civil law.

> The best students studied pure law, or, at most, international or constitutional law. Economics was looked down upon. But that was what I studied, not for tactical reasons, but because of my interest in it. I took not only Gaston Jèze's course on fiscal legislation, but also those of the economist William Oualid, whom I liked and respected, so much so that I asked him to direct my thesis, even though the subject, the fiscal policies of the Poincaré government, was not in his particular area of expertise.

He entered the Faculty of Law in October 1923 and left in June 1926. For the first year he received the overall evaluation of "good," for the second "satisfactory," and for the third "good," which encouraged him to go on for the doctorate.

Simultaneously with his legal studies and his *licence* in history, Mendès France enrolled in 1923 in the Ecole Libre des Sciences Politiques known as "Sciences Po" on the rue Saint-Guillaume. It appears that neither law, "pure" or not, nor the bar was enough to satisfy his adolescent ambitions. It was not that he was particularly charmed by the atmosphere of Sciences Po, which was then a refuge for well-connected and well-to-do young men. But the subject of study there was the world he lived in, the realm where he would display his vitality, the affairs of the nation in which he wanted to act.

We have a valuable document concerning Pierre Mendès France as a student at Sciences Po: his file. It reveals that he was a student at the school from October 1923 to June 1925 in the "general" section (not, as one might have thought, in the section preparing one for "public finance") and that he was fourth in his graduating class, with the notation "very good."[4]

His examiners in 1924 evaluated him as "a good student with an original mind, who can do better," and "intelligent but still young" (he was seventeen). And in 1925 he received the following evaluations: "An excellent candidate who presents his extensive knowledge in clear and precise language." "An obviously superior candidate, very mature for his age." "Very intelligent. An original and already mature mind. Ambitious. Will be successful."

Mendès France's file contains two undated essays. A few excerpts will give a sense of the lively maturity of this eighteen-year-old. The first is an answer to the question: Compare the circumstances in which were promulgated the German constitutions of 1871 and 1919. Mendès France received seventeen out of twenty, with the following comment: "Warm, sharp, demonstrating extensive reading. Bubbling with ideas."

> What a contrast between the Germany of 1871 and the Germany of 1919! In 1871, Germany was brand new, young, a new arrival in the astonished concert of Europe, no doubt surprised itself by its strength and greatness, full of hope and courage, full of confidence in its new and as yet untried power.
>
> In 1919, Germany was already an old state, worn out by fifty years of active, energetic diplomacy that was often clumsy and importunate. Germany was a state that had been conquered by the most formidable of coalitions after the most gigantic battle. The fallen country compared its past greatness with its present weakness and, shattered by such a change, such a collapse, sought its path for a while, and then suddenly burst out in a desperate rage and plunged into the clumsiest form of nationalism, comprehensible to be sure, but ferocious, awaiting the calm that only time could bring. [In the margin, the professor noted: "Eloquent."]

And the young Mendès France concluded:

> In spite of the retreats, the halts, and the accidents we have seen, two facts nevertheless remain interesting because they conform with the parallel evolution that has taken place in other states. There is first an advance toward unity, and second an advance toward democracy, in spite of the constitutional, psychological, or material obstacles that appeared to be serious roadblocks to that evolution.

The second essay is a "history of freedom of the press" that Professor Joseph Barthélemy had asked his students to present in broad outline. It opens with a good comparison between the absence of formal freedoms and the existence of real ones under the *ancien régime:* "After all, Voltaire, Rousseau, and the Encyclopedists were able to publish their works." Mendès contrasted this relative liberty to the rigor of the Convention ("Desmoulins and Chénier were guillotined as journalists") and went on to denounce repression of the press under the Empire and the Restoration and to refer to subsequent battles. He concluded:

> The press plays a more substantial role than ever before. Regulation of the way it exercises its influence is an extremely delicate task that leaves room for much difference of opinion. . . . At the present time, the majority has agreed to allow the press the freedom that it has enjoyed for forty years and that it has apparently not excessively abused.

These two little essays are interesting, although one must be careful not to draw conclusions from early writings produced under the influence of sometimes imperious professors. The first demonstrates a striking serenity about Germany, which was, to be sure, derived from the doctrine professed at the time by the Radical and Socialist left, but was nevertheless interesting coming from a young man who had been educated by very patriotic teachers. Also noteworthy is the sentence on the explosion of "rage" of German nationalism, characterized as "comprehensible." The second demonstrates a rather disconcerting prudence and absence of demagogy. Here was an adolescent who did not feel obligated to erect a barricade of words against the *ancien régime,* who even pointed out that Louis XV treated Voltaire better than the Convention treated Desmoulins, and who placidly observed that, since the beginning of the Third Republic, the press had not "abused" the freedom it had been granted. His mind was sensitive to nuances. Would he have to become a statesman before he took the bit in his teeth?

Certainly not. To look for Pierre Mendès France in his student essays and examinations, the excellent grades of a supremely gifted adolescent devoted to his work, would be absurd. There was also the young man precociously involved in political debate and whose earliest activities can be summed up by saying that he was a "Radical at sixteen." He was a Radical in 1923, at a time when Radicalism meant the left.

It is a strange story of bewitchment, which is hardly comprehensible to those of us who knew the enchanter only when he was old, ponderous, reduced to the condition of a musical brontosaurus. But, one day in 1923, on his way from home to school, Mendès France passed by the old Mutualité (now torn down), where the Radicals were holding a conference. The student entered; Herriot was speaking:

> I had never seen him, but I had heard people talk about him. He was then at the peak of his talent, young and fervent. He spoke in a magnificent style, in a warm, clear voice, about peace, reconciliation with Germany, recognition of the Soviets, disarmament, evacuation of the Ruhr. It was magnificent. For me, it was like love at first sight. I felt as though I were a disciple of the man. He was all generosity, eloquence, youth, total purity.

Conquered by the great man—the great orator, at least—Mendès France wanted to meet him. It turned out that an old uncle, Salomon Hirsch, knew the Radical leader well. Pierre's parents asked him to arrange a meeting. Hirsch was just then organizing a banquet in which Herriot was to participate. He suggested that the young man write a short speech; it would be an opportunity to present him to the leader of the Cartel des Gauches.

Pierre Mendès France went to work, prepared his little paper, and showed it to Salomon Hirsch, who found it good. But, according to his sister Marcelle, "when the time came at the banquet to stand up in front of Harriot, Pierre searched in his pockets but couldn't find his speech. He made a desperate gesture to the family, and then, seizing his courage in

both hands, launched into an improvisation that pleased the great man."
A sign of things to come.

But before joining the Radical Party "in the wake" of Herriot, Mendès France was to discover the organization, or better, the movement, where he could demonstrate his temperament as a student of the school of the Republic and an antiracist democrat. One might also call him an antifascist if the term were not a bit premature, only a few months after the march on Rome. Philippe Lamour, an older classmate at the Faculty of Law, describes him at the time in a lovely book of memoirs.[5] He does not disguise the slightly irritated admiration provoked, from the moment he appeared at the university, by the "strange precocity" of the young, uncompromising, hard-working student.

> His whole existence was exclusively devoted to his political future. He did not see it as a career but as a mission. When he was young, he had dreamed of a life totally devoted to a great work. When our little group dawdled around the Latin Quarter, playing at Rastignac in interminable café discussions, Mendès, always in a hurry to get to a class or the library, looked on us without indulgence. He was dreaming of a career like Disraeli's: "You have time to lose," he would say to us. He didn't.

This phase of the life of Pierre Mendès France would be incomprehensible without a picture of university life in the 1920s, the years when French nationalism, whipped up by the victory of 1918, the election of the *Chambre Bleu Horizon,* and the "old soldier" mentality, held sway. It was a time when, to the cry of "The *boche* will pay!," xenophobic demagogy reigned; a time when the bolshevism of "the man with the knife in his teeth" served as a foil for the conservative right, when popular feeling readily confounded Germanness with Jewishness, immoralism with cosmopolitanism, and the avant-garde with revolution. Finally, it was a time when Action Française preached hatred of the "wogs" as well as of "the Tramp," "the headless woman" (the Republic according to Maurras), and of "democratic disorder."

In the Latin Quarter, and at the Faculty of Law more than anywhere else, the state of mind instilled by Maurras and Daudet had found a spokesman and a hireling, the leader of the Camelots du Roi and of all those who rallied to "integral nationalism": Georges Calzant, a giant with a club foot, endowed with impressive physical courage, and capable, what is more, of tirelessly haranguing overheated crowds. His headquarters were located at 33 rue Saint-André-des-Arts. From there, a mere telephone call would produce squadrons armed with clubs, with their hats stuffed with newspapers.[6]

To cries of "Death to the Yids! Out with the Reds!" the Camelots, sometimes flanked by their comrades from the Jeunesses Patriotes, would march up the boulevard Saint-Michel and gather at the Café d'Harcourt at the corner of the place de la Sorbonne. The usual targets of these punitive expeditions were the Faculty of Letters, a den of "democrats," and La Rivière on rue Monsieur-le-Prince, where the "leftists" gathered. Royalists from below against republicans from above, Faculty of Law against the Sorbonne, for more than fifteen years the boulevard Saint-Michel was the arena of constant battles, with the Camelots and the Jeunesses Patriotes recruiting particularly law and medical students and the left relying on students of the humanities and sciences. It was in this climate of bitter struggle, exacerbated in the spring of 1924 by the accession to power of the Cartel des Gauches cabinet under Herriot, that the university studies of Mendès France and his friends took place. But, in the meantime, they had given themselves the means to retaliate.

In a 1928 interview in *L'Université républicaine,* which had by then become the organ of the movement, Paul Ostoya described for René Georges-Etienne the origins and first demonstrations of the Ligue d'Action Universitaire Républicaine et Socialiste (LAURS), which he had established while a student at the Faculty of Sciences.

> LAURS was founded in 1924. There existed at the time in the Latin Quarter a small group of determined students, the Comité d'Action Universitaire, which had set itself the goal of assuring respect for order at the public meetings of democratic organizations. In early 1924, I came to take on leadership of the committee. It was right after the Camelots du Roi had vandalized the offices of *L'Oeuvre* and *L'Ere nouvelle.* As the elections approached, I had the idea of broadening the activity of the committee and making it a league grouping together all republican elements in the university. . . . LAURS really answered a need. Moreover, I encountered a good deal of sympathy from certain republican politicians and newspaper editors.

The strength and necessity of LAURS, if not its success, were shown during the Georges Scelle affair. This world-renowned jurist, an expert for the League of Nations, had been named professor of international law at the Paris faculty by Herriot's education minister, François Albert, the epitome of the secular militant of the left, in place of his old rival, Louis Le Fur, considered to be a monarchist. Scelle was not a man of the left, but compared to his competitor he seemed at least to be the candidate of the Cartel, especially in the very conservative atmosphere that was then prevalent at the Faculty of Law.

Action Française and the Jeunesses Patriotes seized the opportunity to strike a great blow, and on the day set for his inaugural lecture, they occupied the amphitheaters of the Faculty of Law in order to prevent Scelle from speaking. Philippe Lamour, briefly a sympathizer of the Valois "network" (which was in the process of breaking with Action Française but still carried on the same struggles), describes the battle:

The rebellion in the Latin Quarter was carefully fomented and organized with the slogan: "M. Georges Scelle will not teach his course!" I took the lead with a few classmates. There were marches on the boulevards and a large gathering in the Bullier dance hall. Then we entrenched ourselves in the faculty buildings on the place du Panthéon, with food and ammunition to block the entry of any outsiders. For several days we resisted attacks by the special forces and the hoses of the firemen. We made heroic sorties and seized the police station of the fifth *arrondissement,* locking the police in like moles before retreating to our fortress, as in the good old days.[7]

There was fighting in the classrooms and the corridors. The prefect of police, Morain, in full uniform, managed to slip in through a window opening onto the rue Soufflot and to lead a commando group of "liberators" against the Action Française students.[8] This group joined up with the "internal resistance" led by a student with a pale complexion wearing a startling Phrygian cap, who was to become general secretary of LAURS at the age of eighteen and who was named Pierre Mendès France.

He had been a member of the league from the beginning, in July 1924: his membership card bears the number 10. We do not know whether he was thus committed as the son of Cerf-David the Dreyfusard, the grandson of Jules-Isaac friend of the Communards, the model student of Turgot, the law student opposed to conservative teaching and an atmosphere hostile to the Republic, the adolescent of Sciences Po exasperated by the self-satisfaction of the "sons of archbishops," the dazzled disciple of Herriot, or else as a young Jew more and more aware of the racism that infested the Latin Quarter.

Whatever the weight of each of these elements in his decision, the fact is that, when school resumed in the fall of 1924, Pierre was no longer simply an obstinate workhorse; he was also a militant. He was not yet eighteen, but his choice had been made, and he kept to it. What is surprising is that this commitment to activism in the summer of 1924, far from turning him away from his studies, which he wished to be at the highest level, helped in the precocious maturation of this young mind: We have already seen the sudden flowering evidenced by his performance at Sciences Po in 1925, compared to that of 1924.

In January 1926, the young Mendès was named general secretary of the Paris section of LAURS, which he represented at the Congress of Republican and Secular Youth at Reims the following September. It was there that he met several men who later became his friends: Marc Jacquier and René Georges-Etienne, who were both his successors as general secretary of the league and readily testified to his effectiveness as an organizer and his courage under fire; and Charles Gombault who, before becoming one of his close associates, was already involved in these battles.

Gombault tells the story of a meeting of LAURS on the rue Drouot in 1926 to which Mendès France had come with his father, when the Camelots du Roi interrupted with particular force. Since the police from the nearby station house stubbornly refused to intervene, it was necessary to beat a retreat. In the street, Mendès France's father realized that he had forgotten his hat. Nothing to worry about: the young Gombault went back to the scene of battle to retrieve Cerf Mendès France's hat, receiving a good thrashing along the way.

Mendès did more than simply lead his troops on the streets of Paris. After February 1927, when he was elected national general secretary of LAURS, he was often to be found in the provinces. He delivered a speech at a panel debate organized by the Jeunesses Patriotes at Rennes in April 1928. A few weeks later, in May 1928, *L'Université républicaine* provided him with the opportunity to deliver a report on his term of office. He was at the time national president of the league.

> When I was elected general secretary of the league, I set myself two tasks: to strengthen the Paris section and to develop the league by broadening its activities outside the capital.
> In Paris, the year had begun very badly.
> The Georges Scelle affair was still very much in everyone's mind, along with the breakup of the Cartel in Parliament and the fiscal crisis, all circumstances that impeded our activity. . . . The Camelots, the fascists, and others disrupted Professor Prenant's classes. Since the class was open to the public, every time we were able to attend there was relative calm, and he was able to deliver the lecture. Nevertheless, since disorder persisted, the minister provisionally suspended the course. The Camelots, confronted with unanimous disapproval by hard-working students and the increasing strength of our league, committed themselves to stopping all demonstrations. The course resumed. They had given in. If you remember the Georges Scelle affair, which began in the same way, you can recognize the progress that has been made, how far down the road we have come.

Thus, the president pointed out, LAURS was able to hold its first two national conventions, in Grenoble in 1927, and in Clermont-Ferrand in 1928, the latter including the participation of eleven provincial sections. In the course of four years, the league established by Ostoya in 1924 had become a real force, while Mendès France had established himself as a student leader of national stature, clearly oriented toward the left and already very much in favor of a Cartel-like alliance between Radicals and Socialists (in 1925, the Communists had decided to split with LAURS to form their own organization).

But LAURS was not only a movement of active resistance to the small-scale terror organized by the monarchists and the extreme right in the Latin Quarter, like the Dreyfusard commando unit created and led by

Péguy thirty years earlier for the same purposes in the same place. It also proposed to outline a political and social program, which functioned as a sort of bridge between the program of the Cartel five years before and that of the Popular Front ten years later.

At the conclusion of the Nantes convention in 1929, through its spokesman René Georges-Etienne (a very close friend of the president whose term was ending, and obviously summing up the ideas Mendès France professed at the time), the league launched the following appeal:

> It is in the name of the idea of justice that the league calls on the intellectual youth of France to support the legitimate demands of the working class. The league has recognized that the increasing malaise of our country has as its essential cause the fact that, in our modern society, the capitalist system has placed all power in the hands of the possessors of wealth, who use that power to dominate the world thanks to the support of intellectual workers. Capital can impose its will on labor because labor is divided; on the one hand, manual workers make up an enslaved mass, on the other, intellectual workers who are insufficiently enlightened are too often at the disposal of capital to command in its name.
>
> Against this regime, which is immoral and contrary to human dignity, the league calls on the students of France, who will be the industrial intellectuals of tomorrow, to join the ranks of the manual workers in order to prevent capital from abusing its power.

This clearly situates LAURS, and its outgoing president, well beyond the bounds of Radicalism, even the Radicalism of the time. This manifesto with a socialist flavor, which seems to have been inspired by Léon Blum, if not by Gramsci, raises the question of why, once his initial enthusiasm had passed, Mendès France chose to remain in the camp of Edouard Herriot, whose drift to the right was demonstrated by his more and more frequent alliances with Poincaré and the Bloc National.

This is a question to which we will have to return to on various occasions, but we might suggest for the moment that, in the eyes of the young leader of LAURS, both the structure and the ideology of the Radical Party seemed to be more flexible and open than those of the SFIO. One might argue, without being excessively paradoxical, that the old Radical Party offered him the opportunity to be more freely a socialist than he could have been in the party whose seductive inspiration was Léon Blum but whose rigid organizer was Paul Faure.

LAURS was also a community, a fraternity. It brought together young men with whom Mendès France experienced the kind of camaraderie that was unavailable to him at the Faculty of Law, where he was quickly labeled a "Red," or at Sciences Po, where his classmates were rather cold to a young Jew who was a bit too brilliant. The league in the 1920s and 1930s was a veritable nursery of talents where Mendès

France and his two successors, Marc Jacquier and René Georges-Etienne, rubbed shoulders with Georges Pompidou, Léopold Senghor, Jacques Soustelle, Maurice Papon, Robert Marjolin, Roger Ikor, Léo Hamon, and Maurice Schumann.

Pompidou, then a young socialist preparing to enter the Ecole Normale Supérieure, was an eager editorialist for *L'Université républicaine,* where he attacked the supporters of Action Française, denouncing their methods of argument, their false quotations, the "sophisms of Maurras," their foppish attitudes, and the habit they had of treating "the statesmen of the Republic like a gang of cutthroats and assassins." One can imagine how the second president of the Fifth Republic would have smiled on rereading his article of April 1, 1930, like Aristide Briand, in 1925, hearing again his arguments for a general strike at a Socialist rally in 1899.

No one had a clearer recollection of the young leader of LAURS than René Georges-Etienne, son of the closest associate of Paul Painlevé in the Republican-Socialist Party.

> Mendès France made a strong impression on me. He was intelligent, eloquent, overflowing with fervor and conviction, and his enthusiasm was catching. Once, when someone tried to interrupt a speech, he retorted: "You think I'm an opportunist? I am passionately attached to my ideas and determined to make them prevail." And that sounded right, you couldn't not believe him.

Marc Jacquier, another secretary general of LAURS, and Gaston Maurice, born the same day as Mendès France and a lifelong friend, had similar memories. All of them emphasized the young man's determination, his ability to inspire and organize, his physical courage. Perhaps this young leader, who at eighteen and nineteen encountered all sorts of opportunities and dangers, was too insistent, in too much of a hurry. He took many risks, and he loved to be right. He was called ambitious. But if he had been in such a hurry to "arrive," would he have been so implacably determined to defend a certain idea of public life, and particularly of the public finances? The profession of faith that the twenty-two-year-old student published in *L'Université républicaine* on November 15, 1929, is not of the kind that would gain him favor with the powerful men of the time. The elections that had taken place in 1928 had marked a sharp decline for the left, which was paying for the mistakes of the Cartel governments. The path to a career in that field seemed to be closed. Mendès France nevertheless spoke clearly.

His article, entitled "Les Finances de l'état démocratique" (The Finances of the Democratic State), was an early affirmation of his personality and of his conception of the state. What may now appear banal in his ideas was not banal at the time. The important thing for the moment was not to invent something new, to replace Keynes or Charles Gide, but to take his place in the debate. The young man came out on the side of those who had just lost a battle but who, in his eyes, were right.

His argument was that there are only two basic conceptions of the state's fiscal policy: that of the state as individual, based on the same principles as the management of private property, that is, on profit, the conception of the monarchist state; and that of the state "considered as the public authority responsible for a given state of society and for correcting its injustices." Arguing, of course, in favor of this latter version of the welfare state, Mendès France referred to Gaston Jèze: "Every public expenditure with a social purpose is, naturally and willingly, deficit spending." Hence, it was necessary completely to reconstruct the fiscal system on the basis of a progressive income tax. Dotting the i's, and unafraid of shocking his classical liberal professors at Sciences Po, Mendès France wrote:

> There is thus an opposition between the two broad schools of thought that come to mind when one considers the role of government finances. The first school might be characterized as that of the accountants, the second as that of modern statesmen. At the present time, we are rapidly moving toward the second state of mind. The United States is very close to it. . . . In France, we are in a transitional period. Most . . . of the great politicians who have played a role in our fiscal history, like M. Poincaré, for example, have belonged, consciously or not, to the first school. But the pressure of democratic opinion and of political leaders is pushing us toward a broader understanding of fiscal problems. Democrats have nothing to fear from such an evolution. Their principle of popular sovereignty fits very well with the idea of a tutelary state whose role is to be just and useful.

This represents the earliest version of "Mendésism." It was, of course, a crude, elementary sketch. Personal reflection, the influence of Georges Boris, his reading of Keynes, the experiences of 1938, 1944–1945, and 1954, and his conversations with Gabriel Ardant would all qualify, correct, and deepen these views. But we can say that this was an outline of the managerial morality and fiscal ethics that would provide the backdrop for a half-century of political life.

We can also read the thesis for the doctor of law degree that Mendès France wrote under the direction of William Oualid and defended on March 3, 1928, as a primitive version of Mendésism. It was received with honors, which made it possible for him to publish it under the title *La Politique Financière du gouvernement Poincaré* (The Fiscal Policy of the Poincaré Government). The choice of subject might appear surprising on the part of a man who saw the former president of the Republic, as the article just quoted indicates, as the principal adversary of the kind of economic management he championed. But this is precisely a typical example of Mendès's approach: to consider reality, lived experience, however recalcitrant, rather than what is imagined or desired.

In 1927, more than ideas or doctrines, two practical experiences dominated the debate over economics: the failure of the Cartel des Gauches in 1926; and the currency stabilization carried out thereafter by the Poincaré government. Rather than devoting himself to a study of the reasons for his friends' defeat, Mendès chose to investigate the reasons for the success of their adversaries. Moreover, he admired Poincaré and never entirely ceased to admire him.

In the preface to the book, his new colleague as a lawyer, Georges Bonnet, who was already one of the oracles of the Radical Party, wrote: "M. Pierre Mendès France is not yet a deputy. Therefore, his testimony is impartial." A bizarre formulation. In any event, the "not yet" was encouraging, coming from one of the men who were making careers in Herriot's party. "The author," Bonnet continued, "was a student at the University of Paris a few short months ago. At an age when passions are vigorous and fervent, he has written a study full of intelligence, thoughtfulness, and calm."

However concerned with objectivity he may have been, Mendès France demonstrated his loyalty to the leader of the Radicals by recalling that the panic that swept away the second Herriot government was organized by stock market speculators against the recovery that was beginning to take place under foreign stimulation. Having made this historical point, the young economist drew up a catalogue of the measures taken in 1926 by Raymond Poincaré, who had "admirably carried out the program he had outlined and, all things considered, had derived the maximum possible benefit from it," by consolidating the floating debt and stabilizing the currency, although he had not done it "at the current rate, and immediately," which was necessary. But Mendès France recognized that the technical operation had been "admirably" executed, with a "dexterity" and "ingenuity" that were to assure its success.

The author was thereafter all the freer to explain the real nature of this fiscal strategy, which, instead of placing the burden of a crushing debt on "those for whom the years of upheaval were often years of profit, struck the most disfavored, the most significant, the most productive classes, who had been crushed." And Mendès France, at the end of a very detailed analysis, supported by figures, statistics, and authorities, concluded by locating the debate in the social history of the country.

> Such a conception cannot meet with our approval. Beneath the cold numbers are hidden living realities. While he set out columns of figures and his experts were looking for yet more taxes to increase, M. Poincaré, if he had listened, could have heard the heartbeat of the real life of the country that he was crushing; he saw neither poverty, nor unemployment, nor bankruptcy. Once

again, our politically democratic Republic was not economically equitable. M. Poincaré's technical precision and his very success cannot make us forget the injustices that were committed or increased. . . . We must therefore reformulate the program that will finally bring into being in the economic realm the truly equal and social Republic.

This socialization of the Republic was the sequel that Jaurès wished to give to the French Revolution.

The comments of his professors on this harsh philippic against the "taboo" leader who had, in the course of ten years, presided over the reconquest of Alsace and the restoration of the franc, have not been preserved. The ordinary "honors" given to a work in a class apart from the laborious productions of doctors of law, so often given "high honors," reveals that some members of the jury were shocked. The young Mendès France was all the more pleased to receive the following letter, dated March 15, 1928:

My dear colleague:[9]

I would like to thank you for the interesting work you were kind enough to send me. I have reservations about a certain number of your analyses, particularly about your failure to distinguish between the consequences of inflation or depreciation of the currency and what you claim to be the economic effects of the remedies that were applied. Similarly, in your article of this morning,[10] you make an inaccurate distinction between bank loans under this legislature and the preceding one, by placing June 1924 in the legislature elected in 1919. But apart from a few corrections of this kind, I see no serious imperfections in the work you have accomplished.

Cordially,
Poincaré

Pierre Mendès France did not always encounter the same understanding among his interlocutors, even members of his own party. There is no doubt that the respect he always demonstrated for the former president of the Republic was strengthened by this courteous reception of his substantive criticisms; Poincaré, the head of government, offered only purely formal opposition.

But the very young Mendès did not have to content himself with this sign of understanding from the principal personage of French public life, who came close to treating him as an equal. In the ensuing days, private correspondence and the press demonstrated extraordinarily favorable interest in him. What young doctor of law, who had barely reached his majority, had ever been able to read such enthusiastic letters from such diverse quarters about a first publication? One day, there was a letter from Herriot, who already knew him fairly well; another, from André Tardieu, leader of the "modern" parliamentary right; then, from Philippe Berthelot, oracle of the Foreign Office, a close associate of Briand; or again, from Anatole de Monzie, the most scintillating wit in Parliament, or from Georges Valois, union leader and economist who fluctuated between extreme left and extreme right with equal verve.

And what a press! Not to mention what was written in Paris, Toulouse, or Bordeaux about the young critic of Poincaré, there were press clippings from Germany, Switzerland, Italy, Spain. Few first books have evoked such interest, and even fewer theses. The young Mendès needed all his coolness in order not to lose his head.

Rather than taking himself for Turgot, Mendès France very quickly set to work on a second book. It allowed him to get through the boredom of military service, for which he had received a student deferment at the end of 1927. In his first book, he had approached the problems of national finances and the social aspects of economics, thereby setting out the principles of a very "progressive" hierarchy descending from social, through economic, to fiscal considerations, with the latter reduced to the role of a means. He now took up the question of international settlements, inseparable from the peace that was the principal objective of the left within which he had taken his place.

In May 1930, the Bibliothèque Economique Universelle published his second book, *La Banque internationale* (The International Bank).[11] His publisher was Georges Valois, later a precursor of French fascism, then a resistance fighter who died in the camps, who was at the time concerned with establishing an economic system based on syndicalism. The book's subtitle was "Contribution à l'étude du problème des Etats-Unis d'Europe" (Contribution to the Study of the Problem of a United States of Europe). And it was not merely an intellectual exercise designed to perfect his skills and demonstrate his competence. It was also a manifesto designed to foster his internationalist views and to express the distrust he felt toward triumphant capitalism.

In the very first pages of the book, in a very dense and vigorous manner, Mendès France proclaimed a credo consisting of two elements:

> 1. The principal means of action in the modern world are economic and financial, and are thereby beyond the scope of the archaic framework of individualistic law and old-fashioned politics, both of which must be renewed; 2. Effective solutions to present practical difficulties are international in scope. Since the essential problems have all become international, the organisms needed to solve them must also be international.

This was a rather bold and decisive argument for a Radical lawyer of twenty-three: giving absolute priority to the economy, claiming that individualist law was archaic, and asserting that internationalism was neces-

sary. And he even challenged his recent mentor Poincaré, criticizing him
for being "bitterly" opposed to the creation of the Bank for International
Settlements, although he later joined it. Plainly, both as leader of LAURS
and as a young lawyer under the tutelage of Georges Bonnet, Mendès was
far from timid.

The political ambitions of the young Mendès were clearly not limited
to the conquest of a provincial parliamentary seat.

> In my opinion, it is through the soonest possible adoption of a European
> customs union, the convergence of the diverse Western legal systems, in
> short, the United States of Europe, that we can find effective remedies that
> will calm the anxieties of democrats and pacifists. We must create a new
> Europe, rationalized, organized, and harmonized, so that there may be a
> necessary counterweight to the Bank for International Settlements. If this
> comes to pass, then the bank will become what it logically should be, an
> organism among others, dedicated to the improvement and restoration of
> Europe.

In the course of his argument, with a certain degree of boldness,
Mendès France attacked the international practice of entrusting the defense of the public interest to the representatives of large private interests. In the case of France, he pointed to presidents of banks, mining
companies, and arms manufacturing companies who had been chosen
over representatives of state administrative bodies, whose conception of
the "general interest" appeared to be "more impartial." And he mentioned, as an archetype of these "new men," a certain Dr. Schacht who,
before putting his financial genius at the service of the Nazis, embodied
this multinational banking power.

For the young Mendès, the Bank for International Settlements was
not a conclusion but a point of departure, the "first stone in a structure
that remains to be built," that should daily remind the "citizens of Europe
of their duty to foster reconstruction and unification." For—and this reasoning is symptomatic of Mendès's deeply reformist opposition to revolution—"the race between the two internationals will be heated. We all
know the lead that one of them has taken. There is thus no time to lose."
A Europe already along the lines laid out by Jean Monnet, innovative, run
by experts, reformist, anti-Leninist, allied with the United States, a
Europe of civil servants devoted to "the public interest," this seems to
have been the grand design of the young Radical economist in 1930.

The conclusion has a certain verve:

> Chateaubriand somewhere sums up the history of the nobility by saying that
> it had moved from the age of service to the age of privilege and from the age
> of privilege to the age of vanity. The world of finance, which never should

have left the age of service, is far from ready to be satisfied with vanity. Will democrats and the builders of the modern world allow it to confine itself to the age of privilege?

Mendès's second book received as warm a welcome as the first. The Radical Party's principal expert on financial matters, Joseph Caillaux, who was not known for easy praise, sent him cordial congratulations. His former professor Germain-Martin, who was very influential in this area in the Chamber, offered encouragement. Vincent Auriol, chairman of the Finance Committee of the Chamber of Deputies, praised him warmly for having attempted "to organize finance in a disorganized world." He received similar praise from the young experts Vallon and Quesnay. And the press was superb. At twenty-three, he had all that he could wish for.

At the time he published this internationalist manifesto, Mendès France had been drafted as a corporal and was stationed in Villacoublay, in the "first group of aeronautical workers." When his book appeared, he asked his commanding officer for a leave to "meet [his] publisher," which led him to be taken for an "artist," a very bad image for the barracks. He was nevertheless pleased with his choice of the air force. He had studied the new science of meteorology, and this allowed him to become a very good navigational specialist.

But Minister of the Air Force Laurent-Eynac, a Radical notable, realizing that he had a very gifted young man under his command, appointed him to his staff. Mendès accepted the appointment. Although he could hardly reject so many intellectual and material advantages at the outset of a public career, he nevertheless felt some nostalgia for the world of fliers. He therefore spent several periods in uniform in the early 1930s with a view to becoming an officer. He was appointed second lieutenant in the air force in November 1933, a few months after he had been elected deputy and been automatically transferred to the medical corps, a transfer against which he lodged a violent protest with the minister of war: he did not want to be removed from the air force.

Oddly enough, it was his military training that led him to Freemasonry and the Grand-Orient de France.

> I joined the Freemasons in the late 1920s. Many of my friends were Masons and encouraged me to join them. My father, who had been a member when he was younger, advised against it. Basically, I wasn't very interested. The time came for my military service. There was talk of an assignment to Morocco. I was told that the Freemasons were very influential there, that I was in danger of feeling isolated, and that my membership would provide me with a number of contacts while I was stationed there. So, why not? I joined up. Then I happened to fall ill, with jaundice, which precluded an assignment to a warm country. I didn't do my service in Morocco, but I remained a Mason, but not an active participant.

After the war, I decided that politicians, myself included, were too scattered, belonged to too many associations or groups. In any event, I decided that, as far as I was concerned, I had to put a little order in my life by concentrating on the essential. Thus, I did not rejoin the Masons. Many of my colleagues thought that this was because of a basic disagreement and held it against me. In fact, there was simply a lack of attraction.

There has been much talk of Masonic influence in political life, particularly in the Radical Party. I didn't notice any, either at the time or afterward, either in the form of offers of assistance or in that of obstacles placed in my path. The political career of Chautemps may have been connected to his rank in the Masons, but he was too talented a man to owe his success to some occult influence. *Gringoire* asserted, to ridicule him and perhaps to frighten its readers, that Chautemps held the title of "Sublime Prince of the Royal Secret." That was overdoing it. One day, Jean Zay, himself a Mason, asked him if it was true. Chautemps denied it. Surprised, Zay asked: "Why don't you publish a correction?" "Because my real title is even more ridiculous," sighed Chautemps. "I am 'Knight Cadoche.'"

Basically, it was a mistake, a misunderstanding. I ought not to have joined. Once I had, I should have continued to pay my dues, even though I didn't attend meetings.

Beginning on October 21, 1926, Pierre Mendès France was a "trainee" lawyer in the Paris court. "The youngest lawyer in France" (he was nineteen), he had joined the office of Georges Bonnet, Radical deputy from Dordogne, who had a few months earlier been minister of the budget and was already considered a star of Herriot's party, along with his contemporaries and colleagues César Campinchi and Pierre Cot. Georges Bonnet was not only one of the sharpest minds of the Paris bar, an astute litigator, and a hard worker; he was also one of the few French politicians interested in economic questions. And although he was to achieve his greatest notoriety at the head of the French diplomatic corps, as the moving force behind and negotiator of the Munich agreements, along with Edouard Daladier, he was influential among the Radicals as a specialist in finance.

We have already mentioned the warm preface he agreed to write for Mendès France's first book. But Mendès France had no clear memories either of his collaboration with this brilliant leader when he was head of LAURS or of his activities in the Paris bar. It is clear that his professional activity as a lawyer did not fill him with enthusiasm. And none of his colleagues in the bar—Jacquier, Gaston Maurice, Georges-Etienne, Edgar Faure—remembered his activities during this period.

It was not that he was not gifted for the profession. He was too successful a parliamentary debater for us to doubt his capacity to captivate and convince a judge or a jury, in his sober and logical style. The fact is that in Paris in any case, for the three years that he was a member of the bar, he was not a striking lawyer—because he did not find an appropriate case that would have unleashed his capacity to work and his argumentative energies. What Mendès France seemed especially to remember from his experience as a Parisian lawyer was that the profession at the time did not pay the bills. Still unmarried, and sharing an apartment on rue de la Pompe with his parents (his office was in the apartment), he had no great needs. But he later recalled that "the living conditions of a young lawyer in Paris in the late 1920s were much harder than the young people of today can imagine." An old quarrel.

He had so little money that he resorted to typical family subterfuges. When his mother gave him a car and asked him to teach her to drive, he always arranged for the lessons to come when it was time to fill the gas tank. As soon as Mme. Mendès France had paid for the gas, he would remember an urgent professional engagement at some distance. His sister and his father were very amused: A lawyer, a political figure, a young man, moves around a lot—from *L'Université républicaine* to his lady friends, from the Radical Party to Bonnet's office and the Palace of Justice.

When he left Georges Bonnet, after having done useful work with him and having carried on fruitful debates on French and European economic questions, it was not for political reasons. It was later, after 1936, when Georges Bonnet took positions against the Popular Front, and especially after 1938, when he was one of the protagonists of the Munich policy, that they came into conflict. But by the end of 1928 the young lawyer was thinking of leaving Paris and was looking for an opportunity in the provinces to exercise his profession on a larger scale. Perhaps he was already seeking, more or less unconsciously, to find a local foundation for the political activity which, since he had proved himself at the head of LAURS, had seemed to be his real profession.

He would be neither lawyer nor teacher. His deepest vocation was public service.

3.
A TWENTY-FIVE-YEAR-OLD DEPUTY

Louviers? I came there almost by chance. A party always needs militants to spread the word in the provinces, especially at election time: there is always a shortage of speakers. In 1928, I was sent to speak in Pont-Audemer, a district town in the department of Eure, where I had never set foot.[1] I conducted an ordinary meeting to support our candidate, a very sympathetic and very capable man named Nicolas Leloup. He didn't have a chance, but he was worth supporting. Everything went well. In the course of a verbal duel with the sitting deputy, Henri Le Mire, a large industrialist and an influential man in the Chamber, I scored some points against this local notable. The Radical militants were delighted to see me embarrass the most important conservative in the district. That is why they called on me in similar circumstances. That was how I became connected with the Radical groups of Eure, as a militant, without thinking of anything else.

More or less taking charge of liaison between them and party headquarters in Paris, I found myself a little later in contact with the militants of Louviers, in the eastern part of the department. This constituency had the reputation of being very "right-wing," and no Radical had any chance of being elected there. But they decided that, the more arduous the task, the more self-sacrifice was required, and that they should set to work all the sooner. They asked me to commit myself, not concealing that there was no hope of winning at the next legislative elections in 1932. Failure was so probable that local candidates could be easily discouraged and my nomination assured.

I was still hesitating to throw myself into the adventure when an event concerning my profession changed everything. In 1926, as an economy measure, Poincaré had abolished the court of Louviers, which was one of the smallest in France, employing only three lawyers. The local deputy had naturally attempted, for electoral reasons, to have it restored. He succeeded after the court had been dormant for three years. In the meanwhile, one of the three lawyers had left for the district town, Evreux; the second had died; the third was struggling along by doing consultations. The restoration of the court provided an opportunity for at least one lawyer. Professionally, the idea of moving to Louviers was justified, even though it seemed politically hopeless.

I didn't find it unpleasant to work in the provinces, in a town only about a hundred kilometers from Paris, so that I could frequently come to see my family and friends. The life of a young Parisian lawyer like me was too hard, my future too limited. So I finally took the leap and moved to Louviers late in 1929. To general amazement: when a Parisian buries himself in some provincial backwater, Parisians take him for a lunatic, or for a desperate man. My father, for whom there was no life, no truth, no reality outside Paris, thought that I had an unhappy love affair to forget about.

So, I settled in Louviers, on rue Tatin, across from the church. And only then did I discover rural life, since many of my clients were peasants or small farmers. It was an exciting discovery, and I owe a great deal to it. I was well received, and professionally I had some victories, some satisfactions, a solid success. And then I worked for the party, if only to satisfy the expectations of my Radical friends in the department, who were the origin of the reorientation of my life. I held meetings, I wrote articles, I drew up programs, I had plenty of time: I wasn't even eligible yet, and I wouldn't be until early 1932. If the date of the election had been moved up, as had been rumored, I would have been kept out.

This Parisian intellectual, who had barely left the university, at the top of his class, author of two books (only one had been published, the second was in press), national leader of a very active student movement, militant of a socialist-leaning and internationalist left, already seen as one of the hopes of the largest political party in France, was suddenly transplanted to a provincial backwater in Normandy and fated to become, at first before the court and later in the Chamber, the defender of the apple pickers and the good market ladies of Louviers, in one of the most conservative constituencies in the country.

The department of Eure was not condemned, either because of its socioeconomic structures or its history, to send only dukes or retired colonels to Parliament. Some of its representatives had played a very active role in the Revolution, like the Girondin leader Buzot and the deputy to the Convention Robert Lindet, director of supplies for the

Committee of Public Safety. In 1848, Dupont de l'Eure had led the provisional government. And since then the moderate left had not been without spokesmen, from Arsène Meunier to Modeste Leroy—one of the department's great men until his retirement in 1928, after a half-century of struggle for popular and secularized education. The department even had two Radical leaders: one moderate, Dr. Briquet of Pacy-sur-Eure; the other more combative, Maître Chauvin of Evreux.

But in this world without sharp edges and made up of diverse elements, Louviers was located at the moderate end of the spectrum. The clothing industry was very influential, with its newspaper, *L'Industriel de Louviers,* and its deputy, Alexandre Duval, just as Pont-Audemer had its own in Henri Le Mire. The proportion of the proletariat in the urban area was very small (three hundred out of six thousand inhabitants when Mendès arrived) and the countryside ill prepared to bring its demands, pressing as they might be, onto the political stage.

In a pamphlet he published in 1933, *Le Département de l'Eure du point de vue économique* (The Department of Eure from an Economic Standpoint), Pierre Mendès France pointed out that with a population of only fifty inhabitants per square kilometer (the national average was seventy-two), the region was three-quarters rural (half the land was in grain, with good harvests), but entirely dominated by the power of the millers. Thus, the marketing of grain was of decisive importance, particularly the price of wheat. This was the theme of the two campaigns of 1932 and 1936.

The left was not completely without support in the press. Several papers supported it or were open to it. Although *La Vallée de l'Eure* was in decline, *Le Journal du Neubourg* (an agricultural region around the plateau of the same name) was openly Radical, and *La Dépêche normande* (which had a Louviers edition), directed by Armand Mandle (later an associate of Mendès France and elected mayor of Evreux in 1951), often supported secular candidates.

The church had never played a primary role in political debate in Normandy. In the thesis already cited, M. Rossignol asserts that Bishop Gaudron of Evreux was on very good terms with Action Française and therefore hostile to Mendès France. Mendès France disputed this and maintained that he always had excellent relations with the bishop. We might note in passing that this does not mean that a man of the cloth is any less capable than any other of stabbing one in the back.

As for the political personnel of the department, it included, apart from a cohort of conservative deputies: Join-Lambert, Le Mire, Alexandre Duval; the two Radicals already mentioned: Dr. Briquet and Maître Chauvin; a "republican," Forcinal, who was admired for his heroic behavior during the war and who became a friend to Mendès France. We should also note that, until his death in 1931, Aristide Briand, retired on his property of Cocherel, was not entirely absent from the region's political landscape.

There is no better means than the press to make oneself known to the voters of a constituency. Mendès France chose to address his new fellow citizens with short sarcastic notes published by *La Dépêche* and *Le Journal du Neubourg,* which he ironically titled at first "Chroniques de la prospérité" (Chronicles of Prosperity), and later, more pointedly, "A la recherche de la vie chère" (In Search of the High Cost of Living). In this work as a journalist, he came into contact with a colleague in Evreux, Maître Jean Labéda, and they later formed a team, Labéda dealing with foreign affairs and Mendès France working primarily on economic questions. The pair functioned for many years, well enough so that articles by Labéda on Hitler or Spain might be attributed to Mendès France. The same state of mind produced attacks on price increases and attacks on the crimes of Nazism.

Gradually, the proposition of Mendès's candidacy in Louviers took shape. In 1931, Herriot appeared at his side, flanked by Dr. Briquet, who was to be elected president of the General Council of Eure, thereby consolidating Radical positions as a whole in the department. And on January 31, 1932, the patriarch of Radicalism, Théodore Steeg, came to Evreux to present the party's legislative candidates for the election whose date had just been set for May 1, 1932. In Louviers, Mendès France was indeed named to oppose Alexandre Duval, who had been elected in the first round in 1928. The right-wing press reacted with a sneer.

> Herriot, Steeg, Viollette[2] have come to assure the voters that everything would be for the best if they were to choose whom as a deputy? A very young man, who is barely twenty-five, who two months ago joined the bar in Louviers,[3] where he and his family were totally unknown eighteen months ago and are still too little known today.[4]

The young man conducted a vigorous campaign and continued to receive significant Parisian support. Thus, when former Minister of Finance Maurice Palmade came to lend a hand, he stigmatized the economic management of the right-wing governments led by Tardieu or Laval that alternated with one another at the time and called for a reduction of military expenditures and more widespread tax reductions. His adversary Alexandre Duval, although backed up by a reputable financial expert, Lasteyrie, was outclassed in public debates. One of them, on April 20, 1932, turned openly hostile. Duval failed to appear, and the furious audience came to blows and then laid seige to the offices of *L'Industriel de Louviers,* where he had barricaded himself. This comic battle has left its traces in local history.

The press supporting the sitting deputy took its revenge, in its way. It denounced in Mendès France the "envoy of Israel" and the "millers' man." These attacks—especially the first one—rebounded against their authors, or so it is said today in Louviers. Pressed to answer these attacks by Armand Mandle, who had warmly introduced him to the readers of *La Dépêche,* Mendès France merely wrote a "letter to his friends," in which he asserted: "I will fight only on the level of ideas."

The Radical candidate's statement of principles did not provide anything very new. It defined him as "attached to the principle of private property [which] must be respected by great societies . . . faithful in that respect to the doctrine of the French Revolution, attached also to secularism [which implies that] the state must respect all beliefs and remain neutral."

But the general tone of his campaign, especially when it dealt with the social consequences of the high cost of living, was much livelier than these few generalities. In fact, handicapped as he was by the label of Parisian "outsider," one of the arguments he used made a strong impression: "Win or lose, I am committed to staying." It was a statement he repeated every day.

The electoral campaign took place in an atmosphere of acute crisis. There was first the economic crisis, consequence of the crisis troubling the economy of the West since 1929. It had affected French production as a whole, which had decreased by nearly 25 percent between 1930 and 1932, while many businesses had been forced to close their doors—there were nine thousand bankruptcies in 1932. There was an agricultural crisis, epitomized by overproduction of wine and wheat (harvests increased by 25 percent and 20 percent, respectively, in 1931) that provoked drastic drops in prices on a national scale. Farmers suffered all the more from this decline because the prices of industrial products had decreased by only 15 percent, while their prices had fallen by 30 percent. There was a financial crisis as well. Several banks failed at the beginning of the decade (the Union Parisienne et Nationale du Crédit, for example), and not always for scandalous reasons, while the national budget in 1931, for the first time since the Poincaré government, registered a deficit of five billion francs.

There was also, perhaps most serious of all, a social crisis. Between 1929 and 1932, average income had decreased by 8 percent for the liberal professions, 20 percent in the service sector, 30 percent in retail commerce. As for unemployment, it affected three times as many workers (around 450,000 in 1932) as in 1929. There was a political crisis, which took the form of an exacerbation of ministerial instability (although the mechanical alternation of Laval and Tardieu governments hardly changed the political line of the very conservative majority of 1928) and of profound dissension between Radicals and Socialists, enflamed by Herriot.

There was finally an international crisis. The brutal rise of Hitler in Germany had been manifested by the Nazi success in the 1932 elections: 36 percent of the electorate, thirteen million votes. The seizure of power had not yet taken place, but the danger had become clear. And everything was therefore different.

It was in this bitter and anxious climate that France voted on May 1, 1932. That night in Louviers, the district election officials announced the following figures:

Registered	13,937
Voting	12,287
Duval	5,973
Mendès France	5,834
Haccart (independent socialist)	17
Vimard (Communist)	476

The Radical candidate immediately composed a short article entitled, "In the bag or in the drink?," demonstrating a reasonable and not presumptuous hope. A gap of fewer than 140 votes could be closed, provided the abstentionists woke up, since the Communists were still involved in the suicidal strategy of "class against class."

In the second round, Pierre Mendès France received 6,347 votes, 500 more than in the first, against 6,108 for Duval, and 106 for the Communist candidate. The 370 votes lost by this candidate formed the basis for a legend propagated by a certain "Civicus," who wrote a pathetic pamphlet entitled *Monsieur Mendès France et les communistes*—(Mr. Mendès France and the Communists), according to which Mendès France had always been Stalinism's man; one of the proofs of this was the fact that the leadership of the Communist Party, while having their candidate run in the second round, had "secretly" ordered Louviers Party members to vote for Mendès France, in 1932, at a time when their national platform forbade such transfers of votes. The argument is grotesque. A careful analysis of the voting on May 8, in Louviers and elsewhere, reveals that the majority of the second round, when those who abstained in the first round determined the outcome, contained as few Communist votes in Eure as in Narbonne or Bordeaux, where Léon Blum and Adrien Marquet were elected. And they were hardly in league with the Communists.

Pierre Mendès France was a deputy. What had been unimaginable three months earlier had taken place. A sacrificial candidate, meant to bear witness and to propagate ideas, he found himself, at a little over twenty-five, the youngest deputy in France, victor over a local boss, having won by the vigor of his critical arguments, the force of his ideas, and his inner conviction, the strange credibility commanded by everything he said. Deputy from Eure.

In an interview in *La République* the next day, the young representative declared that his unexpected success was due to a "clearer understanding by the voters of the economic world revealed by the crisis." This "understanding" had been helped by his campaign organized around the theme as well as by the incisive articles published in *La Dépêche*. The crisis had hit harshly the modest people of lower Normandy, who had until then been little affected by large electoral movements. Now, like the nation as a whole, they had moved sharply to the left.

We tend to forget the strength of this shift because of our preoccupation with the two symbolic dates of the Cartel (1924) and the Popular Front (1936). But it was perhaps in 1932 that the French electorate, always so stable, shifted the most decisively: the Union of the Left received a half-million more votes than in 1928 (4,900,000 against 3,850,000 for the right led by Tardieu) and controlled the Chamber with 305 seats to 250 for the right. A Popular Front was then possible, based on the Socialists' "Huyghens" program, which called for a forty-hour week as well as nationalization of the arms and insurance industries. One year before Hitler's rise to power, such an orientation could have changed many things. Neither Herriot, who was then going through his most pusillanimous period, nor the Communists, still locked into their ghetto by a sectarian strategy, would hear of it. And this impressive popular success led into a pitiful period of collaboration by the victorious Radicals, arbiters of the situation, with the forces of the right who had been beaten on May 8, 1932, embodied in Tardieu and Laval.

It is thus tempting to say that Mendès France's appearance on the political stage was ill timed. He had been elected on a powerful wave of popular support, but that was contradicted by a Radical leadership that rejected an alliance on the left and got tied up in a politics of "concentration" with a bloc of "moderates" who were openly reactionary. This attitude of the Radical leaders shocked him all the more because it was that of the two men who apparently exercised the strongest moral and professional influence over him: Edouard Herriot and Georges Bonnet, his former "boss" as a Parisian lawyer. It was a paradoxical situation which strengthened the young man's tendency to accept nothing with his eyes closed, to refuse to bind himself totally to the leadership of a party or to any individual leader at all. Bitter as it may have been, the experience was not lost. And however disappointing it may have been at the time, he remained attached to his party because of the function it allowed him and a few friends—Pierre Cot, reelected in Savoie; Jean Zay, newly elected in Orléans; Jacques Kayser; Gaston Bergery—to campaign openly against the line of Herriot's leadership.

He did not entirely bid farewell to adolescence. At twenty-five, the deputy from Louviers remained in part the sarcastic young man of the

1920s. At the beginning of the electoral campaign, he persuaded his mother that, in case he was elected, she should prepare a speech of thanks for the voters of Louviers and deliver it at the conclusion of a banquet that would be organized by his campaign committee. The prospect was highly improbable. Palmyre Mendès France took the idea seriously. She believed in her son's chances and wrote her little speech. May 8 came, with its success and the banquet, and she was there with her little speech in her pocket. There are two versions of what happened. According to Pierre's sister Marcelle, their mother indeed stood up and, despite an attempt by the new deputy, embarrassed to see his joke go so far, delivered her speech and achieved a resounding success. Pierre maintained that he cut maternal eloquence short, later offering tender apologies to the victim of his joke.[5]

In the Palais-Bourbon, this smooth-faced adolescent at first felt lost in the midst of the bushy beards that decorated the members of the Radical party. So he let his mustache grow, and he was seen with a fine tuft of black hair on his upper lip in an effort to be taken seriously. The first friend he made in Parliament, Jean Zay, had no need for this artifice—he was three years older.

One might think that he would try to make his mark very soon, compensating for the handicap of his youth with his social skill and his eloquence. After all, five years of activity as a militant, his presidency of LAURS, and a masterfully conducted electoral campaign could have emboldened him. But he did not. As he confided later: "At the time, a young deputy walked on tiptoe and was not supposed to be noticed. He was what the English call a backbencher, far removed from the podium. I was like a student."

He thus sat silently on the left for seven months. But he had received a mandate, from the nation in general and the farmers of Normandy in particular. He broke his silence on December 27, 1932, happy that the Chamber was almost empty that night. "The ordeal was thus less trying. I felt surer of myself in front of those empty benches."

It was not Saint-Just's first speech to the Convention, or Jaurès's first intervention before the Assembly. Whatever tone the maiden speaker of twenty-five may have used, what he had to say was certainly useful for the peasants of the Neubourg and even for French peasants in general. But it was not of a nature that would excite our passionate interest today. The subject was a reform of agricultural credit. In any event, the new Radical deputy adopted an acerbic tone to denounce the pitiful character of the credits proposed by the government of Paul-Boncour (who had just succeeded Herriot) for the restoration of agriculture, and especially to attack the attitude of the banks.

It is not without a certain bitterness that I recall here the triumphant communiqués in which M. Tardieu, then minister of agriculture, told us that the question of agricultural credit was settled, that he had finally obtained from the Banque de France the generosity it had always refused to show.

I remember that a well-disposed commentator on M. Tardieu's work said at the time that, since 1789, there had been no reform more important for the peasantry of France. Today we can evaluate the character of that immense reform which was so loudly called to your attention. The problem remains completely unsolved. The Banque de France, despite the often expressed will of the Chamber, in June 1928 and again last month, remains hostile to the extension of credit that we asked from it and that we ask for again.

I beg the government to reconsider this problem and, if appropriate, by proposing the necessary bills, to demand that the Banque de France take the steps that it cannot refuse in the interest of French agriculture as a whole.

Stimulated by applause, Mendès France emphasized the unequal and absurd character of the reform.

You make loans to men who are among those best able to defend themselves. You extend credit to them because they are solid and can wait. But you offer none to those in immediate need, who are threatened with foreclosure, eviction, and ruin. . . . Some large landowners have thus obtained advances at reduced rates and, thanks to these funds, have carried on operations that have only the most distant connection to agriculture.

Finally, the deputy from Louviers, going beyond these criticisms, called on the minister in charge to offer farmers required to stockpile a significant portion of their harvest "an insurance policy against a fall in prices," a proposal that had been rejected by the government but was nevertheless serious and was later to be confirmed. According to the *Journal officiel,* as he stepped down from the podium, Mendès France was "applauded on the left and from various benches." (This notation suggests, from his very first appearance in Parliament, the foundations of "Mendésism.")

In any event, interrupted several times by the minister of agriculture and two of his colleagues, the backbencher of twenty-five had retorted adroitly and courteously, proving that he could go beyond his notes and deal with counter-arguments. He had passed his initial test.

The "youngest deputy of France" had from the outset given the measure of his personality. He had also declared his position for those who, unaware of the tone of the LAURS manifesto, might have doubted his commitment to the left. "I was always very attached to Herriot. But he was making more and more concessions to the right, taking positions that often disappointed me. That was why I became a Young Turk."

They were first called the "young leftists." And they were indeed young, since their first leader, Jacques Kayser—journalist and historian and nephew of Captain Dreyfus, about whom he wrote an excellent book—had been admitted to the ruling circles of the party in 1923, when he was not even thirty, provoking the exclusion of one of the "right-wing" leaders, Albert Sarraut. Then they were called "young Radicals" during the crisis of the Cartel des Gauches in 1925 and 1926. Particularly in 1927, on the occasion of the arrival of "their man," Edouard Daladier, at the head of the party, they were nicknamed the "Young Turks," to indicate their wish for reform and change, first of all within the Radical movement.[6] In the great debate going on permanently in the Party between the partisans of the Cartel (alliance on the left, with the Socialists) and the supporters of "concentration" (cooperation with the right, which was long known as the Bloc National), they were clearly in favor of the Cartel. They revived the old cry, "No enemies on the left!" that Herriot, then leader of the Cartel, had inherited from the great predecessors, the crusaders for secularism: Camille Pelletan, Ferdinand Buisson, and Emile Combes.

In the early 1930s, the Radical Republican and Radical-Socialist Party contained five factions, not including smaller tendencies. There was first a right wing that almost dared to speak its name, consisting of deputies like Marchandeau, Lamoureaux, and William Bertrand, Radicals for practical reasons, because it was par excellence the "party of government." On the center-right there were men like Camille Chautemps and Albert Sarraut, soon joined by Georges Bonnet, while Joseph Caillaux, former leader of the party, with the help of his age, gave their prudence his approval; they were pacifists, and vigorously anti-Communist (Sarraut originated the formula, "Communism, that's the enemy!"), and some of them were later in favor of negotiating with Mussolini first, then with Franco, and even with Hitler.

In the center—which was firmly secularist, socially moderate, and simultaneously patriotic and pacifist—was enthroned Edouard Herriot, surrounded by perennial candidates for ministries like Henri Queuille. The center-left was Jacobin; its leader was Edouard Daladier, accompanied by Yvon Delbos, Théodore Steeg, César Campinchi, and Marc Rucart. Finally, the left was made up of two tendencies: one, ideologically intransigent, including Gabriel Cudenet (who went so far as to break with the party in 1937), along with Jammy-Schmidt and Albert Bayet, uncompromising secularists; and the "Young Turks," not all of whom were politically "advanced." They included men like François de Tessan, Emile Roche, and especially Léon Martinaud-Déplat (whose behavior in the 1930s should not be judged in the light of his colonialist attitude in the 1950s), associated with the Young Turks for reasons that had more to do with the desire to modernize the party and political procedures than with a progressive ideology.

The hard core of the Young Turks was made up, in historical order, of Jacques Kayser (who was in effect the group's ideologue), Pierre Cot and Gaston Bergery, its two "stars," and then Jean Zay, Gaston Monnerville, and Pierre Mendès France. One of the sharpest observers of French political society at the time, Alexander Werth, asserts, "The Young Turks were neither a movement, nor an organization, nor even an ideology, at most a state of mind . . . the desire for a renewal of the party, for a reorganization of France. They were finally in revolt against the old guard, against what is now known as immobilism."[7]

Werth suggests that "the Young Turks were first heard of" at the Angers congress in 1928. Pierre Cot suggested a much earlier date, in the early 1920s. What is clear is that the name was used particularly between 1928 and 1934, when the group launched its most visible approach to the general public, "Adresse des jeunes radicaux au pays républicain." On the eve of the Radical congress of Clermont-Ferrand, Pierre Cot and his friends Jean Zay and Pierre Mendès France, joined for the occasion by a representative of a neighboring tendency, César Campinchi, denounced the fascist threat and violently attacked the Doumergue government, which had come out of the riots of February 6, 1934. But the group was already dissolving: one of its most prestigious leaders, Gaston Bergery, had established the seductive and ambiguous "common front";[8] while a former associate, Bertrand de Jouvenel, drifted temporarily toward the fascism in which another companion of the group, Jean Luchaire, permanently lost himself.

The Young Turks had their moment of glory at the Toulouse congress in November 1932. Led by Pierre Cot and Gaston Bergery, they confronted the party leaders whom the electoral triumph of June had recently returned to power, both in the realm of foreign policy and in the area of economic and financial policy. Gaston Bergery led the attack on the diplomatic orientation of the Herriot government, which had been in office since June 3. The future leader of the "common front," thin and tense, called on the imposing M. Herriot to implement fully the policy of disarmament, and he incidentially obtained significant concessions from the "patriot" wing of the party, resigned to "psychological and material disarmament under the effective control of the League of Nations," which helped lead to the elimination of the government a month later.

It fell to Mendès France to deliver the Young Turks' economic indictment. There on the platform of the Parc des Expositions of Toulouse was the dark-haired twenty-five year old, elected deputy a few months earlier, solid, his hair slick, his complexion even paler than usual. He was addressing the congress of his party, in the presence of Herriot, Daladier,

Delbos, and Steeg, to indict most of these men, whom he admired, beginning with the head of government.

To be sure, the Herriot government had not aligned itself with the deflationist and monetarist strategy of the experts of the right, like Poincaré or Chéron. But its economic policy remained based on the fear of deficits and the obstinate pursuit of a rigorusly balanced budget. It was these imperatives that the young deputy from Louviers attacked, maintaining that what had to be avoided at all costs was "the institution of fiscal measures tending to weaken the country economically." This primacy of economic considerations had indeed been the central theme of his campaign, taken from his 1928 work on Poincaré's restoration. However obvious it may seem today, he created a sensation.

As Mendès France stepped down from the platform, he heard singularly warm praise from the old M. Steeg, the former prime minister who was presiding over the session, and particularly from his comrade Martinaud-Déplat, who, "excited" by the speaker's presentation, declared with a touch of pomposity: "I have applauded the speech of a future great minister of finance, my comrade and friend Pierre Mendès France!" And the next day, in *La France du centre,* their colleague Jean Zay for his part wrote that the Toulouse congress had just revealed or confirmed real "leaders, Jacques Kayser, Pierre Cot, and Pierre Mendès France." For a first speech under the lights, it was a masterpiece.

This man, who was independent by nature and temperament, had found a welcoming structure within which he developed friendships, less with Bergery, whom he found too personal, unstable, and histrionic, than with Jacques Kayser, Pierre Cot, and especially Jean Zay. And also with Gaston Monnerville, who has recounted how the group often met in the early 1930s on avenue de la Grande-Armée, at the home of Raymond Lindon, the magistrate, who was a very active member of the group, like his colleague Boissarie. Everyone was in turn given the responsibility of preparing and defending a report on a subject on which he had some expertise.

Mendès would arrive very punctually, read the most coherent and well-argued presentations, and then put his papers away and prepare to leave. "Don't leave, Pierre, we have to discuss your ideas." "You think so? All right." And he would open himself to challenges, with a touch of surprise or annoyance. In Monnerville's memory, the young Mendès France was more inclined toward monologue than discussion, a shortcoming that a long political life may not have managed to correct.

In any event, his authority had been affirmed, in Parliament first, then in the party, although he spoke infrequently at congresses—except when a great cause presented itself, as, for example, in Biarritz in 1936, when he took arms in defense of the Blum goverment.

It remained to organize his private life, which was not known for any indiscretions. In Louviers, all eyes were upon him. Local history has preserved no traces of any impropriety on the part of a very young deputy—a "Parisian" moreover!—spied on from behind half-closed shutters by all the female supporters of Alexandre Duval. When you live on the rue Tatin, across from the church, you are subject to the guardians of the moral order.

He had not planned to marry as early as he did. Others, of course, were thinking for him. Oracle and vice-president of the Radical Party, before succeeding her father as senator from Gard, Suzanne Schreiber-Crémieux, noticing the new deputy from Louviers at a reception, whispered to her neighbor: "If my daughter weren't so young, there is the husband I would like for her." (It turned out that the girl in question, Marie-Claire, became the second Mme. Mendès France thirty-five years later.)

Pierre's sister Marcelle had a friend of Egyptian origin, Lily Cicurel, who was studying painting in Paris. She was beautiful and gentle. Pierre did not see much of Marcelle's friends, and he was busy with his work in the Chamber, in Louviers, the party, his office. But they were neighbors: she lived on rue Arsène-Mercier, and he on rue de la Pompe, across from the Lycée Janson-de-Sailly.

> We used the same garage. Chance always plays a large role in this kind of story. We met while we were parking our cars. I offered her a beer at the café at the corner of rue de la Pompe. I found her pleasant and asked her if I could see her again. That's how everything started.

Then he fell ill with jaundice. He left for a vacation in Markstein, since he had always loved the mountains in winter. As chance would have it, Lily Cicurel and Pierre's sister Marcelle were also there. It also turned out that they had a mutual friend, Charles Gombault, Pierre's companion in LAURS and a familiar of the Cicurel family. Lily was, of course, less interested than Pierre in political economy, and he didn't share her interest in painting. "I wasn't very artistic, not very well informed on such matters. But I was interested to see her work. She threw herself into it. When she felt inspired, nothing else counted, neither meals nor weekends."

Lily Cicurel was dominated by an authoritarian mother who had been saddled with heavy responsibilities by the murder of her husband in Cairo, for sinister reasons, and she carried them out rigidly. However strong the personality of the man she had just met, Lily greeted him as a liberator. They were engaged, and they married in December 1933. Pierre chose as witnesses Edouard Daladier, his political mentor, and Georges Bonnet, his former professional mentor: Radicals of every variety.

The life of Mendès France did not change appreciably. Married, and soon father of Bernard in 1934 and Michel in 1936, the deputy from Louviers continued to commute between the little town in Normandy that had elected him and where he carried out his absorbing professional activities, and Paris, where he moved from the family apartment to one on avenue Léopold-II. The Chamber and his group of political friends required his presence in Paris two or three days a week. But he spent the bulk of his time in Louviers, spent all his leisure time there, arguing in court and maintaining contact with his constituents.

I sometimes argued cases in Rouen, Evreux, or Les Andelys, at various places in the department, sometimes even in Paris, but mostly in Louviers. There were cases involving peasants, leases, debts, sometimes criminal trials. It all fit in rather well with my political activity. I sometimes set up meetings in little villages with an audience of ten. In criminal trials, the audience was larger, more than a hundred, and they were all on my side. People are always for the defense and against the prosecutor, while in a political debate you necessarily antagonize at least half the audience. My clients? "Respectable" people didn't come to me, they preferred to hire a good lawyer from Evreux or Rouen. That left me the simple people, artisans, shopkeepers, peasants. In normal times, I don't know whether I would have been excited by the profession. But during that time of acute crisis for the peasantry, of structural upheaval in the countryside, when sharecroppers and small farmers were facing ruin because they couldn't pay their rent and were migrating to the cities, the defense of those poor people gave me the feeling that I was useful, and I gave myself to the work with all my heart.

My experience of that poverty might have pushed me further to the left politically, had the Radical Party not been what it was, a meeting place, a crossroads. In it, you could argue for almost any position, on the condition that you tolerated the positions of others. When I reread today what the Young Turks, myself included, were saying then, I say to myself that the party leaders were rather good democrats.

In the Chamber, the deputy from Louviers had inadvertently discovered a specialty that was to open his eyes to the economic conditions of what was not yet called the "Third World."

I became a member of the Customs Committee, which was very influential, since Parliament alone could change customs duties, and these were critical decisions in a period of crisis and protectionism. The committee worked hard, and I worked particularly hard. I presented a whole series of bills to the Chamber, on oil, coffee, any product that affected the colonial territories. This experience provided me with a fairly solid competence in these areas, at a time when no one was really interested in them, except for politicians from the localities concerned; and that led four years later, in the subsequent legislature, to my election as chairman of the Customs Committee.

Although he had found access to newspapers in Normandy, with *La Dépêche* of his friend Mandle and *Le Journal du Neubourg,* he had more difficulty in finding a platform in Paris. He was rather cordially received at *La Volonté* of Albert Dubarry (which collapsed in the Stavisky scandal), and especially at *Temps nouveaux,* directed by Jean Luchaire, who was then his friend. Both papers were clearly left-leaning, especially the second, whose pacifism attracted him. But he was later able to recognize the moment at which that line led to the abandoment of what was essential.

He had made his name in Parliament as an advocate for poor, debt-ridden peasants and as a specialist in customs matters. But he felt the need to assert himself more clearly through an intervention that would express his fundamental ideas, beyond the immediate circumstances. The subject of his speech was not chosen by him but by the minister of finance, German-Martin, his former professor at the Faculty of Law, who in a sense imposed it on him by presenting a plan for fiscal reform intended to be "bold and original," a plan that had been systematically played up by the progovernment press for several weeks. In the left opposition, no one was better armed than he to puncture this balloon. So he once again mounted the podium, but this time he did not secretly hope, as he had two years before, that the benches would be empty.

In fact, he did not like to take the floor, he didn't love to use language, like Herriot or Pierre Cot. He experienced no physical pleasure, no secret delight, in expressing himself, establishing contact with an audience, manipulating his listeners, in the manner of his mentor or his friend. But he was carefully preparing himself to become a great debater. Around this time, for example, while taking a cure at Challe-les-Eaux, where parliamentary speakers often went to care for their voices, he participated in mock trials, held in the hotel garden, against such masters as Moro-Giafferi or Campinchi, who graciously offered him the benefit of their experience.

When he rose to speak before the Assembly on June 27, 1934, he was vigorously applauded by the left as he placed his notes on the lectern. He was confronting the old master of the Faculty of Law, Germain-Martin, whose conservative tricks no longer deluded him, even though he presented himself at first as the master's pupil. But he wished first of all to challenge the minister and his allies on a much broader and more significant subject than fiscal techniques, and to do it boldly.

> The bill that you have submitted to us is deliberately obscure, sybilline, and mysterious. You say as much yourself in your declaration of purposes where you define your conception of legislative work and where you point out that it is up to Parliament to lay down a certain number of general guidelines, leaving to the government the responsibility for applying them. . . . [This

amounts to] granting the government full discretion, a quasi-dictatorial power. . . . The government is today seeking from both houses not a precise mandate but a veritable blank check! One wonders what use there is for the institution of Parliament—which you claim to be preserving, which you even claim to be modernizing—when you ask it in fiscal matters—which is un-precedented—for a delegation of authority that totally and definitively re-moves its power.

This was certainly a way of broadening the debate. We should not forget that these words had particular force in the midst of the great crisis of 1934, when the right thought it was in control of both institutions and the streets, and at least one-fourth of the members of the Assembly ques-tioned the validity of the parliamentary system, a system that had been denounced by André Tardieu, who, after his defeat in 1932, was preparing his return to power by advocating a resort to open authoritarianism. Pierre Mendès France was presenting himself before the public as a whole and dealing with the question of parliamentary democracy itself, within the confines of his particular subject, the budget.

He next turned his attention to the question of the balance of the entire budget.

At the very moment when you are reducing direct taxes, which are, to be sure, imperfect, but which nevertheless are the groundwork for a just and equitable tax system, you are increasing taxes on consumption, which are the most unjust of all. Income tax, which occupies a much smaller place in our tax system than in the legislation of neighboring countries whose civiliza-tion is comparable to ours, Germany, England, or Belgium, has had its place even further reduced. Our budget of government receipts has thus taken on an increasingly retrograde character. Is it necessary to remind you that indi-rect taxes, particularly the tax on business turnover, are a source of the high cost of living?

Focusing his criticisms, he attacked a new, hidden increase in the tax burden on families.

I have read in some newspapers that—from a sense of social generosity which I applaud, but which surprised us coming from a minister of finance, since we weren't used to such feelings—you had granted an additional de-duction to large families of one thousand francs for the first child, and three thousand francs for each additional child, beginning with the third. But they forgot to inform us that you were simultaneously proposing to abolish the five-thousand-franc deduction for the wife.

The minister of finance challenged this point. At that moment, an unexpected ally intervened in support of the speaker. In his delicate voice, Léon Blum read the passage from the proposed bill in which all references to mothers were indeed absent.

Mendès France had only to conclude, and he did so with a rigor that later made him a target for the revenge of the right.

Thanks to [your] policies, there will soon be nothing, or almost nothing, left of the income tax. Transferable wealth and the liberal professions will be officially uncontrolled, income from land and business will be subject to confiscatory taxes. Agricultural revenues . . . let's not even talk about them.

What remains? In the context of the income tax, according to the official forms, there remains only the schedule for salaries, for wage-earners. That you have increased, in the midst of unemployment, at a time when the average of hours worked has declined, by reducing the family exemptions. The income tax will soon be nothing but an even more burdensome tax on wages. Until wage-earners themselves, sickened by this injustice, finally demand its abolition.

Then, one of your successors, pursuing your labors, will definitively replace the income tax with new indirect taxes, by a fiscal system based on class privilege . . . substituting the taxation of things for the taxation of persons.

That is an indexed tax, an indirect tax, the tax of a high cost of living, discouraging the consumer and aggravating the crisis; it is, finally, an unjust tax that we reject!

The government has chosen it, and that is its right. But it cannot expect that we will assist in its nefarious and dangerous work.

On that June 27, 1934, even more than at the Toulouse congress of 1932, the left had heard a vigorous spokesman whose audience was not limited to the Radicals, and even less to their advanced wing. The public approval of Léon Blum, the support he offered to the speaker, and the praise he bestowed afterward, already point to the Popular Front. It was true that the idea if not the label was in the air, launched by one of Mendès's political allies, Gaston Bergery, as the first basic principle of his "united front," and strengthened in many minds by the crisis of February 6, 1934 (and Doriot, the Communist leader who was already somewhat isolated in his Saint-Denis fortress, was doing the same), the "Common Front," later called the "Popular Alliance," and finally the "Popular Front," was a response to the major threat posed by the antiparliamentary "leagues" in early 1934. Mendès France later explained:

It is certain that this movement toward unity on the left was a consequence of February 6, of that spasm of the extreme right that called into question the survival of the Republic. It is difficult to recognize today the seriousness of the threat it faced from Action Française, the Jeunesses Patriotes, and the Croix-de-feu.[9] As for the attack on the Palais-Bourbon on the evening of February 6, I don't remember experiencing a physical fear of encirclement, of being caught in a trap. What I felt was the violence of the frontal attack from the place de la Concorde, at the point when the police were overrun. But I didn't feel as though I were caught in a vice.

Many deputies were afraid that night. But not Daladier, who was then head of government, or Blum, who supported him from the podium. Daladier didn't have Blum's talent, but he was very courageous then, as he was later at the Riom trial, when he and Blum were codefendants against the Vichy government. In situations like that, Daladier reacted with his natural gallantry, even exaggerating in reaction to the challenge. In any event, the great fear of that night was at the origin of the encounter on February 9, when the two processions, Socialist and Communist, rivals at first, joined together and blended in a kind of marriage, for the first time in fourteen years. This scene, which Charles-André Julien recounted very movingly,[10] was in a sense the birth of the Popular Front, which all of us on the left of the Radical Party supported with all our strength.

While anticipating the great electoral struggle of April and May 1936, which everyone, from the rioters of February 6 to the participants in the procession of February 9, already knew would be decisive for the future of French society, the deputy from Louviers, leader of the Young Turks and financial oracle of the left, saw another challenge to take up. Municipal elections were scheduled for May 1935. The Radical committees of Eure obviously thought of the young man whom they had supported in 1932 and who had so soon made a name for himself, locally and in the Chamber. Moreover, they had to resolve a local problem of personalities between the two Radical leaders of the department, Maître Chauvin and Dr. Briquet, who were constantly at swords' point. Giving Mendès France the opportunity to consolidate his position by becoming mayor of Louviers would set up a barrier between the two men and prepare a third man for the future. Thus, Mendès France was asked, and he hesitated only briefly before accepting.

> In 1935, circumstances led me to head up a Radical list in the municipal elections, and I was elected mayor. I hadn't thought of it before, since I was against holding two elected positions simultaneously. But because of my legal defense of peasants and ordinary people, they saw me as a protector. Of course, it was argued against me—in the columns of *L'Industriel de Louviers,* for example—that I was Parisian, a lawyer, Jewish, and very young. But attacks from that newspaper were rather helpful to me among my constituents.

On May 17, 1935, Mendès France was elected mayor of Louviers at the head of a Radical list including one conservative municipal councillor out of twenty-seven, with whom the mayor constantly maintained cordial relations. A small kernel of Socialist schoolteachers strongly supported the new municipal government. Thus, Mendès France's position had been surprisingly consolidated in this reactionary district, where being "on the left" meant being a republican, and where the "whites" were not opposed by "reds" but by "blues."[11]

One of the leitmotifs of my campaign had been: we do not promise everything; but we ask you to remind us of what we do promise in order to keep us to our word, and to keep track of our accomplishments as they occur. It was, in short, like signing a contract. I am very attached to this notion of contract. My constituents rewarded me for it.

During the campaign, the right tried to provoke fear by comparing my policies to the ultrasecularist policies of "old man Combes," ancestor of the Radicals. They claimed that, if we were elected, we would ban Sunday processions, and the nuns would be driven from the hospitals. People soon realized that the nuns had survived very well the victory of the "blues." I even gave one a *légion d'honneur,* which created a sensation. And processions increased in frequency.

The new mayor, who was twenty-eight, was not interested only in the activities of nuns. He attempted to give women in his town their proper place. Since they were not eligible for office, he made them "adjuncts," particularly in the areas of hygiene and social security. It was an advanced attitude that had few imitators at the time, but it made a strong and lasting impression in Louviers.

Pierre Mendès France loved his duties as a mayor because they involved what was real, tangible, factual, and collective. The concept of public welfare was embodied from moment to moment by the installation of street lights, water supplies, and park benches for old people and the provision of social welfare. It would not have taken much effort to make him say that, of all the innumerable and brilliant positions he occupied, it was his work as mayor that gave him the greatest satisfactions and made him happiest.

Everything remained to be done. Louviers was a nineteenth-century town, undeveloped, underadministered, and also underindebted and undertaxed, so that it was relatively easy to find the money to transform it. The town was plunged into a deep crisis, which was not due only to the impoverishment of the peasantry.

At the time, a mayor was more independent than he is today. Not having to turn to a prefect or a minister at every moment, he could take more initiatives and accomplish more things; for example, he could contract municipal debts without having to go through innumerable interagency committees. I confronted these problems directly and with enthusiasm. In the end, being a deputy, sitting on a bench, speaking, sitting down again, is not very exalting. But managing a town means that you are carrying out concrete actions at every moment.

Perhaps it was there that I realized why I was a Radical, even though I was ideologically to the left of the party. It was because the Radicals were directed toward action, national and local responsibilities, the problems of the exercise of power, material realities. The Socialists, with whom I have always felt so many intellectual and moral affinities, have always seemed to me to be a little removed from reality. Among the Radicals, I found a sense of the state, of responsibility, of concrete reality.

But the mayor of Louviers also had to act in other areas. He was seen a little less frequently in the Chamber, where he had courageously presented and defended an amendment to an agricultural bill on March 18 and 21, 1935. This amendment would have granted farmers "ownership" of their cultivation, that is, in case of cancellation of a tenancy, the right to recover expenditures made for the improvement of the property, without having to present a written authorization from the owner for those expenditures. With a little exaggeration, one might see such a step in favor of this form of "ownership" as an initiative leading toward the socialization of the land, analogous to Brecht's "everything belongs to anyone who makes it better." But we should not go so far, nor did Mendès in 1935.

In any event, his speeches as a whole—including, around the same time, a proposed bill to improve cattle transportation—make up a rather coherent program. On the eve of the campaign for the very important legislative elections of the spring of 1936, Pierre Mendès France, deputy and mayor of Louviers, was seen essentially as a progressive advocate for the distressed peasantry.

But the stakes were broader. All of French society was in question, and in motion. From the spring of 1935 on, in response to a call from the Committee for Popular Unity, led by the Socialist Rivet, the Communist Langevin, and the Radical Alain (for once, the Radical spokesman was not the least "intellectual" of the three), the Union of the Left, broader and more ambitious than ever, was at work. On July 14, 1935, there was the great celebration of the Buffalo Stadium, the pledge of popular unity and of struggle in defense of democracy against external and internal fascism. And in January 1936 came the Pact of Popular Unity signed by the leaderships of the Radicals, the Socialists, and the Communists.

The strategy of the Young Turks had carried the day. Pierre Mendès France would fight on the ground he had chosen, for a cause which was above all his own. The Popular Front that was taking shape, preparing for battle, was the force he had dreamt of from the early days of LAURS, endowed with a program that was very close to the one worked out by the student league he had led: the defense of democracy through the union of manual and intellectual workers.

I was very close to Jean Zay, who was one of the strongest advocates of the Popular Front among us. He was a member of all the groups, commissions, and committees bringing together Radicals and Socialists, and later Communists, that were beginning to develop the program for the coalition. Through him, I was therefore very well informed, very "in," and well prepared to carry on the battle, locally as well as nationally. Through Zay, I felt myself totally represented and directly concerned by this politics—which, in the constituency of Louviers and in the department, posed some rather specific problems.

The Radicals of Eure were indeed divided over the Popular Front strategy, with Dr. Briquet, against his rival Maître Chauvin, strongly opposed to any alliance with the Communists. This did not simplify the task of the Radical candidates.

Contrary to what one might believe, Mendès France's campaign was harder in 1936 than it had been in 1932. This was so not only because in 1932, as a young challenger, he had not been a major target of the right, while by 1936 he had established himself as one of the hopes of an effective and competent left attacking the real targets of capitalist power. It was especially difficult because, in the course of four years, the crisis had deepened and enflamed people's passions. Everyone knew the seriousness of what was at stake. Agricultural poverty was turning into destitution. "Empty stomachs" could easily be mobilized against the incumbents, of whatever party.

Against Mendès France the right had replaced the exhausted notable Alexandre Duval with a young, combative, and relatively competent militant farmer, Modeste Legouez, who launched a violent campaign based on demagogic agrarianism against the incumbent. He had other arguments: one day, one of Mendès's supporters was compelled to retort to the insults with a cry of "Long live the Jews!"

The point had not yet been reached, as in the cantonal elections of 1937, when his death was announced between the two rounds and the campaign was conducted through the medium of medical reports. But violence was prevalent. *La Dépêche de Louviers* and *Le Journal du Neubourg* denounced "Napoleon Legouez," which was aiming a bit high, and his "green fascism." He was in fact linked to the Green Shirt movement of Henri Dorgères, a more or less fascist-leaning peasant agitator.

On April 4, *La Dépêche de Louviers* published an editorial calling for a vote for the incumbent. "This campaign will assume a symbolic character. The success of the courageous Mendès France will be the triumph of all that is republican against fascism." Dr. Briquet, hostile to the Popular Front, nevertheless supported his young colleague. "The violent slanders to which he has been subjected prove the importance his adversaries attach to recapturing the constituency of Louviers, where he brought about the triumph of the republican banner four years ago. We place it in his hands once again."

But the support provided by Briquet implied that the candidate would exercise a certain discretion in his references to the Popular Front. It was true that *La Dépêche*, which openly supported his candidacy, had at the end of January 1936 published a detailed account of the Popular Unity program under a three-column headline on the first page. But from that date on it was barely mentioned. In Mendès France's campaign statement, as Georges Dupeux has pointed out in *Le Front populaire et les Elections de 1936,* (The Popular Front and the 1936 Elections), fifty-one lines out of sixty-three were devoted to "local interests." There was only brief mention of the "defense of the Republic against the seditious," of "peace against foreign dictatorships and their supporters," of "democratic reform of the Banque de France," and of the "deflation aggravating the consequences of overproduction of grain." Mendès France later contested the validity of this remark, attributing it to a mistake in the "Barodet,"[12] which confused his campaign statement with an introductory note published in *La Dépêche de Louviers* that announced a second in which the problems of national politics were given more extensive treatment.[13]

Mendès France's campaign was based not only on local questions. Supported in the local press by his friend Maître Labéda, who violently attacked fascism and its domestic allies (notably in a fine article of March 1936, "Le Poing de Hitler" (Hitler's Fist), it focused on the two targets that he had constantly addressed in his own articles for *La Dépêche:* currency deflation, and the necessity of agricultural price supports. He constantly denounced a policy that had led to a collapse of the prices paid to producers of wheat and milk: a hundred kilos of wheat had gone from 162 francs in 1932 to 75 in 1936, and a liter of milk from 70 centimes to 30 in the same period.

But wasn't he the incumbent and, as such, considered responsible for the stagnation? Wasn't the government in power, led by Sarraut, a Radical government? Mendès might very well recall the number and the force of his interventions in the Chamber in favor of the peasantry; Legouez nevertheless attacked him as a representative of an antipeasant government. The audiences were impressive (as many as two thousand people in Louviers in April), and the polemic was very harsh in rural areas, much less so in urban areas.

> As mayor, I had gotten off to a good start. The accomplishments of the city government, in conformity with our promises, made a good impression. These good beginnings in town created a favorable atmosphere for me in the urban area. The inhabitants of the city assured my reelection, thanks to my work as mayor, while the peasant electorate, embittered as it was, and stirred up by Leoguez, was much more refractory.

In short, on April 27, 1936, Pierre Mendès France was in the lead in the first round, with 6,063 votes, against 5,519 for Modeste Legouez, 603 for the Communist Vimard, and 546 for the Socialist Sergent. "Republican discipline" and the agreements to transfer votes signed by the three

Popular Front parties promised an easy reelection, which was accomplished in the second round on May 3, by 6,821 votes to 6,085. It is evident that some Communist votes had been lost. But the margin of victory was ample, and *La Dépêche de Louviers* could be modest in triumph, preferring on May 8 to hail the general success of the Popular Front, which, in this reputedly conservative department, was now represented by three deputies out of five (Mendès in Louviers, his friend Forcinal in Les Andelys, and the Socialist Dupont in Evreux).

Pierre Mendès France was now firmly rooted in Norman soil, a sucessful mayor and a deputy who had been reelected and was already destined for a cabinet post in the Popular Front government, a government that fulfilled his hopes as a citizen and for which his friends the Young Turks appeared to be the cutting edge, the pioneers.

4.
WITH BLUM

Pierre Mendès France was only slightly involved with the popular celebrations of the spring of 1936. He participated in a few marches in Louviers and Evreux, but not in Paris. "I'm more at home in a study than in a demonstration," he observed soberly. But he was deeply happy. Ten years of his brief and already brilliant public life, from the Latin Quarter to Louviers, had found their ideological consecration.

The fact that the Communists had breached the solidarity of the January coalition as far as accepting governmental responsibilities was concerned was, of course, a disappointment. Similarly disappointing was the marginalization of the brilliant Bergery, the Young Turk intoxicated by the ambiguous successes of his "common front," and the drift toward the right (worse was to come) of Marcel Déat's Neosocialists, with whom Jean Zay had for a time felt an affinity.

In June 1936, he could say: "My ideas are in power, along with my friends." The public man for whom he had had the greatest respect ever since Herriot had disappointed his friends, Léon Blum, was head of the government. The leader of the Radical left, Daladier, was vice-premier and occupied the key post of minister of defense, assisted by the Young Turks Pierre Cot, Jean Zay, and François de Tessan. Named to the Foreign Ministry was Yvon Delbos, an old partisan of disarmament converted to antifascism, assisted by another of his friends, Pierre Viénot. And the minister of sport and leisure was Léo Lagrange, one of the deputies whom he most admired and of whom he later said: "I had a good deal of respect for him. He gave off a strong impression of purity and sincerity. I don't know where he stood doctrinally, but he had a truly socialist sensibility. He was a beautiful soul, a man of the highest quality."

One might wonder how Mendès, a man of order preoccupied with efficiency, reacted to the movement of factory occupations. Up to June 11, 1936, when the new government, one might almost say the new regime, took office, the victorious working class was attempting immediate exploitation of the electoral success of the left. The sit-down strikes, an epic of mass spontaneity that intoxicated militants and fascinated sociologists, appeared to the authorities as a kind of direct challenge. At the Riom trial, Léon Blum explained what an ordeal this rank-and-file movement had been for the head of the 1936 government and for his minister of the interior, Roger Salengro, who had the responsibility for containing and channeling it.

Pierre Mendès France was already too much a man of revolution through law and felt too closely connected to the new government not to have experienced, like most elected officials of the time, fear of being overwhelmed by the streets.[1] When legality offered so many opportunities, it seemed risky to give such ammunition to the wealthy classes.

In his study of the Radicals of Eure, Rossignol, relying on a note in the departmental archives that was later lost, asserts that Pierre Mendès France made a speech in which he opposed the factory occupations. The former deputy from Louviers later challenged this notation, or rather wished to qualify it. His attack, he said, was directed against "provocations." In any event, a few reservations expressed about the sit-down strikes—which, incidentally, affected locally his implacable political enemies, the cloth manufacturers of Louviers—do not call into question the strength and loyalty of his support for the Popular Front movement. Others who were at the time devoted to "revolution" and the "dictatorship of the proletariat" also declared that "you have to know when to end a strike."

The deputy from Louviers very soon affirmed his personality and his independence in the early summer of 1936. The Olympic games, which the Nazis were already presenting as a triumph, were about to open in Berlin. There was a question as to whether France should participate in what would be a celebration of racism as much as of sport. Mendès, like the Communists, was in favor of refusing. But when the time came for the appropriations vote in the National Assembly, Thorez and his friends took refuge in absention (the working-class electorate would not understand). Only Mendès France voted in opposition.

No one argued more passionately than he in favor of the work of the first Popular Front government. In the course of a debate organized thirty years later to assess the economic policies of the Blum government, Jean-

Marcel Jeanneny (and Simon Nora, from another angle), developing and modifying some arguments used by Alfred Sauvy, strongly criticized the economic and fiscal strategy of the government.[2] In reply, Mendès France, with retrospective fervor, brought out the contributions of the Popular Front.

In the light of a bitter experience of power, the former deputy from Louviers maintained that almost all the economic mistakes of the Blum government were attributable to social demands that required immediate satisfaction, because the deflationist policies of Laval, Tardieu, and Flandin had driven the working class into the deep poverty and anger demonstrated by the May strikes. The government elected by the masses for radical change could not fail, from the outset, to carry out a redistribution of income, which was, of course, risky in the stagnant condition of the national economy but was in conformity with the mandate received on May 3. For Pierre Mendès France, the failures experienced by this government devoted to justice were essentially due to a bourgeoisie that had not disarmed and that, once the great fear of the spring had passed, systematically sabotaged the attempts at stimulation[3] and revival through distribution, full employment, and restoration of purchasing power attempted by the Blum government.

The argument to which he always adhered has lost nothing of its power:

> Whatever the disappointments, however justified any particular criticism, how can we forget the immense contributions of the Popular Front, the reconciliation between the people and the state, the hope and even the certainty that finally the authorities were acting not against but for the disinherited, that power was no longer in the hands of big capital, but expressed a desire for justice. For the first time in our contemporary history, the people had the impression that the government belonged to them. This is the real historical phenomenon of the Popular Front. This is why Léon Blum and his comrades remain precious in the memories of the majority of French workers.
>
> People often speak of paid vacations and the forty-hour week. And it is true that the condition of the working class was definitively changed by these measures. But, living among peasants as I did, I place highest another Popular Front reform, the creation of the Grain Office, which, without giving it a name, I had been calling for for years and which finally stablized grain prices and saved rural producers from ruin. I see that as the most original accomplishment of the Popular Front, which was able, in my view, to rescue the French peasantry—at least the grain producers—from despair.

However warmly he supported Léon Blum's reforms, Mendès France disagreed with the policies of the first Popular Front government in at least two areas: currency questions, and the Spanish Civil War.

For years, the deputy from Louviers had demonstrated his opposition to a monetarist strategy that gave priority to uncompromising defense of the franc and to balancing the budget. Even before discovering Keynes's *General Theory,* which Georges Boris had him read in 1937,[4] he had argued, in the book on Poincaré as well as in his articles for *La Dépêche,* for expansion, investment, and monetary "flux" and monetary "circuits"; for "economics first," as opposed to "currency first," caricatured by the terrible deflation of which he was a sworn enemy.

And now an antideflation government had come to power, elected by a country exasperated by the straitjacket imposed for years by Tardieu, Laval, Chéron, and Régnier, champions of consolidating the franc by lowering purchasing power. To the franc, Mendès France and his friends preferred the French. And this was also apparently what the oracles of the Socialist Party and the (CGT) (Confédération Générale du Travail) thought: to revive economic activity through exports, the moment had come to devalue the franc.

But it happened that, from the Radical Party (with few exceptions) to the Communist Party, including the majority of the SFIO, the electoral campaign, as far as the economy was concerned, had been conducted with the slogan: "Neither deflation nor devaluation!" In the eyes of most of the old Radical "experts" as well as in the view of labor leaders, devaluation would mean ruin for small savers, doubt in everyone's mind about the national currency, popular capitulation, and an admission that the left frightened people. During the campaign, Socialist speakers generally, including Blum, had guaranteed that "the walls of Paris would not be covered with the white posters of devaluation."

I regretted that we did not carry out the devaluation immediately. That was my hope and that of Boris, who could not make it a reality even though he had great prestige in Blum's eyes and moreover, from his point of view, the virtue of being a Socialist. The government was bound by the electoral promises of the Popular Front coalition. In addition, I think that, deep down, Blum was no more in favor of devaluation than Auriol; that was rather the policy of Paul Reynaud (who advocated it while at the same time observing that perhaps the moment for doing it had not yet come). Some Socialist experts became advocates for it. But Blum and Auriol remained suspicious. So, they implemented distributionist policies without having the means to do so, without giving themselves enough room for action. And they were forced to devalue three months later, too late, making the operation appear as a defensive measure, with a view to correcting the "mistakes" of the Popular Front, whereas, had it been decided in June, it would have appeared as a correction of the mistakes of the preceding governments, a just penalty for them.

Disappointed by the government's refusal to devalue in June, and very conscious of the mistake it made by resigning itself to devaluation only in September, Pierre Mendès France nevertheless came to the aid of the government in October, in Parliament and, a few days later, at the Radical congress in Biarritz, to defend the belated but still necessary devaluation. This required some self-sacrifice: currency manipulation remained unpopular, particularly among Radical deputies. On September 28, 1936, he rose to speak in the Palais-Bourbon, where Auriol and Blum had been dragged through the mud for having finally resigned themselves to reducing the value of the franc.

PIERRE MENDES FRANCE: Listening to some speakers and reading some articles, it would appear that the devaluation whose inevitability everyone recognizes today—

CHARLES DES INARDS: Not at all!

PIERRE MENDES FRANCE: is the result of the policies followed for the last four months, the policies of the Popular Front. . . . At the moment when we are about to vote to ratify it, this is an assertion that we do not have the right to let pass without a categorical answer.

Before the Popular Front and its policies, we went through, as you know, a period of deflation.

MARCEL STURMEL: Under a Radical government!

PIERRE MENDES FRANCE: We cannot forget today the condition in which this deflationary policy left France.

I think that the country will not forget the ruin and the impoverishment that that policy created. It brought about the ruin and disappearance of innumerable small independent businesses, the proletarianization of the middle classes for the benefit of a few industrial and banking trusts that make up what has been called the "protected sector."

Now . . . this economic collapse occurred precisely at a moment when absolutely everyone had already begun to convalesce.

FERNAND WIEDEMANN-GOIRAN: The disease was caused by the threat of the Popular Front.

PIERRE MENDES FRANCE: . . . Once deflation had been condemned, what policy was available to us, in the month of June? For my part, I can say already that, in the state in which the country found itself, precisely because of its weakness, because of the suffering it had endured, immediate relief seemed to me to be necessary, and from that very moment, I thought— regretfully, but firmly—that that relief could come only from an adjustment in the currency.

As early as 1934, M. Paul Reynaud . . . considered devaluation desirable and beneficial, an opinion which could be questioned at the time. In 1936, it had become inevitable; it was no longer an opinion, it was the indisputable consequence of unfortunately decisive statistics. . . .

In these critical hours, certain men, by creating an uproar with a sectarian impropriety approaching defeatism, are providing poisoned weapons to those outside our borders who wish for disorder and misery here at home.

The country, which is wiser, remembers the cruel days of the past.

At the Biarritz congress a month later, he resorted to the same arguments before an assembly as hostile to devaluation as the parliamentary right, and which, inspired by the violent critiques of Radical oracles like Caillaux and Emile Roche, and by the very subtle sabotage of Georges Bonnet, shouted down the name of Vincent Auriol. Bonnet, Mendès France's former "patron," went so far as to express doubts about the honesty of Léon Blum, suggesting that he might have floated a government loan in June while at the same time secretly preparing for devaluation in September.

But even though he came to the assistance of the Blum government, vilified for making a decision that he considered salutary, Pierre Mendès France did not refrain from criticizing it. Thus, on November 26, 1936, he rose to speak in the Assembly in order to comment on the proposed fiscal reform presented by Vincent Auriol, minister of finance in the Popular Front government. Although he recognized that, compared to the previous "reforms" of Poincaré and Tardieu, the system proposed by the Socialist minister would "lead to greater fiscal equality," he believed it

was possible to say that certain intermediaries would take advantage of it in order to raise prices—maneuvers that the government should "energetically oppose."

VINCENT AURIOL: It will see to that.

PIERRE MENDES FRANCE: We have had too many instances in recent years of unacceptable speculations against which the government has not shown all the rigor we might have wished.

We must achieve, by any means, the stability of prices. . . .

[It is] with respect to direct taxes, Mister Minister, that your timidity and the inadequacy of your proposal have been most severely criticized. Above all, and this is praiseworthy, you have sought to simplify, to clarify.

Given that, we expected from you a profound and complete reform of our very complicated system, of our hodgepodge of taxes, rates, and surcharges.

VINCENT AURIOL: Many of them have already disappeared.

PIERRE MENDES FRANCE: In the face of such a situation, you have presented us with only a very modest and very minimal simplification. . . . Hence . . . some of us are disappointed.

. . . In my view, most of the major problems with respect to direct taxes remain. None of the large difficulties has been resolved. . . . The policies followed by the present government seem to be inspired by intentions that we must all approve. But it remains, in a large number of areas, to translate those intentions into realities.

We are confident that the government will accomplish that work, which has only just begun.

LEON BLUM: Very good!

PIERRE MENDES FRANCE: To facilitate its task, we are giving it our votes today, but we remind it that its proposal can be only the beginning of a more

complete reform, the one the country is waiting for, the one we have promised it and which will soon give it the modern fiscal system it needs.
VINCENT AURIOL: Speaking after our colleague and friend Pierre Mendès
France, I would like first of all to pay tribute to his admirable conscientiousness and to his talent.

This autumn of disenchantments was also the season when the Spanish Republic suffered its first serious defeats (especially in the Basque
region) because it had not received the aid it had a right to expect from its
natural allies in Paris—if not in London—and because Moscow was still
hesitating, until November, to come to its support. This sad failure of the
Popular Front government was deplored and criticized by Mendès
France, as it was by his friends Jean Zay and Pierre Cot, who were, along
with Vincent Auriol, Jules Moch, and Léo Lagrange, the most passionate
adversaries of nonintervention in the government. It has often been told
how Pierre Cot, minister of the air force, "covered" by Léon Blum and
assisted in the field by Gaston Cusin, a high-level Socialist civil servant in
the Customs Service, significantly helped to remedy the consequences of
nonintervention by arranging substantial shipments. The young deputy
from Louviers was soon to become involved in his hardly secret plot.

In 1937, Pierre Mendès France, candidate for the General Council of
Eure, had to conduct a very tough campaign, made all the tougher by the
fact that he fell seriously ill with typhoid fever on the eve of the election.
His opponents seized the opportunity, between the two rounds, simply to
announce his death. He was nevertheless elected, since he had remained
very attentive to local concerns; after the war he presided over the General Council.

On June 21, 1937, the Blum government was defeated in a Senate
vote. The upper chamber did not have the constitutional power to remove
the government from office, but drawn up in opposition to Blum by its
leader Joseph Caillaux, oracle of the Radical Party to which Mendès
France belonged, it had greeted the premier with such hostility that he
was obliged to draw the necessary conclusion and to recognize that he
could no longer govern. The episode was all the more bitter for Mendès
France because Caillaux was one of the men he had most keenly admired
from the beginning of his career: Caillaux, the man who had saved the
peace in 1911, the man of the income tax, the man who, before any other
French political figure of the period, had recognized the preeminence of
economic and financial questions.

The young deputy from Louviers nonetheless took a position that his
friend Jean Labéda defined by entitling his comment in La Dépêche: "The
Senate against the Nation." And the designation of Camille Chautemps,
leader of the right wing of the Radical Party, as Blum's successor was not
a choice that he found reassuring. It seemed to be the death of the Popular

Front, of what had been for him, as for so many others, a strong hope and the beginning of the great reshaping of French society to which he had aspired beginning in 1925 as a very young activist in LAURS.

But as head of a government still claiming to represent the Popular Front, Chautemps had no credibility. After refusing the offer of participation by Thorez and Duclos (more inclined to collaborate with this subtle conservative than with Blum), he went so far as to attempt to break off the alliance with the Communists. But making the PCF into an opposition party would have troubled the majority of his SFIO allies. He lost two votes of confidence in the Chamber, in January and then in early March 1938. And on March 10, 1938, the timid President Lebrun was again reluctantly forced to call on Léon Blum. However splintered it may have become, the parliamentary coalition elected in 1936 could find no other leader.

At first, on March 12, Blum attempted to persuade the opposition to join a national unity government, "from Thorez to Paul Reynaud," justified in his view both by the seriousness of the economic situation and by the international crisis initiated, or aggravated, by the Anschluss—the absorption of Austria by the Third Reich that Hitler had just undertaken. But although men like Paul Reynaud and Louis Marin, who placed their antifascism above their antipathy to Blum, and the Communists, for the same reasons, supported the Socialist leader's proposal, the majority of their colleagues rejected it out of hand. Paul Reynaud noted: "This time, it's the right that has refused."[5] In this context, the "moderate" press wrote:

> We have a government. Strangely, everyone speaks of its death and calls for a government of national union and public safety required by the circumstances. This is the formula proposed not only by the press of the right and the center, but even by certain left newspapers like L'Oeuvre.[6]

Léon Blum was virtually forced to resign himself to forming a government similar to the one the Senate had stymied in June 1937.

It was similar but not identical. The central problem was the choice of finance minister. Vincent Auriol, who was aware that he had not measured up to the task in 1936–1937, categorically refused to return to the position. Even though he considered Charles Spinasse a good economist as well as a friend, Léon Blum did not place complete confidence in this specialist, of whom he said: "We are separated, Charles and I, only by the extent of our convictions."

Consequently, ignoring the fact that, in his 1918 book, La Réforme gouvernementale (Governmental Reform), he had maintained that the head of government, in order to devote himself to questions of synthesis, should not accept any particular ministerial responsibility, and because it was, as he said, the "most exposed position," he decided to take on the Treasury (that is, monetary decisions) himself, turning over the Budget (that is, management) to Spinasse. But, very much aware of the burden he was thereby assuming, he decided to appoint an undersecretary and a staff director who were particularly competent. They were Pierre Mendès France and Georges Boris.

Why Mendès?

The few connections between him and the Socialist leader have already been noted. They were not separated "by the extent of their convictions," which were close in many respects, but by the difference between two generations and by the fact that they belonged to two often rivalrous political organizations. We know why the former president of LAURS had not joined the Socialist Party, like many of his friends and the brilliant, slightly older Boris, with whom he was to collaborate. We also know that on several occasions, notably after Mendès's speech in Parliament on fiscal reform, Léon Blum publicly expressed his respect for him. Curiously, he owed his call to serve in the councils of government, at thirty-one, as much to the difference in political allegiance as to Blum's respect. As Mendès said:

> I deserve no credit for being chosen. I benefited from a kind of automatism. The rules for constructing a cabinet were the following: When a minister was a Socialist, the undersecretary had to be a Radical, and vice versa. Blum had resigned himself to taking over the Treasury, and he needed a Radical young enough to be only an undersecretary, but adequately informed on the subject and a hard worker, since he had little time for these questions himself. Looking back on it today, he had little choice. I was in some sense inevitable: Blum was led to me like a train on a track.
>
> Moreover, he was a man who liked young people, who was particularly fond of working with them. And he savored the spice of our difference in temperament. I was called rather pessimistic. I was often troubled or anxious. However perceptive he may have been, the optimist liked to reassure me: "You'll see, my dear Mendès, the worst doesn't always happen." Indeed, I received his summons with a certain surprise. But it rescued me from a very troublesome situation. I had been very ill in 1937, with the typhoid fever that almost eliminated me from the local elections. Today, that illness is no longer considered serious. But at the time it was often fatal. I had not fully recovered. Then I had an appendicitis operation. In early 1938, I was weak, gloomy, discouraged. The call from Léon Blum to work with him gave me a lift. The anticipation of confronting a task like that didn't depress me, but on the contrary invigorated me and put me back on my feet.

From the very beginning, the division of labor between Treasury and Budget that had been arranged by Léon Blum surprised the new undersecretary. Why had the head of government, minister of the treasury, insisted on taking complete control over customs? Was this because Mendès France was an "expert" in the field, as member and then, since May 1936, chairman of the parliamentary committee—which might provide further explanation for Blum's choice of him? The premier very clearly indicated that this was not the reason: Customs was to remain under their joint control because on it depended a great deal of the aid to Republican Spain.

High-level civil servants who, in the last two years, had changed themselves from border guards into smugglers (closing their eyes to strange convoys passing through Port-Bou or winking at bizarre labels indicating the fictitious destination "Mexico" for goods really intended for Valencia) had to be able to continue their game with the assurance that they were "covered." The chief example was Gaston Cusin, director of customs, who, thanks to Auriol and Blum, had done a great deal to bring materiel in principle prohibited by the nonintervention pact to the troops of Miaja and Rojo.

Thus, Pierre Mendès France was introduced to this traffic, and, as undersecretary of the treasury, he was obliged to cover if not to foster it. Despite the shift of Pierre Cot, the most determined ally of the Spanish Republic, from the Ministry of the Air Force to that of Commerce, it was during the spring of 1938 that the "relaxation" of nonintervention was most significant. But the Blum–Mendès team remained in place for too short a time to enable the mechanism invented by the leader of the Popular Front to bear fruit.

At least the young undersecretary found the opportunity to put his ideas into practice and to verify that Léon Blum was not, with reference to Spain, the abstentionist denounced by his enemies on the left.

The fact that Léon Blum called on Georges Boris as staff director for the Ministry of the Treasury is no more surprising than his choice of Mendès France as undersecretary. What may be surprising is the fact that these two choices for such difficult positions gave birth to such a deep and enthusiastic friendship on both sides.

At fifty, the director of *La Lumière* was one of the great French journalists of the day and one of the keenest observers of the world economy. After having been a very vigorous critic of the economic strategy of the right-wing governments from 1926 to 1936, he had established himself, even though he was a Socialist, as a lucid critic of the fiscal policies of the first Popular Front government. His cultivation, his connections, and his authority were steadily growing.

At first sight, he might have seemed a dilettante. The son of an inhabitant of the area of Lorraine annexed by the Germans who had chosen France in 1871 and had then run a large import-export business on the rue de la Victoire, he had traveled at a very young age to take care of family business, to Brazil first, and then to Ceylon, where he directed a tea plantation—his first direct experience of human misery. A Socialist at sixteen and a participant in violent demonstrations, he said that he was "born on the left." Thus he was protected from Epicureanism, although he adored Bach and Stendhal, was a friend of the poet Henri Franck, a connoisseur of Oriental art, and a dazzling conversationalist, informed about almost everything and curious about everything else.

Exempted from military service in 1914 because his health had been impaired by his long stays in the tropics, Boris had been assigned to the commission directing the blockade against the Central Powers and then named as an expert for the French delegations in the postwar economic negotiations. Rejecting an appointment to the foreign service, he became for a while an associate of the Belgian banker Alfred Lowenstein, managing an artificial silk business for him and leaving when he learned about some questionable operations.

Georges Boris was above all interested in the economy as a whole and in theoretical economics. Since the press was an incomparable tool for analysis and education, he became a journalist, writing his first articles for Henri Dumay's *Progrès civique*. In 1923, when Dumay proposed that they establish a left-wing daily funded by subscriptions ("the newspaper founded by seventy thousand honest people") that would reject any pressure from big business, particularly in the form of advertising, Boris enthusiastically agreed to join the enterprise. The paper was named *Le Quotidien.*

Boris was a man of character. When he discovered that the director of *Le Quotidien,* which he had helped launch on a foundation of intractable moral rigor, was making it a tool for the victory of the Cartel des Gauches in 1924 and was accepting hidden contributions from a railroad company, he left the paper whose general secretary he had become, taking with him its most prestigious contributors—Alphonese Aulard, Albert Bayet, Salomon Grumbach, Georges Gombault. It was then that he fulfilled his dream of establishing a militant weekly, *La Lumière,* where he brought together his best associates from *Le Quotidien* and which was one of the three or four most influential organs of the left in the late 1920s and the 1930s, one of the pioneers of the Popular Front.

Boris had met Mendès France for the first time in the offices of the family bookstore on the corner of the boulevard Saint-Germain and the rue Saint-Jacques, a few steps from the Collège de France. The young deputy strongly admired the journalist for his talent, his ideas, and his competence in economic and fiscal matters, to which he himself devoted his principal energies. The first works of the president of LAURS on Poincaré and on the Bank for International Settlements, his affirmation of the primacy of economic over fiscal considerations and of the worldwide, interlocking character of all monetary problems, owed a good deal to the specialist of *Le Quotidien* and director of *La Lumière*. When he visited Boris, Mendès France was aware that he was paying a debt. They did not become immediate friends. Boris was nearly twenty years the elder, but as Mendès observed: "He was a man whose courtesy and generosity quickly bridged distance; he liked young people and made himself liked by them."

In any event, it was Léon Blum who brought them together and changed their cordial relations into a friendship.

"At the beginning," Mendès half-smilingly suggested,

> Boris did not take me particularly seriously: an undersecretary of thirty-one. But we worked hard together and confronted the same challenges. We saw each other ten times a day. Blum spent very little time in the rue de Rivoli offices; he came in the morning around eleven and stayed for an hour or an hour and a half. All the rest of the time, we were alone, Boris and I, in charge of that intimidating office where everyone was hostile to us. Neither one of us was an *inspecteur des finances:* a journalist and a minor deputy from Louviers. I exaggerate a little when I say that everyone was hostile. But among the high-level civil servants, two years earlier Blum and Auriol had removed Baumgartner, who would have been more favorably disposed toward us than Rueff—at least in terms of loyalty, because as far as ideas were concerned, there were no great differences between them: both of them were "classical" economists. Boris and I had to rely on each other, constantly. That creates bonds.

One can imagine that the designation of the Young Turk Mendès France alongside Léon Blum enchanted neither the conservative parties nor financial circles. We need not comment on the anti-Semitic articles, of which there was a flood, with remarks like: "Three Jews to guard the French Treasury!" It is more interesting to quote a subtler, more insidious article that refrained from insults and preferred to insinuate doubts while showing a certain consideration for the manifest talent and the courage of the new undersecretary. The article was published on March 20, 1938 by the "apolitical" weekly *Commentaire*.

> In the Ministry of the Treasury, M. Léon Blum has chosen M. Mendès France as his undersecretary. The young deputy from Louviers has thereby become the real minister of finance . . . since M. Spinasse is content with managing the Budget, and since M. Mendès France has moved into the rue de Rivoli while M. Léon Blum remains in the Hôtel Matignon.
> M. Mendès France is thirty-one. He is the youngest member of the government, as he was one of the youngest deputies in the previous legislature, [where] he soon developed a reputation as a technician in financial matters: in the kingdom of the blind. . . . In fact, M. Mendès presented some

good reports on behalf of the Customs Committee. He continued to be a "militant" of the left wing of the Radical-Socialist Party. His reputation as an expert and his verve as an advanced militant have finally earned him the recompense he has hoped for since he entered the career: to participate in the councils of government.

M. Mendès France is certainly ambitious. This is why we can both hope for and fear a good deal from him. He lacks neither talent nor definite ideas. . . . For our part, we will express only one wish: that M. Mendès France have the courage to renounce his past mistakes on the day when, in contact with the realities, he senses that one does not govern with illusions.

"Illusions"? We shall see that Pierre Mendès France and Georges Boris, far from renouncing their "past mistakes," that is, the intervention of the state in the direction of production and exchange, attempted on the contrary to put them into practice. At first, however, they had to establish themselves at the head of the ministry and prepare the ground for the proposed reforms.

It was exhausting work, carried out in a climate of suspicion that didn't make things any easier. And then I had contacts with Parliament to maintain. Blum lived in a state of alert. He was known to be uncertain in fiscal matters. In the Chamber, he measured up courageously. But in the Senate. . . . His relations with Caillaux remained tumultuous. That was why I served as a cushion, an intermediary between them. Caillaux received me rather cordially, as a young novice. I don't claim to have influenced either man, or to have played an important role. I softened a few blows, that's all. When Blum needed to negotiate with Caillaux on a point of detail, I sometimes took it in hand. It was a rather exhilarating task, but it was so soon interrupted. We knew from the beginning that the experience would be brief, perhaps six months. It lasted less than a month.

Undersecretary Mendès France took part in cabinet meetings only when economic and fiscal questions were under consideration, but this was almost always the case. He had the right to speak, like Spinasse, but did so infrequently. Blum was the "boss" and assumed the functions of spokesman for the team. In fact, in cabinet meetings, as in his office, Mendès felt himself very much an "adjutant," very much "at the service of Blum."

The premier was so seldom present at the ministry that Boris and Mendès were unable to influence him significantly, to make their view prevail after the indispensable long discussions. Blum did not have the time. Boris and Mendès prepared the dossiers for him, and he made the decisions. From that point on, his colleagues, whether or not they agreed on every point—and Mendès later let it be known that he did not always agree—did nothing but execute orders. They lacked the improvised exchanges in the course of a day, the kind of interchange among members of a team that would allow them, in consultation with the minister, to mature, polish, and change the measures that had been or were to be taken.

This was all the more the case, as Mendès France pointed out, because Blum, despite his reputation for flexibility and the shifting character that was attributed to him, was inflexible once a decision had been made.

> Once he had settled on something, there was no one in the world more stubborn than he. Aside from that, he was very open, ready to listen to any theory or argument, even if they contradicted his own or those of his party.
>
> How much his party meant to him! It was really his family. Those who didn't belong to it, no matter how great his friendship for them (like me), remained more or less apart from him. They did not belong to the intimate circle in which he had made his career and his life. Even those who were in disagreement with him, like Marcceau Pivert—whose ideas were further from Blum's than mine were, for example—had in his eyes the incalculable virtue of being "in the party." But the sympathy he showed me was strong and exhilarating. I was proud of it.

Of the two important points of disagreement that had separated the young Mendès from Léon Blum during the first Popular Front government—the refusal to devalue rapidly, and the refusal to give massive aid to the Spanish Republic—the first had disappeared, as we have seen. As for the second, it had become attenuated to the extent that, on his return to power, Blum had not only decided to "relax nonintervention," closely associating Mendès France, as we have seen, with this strategic change, but he also considered intervening militarily with a "lightning" operation to save Barcelona. Mendès France did not participate in the discussion of this plan, which took place on March 16, 1938, not in a cabinet meeting but with the Permanent Committee of National Defense, in the presence of Marshal Pétain and General Gamelin.[7] But he supported the initiative with all his force.

> I remain convinced that it was necessary to intervene, that Clemenceau, Poincaré, or De Gaulle would have done so by July 1936. Obviously, confronted with the resistance of the majority of the Radicals at home and of the English abroad, it was very difficult. It would have taken a lot of "stomach" to confront the English and the Foreign Ministry with a *fait accompli,* especially after international commitments had been made. In any event, I was hardly kept informed about the intervention plan of March 1938, which appeared to be very belated.

But the great affair of the second Blum government, and more precisely of the Mendès–Boris tandem, was not Spain but what must be called the "Plan," which Alfred Sauvy characterizes as the "Socialist project." In the light of the disappointments and failures experienced by the first Popular Front government, there had developed a convergence among a group of economists and technicians from the CGT who had long been in favor of economic planning, certain experts from the SFIO like Georges Boris, Jules Moch, and Gaston Cusin, and men like Pierre Mendès France.

Léon Blum was personally rather suspicious of systematic economic planning, in which he saw the germ, or the risk, of a certain totalitarianism. Indeed, those of his former comrades, like Déat and Marquet, whose brutally statist tendencies had "appalled" him in November 1933 were the warmest supporters of planning. But Jules Moch and Georges Boris made him modify his prejudices. During the winter of 1937–38, the plan prepared by the CGT economists was revised by Boris; when Blum set up his second government, the proposal aiming to reshape French production with the goals of full employment and rearmament was quickly adopted as the fundamental basis of the government's economic strategy.

In 1933, Georges Boris had published a book entitled *La Révolution Roosevelt* (The Roosevelt Revolution), in which he argued that only a social revolution led by the state could save the West from the crisis, but also that such a revolution was not incompatible with the maintenance of the democratic system. The application of John Maynard Keynes's ideas by the strategists of the American New Deal, who were grappling in 1932 with a crisis that was more violent than the one troubling the European economy, had appeared persuasive to him. Convinced, moreover, that by 1936 the Western democracies had "entered a war economy," Boris, on the basis of the CGT plan, developed a way of connecting the two phenomena and attempting to place the revival of production and employment at the service of a determination to resist fascism. Since unemployment had allowed Hitler to recruit large numbers of shock troops, the basis of his power, the pursuit of full employment, should allow the democracies to prepare their defense.

Mendès France later remarked:

> Boris had measured the economic effects of capital flight and had attempted to find the means to guarantee the functioning of a domestic financial circuit in order to revive production. On the basis of Keynesian theories and the experience of the New Deal, he recommended a public works program to reduce unemployment and revive production. And although he was a pacifist, he had understood that against enemies like the Nazis it was necessary to oppose the strength of free peoples, that is, to rearm. These were the bases of the plan that was perfected in those weeks of March 1938 and presented at the time to the Parliament by Léon Blum.

Of the "declaration of purpose" of this bill, written by Georges Boris and Pierre Mendès France (a few of its formulations reveal the hand of Blum), the *Times* of London wrote that it was a "masterpiece of economic

thought at the service of a government." The Plan, which included measures that were extremely unpopular in right-wing circles—levies on
capital, exchange controls (to which Mendès, at first reticent, had
agreed)—was formulated in terms likely to appeal to presumably patriotic
public opinion.

> The measures proposed are governed by the immense obligation to assume
> the defense of the country. We shall show that the free peoples can live up to
> their duties, that the democracies are capable, through freely accepted disci-
> pline, of displaying the strength that is obtained elsewhere only from blind
> obedience. We shall proceed in such a way that a coordinated economy built
> around the manufacture of armaments will be the basis of enlarged produc-
> tion in every area.

The Blum–Mendès Plan was made up of a set of economic, financial,
and fiscal measures which today appear prudent but at the time provoked
cries of "inflationist" revolution:

> —Economic: price controls, increased hours in businesses working for
> national defense.
> —Financial: a two-year suspension of amortization of the public debt,
> authorization to the government to require the national bank to issue a new
> advance of ten billion francs, reevaluation of the gold holdings of the Banque
> de France on the basis of domestic prices, practical establishment of ex-
> change controls by requiring buyers to provide reasons for their operations.
> —Fiscal: levies on capital (up to 17 percent), general increase of income
> tax and taxes on businesses working for national defense, deductions for
> small retailers and manufacturers, energetic measures against fraud.

In the course of the debate that took place, while the Plan was being
put into final form, among Blum's colleagues, management, and the unions, "the right," according to Alfred Sauvy,

> was much less concerned with increased hours than with the restoration of
> public order, that is, the authority of the owners of goods. The national
> economic perspective escaped it yet again. The workers never refused to
> make an effort, but they did not see any necessity for it; the most perspica-
> cious demanded, in return, a sacrifice on the part of property owners. But the
> latter, sensing a change in the wind, were very far from a night of August 4.[8]

In the Chamber on April 6, Léon Blum, with Mendès France beside
him on the government bench, had the bill adopted, and the right-wing
press ("foolishly," according to Sauvy) characterized it as "Marxist."
Then, on April 8, the Senate of Joseph Caillaux made it plain to him,
danger of war or not, that the time had not come to place capital under the
tutelage of the state. And once again the upper chamber forced Blum to
resign a few days later.

Mendès France's first trial in government had not even lasted a month. But the breadth of the tasks undertaken, the vigor of the resistance encountered, and the boldness of the proposed plan had given exceptional meaning to the experience, reinforced by service alongside a man like Léon Blum and the now fraternal cooperation with Georges Boris.

The government had to dissolve. The evening he had been "executed" by Caillaux (the word he used), Blum submitted the resignation of his government, the members of which went with him to the president of the Republic. "M. Lebrun," according to Mendès France,

> gave us a rather ridiculous little speech. When the government had been set up, he had served champagne. That day, he offered us only orangeade. As for Léon Blum, I think I asked to see him in order to thank him for the confidence he had shown in me. We remained in contact. Every morning, I read his article in *Le Populaire,* and I agreed with it nine times out of ten. He helped me to see clearly and to articulate my positions precisely.

Was this also true of Munich? Three months after the fall of the second Blum government came the Sudeten crisis, threatening war clouds, and in September the quadripartite conference and the Munich agreement, which opened to Hitler the west flank of a now defenseless Czechoslovakia. The director of *Le Populaire,* on that occasion, allowed himself to speak of a "cowardly relief." What did Mendès France, a resolute antifascist, think of that?

> Basically, what Léon Blum expressed that day was what everybody felt. Even opponents of Munich like us—the "warmongers," as the right-wing press called us—felt seized by a "cowardly relief" when we saw war move away. The articles by Georges Bidault in *L'Aube* had the same ring. Paul Reynaud himself said nothing against the agreement. The only ones who did not stop protesting were the Communists, and Henri de Kirillis. Must we talk of a "crime of Daladier" in Munich? What would I have done if, by some unlikely chance, I had been called on to replace him that day? The crime was the one that had been perpetrated during the preceding six months by all French authorities, allowing Hitler to act with impunity. The day of Munich itself, it was too late. On what step of the staircase should we have stopped: the Rhineland, Spain, Vienna, Prague? Munich was only a stage in that long descent into Hell.
>
> I remember the visit I paid to Daladier at the Ministry of War a few days after his return from Munich. In the room next to his office there were piles of gifts that all of France had sent him in gratitude: bouquets of flowers, *objets d'art,* boxes of cigars, knick-knacks of all kinds. It was overwhelming: it looked like a display of gifts at an old-fashioned wedding. Daladier opened the door and found me there, contemplating these proofs of a popularity at its zenith. I didn't really know what to say to him, but I went ahead: "It must be moving for you, all these demonstrations of popular gratitude." And he

looked at me with a dismal air, shrugging his shoulders: "What asses." He wasn't taken in then, but he was later, when he'd breathed in too much of that tainted incense.

Pierre Mendès France was taken in neither then nor later. In *La Dépêche,* the articles by his alter ego, Jean Labéda, showed no indulgence: "We have, provisionally, saved our lives. But at what cost?" In his department, Mendès appeared more and more as an "anti-Munichois," along with his colleague Maître Chauvin, mayor of Evreux, whose Municipal Council passed a resolution against the September agreements. In the Chamber, the first time, on October 4, the deputy from Louviers voted for Daladier, like all the Radical deputies, including the Young Turks. But in December, after the general debate which allowed the Assembly to assess the operation, he abstained.

He was all the more inclined to do so because the general political orientation of the government was moving further and further from the Popular Front program on which the majority of the Assembly had been elected. Paul Reynaud, minister of finance, pushed through bills that gradually reduced the gains of the two Blum governments. In January 1939, Mendès France protested against "these decrees contrary to social justice as well as to financial recovery."

But general concerns were already turned elsewhere. Everyone thought about the coming war, announced by Hitler's every word, every action, every measure. In March, seizing Prague, which had been disarmed by the Munich agreements, the Nazi dictator openly flouted those he had negotiated with in September. From then on, there was time to think of nothing but how to confront the threat. At that point, Blum's former undersecretary even reproached himself for not having been interested enough in military questions, not having given them enough of his time. Several of his friends in Parliament, from Philippe Serre to Léo Lagrange, had read Colonel de Gaulle's books and tried to interest him in them. Like Boris, he had thought only about the "war economy," which was indeed his "niche."

As a citizen, he had prepared himself. We have seen how keenly interested he was in his original branch of service, the air force, in its various forms, of which meteorology is not the least important. He had done periods of military service, enough to be promoted to the rank of lieutenant (not airborne) in 1937. He wanted to transfer to the flying force. But, past thirty, he was already too old. It would take the exceptional circumstances that were coming to enable him to fulfill his wish.

In 1939, Pierre Mendès France was thirty-two. His wife Lily had given him a second son, Michel, in 1936. Former undersecretary, deputy from Louviers—by now very solidly established—mayor of the town, general councillor of Eure, spokesman for the left wing of the Radical Party for economic and financial questions, chairman of the Customs Committee in the Chamber, he would already have been destined for a long and prestigious governmental career had he not been so solidly anchored on the left, especially in matters of foreign policy. A journey to the Soviet Union with Herriot in 1934, his steps in favor of active support for the Spanish Republic, and his criticisms of the Munich agreements had placed him, in the eyes of the right-wing press, along with Blum, Reynaud, Mandel, Cot, Zay, and the Communists, in the camp of the "warmongers." And there were many who wanted to make him pay for that.

Nevertheless, his position as a lawyer provided him with a comfortable income—less than what he earned after the war, after he had practically stopped his activities as a lawyer, in the international arbitrations for which his character and his competence made him so suitable. As much for pleasure as to deepen his knowledge, he taught economics and finance at the Ecole Supérieure des Hautes Etudes Sociales.

At the Radical congress in Marseille he spoke little, only on technical questions. What restrained him from expressing himself was the reserve imposed on him by his profound disagreement on foreign policy questions with the leaders of his party, who had provided friendly patronage for his professional and political life, Georges Bonnet and Edouard Daladier, signatories of and now advocates for agreements that he, Mendès France, like his friends Pierre Cot, Jean Zay, and Jacques Kayser, disapproved. What good would a skirmish in a congress do, when it would soon be necessary to rise up in arms?

> Would it be in three weeks, three months, three years? Would Hitler first seize Poland, Denmark, the Ukraine, or what? One might be surprised by a particular event or a particular headline, one morning; but everyone knew what was at the end of the tunnel we were traveling through.

THE WIND OF FREEDOM

5.
THE INSULT AND THE PITY

Pierre Mendès France recounted what he lived through from September 1, 1939, to the liberation of France in 1944 in *Liberté, liberté chérie,*[1] a book whose sincerity is complete. Whether he is talking of the abject trial to which he was subjected, his escape from the Clermont-Ferrand prison, his tribulations in occupied France, or his battles in 1942 and 1943, the narrative rings true. Published in New York in 1942, and revised thirty-five years later for its Paris publication, it retains the slightly harsh and breathless spontaneity of on-the-spot testimony. As such, it is a particularly valuable source of information about the experiences of a man of character in the innumerable vicissitudes of war. It will be our principal source here, supplemented with others as necessary.[2]

To fight, rejecting the opportunity granted young deputies to receive a commission without risk and close to Paris, this was the first rule he adopted for himself. He chose this path first of all because he felt totally committed to the war as a patriot and as a militant of the left: Beyond a classic confrontation of nationalisms, as in 1914, he saw the war as a battle against aggression, racism, and barbarism. Moreover, he was what was then called in *L'Action française, L'Oeuvre,* and *Je suis partout* a "warmonger," a man who called for taking arms against Hitler. When one has taken such positions, it is hard not to put them into practice. He felt obliged to accept his responsibilities, take risks, provide an example, in short, to fight. And to fight alongside the fliers, to whom he felt very close.

But the talk around him was, particularly from his friend Daladier, that the fortification systems, Maginot Line against Siegfried Line, were such that fighting in Europe would be stagnant for a long time. It would be a long war of attrition, of economic exhaustion through a blockade. On the other hand, a real battle was shaping up in the East, where an ambitious expeditionary force had been sent under the command of General Weygand, presumed to be the most competent French military leader. He decided to attempt to participate in the vast operation of encircling the Axis through the Balkans that was being set up in Beirut, an operation involving some of the best officers of the French air force.

Mendès France was thus assigned to the Levant. In the plane en route to Beirut on September 29, 1939, he met Colonel Lucien, a "splendid fighter of 1914," according to Mendès, who had become leader of the French air force in Lebanon—and Lucien naturally assigned Mendès to his headquarters staff. But Mendès thought only of fighting, that is, of flying. He made persistent requests to be transferred to the airborne branch, and he was met with the objection that what the air force lacked was "planes, not men," especially men of thirty-three. Once the request was made, his file sat in Beirut and then in Paris, where Lieutenant Mendès was sent on leave in January 1940 in an attempt to compel a decision in his case from the minister. He was also given the task by Colonel Lucien to speed up the deliveries of up-to-date materiel to the Levant.[3]

As a soldier on leave in Paris in early 1940, Mendès found the capital only moderately concerned, with the head of government, Daladier, asserting that he "had confidence in the military leaders," and the ladies of the sixteenth *arrondissement* preparing flower arrangements for the army. Mendès France cut his leave short, since he had seen his family, been assigned to a training program in the airborne division, and received promises of delivery of modern aircraft for "the eastern Mediterranean theater of operations."

By the end of January, he was dividing his time between the headquarters staff of Colonel Lucien and the base at Rayak, near the Syrian border, where he was following the training program for navigators under the direction of Colonel Le Coq de Kerland. On April 22, even though he had joined the course two months late, he received his certificate as navigator, first in the class (as usual) with a grade of eighteen out of twenty and the congratulations of his instructors. He was now ready for battle.

On May 3, Lieutenant Mendès France, with leave granted by Colonel Le Coq de Kerland, flew to Paris and then traveled to Louviers, the official destination for his leave—he had to attend a session of the General Council of Eure. Immediately after landing at Le Bourget, he set out for Evreux and then Louviers, where he stayed until the eighth. On the ninth, he was back in Paris, shocked by the prevailing climate of indolence. But the operations in Norway seemed to be a prelude to a real outbreak of war. To fight against Nazism at last, he had to be assigned to Scandinavia. With this in mind, he called for an audience with the minister of the air force, his friend Laurent-Eynac, for the morning of the tenth.

That morning he was awakened by air raid sirens and the sound of anti-aircraft fire. But he paid little attention, since the phony war had been punctuated by such sounds. He was calm when he arrived at the ministry on the boulevard Victor at nine o'clock, where Laurent-Eynac was waiting for him. The conversation was normal at first. The visitor spoke of the Levant, of his proposed assignment to Norway. "Considering what is happening now," said the minister, "I don't know whether we can send planes there." "What do you mean?" "You mean you don't know? Last night the Germans invaded Belgium and Holland."

Mendès rushed to Colonel Lucien, who had been transferred to the post of head of personnel at the Ministry of the Air Force, to have himself assigned to a unit fighting on the Belgian front. But his certificate was too recent, and the Potez in which he had passed his tests were old planes. According to Colonel Lucien, he needed seasoning on more modern planes before he could be risked in a fighting unit against the redoubtable Messerschmitts. That meant that, for now, he had to undergo training at Romilly or Mérignac, the Bordeaux airport where a retraining center had just been set up.

The obstinate Mendès did not give up, and in the succeeding days he tried all sorts of tactics, particularly approaching his instructor from Rayak, Colonel Le Coq de Kerland, who had also been recalled from the East to serve in the ministry, in order to be assigned to a fighting unit before the end of his leave. It was a wasted effort.

At lunch that day with the anti-Nazi writer Emil Ludwig, Mendès France met Henri de Kerillis, a journalist of the right who was nonetheless a leader of those opposed to Munich. Kerillis assured him: "In a month, the Germans will be in Paris or we will be in Berlin. This is not *one* of the battles in the war, it is *the* decisive battle." This could only encourage him to step up his attempts to be assigned to the northern front. Staff officers of the Ministry of the Air Force convinced him to wait in Paris for his new assignment; in any event, they pointed out, the order for all soldiers on leave to return to their units immediately did not apply to the army of the East.[4]

It was difficult to wait. By the thirteenth and fourteenth the news had become tragic.

On May 16, the day the Assembly session resumed, there was the beginning of a panic, which was probably not spontaneous. One minister advised his friends, particularly the Jews, to leave the threatened capital. The corridors of the Palais-Bourbon were choked with a feverish crowd. Members of the government hinted that the Germans would be in Paris that very evening. An officer from the headquarters of the commander-in-chief announced that a column of German tanks had broken through the front near Laon and that there was no obstacle between them and Paris.

It was about time for Mendès France to discover, through his friend Philippe Serre, that five months earlier a certain Colonel de Gaulle had distributed a memorandum demanding the activation of autonomous armored divisions supported by a powerful air force.

Blocked from participating in battle, he fully assumed his responsibilities as mayor of Louviers, where he had settled his wife and sons at the outset of the war. The little town, at first traversed by French and British units advancing to the front, was suddenly inundated by refugees. Mendès France evoked the scene very powerfully in *Liberté, liberté chérie.*

> Then came the heavy horse-drawn carts of the peasants from Nord; they advanced slowly, loaded with the sick, children, old people, agricultural tools, furniture. Everything that could be piled on, everything that could be torn from the earth to keep it from the enemy, had been carried away. Surrounding the carts, there were sometimes horses and cattle. . . . Generally a village had moved off as a whole, with the mayor, the priest, the old schoolmaster, the rural policeman. It was a colossal uprooting, an avalanche of one region falling on another.
>
> At the beginning there were no soldiers in this dramatic convoy. Later, a few isolated uniforms, Belgian first, then French, appeared. In the end, whole detachments, military cars, and trucks mingled with the great wave flowing south and west, and they added to its strange variousness. My friends in Louviers did their best to help these poor people, who had been cast out on the roads, headed toward an unknown fate. But the problem was superhuman. The convoys, which were at first intermittent, became continuous; covering dozens, and then hundreds of kilometers, the river of refugees overflowed, irresistible, uninterrupted, without a break or a breathing space; half of France was flowing into the other half.[5]

Every day he did not spend in Louviers he went to the Ministry of the Air Force to request a new assignment from Colonel Lucien, who, exasperated, finally promised him that he would be accommodated on June 10, as long as he agreed to undergo the required extra training before being assigned to a combat aircraft. On the ninth began the evacuation of Louviers, in imminent danger from German tanks. He rushed toward the town, but he had covered only half the distance when he came upon

Verron in flames. And as soon as he entered the town, on the south bank of the Seine, he came under fire from the German tanks holding the north bank. The bridge had been blown up, but without any artillery, the small French unit stationed there could not hold out for long.

His car, riddled with bullets, was useless. Mendès set out in search of another vehicle: if Louviers was occupied, he had at least to return to Paris. At that point he received a shrapnel wound in the shoulder: "Not a serious wound," he pointed out soberly, but it was to trouble him in the course of the dramatic events of the succeeding days. A military truck transported him to Evreux, where a merchant fleeing to Paris took him into her car. Under constant bombardment, short of gas—they ended up siphoning fuel from an abandoned car—he reached the capital at dawn, having already experienced the debacle in his own flesh.

On June 10, after treatment and X rays at a Paris hospital, he was received by Colonel Lucien at the ministry with the news that no decision had been made about him. But Colonel Lucien, whose staff had already been evacuated, prepared a handwritten order directing "Lieutenant Pierre Mendès France, of the French air force of the eastern Mediterranean, to report to the navigators school in Bordeaux, where he is assigned to complete his training."

Mendès France had decided to send his wife and children, who had been evacuated from Louviers a week earlier, to Jarnac, where he had bought a little house a short time before. He stayed put for three more days, for medical treatments and to spend a little time with his parents, who had decided, in spite of everything, to stay in Paris. It was only on the thirteenth, at the very moment when the first enemy contingents were entering the capital, that he took the road south in an old car he had borrowed from a cousin.

In the tragic rout and under fire, driving with difficulty because of his wound, he took four days to reach Jarnac, exhausted. Lily and the children had, with great difficulty, arrived two days before. He had his wound treated, slept a little, and, on the seventeenth, left for Bordeaux, where he learned that the Reynaud government had just resigned, giving free rein to Pétain, who was known to favor an immediate armistice. He had just seen France defeated; he had yet to see it degraded.

Mendès entitled the chapter on the Bordeaux episode in *Liberté, liberté chérie* (a book written in the midst of war, struggle, and anger) "Les Traîtres" (The Traitors), coarsening outlines a little, simplifying perspectives and problems. But the indictment is powerful.

> More often than not, the supporters of the armistice were motivated by domestic political concerns. France had to expiate its sins. It needed a defeat in order to be regenerated, to build a new regime on the misfortune it had deserved. A victory would have consolidated the old regime. Wasn't it finally

a good thing that it had been refused that victory? The men who thought like this knew that the cessation of hostilities would involve a more or less substantial surrender to Hitler's Germany, a reversal in domestic politics, and a break with the democracies. This was exactly what they wanted, and they now proclaimed it without restraint. The perennial enemies of republican government, the politicians who had been seeking revenge since 1936, bankers in search of business (they were already talking of "reconstruction"), the fascists who had been systematic "conscientious objectors" since September 1939, right-thinking great ladies (they recommended a government made up of military men, whom they considered the only ones capable of restoring order and putting down communism), academicians whom no one read in France but who had lucrative contracts with German publishers—all joined together in a conspiracy that insinuated itself, infiltrated, slipped in everywhere, in the press, administrative offices, the army, and the goverment.

Pierre Mendès France, attracted by Churchill's proposal to join France and Great Britain into a single nation against the Third Reich, devastated by the request for an armistice, was among the small minority of the French who listened to General de Gaulle's appeal on June 18: "passionately," he said later. But, at that point, he did not consider going to London. He agreed with Colonel Lucien, whom he met again in Bordeaux and who disapproved of De Gaulle's attitude that the fight should continue in North Africa. Lucien accompanied Mendès to the base in Mérignac, where he was to join the unit to which he had been assigned.

In the indescribable chaos that submerged the airport, it was impossible to find the training squadron to which he belonged. A group of noncommissioned officers informed him that his new commander, Colonel Bonneau, had flown to Morocco, where the unit had been transferred. From all sides came assurances that General Vuillemain, head of the French air force, was for resistance and that he had given all necessary instructions to continue the struggle alongside the English. The order circulating was: "As many planes and as many men as possible to North Africa!"[6] And one of Mendès's informants concluded: "You're on your own!"[7]

June 19 was the day when the government decided that the president of the Republic and the whole government, led by Vice-Premier Chautemps, since Philippe Pétain refused to leave the national territory, should leave for North Africa. The members of the executive were to leave from Port-Vendres, the legislators from Bordeaux. Admiral Darlan had chosen as transport vessel the auxiliary cruiser *Massilia,* which was to cast off on the twentieth. Since the Gironde was mined, the ship had anchored off Verdon, where embarkation was to take place.

Returning from Mérignac, Mendès France met one of his Radical colleagues, Chichery, minister of commerce, who informed him of the

Massilia's sailing and encouraged him to get on board. As a soldier, he would then find a way to join his unit in Morocco. He would be able to bring his family, still refugees in Charente, with him; official orders recommended that departing political figures not leave their families on French territory because the Nazis might use them as hostages. He decided immediately. With his papers duly stamped by the central military transit office, he set out for Jarnac, where everyone piled into the old jalopy. They arrived in Verdon on the evening of the twentieth; there he met General Michel, commander of the guard at the Palais-Bourbon, who assumed the same functions during the crossing, and his friends from Parliament who had decided, as he had, to wear their uniforms and to continue the war: Pierre Viénot, Alfred Wiltzer, and Jean Zay.

The ship was soon boarded by Daladier, Mandel, Campinchi, Delbos, Le Troquer, Paul Bastid, Jammy-Schmidt, Salomon Grumbach, Perfetti (Assembly finance officer), Jacques Ibert, Julien Cain, Suzanne Schreiber-Crémieux and her daughter (who was to become Mendès's second wife). There were about a hundred people, who had been subjected to Luftwaffe attacks on the night of the twentieth. Herriot and Jeanneny, the presidents of the two assemblies, remained on land. The passengers on the *Massilia* legitimately wondered why. They had not been informed of the reversal that had taken place in Bordeaux: No matter what the provisions of the armistice that had been demanded, the government would remain on metropolitan soil, thereby placing itself at the mercy of Hitler's *diktat.* This decision made the *Massilia* passengers appear as runaways (others were already calling them deserters). The Pétain government was in any event now rid of the "resisters." The ship sailed on the twenty-first.

The next day, Laval and Marquet joined the government, the former as vice-premier, the latter as minister of the interior. And the day after that, the armistice was signed—it included a provision turning anti-Nazi refugees in France over to Hitler. The deputies on the *Massilia* immediately held a meeting to debate whether they should turn back, in order to oppose that policy in person, or because the continuation of the war was now useless and illegal.

Irritated by this palaver, Mendès France took no part; his parliamentary reflexes were overcome by his will to fight. As far as he was concerned, the question did not arise: he was in a hurry to join his unit in Morocco. Moreover, legality and honor seemed to him to be on the side of those continuing the struggle alongside the allies of France against the armies occupying the national territory. This was also the opinion of the majority of his friends on board: Viénot, Zay, Campinchi, and others. Cutting the debate short, Major Ferbos relied on a wartime regulation to maintain the course for Casablanca.

They landed on the twenty-fourth amid freighters unloading cases of American materiel. This created a good impression: they would find a means there to continue the war, all the more because the climate seemed favorable. Although General Noguès, resident general in Rabat, who had just been named commander-in-chief of all North African forces and to whom De Gaulle had just addressed an appeal full of hope, was unable to meet the travelers, he sent his general secretary from Rabat, Morize (who affirmed his conviction "that North Africa could not possibly desert the cause of the Allies"),[8] and seven generals, who, with Daladier and Mandel, participated in an improvised conference on the strategic perspectives open in the Mediterranean sector.

On the twenty-fifth, while Mendès France went with Campinchi and Jean Zay to the Jewish Circle of Casablanca (a gesture that provoked a lot of talk, but that allowed the visitors to verify the depth of the attachment the Moroccan Jewish community felt for France), Daladier, Mandel, Delbos, and Viénot went to Rabat to make political contacts. Mandel spoke with the British consul, who immediately began arrangements for a conference with two important English figures, Lord Gort and Duff Cooper. But when these two landed in Rabat the next day, on board a hydroplane into which Churchill had literally thrown them, they found that Noguès had forbidden them all contact with the people from the *Massilia,* which he had sent out to anchor off the coast of Casablanca. The general had chosen his camp. The North African war would not take place, not yet.

The next day, once the English emissaries had left, the *Massilia* returned to port, and everyone debarked. Georges Mandel had no sooner set foot on land, flanked by his companion Béatrice Bretty, an actress at the Comédie-Française, and their daughter Claude, and carrying the bronze bust of Clemenceau in his arms, than he was arrested. Brought before the director of the Sûreté, he simply said: "Sir, I will remove you. In six months or in six years, I will remove you."

The arrest of Mandel was only one sign of what was being prepared for the "runaways" of the *Massilia.* Another was a speech delivered in Bordeaux by the new minister of information, Jean Prouvost, denouncing "the cowards who have fled the fatherland," to go to Morocco; the press naturally followed the minister's lead. The campaign thus unleashed against people who had set sail in order to continue the struggle increased and grew more venomous for the next few years.

Pierre Mendès France had no other concern for the moment but to rejoin his unit. In Rabat, he presented himself to the regional air force commander, General François d'Astier de La Vigerie,[9] whom he found very cordial. He learned that his new unit was stationed in Meknès. But since all flights were suspended, the general preferred to keep him on his staff. He was thus reassigned to Rabat, under a leader of whose sympathy and respect he was assured.

But what was he to do? Many things were played out in Rabat in the course of the last few days of June 1940. It was then that General Noguès decided to rally to Pétain, to the politics of the armistice and everything that that implied, rather than to lend his authority—and the support of his very significant resources—to the strategy proposed by De Gaulle. Noguès later pointed out that it was the recognition of the Pétain–Laval government by the United States, legalizing the "*coup d'état* in defeat" perpetrated in Bordeaux, that led him to the "abdication against his deeper feelings," to use Mendès's terms.[10] But although the path of resignation had been chosen at the top, the officers of the air force were animated by a totally different spirit. Escapes to England by way of Gibraltar proliferated, "covered" by the headquarters staff of General d'Astier.

On July 3, however, the Mers el-Kébir massacre widened the gulf between London and a significant number of the French, who thought only of joining with their allies. In *Liberté, liberté chérie,* Mendès France nevertheless asserts that, after Mers el-Kébir, although "the navy took sides against the English, the air force as a whole understood the reasons for their intervention. In Casablanca, there was a brawl between sailors and airmen."

There were, however, air force generals who agreed, in cooperation with the navy, to a reprisal against Gibraltar. On July 16, Lieutenant Mendès France was "officer of the day" in the headquarters of General d'Astier (who had refused to lead the operation). He was alone in the offices from noon until two. The order to unleash the operation, demanded by Laval, Darlan, and Weygand, but that other members of the government were trying to prevent, was expected from one minute to the next. "What should I do?" The answer came immediately: "Do not transmit it. That would create a delay of a few hours which might change everything by allowing the moderates to regain control. Once bombardment had begun, the situation would be irremediable."[11] Shortly after two there came a delaying message, soon confirmed by the Algiers offices. Thus Pierre Mendès France, on that July 16, did not have his own version of June 18.

Because Mendès France had long served as *rapporteur* for questions relating to oil in the Customs Committee of the Chamber, General d'Astier gave him the task of preparing a report on Morocco's fuel needs, in anticipation of new developments in the war. In the minds of the military leaders in Algiers, there was obviously the hypothesis of a conflict with London. The report of Lieutenant Mendès France must have caused more than one raised eyebrow in Weygand's entourage.

France and its empire, Morocco in particular, have based their oil policy on imports, that is, in the end, on the Anglo-Saxon world, master of the oil wells and of the maritime routes. They cannot, from one day to the next, in the midst of an international crisis, reverse that policy and seek autonomy, which is unattainable through the use of their resources alone. . . . There are raw materials, of which oil is a prime example, that nature has distributed in such a way that, for them, despite everything, we will remain dependent on the Anglo-Saxon world. It is up to us to draw the necessary conclusions from this fact.

And he punctuated the assertion of his position with these formulations: "One can only, in Morocco and elsewhere, follow the policy of one's means. One can only fight the war of one's resources."[12] These words would be heard again.

Even if we presume that it was slightly softened by General d'Astier before being transmitted to them, such a report was not of the kind that could help Mendès with the masters of Algiers. They had no doubt heard the reply he had given to one of his commanders in early July, who asked whether he intended to ask for leave to participate in the National Assembly session in Vichy:

The Assemblies no longer have any real power. They will not even be consulted on the essential thing, that is, the armistice. A constitutional abdication will be dragged out of them. The Third Republic is dead. While we wait for the return of a democratic regime, France will be governed by people chosen directly or indirectly by the enemy. I will not participate in the comedy to be performed in Vichy.

Moreover, for the last few weeks, he had heard around him a kind of obscene murmur, a slippery rumor: the *Massilia* passengers were runaways. At the Assembly podium in Vichy, Herriot had protested against this assertion, and Laval had noted his protest. But these debates were barely reported in Rabat. Around July 20, a newspaper published his photograph with the caption: "Deserting Officer." And on July 26, a dispatch distributed by the Havas agency announced that the four deputies in uniform who had sailed on the *Massilia,* Jean Zay, Pierre Viénot, Alfred Wiltzer, and Pierre Mendès France, would be "put before military tribunals for abandonment of their posts in the face of the enemy." General d'Astier, who considered himself attacked by the disgraceful accusation brought against an officer he had chosen for his staff, summoned him immediately and went over the dossier with him. "They made a mistake in your case," he concluded. "In good faith, I'm convinced of it. Prepare a report, and I will transmit it as quickly as possible."

It seems evident that D'Astier was "covering" him and would refuse to sign the order, without which he could not be pursued. But in Algiers, Noguès and General Pennès, commander of the air forces of North Africa, mislaid or buried the protest of Lieutenant Mendès France, whose fate now depended entirely on General d'Astier. Should he escape, like a number of his comrades, and go to Gibraltar and London? He was more inclined to stay put, scorning a way out that would, provisionally, suggest a confession of guilt. Maître Mendès France was even then steeped in juridical attitudes. How confident he was in the legal procedures and the justice of his country, even though he knew all the mechanisms of the Dreyfus affair. D'Astier advised him along the same lines: "You ought to stay to defend your honor. You do not have the right to doubt military justice."[13] And he demanded his word of honor that he would not leave Rabat.

His life there was not unpleasant. With his wife and two sons, he had moved into the Hotel Balima, in the center of the city, along with most of the "immigrants" of June, notably the Zay family. The hotel was reasonably comfortable, and the food acceptable. There they met Henri Fouques-Duparc, who had been Mendès's squadron leader in the Levant, and his wife, who became friendly with Lily.

But the circle of hostility was closing around them. General Bouscat, whom he had known as on the left in Paris, and who was trying to make up for it, refused to recognize him in the corridors. A captain let him know that if he met him in the Balima bar he would kick him out. In return, Mendès's friends let it be known that, if necessary, they would force their way in. The captain was urgently transferred out of Rabat. A lawyer who had been asked to defend him in the event his case came before the tribunal begged off because he had received threats from headquarters. It was the atmosphere of the Dreyfus affair, or worse. When Jean Zay, whose wife was about to give birth to their second child, went to get the midwife he had retained, she excused herself—she, too, had been threatened. The carriers of the plague should not even be allowed to have children.

On August 12, Jean Zay was arrested. Why he alone? He had taken on more significant political responsibilities than others and therefore provoked more intense hatred. (It should be noted that Zay was not Jewish according to Jewish law. His father was a member of the Jewish community of Orléans, but his mother was Christian, and he was baptized a Protestant and was, moreover, agnostic.) The protection of General d'Astier continued to work in Mendès's favor. But because he refused to sign the order of indictment against Mendès France, and also because this monarchist did not hide the fact that he remained loyal to his Jewish friends (which earned him in Rabat his nickname "D'Astier de la juiverie"), he was relieved of his command on August 22. Thereafter, the proceedings against Mendès France could get under way. "On August 30, I learned from an indiscretion that I would be arrested the next day."[14] He took advantage of his last hours of freedom to visit Jean Zay's wife, who had just given birth to a girl: if he, too, was transferred to Clermont-Ferrand, he would be able to describe the child, whom the father had not seen.

On August 31, at six o'clock in the morning, at the Hotel Balima, the captain of the Rabat gendarmes came to ask Pierre Mendès France to accompany him to the barracks to be given "a letter concerning him." The letter indicated that, by virtue of "a telephone order from Algiers," he was under arrest. The illegality was complete, down to the slightest details. After a brief visit with his family and the announcement that he would be incarcerated and judged in Morocco (near his family and at some distance from the pressures of Vichy), he was taken to the military prison in Casablanca, an old sordid building on the rue de Tunis, where the cell in which he was put was illuminated only by a tiny grill in the door. Through that, he saw the arrival of Philippe de Rothschild, whom he knew only slightly, arrested at the same time and whose indictment had, so to speak, nothing to do with his own. No relationship except the abject pursuit of the Jews.

It is useless to attempt to imagine the first of the three hundred nights of Mendès France as a prisoner; he has described it himself with restrained emotion.

> I think of my old parents to whom I cannot write, since the demarcation line separates us. They will learn of my arrest from the newspapers. I think also of all those who have had confidence in me for years, who will not learn the truth about my affair, because the press will unanimously deceive them. Will they doubt me? Will they believe that I was capable of committing the cowardly crime of which I have been accused and for which I will be condemned?
>
> Not for an instant do I consider the possibility of having the charges dropped or being acquitted; the chances of my receiving justice are infinitesimal. No matter, I will have to fight as though the game were fair, as though justice were just, as though the judges were free, as though I could have a little confidence in the men who hold my fate in their hands. I sense that they hate me. I know that one discusses nothing, demonstrates nothing, proves nothing, against hatred.
>
> For a long time, I dream, I reason, I reflect. I consider my affair from the beginning, day by day, hour by hour, I relive the adventure that has brought me here, and I try to find the crime that, involuntarily, I might have committed. Of course, once the armistice was signed, I would have deserted if necessary, to join the army of Free France. But on June 20, when I embarked in Bordeaux, I did not have to desert. I committed no infraction, not even apparent, not even formal.
>
> What will become of my wife, alone in this foreign country? What will become of my little boys?[15]

Material problems were pressing. Lily had finally been able to sell her few jewels. But, Mendès France later observed, "the banks were ignoble, even before my arrest and the official proclamation of the racial laws, although the Banque de France was less guilty than others." Some friends did come forward, particularly in the Jewish community. The Scemama family of Tunis, for example, offered their services and invited Lily and the children to come to stay with them. The offer was not accepted, but it gave evidence of a state of mind that allowed the prisoner and his family not to despair when they read in one of the newspapers that always manage to get through prison walls: "Arrest of the Jewish deputy Mendès France who deserted during the campaign in France."

The prisoners were allowed a half-hour visit each week from their closest relatives. Lily would come from Rabat with the two boys. But the entrance hall of the prison was even dirtier and more foul-smelling than the cells. The guards were present, and they took part in the conversations and dared to beg for "their" share of the food brought by the visitors.

> I was ashamed for my wife every time I met her in such circumstances. And seeing the boys in that sordid hole, in front of the coarse guard, did me more harm than good. I had the impression that it was dirtying them, contaminating them. I asked my wife not to bring them anymore.

There were a few friends with him: in addition to Philippe de Rothschild, who taught him to play bridge and belote, there was Philippe Michelin, arrested when he attempted to go to Gibraltar, and Pierre Viénot, a perennial military volunteer, who had been wounded in 1914 and was nevertheless accused of desertion as well. On September 4, he was visited by the examining magistrate in charge of his case, Captain Voituriez, a minor functionary whose superiors soon recognized that he was no match for Mendès. They therefore removed the case from this amateur and gave it to their cleverest examining magistrate, Colonel Leprêtre, which meant that the dossier and the accused would be transferred to the tribunal of Clermont-Ferrand. On October 4, it was learned that that court had condemned Jean Zay to deportation for life. Mendès was warned. He was not being sent before judges but before prosecutors, with no concern for legality.

The transfer to Clermont-Ferrand posed a new family problem. Lily immediately decided to follow him, with the boys. He was against it, as Jean Zay had been in similar circumstances, for two reasons: first, in reach of the judges and police of Clermont, the families could more easily be used as hostages; second and more important, the two former colleagues of Léon Blum thought that the invasion of all of French territory was inevitable. In that event, those who were still in a position to do so should be able to flee to America, which could be more easily accomplished from Casablanca than from Clermont-Ferrand. Zay and Mendès had urgent exchanges of letters with their wives. Mme. Zay finally joined her husband, confronting him with a *fait accompli* (Mendès France thought that this was the reason Zay never tried to escape), while Lily finally allowed herself to be convinced to wait in Morocco, from which she was able to take her sons to the United States in 1942.

Casablanca, Oran, Marseille, Clermont-Ferrand: it was a sinister journey in the company of four gendarmes. The Auvergne prison was a little more decent than the Moroccan. He was no longer at the bottom of a stifling well, and, from the window with one pane missing (it was already cold in October), he could see mountains beyond the factory smokestacks. But he was in solitary confinement. He had the right to communicate neither with Zay, already found guilty (they had only two furtive encounters), nor with Viénot, who had arrived before him. And there was starvation, the food was disgusting and hygiene nonexistent. Most of the prisoners, who had been crowded together for more than a year, were tubercular. In his cell, he suffered unspeakably from isolation.

In December, after Viénot had been given an eight-year suspended prison term, Wiltzer had been granted a dismissal (he was the only one on the *Massilia* whose situation was not entirely regular, but he belonged to a party of the right), and Zay had been transferred to Marseille and then to Riom, Mendès was the last of the *Massilia* passengers incarcerated in Clermont. Tragically abandoned as he felt, he had to find a defender at any cost. After the president of the Clermont-Ferrand bar had courageously declined (defending a Jew, even if he was a colleague victimized by political and judicial machinations . . .), Mendès was visited by two courageous and talented men, Rochat of the Clermont bar and Fonlupt-Espéraber of the Strasbourg bar.

A visit from his father, who had managed with great difficulty to come from Paris, provoked more anger than it provided comfort. A guard greeted the old man with insults. Mendès's reaction was typical of him: "I will forgive many things. But I will never forget Officer Montagne, who was cruel and nasty to an old father overwhelmed by seeing his son in prison and deserving of pity and respect."

He was released from solitary confinement at the end of December, and he felt as though he had come back to life. He finally had contacts with other prisoners, Gaullists like himself for the most part, among them the future General Biroche and Vincent Monteil, who later became a noted specialist in Arab affairs and whom he sent to Algiers in January 1955 along with Soustelle. His most surprising encounter was with Georges Valois, old union official, former editor of *L'Action française,* founder of the *Faisceau,* who had become a publisher and issued Mendès

France's second book, *La Banque internationale,* in 1930. Having quarreled with Maurras, he was evidently there as a victim of the rancor of the old leader of Action Française; he maintained that he had never had the slightest contact with the Gaullists. He died in the camps in the following year.

In early 1941, the deputy and mayor of Louviers received in prison a circular addressed to all members of Parliament specifying that the Jews were henceforth deprived of their elected positions; those affected by the measure were supposed to send a statement to the head of state. Invited to write to Pétain, he did so in a vehement tone, simultaneously denouncing this crudely racist decision and the insulting procedure that had been undertaken against him, demanding that it be brought to an end. To be more certain that the letter would be read, he addressed it to Pétain's chief of staff, Du Moulin de La Barthète, whom he had known for a long time and considered as a "loyal adversary." The answer was sent by Du Moulin to Mendès's lawyers: it indicated that the marshal had taken note of the letter and had been "very moved by reading it." Moved, not outraged?

Preparations of the trial dragged on interminably. On October 16, four days after his arrival at the Clermont prison, the accused had been summoned to the office of the man on whom Vichy was counting to bring in a guilty verdict. Colonel Leprêtre was the best military specialist in this kind of procedure; he had been in charge of the cases, successively, of Reynaud, Mandel, Zay, Viénot, Colonel d'Ornano, and General Leclerc.

> He was a short, thin man, discreet, a little timid, rather distinguished in appearance, in speech, and in style. He had a soft face, with delicate features, rather sad, and a pepper-and-salt mustache. A former student of the Ecole Normale Supérieure, he wrote well, with a certain elegance. He knew his job admirably well. In my case, he had studied everything, sifted everything, probed everything. While the proceedings lasted, personal letters from my wife were intercepted by the censors, photographed, and added to the file; he exploited them with Machiavellian cleverness. My lawyers themselves were watched, followed, spied on. His methods were so shocking that he was summoned to Royat by his superiors in the military justice system and reprimanded, not so much for having broken the law as for having done it too flagrantly. He did not forgive me for this slap in the face.

Against this implacable enemy, he had vigilant allies, first of all his lawyers. Jacques Fonlupt-Espéraber, a luminary of the Strasbourg bar, former general secretary of the Alsace-Lorraine Association, did not conceal from Mendès when he immediately accepted his case that he was "blunt, impetuous," and that he "could not be counted on to smooth things over"; to which the accused retorted that he had few illusions about the judicial system and that he wanted to "fight." Rochat was much

younger and less political. But the baseness of the file and Colonel Leprêtre's methods made him join in with Fonlupt. And Mendès soon found
other support, notably from Lucie and Edgar Faure, who had taken refuge
in the region and were very attentive to him and paid him frequent visits
and whose presence was very comforting.

Leprêtre, who had begun the proceedings on October 14, slowly built
up the file and then tested the accused with a few visits to his cell,
occasions for apparently anodyne, undirected conversations, finally got
to the heart of the matter on December 17, when he carried out a thorough
interrogation in his office. It turned out, according to the theory he had
constructed, that Mendès was guilty not of one but of three desertions: on
May 10, 1940, when leaves were canceled and he did not immediately
return to his unit in the Near East; on June 10, when he had received
orders from Colonel Lucien to join his new unit in Mérignac and had not
reported to the base until several days later; and finally on June 20, by
sailing on the *Massilia:* whatever his intentions may have been at the
time, he did not have the right, said Leprêtre, to "choose his battlefield."

Did Colonel Leprêtre really believe in the solidity of this indictment?
When Mendès France's lawyers asked for his conditional release at the
end of December, the examining magistrate objected that it was useless to
complicate matters: imminent dismissal of the charges was probable. And
he confided the same thing to Colonel de Margueritte, military commander of Clermont. It was true that immediately after Laval's disgrace
and the formation of the Flandin government, the atmosphere in Vichy
was moving toward moderation. But when Darlan replaced Flandin a
month later, the orders that came from Vichy encouraged Colonel Leprêtre to return to his original rigor and to pursue it to the infamous end.

On January 13, 1941, he sent to the air force minister in Vichy a
request for "information" on the personality and the morality of the two
principal witnesses, who, he knew, would refuse to give evidence against
Mendès: General d'Astier and Colonel Lucien. By return mail he received
a letter signed by General Bergeret, minister of the air force.

Bergeret's letter was a mass of vile informers' reports concerning all the men
who had committed the wrong of speaking the truth from the beginning of the
proceedings. Most of my former superiors were dragged through the mud in
the most outrageous manner. Their private lives, their families, their pasts,
were denigrated with incredible indiscretion and vulgarity. Out of respect for
them, I cannot sum up this dishonorable document. Fonlupt, in the indignant
protest that he immediately registered, could write that "in thirty years of
professional experience [I] have never seen such a document over a respected signature." . . . From that point on, before Leprêtre and later before
the tribunal, it was impossible to invoke the statements of any of the witnesses without an immediate objection about his mistresses, his intimate life, his
too rapid rise, his supposed political opinions, past or present.[16]

On March 31, the examining magistrate concluded the first phase of the proceedings with the formal charge against Pierre Mendès France. His lawyers immediately notified the military appeal court of Lyon, which, on April 11, confirmed that the accused should be tried by the court of Clermont, but removed from the indictment the first charge brought up by Leprêtre in the preliminary proceedings, the so-called May 10 affair.

On May 3, 1941, Mendès France was summoned before Colonel Degache, government representative, the man who had asked for the death penalty against De Gaulle and Leclerc, to hear the indictment read. From embarrassment or contempt, the colonel did not deign to go through with the reading but simply handed a copy of the text to the prisoner, who read it in his cell, "with amazement." He was no longer accused for his "desertion" on June 10 (the delay in joining his unit in Mérignac), but the "May 10 affair" and the *Massilia* story were developed at length.

There was a final battle before the trial over the calling of defense witnesses. During the preliminary proceedings, Leprêtre had already for a long time refused to call one essential witness, Mendès's chief of service in the Near East, Colonel Alamichel. Now it was Degache who multiplied delaying tactics, refused to look for the addresses, and, in the case of people living in the occupied zone, who therefore needed a German *Ausweis* to cross the demarcation line, refused to ask the occupation forces for them. The lawyers insisted:

"These witnesses are not useful to the prosecution," said Degache.

"But," retorted Fonlupt, "they are useful to the demonstration of the truth. Are you seeking to learn the truth, or to make certain of a conviction at any price?"

"Interpret it as you like. I refuse to subpoena these witnesses; they have only to cross the demarcation line secretly."

On May 9, 1941, shortly after eight o'clock, Pierre Mendès France, dressed in his uniform as lieutenant of the air force, tense, very pale, thin (he had lost more than thirty pounds in six months), with flashbulbs popping around him, penetrated into the military courtroom of Clermont-Ferrand jammed with an excited crowd. The trial was public, but "to avoid any incidents" an invitation was necessary to attend. The prosecution had received three hundred cards, the defense six. There were rumors that, in a nearby café, invitations were being resold for twenty francs.

While the clerk was reading the indictment, Mendès looked at the chief judge, a massive and lantern-jawed colonel named Perré, member of the tribunal that had pronounced a death sentence on Charles de Gaulle, whose unfortunate rival he had long been in the armored division of the army; the prosecutor, Colonel Degache, who appeared to be asleep beneath an enormous photograph of Marshal Pétain; and the public. He recognized a few friendly faces: Emile Kahn, president of the League of

Human Rights; and Edgar and Lucie Faure in the first row. But most of the faces were hostile, notably that of a lady writer who published, under the pseudonym of André Corthis, works that have happily sunk into oblivion and who constantly showed her hatred throughout the trial. In a corner, almost hidden, was Colonel Leprêtre, the stage director of this lugubrious farce.

The accused was, of course, asked to explain himself with respect to the indictment. He approached this ordeal, for which he had been passionately preparing for months, certain of his right, strengthened by his innocence as much as by his talent, with a kind of awkwardness, exasperated by the constant belligerent interruptions by Colonel Perré. Piece by piece, he destroyed the argument of the prosecutors and felt the audience shaken by his proofs, notably with respect to the May 10 affair and the soldiers on leave from the army of the East (he pointed out that Colonel-Doctor Bergeret, brother of the minister who had accused him, was in precisely the same situation as he). But, returned to prison at the end of the first session, he felt unhappy with himself.

> I felt embarrassed and rather tired. Was it the position of defendant that had paralyzed me to that extent? Or was it the belligerence of the chief judge and the hostility of the public? On a hundred occasions in the past I had been able to defend successfully cases to which I had not attributed equivalent importance. That day, I had not dominated the physical and psychological difficulties that took hold of me at the beginning of my explanations. And then, in my conclusion, I hadn't been firm enough, I hadn't taken the offensive. I had promised to conduct this battle energetically, and I hadn't done enough.

In the afternoon, it was the turn of the witnesses. The direct superior of Mendès until June 10, 1940, Colonel Alamichel, explained that the soldiers on leave from the Near East were not recalled on May 10, 1940, and that he had acted like all his comrades. Mendès could even supplement this statement with the reading of a letter of May 1940 (which he had retrieved on the very morning of the trial), in which Alamichel told him to stay in Paris. The testimony and the letter reduced the "May 10 affair" to nothing: the accused had acted on a precise written order from his superior.

Questions from the defense: "What was Mendès France's conduct in the service like?" "Excellent. He never stepped out of his role as an officer, never tried to take advantage of his parliamentary position." Another question: "You know Mendès France, since he was under your orders. Do you think he is capable of running from the enemy out of cowardice?" "He is incapable of doing that."

The following witness, Lieutenant-Colonel Faÿ, chief of staff of the air force in the Near East in 1940, presented identical testimony, equally clear and positive. But then came the third witness, Colonel Bailly, member of the staff of the Radical minister Laurent-Eynac in 1940, who had since joined Darlan's government. He accused the defendant: "I saw Mendès France in June 1940 in Bordeaux, running away. I warned him that if he went on board the *Massilia* he would be reported as a deserter and would be called before the War Council." "It was prophetic!" the chief judge chimed in.

The defense had decided to respond only with contempt to this officer. Mendès, outraged, stood up and recounted in detail the signs of obsequiousness that Bailly had repeatedly shown him in May and June 1940, recalled his intrigues in parliamentary circles, and his membership in the Masons. Bailly, as his only answer, asked the chief judge to allow him to leave. "Admiral Darlan is waiting for me." Perrè hastily got rid of him.

Next came General d'Astier de la Vigerie. No sooner had he reached the witness box than the chief judge said to him: "On the basis of the way you testify, the tribunal will arrive at an opinion about the patriotic feelings that inspire your family."[17] It is hard to imagine a blunter form of blackmail: the general's oldest daughter had just been arrested for her activities in the Resistance. D'Astier did not bend. He was about to go on when Perré again interrupted him: "You took Mendès France onto your staff in Rabat in June 1940. That was a political action." D'Astier: "If I had given in to the temptation to pursue politics in the army, it would have been in a very different way. I have always been an adversary of the Popular Front, and I sometimes happened to suffer the consequences for that. I am ashamed to be obliged to recall that in this place!"

This was the moment chosen by Fonlupt to reveal to the witness and the dumbfounded public the slanderous report prepared about him under the direction of General Bergeret. Either because Perré did not give him the time or because so much rancor disconcerted him, D'Astier did not, that day, make the statement: "It would have been by not taking the *Massilia* that Mendès France would have deserted!" But it hovered over the trial.

Colonel Lucien, a crucial witness who had been involved in all the episodes of the affair, from May 10 to June 10 and 20, could not hide his disturbed feelings. In the course of the preliminary proceedings, manipulated by Leprêtre, he had hesitated and contradicted himself, admitting that he had forgotten the details of rather minor events that had taken place in the midst of the debacle. But what was at stake on that day was the honor and the freedom of a man whom he respected. He overcame his confusion.

On May 10, Mendès France asked me to send him to the front. I refused. He came to see me again. I can completely vouch for his behavior throughout the entire period. On June 10, I gave him a transfer order for Bordeaux, where he was to report within a few days. He did not in any way disobey the orders I gave him. I found nothing at the time, when my memory was fresher than it is today, to reproach him for.

Afterward, in reply to a question from the lawyers, Lucien declared himself as certain as his predecessors—except for Bailly—that Mendès France was "incapable of fleeing, of deserting.

But none of the witnesses was warmer than Colonel Le Coq de Kerland. It was not so much testimony as an argument for the defense. Very well informed about the affair, he remembered Mendès's training program in Rayak, where he had come at the head of the class, as well as his requests to fight in Norway, and later on the French front. He explained that, although he was not present on June 10 when Colonel Lucien gave Lieutenant Mendès France the order to report to Mérignac, he and the colonel had spoken of it in Amboise and that, in any event, the accused had not committed the slightest infraction. "I will answer for his character and his patriotism. He is a man who does not desert. Whatever may happen this evening, Mendès France has and will maintain my esteem." At that point, unexpected applause broke out, and the chief judge threatened to restore order by closing the trial to the public.

After a second recess, it was time for the prosecution's case. Colonel Degache centered it around the principal charge in the indictment, the defendant's delay after June 10 in getting from Paris to Bordeaux to report for his new assignment. He conceded that, given the circumstances, the journey could not have been made in less than three days.[18] "In that case," interrupted Fonlupt, "how much of the delay makes up a desertion?" Degache did not answer. He would have to admit to insignificant figures, a few hours, even presuming that Colonel Lucien's transfer order contained a precise time. For those few hours, Degache was calling for eight years in prison for Mendès France and the deprivation of all his civil and familial rights.

The lawyers simultaneously had an easy road (their client was an odd deserter indeed, constantly asking to fight at the hour of battle; and the trial was so obviously motivated by political rancor and racism) and an impossible task: the tribunal and the prosecution ostentatiously ignored their arguments. Consider this curious passage from the vehement closing argument by Jacques Fonlupt-Espéraber, which must obviously be placed in its historical context:

> Mendès France has a family past that deserves respect. Since his mother is my compatriot,[19] I may be allowed a personal observation. I know the incomparable services that our brothers from Alsace, among them those who are of the same faith as Mendès France, performed for us during the 1914–1918 war. Because, gentlemen, there is not a single drop of blood in my veins that is not

Christian, I can speak freely, I can pay tribute to them with respect and sincere admiration, and I can say that they were among the best defenders of our French traditions.

As soon as Fonlupt had concluded his argument ("admirable," according to Mendès, "for its verve, insolence, and talent"), the chief judge asked Mendès whether he had anything to add in his defense. He contented himself with denouncing "the shame of this undeserved trial" and proclaiming his pride in having heard his superiors, all the superiors under whose orders he had served, testify so forcefully in his favor.

He was led into a small adjoining room. The verdict was delivered in his absence. He was alone. A few seconds later his lawyers and friends appeared, with such a mournful air that he understood: he was sentenced to six years in prison. He had expected it. It hardly mattered whether it was four, six, or ten years; his liberation could only be tied to the liberation of the country. He was again in the courtroom dominated by the portrait of Pétain, confronting the Mussolini-like face of Perré, the lifeless face of Degache, and the almost fraternal gaze of the young soldiers of the guard.

The clerk, Captain Cadenat, began reading the judgment in a toneless voice. I barely heard. I caught in passing the formulas I had often heard in another time, when I was a lawyer:

"In the name of the French people (alas!). To the first question, presented as follows: 'Is Lieutenant Mendès France guilty of having deserted?' the tribunal has answered 'yes.'"

I interrupted: "The tribunal has lied."

The government prosecutor seemed not to have heard.

The clerk halted, disconcerted, incapable of imagining that such an outrage would not be answered. A second of silence. Then he went on: "To the second question . . ."

"I heard: "Six years in prison . . . loss of rank . . . deprivation of civil, political, and familial rights for ten years."

Finally he stopped. I turned toward the guards. The soldiers were pale. I said to them: "An innocent man has just been condemned out of political hatred. This is not the justice of France, it is the justice of Hitler. Do not despair of France."

Then I moved toward Degache, who stubbornly looked at his feet: "Mister Prosecutor, I wish you an untroubled conscience. You have done well for Hitler—and for your advancement."[20]

By the next day he had signed a notice of appeal. As a lawyer, in spite of the circumstances, he had to exhaust all legal remedies. Afterward, if necessary, would come the time to rebel. He told the director of the prison: "I will not submit to what is not a judgment but a political assault. I will not remove the stripes from my uniform, I will not pay the costs of the trial," practically announcing his decision to escape. It was true that as soon as the appeal procedure had been concluded he would be subjected to more severe regulations, those applied to prisoners who had been found guilty, making escape more difficult.

The censored press was able to publish only a twenty-line item summing up the indictment and the trial from the official point of view. But Mendès France very soon heard echoes of the indignation provoked almost everywhere by the denial of justice of which he had been the victim. A few days after the trial, Rochat was visited by René Giscard d'Estaing, *conseiller d'état,* uncle of a young man named Valéry, and member of a family with little sympathy for the ideas of Pierre Mendès France. He came to say that, having happened to attend the trial, he was "revolted" by it and planned to say what he thought of it to his friend Philippe Pétain. He asked Rochat for a transcript of the proceedings.

The military appeals court had substantial grounds for a reversal. It took Jacques Fonlupt-Espéraber only a few days' investigation in Lyon of the whole dossier to discover irregularities that made the conviction of Mendès all the more scandalous. He noted that, contrary to the provisions of the Military Code, the members of the tribunal had not been chosen according to the list, without consideration of political opinion or rank, but arbitrarily chosen by General Bergeret. And, infinitely more serious, a circular distributed in February 1940 granted every officer who had been transferred more time to report to his new command: in the case of Mendès, two weeks. He could not have been accused of desertion before June 25, in Bordeaux, a week after he had reported to his superiors. The whole substance of the trial! And this document had knowingly been concealed from the defense by Degache and Leprêtre. Dreyfus's judges and Colonel Henry had found disciples.

On June 20, 1941, after six weeks of deliberation, the tribunal of Lyon rendered its decision, which can be summed up as follows: In the present circumstances of French life, it is impossible to respect scrupulously the rules of the Code and the protections of the defense. And in this particular instance, there is no reason to believe that the irregularities noted were due to malice toward the accused.

And Mendès France concludes his narrative with Stendhalian brevity: "I expected nothing different. The following night, I removed from my window a bar that had long before been sawn through, and I escaped."[21]

He had wanted to confront his judges in a full-scale debate. He had wanted to present his proof and denounce the military tribunal's abuse of its authority. He had wanted his trial to become a scandal, which was soon to happen at Riom, where Blum and Daladier were to confound their accusers. Then the transcript of his trial, as it was distributed, would become a Resistance tract. Now that this political mission had been accomplished, he had to recover his freedom to assume his military tasks.

But to sum up his attitude in May 1941 in this way might be to rationalize it a little too much, to reshape after the fact what was at first a manifestation of patriotic legalism and then a reflex of wounded dignity. There was first of all his naive desire to place his confidence in French judges, military ones at that. Like François d'Astier, he could not bring himself to prejudge their infamy. A lawyer and a Jew, and thereby doubly patriotic, he refused to despair of the successors of the judges of Rennes, who, once Dreyfus's innocence had been proven and Esterhazy unmasked, persisted in finding the captain guilty, but "with extenuating circumstances." This description might also involve some neglect of psychological factors, of the burden of humiliation. "I was wrong to take the proceedings tragically," he said later. "I was on edge. I had to escape and fight in order to cleanse myself, to feel cured of that wound. I find that a little foolish now."

In any event, he had to escape. As he wrote later,

> Escape is the prisoner's permanent preoccupation. When he is locked into his cell for the first time, his first concern is to sound the walls, to test the solidity of the bars, the security of the locks. Then he spies on the guards, their habits, their quirks, their distractions. He looks, he observes, he keeps watch. The prisoner keeps much closer surveillance over his guards than they do over him.

Two months before the beginning of the trial, he had discovered, half-buried in the prison exercise yard, a piece of a lightning rod that had been torn down in a storm. It was two yards long with several parallel projections. It was a ladder. Later, against the exterior wall, he noticed a hutch that could be used as a base for the ladder. A few days later, the shaft of the lightning rod had disappeared.

While waiting for the trial, the prisoner continued to accumulate the tools of his escape. One day he found an old hacksaw lying around in the repair shop. He concealed it under some wood shavings and two months later carried it off. There followed an old sweater and a pair of glasses left behind by a released prisoner; a nest egg made up of small bills and loose change; food (chocolate, dried figs, sardines) slowly collected; even a ration card stolen by another prisoner that he bought by giving up his bread ration for several weeks. There was a little mascara to blacken his face borrowed from a visitor to a fellow prisoner and an old rubber stamp that he used, unskillfully, to fabricate parts of false papers. Everything was concealed in the stove pipe in his cell, which, with the approach of summer, might be dismantled or cleaned out at any moment.

He methodically undertook physical training to become capable of long runs, jumps, and even fights, which did not come naturally to him. Like an ant, he amassed little vials, bits of string, nails, useless utensils, anything that could cut, tie, or hold something else. If it was noted that he traded a lot, he wrote later, "it must have been attributed to my Semitic origins." And then his cousin Jean Stamm,[22] who had come to visit, gave him a map and a train timetable; his plan was to reach Grenoble as quickly as possible and from there the Swiss border. From Geneva, London would be within easy reach.

When he learned that his trial was set for May 8, he calculated that the appeal would be decided on the sixteenth and that he therefore had to be ready by then. In fact, he had constantly to revise his plans. In any event, he had decided that a transfer to the infirmary would not only facilitate his attempt but, in view of the energy he would have to expend, would allow him to restore a little of his health that had been undermined by privations, the sanitary conditions of the prison, and his anxiety. Three days after the sentence, on May 12, he went on sick call. The doctor found his liver to be "very large" and decided to hospitalize him in La Providence, an annex to the military hospital of Clermont-Ferrand reserved for civilian and military prisoners.

Transferred on May 13 to this former convent that had been turned into a prison hospital, he demanded, as an officer, to be put into an individual cell, and he finally prevailed. It was a room next to the guard post. A sentinel was posted in front of the door, which was bolted shut. The barred window gave on a deep ditch, which was traversed by a footbridge opposite the guard post. Alongside the exterior wall, an iron ladder climbed from the ditch to the footbridge. From the bottom of the ditch to the top of the wall, the distance was eight yards, but it was only half as far from the footbridge to the top of the wall. And a little farther along was a break in the wall that lowered the top by a yard, offering a better chance for climbing and a less risky jump—all the more because the street was at a higher level than the prison yard.

After studying the location, he examined the schedule. He was awakened by coffee delivered by the nurse on duty (one of whom, Mlle. Lourde, very soon showed herself to be an ally, almost an accomplice) at seven-thirty. He soon gave up coffee on the pretext of stomach troubles— the alarm would be given a little later. The doctor visited between nine and ten. Lunch at eleven, another visit from the doctor, dinner at five, and a last round by the nurse, followed by the guard, at ten. There was no further observation during the night, but there were guard patrols outside. From ten on, the shutters on the guard post windows were closed. There were sometimes unexpected patrols, but he should be able to pass between ten-fifteen and dawn. The street outside was almost always quiet.

At night, around eleven, there was a little disturbance, probably from a nearby movie theater.

In addition, his study of the timetable had led him to decide to take the eleven-twenty-five train for Grenoble. He therefore had to move between ten-fifteen, when the guards closed up, and eleven, when the adjacent street began to come alive.

His first task was to saw through the bars of the window with the large file he had stolen from the prison shop. It seemed to be simple, but he had not thought of the resonance of the steel bars, which vibrated like violins in the night. Terrifying. But he noticed that at certain times the snoring of the guards covered the noise of his work, provided that his movements followed the rhythm of their breathing. At that rate, it took two weeks before the bar was holding by a single thread. And in order to conceal the cut, he made a black powder out of stone dust and mascara.

There was a severe setback at the medical inspection of June 4, when Dr. Gagnepain announced that the prison authorities demanded his return to the prison and that he had had to agree to the transfer, which, though regrettable from the point of view of Mendès's health, did not place him in immediate danger. Mendès was forced to accept, and everything seemed to have been in vain. In prison he saw his lawyers again, and they told him that the appeal court would render a decision on June 20. According to them, Degache was in a panic. They were optimistic despite the pressure being put on the Lyon judges. Mendès refused to believe in a miracle. On June 15, there was another medical inspection. This time he was examined thoroughly, by a young intern: "Your liver is in bad condition. You have to go back to La Providence."

There were only five days left. If the tribunal of Lyon was to deliver the final judgment on June 20, after which he would be stripped of his rank and transferred to an ordinary cell, he had to act on that day or the next. That night, he was on the alert, ready to move. He prepared to tie his sheets into a rope. But the nurse on duty, who had come particularly late (it was not the friendly Mlle. Lourde that night), suggested to the guards next door that they keep their shutters open because of the heat. It would be impossible to jump, climb, and crawl over the wall under their eyes. A decisive night had been lost.

The next morning, the twenty-first, there was another setback. They brought a seriously ill Gaullist prisoner named Douket into his room. And that complicated everything. But it was too late to turn back. In the afternoon he was visited by Fonlupt and Rochat, and he let them in on his plans. In return, they very loudly set up a meeting for the following Monday. Then he wrote a series of letters addressed to his wife, his parents, his lawyers, his friend Jean Zay, and Marshal Pétain. The letter to Zay has a sober eloquence.

My dear Jean,

I am using the last means of protest left me after the rejection of the appeal. To resist, to fight, to defend myself to the unfortunately limited extent that is still allowed to us. But not to accept. This is what has led me to a decision which may surprise you, but which I will doubtless not regret no matter how things turn out later. I will regret not being able to maintain the contact with you that was very important to me. But it is after all difficult for me to give you my address.

The message to the "head of the French state," in strained, convulsive handwriting, portrays the trembling anger and militant rage of the Mendés France who had been deeply wounded by the trial.

I patiently withstood nine months of pretrial detention; I suffered from atrocious press attacks to which I was forbidden to reply. I have exhausted the judicial appeals that were available, wishing to believe to the end in the courts of my country. I was mistaken. They have convicted me although I know absolutely that I have committed no crime. It would be beyond my strength to give in to their decisions.

They are not decisions based on justice. In my conscience, I am not obliged to obey them.

It is, of course, illegitimate to judge oneself, but only on the condition that institutions provide the means to have one's rights recognized and to defend one's honor.

I cannot accept the infamy of a shameful verdict proclaiming that I failed in my basic duty as a Frenchman when the fatherland was in danger. I cannot allow the affirmation of my dishonor without using the only means of protest left to me, the most solemn and most spectacular: I am reclaiming the liberty to which I have never ceased to have the right. . . .

If I manage to evade the search which I proclaim to be illegitimate, I commit myself from this day to present myself to the authorities if France once again calls on her sons (I will then ask for authorization to serve in the most exposed position, as I did in 1939–1940) or if, tomorrow, the law or the circumstances offer the possibility of correcting my trial.

This is an exalted patriotism, made up of a sense of honor in the style of Corneille, Danton's Jacobinism, Poincaré's legalism, and Clemenceau's pride. We do not know what the old marshal thought of it, although he must have thought that the young man was going to great lengths and taking many risks for a simple question of honor.

It is 9 P.M. on June 21. Douket, his new cellmate, wakes up. Mendès, who has told him of his plan, has him take an extra dose of sedatives for the night. He will be groggy enough the next morning to be able to say that he noticed nothing. At nine-forty-five, after the guards next door have finally closed their shutters, the friendly nurse, Mlle. Lourde, goes by. Thanks to her, he will have as much time as possible. He has a little less than an hour to act, time enough to make a rope out of his sheets, to shave (his beard, but not his mustache, which will be an element of his disguise), and to wrap his shoes in rags to muffle their sound.

"Sitting on my bed, already shaved and dressed for flight, I now feel my courage abandon me. Will I succeed? This night, which I have so passionately awaited and prepared, suddenly seems to me hostile, an enemy."

Ten-thirty. In ten minutes he will have to rip out the bar, attach the sheets to the window, suspend himself on the wall. He will then have a quarter of an hour to get outside the walls.

> Again, I go to the window. The guards' path frightens me. In a few minutes, won't I run into a patrol, a late kitchen helper, a nurse hurrying out? The great silence surrounding me upsets me. Time flows with desperate slowness, and yet I would give years of my life to delay, for a few minutes, the approaching moment.

It's now or never. He grasps the bar. It is the irremediable act. It is torn out. A space gaping onto freedom. Slipping, jumping (clumsily, on the valise), stumbling, getting up with a minor racket, hastily climbing the stone steps up the outside wall to the footbridge. No one on the guards' path. The guards' shutters are dark. There are three or four yards of the wall left to scale. But he has scrutinized this stone wall for so long, for hours at a time, that he seems to be grasping familiar handholds. A pull-up (thank God for his prison exercises) and he is lying on top of the wall. He crawls to the break, where the ground outside is five or six yards below. The time has come to jump. But what's this?

> There, hidden beneath a tree, two lovers. They are talking about what to do with their evening. He has a very clear idea. She hesitates, she resists. It lasts for a century, I mean ten minutes. And those ten minutes may become tragic for me. At eleven o'clock, the movie theater lets out, and that will make the street very active for a while; besides, if a patrol passes on the guards' path, it will easily see my silhouette on top of the wall against the very clear sky. . . . The turtle doves are still debating. This boy lacks authority! Finally, she says yes. Dear little unknown lover, perhaps you will someday read this book in which you play an unexpected role. Remember, it was the night of June 21, 1941. I want you to know how I cursed your virtue and how I blessed your weakness.[23]

Knees next to his chin, as friends have advised him—like a real parachute jumper—he jumps, hurts himself, but recovers; nothing broken. He is ready to walk.

> The avenue is completely empty. A car passes on a cross street. In the distance, I can see the softened light and hear the muffled music from a café. It is very warm, but a slight unexpected breeze caresses my face, a gentle little breeze that never blows in prison.

The prisoner has been replaced by the hunted man.

He knew the railroad station was nearby, down the hill toward the right, a few hundred yards away. He had more than half an hour before the departure of the train to set the pursuers on false trails. He walked up the avenue throwing some things—his jacket and the handsaw—into a side street, and then persuaded a café waiter to mail his letters the following morning—the investigators would then think that he had stayed in Clermont until the morning of the twenty-second. He reached the station; there was a line in front of the ticket window. But the train for Lyon and Grenoble was, of course, late. A female employee took his ticket, and he was thus able to avoid the inquisitive glances of a few policemen he had seen at the trial and who might have remembered him, however thick his makeup. The train was, of course, packed; there were ten people in his compartment, among them a group wearing the uniform of the Chantiers de la jeunesse, an organization of the "national revolution." It appeared to be an unfortunate encounter, but they spoke only of the misdeeds of the occupying forces, who "took everything." It was a useful observation for the escaped man.

It was 1 A.M. when the train reached Vichy—where too many people he knew got on—eight when it got to Lyon, and nearly ten when it reached Grenoble. It was already very late. The alarm had certainly been given, but had it come this far? He left the station without incident and, avoiding the center of the city, walked toward a nearby village, La Tronche. Too many people he knew lived in Grenoble, and police checks were frequent. He hoped to escape observation in one of the little tourist towns full of vacationers during the summer. He presented himself at the Richmond Pension as a lawyer's clerk named Séoyer, a native of the Ardennes, recovering from an illness and come to spend a few weeks of convalescence in the Alps. He was put in a garrett, and, determined to be forgotten, he spent his days in long walks, reading the newspapers for the slightest sign of the search that must have been organized.

The nurse on duty had given the alarm shortly before 8 A.M. June 22 was a Sunday, and the whole repressive machine was thereby slightly delayed. At eight-forty-five, the Sûreté nationale in Pau sent out a description of the escaped man for the border posts. The information minister, Paul Marion, and Admiral Darlan, head of the government, were informed around ten. The admiral was furious and immediately ordered total censorship. But the North African press was forgotten, and it published the news the next day: Lily Mendès France was thus very quickly informed. As for the Paris press, it paid no attention to orders from Vichy. On June 23, *Le Petit Parisien* published the following dispatch:

Recently convicted by the Clermont-Ferrand court for desertion on the home front in time of war, the exdeputy and reserve lieutenant Mendès France had been admitted to the auxiliary hospital La Providence for reasons of health. These "reasons of health" were probably only a new ruse by the deserter to escape justice after having shirked his duty. Indeed, it has been learned that yesterday, Sunday, early in the morning, and no doubt with the help of accomplices that his large fortune allowed him to bribe, the Jew Mendès France succeeded in escaping from the hospital.

On the afternoon of the twenty-second, a sort of council of war was called together by the general in charge of the Thirteenth Military Region; it included the prison commander, the commander of gendarmes, the police supervisor, and Colonel Leprêtre, who, with complete candor, suggested the arrest of Lily Mendès France to serve as a bait for the fugitive.[24] The presentation by the inspector in charge of the affair was summed up by Mendès France in *Liberté, liberté, chérie.*

Mendès France was seen for the last time on Saturday evening around nine-forty-five, during the rounds of the night nurse, Mlle. Lourde, who claims to have talked to him. He was getting undressed. From that point on, we know nothing for certain. Nonetheless, in a letter left in his cell by Mendès France intended to inform his wife of his escape, he says that he will go through his window 'just before dawn.'[25] . . . In these circumstances, he may have hidden in Clermont-Ferrand itself, or he may have been taken off by a friend waiting in a car, or else he may have taken one of the trains that leave Clermont-Ferrand between four and six in the morning. Searches are under way in the major cities served by these trains, but it does not seem probable to me that he used the railroad. . . . It is possible that Mendès France intends to enter the occupied zone by secretly crossing the demarcation line. This would be rather clever on his part, since he might presume that we would not think of looking for him in the occupied zone. Given this hypothesis, there is reason:
  1. to inform the German authorities;
  2. to carry out surveillance by the police forces concerned to whom we have already transmitted instructions;
  3. to place his parents and known friends in the occupied zone under surveillance, particularly his constituency, where he may find many accomplices. . . .
His aim can only be to reach England. In these circumstances, we are keeping particular watch on the Spanish border, where his photograph has been sent and two inspectors have been specially delegated to organize surveillance. Mendès France's photograph will also be sent to the Spanish and Portuguese police. It is possible that he will try to reach England through Morocco. His wife, who is living in Casablanca, will be placed under rigorous surveillance.[26]

Lily Mendès France, who in April 1941 had received an order of expulsion, later revoked, was indeed harassed for months, from June to

December, in Casablanca. She was searched, interrogated, followed, and subjected to suspicious visits by entirely too amiable informants and had her mail confiscated. Tired of resisting, and following pressing demands from the fugitive, she asked for a visa for the United States. The police official from whom she requested her exit visa, named Bourrel, went even further in brutality and vulgarity than his colleagues. He boasted of having deported a number of Jews to the south and of having arrested some Gaullists. When the visitor stubbornly refused to reveal anything about Mendès France, he covered her with insults and threats.

> For seven months, my wife never uttered a word that could put the police on my track. Never did they discover, where she was living or among her friends, the slightest indication that would allow them to find my trail. She knew perfectly well where I was and heard from me at rather regular intervals.[27]

Lily Mendès France obtained an entry visa for the United States thanks to Pierre Cot. Since General de Gaulle had not wanted him in London—although he was to make Cot's closest friend, Jean Moulin, head of the Resistance in France—the former air force minister had gone to New York. He gave his friend's wife and two sons the financial guarantee without which they would not have been admitted to the United States: immigrants could not become dependent on the U.S. Treasury. A Jewish organization, the "Joint," took charge of their exodus, embarking the three members of the Mendès family on one of the little Portuguese boats that it chartered to travel between Casablanca, Lisbon, and New York, in accordance with strange, tacit agreements between the English and the Germans. These ships were often under surveillance by Nazi submarines, but they were usually allowed to pass, in return for the liberation of a pilot or a Nazi agent.

In New York, Lily Mendès France received a warm welcome from the majority of the substantial French community, even though there were very few Gaullists among them. To distract herself from her anxiety, she devoted herself to painting, while her two sons became perfect Yankee schoolboys.

It was not long before politics, or rather history, once again took hold of the fugitive. His landlady, while making his bed, told him what she had just heard on the radio: the armies of the Reich had attacked the Soviet Union. Thus, at the moment he had recovered his freedom, the nature of the war had shifted: Russia in the conflict and the United States in the wings. Everything would be changed. Hitler had not been able to resist adventurism, and that might very well lead to his defeat.

For the moment, Mendès had two objectives before preparing to cross into Switzerland (for which he had, prudently he thought, allowed himself six weeks): to fade into the background and to obtain acceptable papers. He had as yet only a few miscellaneous cards, including two ration cards: the one he had bought from a fellow prisoner and his own, which he had gotten from the prison clerk on his transfer to La Providence, which indicated the address of the bearer as the "military prison of Clermont."

He had to go to Grenoble to get the materials necessary to fabricate his papers: duplicating paper, rubber stamps, correcting fluid. He threw avarice to the winds and, scratching, copying, cutting, and pasting, he made himself three identity cards with three different names: Séoyer, Laurent-Jean, lawyer's clerk, born in Montherné in 1897 (adding ten years to his age); Grassct, Jean-Philippe, born in Amiens in 1906; Besson, Jean-Auguste, office worker, born in Abbéville in 1908. Although the birthdates varied, the birthplaces had in common their location in the "forbidden" zone, where the occupation forces would make any checking impossible.

Without playing on words, it can be said that the modest country photographer of La Tronche had not flattered him. With his thick glasses, hair parted in the middle, a black mustache drooping over his pursed lips, and his pale complexion, he looked like a lawyer's clerk, an office worker, or an accountant who did not have an easy life. It was easy to imagine that he was badly married, had liver trouble, and was frugal. He seemed to be a man more to be pitied than criticized, and he was likely to appeal to the sympathy of local gossips and country policemen.

Was this the notable figure of the Third Republic whose "large fortune," according to *Le Petit Parisien,* had enabled him to escape? The man who had taken refuge in the Richmond Pension looked so much like a modest milquetoast that the employees at the town hall did not hesitate to add to his collection of false identity papers an authentic card, duly signed by the mayor, a personal protégé of Darlan.

But he could not stay forever in the Grenoble region. He encountered too many familiar faces: one day, for example, André François-Poncet, former ambassador to Berlin, whom he had known slightly in the past. And the following day, a mailman distributing Gaullist tracts had been arrested in La Tronche. He had to clear out, speed up his flight from the country. At the Grenoble station, he bought a rail pass that would give him more flexibility of movement and chose Chambéry, first as a place of retreat and then as a jumping-off point for his attempt to cross the border.

The fugitive found lodging in Chambéry with a very amiable old lady, a supporter of Pétain, which he found ordinary, but who hoped for an English victory, which surprised him a good deal. He would have to get used to the unusual combinations of those troubled times. A census was in progress, no doubt for the manpower services. Among the dozens of questions on professional and linguistic aptitudes, there was this one: "Are you Jewish?" Tempted to react to this contemptible challenge, he wrote, "No," "a little shamefully." At a secondhand clothes shop he bought an old, worn suit for an extravagant price, but, as a bonus, he was given a Basque beret, at the time a sign of bourgeois respectability.

One evening, he was a dinner guest of neighbors on his floor. They had also invited a traveling salesman friend who had recently returned from Paris, where he had visited the anti-Jewish exposition organized by *L'Illustration* at the Berlitz palace. He showed them the catalogue. And the humble Séoyer, lawyer's clerk, was astonished to observe that, among the mannequins displayed in this wax museum of racism, including the most "nefarious" figures of each country (Basil Zaharoff for Greece, Hore Belisha[28] for England, Litvinov[29] for Russia), it was he, Pierre Mendès France, who embodied French Judaism. The traveler's tale deserves some attention.

> Standing in the hall where I had been prematurely turned into a statue, the visitors would have stopped in front of me, and one of them would have said: "Why did they choose Mendès France? He never played a principal role; they should have put Léon Blum or Mandel."
>
> Then there was a conversation about me and my conviction. One of the traveling salesmen told the others that I had escaped (he had read it in *Le Journal de Genève*). He knew from a very good source that I was in England, in General de Gaulle's army. Several people present approved of my conduct.
>
> It was the first time for many weeks that I had heard my name spoken. I was delighted to receive good news about myself, to learn that I had already arrived in London, and that people thought I had done right to join De Gaulle.

To join De Gaulle. He marked time, going from Chambéry to Annecy, and then twice to Marseille, where he had friends (but he decided not to visit Colonel Lucien, for fear of compromising him; Lucien later joined the Maquis (underground). He found the situation there more tragic, the poverty more oppressive, and the atmosphere more sinister than anywhere else. And corruption, inequality, and the black market were even more scandalous. Doriot's henchmen, led by Simon Sabiani, were in complete control. In any event, his contacts in Marseille produced no results.

Another friend, Gaullist and Catholic, might be more effective. But he lived near Rennes. To make contact with him, he would have to cross the demarcation line, traverse occupied France, and risk German patrols. He decided to take the risk, left Chambéry on November 2, crossed the Saône (which served as the demarcation line) on the fourth, with the help of a smuggler, avoided Wehrmacht identity checks, and found himself in Brittany on the sixth. His arrival astonished his friend, who, knowing of his escape, thought he was in London. His one-week stay with the family was the first happiness he had experienced in many long months.

Perhaps he gathered information there that was too optimistic on the state of mind of the French in late 1941, seeing less resignation and less complicity with the occupying forces than most other witnesses and historians. The reportage on the France of those months in *Liberté, liberté chérie* shows the effects of this. But he was perhaps less naive than the reader of today might think. Published in the United States in 1943, the book was not only an eyewitness report, it was also an appeal to the sympathy and the confidence of the American people. He explained himself on this point quite clearly.

> In 1941 and 1942, I lived chiefly in Dauphiné and Savoie, where popular reaction was, from the very beginning, sharper and more vigorous than anywhere else. No doubt I would have had different impressions in different regions among different people. My testimony can give only a partial image of the reality of the time. I also admit that I have written above all for foreign readers; although I have been careful to say nothing that is not strictly accurate, I have not had the courage to emphasize as much as I should have aspects that I found too shocking or degrading: the passionate collaboration of some, anti-Semitism, surrender to the enemy of men who had taken refuge with us, trafficking, and so on. . . . What I heard and recorded, in the darkness, were the echoes of a refusal and a revolt that later took on the size and the vigor of the Resistance.[30]

In any event, when he recrossed the demarcation line on November 13, in the midst of a group of workers, on bicycles like himself, he had still not perfected his plan of escape to London. It was clear that the road through the Alps to Switzerland presented the best chances. In Chambéry he had met a Radical colleague and friend of Pierre Cot's, Senator La Goutrie, who advised him to head for Thoron. He moved to Thoron, where several Resistance groups were operating.

But chance would have it that he never established contact with an organized group. His reserve, his prudence as a hunted man, made him appear cold to others. The numerous anti-German sentiments he heard never went as far as an offer of help. It is true that his odyssey took place before the establishment of the great Resistance network in the summer of 1942. In any event, this bitter traversal of humiliated France would never encounter the France of active refusal.

In January 1942, in the court report of an old Chambéry newspaper, Mendès France read the story of the adventures of a smuggler—a Swiss fisherman on Lake Léman and a former legionnaire—who he was told was still active and might also be a smuggler of men. Mendès went to see him in Thoron. The fisherman received him very badly but suggested that he speak to a "colleague," Louis Duchêne, who agreed to take him on his boat. Mendès was transformed into a deckhand on board the *Oncle-Paul,* a punt anchored in the little port of Rives. They traveled at night, rowing at first as long as they were in sight of the French shore, then turning on the motor. There remained the risk of the Swiss customs men, but the fugitive shrugged it off. They landed to the west of Lausanne, on the outskirts of Saint-Prex. Free soil. At this point, did Pierre Mendès France cease to feel hunted?

In Geneva, where he stayed at first with the Toriel family, his wife's cousins, he made contact with a certain François Berthelot, known as "Robert," an old friend of Republican Spain and now of the French Resistance, who constantly went back and forth across the border and took Mendès with him on several occasions, over the mountains near Saint-Gingolph. But this was not the journey he wanted to undertake. He presented himself at the British Consulate in Geneva, where he was very coldly received—there were so many *provocateurs.* At the American Consulate, on the other hand, he was very cordially received and finally given the means to send news to his wife.

He was especially warmly received by the Socialist deputy Rosselet. Hoping to obtain help for the fugitive, he went to see the justice minister, von Steiger:

"Do you know that the former minister Mendès France has arrived clandestinely in Geneva?"

"We have been informed," answered the other, "but we prefer not to know. Let him arrange to remain invisible; otherwise we would be obliged to hand him over to Vichy."[31]

It was through an extraordinary character named Silberscheim, former Bund[32] deputy in the Polish Diet, that Mendès France obtained the false papers indispensable for the trip to London. Silberscheim gave him what he needed to travel with a Polish identity. He thus became Jan Lemberg, Polish refugee, en route to Havana, carrying a transit visa through France and Spain and an authorization to live in Portugal until the ship for Cuba was chartered.

On February 20, 1942, he met the group of Polish emigrants in the Geneva station. It was forbidden to get off the train for the two days that it then took to cross France, from Annemasse to Port-Bou, where Franco's Guardia Civil was, of course, surly and punctilious: several Poles were turned back. They had to change trains at Barcelona. It took only five days to cross a thousand kilometers of Spain, where Lemberg and his companions even avoided the temporary internment that was then common. On February 28, the Poles were in Lisbon.

In other circumstances, Pierre Mendès France would have felt some emotion on discovering the Portugal of his ancestors: Lisbon, Portel, Vila Viçiosa, Evora. We know that the genealogist in him had shown himself as early as 1935. But Lisbon for the moment was only a port of call, still dangerous: André Blumel, a close colleague of Léon Blum's, had been arrested there a few months earlier. While waiting for the "ship for Cuba," Mendès went first to the delegate of Free France in Lisbon, Gorlier, then to the representative of the English Special Services, Colonel Schreiber, responsible for arranging liaison with London. He was well received, he had only to be a little patient. Three days later, an appointment was made for that night at one in the morning: a hydroplane would fly him to London.

That evening, as he was finishing dinner in the hotel, he was asked for at the reception desk. A young, rather pretty blond woman asked to speak to him in private. A little worried, he agreed. "You are Pierre Mendès France." Jan Lemberg poured forth denials, hidden behind his mustache, his glasses, his old overcoat, his Basque beret. To no avail. "And you, who are you?" "A journalist, a correspondent for the British press in Lisbon." And she recounted his life in detail, his trial, his escape. "That's a marvellous story. What reporting! Help me to come a little closer to the truth." In fact, she was unaware of only one thing, that his departure was set for the coming night.

> Then, to hold her back, to keep her from talking before I left, I invited her to spend the evening in a night club. We danced, I flirted with her, I kissed her on the neck, and I found out that what she knew she had heard from Colonel Schreiber, the agent of the Intelligence Service in Lisbon, with whom, she said, she was on intimate terms. Around twelve-thirty, a half-hour before my appointment, I called a halt, claiming to be tired. We'll meet tomorrow, to get a little better acquainted.

At one o'clock he was at the airport. At two o'clock the hydroplane took off. The fugitive arrived in London on the same day, and he lodged a complaint against Colonel Schreiber for the serious leaks attributable to him. After an investigation by the English Special Services, Mendès learned that the "journalist" in question had gotten her information from other sources (perhaps from the Gaullists, who had the reputation among the English of being a little too talkative) and that she was in fact a spy working for the Nazis. He had barely escaped: the morning after his flight, his hotel room had been searched. He had almost suffered the fate of André Blumel.

6.
I GO TO WAR

London, at last! First of all, of course, he had to make contact with General de Gaulle. But he also wanted to find the friends who had chosen to continue the struggle, in the most varied forms.

On March 1, 1942, Charles Gombault saw, "arriving from Portugal, a character out of Chagall who had barely escaped from the ghetto, looking hunted, rumpled, pallid, exhausted, and who moreover said his name was Lemberg! A real stage performance. It took me a moment to recognize in him Pierre, my childhood friend."

But where was Georges Boris? Mendès had heard his former colleague in the Blum government speak several times on the BBC. But now Boris was there, eloquent, precise, describing, with admirable control over the details, the course of the war, the balance of forces, the hopes, and also the conflicts around and about De Gaulle, whom he supported without reservation.

As a liaison officer attached to a British division in 1939, Boris had joined it in the retreat from Dunkerque and found himself in London in June 1940. On the morning of the nineteenth, he was among the first dozen volunteers who presented themselves at the little office of the Free French on Seamore Place, where Geoffroy de Courcel gave him the job of answering the telephone. That very evening, the general summoned him to a private meeting and calmly explained to him why he had chosen to continue the struggle and how, if Hitler's attempted invasion of the British Isles was repulsed, the Allies would win the war.

Georges Boris would never forget that "clear French lesson in logic and cool-headedness, strength and honor."[1] He recalled that, greeted with such warmth and confidence by the general, he was the one who, the next day, asked De Gaulle to let him fade a little into the background, in order not to compromise him or give him a "left-wing" aura. He then left for two weeks to visit the camps where the French soldiers who had retreated from Norway were stationed to convince them to rally to Free France. For an entire year, he was content to prepare the press summary for De Gaulle in a modest office in Carlton Gardens. The imprint of this "historic Gaullism," received so early by Boris, could not fail to have repercussions on his friend Mendès France.

> I will never forget my first night in London in 1942, with Germaine and Georges Boris, when he spoke to me for a long time about his work, his concerns, the leader to whom he had attached himself. As early as 1942, we were both passionately concerned with the tasks of reconstruction; we sketched out a global politics, the Plan, full employment, a just division of sacrifices to be made and wealth to be created.[2]

Mendès France needed neither Boris's argument nor even the meeting the general granted him on the very day of his arrival to feel himself totally a Gaullist. But the statements of the friend for whom he had the greatest respect supported his immediate impulse. Of course, the reservations, and even the opposition of his friends in London, like Louis Lévy, Comert, and the Gombault brothers, who had made a different analysis and saw in De Gaulle, beyond the war leader, a potential dictator, did not leave him indifferent. But first the war had to be won. And no one better than De Gaulle could fully utilize the still slender resources of Free France and galvanize resistance.

However voluntaristic the escaped prisoner's analysis of the situation in France, and however optimistic his report to Boris, the fact remained that De Gaulle was the symbol for both of them and that they thought everything should be done to consolidate his position in French public opinion. Moreover, Boris was able to point out to his friend that the man the two of them respected above all others, Léon Blum, had made the same analysis and drawn the same conclusions from his prison cell—not without a little help from a letter from Boris in June 1942.

We should allow Mendès France to narrate himself his first meeting with De Gaulle. Even in 1980, he spoke with strong feeling.

> On the very first day, conducted by Boris, I asked for an audience at Carlton Gardens, where the general had set up his office. I was a little ashamed to

present myself in such a state, rumpled and seedy. And besides, seeing De Gaulle was a moving and extraordinary event. I was told that he was on an inspection tour outside London, but that he would return that evening and, knowing that I had arrived, he expected me for dinner. In the restaurant, he was accompanied by his aide-de-camp and by René Pleven, then representative to the colonies. It was explained to me the next day that he had brought along Pleven, in whom he had more confidence than anyone else, because he attached particular importance to the conversation.

Mendès France's memory of the dinner was quite precise.

He was naturally interested in everyone coming from France, and he had me talk for quite a while, giving my impressions and my information. And then, suddenly, he began a monologue. It was very moving, and surprising as well. We were in the midst of a crisis with the Americans over Saint-Pierre-et-Miquelon. Seen from France, or by someone who had just come from France, it didn't seem very important. But he was distraught, all the more because he had just come through a much more serious conflict with the English over Syria. He began to speak, to pose rhetorical questions, seemingly directed to me, but really addressed to himself:

"Was I right about Saint-Pierre-et-Miquelon?"

"I don't know the situation well enough to judge, but since you have gone there, you cannot give in to pressure by evacuating."

And he continued, with a kind of anguish:

"Was I right about Syria?"

And then there was a whole series of questions concluding with an astonishing one that requires some effort to understand:

"Was I right on June 18?"

Of course, that did not mean: "Was I right to choose as I did between the Germans and the Allies?" He had no doubt about that. He meant rather: "By taking this position, I have offered a guarantee to the French people that they could count on the Allies and that, if the Allies won, France would recover all its rights and its grandeur, its empire, its gold. Was I right to trust the English?"

Was it reasonable to entrust the fate of France to them, to make this crucial political gesture, while it was daily becoming clearer that the Allies, quite naturally, placed their national interests above French interests? In Syria, for example. For General de Gaulle, guarantor of the future of France, this was tragic. From the military point of view, the strategist in him was confident in his choice. That was his job. He had acted accordingly, and he was sure of himself. But with respect to the political aspect of things, the trust placed in Churchill and Roosevelt, he had doubts and questions. It was an echo of that anxiety that I heard that night in London.

De Gaulle was all the more cordial to me because I asked nothing of him but to fight. But, come to think of it, I did ask him for one thing, to be allowed to meet with him whenever I asked. Knowing that I would not abuse the privilege, he immediately accepted. Thus I must have seen him about ten times between early 1942 and late 1943, when I became his finance minister. As soon as my arrival became known, there must have been a little concern in his entourage. Was I going to solicit some post of responsibility? Diethelm, commissioner of war for the CFLN,[3] on learning that I was asking only for a combat role, declared: "That takes care of everything."

Things did not appear the same way to De Gaulle. He anticipated no particular complications from my arrival in London; I did not trouble him in any way. But the fact that I wanted to fight gratified him. He thought that was "good." He was happy that one of the men who had rallied to his cause preferred to fight in the hour of battle.

"What do you want to do," he asked me, "and where?"

"I am in the air force, I want to rejoin my service, and in a fighting unit."

There was only one fighting unit in the Free French forces, the Lorraine group, based in Syria. Indeed. But the geography of the time was not, or was no longer, the one that we know. Going from London to Damascus meant going around the world, passing through the Cape of Good Hope. So I was pacified a little, and I became acquainted with the ruling circles of Free France.

He was generally well received, since a large fraction of the microcosm of Free France had its heart on the left—both the "critical" branch of Gombault, Labarthe, and Comert and the "knights of the round table" like Boris, Brossolette, and Schumann. With a few others, this latter group ran an Executive Committee for Propaganda. It was there that Maurice Schumann announced one day that Pierre Mendès France had escaped and reached London and that he should be given an appropriate welcome.

"Les Français Parlent aux Français" (The French Speak to the French) on the BBC thus announced that Blum's former cabinet minister had escaped and joined the Free French. And a few months later, on November 18, 1942, Maurice Schumann, in the name of General de Gaulle, paid real tribute to the escaped prisoner.

Where does Pierre Mendès France, national commissioner of finance, come from? Not from one front, but from two. Arrested and tortured by the anti-French, convicted as a deserter for having crossed the Mediterranean in June 1940 in the hope of continuing the struggle on the soil of the empire, he succeeded, after two fantastic and dangerous escapes, in rallying to General de Gaulle. Hardly had he arrived on British soil when this thirty-five-year-old deputy, who had already sat in the councils of government, demanded and obtained a front-line combat post.

In London, before he joined his unit, and later on leave, he spent most of his time with Boris and his wife, who created a family atmosphere for him, and with whom he rediscovered the passionate exchange of information and ideas of which he had been cruelly deprived for two years. As the war continued its course, Boris and Mendès confirmed the validity of the arguments that associated economic growth with state activity. They saw England at war, wounded to the quick, rise to the terrible challenge by virtue of economic as well as military mobilization, through "war planning." Above all, they saw the United States, as soon as it had been thrown into the conflict, set in motion the formidable industrial machine prepared by the "Roosevelt revolution" and develop into a gigantic steam hammer to crush Nazism and Japanese militarism. The evenings in London with Georges Boris counted a great deal toward the maturing of his theoretical understanding and to his more and more definite commitment to democratic planning.

He also saw a number of people at L'Escargot and the Petit Club, a London restaurant run by a lady who gave the illusion—at least to herself—of preparing "French" cooking. It was there, on Christmas night 1942, that he learned of Darlan's assassination. At first he refused to believe it, since the word came from a friend who was a little tipsy. But he was finally convinced. The outcome of the war was not changed, but the rhythm and the methods of the liberation of the country and relations between France and her allies were.

By the end of April 1942, after a little less than two months in London, where he had begun to restore his health, which had been undermined by prison and the privations of clandestine life, Lieutenant Mendès France was prepared to rejoin his unit. But how? He had learned that by going to the United States he had a chance of avoiding the interminable sea voyage and that he could find an air connection with the Middle East.

He managed to follow this rather exceptional course. Going through New York would mean that he could see his family for the first time in two and a half years—and what years. But if he thought that going through America would be easy, he was wrong.

> It was tragic. How many weeks did it take us to cross the Atlantic? Our convoy of twenty-five freighters, protected by small escort ships, moved with exasperating heaviness and slowness. We were sent off course and found ourselves off the coast of Greenland. Finally we reached New York, where I had the happiness of seeing my wife and sons in good health.

He saw many people in New York, among them his old friend Pierre Cot and the representative of Free France, who did not have an easy life. The U.S. administration, which continued to maintain an embassy in Vichy, gave him the cold shoulder; he was forbidden to fly the tricolor, and the French colony snubbed him. But he had many contacts, friends well placed in the press, the political parties, and New York Jewish circles. He was well informed, cordial, invigorating.

Another of Mendès France's connections during his American stay was Alexis Léger. The former secretary general of the Foreign Ministry, who was then much better known for that than as Saint-John Perse, author of *Anabase,* had retreated to Washington, where he lived like an ascetic, with a little job as secretary in the Library of Congress. Enough to survive. But, Mendès said later,

> He had a great reputation with the Americans, who consulted him constantly. Newcomers to great world affairs, unfamiliar with foreign problems, they had at hand a man who knew everything. So they made him spout forth on almost anything, Bulgaria, the Peloponnesus, the occupation of the Ruhr.
>
> Unfortunately, he had bad relations with De Gaulle. He thought of him as one of "Paul Reynaud's men"—Reynaud had peremptorily dismissed him from his post as permanent secretary of the Foreign Ministry. De Gaulle, on the other hand, thought that Léger was a creature of the Americans. This was very unfair: I know of instances in which he succeeded in staving off attacks that Washington had prepared against the general. But he refused to rally to Gaullism. I did everything to try to bring them together, which would have changed many things. I failed.

And then Lieutenant Mendès France, still wanting to leave for Syria—the delays in transit were, in this case, of the kind that would have infuriated Colonel Leprêtre—learned that, in conformity with military tradition, his orders were countermanded. The Lorraine group was to leave the Near East for London. To rejoin his unit he therefore had to retrace his steps to London. But a direct route from New York to London would be too simple. He had to go to Canada and wait there for the convoy that would return him to his point of departure.

He was back in London in September 1942. He asked for a meeting with De Gaulle, not for one of those free-swinging conversations they had sometimes had, in the course of which the general would allow himself to think out loud as he did with those he trusted. But this time, Mendès felt that he had something important to tell the leader of Free France. On the basis of rumors that he had checked, particularly with Tixier, he had arrived at the conviction that the Americans were preparing a major operation for October or November. A landing, for example. He could not say where, and he had no means of knowing of the great debate in progress between Eisenhower, who preferred a landing in North Africa, and Churchill, who favored operations in Yugoslavia to prevent the Soviet Union from taking control of Eastern Europe and the eastern Mediterranean. But what he said was enough to hold the attention of Charles de Gaulle.

Feeling closer and closer to the leader of Free France, Mendès at the same time continued to strengthen his pro-British feelings. Although it is true that, of all the duties he performed in his life, those as mayor of

Louviers gave him more satisfaction than any others, and although it is true that, of all the men whom he came to know, De Gaulle impressed him the most (despite their fervent disputes), it is no less true that, of all the communities whose life he witnessed, he felt the strongest admiration for the English at war.

> First of all, there was the extraordinary behavior of this people under fire; they made no display of their civic sense since it was so natural to them. They were fighting because it was unimaginable or intolerable that the Nazis might win. They were holding on, they would hold on, and that was that. After every bombardment, they calmly put out the fires, they serenely buried the dead, and life resumed. The women, especially, demonstrated admirable stoicism and effectiveness.
>
> And also, I admired the operation of their democracy in wartime. I seldom went to the House of Commons, but I saw, through the press, the radio, and the contacts I had, the operation of the mechanisms of government and opposition, free debate, and respect for divergent ideas. In the midst of war, under the bombs! Churchill was "making war," like Clemenceau, but without touching any democratic guarantees. I sometimes saw him, thanks to his chief of staff, Major Morton, a friend of Pleven's. He had formidable serenity. Are you surprised, given all that, that I became—and remained—an Anglophile?

Lieutenant Mendès France was enabled to foster this Anglophilia through his contacts with the British at war. The Lorraine group was not, of course, integrated into the RAF: De Gaulle would have been fiercely opposed to that. But although he was in the Free French and therefore officially responsible only to the Carlton Gardens headquarters, Mendès was nevertheless operationally closely associated with the Royal Air Force.

The Lorraine group, which he joined after a two-month training period, was based at Hartfordbridge, an airport located a little more than fifty miles to the west of London, which meant that he could use his leave every ten days to reimmerse himself in the friendly political and intellectual atmosphere of the capital. In technical terms, it was a "bombing group with a medium range of action"; a typical target was the Ruhr. It was made up of two squadrons and under the command of Lieutenant-Colonel Rancourt, who was thirty-three.

The camp—a few huts, two tents for the offices and the work room, two light camouflaged hangars—where the two squadrons of the Lorraine group were installed was at the edge of the runway and surrounded by the planes covered with canvas for the night. They lived in a state of alert, dedicated to combat. The planes were Bostons, peculiarly constructed so that the members of the crew—the pilot, the navigator (Mendès), and the two gunners—were totally isolated, never saw each other in flight, and could communicate only through an intercom whose correct operation was vital. The lieutenant-navigator was installed forward, in a kind of glass cage, surrounded by his sights, his rulers, his protractor, his life jacket, and his raft.

On days without missions, we fretted with impatience. The English, who were excellent fighters but were also disciplined, calmly awaited their orders and obeyed impeccably. The French, on the contrary, charged ahead, exaggerated. One day, Colonel Rancourt refused to give me a mission; I grumbled insolently. The result: I was confined to base for two weeks. It was my only military punishment. My comrades were all like that. There was a sortie on the same day I was named as a minister in Algiers. My pilot, upset, thought for a minute that I wouldn't go, and that it would be taken away from him. Of course, I was determined to accomplish the mission—it was against the V1 launching pads in Pas-de-Calais. But it was the last one for me.[4]

Romain Gary sketched an ironic but friendly portrait of Lieutenant Mendès France in the Lorraine group in a book of memoirs:

Mendès was in my squadron toward the end of the war. He was unbeatable "in class," on paper navigation exercises. But one day, he was in my plane on a training flight. In spite of his calculations, he got lost, he no longer knew where we were and asked me to show him my navigation figures. I hadn't done any: I knew the "triangle" by heart, I was commander of the plane, the weather was fine, and I was navigating by sight. I told him so. He flew into a black rage, yelled at me that I was refusing to show him my calculations; I think he took me for an "anti" and was going through a little psychological storm. . . . I showed him the village we were flying over, told him it was Buckingham and that all he had to do was start from there. He looked at his calculations and said: "It's Odiham." I said: "Buckingham," showing him on the ground the two green water tanks I recognized. He stuck his papers under my nose and repeated: "Odiham." I asked to have our position plotted from the ground and showed it to him with material proof in support: "You see, it's Buckingham." Mendès looked at his figures again, smiled at me, and repeated: "Odiham," and walked off. Of course, there was that touch of amusement and the smile, but also an excessive confidence in abstract calculations.

Of the dozen major bombing operations in which he took part, from October 1942 to November 1943, the date he was asked by General de Gaulle to join the Liberation Committee in Algiers, Mendès France chose to narrate one, in an article reprinted as an appendix to the 1977 edition of *Liberté, liberté chérie.*

On October 3, 1943, the airmen of the Lorraine group, among them Mendès France, who had just been promoted to captain, heard from a British colleague that they were going to be involved in a "bloody good show," perhaps over France. (It was an old debate. Did they have the right to bomb the French? But who would be more willing and able than they to limit the losses by taking the extra risks of low-level flight that made the bombers more vulnerable to some, not all, forms of enemy defense, but would also allow them to avoid spraying civilian targets?)

Meeting in the operations room. A shock: they were being sent over Paris. After so many years, they were about to see again "its houses, its bridges, its streets, its domes, breathe a little of its air." They had sometimes dreamed of it, but they had said to themselves, it's the "kind of thing that doesn't happen."

Lieutenant-Colonel Rancourt gave the briefing:

> We are going to attack the power station and the transformer in Chevilly-Larue, north of Villeneuve-Orly, near Paris.[5] It is a very small target, difficult to find and to hit without scattering bombs. We will therefore make the attack at a very low altitude. We will have three formations of four planes each. I will lead the first four, which will be hedge-hopping throughout; the crew of the "N"[6] will lead the eight others, which, eight kilometers before the target, will rise to five hundred meters, drop their bombs, and dive again toward the ground to return behind us and complete the mission at hedge-hopping level.

Whatever the circumstances, they had to avoid attacking a target without verification, and above all to avoid dropping the bombs if the target did not appear exactly in the crosshairs of the range finder. In that event, it was better to bring them back. And there was a special order: At all costs, avoid hitting the apartment houses and the workers housing in Chemin-Vert, very close to the target.

They took off at 12:55 in good weather. They reached the French coast at 13:32, met by a few German machine guns.

> Why is the countryside rushing beneath me more beautiful than any other? I try to define what distinguishes it from the English soil I have just flown over. There is no real difference. And yet, I would recognize it among a hundred others. It has a look, an atmosphere that are ours. . . the wind pushes us a little off course, there's Geneviève-en-Bray, near the sources of the Andelle (are there such gracious names anywhere else?). Peasants stop to look at us, wave their arms to signal to us. These signs of encouragement and approval are proof that we are right. We are in the department of Eure, my department. A few kilometers away is my house. If, instead of sticking to the ground (to the point that we sometimes almost touch trees and houses), if we were to climb to five or six hundred meters, I would see Louviers in its valley, toward the Seine, and right next to it, the little hamlet of Monts with my house, my garden, my apple trees.

At the moment they arrived over Paris, he would have to give the order to the eight last planes to raise altitude to avoid being blasted by the bombs of the first squadron. He gave the order (a little too soon?) at the moment when German fighters appeared over Toussus-le-Noble; oddly, they didn't attack. They passed the peripheral railroad tracks, Fresnes prison, Orly. At six hundred meters, a sort of silvery fog obscured the ground a little, but he could make out the highway leading to Chevilly. The pilot opened the bomb-bay doors.

There was heavy fire from machine guns and the eighty-eight-millimeter cannons of the German anti-aircraft forces. The sky filled with black flakes. The four planes of the first squad dropped their bombs, setting off at first showers of sparks from short circuits, then an enormous explosion and a stream of orange flames. Mendès aimed for the station's cooling tower. Four pushes of the button, counting out loud (each push set off, along with the bomb, a camera to record the results: he verified later that the target had been destroyed and the Chemin-Vert neighborhood spared).

Once the number four had been spoken and the bombing ended, the pilot took charge of maneuvers, initiating evasive actions in the midst of heavy anti-aircraft fire. The lead group was flying down below, already at the house tops; but one of the planes had been hit and, following orders, headed toward the Seine, where it crashed. Another plane, navigated by Jean d'Astier de La Vigerie, seemed to be having trouble keeping up. They flew over the center of Paris, the Gobelins, place de la Nation, Vincennes, where there were soccer players, Ivry. They slowed down to wait for d'Astier's plane, but the fighter planes that were to take them under escort over Crèvecoeur could not wait. D'Astier had to be left behind to save the others—but he managed to make it back.

And then, marking the limit of the Paris urban area, isolated in the middle of the fields, there was a little hamlet he didn't know, Roissy-en-France. A village in France. The name and the minuscule town gathered around the church touched him so strongly that he made it a symbol of the mission and the title of his moving narrative.

They landed at 15:16. One crew and two planes out of twelve had been lost.

> The "N" comes to a stop. I put away my papers, my maps, my rulers. An immense silence falls over me: the motors have just stopped. I hear the exclamations of the ground crew: they are examining the damage caused by an artillery shell to the gun emplacement on the left wing.
>
> I detach my belt, and I open the passage beneath me so I can get out of the cabin. I take off my parachute straps and my helmet. I jump to the ground.
>
> I am tired; I have the impression that it's very cold, suddenly.

Cold, perhaps. But he felt above all liberated, cleansed of the stain that had been inflicted on him. The "deserter" had proved himself in arms, demonstrated the bravery that the judges in Clermont-Ferrand had refused to accept. But he did not yet feel available for other duties. Soon thereafter, when General de Gaulle proposed that he join the Consultative Assembly he had set up in Algiers, where the general had taken up residence in May 1943, Captain Mendès France refused. Why should he palaver in the sun when his comrades here wished to keep him at their head?

In short, Mendès preferred Hartfordbridge to Algiers. Three more missions would take him over the continent, to Langer, Barden, and Krasker, in the windowed cabin of the *Lieutenant Sandré*. But war strategy was not only military, and he had spoken too much about economic mobilization, with Boris and his English friends, not to know that, sooner or later, the fight would take on other forms.

In early November, his friend Pierre-Bloch, who had just escaped from France and arrived in London, called Mendès at Hartfordbridge: "There's a man coming from France, Leroux, one of my Socialist comrades. He was sent by the clandestine party to De Gaulle in Algiers, whom he advised to make his staff younger. He wants to see you." The next day, Mendès, contacted by Leroux, started by yelling at him: "Mind your own business. Let me fight." Then he listened to Leroux's account of the conversation with De Gaulle.

> "I pointed out to him that the National Liberation Committee, that will sooner or later have to change into a provisional government, should stop being a collection of generals, prefects, and treasury officials, and become representative, politicize itself. It's the left that's fighting in France, and it has to be more closely associated with the leader of the Resistance. That's why I mentioned your name. The general did not say no. He is going to contact you. Accept!"

(The traveler was so anxious to convince Mendès that he did not report that at the beginning of the conversation, when he first mentioned his name to the general, De Gaulle murmured: "Another Jew!") In short, the conversation between Leroux and Mendès turned out rather well.

> This Leroux was Gaston Defferre, whom I did not know. I found him likable and almost convincing. I answered that I found his offer very flattering, but that there was no question of my accepting, that I belonged to a fighting unit from which I could not take a leave as though it were a vacation (and I ought to know!). We separated on friendly terms. And I heard nothing further for some weeks. From Algiers, we heard nothing but rumors of machinations, squabbles, and rivalries, in which I was not at all tempted to become involved. Suddenly, toward the middle of November, I received a telegram from De Gaulle in approximately these terms:
> "I need you in the Finance Ministry. I know that this was not your idea, but you have entered into a commitment. A soldier does not choose the

location of his fight. As your leader, I have assigned you to a position with me in Algiers."

The tone was simultaneously authoritarian, warm, and gracious. In fact, I was at the end of what was called a "tour of duty," and I knew that I would not stay for long in the Lorraine group. De Gaulle knew it, too; I couldn't quarrel with him in this area as I could with Defferre. I had no choice. So I went to Algiers in late November 1943, and became commissioner of finance in the CFLN, which had been established in June 1943, recognized two months later by London, Washington, and Moscow, and would become the "provisional government" on May 15, 1944.

When Mendès France landed in Algiers, De Gaulle had, over the course of the preceding five months, established his preeminence, gradually eliminating Giraud and imposing himself on the English and Americans, not without a struggle, as is well known. In the new cabinet, he had kept a few supporters of Giraud, like René Mayer and Jean Monnet, but not Couve de Murville, for whom he nevertheless already felt a great deal of respect. It was Couve whom Mendès France succeeded, with broader responsibilities; but De Gaulle said to him on his appointment: "We have to find something for Couve."[8]

Installed in rather uncomfortable and modest quarters in the Lycée Fromentin—he was known not to care about nonessentials—Mendès had only a small staff, clearly dominated by the director of the budget, Didier Gregh, a workhorse like him and an excellent specialist in financial management, along with some good technicians. Everyone set vigorously to work on their first task, preparation of the budget. In fact, according to Mendès,

> they had created a Consultative Assembly, but with little idea of what to submit to it. It is hard to imagine De Gaulle submitting his strategy to detailed critique by Pierre Cot or Fernand Grenier. So we were asked to improvise a budget that it could debate. It was a strange budget; it was printed in the *Journal officiel.*

During this stay in Algiers, Mendès France established friendships with two fellow members of the CFLN (French National Liberation Committee) who initiated him into Algerian politics, a lesson that was not entirely lost: René Capitant, son of his former teacher at the Faculty of Law, who had opened the gates of Algiers to De Gaulle; and General Catroux, one of the men he most admired in a career rich in friendships and debates.

> I consider Catroux as one of the great figures of this period, and I think that De Gaulle treated him shabbily. As a general of the army, with his five stars, he had been capable of giving way before the extraordinary personality of the

brigadier general on a temporary appointment. Having recognized him as leader, he always conducted himself toward De Gaulle with chivalric fidelity. Ten times, the Americans and the English tried to set him against De Gaulle or to offer him his place, much preferring to deal with this accomplished diplomat. Ten times, he cut them short.

Governor-general of Algeria and at the same time commissioner of Arab affairs in the CFLN, he had admirable knowledge of the problems of the region, and most of my knowledge in the area I derive from him. Determined to improve the condition of the Algerians, he had elaborated a vast plan of social and educational reforms, for which he needed a lot of money. He came to see me, and that is how we became friends.

Mendès tried to fight for the establishment of a broad Ministry of the Economy, coordinating production and trade as well as the treasury and the budget. Diethelm, commissioner for production and supply, who knew his own lack of competence and who did not want to be swallowed up, opposed his plan. Mendès gave in, recognizing that everyone was working as well as possible in his particular area and that at that time structures counted for less than action. Thus, theoretically a member of the cabinet, Jean Monnet, who spent most of his time in Washington at the head of the French purchasing commission without a very precise mandate, rendered invaluable services. And René Pleven, commissioner for the colonies, which was very important in view of the territorial bases of Free France, was involved in many other matters, for De Gaulle had more confidence in him than in anyone else.

Mendès France set himself the dual task of reestablishing order and preparing for reconstruction. The French Treasury was made up at the time primarily of the product of taxes on territories under De Gaulle's control (which did not amount to much), and the contributions, gifts, or loans that came from many sources, including individuals, to Free France. All of this had to be organized and classified, and two of his staff members were particularly qualified for the work. As for future plans, that was what chiefly occupied Mendès, who was more a planner than a manager.

But he was not contemptuous of day-to-day management, and he did everything to make it as rational as possible in the strange pre-Gaullist republic of Algiers. Barely had he assumed his position when, on January 4, 1944, he delivered a speech to his colleagues in the Consultative Assembly, legalistic, and imbued with the idea of democratic control:

Why a budget? . . . By force of circumstances, the necessary appropriations must be foreseen, ordered, distributed, and accounted for. But these budgets—and this is the essential point—have not been public or submitted to any control or any preliminary discussion. The great interest of the effort that is demanded of you today is precisely that it throws a little light on these complex and difficult accounts.

Concerning his thinking and his plans at the time of the Algiers government, we have a significant internal memorandum composed in the second half of February 1944; it constitutes a sort of breviary of Mendésism at the end of the war and was often referred to in subsequent years.

Two themes ordered his thinking: the ruin of the economic market, and the plethora of monetary instruments. On the basis of these two inescapable observations (the first based on the destruction brought about by war, the rapacity of the occupiers, the aging of the productive apparatus, and the expenditures incurred because of the pursuit of hostilities; the second attested to by the tripling of bank deposits and of paper money circulation), Pierre Mendès France and his colleagues sketched the broad outlines of what was to be the economic strategy of France at the hour of its liberation.

Treating first the question of restoring supplies (through production and imports), his memorandum proclaims the "impossibility of reestablishing the free market," and the necessity of a "general plan" organizing a "single policy defined by a central economic authority prefigured by the General Commission for National Supplies, which is now functioning in the de facto government of Metropolitan France[9] and which can become a genuine bureau of the Plan," taking its inspiration from the British precedent and coordinating French production with that of England, Belgium, and Holland. In any event, to avoid having the poor bear the major burden of shortages, "severe restrictions will clearly continue to be necessary." A choice will have to be made, if not between "guns and butter," at least between "well-being and grandeur."

Considering next ways to correct for the effects of excess currency, with the aim of "reestablishing a relative equilibrium between the average total volume of money and of merchandise," the February 1944 document advocates the "freezing of bank accounts" and the "exchange of currency," inspired by the "experiments carried out in Tunisia and Corsica," which had shown that this operation would enable "a massive reduction of currency in circulation," while at the same time invalidating the reserves held by the occupiers and allowing the identification of "abnormal profits" realized during the war. According to Mendès France's staff, this currency manipulation should be supplemented by "severe fiscal measures," "taxation of surplus profits," while "exempting productive activity and the least favored categories of the population, notably prisoners, repatriated soldiers, the unemployed, and disaster victims."

In a third section, the February 1944 memorandum insists on the necessity of a radical change in the orders broadcast from London, Algiers, and Brazzaville in order to prepare public opinion for austerity and sacrifices (provisional wage and price freeze, which can only be lifted very slowly, as a function of gradual improvements in supplies, the objective being to create "an equilibrium of prices, wages, and charges comparable to that of 1939"). And the memorandum concludes: "We are not unaware of the unpredictable elements involved in the working plan that has just been summed up. But it is the only one that offers some chance of avoiding the collapse of the national currency and large-scale social convulsions."

Even though the expression contrasting "well-being" to "grandeur" was used by the authors of the report only in a footnote, quoting an earlier document from the Conseil National des Etudes, these few words indeed sum up this sort of manifesto of Mendésism at the moment when his second ministerial career was beginning, when he moved from the Popular Front to Free France. It seems to express in depth the thinking of Mendès as he emerged from military combat to plunge into economic combat and illustrates in an almost excessive way the community of reflexes and of thinking that had been established between the commissioner of finance and his "boss," De Gaulle. No statement could be more Gaullist than that one, and it makes still more mysterious the choice the general made a year later of "well-being" over the "grandeur" whose paths had been traced by his austere finance minister.

Concerning the debates and plans of this period, we have an unfortunately fragmentary unpublished correspondence between Pierre Mendès France and Georges Boris, who was then reponsible in London for propaganda broadcast to France. A few excerpts give the tone of the correspondence:

London, January 4

My dear Pierre,
    I have received your kind letter of December 1 after the delay you can imagine, and I am deeply touched by your understanding and affection. At the same time as your letter came a few cordial and encouraging lines from the general. I know that you had something to do with this comforting letter, and I thank you for it. . . .
    You pride yourself on having treated us well from the budgetary point of view; I don't know much about it, not having seen the final figures, but what I have heard concerns me a little, I must admit. Beware of collective futures! . . .
    The latest international vicissitudes seem more favorable to us, but I wish we could avoid illusions and especially not persist in expecting from the West what the West will not give us.[10] And we should especially avoid putting off the inhabitants of this island,[11] who, although some of them are hostile, know us better, know what we need, and are beginning to feel a sense of European solidarity. I am now touching on one of my principal objects of concern, and I would like it to be known how many sincere and useful supporters I have found in important positions, people whose support is not due only to sentimental reasons, sometimes just the opposite, deriving from a

sense of the realities. I have no doubt that your beneficial influence will operate in the right direction. . . .

Algiers, March 27, 1944

My dear Boris,

I am very concerned with the dangers created by certain blunders made in radio propaganda broadcast to France. We have noted in Algeria, and even more in Corsica . . . how dangerous the illusions created by this propaganda have been in the occupied countries over the last four years.

Every day, the French are promised, at liberation, a standard of living—particularly with reference to food—that we will unfortunately be unable to provide. Thoughtful people estimate that the period immediately following liberation will be, from the point of view of food supplies, for example, much harder than the current period, especially in regions far from the ports and connected to them by transportation systems that may be destroyed by the enemy, by saboteurs, or by the Allies. . . .

Algiers, March 30, 1944

My dear Boris,

It is very comforting for me to realize that we are in such total agreement even on questions we have not discussed for years. I am distressed that you are now devoting yourself to something else. Your presence here would be very helpful at the moment when I am defending my proposal against just about everyone.

You have understood, on reading the general's speech, that it was delivered in my support, but this is only an apparent success, whose only effect was to oblige me to withdraw the resignation[12] I had submitted a few days earlier, in the face of the resistance that had come up from every direction. Tixier,[13] who you seem to expect to support me in this matter, has let himself be completely captured by the representatives of the CGT, who, for their part, want to be no less demagogic than the Communists. The result is that I have come up against great difficulties with Tixier that I didn't need, far from it.

Strangely enough, I have been able easily to work out the agricultural aspect with Queuille, thanks to a very clever formula he developed. But there are more ardent defenders of agriculture on all sides—among them the general—who are terrified at the idea of seeing, when the time comes, protests or complaints. No one wants to run the risk of unpopularity. What will it be like when we are in power?

The general-president often saw his commissioner of finance. Of necessity, as much as because of De Gaulle's tendencies, they willingly avoided financial questions in favor of discussing the broad perspectives of international politics. Mendès—having discussed with an envoy of the Belgian minister Camille Gutt the conditions under which the currency exchange had been carried out in Corsica under the direction of Gabriel Ardant, an exchange Gutt later successfully carried out in Belgium—asked De Gaulle in the spring of 1944 to what extent they could envisage a coordination of the economic policy of France with the policies of its neighbors within a European framework. The general answered:

> Europe? Of course, it has to be set up. With Belgium, Holland, and Italy to begin with. Spain will follow when they have gotten rid of Franco. Germany? There will no longer be *one* but *several* Germanies. We shall see, when it is divided, and the Ruhr is placed at the disposal of the victors, what to do with it. England? No, I don't see it participating in a European enterprise. In any event, for every federation, there has to be a federator. It will be France, and the group thus established will allow us to maintain our independence and to escape from the co-dominion of the Americans and the Russians.

The commissioner of finance of Algiers could not remain fixed in his offices of the Lycée Fromentin. He was sent on foreign missions, particularly to the United States. In early June, he represented France at the financial conference in Bretton Woods and negotiated in Washington the financial conditions of the landing scheduled for the coming months and the rates of exchange that would be established between the dollar and the Allied currencies. He left again for the United States in July, after the landing, to participate in the conference in which the author of *La Banque internationale* saw sketched out—very badly at first because of the excessive superiority in fact of the United States—the application of ideas that had always been dear to him: harmonization of growth, monetary coordination, rationalization of exchange, development of the nonindustrialized world, creation of a veritable world bank.

Pierre Mendès France was then involved, in Washington and New York, in many Franco–American negotiations, alongside the general or in the background. De Gaulle, glowing as he was with the welcome the people of France had given him near Bayeux after the landing, "consecrated" by the acclamation of the crowd in Normandy, was an object of special consideration in Washington. President Roosevelt received him courteously, but considered him "essentially egotistical." Aside from Morgenthau and McCloy, all the American leaders were hostile or suspicious, and this aggravated De Gaulle's antipathy toward them.

On July 7, when he thought he could derive some benefit from some Washington colleagues whom he had finally found well disposed toward him, Mendès France received a letter from De Gaulle that clearly expressed the distrust the visitor felt toward his hosts.

Blair House, July 7

My dear friend,
> Things are not going badly here. Morgenthau and McCloy, it appears, have had the president accept a paper that comes very close to the Viénot-English paper,[14] notably with respect to currency, buried in a lend-lease

agreement. I expect the president to show me this paper tomorrow. I will answer that we will examine it calmly in Algiers. And you must take the same position. If Morgenthau approaches you, do not negotiate yourself, at any cost. The diplomatic channel is open, and it is the only one that allows us to operate with care, reserve, and without surprises. I shall see you soon.

Cordially,
C. de Gaulle

This is a very curious letter that expresses both significant suspicion of his hosts and real cordiality toward his minister.

But in New York, where De Gaulle then went, it was an entirely different story. He was greeted by the little mayor, Fiorello LaGuardia, who was taken with him and brought out in force his Democratic Party supporters, that is, the immigrants and the disinherited of all kinds, the anti-Nazi refugees from Europe, the blacks. For them, De Gaulle was the man who had refused to compromise with Hitler, the man of antifascism— the King of Denmark, Tito, Sikorski, and the Dolomite partisans rolled into one. He was the Europe that had rejected Hitler, Mussolini, and Franco, from whom many of them had had to flee.

Overwhelmed, Pierre Mendès France, who followed De Gaulle like his shadow and arranged useful contacts for him, was enchanted to see him acclaimed by these New Yorkers in a delirium of affection, from the West Side docks to Times Square. The general turned toward Mendès, half-seriously: "In short, my supporters are the blacks and Puerto Ricans, the deformed and the cuckolds, immigrants and Jews?" "Yes, indeed, you will have to get used to it, *mon général:* now you are the leader of the Popular Front." (And when he told this story thirty-five years later—"It is one of the memories that counts for me"—Mendès France did not speak with much more corrosive irony than he had in the taxi bringing them back from the rally of "cuckolds" LaGuardia had organized at their hotel. He did not forget the close communication he felt then with the man of June haunted by his paradoxical fate.)

And then there was Paris. Not on August 26, 1944, for Mendès France. He was not beside De Gaulle on the Champs-Elysées, moving through the sea of people with Bidault, Parodi, Le Troquer, Leclerc, and Juin. Neither a soldier nor a member of the internal Resistance, he was civilian staff and therefore had to follow at a distance. Simple ministers like him had been embarked on the cruiser *Jeanne-d'Arc,* which transported them slowly from Algiers to Cherbourg, from August 28 to September 7. He found a car in Cherbourg in ruins and raced toward Paris without going through Louviers.

He hurried to the rue Saint-Dominique, where De Gaulle had settled in, four years and a few weeks after being driven out. The general, who had succeeded in forestalling the attempted seizure of power he had expected from the Communists, said to him at the outset: "There is no longer a question; we now have only problems."

7.
MINISTER OF RIGOR

Paris was overwhelming. It was summer. The weather was extraordinary. There were tricolor ribbons and flags everywhere. A great deal of joy. Even privations were barely felt; of course, everything would be arranged. Because transportation was lacking, no one could travel, everyone lived in the street, in front of his door, everyone talked to everyone else. A great celebration!

Thus spoke Mendès France in 1980. But in early September 1944, he wrote to his wife: "There is nothing. No electricity, no mail, no gas, no transportation. Only the telephone, which we abuse."

His apartment on avenue Léopold-II had been confiscated and remained unusable. He was moved in with a few other members of the government to the Hotel Claridge, which, still occupied by the Germans a few days earlier, had not had its current cut off. In the luxurious suite put at his disposal he was shocked to find, carefully hung in the closet, a Nazi uniform.

He asked himself the question of whether he would resume his political life, or at least his parliamentary and ministerial life.

The ordeals of the war had tired and tried me. I had a thousand things to do, I wanted to see my children again. My house in Louviers had been gutted by bombs. My responsibilities as mayor of that city that had been severely tried once again seemed to me to be the first priority. And in the government, I felt that I would have the greatest difficulty in getting through a policy that was both innovative and reasonable, in opposition to a man like Adrien Tixier in Social Affairs, who was asking for the moon, and against people like Pleven and Diethelm, who were terribly conformist. So I was tempted to withdraw, at least for a relatively long period.

And then De Gaulle summoned me and said: "I am reorganizing the government. But you, you have to stay." No longer hoping that he would give me the Ministry of Economic Affairs, whose creation I had long advocated in Algiers, I thought he was going to ask me to stay at Finance, and I was preparing to make objections, when he said to me: "You have been talking for months about a great Ministry of the Economy. Very well, take it." But I quickly realized that this "great" ministry of coordination was only a fragment of the Ministry of Finance, and the least important in his mind.

At bottom, there were for him serious portfolios—Army, Foreign Affairs, Interior—and then the more abstract, more theoretical departments, where idealists and dreamers should excel, likable men of the left. In the event, the Ministry of Finance (the "purse strings") had to be given to a prudent and thoroughly trustworthy figure—Pleven, for example—while in "economic affairs" a social experimenter like me could give free rein to his imagination. It was not quite a consolation prize. He was quite attached to me, I'm convinced of it, and he thought my conceptions were salutary, my way of thinking and acting, my concern for justice, and my concern for the "long term." But he was a little suspicious. Besides, he explained very clearly to me that there were rumors everywhere that I was preparing a currency exchange—which was true—and that if I was put in charge of Finance, that would make everyone get rid of his currency and that would ruin the chances of the projected government borrowing. In short, I made people afraid, but he was attached to me. Not immediately grasping all the implications of what he was saying, and because he was cordial and even friendly, I gave in.

But it was not Pleven who went to the Ministry of Finance. He rejected De Gaulle's offer after having also declined Foreign Affairs, where he practically imposed the appointment of Bidault. He did not want to leave his Ministry of Colonial Affairs, where he was doing what interested him, where he thought he had many things to set in motion, and from which he could exercise influence in other areas. De Gaulle gave in to his arguments and, on his insistence, chose for Finance a man from Nord who had worked for one of the great private banks, Aimé Lepercq. He was a member of the Resistance and a leader of the Paris insurrection. He had been in the first rank of those who seized the Hôtel de Ville on August 23. Pierre Mendès France immediately felt comfortable with this likable and very open figure.

"I know nothing about public finance," Lepercq confessed to him. "Up to now, I have had to do only with private business. We have to work together very closely. Find me a good expert to be a liaison between us."

Mendès selected one of his colleagues from Algiers, the *inspecteur des finances* Riquebourg, responsible along with Ardant for the currency exchange in Corsica. And he retreated to his semi-ministry, where he appointed, with the discreet title "head of mission," the loyal and indispensable Georges Boris, who was later in charge of the Plan.

The severe Mendès France of the last months of 1944, returning from Algiers to the "château" on the rue de Rivoli that he had tried to govern in 1938, now moving from Finance to Economic Affairs (already placing his imprint on a brilliant generation of young civil servants who were to create the Plan and prepare the conditions for economic recovery in the early 1950s), was perhaps best described in an anecdote related by one of his disciples of the time, François Bloch-Lainé.

> After the Liberation, when Pierre Mendès France arrived at Finance (before De Gaulle appointed Aimé Lepercq), he called me in and said something like: "I need to know, from the mouth of a witness I trust, how the civil servants here conducted themselves, who was very good, very bad, or in between." And Bloch-Lainé answering that he couldn't play informer and that in his opinion "most of them had done their duty, without heroism or disgrace." Mendès exclaimed, without real indignation: "You're all the same, the pure servants of this place. In Algiers, Guillaume Guindey said the same thing. This morning, the chauffeur they've given me, when I asked what he had done for four years, said: 'I drove Bouthillier,[1] I drove Cathala,[2] and now I'm driving you.' All the same, from top to bottom!"[3]

They were not all alike. There were those in whom he placed his confidence, and the others. Among the former, in addition to his colleagues from Algiers—Largentaye, Guindey, Riquebourg, Gregh, Goetz—and the liaison with Jean Monnet—Hervé Alphand and Olivier Wormser—there were those who had acted in Paris—François Bloch-Lainé and André Postel-Viray. And then, from Algiers through Corsica, the man who—except, of course, for Georges Boris—was to play the most important role at his side: Gabriel Ardant, still decked out in his uniform of colonel of Free France.

The great battle broke out immediately. Mendès France, Boris, Largentaye, Guindey, and Ardant, among others, wanted to make policy on the basis of the February 1944 Algiers document. It was their charter for action. Austerity to assure justice in a period of penury, currency reduction to reestablish the balance between production and the means of exchange. It was to obtain the realization of these principles that Mendès, very briefly as minister of finance, a little longer as minister of the economy,[4] fought uninterruptedly, against those who wished to believe that time, the regulatory effects of the market, and the excellence of human resources always arrange things for the best.

The battle was not between the "free marketeers" of Finance and the "planners" of Economy. That would be too simple. But it is true that the planners, with Mendès at their head, were a majority at the Economy and the marketeers a majority at Finance. Aimé Lepercq was not a planner by nature and, trained in traditional banking, was rather inclined toward simple procedures. Freezing bank accounts, what audacity! But the Resistance had made him evolve. He had developed some hostility against the members of his profession. Moreover, he was influenced daily by the Mendésist Riquebourg. In short, he wanted above all to be informed before making the necessary decisions. Every Sunday morning, he held a meeting of his associates and some of his colleagues from the Ministry of the Economy. Ardant and Guindey were the most ardent supporters of intervention, of controls, and of freezing accounts.

It was less Lepercq, it seems, than, in the background, René Pleven, still minister of colonial affairs and De Gaulle's most trusted adviser (supported by Emmanuel Monick, the new governor of the Banque de France, and by René Courtin, a professor of law who had been very active in the Resistance, cofounder of *Le Monde,* and oracle of the Resistance for economic matters), who decided the fate of what could be called the first leg of the battle: the floating of a government loan. It was a measure exactly contrary to the spirit of the Algiers memorandum, by reason of the fact that it was based on the credibility of a currency that ought to have been subjected to radical surgery. This was all the more true because, even before Mendès France was appointed to Finance, immediately after the Liberation, a large increase in wages had brought about a further expansion of currency in circulation.

By rallying to the idea of the great "Liberation loan," a painless but half-illusory procedure that De Gaulle had allowed himself to be sold on by Pleven and his friends (and that was, incidentally, a success), Aimé Lepercq did not know that he was racing to his death. While he was crisscrossing the department of Nord along with some of his colleagues to promote the loan, his car fell from a destroyed bridge into a canal. All the occupants were drowned, including Lepercq and Riquebourg.[5]

The problem of selecting a successor took on the character of a decisive test of French politics, to the degree that it took place in the heat of the debate between the opposed clans of the austere and the flexible. In December 1944, De Gaulle was in the grip of problems that he found much more interesting and weighty: the counteroffensive of Rundstedt from the Ardennes, which was growing and threatening Strasbourg; and his journey to the Soviet Union, in the course of which, in order to establish a counterweight to American influence through an alliance with Russia, he had had to concede to Stalin the recognition of the puppet Polish government of Mikolaïcjik, abandoning his nationalist friends in London, who had been the very first to recognize him. Compared to such problems, in the general's view, Lepercq's succession had only marginal significance. "Would he give me another chance?" Mendès later commented.

He had thought of it. But the loan had been floated, and my face was not the kind that would encourage subscriptions. The general thought of René Mayer. I suggested Paul Giaccobi, with whom I got along well. Former chairman of the Senate Finance Committee, he was minister of supply. He was a very courageous and honest man, a Corsican Radical who had fought with exceptional bravery, first in the Resistance, and then with Gabriel Ardant for the currency exchange in Corsica.

On one particular day, the general summoned me and said: "You are interim finance minister. I am leaving for the front with Churchill. When I return, we will make a decision." I don't know what happened then. Perhaps Churchill's influence worked against me, because, in his eyes, despite the cordiality he showed me, I looked like a Labourite of the Stafford Cripps variety, while Pleven, whom he also knew better, satisfied him from every point of view. In any event, I remain convinced that he and De Gaulle brought up the question in the course of their journey.

While the succession in the Finance Ministry was being debated in Alsace, in the face of the tanks of Rundstedt, Mendès and Pleven had gotten together. And Pleven said to him: "I have no desire to go to Finance. I'm fine at Colonial Affairs. My intentions are the same as they were three months ago." Even in 1980, Mendès France said he was convinced that Pleven was sincere and did not wish to assume the crushing responsibility of Finance, preferring to exercise a lateral—and decisive—influence on French financial policy. As a former unsuccessful candidate for *inspecteur des finances,* he may also have had a certain inferiority complex toward all the successful candidates he would have under his orders. In short, he preferred to remain at a distance. But as René Pleven himself informed us,[6] shortly before his death, Aimé Lepercq had told the general that if he (Lepercq) could not complete his task, the general should call on Pleven.

Thus, to the surprise of most of those involved, the name of Pleven came out of the general's hat. And the choice, apparently the most anti-Gaullist possible, implied facility against austerity, laissez faire against discipline.

"From that point on," said Mendès,

it was clear that we were confronting new difficulties. Pleven and I were not on bad terms, on the personal level. We had respected each other in London. Our wives had met in New York. But we still disagreed about everything. There were dozens of disputes, notably about holdings of Alsace and Lorraine banks that had been seized by the Germans over the Sarre dispute. Moreover, in most of these debates, I found myself opposed not only by

Pleven but also by the majority of Socialists: Robert Lacoste, minister of production; Tanguy-Prigent (whom I particularly respected), for agricultural reasons; and even their colleague at Social Affairs, Adrien Tixier, for reasons related to the workers. Not to mention the Communists, who, quite obviously, had no desire that a left-wing policy be carried out by anyone but them.

Thorez had declared, not to Mendès but to André Philip, who had spoken of reforming the distribution system: "We are for revolution, tomorrow. In the meantime, today, we want the capitalist system to function according to its own laws, which must not be attacked. We are not going to help the capitalist system improve itself."[7]

These principles were applied with particular rigor to Mendès France, for example with respect to the Alsace and Lorraine bank affair. When they annexed Alsace and Lorraine, the Nazi leaders had compelled the owners of banks or banking agencies of those regions to sell to them. With Liberation, Pleven declared himself in favor of pure and simple restitution of these holdings. Mendès France on the contrary objected first that the bankers in question had received payment from the occupiers, and further that, since the government had decided to nationalize the largest banks, it would be appropriate to place these enterprises under temporary government control in order to allow the state immediately to manage a banking sector while waiting for the nationalization laws.

The Communist leaders supported Pleven, in order to avoid the transformation of "a principle, the nationalization of the banks, into a local problem." Annoyed, De Gaulle turned to Mendès: "Well, what of those structural reforms?" "*Mon général,* you have often argued against me that we . . . are the managers of affairs. But I have prepared a file, and I am ready to submit it to you."[8] He quickly learned that the file submitted to the head of government was subject to Communist Party attack, accusing him, because he had established a hierarchy of urgent tasks and designated the enterprises that were to be nationalized first, of wanting to "protect" broad sectors of the private economy. And because, in his file, the minister of the economy recommended that nationalized enterprises be treated with the same rigor as private businesses, he was accused by the spokesmen of the PCF of condemning the public sector that was in the process of being created to failure or paralysis.

Among the Socialists, at least those who were not in the government, there were currents much more favorable to Mendès France. In his *Journal du septennat* (Diary of a Presidency),[9] Vincent Auriol asserts that he helped develop the Mendès France "plan" in Algiers and continued without interruption to support it thereafter. On November 17, 1944, a Socialist delegation made up of Daniel Mayer, then general secretary of the party, Jules Moch, André Philip, Edouard Depreux, and Vincent Auriol himself, went to see De Gaulle to argue for structural reforms, notably for nationalization of the banks. The head of government answered that "what Mendès France is preparing is along those lines should fully satisfy you." The visitors refrained from asking for details, impressed as they were by what seemed to them to be the general's agreement with Mendès France's arguments against those of Pleven.[10] But within the government, the only colleague who continuously supported the minister of the economy was Augustin Laurent, known as the "pope" of the SFIO because of the moral authority he held over his comrades.

But it is in the end difficult to sum up this great debate that legend has reduced to a conflict between Mendès and Pleven. It was that, but it was also something much broader, a confrontation of two policies, two economic strategies, and two conceptions of the role of the state in the life of the people. Considering only the obvious measures, we may recall the four or five essential decisions advocated by the Mendès report of February 1944: restriction of consumption; wage and price controls; freezing of bank accounts; currency exchange tending toward a sharp decline in the money supply; rigorous discipline imposed by the state on various activities of production and exchange. This is in outline what was called at the time the "Mendès France plan," summed up in the word "rigor," as opposed to "laxity," the word his supporters used to characterize the policy Pleven first advised Lepercq to follow and then put into effect himself.

René Pleven later challenged this presentation of the situation.[11]

Rigor versus laxity? That's too easy a way of locking people and events into simple formulas. Mendès France did not have a monopoly on rigor in thought and management. I do not recognize myself as a "laxist." Many Socialists and advocates of planning supported my point of view, which wished to avoid crushing the French people, who were emerging from the cruelest of ordeals, by imposing too heavy a burden on them. The French had the right to breathe a little. The country was covered with ruins. But we still had a healthy population and an industrial apparatus that was partially functional. Our country is rich and fertile. We could be confident of success by directing and controlling efforts. Between Mendès and me, the conflict was not one of rigor against laxity, but of dogmatism against realism, interventionist theory against the spirit of practicality.

I was not hostile to the Plan. In fact, I collaborated closely with Jean Monnet. My difference with Mendès had to do with the intensity and the rhythm of intervention. Indeed, one might say, by analogy with two pianists, it was a difference of "touch." I was hostile to an interventionist "fortissimo."

Besides, as a Breton, I knew how strongly our peasants were against too heavy an intervention by the administration. We risked seeing established the withholding of production and deliveries, starving Paris. With more or less success, I decided to have confidence in the French. Mendès wanted to impose the direction to follow on them, a rigorous discipline. On top of all the restrictions they were suffering from, I did not think it was a good idea to add the rationing of currency.

I do not claim that we were 100 percent correct. But I remain convinced that what he wanted to impose, with all the force of his will, his imagination, and his honesty, was unbearable and would not have been borne.

François Bloch-Lainé, a Mendésist at heart, but at the time a "Plevenist" by reason of his position in the ministry, can serve as an arbitrator.[12]

It is too simple to say that Mendès was entirely right and Pleven entirely wrong. The arguments put forth . . . by the advocates of the harsh method did not seem decisive to me. In my personal opinion, they were decisive for reasons of principle, but not for reasons of fact.

The free market solution was absurd. To count on the loan to absorb excess liquidity, to fear an inventory of holdings and interference with transactions was to underestimate the scale of the evil and to place the tranquility of the wealthy before everything else.

But recalling that the operation carried out in Belgium by Camille Gutt had demonstrated the virtues of the operation advocated by Mendès and his group, Bloch-Lainé observes that the counterindications in France were not negligible.

In his view, the least convincing argument on Pleven's side was that "it was too late," and that because there had been no resistance to the demagogic wave immediately after Liberation that had brought about a brutal rise in wages and prices the plan was inoperable.[13] A "fallacious argument," according to Bloch-Lainé. Of course, constraints would have to be all the more rigorous and painful, but they were possible.

The second counterindication seems more serious to him. The dimensions of French territory, compared to Belgium, the contradictions among various de facto power centers immediately after Liberation, the fact that it was impossible for Paris to be heard and obeyed, if only for material reasons, from one region to another of the territory, terribly weakened the virtues of a Jacobin strategy of rigor directed from the center.[14]

Finally, the third argument seems to him "almost conclusive." He formulates it in this way:

How could an exchange be carried out without possessing enough means of substitution? Now, the Allies, denying to the Free French—which they hadn't done to the Belgians—recognition as a regular government, had refused to print new bills for them outside France. Where could we find enough currency to satisfy a population that was eager to revive?

Thirty-five years after the event, Mendès France considered only the second objection as more or less serious. How could a plan of austerity be applied when the control mechanisms of the country were not certain to respond? In this connection, he recalled that in late 1944 and early 1945, the *commissaires de la République* were veritable viceroys of the great provincial capitals, that in cities like Lyon or Marseille, Yves Farge or Aubrac were subject to formidable pressure from liberation committees and the PCF, interpreting the directives from Paris according to this balance of power: "On one occasion, Farge, in Lyon, published only articles 3, 9, and 28 of a law promulgated in Paris in the *Journal officiel*."

But on the question of disposable currency, Mendès recalled that in November and December the operation had been carried out "with the means at hand" in Tunisia and Corsica, smaller territories of operation to be sure, and thereafter American industry had begun to deliver bundles of tricolor bills whose production could have been accelerated. He also pointed out that stocks of bills printed by Vichy—in the bizarre denomination of three hundred francs—were available and could have been surcharged.

As for General de Gaulle, in his *Mémoires de guerre,* he summed up what he called the "strong approach" of Mendès France.[15]

> In the face of inflation, let us take the bull by the horns. Let us carry out a radical reduction in liquidity by decreeing suddenly that present bills are no longer valid, that their bearers must without delay exchange them at public offices, and that they will be given in return new bills worth only one-fourth of their holdings. Let us freeze accounts. Let us block prices. Let us establish, besides, a large tax on capital. These arrangements are harsh. But, provided General de Gaulle puts his authority behind them, they will allow us to overcome the crisis.

And De Gaulle adds a comment that explains many things.

> In economics, as in politics or strategy, there does not exist, in my view, any absolute truth. But there are circumstances. It is the idea I have of the circumstances that determines my decision. The country is sick and wounded. . . . Why throw it into dangerous convulsions when in any event it is going to recover its health?

Ten years after the crisis, in a conversation with Pierre Mendès France, who was then premier, De Gaulle justified his choice in 1945.

> Pleven was mistaken in his laxity, and you in your excess of rigor. If I had agreed with you, if you had been able to freeze bank accounts and withdraw currency, I would have been done for, for we would have had no more supplies, the markets would have emptied immediately, the butchers would have closed up shop. We would have been done for, I repeat.[16]

Although he was not aware at the time of this lack of comprehension on the part of the head of government, Mendès glimpsed some of its effects in various places. And the contradiction between Pleven and him, and the support given his opponent by the majority of ministers, reached such a point that he wondered about the meaning of his mission. What did governmental responsibilities mean if they had no effects? If he was, in reality, next to the "serious people" of the ministry, holders of the real power of decision and means of action, only a simple social experimenter, a delegate for ideas of the future, the house utopian, the bad conscience of the government resigned to allowing itself to be dominated by the demagogy of some and the appetites of others, what was the meaning of his position?

It is true that his presence in the government gave him the opportunity to appeal to public opinion by weekly radio talks, quite original at the time, although they had been inspired by Roosevelt's "fireside chats." By offering him this opportunity to express himself, De Gaulle—having refused him the realities of power—gave the measure, if not of the confidence he placed in him, at least of the interest he took in his suggestions. These lessons in civic morality and economic rationality for the use of the French are very revealing of the pedagogue, the teacher to which, inaccurately of course, one is sometimes tempted to reduce the figure of Pierre Mendès France. Take, for example, this talk from November 1944:

> If we are content with the rhythm of activity, the humdrum pace of the prewar period, it will take us fifteen years—yes, fifteen years—just to rebuild our ruins. . . . On the other hand, if every Frenchman provisionally gave up consuming the equivalent of what is produced in ten hours of average labor, then ten more hours, that is twenty hours in all, would be devoted to reconstruction, which would be completed twice as quickly, in seven and a half years instead of fifteen. . . .
>
> Thus, if we want to win the third battle of France, the one that is beginning for the reconstruction and renovation of the country, productive effort and simplicity of life are necessary, not for a single class of the population, but for all.
>
> I have the task—some would call it "thankless"—of having to speak of sacrifices. But our country understands that if it must agree to sacrifices, they will be much less than those involved in defeat, and also that they are the price to be paid temporarily and *by everyone,* without exception, for a considerable improvement in the well-being of *everyone.*

A week later he argued for price controls, knowing that he was incurring the hostility of certain categories of the population. On December 9, he called on peasant producers to give up supplying the cities at black-market prices. On December 30, he hailed the miners of the Loire basin who had decided to work an extra day in order to supply coal to a population that was numb with cold. On January 27, he rose to the defense of regulations—tickets, formalities, paperwork—that he had heard reviled everywhere. But, he objected, the regulations are aimed at "equity." He nevertheless admitted that discipline functions only if it is "consented" to, because it has been "honestly explained."

Identifying steel as the key industry on which the productive capacity of the country in every area depended, on February 24, 1945, Mendès France proposed the accomplishments of the Soviet plan in this area as an example. And on March 10, drawing in broad outline an assessment of the "hard winter" that would leave "cruel memories," he recognized that "the French have no taste for hearing prescriptions for what they must do," but that his dearest wish was that "the initiative of those concerned" would tend toward constantly increasing solidarity—particularly between rural producers and urban consumers.

On March 24, finally, he presented a new assessment, emphasizing the decline in unemployment and the growth in electricity consumption and in steel and automobile production. He admitted that the patient was not cured, that he remained "discouraged, irritable, and impatient." But, he added, "the man who, at his bedside, has not tried to gloss over his suffering and has refrained from announcing a premature cure, has earned the right to say to him that now is not the moment, after courageously going through so many ordeals, to despair."

Why this assessment and this discreet argument *pro domo?* Because he knew that his mission was completed and that he had to withdraw.

On January 18, 1945, he had sent to the head of government a letter that, within the forms of respect and admiration, was a veritable indictment, not only against Pleven, but also against the orientations attributable to De Gaulle's judgment. The surprising thing is that De Gaulle decided to publish this document, that is so harsh to himself, as an appendix to his own *Mémoires.*[17]

> *Mon général,*
> . . . The government had decided in Algiers, and more recently since the Liberation, to practice an active policy of reconstruction and stabilization of our finances. To this end, it had appeared necessary to it, notably, to attack without delay the plethora of currency. . . . [My] propositions, with a few changes of detail and after long and hard debates, had been approved. . . . When you asked me to take the portfolio of the Economy, I thought that, in full agreement with yourself and with the government as a whole, I had prepared, on the financial level, for the creation of the necessary conditions for success in the economic realm. . . . Now, the government has taken since then a series of measures that are in contradiction with the policy I had proposed. . . . For the necessary rigor, it has substituted laxity. . . .
> M. Lepercq had decided that the currency exchange would be possible by September 15. M. Pleven asserts that it will not become possible until

March or April. I affirm on the contrary that the operation is possible right now, on the condition, of course, that we keep . . . to a limited exchange along with a partial freezing of accounts (at least temporarily). The government turns away in horror from this method, which would for a time deprive the French of resources they can use only on the black market; it seems that this deprivation would be more unbearable for them than all the others they are now suffering. . . . The longer we wait, the less effective the operation will be; every day lost gives the enemy the opportunity to place into circulation bills that he has carried off or that his agents have kept in place. Every lost day provides new opportunities for the profiteers of disaster to conceal their holdings. . . .

This policy has a name . . . inflation [that] satiates speculators automatically enriched by constant and certain price increases. . . . In this system, one class is completely sacrificed, the class of ordinary people with fixed incomes, and your daily mail has certainly brought you pathetic testimony of this sacrifice. . . . To distribute money to everyone without taking any back from anyone is to foster a mirage . . . but the more we grant nominal satisfactions, the less we are able to give real satisfactions. . . .

I am afraid, *mon général,* that through a very understandable concern for evenhandedness, you are inclined to facilitate, or at least to accept, compromises. But there are areas in which a half-measure is a countermeasure, who knows that better than you? . . . The difference between my opponents and me is that, consciously or not, they are counting on a balance that will be achieved through increases, without any intervention, that is, on a miracle . . . it has to be said very clearly: the choice is between calling a halt voluntarily and the acceptance of an indefinite devaluation of the franc.

. . . France knows that it is sick and that it will not be cured through euphoria. It knows that it will restore itself only by a long, difficult, and painful effort. It is waiting for someone to call it to make that effort. I receive evidence of this every time I have the opportunity to express the opinions to which I am attached. I even think that I have noticed that the most ardent, the best, the "Gaullists," are disappointed by the silence of the head of government on this issue. *Mon général,* I call on you, on your inflexibility, on everything that has led the French to have confidence in you, to take measures for the public safety.

. . . I decline the responsibility for the weighty decisions which I have opposed in vain; I cannot accept solidarity for measures that I consider nefarious. I ask you, therefore, to allow me to resume my freedom. . . . I consider that I have as of now resigned, after fifteen months of work in which I have been supported only by the pride of being your collaborator. . . . I ask you to accept, *mon général,* my sincere and respectful affection.

De Gaulle, who was not accustomed to receiving such reprimands from his collaborators, accepted it and attempted to mollify the critic. He pointed out that France was still at war, that he needed Mendès as he had in London or Algiers, that he rejected his resignation and preferred to keep the letter of January 18 to himself. And he invited Pierre Mendès

France to spend the following Sunday with René Pleven and him in the residence that had been placed at his disposal in the Bois de Boulogne. The two ministers argued their cases before De Gaulle, Pleven for twenty minutes, Mendès for more than two hours.

"It was probably the only time in his life that he devoted an entire day to political economy, an entire day that must have been one of the worst in his life," Mendès observed years later. As for De Gaulle, according to Louis Vallon, when he related this contest, and particularly Mendès's argument, he concluded: "I will never again allow anyone to speak to me for three hours about economics." This may, in the end, have contributed to the victory of the concise lecturer over the loquacious professor.

Since the personal intervention of the general had allowed him on that day to extract some promises from his colleague at Finance with respect to the currency exchange, if not the freezing of bank accounts, Mendès agreed to continue his task for a while. But the balance of power remained the same. De Gaulle refused to join with him clearly, before the country, to call for the necessary sacrifices. And it became more and more evident that Pleven was going to carry out (in June) the currency exchange as a simple technical measure permitting the apprehension of a few large war profiteers (although many of them had found straw men), but not as an operation of currency reduction bringing about a long-term rectification. He was encouraged in this by the Communists, who did not want too radical a manipulation, which would have absorbed the war chest they had amassed in the Resistance and at Liberation. (Near Aurillac, for example, their maquis had seized five billion francs from the Germans—enough to finance quite a few campaigns and newspapers.) Thus, on April 5, Pierre Mendès France decided to make his January decision public and to resign.

Three days earlier, he had sent another letter to General de Gaulle, explaining his decision to resign in this way:

Mon général,
Since coordination of financial policy with economic policy is a condition for the country's recovery, I thought, three months ago now, that, in the public interest, it was appropriate that I submit to you my resignation from the position with which you had honored me. You asked me at that time to delay my decision, in the hope that it would be possible to harmonize these two policies.

The positions that have just been adopted by the government, in conformity with the propositions of the minister of finance, demonstrate that that hope had no basis. The persistence of a fundamental divergence on the means of reviving production and avoiding inflation could only hinder government action and harm the country.

You will certainly understand that, in these circumstances, I consider it my duty to repeat a resignation whose motives remain unchanged. . . . If, in the course of eighteen months' work, I have been supported by the pride of being your collaborator, today I have the impression that I cannot usefully assist you in your mission.

General de Gaulle commented in his *Mémoires de guerre:*

As was natural, Pierre Mendès France left the government, at his request, in the month of April. He did so with dignity. Thus, I kept my respect for this collaborator of exceptional value. Moreover, although I have not adopted the policy he advocates, I do not at all exclude the possibility of doing so one day, if circumstances have changed. But in order for Mendès France to be in a position, possibly, to carry it out, he must know how to remain faithful to his doctrine. In this way, the departure of a minister can be a service rendered to the state.[18]

There were only two Socialist ministers in the government—Augustin Laurent and Adrien Tixier—who clearly took sides with the resigning minister. Not one Communist. The MRP ministers were divided. But in *L'Aube,* Maurice Schumann had supported the Mendès France plan, thereby for the first time taking a position against a decision by the general. In the Consultative Assembly, it was again in the Socialist Party that voices were raised—those of Jules Moch and André Philip—to deplore the fact that the strategy advocated by Mendès had not been adopted and supported by the government.

The Communists were openly pleased by the exclusion of this troublesome figure. Mendès later commented: "Consider that the CGT was demanding that the minimum wage not be calculated according to official prices but according to black-market prices, relying on this argument: There is no reason why only the rich, and not the people, should be able to buy on the black market!"

It remains to elucidate the general's strange choice. It has already been suggested that it was the least consistent with his vision of the world, his political morality, his temperament. Follow the current, rather than fight against it? Among all the reasons that might have tipped the scale on the side of Pleven and his "soft strategy," let us isolate two.

The first has to do with the past, with the history of Free France. It is impossible to overestimate the role that René Pleven played for Charles de Gaulle or the strength of the ties that developed between them at the time. From 1940 to 1944, Pleven was the most trusted adviser, the lieutenant, the "vicar." Moreover, the general always arranged not to take the same plane as his adjutant. This kind of relationship would naturally shape his later decisions. Between two candidates, how could he not choose the one who, in the heroic times, had been his first lieutenant?

It will be said that this was a matter of a debate not only between two men but between antithetical policies, one of which, that of Mendès, fit much better with the character, the myth, and the ideas of Charles de Gaulle. Perhaps it is necessary, then, to consider more attentively the man De Gaulle in power, in the exercise of his functions. What interested, excited him, held his attention, was strategy (the war was not over) and foreign policy, more precisely, the place of France in the world. Economic questions bored and annoyed him.

Mendès France was a man who tried to involve him in those questions, who summoned him to become involved, who demanded from him decisions having to do with prices and wages, the Plan and currency, who wanted to draw him into the firing line by his side. Pleven was more discreet. With him, the economy was obscured, dissolved in the general movement of "affairs," became once again mere stewardship. With him, De Gaulle would be unburdened, liberated from such questions. Mendès represented dismal economics, Pleven economics without tears. A minister who was less burdensome to the French, he was also and above all less tedious for De Gaulle, who therefore could devote his time to "serious" matters, to Germany and Asia, to relations with Churchill and with Moscow.

For De Gaulle, the choice was not between two men, or even between two economic policies, but between two ways of establishing a hierarchy of problems. He gave preference to the minister and the policy that left him free to be, in the face of Roosevelt and Stalin, a "full-time" General de Gaulle.

Before allowing him to leave for good, De Gaulle had tried to keep Mendès, not in the Ministry of the Economy, where he clearly could not stay, but in a position he would choose himself: "Whatever you wish." Mendès had allowed himself to be won over twice. This time he stood firm and resumed his freedom.

However loyal he may have wished to be to the general, and however concerned not to aggravate, through any outburst, the ordeals the country was going through, Pierre Mendès France owed explanations to a public opinion that he had been addressing familiarly for six months about his programs and their common problems. On the morning of April 6, 1945, he called a press conference at the ministry to present the reasons for his resignation.

The first had to do with the "insufficient powers of control" of the minister of the economy. From the moment that, in the case of conflict, the minister of finance took precedence over his colleague, and one had either to submit or resign, the solution in his view was to join the two ministries—which gave him the opportunity to praise in passing the "eminent qualities" of M. Pleven.

The policy that he had not been allowed to carry out, continued Mendès, was "the reform of the currency in order to lay the groundwork for economic development." With a view toward averting inflation, he had advocated the "exchange of currency along with freezing bank accounts," which would have permitted an "inventory of wealth," the levying of a kind of "tax on capital," and the "recovery of unlimited profits." But these plans, according to him, had come up against "numerous reservations," particularly on the part of the Banque de France.

Regretting that he had not been permitted to reduce public expenditures, he had recently "resigned" himself to an "upward revision of wages and prices," on the condition that that "reordering" be accompanied by "stabilization measures." It was because these measures had been rejected that he thought it necessary to resign. He did so while expressing his "joy and pride in having worked alongside General de Gaulle for the grandeur of France."

He therefore "fell" on a question of wages and prices, on the theme of stabilization and austerity. In the interview he granted me in May 1980, M. Pleven criticized Mendès, not for having resigned, not for having chosen that moment and that pretext, but for having subsequently "given himself too good a press, thanks to Georges Boris." Yet it was not Boris who prompted the historians of the last thirty years to conclude that the direction that was then taken, free rein given to prices and wages, was, along with the colonial wars, the source of most of the infirmities that undermined the Fourth Republic. A reading of the press, and particularly of papers like Le Monde, where the minister of the economy enjoyed solid support, reveals no "campaign," no orchestration. One might even say that the resignation of a figure as well known and controversial as Pierre Mendès France was carried out in April 1945 in semi-indifference.

The time had come, not to think of his family, which he had never ceased doing, but to take care of them—his parents, his wife and sons, and of his house—and to think of all the members of his family who had not returned from the Nazi camps. It was a time when, in the Jewish community even more than in others, the dead were counted. There were many in the Mendès family. But he was fortunate enough to know where and how to reach his mother and father, who had been able to escape from repression; they had been released after their arrest in 1941 near the demarcation line, on the outskirts of Angoulême (they had been trying to visit him in prison); they had then escaped from Paris in 1944 with the help of a friend of Pierre's, and reached Switzerland by bravely crossing the snow-covered mountains. He wrote to them from Paris on September 23, 1944.

> I have just now learned that you received one letter from me out of the three or four that I sent. . . . It did me a world of good to receive mother's letter,

brought by de Leusse. I have not seen her handwriting for years, or father's either. . . . Someone saw Marcelle . . . in Toulouse about ten days ago. . . . Lily and the children are well. The boys are growing and becoming Americanized. All three of them are impatient to return to Paris, but, unfortunately, transportation is not easy. We may have to wait for several months—it's a long time.

I do not advise you to come back immediately, despite my impatience to see you again after so long and terrible a separation. Complete your recovery and rest . . . in the healthy air of Switzerland. . . . Within a short time you will be able to take a train from Geneva to Lyon, and I will find you a place on the Lyon-Nevers-Paris *micheline*. Probably within six or eight weeks.

A lot of work, but in harsh and difficult conditions. I have done everything not to stay in the government, but De Gaulle has practically forced me. However, after a period like this, I look forward finally to some relaxation with all of you, my little ones, and Lily.

I went to Louviers. Enthusiastic welcome. But how many empty spaces! My love to the Stamms.[19] I share their sorrow and their hope.

Cerf and Palmyre Mendès France returned to Paris before the end of the year. But Lily and the children stayed longer in the United States: Lily and Bernard until 1946, Michel until early 1947. They liked their life in New York, in an apartment on Eightieth Street. The two boys had gone at first to the neighborhood school, becoming real New York kids and forgetting their native language, and had then gone to the Lycée Français, where Bernard accumulated successes as his father had before him at Turgot. Lily had made many friends. She continued to paint avidly, and had it not been for Pierre's absence and the risks he ran, she would have been happy during those years.

One evening in 1942, she had some shopping to do in the neighborhood and told the boys to go back to the apartment before her. They came face to face with an oddly dressed man, and ran downstairs to tell their mother, who was waiting for the elevator: "There's a man in our apartment!" Then Pierre Mendès France explained to his sons why their last meeting had taken place in the prison of Casablanca, why he was held there. Everything had to be told, explained, justified.

Lily had avoided talking about political questions with her sons. Only once had she shown them a swastika and a cross of Lorraine, telling them that the former was "evil" and the latter "good," and asking them to think no more about it—and not to draw either one on the walls. By 1945, at the age of eleven, Bernard had become a real American patriot, standing and saluting whenever the "Star Spangled Banner" was played. Both in the neighborhood school and in the *lycée,* Bernard and Michel had excellent relations with American children, who were Francophiles, very protective, and eager to show their solidarity in the ordeal.

The warmth of the welcome Mendès had received in Louviers in

September 1944 increased his desire to devote the bulk of his time to the mayoralty of the little town from which the Vichy regime and the judges of Clermont-Ferrand had tried to expel him. He rediscovered the charming eighteenth-century town hall covered with climbing ivy that he had planted. And he set to work. Although a part of the town had been spared, the old quarter had been annihilated. Louviers was one of the most devastated towns in France. It was necessary not only to reconstruct, heal wounds, restore warmth and confidence, but also to reorganize the economic structures of the municipality, put an end to the monopoly of the cloth industry, and establish industries of a new kind, electronics, for example, to make the population less susceptible to fluctuations in the textile market and the consequent unemployment.

But before the elections that would certainly restore his offices, was he still mayor, deputy, general councillor? A Vichy decree had stripped him of all titles and offices. Would he be content with the law promulgated by De Gaulle in early 1945 that abrogated all these decrees, vacated the judgments rendered by the Vichy courts, and declared illegal the convictions that had sanctioned, from 1940 to 1944, acts carried out in the interest of liberating the country? He had been accused of three crimes or misdemeanors: the "desertion" of 1940, the "damage to a public building" at the time of his escape, and his joining Free France. He could have been satisfied with the general law that restored his honor and his public and private rights.

He could accept this for the "damage to a public building" (the bar sawed through in the prison hospital of Clermont) or his joining Free France. But for the "desertion" he demanded more, as a lawyer, as a moralist, and as a patriot. He needed a judicial decision that abolished any trace of or foundation for the judicial insult inflicted on him in Clermont-Ferrand. He had to obtain a declaration that the operation carried out by Leprêtre, Degache, and Perré was illegal and baseless. It was a long-term enterprise that took nearly ten years—despite the diligence of an honest magistrate, Councillor Patin, a total revision of the procedure, a kind of counter-investigation and counter-trial—to achieve, in April 1954, on the eve of his accession to the premiership.

In the meantime he had been reelected mayor of Louviers in May 1945, elected councillor of Pont-de-l'Arche Canton in September, and then president of the Eure General Council and deputy to the Constituent Assembly in 1946 and the National Assembly in 1951. And he soon found himself holding the presidency of an institution he had done a good deal to create, the National Accounting Commission, where he worked with men for whom he had particular respect, like Claude Gruson and Paul Delouvrier. He had overcome his hesitation to return to the political arena that he had expressed in the letter to his parents of September 1944, and succeeded in combining a very normal career for a noted international expert with his municipal and parliamentary obligations. He assumed the former with unfailing delight, the latter with growing detachment. His appearances in Parliament became less frequent (he was often "absent on leave"). Active in committees, he only spoke once or twice a year from the podium, presenting often technical speeches, listened to and applauded, but apparently without effect.

It was true that he could hardly count on the Radicals to promote his declarations and assure their development and execution. His relations with the party of Herriot and Daladier, as we know, had always been unusual. Having joined the "organization" at sixteen, he had remained very attached to it, attracted by the liberalism of its leadership, the pluralism that inspired its debates, and the almost familial atmosphere that pervaded it.

Had it not been for the war, the problem of his loyalty to the party would not have arisen for him. But the ordeal of 1940 to 1944 had deepened many divisions, less in experience than in consciousness. More than half the Radical deputies had voted for Pétain and Laval in Vichy on July 10, 1940. Chautemps had been a collaborator of Pétain's during the early months of the regime of the "French state." Herriot had appeared momentarily in August 1944 to support a maneuver by Laval attempting to establish a provisional government in Paris, between De Gaulle and the Nazis. During the same period, Mendès France had been one of the closest and most important of General de Gaulle's collaborators, and De Gaulle had little affection for the Radical Party. Mendès had been a part of organizations and governments in which Socialists and orthodox Gaullists were more numerous and influential than the Radicals.

Then how could he renew ties with the party at the very moment when he was breaking his last connections with the Masons? However distinguishable the two organizations may have been, it was difficult not to think of one at the moment of making a decision about the other. It seems that Pierre Mendès France planned, immediately after the Liberation, to leave this marginal and exhausted party.

I was in no hurry to rejoin the Radical Party, which seemed anachronistic to me. After the Liberation, I seldom saw Herriot, whose behavior in the course of the preceding few years had not delighted me. But I was visited by a comrade whom I respected and who had been very active in the Resistance, Mazé, a former deputy. He told me that he was going to reconstitute and rejuvenate the Radical Party and that he was counting on people like me to do this. He touched me. He was general secretary, and he was doing his job, but he did it with spirit. In short, I let myself be persuaded and at the moment of important decisions, like the referendum of 1946 on the Constitution, I voted "no-no" with the Radicals.[20]

Thus the pattern broken by the war was reconstituted: mayor, general councillor, deputy, notable of the Radical Party. All that was lacking was the role of professor, which he had always longed for and which he had exercised before the war at the Ecole Supérieure des Hautes Etudes Sociales. The opportunity soon presented itself: The Ecole Nationale d'Administration, promoted by Michel Debré, and dedicated to the training of high-level civil servants, offered him a position teaching a very practical course closely connected to his experience. He was to present to future leaders of the nation an analysis of the fiscal and budgetary problems posed by planning and reconstruction.

Mendès France taught this course during two winter semesters (1947 and 1948) to about twenty young geniuses—among them Valéry Giscard d'Estaing, who never lost an opportunity to point to this intellectual connection. The former minister of the economy confessed that this teaching wore him out because the subject had so many implications that were simultaneously theoretical and practical, and he asserted that, although he was not certain that he had taught much to his listeners, he himself learned a great deal in preparing his lectures.

The fact is that this teaching helped to establish connections between Pierre Mendès France and the most promising managers on the French economic scene. For those of the generation immediately preceding his students, who were generally younger than he, he was already, more than the too simple, too empirical, and too "American" Jean Monnet, the leader, the man who had attempted to reshape the system of production and exchange along the lines of rigor, justice, and productivity.

But for his students at the ENA, some of whom were young enough to be his sons, and some of whom became his collaborators even before the 1954 government, he was not only the courageous reformer of 1944 but also the author of the 1938 Plan, the man who had introduced Keynesianism into French public life.

Some of them may have found him too reformist, too legalistic, insufficiently detached from the capitalist world view—like Simon Nora, who was then a Marxist. But they all respected him and followed his actions and his words with attention and hope. A man without a real party, he was no longer without real supporters.

8.
CASSANDRA AND INDOCHINA

At the moment when he allowed Mendès France to leave on April 5, 1945, General de Gaulle said to him: "There are tasks outside the government that require skills like yours, in America especially, in financial organizations and in the United Nations. Go and represent France there. You will be making the best use of your abilities, while maintaining your distance."

International organizations, currency questions, and America, where his wife and children were living—he accepted, and soon arrived in Washington, the headquarters of those organizations. In 1944, he had participated in the work leading to the Bretton Woods agreements establishing the World Bank and the International Money Fund. He thus appeared as a founding father and was elected as a member of the Executive Committee of the IMF and the World Bank. In this academy of financiers, bankers, and economists, one figure fascinated him: Lord Keynes. For a few months before his death, the author of the *General Theory* represented Great Britain and, indeed, all the countries indebted by the war.

Pierre Mendès France joined with this almost legendary man, whom he had greatly admired for ten years, to obtain for France and the United Kingdom a position other than that of humble beggar in the international monetary system set up by the American experts. Like Keynes, he argued for the establishment of mechanisms that would not automatically work in favor of the Americans as lenders and as holders of the largest stock of gold in the world (France had the second largest holding, thanks in part to its "avarice" of the last few months).

John Maynard Keynes could not persuade the American giant and suffered what he himself called a "strategic defeat."[1] Although some of their colleagues, like Morgenthau, tried to encourage them to defer to the susceptibilities and opportunities of their wartime allies, Harry White and Fred Vinson, the principal American negotiators, thought only of imposing a system which, on the pretext of making gold the basis of the international monetary order, ended up by promoting the dollar as the only reserve currency and establishing the United States as the arbiter of the world economy. Neither Keynes nor Mendès was able to avoid the establishment of the American monopoly. The representative of France retained a very vivid memory of the stinging humiliation experienced and displayed at the time by his illustrious British colleague.

Another battle unfolded at Bretton Woods over the creation of the World Bank, an old dream of Pierre Mendès France. For the Europeans ruined by the war, this organism ought to have been called the Bank "for Reconstruction." But other delegations, particularly from Latin America, were also heard, and they used a term that was unusual at the time: development. For them, the new bank could only be placed under that sign. Days of debate were taken up with the question of whether development should take precedence over reconstruction. It was a debate about words, but it went far and anticipated many conflicts. They finally created the Bank for International Reconstruction and Development (BIRD).

There, as in connected organizations like the IMF, Mendès France familiarized himself with concepts, problems, and men that he still knew only vaguely and came into contact with the Third World, which had not yet received its name.[2] At Bretton Woods, he listened to spokesmen from India, Mexico, and Egypt on the theme of development. A veil was lifted from his eyes. To be sure, on the Customs Committee of the National Assembly he had had to consider underdeveloped populations. His friend Boris, who had had early experience of the Indian world in Ceylon, directed him toward the study of these questions. But the negotiations of Bretton Woods had played the role of a revelation for him.

This revelation was soon deepened on the Economic and Social Council of the United Nations. Pierre Mendès France agreed to represent France in this body after having resigned from the administrative council of BIRD. As French delegate to this key organization from 1947 to 1951, Mendès encountered the best specialists in development, from Gunnar Myrdal to Raul Prebitsch. The problems of decolonization had already been posed, along with the closely connected problems of underdevelopment. And it was because to one of these problems, the Indochina question, France proposed only a military solution, that in 1951 Mendès left the council, where he had found himself in the untenable position of spokesman for a nation whose policy, on an essential point, he did not approve.

But before carrying out these American missions, Pierre Mendès France had once again been confronted with the responsibilities of power. It was De Gaulle who had called him to power in November 1943, taking him away from combat. It was De Gaulle's departure that gave him the opportunity to attempt the experience once again, early in 1946, when he seemed to have structured his life around distant and technical responsibilities.

On Sunday, January 20, at noon, Charles de Gaulle summoned "his" ministers to inform them of his decision: he was withdrawing, disheartened by "the exclusive rule of the parties." There was stupefaction, due less to the resignation than to the accompanying reasons. According to the terms of a speech broadcast that evening, the general considered his task accomplished, so favorable was the situation of France: "The train is on the tracks." This was not, in any area, the opinion of the experts. Naturally chosen, as president of the Constituent Assembly, to "succeed" (if that term can be used) De Gaulle, Félix Gouin hastily drew up a provisional assessment and was obliged to observe that, on the "track" where it had been placed, the train of France could not continue on the same path without serious damage.

To correct the mistakes, he naturally thought of the man who had been excluded from the center of power for nearly a year: Pierre Mendès France, who could point out that the anemia of the French economy was due to the choice the general had made despite him. From the observation posts De Gaulle had arranged for him in Bretton Woods, Washington, and New York, the former economics minister was in a better position than ever to measure the infirmities of the French economy and the tragic risks of a continuation of the journey without navigational corrections.

On January 24, 1946, Pierre Mendès France, who had many supporters in the SFIO, the premier-designate's party—André Philip, Jules Moch, Daniel Mayer, and Edouard Depreux, among others—met with Félix Gouin. With Boris, he had hastily put together a program that he demanded the government accept as its charter. According to its terms, as minister of the economy, he would have "plenary power" to apply it. The plan was rather different from that of 1944 and no longer contained a proposal for manipulating the currency: Pleven had in the meantime carried out the currency exchange (without freezing bank accounts), which had made a similar operation impossible. It involved essentially a brutal reduction of nonproductive budgetary expenditures (beginning with military expenditures), gradual elimination of subsidies, wage and price controls, and finally the establishment of a real tax on capital. It was the very archetype of what is called an "austerity plan," comparable to the one imposed at the time, with some success, by Sir Stafford Cripps on the British.

The brutality of the remedy soon alienated from him the leaders of several parties, beginning with the Communists. In some sectors of the Socialist Party there were signs of rejection, less against the content of the plan than against the demand for "plenary powers" formulated by Mendès France. Among the Radicals, his "friends," there were only a few, like Pierre Cot and Dreyfus-Schmidt (already closer to the "progressive" group than to their own party), who asserted that only "the Mendès France plan can safeguard the interests of the country."

The day following an exhausting day of negotiations with Félix Gouin, who was supported by experts from the Ministry of Finance, Mendès France, without illusions, contented himself with stating: "The lessons of the past have taught me to stand firm on my positions. I refuse to modify any particular point of my program on the insistence of any particular individual."

In response, the economic specialist of Le Monde, Marcel Tandy, wrote unsympathetically: "When he left the Ministry of the Economy, M. Mendès France complained that he had not received the powers of command that he claimed to need. He demands them today. Will the parties agree to make him a veritable dictator over the economy and finance?"

The answer was no. Despite the support of his former "patron" Léon Blum, who was active not only in Socialist circles but also in the very various political milieus where he had some prestige, enhanced by the ordeals of war; despite a rather favorable immediate reaction from Georges Bidault in the name of the MRP, the former minister of the economy was refused the blank check he demanded to carry out a new campaign of reductions. The unlimited authority that De Gaulle had refused to grant him was also resisted by the party government that had provisionally triumphed over the general. Why should they have deposed the "dictator" in uniform only to submit themselves to such an implacable "controller"?

In the absence of the powers he had asked for, Mendès France refused to join the government, even though Félix Gouin had told him that it would carry out the essential aspects of his program, while respecting parliamentary norms. André Philip, the most Mendésist of the Socialist leaders, was to hold the economics portfolio in the Gouin government. And Léon Blum urged his former colleague to join the new government, in no matter what capacity, to contribute his personal prestige and to provide the benefit of his advice. Mendès refused, objecting that he could not "play a fourth tune in an orchestra whose musicians were already playing three different tunes."[3] He nevertheless agreed to participate in the development of André Philip's program and in drafting the economic section of Gouin's investiture speech.[4]

This time it seemed that, as for Charles de Gaulle a week earlier, Mendès had entered on his "sojourn in the desert." But it was not the same sojourn. The general, surprised and irritated that his departure had been so easily accepted, quickly launched a campaign to denounce the constitutional proposals formulated successively by two friends of Mendès, Pierre Cot and André Philip, and then threw himself into the adventure of the RPF (Rassemblement du Peuple Français), an adventure with which he wished to associate his former economics minister. There was no lack of intermediaries between the general and Mendès. Directly asked to give his support to the RPF, the deputy from Louviers refused, courteously, but firmly enough that the general and his lieutenants considered the question closed.

This solitary man, so often far from Paris, was nevertheless not forgotten. He was consulted, directly or indirectly. On various occasions between 1946 and 1951, he was considered for the posts of premier and minister of finance, and rejected because of opposition from Radicals, Communists, or independents, depending on the circumstances. In the middle of 1951, faced with one of the recurring cabinet crises, the president of the Republic, Vincent Auriol, noted: "Mendès France, whom I had thought of for his dynamism and his qualities, is impossible because of his position on Indochina and military appropriations." These significant words defined the situation of Pierre Mendès France for a long time.

Indochina. At the outset, the Jacobin Mendès France was not fated to liquidate French control. As a Radical, he was not "programmed" to follow either the colonial tradition of Ferry or the anticolonial tradition of Clemenceau. His true ancestor in this school of thought, Joseph Caillaux, was the man who had refused to go to war over Agadir, but also the man who had not been afraid to use the Congo as a bargaining counter with Berlin. And as a minister of General de Gaulle, he had been able to recognize the strategic importance of the empire.

However, he had been subjected to three influences that had oriented him toward anticolonialism. First, in 1943 and 1944, in Algiers, General Catroux, who had been governor general of Indochina in 1939, had communicated to him his conviction that, in Africa as in Asia, the colonial system was ephemeral and that the dominated peoples would soon rightly demand their emancipation. Then Georges Boris, long aware of the cruelties of the exploitation of the underdeveloped world, drew his attention to this kind of problem, to the fragility and the unjust basis of the colonial edifice. Finally, in the Economic and Social Council of the United Nations, these questions confronted him to their full extent, no longer formulated by intelligent and generous European, like Catroux and Boris, but by those who had most recently been decolonized and by the most eloquent of the "underdeveloped," Indians Mexicans, and Egyptians.

Thus, from his appointment to the Economic and Social Council in 1947 on, Mendès France was in contact with the colonial question, often summed up by his Asian, African, or American interlocutors by the word *Indochina*. War had broken out in late December 1946, despite the efforts of General Leclerc and Jean Sainteny (and, in Paris, Léon Blum and the Communists) to avoid it. France was conducting a colonial war, denounced as unjust and immoral by most members of the council, by the Indians who offered the example of British policy in their country (an argument that powerfully affected the ardent Anglophile Mendès), and by the spokesmen of the Eastern bloc who advocated the federated system of the Soviet Union (a less probative example in the eyes of the French delegate, but one that his friend Georges Boris considered worthy of interest).

As for the essence of the problem, the Mendès of the late 1940s was thus a man who was deeply troubled by his country's policy in Indochina, with respect to principles, prestige, and diplomatic relations. He had enough contacts with American ruling circles to sense that, although at the head of the State Department Dean Acheson and his closest advisers had decided to forget Roosevelt's precepts and to resign themselves to France's Indochina policy in order not to alienate a useful ally in Europe, Congress, the Treasury Department, and the press considered this policy immoral, costly to American taxpayers, and a dead end.

But Pierre Mendès France was first of all a French citizen and an economist. And in these areas, his condemnation of the Indochina operation was still more implacable. Thirty years later, he recalled the manner in which he had reached a decision about Indochina.

> Since my experience in the Finance Commission in Algiers, I had become aware that, although every affair does not resolve itself into a budgetary problem and has many other implications, it must necessarily go through that phase. Every problem is not financial, but it becomes one day financial. This was true of Indochina. Badly begun politically, militarily, and morally, it was even worse in budgetary terms. Studying the position of France from the observation posts where I was placed, from the International Monetary Fund to the Economic and Social Council, and from BIRD to the Commission des Comptes (National Finance Council) in Paris, I always came up against the

question of Indochina. Whether it was a question of stabilizing the franc, investing in industrial equipment, or increasing our contribution to some international effort, the answer was always: "But there is Indochina!"

This obsession was nowhere more weighty than in the Commission des Comptes.[5] Most of its membership considered the Indochina expedition a budgetary abyss, particularly the young general secretary, Simon Nora, formerly a Communist sympathizer. Although he had established his distance from doctrinal Marxism, he nevertheless seized every occasion to emphasize the extent to which the war in Asia posed an obstacle to the effort of planned development of the French economy that they were preparing in common. As president of this organism, Mendès France saw himself placed in the role of a prosecutor in the "Indochina affair."

He heard arguments from all sides, especially from the military. Two generals whom he had known for a long time, Jacquot, Daladier's former chief of staff at the Ministry of War and an old Radical militant, and Faÿ, who had been his commander in the near East and had courageously testified in his favor at the Clermont-Ferrand trial, enlightened him on the difficulties their colleagues were experiencing in Hanoi and Saigon. The air force, in particular, was pessimistic. From late 1947 on, they had been pointing out that American aid was not increasing at the rhythm of the Vietminh war effort. And in late 1949, the arrival of contigents from Mao Zedong's Red Army on the Tonkin border made it clear to the most lucid among them that the fate of the expeditionary force engaged eight thousand miles from home was sealed.

At the time, Mendès France did not see General Leclerc,[6] whom he had known in Algiers and considered a trustworthy and kindred spirit. But he was not unaware of the fact that this intrepid fighter, before leaving his post as commander-in-chief in Saigon—more or less forced out by the high commissioner, Admiral d'Argenlieu, who believed in fighting to the end and called Leclerc a Munichois—had written a report that concluded that the operation could succeed only through political means. Mendès did not yet know the text of this report, which spoke of "independence," but it was communicated to him at an appropriate time.

Before most of his colleagues, he became aware of the totality of the burdens that this affair placed on the functioning of French democracy, consolidating the system of lobbying that the major interests of North Africa had already introduced. Well informed by young administrators returning from Saigon armed with persuasive experience, he had penetrated the systematic and logical activities of the large French enterprises that were profiting from the situation—the Banque d'Indochine was the best example. Bankers, brokers, exporters and importers, transporters, and open or clandestine intermediaries in the territory had bound the Bao

Dai government in their spider web, preventing it from asserting itself in the national arena, and, in Paris, they had made certain of their ability to shift the few votes in the Palais-Bourbon on which the governments of the Fourth Republic depended.

In political circles, the deputy from Eure was obviously not alone, along with the Communists and his "progressive" friends Pierre Cot and Emmanuel d'Astier, in criticizing the war. In the government, men like Robert Schuman, who held the post of foreign minister on several occasions, agreed with him that the operation was ruinous and leading nowhere. It even happened that Bidault himself agreed that it would be wise, one day, to seek a negotiated solution. But when? And with whom?

As soon as the Korean War broke out in June 1950, the colonialist faction could easily argue that "Communist aggression" was the same, in Southeast as in Northeast Asia, and that it had to be opposed in both places. These arguments did not fail to affect a man like Mendès. The expedition was an act of folly, but how could it be brought to an end? To Roger Stéphane, who said to him: "Simply by recognizing the independence and the unity of Vietnam," he replied: "Is it that simple? What do the Vietminh want, and whom are they working for? Is the unity of the three parts of Vietnam so obvious?" He thought of gradual, evolutionary formulas. He was a man in search of the truth.

But the facts were to speak more strongly than the questions. At the end of September 1950, the line of positions held by the expeditionary force along the Chinese border, from Cao Bang to That Khe and Lang Son, collapsed under assault from the Vietminh, who had already begun to receive constantly increasing aid from their Chinese allies and were to receive even more as soon as they had eliminated all the obstacles to convergence between the two "revolutionary" wars. There was a catastrophic retreat, with fifteen hundred men left in the hands of the enemy— a disaster.

On October 19, 1950, on the occasion of a budgetary debate that gave no indications of being dramatic, the deputy from Eure mounted the rostrum of the Assembly. René Pleven, his old adversary (with whom his relations were always courteous), was on the government bench, resigned in advance to the indictment that this implacable accuser traditionally directed against his "laxity" and already prepared to oppose these frontal attacks with clever evasions.

But that day something else was involved. Very quickly, Pierre Mendès France broadened the debate, sharpened his tone, and denounced to the fullest extent the evil, the wound out of which was flowing the blood and the wealth of France: Indochina. And he was not content with saying that the war cost too much. He raised political and military as well as financial questions.

It is the entire conception of our action in Indochina that is false, for it is based on a military effort that is insufficient . . . to bring about a solution by force and on a policy that is incapable of assuring us the support of the people. Things cannot continue like this. . . . There are only two solutions. The first consists in realizing our objectives in Indochina by means of military force. If we choose that, let us at last avoid illusions and pious lies. To achieve decisive military successes rapidly, we need three times as many troops in the field and a tripling of appropriations, and we need them very quickly. . . . The military solution is a massive new effort, sufficiently massive and sufficiently rapid to anticipate the already considerable development of the forces opposed to us.

Before a Chamber that was suddenly full, in a tense silence broken by brusque exclamations of incredulity or anger, confronting the government bench where René Pleven, suddenly disabused, gave signs of growing impatience, Mendès France enumerated the sacrifices that would have to be accepted in order to give this policy a chance—new taxes, a slowdown in productive investment, a weakening of national defense in Europe, and the consequent impossibility of opposing the German rearmament called for by the Americans—and he finally came to the "constructive" part of his speech.

The other solution consists in seeking a political agreement with those who are fighting us, obviously. . . . An agreement means concessions, broad concessions, without doubt more significant than those that would have been enough in the past. One may reject this solution. It is difficult to apply. It will embody painful renunciations and bitter disappointments. But then, we must speak the truth to the country. We must inform it of the price that will have to be paid to bring the other solution about.

The reaction was vigorous on the benches of the Assembly. Even among those who saw in the speech only sophistry or defeatism, the call for a politics of "truth," after the disaster of Cao Bang, had had an effect. René Pleven rose from the government bench. He refused, he said, to mount the rostrum to answer substantively such an improvised attack. He retorted that the country knew the truth, a painful truth, and, knowing it, aspired only to remain united around its soldiers in danger. Applauded on all sides, he had, for the moment, saved the situation. But, as Mendès France had formulated it, the problem remained unresolved, going far beyond the person of the premier and the survival of his government.

"What shocked me that day," René Pleven said thirty years later,[7]

was Mendès's procedure, attacking me suddenly on that terrain on the occasion of a financial debate, without having warned me, although we had good relations. Had I been prepared, I would have spoken broadly along the same lines, and the debate would have been useful for everyone. At bottom, I agreed with him on many points. I had not been a deputy when the war started. Since then, I had argued that we had blundered. As an intimate friend of General Leclerc since 1940—I am his children's guardian—I had been more struck than anyone by the arguments of his 1946 report. But in the ordeal we were then going through, neither Mendès France's arguments, nor the procedure he had adopted, seemed to me to be appropriate.

To which Mendès France answered:

A man as intelligent as René Pleven could not have been unaware of the impasse into which France had blundered, but he was among the many parliamentarians of the time who, every time they were approached on the subject, sighed: "Negotiate, yes, but now is not the time." Sometimes we were to weak to accept concessions, sometimes we were too successful to consider giving in. I therefore chose the method of an electric shock.

Asked by some to be more precise, called on by others to explain himself, and suddenly surrounded by the attention of everyone who thought it was possible to seek a political solution without capitulation, he hastily prepared another speech in which he would present a kind of program envisaging an alternative to war. On November 22, 1950, a full-scale debate on Indochina opened in the Palais-Bourbon, in the course of which, following his example, the spokesmen of all the parties were to speak. In the wake of the disaster, should the combat be continued?

The deputy from Eure had discovered a prestigious supporter:

"We have to avoid," wrote General Leclerc in 1946, "an adventure that exceeds the present capacities of France. Ambitions must be commensurate with our means, or else there will be a catastrophe. It is no longer a possibility to impose ourselves by force on masses who wish for evolution and novelty. France will no longer stifle by arms a grouping of twenty-four million men that is taking shape."

To which the premier retorted:

General Leclerc . . . recognized the necessity of a political solution, but I do not think we should make the dead speak and transpose a report from 1946–1947 to a period that has seen the aggression in Korea, and in the face of the magnificent movement of solidarity that has united democrats against totalitarianism.

Mendès France was not content with "having the dead speak":

To this day, we have devoted much more to Indochina than to reconstruction. Now, whatever more we do for Indochina, we will do that much less for European defense and for the security of the national territory. We have to choose and not let the French believe that everything is possible at once. Outside the military solution, outside the solution through force, there is only one possibility: negotiation. Do we have the means to avoid the result after having ourselves made it inevitable by our mistakes and our errors?

Then Mendès France did what was expected of him in the Assembly, and even more than that; he enumerated the conditions for what he considered a possible settlement: unconditional recognition of the independence of Vietnam, free elections under the control and the guarantee of bipartite or neutral commissions, gradual evacuation of French troops according to a schedule to be established. The Vietminh (or the Democratic Republic of Vietnam) would be able to enjoy the status of a neutral state and would sign agreements for economic and cultural cooperation with France.

This was a radical change of direction. It was an absolute challenge to the current leaders of France, from Vincent Auriol to the MRP, from Pleven to the majority of the SFIO. It was a total liquidation of the "Bao Dai solution" and a bold wager on the Vietminh, as Jean Sainteny had done four years earlier, with the support of General Leclerc and General Salan.

It was certainly possible to formulate reservations about his plan, to question him about the possibilities of "free" elections in a country that had been so disrupted by war, of the chances that a Communist Vietnam, now protected by Maoist China, would adhere to a neutralist system— even though Ho Chi Minh had spoken along those lines in an interview with an American journalist eleven months earlier. But in the end, the plan had been presented from the rostrum of the Chamber by a former companion of General de Gaulle, by a public man who enjoyed prestige inside and outside France, who was known to be in contact with high-ranking military officers and with particularly well-informed international civil servants. This speech changed perspectives. It offered an alternative, uncertain, vague, costly, but at least perceptible.

Pierre Mendès France, who had now left his American "retirement" and was to find himself in the center of the French political maelstrom after resigning his United Nations position in February 1951, could not possibly confine himself to the role of a Cassandra about Indochina. In fact, the government hardly listened to him. Far from turning away the war, the government appointed General de Lattre to win it. The more and more pressing interventions of the deputy from Eure concerned the general orientations of French economic policy as well as the problems of national independence.

In the course of the years 1951 and 1952, the theme of national independence became one of his leitmotifs, as it was of General de Gaulle and the leaders of the RPF. But Mendès made a totally different use of it; in fact, he pointed out that French dependence on the United States was due less to the Atlantic Alliance—he had not voted for ratification of the 1949 treaty, since he was "absent on leave," but later voted for the accompanying legislation and never placed it in question—than to the Indochina expedition.

An attentive examination of the evolution of the defense budget, compared with a study of the growth of U.S. military assistance, led him in fact to observe that the effort undertaken in Indochina was more and more directly financed by the United States: 20 percent in 1948, 30 percent in 1949, 40 percent in 1950, 50 percent in 1951. How could one characterize a policy that was financed by a foreign government, while the human losses were reserved for the young men of France (or of the "colonies" or the "associated states")? Thus, whether he studied the structure of the budget, public morale, economic strategy, monetary health, or diplomatic independence, he always encountered the Indochinese obstacle.

He returned to the charge three times in 1951, with all the more vigor (and virtue) because public opinion, dazzled by General de Lattre's successes in Tonkin and by the new tone and style he gave to the war, had fallen into the illusion of a possible victory.

In early July, he gave an interview to René Dabenat of *Le Monde:* "What must be done? We must choose among the tasks that make demands on the economy and our finances, for we cannot do everything at once: reconstruction, industrial investment, housing, domestic rearmament, social reforms, living standards, the Indochina war."

And, referring to military expenditures:

A more rigorous management of appropriations for national defense is necessary. We must review programs in a realistic way and present only demands with solid economic and technical foundations. And then, there is Indochina, the war "without end and without hope" into which we are sinking resources that might be necessary in Europe.

And he spoke again in October, at the Radical congress in Lyon, and then, with particular brilliance, in December in the Chamber. The Lyon congress was not predisposed in his favor. Emile Bollaert, a respected figure in the city where he had led the Resistance, and in the party of which he was a notable, was also one of the architects of French policy in Saigon, where he had been high commissioner from 1947 to 1949. Many of the party's "bigwigs" were still tied to the colonial tradition, if not to overseas big business. Declaring that the "hemorrhage of Indochina" was preventing France from organizing its defense in Europe and that he would no longer vote "for any government that refused to make the necessary choices," Mendès was strongly applauded. Auriol noted this in his diary, but he added: "He does not realize that were a government to apply his ideas and abandon Indochina . . . it could not exist."[8]

On December 30, 1951, the National Assembly heard the third of Pierre Mendès France's attacks against the war. It was his most violent indictment, the boldest synthesis he had developed against the government's Indochina policy, tying together in a single attack his arguments of 1945 against laxity and social disequilibrium, his criticisms of 1950 against unproductive expenditures and fiscal injustice, and his most recent appeals to national pride. A veritable "symphony of lucidity and indignation," according to Alain Gourdon,[9] it was this speech above all that earned him the name of Cassandra—especially in *Le Monde* (which knows all about it, General de Gaulle would have said).

Two unexpected observers were sitting in the press gallery: one of the most celebrated Parisian journalists, Françoise Giroud, who at the time seemed more interested in literature and fashion than in the doings of the MRP and the SFIO; and the young head of the foreign service of *Paris-Presse*, Jean-Jacques Servan-Schreiber, peremptory and combative, in whose eyes political genius had its source in the Cambridge economists and reached fruition in the political scientists of Harvard.

For several months, Servan-Schreiber, whose criticisms of the diplomatic situation of France had led him to study Mendès France's analyses, had been fascinated by their logical rigor. A man who had entered on the career of international observer as a champion of the American alliance, he was shaken by the arguments of General de Gaulle's former minister and all the more charmed because Mendès did not put in question the principle of the Atlantic Pact, but was fighting against the involvement of France in a postcolonial war which was transforming its proper cooperation with the United States into a humiliating subordination.

A week later, the austere deputy and mayor of Louviers made an unexpected appearance in *France-Dimanche.* Between those of Sagan and Camus, Françoise Giroud had devoted her portrait of the week to him. Departing from the amiable sarcasm which usually gave her Parisian sketches their charm, with a neophyte's fervor, she drew a portrait of the anti-star.

> Suddenly, toward a quarter to six, we heard: "M. Mendès France has the floor." Then a slight tremor ran through the audience. . . . Heads were raised, murmurs were stilled. A short, dark man with a pale and almost sorrowful face . . . calmly mounted the rostrum, opened a thick file, and began to speak. Two hours later, he was still speaking. . . . With the pure voice of those who are certain they are right, the deputy from Eure soberly and clearly developed an argument whose originality seemed to stupefy all his colleagues. "You are once again," he said in substance, "preparing to spend fifteen hundred francs when you have only a thousand." . . . Mendès France was listened to with religious silence. One may be certain that there was not one of his listeners who did not say to himself: "I would like to have the courage of that man when I have to defend a cause I believe to be just."

The speech and the article established an alliance that was very important to the life and career of Pierre Mendès France. From that day on, first without his knowledge, and then with his agreement, was forged the press arm which for ten years gave impetus and often color, for better and worse, to his political action.

The speech also put him back in the running for the premiership. Relating a conversation he had just had with Herriot, in search (once again) for a successor to René Pleven, whose fall had been helped along in no small part by Mendès's speech, the head of state noted: "I will call Mendès France, who was unanimously applauded; let him defend his ideas." And a little later, he said to Paul Reynaud: "I will call Mendès France, and it will not be for consultation this time. . . . Mendès France was applauded from all sides, he is at the juncture of the two majorities."[10] After which Edgar Faure was called, elected, and then quickly defeated, to be replaced by Antoine Pinay.

Mendès France devoted much of his time in the year 1952, which saw the rise of the rather pallid star of the mayor of Saint-Chamond, to other questions besides Indochina. This was not because the situation had stopped changing after the death of General de Lattre in January, but because other serious matters occupied his attention and his concern, notably the increasingly bitter crisis in Tunisia: Habib Bourguiba was arrested in January; in March, most of the ministers of the Cherik cabinet were arrested; and in August the French government was about to deport the inoffensive Lamine Bey, as General de Gaulle had done seven years earlier to his predecessor Moncef.

Tunisia was a country that Mendès France knew and where he had friends. He thought that this small state, endowed with old political structures, a bourgeois dynasty, and a modern and coherent party headed by a popular leader, could serve as a test for a broad policy of contractual decolonization and emancipation through law. Thus, when Tunisian friends asked him to come to defend three brothers, arrested under illegal and brutal conditions, although he hardly practiced his profession as lawyer any more, he immediately agreed to argue before the military tribunal of Tunis, knowing that this gesture would signify a political and moral commitment.[11] He was now involved in the Tunisian "hornets' nest," after having thrown himself into the Indochinese "quagmire."

There had also just appeared on the French political horizon the question of the CED (European Defense Community), which was for three long years to excite political circles and public opinion even more violently than the Indochinese tragedy. From the North Korean aggression of June 1950, which had unleashed the second Asian war and provoked the intervention of the United States, American leaders and a substantial number of their European colleagues had drawn the conclusion that only the reconstitution of a German army would be capable of balancing in Europe the Soviet power that had just "shed its disguise" (which was, incidentally, to simplify the role that Stalin and his lieutenants had played in the affair, since their Korean and Chinese comrades had gone over their heads).

To make the reconstitution of German military potential tolerable to French public opinion, five years after the liberation of the country, René Pleven and Robert Schuman had invented the idea of blending it into a combination of forces, the European Defense Community, a formula which, to be sure, had the virtue of avoiding the rebirth of the *Wehrmacht* itself, but one which on the other hand forced France and the other European states to drown their military, if not governmental, personality in this intra-European amalgam.

This dilution of the French army was sacrilegious in the eyes of General de Gaulle, all the more because this "integrated whole" would be able to act only within the sphere, if not under the direct orders, of the U.S. joint chiefs, who had already been given the supreme command of the combined forces of the Atlantic Alliance. At the other end of the spectrum of opinion, the Communists launched a campaign against this disguised form of a rebirth of "revanchist German militarism," anathema in their eyes and a constant target of Soviet propaganda.

In the Parliament elected in 1951, made up of three blocs—Gaullist, centrist (Socialists, MRP, moderates), and Communist—the first and the third came together, sometimes actively, in resistance to the CED. Only the second, the group in power, to be sure, supported the Pleven plan— with some notable exceptions: Socialists like Jules Moch and Radicals like Edgar Faure declaring themselves against the European Defense Community—which was ardently supported by Washington.

In this stormy debate, Mendès France, who was usually so quick to take a position, had difficulty in deciding. European in heart and mind since his adolescence, aware of the fact that Germany with a democratic government could not for long remain disarmed,[12] exasperated by the nationalistic demagoguery of the Gaullists and the Communists, he balked at a proposal in which he found the subtle and sinuous spirit of René Pleven, with whom he decidedly had a great deal of difficulty in seeing eye to eye. Of course, he had a great deal of respect for the other sponsor of the CED, Robert Schuman, whose plan for common development of European coal and steel had seemed to him "a new idea in Europe." But the proposed community was a strange combination. And especially, why should the extremely fruitful idea of Europe be structured around a military objective? Wouldn't that expose it to dubious conflicts?

Mendès France at the time was defending "civil" Europe, the Europe of economic and customs unification, in an unusual forum, at the international conference of Mexico City in September 1952. Asking, in the name of France, for closer cooperation between the International Monetary Fund and the European Payments Union, "whose objectives were in no way incompatible," Mendès suggested that the IMF facilitate the expansion of regional multilateralism by granting credits to the members of the EPU as frequently as possible. According to him, monopolistic tendencies were the result of limited markets.

> Weak enterprises would be in danger of succumbing to American competition if they were exposed to it without preparation, while if national markets are integrated within a regional framework, one may hope that the enterprises will thereby be strengthened to the point of one day being able to confront their trans-Atlantic competitors. These considerations, which inspired the Schuman plan, find a vast field of application in Europe.

This was doing more for Europe than many conferences of the military "Eurocrats."

The great quarrel of the CED, however, did not make him forget the Indochina emergency. Beginning in 1952, governments, from Edgar Faure to René Mayer, were looking for an "honorable way out," as they said at the time ("honorable" meaning no direct negotiations with Ho Chi Minh). Everyone, from Reynaud to Schuman, and from Pleven to Pineau, murmured that an international conference would take care of the matter. Even Letourneau, the MRP minister in charge, whispered that, if the negotiations on Korea undertaken in 1951 were to be broadened into a conference, France would do everything in its power to add the Indochina conflict to the negotiations on Korea.

Sophistry, idle arguments, specious detours, attempts to save face while time and human lives were being lost, thought Mendès France. In a lecture to Radical students on March 6, 1952 (sixth anniversary of the Ho Chi Minh–Sainteny agreements, the "lost peace"), he pointed out that the best way to put an end to the war was to negotiate directly with the enemy and that, according to his information, the Vietminh were not fundamentally opposed to that.

The situation became more and more pressing. In late March 1953, while in Indochina the conflict was spontaneously internationalized, overflowed the borders of Vietnam into Laos and, ceasing to be a battle for the Tonkin delta, became (much more dangerous for world peace) a war for the Mekong, at home the René Mayer government confronted an unprecedented parliamentary offensive. The Socialist Party members of Mayer's majority had now adopted Mendès France's arguments; on March 24, 1953, Jules Moch said to the head of government: "You are presiding over a bankruptcy!" But, independently of the Communists, it was once again the deputy from Eure who struck the hardest blows against the government, denouncing its "cowardice" (a word that René Mayer would never forget) and explaining:

> A constructive politics should follow two great principles. First, to reduce sterile expenditures, electoral and demagogic expenditures, to reduce our military burden to a bearable level, in order to provide appropriately for fruitful expenditures—industry, education, housing. . . . Of course, the measures that have to be taken will be painful. New taxes are painful, savings are painful. You will need, we will need, courage. But why delay?

The time for decision had arrived. And for those who thought them possible, who had the courage to see them in the present and to take them on in the future, the time for assuming responsibilities had also arrived. For Mendès France, a sort of budding or germination took place at the time, both for him and for others. First of all, encouraged, whipped into action, so to speak, by the publication of *Technique de l'état*[13] by his friend Gabriel Ardant, he felt the need to formulate the questions in a broader perspective. Beyond technical economic and financial questions, beyond colonial and military urgencies, he had to pose the problem of the state, its vices, its functioning, its reform, and ways of taking charge of it. He did this in the form of a sort of manifesto that he published in *Le Monde*.

Despite his reservations about the "neutralism" that Hubert Beuve-Méry had made, not the diplomatic doctrine, but one of the themes of the editorial policy, of the newspaper, the deputy from Eure was more and more seen by contributors to *Le Monde* as the man of peace in Indochina, that is, of the preliminary to any effort to reconstruct the state. This was the subject of the article published in *Le Monde* on April 10, 1953:

> What is necessary for France today—for its leaders as for the nation as a whole—is, on the one hand, the indispensable qualities of imagination to determine solutions, and on the other, the acceptance of certain discomforts and certain risks; any solution involves them, especially at the beginning, and they must be carefully foreseen and calculated and, if necessary, accepted. That requires both institutional modifications and changes in psychology, habits, and customs. . . .
>
> What is important, more than improvements in laws, are the much broader and, let us admit it, more difficult changes that concern men and their actions. Men in power to begin with, and also those who, throughout the country, make up the administrative, political, social, and military leaders of a generation that has now been abandoned to the kind of generalized disorder and discouragement, whose effects could be disastrous in the short run. . . .
>
> It is up to statesmen, real statesmen, to take the initiative and give an example.

We have used the word *manifesto*. Mendès France did not compose it entirely in that spirit. But public opinion received this call for "initiative" from "real statesmen" as a manifesto. Since they were not legion in the France of the spring of 1953, it was possible to see it as a declaration of candidacy. Did the deputy from Eure already have this in mind? In any event, it was in the minds of a number of young people who, from that point on, placed in him the hope for a much more fundamental renewal than the one that would aim for peace in Asia, fiscal reform, and the establishment of a policy for productive investments.

It happened that these young people had not only hopes and ambitions, for themselves and for Pierre Mendès France. They were in the process of creating a weapon of battle, and they had offered to put it at his disposal. It was a newspaper, *L'Express.*

Combative and worldly, lucid and partial, scintillating, discontinuous, inventive, snobbish, and provocative, *L'Express* in the end expressed ten years of French political sensibility, from the Indochina war to the end of the Algerian war. It brought together the most striking talents of the age, from Mauriac to Camus, from Sartre to Mitterrand, from Viansson-Ponté to Jean Daniel, but finally it resembled very little the man whom it had been created to promote and support.

From the outset, in fact, Mendès France was at the center of the enterprise. Servan-Schreiber had not had much difficulty in convincing his father to help him launch the new weekly. But his Uncle Robert, the elder, the head of the family, was more reserved. What was the reason for the paper? "To bring Pierre Mendès France to power." "Then, I have no further objection." Thus, at the end of the year 1952, the deputy from Eure, removed from the highest positions for many years and a little eclipsed in the eyes of the public as a vaguely miraculous solution by the figure of Antoine Pinay, was chosen as leader and as a candidate for power by a group of intrepid young people and experienced old professionals. At first, Mendès was skeptical. The Parliament of 1951 would never elect him. And he was not one to act outside Parliament. But Jean-Jacques Servan-Schreiber was so ardent, so convincing:

> He came to see me several times. He even had the charming idea to propose that I be the director of the future newspaper, swearing to me that he would be entirely obedient. I had the wisdom to say no. I may have changed my opinions about him, but never on one point: he is uncontrollable. Having said that, he was remarkably devoted, courageous, and effective.
>
> From the very first issue, I was involved in the adventure. They asked me for the interview that served as the feature for the first issue. Did *L'Express* give me the decisive impetus, or did my first attempt to form a government, in June 1953, give it a lift? I couldn't say. In any event, *L'Express* rendered enormous services to me, and I am grateful to its editors.

9.
IN THE ANTECHAMBER

On May 16, 1953, the kiosks displayed a weekly of modest size and sober layout. This was *L'Express,* under the direction of two publishers, Jean-Jacques Servan-Schreiber and Françoise Giroud, and an editor-in-chief, Pierre Viansson.[1] On page six was the interview with Pierre Mendès France featured on the cover and on posters put up everywhere; most of the interview was reprinted in *Le Monde.*

He had nothing new to say, but, under a fine title, "France Can Bear the Truth," there was a judicious presentation of his favorite arguments, formulated in very simple terms.

> Today there are no longer any particular remedies, we must consider the totality of the problems; their solution can only be achieved as a whole.
>
> 1. We cannot approach the problem of economic recovery without resolving the problem of unproductive costs like rearmament and the Indochina war;
>
> 2. On the other hand, without economic recovery, we will not have a valid foreign policy;
>
> 3. Without a coherent foreign policy, we will not resolve the problem of unproductive costs. Everything is linked to everything else.

Of course, the publishers of *L'Express* had asked him to explain his ideas about Indochina.

The facts long ago led us to concede that a military victory was not possible. The only solution therefore lies in negotiation. Our negotiating position was better two years ago than it was last year; better last year than it is now; it is probably not as bad now as it will be next year.

A week later, the René Mayer government fell. President Auriol called on Guy Mollet, who declined, as did the Gaullist leader André Diethelm. Paul Reynaud agreed to attempt to form a government. Refusing to consult organized groups and establishing a bold prerequisite for any such attempt—a revision of the Constitution strengthening the executive—he was heavily defeated: 274 votes against 295.[2] The next day, May 28, Mendès France was called to the Elysée. The head of state greeted the deputy from Eure with a reminder that the two primary questions were, first, financial, and second, diplomatic—the representation of France at the Bermuda conference, scheduled for two weeks thence, to which President Eisenhower had invited the heads of the British and French governments—and, as a consequence, he asked Mendès to form a government.

The ensuing exchange of views, as noted by Vincent Auriol,[3] says a great deal about the two figures, about the style and the political procedures of the period, if not about the president's real intentions.

AURIOL: I would like to go off the beaten path. As a young man supported by the young, you can create a new majority with a bold program.

MENDES: I am hated by those who are called the "great" political men of this country. That doesn't concern me. On the other hand, I have received much encouragement from the young, and that is what counts. One ought to use men who have the greatest opportunities. I would like to serve a useful purpose. I am a little card, but I would not like that card to be used up. [After Reynaud's attempt], a second tough program is in my opinion useless and harmful. If you force me to do it, I will do it, but I will get between 180 and 200 votes. How can you imagine that I will get 314 votes if I seize the bull by the horns, when Reynaud did not get them? With Indochina. . . . At this moment, I can only help you gain forty-eight hours from which some old hack will benefit.

AURIOL: I did not call on you to amuse myself: I refuse to play games merely to gain time. There are moments when one must have the courage to speak the truth.

MENDES: You have to give me a really serious opportunity!

AURIOL: You seem to me more and more indecisive. The last time I wanted to propose you, you let me know that you considered it an insult! Perhaps I will no longer call on you. For we have brilliant men in the Chamber, courageous men.

MENDES: I am simply a man sickened by what he sees happening.

AURIOL: We will be forced to come to extreme solutions and to dissolve the Chamber.

MENDES: You can't give me a few days? You will break my back immediately, in any event.
AURIOL: That's the third time you've used that expression!
MENDES: Mister President.
AURIOL: Call me Auriol, as you used to, since you're yelling at me.
MENDES: I have not forgotten who you are, and I am well aware of the seriousness of a conversation of this kind. It is serious for a whole career and perhaps serious for the country.

The next day, May 29, at four-thirty, Auriol noted: "Mendès France accepts. He thinks I am sending him to the sacrificial altar. Party colleagues have told him so." (Herriot had told Mendès: "It's a trap. Auriol is not nice: he should have called on a professional!")

It is not clear that Auriol had gained Mendès's confidence. Twenty-seven years later, the premier-designate of 1953 said the following:

He thought the time had come for a center-right government, like Pinay's. Beforehand, he had to "dispose of the Radical option," as the politicians of the time said. He could have chosen a more representative Radical! But in calling on me, he simultaneously dealt with the Indochinese challenge ("You see that a policy like yours is impossible"). That is why he called on me, asked me to "go on stage," to "do my number"—those were his expressions. Without really believing in my chances, he threw down a challenge to me, even calling into question my good faith, my sincerity. I gave in.

The interpretation is perhaps too narrow. The tone of Auriol's journal has, in its sly vulgarity, an excitement and a warmth that locate his use of the "Mendès ploy" of 1953 somewhere between the bold originality he claims for himself and the short-sighted cynicism that Mendes attributes to him.

Mendès was on the "hot seat." With the help of Georges Boris and Servan-Schreiber, he had had four days to prepare for this decisive encounter where, against his will, his political credibility was at stake.

On June 3, at ten o'clock, next to a glass of milk, he set down the forty-two pages of a speech that everyone knew was a veritable government program, for a government that many thought would never see the light of day.

In fact, it is from that point that we can date what was later called Mendésism. Why? It has been observed that on none of the six principal points of this programmatic speech—the independence of France within the Atlantic Alliance, a vote of confidence on the CED, reduction of military expenditures, development of a plan of negotiation in Indochina, resumption of the dialogue in North Africa, and more rigorous management of national enterprises—did Mendès France have anything very new to say. But because what he did say sounded right and strong, because he had the surprising gift of fostering belief in what he said, and because he was also throwing down a challenge to the accepted banality of the government, it was something new. His remarks were frequently interrupted by applause. And his peroration—of which the London *Times* said the next day that it had "the accents of genius"—finally brought around an audience filled with vigilant enemies as well as friends.

> Ladies and gentlemen, since I became interested in public life, three men have left an indelible trace in my thought. As a very young man, I admired in Raymond Poincaré the statesman worthy of the France he governed. As a deputy, I was asked by Léon Blum to be a part of his second government; a wave of popular enthusiasm exalted his generosity and his intelligence. And five years later, it was General de Gaulle, symbol of French continuity and inspiration of the Resistance, who ordered my transfer and called on me to serve in the Algiers government. Why, at this moment that is very moving for me, am I led to associate the names of these three very different men? It is no doubt because, under the aegis of love of country, their example taught devotion to the public welfare and the sense of the state. . . .
>
> If I do not obtain the decision I wish for from the Assembly, without joy but with complete serenity, I will feel no bitterness. I will remain convinced that I have served the country by presenting from this platform truths that will, in any event, finally prevail; the only question is to learn whether you will make them prevail today in a spirit of disinterested patriotism, or else whether they will impose themselves later, after new sufferings that we can avoid. . . .
>
> Let us think of the young whose fate is what is really at stake in our debates, and of the anxious country that is observing and judging us.

When Mendès France descended from the podium at eleven-thirty, he received extended applause from all sides except the Communists and some of the right. In *Le Monde,* Raymond Barillon spoke of a "considerable personal success," of "a deeply moved Assembly," and of the public very significantly adding its applause to that of the deputies.[4] Many years later, Mendès France still wondered about the reasons for this stunning success.

> I mount the podium, I say a few banalities, I explain that we have to introduce some order into the nationalized sector, things that others had said before me—and the audience bursts into applause. Why? I have no idea. The call to the young was more novel. But even so! It was like an electric shock. Incredible.

No less incredible was the cabal that was immediately organized, not only among the leaders of *all* the parties, but even more, in the corridors, where there was a sudden pullulation of "sinister fauna"[5] of informers spreading gutter-level rumors about Mendès and his "crypto-communism" (so crypto that the PCF was alone preparing as a bloc to vote against him). Messengers of panic stirred up the members' lounge against "the Jew who wants to stab the expeditionary force in the back."[6]

Before answering his critics, Mendès, in a few sentences, gave the "sinister fauna" a slap in the face.

> The exchange of views that has taken place at this podium, whatever its result may be, will have been useful for the country. I will not say as much for the agitation that has taken the corridors as its stage. Rarely, in the twenty-five years that I have been sitting in this chamber, I can testify to it, has the Assembly been besieged by such a swarm of officious informers. . . . Everything that has been echoed at this podium is worthy of being discussed. Everything that stayed in the corridors is contemptible. I would be under-estimating you and diminishing myself were I to respond to that.

This time it was not a majority of the Assembly, but a near unanimity of the deputies that acclaimed this call to decency, as though to cleanse themselves, including, of course, some of the organizers of the rumors. The campaign did not, however, subside. And yet, at the conclusion of a debate that had taken on exceptional density and dignity, Mendès France did indeed obtain a majority, completely unexpected a few days earlier, of 301 votes to 119 (the Communists and a few isolated individuals), but not the 314 the Constitution required to form a government.

The next day, Jacques Fauvet wrote in *Le Monde* that it was "the event of the legislative session," and, deepening his analysis: "The pessimism of M. Mendès France is real; that of his opponents is worse. He does not despair of his country in the long run; they doubt it daily. He claims, rightly or wrongly, that to be reborn we must first, if not die, at least withdraw; they prefer a slow, sure, but painless death."

The press was swept with unprecedented emotion. From *Le Parisien libéré*, which spoke of "a date in parliamentary annals," to *Les Echos,* which saluted "a statesman," and *Franc-Tireur,* which was happy to have heard "at last the doctor and not a sorcerer," the opinion makers were not mistaken: nothing would ever be the same. A certain kind of falsifying drone was thenceforth condemned—with a suspended sentence. Another language, another kind of demand had shown themselves, changing, in the medium and long term, the laws of the political class.

The reaction of Vincent Auriol to this operation that he had had, in any case, the virtue of unleashing was pungent.

> What a fellow! This morning in *Le Figaro,* Mauriac congratulates me for calling on him. I did it against everyone. Enormous effect in the Chamber. He has just struck a formidable blow, that classes him among the greatest. The country is certainly going to be agitated, and that's the important thing.

And to the loser covered with laurels, who had come to give a report of his mission, asserting that he had not thought he would be able "really to get so many votes," the president declared with a kind of exaltation: "With my young heart, I embrace you. You cannot stop there. The impetus has been given and you must continue. The country is waking up. I say with Mauriac: Stay in the antechamber!"[7]

Although its majority had given in to the strange intoxication of admiring, in one of its own, the body capable of producing (or of not assassinating without hearing him) a figure of this caliber, the political class was nevertheless not miraculously transformed. We have already pointed to opposition within the leadership of the Radical party. There was some minority support on the right, and the MRP was divided, particularly over the question of the CED. On the left, Guy Mollet opposed the support given by much of the leadership of his SFIO, and Mitterrand had some success in assuring the support of his UDSR (Democratic Union for the Socialist Republic).

The most disconcerting development provoked by the achievement of the deputy from Louviers was the shock wave unleashed within the Communist Party. We have indicated that the votes against Mendes in the Palais-Bourbon were above all those of the ninety-five Communist deputies and their four progressive fellow travelers (one of them, his old friend Pierre Cot, had abstained). From the podium, Jacques Duclos had proclaimed: "It's an attempt at deception! We are to swallow, in slightly different language, old reactionary policies!" But it soon appeared that, among the masses, this veto against a man who then symbolized negotiation in Indochina had been badly received. As is usual in such circumstances, we have little precise information. But Pierre Mendès France was not a man to make up fables. Commenting on this episode, on the basis of solid indications, he told us: "If Duclos and the leaders who had cut short my attempt in 1953 had to change direction a year later, this was because they had been taken to task by their voters and their rank-and-file militants."

Here and there, in any event, from the leadership of the RPF to the rank and file of the PCF, something had shifted, as it had in public opinion. However partial and hasty its judgments may have been, *L'Express* was not mistaken when it quickly replaced the disappointment of June with the hopes of the summer. It was under the sign of Mendésism[8] that there developed at the time a link between Servan-Schreiber's petulant weekly and the most prestigious journalist of the period, François Mauriac, who left *Le Figaro* the following year to join that effervescent avant-garde.

As for Mendès France's contemporaneous judgment of the success he had achieved almost in spite of himself, a quarter-century later, he laid no claim to any factitious lucidity.

A certain number of things were suddenly revealed to me. First, that I was *papabile;* that although, in all the parties, and particularly in the MRP, the leaders, the "union of premiers," were against me, the rank and file, the foot soldiers, the backbenchers were for me: they came to tell me so in secret. And then, I realized that Indochina, even more than I thought, was at the center of the debate, that it was making "the situation ripe," that I should therefore make it my first priority, even more than economic and social questions.

For him, then, Indochina took precedence over any other problem. Of course, all the speeches, actions, and initiatives of Mendès France, confined in the antechamber of power where Mauriac and Auriol situated him from June 1953 on, were not devoted to Indochina. The speech he delivered to the Radical congress at Aix-en-Provence in September went well beyond that. He outlined a bold portrait of the France of tomorrow, "more austere but happier," concluding with the famous cry: "We are in 1788!" which soon led Herriot to compare him to Necker. He did not forget that he was chairman of the Assembly's Finance Committee. It was particularly in this capacity that he wrote an article for *Le Monde* in February 1954 entitled, "Are We on the Verge of an Economic Crisis?" in which he adopted the idea of an imminent and profound disturbance of capitalist society and drew from this an argument for posing the problem in terms of government.

> What value can our opinions have as long as we present the spectacle of increasing disorder, stagnation, and dependence? . . . It is no longer only a domestic condition of the country that demands it; international perspectives confirm the necessity and the urgency of the effort of restoration that has taken entirely too long.

The election to the presidency a few weeks earlier of the discreet René Coty as successor to the warm Auriol had done nothing to restore confidence in the vigor of the system.

But Indochina was no longer in the center or the background of all French political debates. In a more and more obvious fashion, it was moving to the front of the stage. In the month of November 1953, while General Navarre was undertaking Operation Beaver, that is, the occupation by six battalions of parachutists of the valley of Dien Bien Phu, where the fate of the war was to be sealed, Ho Chi Minh declared that his government was ready to study any proposal that might lead to a cease-fire.

Bidault, minister of foreign affairs in the government of Joseph Laniel, whom Auriol had resigned himself to naming in place of Mendès France, might very well reply that "France does not conduct diplomacy through classified ads." Mendès's arguments were suddenly strengthened. Whether or not they were preferable to collective initiatives, direct negotiations were possible. Pleven was so struck by this that he asked the Socialist deputy Alain Savary, whose liberal positions on colonial questions had gained the respect of African and Asian militants, to make contact with the Vietminh leaders in the jungle. Bidault's veto aborted the plan.

On February 7, 1954, when the four-power (the Soviet Union, the United States, Great Britain, and France) conference opened in Berlin, considered in Paris as an opportunity to float the idea of an international conference on Asia, linking the Indochinese and Korean questions, the *New York Times* revealed that Washington was no longer opposed to an Indochinese negotiation as it was envisaged in Paris, that is, in a multilateral framework, adding: "Paris is of the opinion that if the United States has been able to negotiate an armistice in Korea, there is no valid reason why the French should refrain from doing the same, if they can, in Indochina."

Pierre Mendès France, as we have seen, was hardly in favor of this procedure, which consisted in seeking a settlement by drowning it in a vast international bargaining session, as though the better to dilute everyone's historical responsibilities. He said at the time:

> What's the use of going through Washington and Peking in order to invent peace between France and the Vietminh? Where is France's interest? Do people think that the Chinese need us to talk to Washington, to join the UN, to buy capital goods? Do they think that in exchange for a few railroad tracks Mao will play the role of benevolent intermediary? And do they think that, in order to negotiate, the Vietminh are determined to work through Chinese mediation?

A few days later, on March 4, 1954, the National Assembly was summoned to examine the perspectives opened by the convocation of an international conference on Asia, to be held in Geneva on April 15, decided on at the end of the Berlin four-power conference. Thus, the path to negotiation had been opened. The debate was no longer between supporters of war or peace, but between advocates of the two forms of negotiation: bilateral and multilateral. Mendès France might be expected to be exultant. But he was not, less because his austere character was little suited to jubilation than because he thought he had detected, in public and private statements by Georges Bidault and his collaborators, aims that were very far from a real peace settlement.

For him, the Laniel–Bidault government had devised the Geneva conference with two alternative objectives in mind. The first consisted, in return for a few concessions and by relying on the threat of American intervention, to extract from Moscow and Peking an agreement to abandon the Vietminh. If the Russians and the Chinese could be persuaded to abandon Ho Chi Minh, as Stalin had forgotten the Greek Markos in 1947, France would avoid a military defeat and could impose on the Vietminh a compromise beneficial to French policy. If this objective could not be obtained in Geneva, the French negotiators would aim for a second one: to associate the Americans with a war that had been internationalized in the Korean style of 1950.

Were these really the innermost thoughts of Georges Bidault on his way to Geneva? It has always been impossible to find out with any precision. He hardly knew himself, torn as he was between his rancor and his dreams. Did he think he was in a position to persuade the Soviets that they had to abandon Ho Chi Minh? It is hard to see how the French premier could detect the slightest sign pointing in this direction. The clarifications formulated in Moscow, after the publication of a few rumors on the subject in the Anglo-Saxon press, do not seem to have unsealed his eyes.

Nevertheless, relying on this chimera, on his return from the Berlin conference in February, he told a former Resistance companion who was then writing for *Le Monde,* Georges Mamy: "Finally your boss⁹ is going to be satisfied with me: I am preparing to make peace in Indochina, to put an end to this terrible war. You can tell him from me: I have finally found the grounds for an honorable compromise."

He remained convinced that Ho Chi Minh would soon be abandoned by his allies in Moscow and Peking, apparently unaware of the price he would have had to pay in exchange for such an enormous concession, which could only have been French opposition to German rearmament— what he himself had called "planetary bargaining," imputing it to Mendès France.

The latter's description of his predecessor's Indochina strategy nevertheless seems severe. But his argument at the podium of the Assembly on March 9, 1954, six weeks before the opening of the conference, was impressive.

> Some want to continue the war after pretending to seek peace, after giving themselves an alibi. Yes, continue the war, but with a considerable change, with the hope that the new conditions will finally permit them to obtain a United States military presence in Indochina.
>
> But have you forgotten that American intervention would certainly mean Chinese intervention and, perhaps, general war? Can you lightheartedly play that game and take that risk?
>
> In any event, when I consider, as I have just done very rapidly, the general picture of the Geneva conference, I see very clearly what peace and France can both lose there, but I do not see what they can gain.

There is only one solution, and you will come to it: a difficult solution, a painful solution, a solution that is cruel and, in certain respects, unjust: direct negotiations.

In fact, although the third parties whom you involve in negotiations have objectives and political views that are different from ours, there are two peoples in the world who aspire to peace in Vietnam, because, for eight years, they have been bearing the bloody burden of war. Yes, there are many differences between the French and the Vietnamese, many painful, sometimes atrocious, memories that divide and oppose; there is hatred, there is rancor; but they also have one thing in common: the will to end it, the need to restore peace.

You sometimes say that Ho Chi Minh is not free, that he takes orders and instructions from elsewhere. For my part, I know nothing about it. But I know that negotiation through Moscow and through Peking can only increase his subjection, while our policy ought to consist in liberating the Vietnamese people from the burden weighing upon them, in touching them, reaching them directly and without any barrier or intermediary. We should appeal to their national and even nationalistic sense, not push them toward a dependence that many Vietnamese, even the Communists, would like to avoid. We should show the Vietnamese people that they can have peace and independence, that they can receive them from us, and not from Moscow and Peking; that is indeed the best investment. But if we subject them more thoroughly to other influences, we shall give them new causes for complaint against us.

The fundamental irony of history willed that the man who had thus warned public opinion against the Geneva conference was to make it the instrument for peace. To be sure, a procedure is only worth what one makes out of it. But all the same, Cassandra was painting too somber a picture. A few days after this indictment, *L'Express* spoke with a different tone (not without advice from its political oracle): "This conference is highly desirable: it can contribute to general détente in Asia."

Thus, when the time to assume his responsibilities came, Mendès was able to use very cleverly the multilateral procedure invented by his predecessors, to make it the framework for his own approach, which was essentially bilateral. But he was obliged to recognize (at least privately) that this framework was sometimes very useful; that the American presence in Geneva, as a deterrent threat—which Mendès was at pains to make clear—was not without effect; that English good offices were salutary; and especially that the combined pressures of the Soviets and the Chinese on their Vietnamese allies were, at certain moments, decisive. Isn't politics the art of making do with whatever material is available, even of what you have at first considered useless?

We should also point out, in order to refute the simplistic or ironic opposition between the "anti-Geneva" Mendès France of March 1954 and the negotiator of July, that the very structure of the negotiations was changed from top to bottom. In the minds of Bidault and his American friends agreeing to extend the negotiations to Indochina, it was still a matter of a four-power conference (the Soviet Union, United States, Great Britain, and France), or perhaps five, including China. But there was no question of inviting our Vietminh opponents, "those who were fighting."

It was here that Mendès's diagnosis remained valid. And it was because the inventors of the Geneva meeting finally recognized the correctness of his argument in favor of a bilateral conversation, inserting his procedure into the one that had been initially foreseen, and associating the Vietminh with the negotiation of which they became the pivot, that the enterprise was able to succeed.

The situation became more and more dramatic. In early March, the mission to Indochina conducted by René Pleven, minister of defense, annihilated the last military illusions; by the fifteenth, the fortified camp of Dien Bien Phu, where French strategists had promised themselves they would break Giap's fighting force, was doomed. A precipitous evacuation, recommended by most specialists,[10] had become practically unrealizable. It was no longer a question of winning, or of shaping the defeat, or even of opposing enough force against the enemy to maintain a superior position in the negotiations, but of saving men. And this is why Pleven recommended an appeal to the United States: only an intervention by their air force would permit an evacuation of the fortified camp. And it was always possible that the Americans, once involved in the war, would change the outcome.

From March 27 to April 29, the eve of the opening of the Geneva conference, there was a flurry of contacts between Paris and Washington with a view to launching "Operation Vulture," which would have consisted of the bombing of the Vietminh positions around Dien Bien Phu by a squadron of two hundred U.S. air force planes based in Manila. This operation of open war, recommended by Secretary of State John Foster Dulles, was vetoed by Admiral Radford, Vice President Nixon, and the majority of the Senate (in the first rank of which was Lyndon B. Johnson), in agreement with President Eisenhower. At the same time, in London, on April 27, speaking in the House of Commons, Winston Churchill staked his prestige and his reputation as an inflexible fighter on the theme: "Do not ruin the chances for negotiation: priority to the Geneva conference!"

At first devoted to Korea—where an armistice had been signed two months earlier at Panmunjom after interminable discussions—the conference opened on April 27 on the banks of Lake Léman. The sensation it created was due first of all to the participation of the People's Republic of China: John Foster Dulles had finally agreed to sit for a few hours at the same table as the "Reds" from Peking. History finally recorded that the four were now five. The Korean prelude hardly stirred public opinion, or even the delegations, who lived in expectancy of the Indochina episode that had been dramatized by the intensification of the fighting around Dien Bien Phu. Although the specialists had known as early as March 15 that the battle was lost, by April 21 public opinion could no longer ignore the imminence of the disaster. Would the last outpost hold out until a cease-fire was signed?

The answer was no. On May 7, on the eve of the opening of negotiations on Indochina, the fortified camp, crushed by artillery and submerged by the human wave of attackers, had stopped answering calls from General Cogny in Hanoi. At that point, the French negotiators had in hand only "the two of clubs and the three of diamonds," sighed Georges Bidault, whose perspectives were placed "between the inaccessible and the unacceptable." To be sure, on the fourth, fifth, and sixth of May in the Assembly, confronted with an oratorical offensive of uncommon violence in which, accusing Bidault of "forfeiture," the Gaullist Louis Vallon had stolen the role of prosecutor from Mendès France, the Laniel government had won a vote of confidence by 311 to 262. But, in Geneva, Bidault was now only a minister with a reprieve whose survival depended on a rapid conclusion of the negotiations.

In the "antechamber," where the prestigious failure of June 1953 had set him, Pierre Mendès France now appeared as the heir apparent to the government, since everyone saw in him the man of the alternative, the one who, on the road to negotiation where the future of the country was being played out, and on which the Laniel government had set out against its will, would be able to commit himself without reservation. Thus, even before taking the negotiation in hand, he had won a capital point on the fundamental issues: neither Washington nor Bao Dai had been able to prevent Molotov and Chou En-lai from forcing the invitation of a Vietminh delegation to Geneva; it landed on May 4, under the leadership of Pham Van Dong, Ho Chi Minh's preferred colleague. Thus, even before Mendès came on stage, and within the framework of the multilateral conference, the conditions for the direct negotiations that he had constantly advocated had been created.

But what would Bidault make of this opportunity? His strategy, defined in the speech he delivered at the opening of the conference on May 8, was that of a victor: the cease-fire must be declared according to the "leopard skin" formula (the irregular outline of territorial zones controlled by the opposing forces), without any recognition of the adversary. There was no question of discussing the political future of Vietnam in this forum. Bidault confined himself to the military aspects of the debate. And in carrying out this unrealistic dissociation, the French minister came close to demanding the surrender of the Vietminh units—twenty-four hours after the fall of Dien Bien Phu.

But even more disconcerting than this intransigence on the substance was the professional behavior of Bidault, who stubbornly refused to meet Pham Van Dong. "I am not used to associating with assassins," he declared haughtily, adding: "What do I have to hear from him? I know that he has only one idea: to kick us out the door." Nevertheless, however strong the repulsion of this diplomat for the adverse party, he was obliged to authorize one of his colleagues, Colonel de Brebisson, to establish contact with his counterpart, Colonel Ha Van Lau, for the purpose of organizing in common the evacuation of the wounded from Dien Bien Phu.

This first direct contact between the French and the Vietminh immediately showed itself to be positive. While the collective negotiations were still occupied with the exchange of abstract plans and outdated historical and ideological arguments, in a few hours these men from the field, representing the real combattants and the two peoples who, as Mendès pointed out, wished for peace more than anyone else, were to open the way to the real face-to-face negotiations, which were to begin on June 9.

In the meantime, a perspective had been opened (or hinted at) in a conference session on May 25 by Pham Van Dong. To the French plan of regrouping the two enemy forces "in a leopard skin" (irregular zones with such extended borders that surveillance would require, it was suggested, 800,000 men), the Vietminh minister replied with a plan according to which, thanks to "exchanges of territory," they would create vast "zones under single command," facilitating, on both sides, control, transportation, and administration. One French diplomat, Claude Cheysson, excitedly followed this presentation and feverishly took notes. Leaving the session, he grasped Colonel de Brebisson by the arm and said: "This time, colonel, it's division—and he is the one who is offering it."

All serious observers, from Walter Lippmann to Robert Guillan, from the *Times* correspondent to the editorialist of *Le Monde,* had the same reaction as Cheysson. The path was laid out, but who would dare to set off on it clearly? Bidault was content with one of those incongruous remarks that summed up, for ten years, his diplomatic genius: "Cut the pear in half? On condition that we keep the stem."

Was this what he called recourse to the Americans? During the last days of May, he attempted, through the intermediary of the French ambassador in Washington, Henri Bonnet, to obtain a solemn promise of intervention by the U.S. air force and the marines in case his interlocutors in Geneva remained intractable; there were again a few rumors about nuclear weapons. Did Bidault expect that his interlocutors in Geneva would confess themsleves intimidated by these more or less veiled threats? When Molotov spoke in the public session on June 8, the French minister had to back down. Not only did Molotov show no anxiety (all the less because, in Washington, Dulles had just indicated that the United States was not considering any military action in Indochina), but his attack was a kind from which an adverse negotiator could not recover.

The next day, June 9, Bidault was in Paris to present to an exasperated Assembly an assessment of the first month's negotiations, while every passing hour had worsened the situation of the expeditionary force, decapitated and trapped in the Indochinese rice paddies. Accused by Raymond Aron of "diplomatic somnambulism," he responded boldly:

> Some have spoken of a double game at Geneva, where negotiations are supposed to have been undertaken only in the hope that they would fail. If someone can report that I have accomplished a single act contrary to peace or favorable to war, I calmly wait for him to rise and speak. If you think that another negotiator would have more chance of success, I am ready and willing to surrender the task and the responsibilities to him.

This challenge by the foreign minister was directed at Mendès France more than anyone else. Mendès had sent Joseph Laniel a very harsh letter on the conduct of the negotiations on May 21, and on May 27, had felt attacked by the seizure of *L'Express,* which was accused of revealing national defense secrets.[11] He could not fail to take up the challenge. Not content with a harsh denunciation of Bidault for his lack of interest in meeting with interlocutors who were indispensable in the search for a solution, the deputy from Eure accused the minister of having played a "diabolical poker game" with the Americans by asking for the intervention of their air force, for, he said, there was a great temptation to subsume the Indochinese disasters within a general war. Listened to with even more concentrated attention than usual, Mendès France added: "We will be all the stronger if we cannot be suspected of hiding our intentions or of maneuvering. We must have done everything to obtain peace."

Some of his supporters, however, found him "aggressive," too partisan, too personal toward Bidault. Robert Buron, an unorthodox MRP who admired Mendès enough to risk his political career by his side a few weeks later, considered the speech "maladroit" and reported this statement from one of his friends: "PMF makes one think today of a young girl whom everyone found charming at her debut and who has been told as much. On later occasions, she feels all eyes glued to her, becomes awkward, stiffens, and even catches her feet in the rug."[12]

"Maladroit" or not, Mendès's speech was decisive. On the night of

June 9, the Laniel government was placed in the minority by a vote of 322 to 263. Since a vote of confidence had not been taken, it could have attempted to remain in power. It was at that point that an astonishing figure intervened. Frédéric-Dupont, whom a sarcasm of history had made a few days earlier "minister of the associated states" (of Indochina), attempted to save the government by asserting at the podium that a significant event had just occurred in Geneva and that peace was imminent. He was referring to the proposal about the conditions of territorial division made by Colonel Ha Van Lau to Colonel de Brebisson to which we have already alluded. But such an initiative was promising only on condition that it remain secret so that the French minister might reply in the same spirit. Bidault had the honesty to deny—in parallel with the Vietminh delegation—the "revelation" of his indelicate colleague. And the Laniel–Bidault government fell, by a vote of 306 to 296, on June 12.

However irresponsible Frédéric-Dupont may have been in revealing it, a negotiation had indeed gotten under way on June 9, during the second private meeting between Ha Van Lau and Brebisson, where they had been joined by their direct superiors, Ta Quang Buu and General Delteil. That evening, between ten and midnight, an extraordinary conversation took place in a villa on the outskirts of Geneva.

A former scout leader, a professor of history well informed about military problems, Ta Quang Buu came directly to the point. Brusquely unfolding a map of Indochina, he placed his hand on the Red River delta with an imperious gesture and declared: "We must have this. We need a state, we need a capital for our state, and we need a port for our capital." Astounded, Delteil and Brebisson tried to redirect the conversation: Could Buu explain more clearly. Did the gesture, the references to the North, a capital, and a port, refer to Tonkin alone, Hanoi and Haiphong, without the Center and the South?

Cutting the debate short, Buu insisted on the advantages of this discreet bilateral procedure, pointing out the drawbacks of the conference and of supervision by the great powers, and recalled the secret nature of the conversations that had been undertaken. Aware that these were the most novel and creative propositions that had been presented since the beginning of the conference, the two French officers immediately reported to the head of their delegation; and two days later, they thought that Frédéric-Dupont's revelations were going to ruin these clandestine negotiations. But on the twelfth, their interlocutors resumed contact, which was to deepen after the twenty-second, since power had changed hands in Paris.

Although the Franco–Vietminh dialogue wished for by Mendès France had already gotten under way, the full conference was gradually sinking into posturing and useless polemics. On June 12, *Le Monde* wrote, "Bidault's refusal to discuss political problems has doomed the conference to failure, at least in the immediate." On the fifteenth, the *Times* announced: "The conference will close before the end of the week." And the American delegation was preparing to leave on the twenty-fourth. It seemed to have been a failure.

At that point, Chou En-lai, of all the principal figures of the conference the one who provoked the greatest curiosity while maintaining the greatest discretion, stepped forth. He seemed to have been caught short. A mask seemed to fall from his admirable, pale copper face. This dispassionate diplomat showed signs of intense agitation. He had foreseen an interminable negotiation that would be the occasion for numerous contacts and deep penetration of the West by Chinese diplomacy, and that objective now seemed about to be frustrated. On June 16, he spoke privately to Anthony Eden (Great Britain was the only Western state that had recognized the Peking government) to inform him that he was in favor of dissociating the questions of Cambodia and Laos from the question of Vietnam.

This important initiative answered to a desire of Western diplomats that their colleagues from the East had until then appeared to ignore. If their losses could be cut in Vietnam, without drawing Cambodia and Laos into the same outcome, the perspectives would shift (and we understand better today that Chou En-lai, by thus appearing to "grant" an important concession to the West to save the endangered conference, was serving above all the interests of China by preparing the dissociation of Cambodia and Laos from the future of Vietnam).

The general view was that the Chinese minister's action offered the conference a second wind. The framework for a settlement existed. There lacked the will to make peace finally a living reality, after the rumblings of American thunder provoked by Bidault, Molotov's brutal remonstrances, and Frédéric-Dupont's gaffe, not to mention the hidden sabotage fomented by the U.S. delegation.

The Geneva conference had survived the intrigues of the skeptics and the warmongers. It remained to give it the decisive impetus.

THE FIRE OF
ACTION

10.
PMF

In the later afternoon of Sunday, June 13, Pierre Mendès France was called to the Elysée. He could not have been surprised: No one had contributed more than he to the fall of the Laniel–Bidault government, and it is good democratic practice to choose an alternate government by recourse to an alternate politics. The country's chief concern was the Indochina war, and Mendès was the preeminent advocate of peace. He had just proclaimed to the country that Georges Bidault had not done everything to put an end to the fighting, that he had on the contrary risked widening the war. He had seen himself challenged on the floor of the Assembly by the minister responsible to do better. In this extraordinary struggle of men and policies, what other solution could the head of state find but to call on the man who offered a *different* opportunity?

There were times when Mendès France suspected the deep motives that impelled René Coty at the time, as he had suspected Vincent Auriol a year earlier. It might be another ambush, designed to "dispose of the claim of the left," in order to promote the access to power of a political friend of the president's from the moderate right, like Pinay—or from the center, like Edgar Faure.[1] Coty and Mendès were acquainted. The senator from Seine-Maritime and the deputy from the neighboring department, Eure ("which the people of Rouen look on as colony"), had often confronted one another at electoral meetings where, against the candidate of the left from the "colony," Coty supported the spokesmen of the right, but, Mendès emphasized, "without ever departing from the greatest courtesy." In sum, he pointed out, "René Coty showed me a certain consideration, but he considered me a leftist, a particularly aberrant type in Normandy." Mendès France would soon recognize that this astonished consideration could be of more use to political cooperation than the exuberant cordiality that often governed in such affairs.

On this Sunday, June 13, however, he resisted Coty as he had resisted Auriol the year before. "I fought like a tiger all night long," he told us in 1980. But the president's arguments were too strong, especially those inspired by democratic principles, the sense of responsibility, and finally the situation.

The Radical deputy might very well argue that from the parliamentary point of view, the perspectives would be better after the failure of a candidate from the right; the head of state—who, in six months at the Elysée, had been able to get an idea of the disaster threatening in Indochina—could easily answer that the time for tactical maneuvers had passed, that every minute counted, that the expeditionary force in the field and the Geneva conference close to home could no longer wait for the merry-go-round of the trained horses of the Palais-Bourbon.

In short, after three hours of debate, Pierre Mendès France left the Elysée as premier-designate, invested with a "sacrifice mission," and instructed by Coty to act quickly. His first telephone call on the morning of the fourteenth was to Joseph Laniel, the incumbent premier. He had to meet the military leaders as soon as possible in order to have at his disposal the elements of the Indochina question before presenting himself as a candidate to the National Assembly.

To Mendès France's great regret, General Ely was not present. Two weeks earlier, Ely had accepted a sacrifice mission even more difficult than his own, to succeed General Navarre in Saigon. This lucid and scrupulous man, whom he had known in Washington when he represented France at the International Monetary Fund and Ely was in the standing group of chiefs of staff of the Atlantic Alliance, and who had not hidden from him his apprehensions about Vietnam, was not there to enlighten him.

In the absence of Ely, the military spokesmen were Chief of Staff Guillom and the leaders of the army (Blanc), navy (Nomy) and air force (Faÿ). It was from the latter that he expected the most serious revelations. It was known that the air force troops, short of supplies and held in check by the Americans, were particularly pessimistic. But it was General Blanc who was the most eloquent.

Three ideas stood out from his presentation on June 14. First, one month after the fall of Dien Bien Phu, the delta of the North was deteriorating from day to day, and the situation of Hanoi was almost as serious as that of the fortified camp had been in March. The road from the port of Haiphong to the capital of Tonkin was constantly in danger of being cut, not for a few hours, which had already occurred, but permanently. Thus, General Ely, shortly after his arrival in Indochina, had prepared for the evacuation of Hanoi, which risked taking on the form of a costly "sortie" in the coming weeks.

A second theme of General Blanc's presentation was the risk of desertion by the Asian units in the expeditionary force, now made up of only 30 percent of soldiers from metropolitan France. As the disaster grew, it was to be feared that Bao Dai fighters, to redeem themselves in the eyes of their Vietminh compatriots, would unleash a Saint Bartholomew's Day massacre against their European and African fellow soldiers. To allow a further deterioration in the situation of the forces in Hanoi and Saigon would be to run this terrifying risk.

This was why, General Blanc concluded in substance, it was important, as General Ely advocated, first of all to make French forces locally supremely powerful, by rapid regroupment, tactical retreats, and reinforcements. Then, they should obtain, with extreme urgency, an end to the fighting. Quickly, very quickly; it was now a matter of weeks.

However informed he had been for years about the course of events, Mendès France was stunned. The situation was even more tragic than he had thought. In sum, he suggested, we have to end it very quickly, within a month? To which his military interlocutors retorted that a month is a long time. They didn't know if they could hold out that long.

He had to act quickly, very quickly, that was all, and avoid letting the negotiations drag on, "Asian" style, like those in Korea two years before. Wasn't it in the interest of the Vietminh to let time work for them?

This was the origin of Mendès France's idea of setting a deadline of one month for concluding an agreement, the minimum needed to get a vote of confidence, form a government, organize a military deterrent, run to Geneva, persuade his allies, impress his opponents, and allow consultations with various governments—including the Vietminh—to develop.

In addition to seeking the advice of military leaders, the premier-designate consulted various economic advisers, carefully scrutinized the telegrams from Ambassador Chauvel, who continued to lead negotiations in Geneva, and visited Georges Bidault and Frédéric-Dupont. The foreign minister, with whom he had been rather severe, greeted him rather cordially, saying simply: "It is more difficult than you think. You have illusions about those people."[2]

Everything conspired to persuade him to hurry. He was to appear before the Assembly on the seventeenth; by the night of the fifteenth he had begun preparing his speech, assisted by Georges Boris and Simon

Nora, and occasionally by Jean-Jacques Servan-Schreiber. And he was taking steps, if not to form his government (he already knew, in any event, that he would call on François Mitterrand, Paul Bacon, and Robert Buron from the MRP, the Socialists Gaston Defferre and Alain Savary, and the Gaullists Jacques Soustelle and Jacques Chaban-Delmas), at least to set up his team of close collaborators.

On the fifteenth, he spoke to the press, careful not to reveal the most dramatic elements of the situation, but declaring himself determined to act very quickly and just as determined not to consult the political groups of the Assembly in order to develop his program and, in case of need, to form his government. Parliamentary observers, once again charmed by the man, his precision, sobriety, and conviction, gave very slim odds on his attempt, which they considered, as he had in speaking to Coty, tactically "premature."

Thus, on the eve of the investiture debate, three of the journalists who were the most favorably disposed toward him and as aware as he was of the Indochina emergency—Jacques Fauvet, Jean Ferniot, and Georges Altschuler—scarcely concealed their skepticism. The first wrote: "Without the votes of the extreme left,[3] M. Mendès France would have little chance of putting together a constitutional majority." The second: "M. Coty called M. Mendès France only because any other majority (aside from the one that had supported Laniel) was impossible." The third: "M. Mendès France's nomination has been seriously compromised." These careful observers in fact realized that, Dien Bien Phu or not, the veto of the "union" of presidents and general secretaries remained poised against Mendès and that the movement toward him among the Gaullists would not be enough to make up for the votes lost in the MRP by his lack of enthusiasm for the CED.

Pierre Mendès France was nevertheless elected before dawn on June 18, 1954, after the dramatic events we have narrated, by one of the strongest and most complex majorities in the history of the Fourth Republic. Between his appearances at the podium and on the government bench he had already brought together a group of advisers led by two powerful figures, George Boris and François Mitterrand, to hastily set up a government of which he had said that it would be made up of persons and not delegates of the parties, solely on the basis of the homogeneity he could hope for from them, their probable effectiveness, and their loyalty to the program outlined in his speech of candidacy.

The presence of Boris by his side in those hours was a matter of course. That of Mitterrand was more novel. Their relations had long been cordial. The fact that both contributed to *L'Express* had brought them closer together without making them intimate friends. But Mendès had discovered in his young colleague a parliamentary zoologist of incomparable skill. No one was more knowledgeable about the deputies, their talents and their weaknesses, their past performance, their secret aspirations, and their connections.

Aware of his parliamentary naiveté as an expert of the IMF and a devourer of dossiers, Mendès Frances had chosen Mitterand to obscure that naiveté ("he knew everything and everybody; in Parliament, he was like a pianist at the keyboard") and later to give him significant responsibilities. It was thus that, from time to time seeking the advice of another parliamentary virtuoso, Edgar Faure, Mendès and Boris drew up the list of government officers between the seventeenth and nineteenth.

The selection did not take place as freely as Mendès France would have liked. The SFIO, which contained the bulk of his supporters, did not participate because he had refused the usual procedure of designation by the group, and also because party divisions over the CED posed a risk of breakup if it were submitted to the test of power. Guy Mollet prohibited all of his comrades, under penalty of exclusion, from participating in the government of the "best of the others." The leadership of the MRP, irritated by the support that a number of its deputies had given Mendès, made the same decision, but discipline was not as strong as in the SFIO. While Paul Bacon refused the major Ministry of Economic and Social Affairs that was offered to him, Robert Buron and André Monteil broke ranks, for which they were excluded, not from the party, but from the MRP parliamentary group.

There were fewer hesitations among the Gaullists. Although Soustelle, believing he was intelligently interpreting De Gaulle's silence, rejected an offer, six prominent Gaullists joined the government.

The moderates—independents, peasants, ARS—who had played an important role, as we have seen, in voting in the government, had a sustantial representation. The Radicals, the party of the head of government, were less well endowed, with only three ministers. As for the UDSR, from its ranks came not only Claudius-Petit, who had been given the Ministry of Labor because he was the only former worker of the group, but especially François Mitterrand, who from the outset appeared as the third man of the government in which Edgar Faure played the role of brilliant second.

There was, however, one setback in his task as selector. Having decided to take charge of the Ministry of Foreign Affairs, and knowing that he would be preoccupied for at least a month by the Indochina affair, and long afterward by the CED and North Africa, he had wanted to find an alter ego, what the English call a deputy, a substitute who in his absence would take on his full responsibilities, at least before the Parliament. For this purpose, he had thought of Gaston Monnerville, an old comrade from the days of the Young Turks, president of the Senate,[4] a prestigious parliamentarian who had never participated in any government.

Monnerville refused. The reasons he offered were not personal but constitutional. The spirit and the letter of the 1946 Constitution personalized in the extreme the role of the premier: he was the one, *intuitu personae,* who was elected. No "vicar" could substitute for him, enjoy his authority, assume even episodically, his responsibilities. Mendès's idea, attractive as it was, would not stand up, especially with a president like Coty, a scrupulous jurist and a constitutional expert, concluded Monnerville, who was surprised to see the new premier, who was exhausted and enerveted, create a scene: "So, you, too, are forsaking me, an old friend!"

In fact, during the Geneva conference and at the that time of Mendès's various trips to Brussels, Washington, and London, it was Edgar Faure who played the strange role of double, with the ease of a virtuoso and enjoying the confidence of his old classmate. And in January 1955, Faure took Mendès France's place in the Foreign Ministry.[5] Relations between the two men were sometimes difficult on economic and financial questions, but not on Faure's exercise of surrogate authority.

Pierre Mendès France had chosen to assume the Foreign Ministry because the task to which he had given priority—making peace in Indochina within a month—was essentially diplomatic. Moreover, he thereby had the sense that he was making the conduct of foreign affairs the essential public business, placing it before the public who had elected him and to whom he freely expressed himself in his weekly Saturday radio broadcasts.

This kind of enterprise marked by urgency and innovation demanded not only a government shaped like a team around a leader. It also required a small and closely knit circle, his staff. In fact, Mendès France had three, in addition to the official one. And it was the fourth that played the most significant role.

There was the premier's staff, the staff of the Foreign Ministry, and the unofficial staff associated with *L'Express.* But in the early stages, there was a fourth staff, which played the most active role: the team of negotiators that Georges Bidault had left behind him in Geneva and that Mendès changed only at the request of some of its members.

Considered for twenty years in the Foreign Ministry as a diplomat of international standing, equal to the most important negotiations, Jean Chauvel continued to show himself at Geneva as one of the most brilliant shapers of the course of the conference. This diplomat in the classic tradition had found an international negotiation of the kind that seemed to have disappeared with the nineteenth century. And he conducted himself with sovereign talent.

Pierre Mendès France obviously kept him at the head of the "fourth

Jules-Isaac Mendès France, a grandfather with his
sympathies on the left

Cerf Mendès France, artillery man

Isidore (with an *e*) Cahn and his family: the wise man
of Strasbourg.

A pampered little boy, with his mother, grandmother, and great-grandmother

Pierre with a hoop: the "first in the class" does not look timid.

The war comes to an end: Palmyre, Cerf, Pierre, and Marcelle in the country.

Jean Zay, the friend assassinated by the French Nazis.

With Marx Dormoy (on the left) and Georges Boris, under-secretary of state Mendès France leaving Matignon, at the time of the second Blum government, March 1938.

Lieutenant Mendès France at the Clermont-Ferrand trial. The prosecutor is seated beneath the portrait of Philippe Pétain.

The war is over: Lily, Bernard, Pierre, and Michel Mendès France finally reunited.

A mustachioed underground figure named Laurent Séoyer—unrecognizable?

he mayor of Louviers greets General de Gaulle in the
idst of the ruins.

Between Léon Blum and his son Robert,
a future Socialist militant,

In Geneva, Pham Van Dong and Pierre Mendès France on the road to peace.
Between them, Guy de la Tournelle (an aid to Jean Chauvel) and Georges Boris.

In Carthage, July 30, 1954, before Lamine Bey and two generals of his court.

At Chartwell, Sir Winston Churchill greets a European in search of friends.

The "no" to De Gaulle, September 1958

Electoral campaign of 1962 with the Radicals of Normandy. The "châteaux" were the stronger party.

With François Mitterrand: a question of wavelengths

On the way to Charléty, a stop at the place d'Italie, with Georges Kiejman, Jean-René de Fleurier, Harris Puisais, and Michel Rocard.

With Marie-Claire Mendès France on the ski slopes

cabinet," assisted by Claude Cheysson, a young diplomat who had acquired a thorough knowledge of Indochinese affairs in Saigon but had remained up to that point confined to a technical role. He soon affirmed his vigorous and imaginative personality and was called upon to play a key role in the Foreign Ministry after leaving Geneva.

The first indications from Geneva, on the day of his election, were very favorable to the new head of government. The correspondent of *Le Monde* spoke of an "enormous sensation" and of "passionate interest." Everyone, he added, "expects a renewal of the conference" thanks to the succession of Mendès France to Bidault, whose "hostility to linking military and political questions put a brake on the progress of the conference."

But despite Bidault's hidden agenda, his indecision, and his lack of realism (characterized by Raymond Aron as "somnambulistic"), the first six weeks of talks had left for the new French negotiator certain accomplishments. The official conference had produced hardly any tangible results, except in the last few days, when Chou En-lai had agreed, on June 16, that the problems of Laos and Cambodia were of a different nature from those of Vietnam and should therefore be treated according to distinct principles and procedures. This was a fundamental concession to the arguments of the West, of Phnom Penh, and of Vientiane.

For his part, as early as May 14, the Soviet minister had agreed that military problems could take priority over political ones, on condition that the two were not dissociated from one another.

Thus, on two important points—priority for a cease-fire and separate consideration of the problem of Cambodia and Laos—agreement had been vaguely sketched out. But they were far from a resolution of questions that were to appear—already had appeared to the best-informed observers—as the most important: the military (and thus provisional) division of Vietnam, and the date of the elections that were to allow the ultimate reunification of the country.

With respect to the division, on June 9, as we have seen, the Vietminh delegation had made an overture that could be considered the major event of the conference. But this offer still had only limited value, for the good reason that the French delegation had not agreed to the very principle of division, even temporary, and held officially to the arguments of Laniel and Bidault: regroupment zones in a "leopard skin" pattern. This formula signified only a military truce allowing resumption of hostilities at any moment, while division according to political criteria would require a reciprocal retreat of armed forces that would make a return to warfare much more difficult.

As for the crucial question of the line of division, it had only been touched on glancingly. During the June 9 meeting, Buu had appeared to demand Tonkin alone, which would have located the line near the eighteenth parallel. But since then Pham Van Dong's advisers had spoken of the thirteenth parallel, which changed everything. In fact, everything remained to be done in this area, and it seemed to be terribly arduous.

On the question of the time foreseen for elections to reunify Vietnam after the "provisional" division, Pham Van Dong had spoken of six months, which seemed totally unacceptable to the West. It seemed to be necessary to place the Bao Dai regime, apparently destined to be the regime of the South, in better condition to confront the electoral ordeal, that is, competition with the magical name of Ho Chi Minh.

This assessment did not encourage optimism. Everything was in process. But a preliminary clearance had been made from which emerged elements of negotiation that were useful, provided a man as determined to conclude as Pierre Mendès France took them from the hands of Georges Bidault, whose inclinations toward peace were still overborne by a desire for revenge.

There was another antithesis. While the diplomacy of Bidault was of the secret variety, based on the personal talents, the historical culture, and the network of relations of the minister, the diplomacy of Mendès France attempted to rely on public opinion, on popular aspirations for peace. Not only did the new premier speak to the French public every week on the radio, but he played on this factor in his relations with the adversary. In Geneva, the new head of government gave voice to the murmurs of the citizenry, making clear in the eyes of the world the will of France for peace.

11.
THE GENEVA RICE PADDY

On the evening of June 19, after his government had been presented to the head of state and to public opinion, when Pierre Mendès France consulted the Indochina file of which he had had until then only partial knowledge, he observed that the situation had continued to worsen in the course of the last few days. On June 18, a few hours before his own investiture, a contrary maneuver had taken place in Saigon: Bao Dai had just replaced the flexible Prince Buu Loc as prime minister with a fanatic determined to fight to the end, Ngo Dinh Diem, from whom no understanding could be expected: he did not conceal the fact that he would do everything to sabotage a compromise.

At the same time, Mendès France learned of an operation in progress that had until now been concealed from him. Named "Auvergne," it involved the evacuation of the two bishoprics of the southern Tonkin delta. This was distressing news, first of all because it improved the "war map" of the adversary negotiators, and also because it would have a tragic effect on the Catholic population. This was something that would increase the bitterness of the MRP against him, although he preserved the warm support of François Mauriac by explaining the situation.

Finally, on June 20, the new head of government learned that the leaders of the British and American delegations, Anthony Eden and General Bedell Smith, were preparing to leave Geneva. Eden, on his way through Paris, gave assurances that he would return to Geneva before the fateful date of July 20. But Smith declared that the presence of Ambassador Alexis Johnson at the head of the delegation would be enough to display the participation of the United States in the talks. This was a serious disappointment to Mendès France, since he was convinced that an American presence at the highest possible level (Bedell Smith was an undersecretary of state) would be necessary for the equilibrium of the negotiations, because the two Communist powers were represented by significant figures.

Less than a week after taking over the government, Mendès France decided to reverse direction by demonstrating how much his ideas differed from those of his predecessor. Consulting Chauvel about the benefit that might be derived from a brief preliminary contact with one of the Geneva negotiators, he was advised against a conversation with the head of the Vietminh delegation. But the ambassador—who himself had an appointment with Pham Van Dong for the twenty-second—pointed out that there would be much to be gained from a conversation with Chou En-lai, who had expressed the wish to meet the new French premier.

Since the head of the Chinese diplomatic corps could not go to Paris as long as the Peoples Republic of China was not recognized by France, and since Mendès France thought it still a little premature to enter the cycle of the conference in Geneva, they agreed to meet in Bern, on the pretext of thanking the president of the Swiss confederation for providing a site for the negotiations. The meeting was set for the afternoon of June 23, in the French Embassy.

A man of celebrated charm who, both before and after this meeting, enchanted so many visitors, negotiators, and adversaries, Chou was not yet intent on charming his interlocutors. Recently admitted into the diplomatic arena, he still often behaved as a bitter challenger, representative of a revolutionary state disdained by most of the great powers. Several observers were struck by the insulting brutality with which he treated the American delegate at Geneva, Walter Robertson, one of the men responsible for the U.S. China strategy. Chou seized every opportunity to cover him with sarcasm, reminding him of the errors of judgment made by his predecessors and colleagues about Chiang Kai-shek and about his own comrades.

However familiar Chou was with Mendès's reputation, he did not at first use a much more cordial tone than he had with the Americans; he even made a point of observing at the outset that China feared neither threats nor provocations and did not recognize them as negotiating techniques, which Mendès France knew enough not to take personally.

Having thus expressed his anger, the Chinese minister began by pointing out that, in his view, and in conformity with the wishes of France, military questions should have priority over the political aspects of the Indochina question. He then defined his government's policy with respect to each of the three countries of Indochina in such a way that Mendès France could note for the future of the negotiations that Chou had not only accepted the separation of the question of Cambodia and Laos from that of Vietnam, but also, indirectly, the existence of "two governments in Vietnam."

Chou En-lai declared that his government—like that of the Democratic Republic of Vietnam—intended to move toward recognition of the two kingdoms of Vientiane and Phnom Penh and to adopt a policy of nonintervention toward them. He even appeared to consider favorably the attachment of the three states to the French Union, "which could encourage relations between China and France," but pointed out that the respect by China and Vietnam of the independence of these countries should not lead other powers to transform them into "bases for American aggression." He added that the two royal governments should recognize the resistance movements—Khmers Issarahs and Pathet Lao—with the latter even being granted a zone of administrative control.

Mendès France, who sensed that Ambassador Chauvel was as pleased as he was with the direction of the conversation, began by recalling that he had, from the beginning, expressed his preference for bilateral proceedings, a choice that was amply justified by the present conversation. Then he asked Chou En-lai if he, too, was indeed in favor of the formula of military regroupment in "very large areas" (meaning a division of the country).

At first very circumspect on the question, the Chinese minister declared himself in favor of "large sectors" as well, asking whether his interlocutor had "concrete ideas on the subject." To this the French premier responded prudently that it was a question of "a horizontal division" that the spokesman of the Vietminh located, it appeared, "farther south than the actual situation would justify." In any event, he pointed out, this was "the problem which was much more important than any others." Chou agreed. Then, without the slightest appearance of irony in his expression, he voiced the wish that the military negotiators could find a basis for agreement within three weeks so that they, the politicians, could meet again usefully in Geneva.

Three weeks; that was July 15. Mendès France considered it a little discourteous to be thereby trapped between this meeting and his own deadline of one month. He realized that, although by setting July 20 as a limit he had had a great effect in Paris, he was perhaps not taken seriously enough by the opposing parties.

Before taking his leave, the Chinese diplomat expressed the hope that Mendès France would soon meet his friend Pham Van Dong. The head of the French government recalled that "Ambassador Chauvel had spoken again with Mr. Dong the day before" and that he did in fact intend, as he had often said, to establish direct contact with the representative of the Vietminh.

With that, the two negotiators separated, agreeing that they had "understood" one another "well." Landing that evening in Paris, Mendès France told the press that one could look on the remainder of the conference "with optimism." What Chauvel had told him about his first official private conversation with Pham Van Dong did not in any way contradict his conversation in Bern. Agreement no longer seemed beyond a reasonable grasp, on condition that the price of peace was clearly established and the means were brought together to pay only that price. The next day, June 24, the premier, meeting with General Ely, who had returned for a few days from Saigon; Guy La Chambre, new minister of associated states; Alexandre Parodi, general secretary of the Foreign Ministry; and Jean Chauvel, was able to establish once and for all the broad outlines of his diplomatic strategy in Geneva.

Jean Chauvel, having pointed out that the military division of Vietnam was inevitable, obtained General Ely's acquiescence. It was agreed that the eighteenth parallel, at the level of the "gate of Annam," would be the ideal solution, for military as well as political reasons, but that it might be necessary to compromise. As for the date of subsequent elections, the ambassador expressed the hope that everyone would be satisfied to accept the principle—which was rather optimistic. Guy La Chambre pointed out they could no longer confront Bao Dai and his supporters with *faits accomplis* and that they had to organize a better system of mutual communication or else they would be faced by serious misunderstandings. Mendès considered this quite pertinent. As for General Ely, he emphasized the threats weighing on the expeditionary force in a period of withdrawal and thus the necessity of placing it in a state of "supreme security"—which implied sending draftees to Indochina, something already considered by Mendès.

He asked Chauvel:

"Is that your opinion?"

"Yes, the announcement of such a decision would have interesting effects. And the time we have at our disposal is so short that only a few people would in fact be moved."

"But wouldn't it be simply banging our fist on the table?" objected the premier. "Wouldn't the effects on the diplomatic level be the opposite of what we wish?"

And turning toward General Ely:

"Couldn't we reestablish an airlift to Indochina to send reinforcements taken instead from among professional soldiers?"

The general suggested that the two kinds of measures could go together, and he insisted on the idea that the Indochina army should feel the support of the country and that nothing could be a more concrete expression of that support than sending, even in limited numbers, units of draftees.

"I will, then, assume my responsibilities," concluded Mendès France. "The difficulties will be great before the Parliament. But I will pose the problem at the next meeting of the Committee of National Defense, next Monday."

Choice of an *objective:* division, at least provisional; choice of a *procedure:* dialogue with the Vietminh, in the framework of the Geneva conference; choice of a *pressure tactic:* the possible sending of draftees. Thus was defined the policy of the Mendès France government—at twenty-six days from the deadline the premier had set for himself.

"We could come to a conclusion in about ten days," Pham Van Dong declared amiably to Chauvel on June 25. But the next day, in a conversation characterized as "official and secret," and which everyone in the French delegation expected to be even more important than that of June 9, the French military negotiators were terribly disturbed. From the outset, their negotiating partners Ta Quang Buu and Ha Van Lau complained that the Vietnamese delegation was not treated on the same footing as the Chinese delegation and that it had not even met in Geneva with a representative of ministerial rank. Then they entered into the heart of the matter by proposing to trace the "provisional border" slightly to the north of the thirteenth parallel, along "Colonial Route 19." The French officers were startled; they could not imagine that between the two propositions there would be six hundred kilometers and four million inhabitants. At this point, General Delteil could only observe: "In these conditions, the negotiations are hopeless."

Why this sudden hardening? It can be attributed to the reputation the right-wing press had given to Mendès France as a simple "liquidator," ready to concede everything in order to reach agreement, to "win his bet," and also to the evacuation of the Tonkin bishoprics, which revealed to the Vietminh the weakness of French resources around the eighteenth parallel. Since in any event the French army would cede these territories on its own to the Vietminh, why not demand more in negotiations? In short, this whole phase of the negotiations was dominated less by the participants, their intentions, and their initiatives than by what the spokesman of the Vietminh called with insidious irony the "fluidity of the military situation."

Moreover, it was possible to measure here the relative lack of realism of Mendès France's argument in favor of direct negotiations with the

Vietminh. Confronting these spokesmen of an army puffed up by its victories, the French negotiators needed this dialogue to be set in a pluralist framework—bringing together not only their allies but also those of the Vietminh, the Chinese as well as the Soviets. It appeared, in the course of the conference, that it was the "advice," in fact the heavy and insistent pressure of Moscow and Peking, that forced Ho Chi Minh and his comrades to accept concessions they had not anticipated agreeing to.

What were the reasons for this pressure? Reflecting on these questions a quarter-century later with Pierre Mendès France, we came to the following conclusions. On the Soviet side, there appeared to be a sort of permanent, though unwritten rule: never treat two affairs simultaneously. At the time, it was Europe and the CED that interested them. Shortly before, they had convinced the Chinese to cut their losses in Korea and wished to stop them in Indochina, hoping that this "feather" for French diplomacy would incite it to be "reasonable" about the CED. On the Chinese side, Taiwan was then the major preoccupation.

And also, more broadly, there was a fear of the organization around them, on the basis of the neighboring states, of an American *cordon sanitaire,* the establishment of a system of bases on the continent and the neighboring islands that would encircle them. For them, the prolongation of the conflict involved heavy threats of this kind. They had gotten wind of the discussion of Operation Vulture. During the conversation in Bern, Chou En-lai had more than alluded to the refusal of his country to accept the installation of foreign bases in Cambodia or Laos. Thus, the end of the war, under conditions such that the Americans would not wish to intervene or prepare a counterattack—and perhaps such that Vietnam would not come out too strengthened—was a reasonable objective for Peking.

In short, at the conclusion of the bitter meeting with the Vietminh, the French negotiators had grounds for raising questions, but not for despair. It was that evening, when he had just learned from Chauvel in Geneva of the stiffening of the Vietminh, that Mendès France inaugurated the series of his Saturday radio talks that were to establish ties between him and public opinion warm enough to exasperate the majority of the political class.

> My intention is not to give you major news or to announce important decisions to you. . . . Decisions . . . I must present first to Parliament. No, the principal object of this talk is to tell you of my intention to address you regularly. . . .
> You can feel very close solidarity with a government which promises only what it believes it can deliver, but which is bringing about what it has announced. Tomorrow, Sunday, will be a day of rest for you, a rest which I will not yet be able to share this week. I ask you not to let this Sunday pass

without having thought, at least for a few minutes, about the appeal I have just made to you about the help that each one of you should offer me.

This tone of rather insistent confidentiality did not please everyone. But it located the bold enterprise of the head of government in a climate of stubborn confidence capable of impressing the other participants in the negotiations. The same tone suffuses the letter he sent to Jean Chauvel on July 2:

> We recognize all the obstacles you confront and we are happy that you are not growing weary, in spite of the uncertainties and the complexities of the negotiations. It seems to me, as to you, that for the moment we have to "hold on" without revealing excessive enervation or impatience. It is obvious that our interlocutors are speculating on the July 20 deadline. They think that we are pressed. That is true, but not to the point of accepting anything at all (for example, the thirteenth parallel). I am not disturbed, consequently, by the difficulties of the past few days nor by the de facto break that has resulted. At the worst, we will resume that on the twelfth, perhaps even later. On the night of the nineteenth everyone will finally lay down his cards!

The game would be played in a few hours, but the cards would be distributed between now and then. The disappointing dialogue with the Vietminh on June 26 had not been useless: it had particularly allowed the French negotiators to measure the importance of a tightening of alliances at the hour of decision. It did not appear as a demonstration of the superiority of the procedure of the conference over that of bilateral conversations, but rather as a reminder of the multifarious character of any negotiation and of the necessity that any policy be based upon the realities.

A tightening of alliances? Although it slightly startled the Americans, while on the other hand encouraging the British, Mendès France's imaginative boldness contributed to this result. The agreement reached between Eisenhower and Churchill in Washington on June 29 had a very Mendésist basis. It contained the following points, on which the two allies of France conditioned their approval of the solution that would be negotiated by the head of the French government in Geneva.

1. Preserve the integrity and the independence of Laos and Cambodia by assuring the withdrawal of Vietminh forces from the two countries.

2. Preserve at least the southern half of Vietnam and, if possible, an enclave in the delta, with the demarcation line not located south of Dong Hoi (north of the seventeenth parallel).

3. Impose neither on Cambodia, nor on Laos, nor on the southern part of Vietnam any restrictions on their ability to maintain stable non-Communist regimes—notably on their right to dispose of sufficient forces for internal security, to import arms, and to call upon foreign advisers.

4. Contain no political clause of a kind that would bring about the loss to the Communists of the preserved zones.

5. Do not exclude the possibility of an eventual unification of Vietnam through peaceful means.

6. Allow the movement, in humane and peaceful conditions and under international control, of all those who would like to go from one zone of Vietnam to the other.

7. Make provision for an effective system of international control.

Pierre Mendès France could not have read this astonishing text without satisfaction, since it prefigured the agreements of the following month. It hardly differed from the instructions given to Jean Chauvel on June 24 and amounted to an acceptance by Washington of the principle of division—less exigent than the French arguments with respect to the demarcation line between North and South. It therefore offered rather extensive room for maneuvering to the French negotiator and allowed him to turn to the Bao Dai leaders and have them accept—with American support—the indispensable concessions.

Thus Mendès realized that American diplomacy was not hostile to him, whatever may have been the suspicions maintained, through a well-orchestrated campaign, by a certain number of "French specialists" in the State Department, notably Douglas MacArthur, Jr., the general's nephew, admirer of Bidault and advocate for Operation Vulture. Why should he not attempt to associate Washington more closely with the negotiation, try to persuade John Foster Dulles himself that what he, Mendès, was looking for was peace, not capitulation?

The two men finally met in Paris on July 13. Handling with dexterity the English he had perfected in twenty international monetary conferences, the premier immediately focused the attack on the point of primary interest to him: the dispatch of a high-ranking American personage to Geneva.

"We want above all to avoid appearing to abandon France," said Dulles. "The reason I have come to Paris is to show the opposing side that there is no misunderstanding between us. And then to convince you that the best role that we Americans have to play in Geneva is that of the 'wicked partner' of modest rank."

"But do you know that the absence of an American minister in

Geneva delights the delegations from the East? Do you know that the mere announcement of your arrival in Paris has sown confusion among them? Your presence in Geneva would strengthen the West's position."

"In any event," grumbled Dulles, "what you sign in Geneva will be bad. We do not want, by our presence, to encourage a new Yalta."

"But," retorted Mendès, "we want your presence precisely so that the agreement will not be bad! So that it will conform to your seven points of June 29."

Then the head of the French government took a map, unfolded it, and, pen in hand, asked the secretary of state to consider it carefully:

"This is already where they went to draw the demarcation line, there, near Faifo. And this is where we hope to end up. There, very near the eighteenth parallel."

"What? Isn't the map upside down?" said Dulles, taken aback. "I don't understand. Your line is farther north than mine. You're asking for more than we are?"

Mendès France could not suppress a smile: on certain points, the French plan was more demanding than the Anglo–American one (which does not at all imply that it was more judicious).

An appointment was made for the next day at the Foreign Ministry to work out the terms of the communiqué. But they did not take leave of one another before Dulles had made the anticipated promise: if his health did not make it impossible, General Walter Bedell Smith would represent the American government during the last phase of the Geneva conference. Thereby announcing to Mendès that he had won his point, the secretary of state added with a grimace that lengthened his face: "This guy is terrific!"

The next morning Mendès France sent Dulles a letter noting the recognition by the secretary of state of the "primary right of France and the Associated States to decide the conditions of settlement of a war in which they are the only belligerents on the non-Communist side." The Franco–American memorandum drawn up on his return from the Bastille Day ceremonies stipulated that the United States would adopt toward a "respectable" agreement an attitude analogous to "that imposed by a commitment deriving from the United Nations Charter"—which was, in American terminology, very strong, and powerfully validated the position of the French negotiator in Geneva.

Two days later, in Geneva, Mendès received a still more comforting letter from Dulles:

> I admire and respect the rectitude with which you approach the vital problems that confront us today. Indecision is the worst of evils, and you have done a great deal to dissipate it. At the moment when you are going to have to make historic decisions in Geneva, you should know that all the many

friends of France are supporting you with their prayers. And I am happy that we have found a way in which, without, I hope, any violation of our principles and without risk of subsequent misunderstanding, we may clearly demonstrate in Geneva the support that we bring to you.

From that point on in Geneva, time was measured not in days but in hours. At the end of June, everyone except Pham Van Dong had left to deal with other matters or to consult with his government, but because Mendès's challenge was finally taken seriously, everyone had decided to return to Geneva ten days or so before the fateful hour. Molotov returned on the eighth, and Eden was expected on the twelfth. Chou En-lai, after an extensive trip to Asia that had allowed him to speak with Ho Chi Minh, landed on the tenth. This was the day that Mendès France chose to engage the battle. But it was Saturday: before leaving he had to address the country.

"In a moment, I am going to leave my office in the Foreign Ministry to take the plane for Geneva. This evening, I will meet there the minister of foreign affairs of the Soviet Union, Mr. Molotov."

One cannot fail to note how much a man addressing his fellow citizens in this tone of warm candor would gain by this informing public opinion. By speaking of his desire for peace, recalling that three days earlier he had informed the Assembly of the measures taken to send draftees to Indochina should the negotiations fail, even by expressing his doubts about the outcome, and finally by addressing the young people of the country, he added to his undertaking a little more popular support.

His conversation with Molotov went directly to the heart of the matter: the division, and hence the location of the border. Pierre Mendès France argued strongly for the eighteenth parallel, in conformity "with reason, the laws of geography, and the interests of everyone."

But Molotov objected that the Democratic Republic of Vietnam had controlled several provinces south of the eighteenth parallel since the beginning of the war. Mendès retorted:

> The present situation is less important than the political balance to be established. What is needed is to draw the line least likely to provoke frictions, that is, the shortest line possible. And that is close to the eighteenth parallel. And we should not forget this: we will have to have all the participants in the conference accept the agreement. It is hardly likely that all nine can come to an agreement on another line.

The Soviet minister seemed interested but not convinced. Refusing to commit himself further in an area where he sensed that his interlocutor was better informed than he, he shifted to the subject of Europe, indicating that he would be happy to discuss with the French premier questions going beyond those under discussion in Geneva. This appeared to be a hint of the "global bargaining" the idea of which Bidault had rejected even before it was proposed to him (abandonment of the CED by Paris in exchange for a "good" peace in Indochina). Mendès France cut him short, putting off until later any subject other than Indochina and speaking of an order of urgent questions.

On the morning of July 11, Mendès France was able to discuss the latest developments with his entire team: Chauvel, Cheysson, Folin, Delteil, and Brebisson.

Ambassador Chauvel reported on his conversation of the day before with Pham Van Dong, who was scheduled to visit the head of the French government the next day. He had found him very cordial, but at the same time his military colleagues were more unyielding than ever. In any event, the climate was rather good. And Mendès France reminded his colleagues that he would steadfastly use the threat of sending draftees to Indochina in case of failure. To substantiate the threat, young recruits in Marseille had for the last week been inoculated against Asian diseases.

On July 11, the private conversation between Mendès France and Pham Van Dong finally took place. When he got out of his car, Pham Van Dong seemed in the grip of unbearable emotion, as though he were suffocating. He seemed, according to Claude Cheysson, "almost incapable of speaking, so greatly did the physical sensation of an historic moment grasp him by the throat." But he quickly recovered. Mendès France was hardly less sensitive to the symbolic value of the meeting as he watched Pham Van Dong approach on the lawn beneath the trees.

The Vietminh minister of foreign affairs had barely anything more to say than he had to Chauvel the day before, or than his military colleagues had to General Delteil the day before that. In personal terms, the contact was good. But on the essential, Mendès France observed that his interlocutor was not accommodating: in answer to his argument for a division at the eighteenth parallel, Pham was content to point out that his military colleagues had just made a concession by proposing to move "their" line from the thirteenth to the fourteenth parallel. And with respect both to the time for evacuating French forces and to the methods of regrouping, the Vietminh minister made arguments further from French proposals than those he had recently made to Chauvel.

The next day, for the second time, Pierre Mendès France met Chou En-lai, who had returned from Asia. This led the French premier to ask if his conversation with "Uncle Ho" had been fruitful. "I have found among all those I have spoken to an equal desire for peace," answered Chou, with a placid smile.

Like Molotov two days earlier, the Chinese diplomat immediately directed the conversation toward the question of the demarcation line in Vietnam. "Why not demonstrate good will?" he said in a gentle tone. To which Mendès, full of a subject that he had been furiously working at for several days, answered by repeating his argument, by now in very good form, in favor of the eighteenth parallel. "Look at the map. You object that the Vietminh control a zone situated between the thirteenth and the sixteenth parallels? But we control provinces located between the sixteenth and the eighteenth. So that, if we accept a break at the fourteenth or fifteenth parallel, the Communists will receive nationalist regions, and the nationalists Communist provinces."

Chou En-lai listened impassively and resumed: "It is nevertheless necessary that each of the two parties take a few steps toward the other," and he added: "That does not mean that each one has to take the same number of steps." There is every reason to think that, however ambiguous it may have been, this second conversation between Chou and Mendès was at the origin of the evolution of the position of the Vietminh, who on the thirteenth accepted the possibility of a division "near the sixteenth parallel."

That day, or perhaps a little later, occurred the episode of the *petits suisses*. Chou and Mendès had lunch together at the residence of the French delegation. At the end of the meal, for local color, they were served the little pieces of cheese wrapped in the fine paper that traditionally covers them. The Chinese prime minister stuck one, paper included, into his mouth, then another. Western food is bizarre. Everyone looked at Mendès. Stoically, he too swallowed the little packaged cheese, immediately imitated by the entire delegation. A Vietnamese parallel is clearly worth one Mass.[1]

12.
SIX DAYS THAT REASSURED THE WORLD

Late in the afternoon of July 15, Pierre Mendès France landed for the second time in Geneva, strengthened by his "American" success in Paris and accompanied by the very friendly and comforting Eden. But on the shores of the lake things had hardly moved forward. In his absence, the conference was nothing but a complicated ballet around a body of water, a ballet made up almost entirely of pas de deux. But that day, one of them prevailed over all the others: the one began after dinner at the French residence by Pierre Mendès France and Vyacheslav Molotov.

Once dinner was over, the two men crossed the lawn to a table under the lime trees. Between them were a red lamp, a map of Indochina, and the interpreter. Grouped in the salon of the villa, their respective colleagues followed from a distance a conversation that was evidently interrupted by long silences.

"Mr. Molotov has an extraordinary capacity for silence," said Mendès many years later. "He can, I think, remain for hours without speaking. Which is, for his interlocutor, rather painful. I had presented my arguments to him, he sat there, smoking one cigarette after another, without replying. It was exhausting." Molotov did not get up until one-thirty, after more than three hours of this strange tête-à-tête.

Nothing creative came from these silences around the scarlet lamp in a swarm of mosquitos that the cool air coming from the lake did little to dispense. The visitor patiently maintained that the sixteenth parallel would be the best border, allowing for "special arrangements" for Colonial Route 9 from southern Vietnam to Laos. There seemed to be no cracks in this rock of courteous certainties.

"This conversation produced no concrete results," Jean Chauvel cabled to the Foreign Ministry one hour later. But when one of Mendès France's colleagues met a member of the Soviet delegation the next day and referred to the conversation with a touch of bitterness, his interlocutor looked startled and replied that, for his part, his minister was "enchanted" by his contact with the French premier.

In any event, that evening, July 16, the two men met again along with Anthony Eden to clarify the situation by comparing their respective memoranda summarizing the positions of the two camps on all points. The head of the French government pointed out the divergences on the demarcation line, with two parallels still separating the parties. Then he came to another subject of disagreement, the date of elections, noting that the latest Soviet plan proposed the end of 1955 as a date. For his part, he judged that it would be better not to set a deadline but rather to have a multiparty authority set the date according to the situation.

The Soviet minister insisted that a date be set for the Vietnamese elections, and he returned to the question of the demarcation line, insisting on the magnitude of the concession made by the Vietminh, who—according to him, but nothing of the kind had yet been formulated by the principally interested parties—had withdrawn from the thirteenth to the sixteenth parallel, and recalling that this line had been drawn in 1945 to separate the Kuomintang and British "zones of influence" after the Japanese surrender.

Late in the afternoon of the seventeenth, when the Vietminh delegation was again at the French residence, it was remembered that it was Saturday, the day of the premier's weekly radio talk. The microphones were there. Mendès went into the next room, partly to read and partly to improvise the most moving of his messages to the nation.

> I am speaking to you tonight from the villa on Geneva's lake that the press has described to you. At this very moment, our consultations and discussions are going on in the next room. I have asked my interlocutors to be kind enough to excuse me for a few minutes so that I might speak to you. For whatever may be the outcome of this conference, every French citizen should know, as clearly as possible, what may have been the reasons for success or, in case of misfortune, the causes of failure.
>
> It is no longer so much a question of work as it is one of will. I have no doubt that all the delegations now meeting in Geneva desire peace—and I

mean all of them. After many exchanges of views with the leaders of each one of them, this is a conclusion that I have reached. There is no one here, I am convinced of it, who is a saboteur of peace; there exists nowhere a will to fail or to create failure. However, the wish to conclude, however universal it may be, is not enough.

I would like to name the enemy, the great enemy, against which I have always fought. It is called lack of trust. Among the men who are seeking peace here together, one can recognize a profound and painful mistrust, which you can understand only with difficulty unless you have experienced it directly. It is the heaviest burden weighing on our labors, it is the most serious threat, present and future, against the preservation of peace. Now, I am going to return to the room next to this one from which I am speaking to you. I am going to rejoin my interlocutors, who this evening, like me, I am sure, have the intense feeling that they carry the hopes of men, of the men who are fighting, and of whom we think with affection, and also of all the men and all the women whose life and happiness for years will depend on the result of our negotiations. As for me, the fact that I have come into your homes at the dinner hour when you are gathered with your children around the family table, after the work, the cares, and the anxieties of the week, the fact that I have come close to you just for a moment will give me a still stronger conviction that I am speaking in the name of all of you in the final and, I assure you, difficult effort I have yet to make.

And, in spite of the obstacles that remain, I hope with all my heart, with all my energy, with all my will, that within three days, mistrust will in the end have been weaker than peace.

The next morning, Sunday, July 18, the delegations were called into plenary session at the Palais des Nations at Molotov's request. What did the Soviets want? In fact, Copresident Molotov said nothing that was not approved by his counterpart Eden, and even by the American delegate Bedell Smith, who had finally arrived two days earlier. But suddenly an unexpected delegate, Tran Van Do, minister of foreign affairs in the Diem cabinet, rose and, in a restrained but pressing tone, in a voice constricted by emotion, registered a solemn protest against the division of his country and the manner in which "they" were determining the fate of the Vietnamese. The relief provoked by the benign tone of Molotov's speech was so profound that no one paid much attention to the touching intervention of Bao Dai's minister.

That Sunday evening, Pierre Mendès France felt possessed by a kind of lassitude. To be sure, his colleagues told him that Radio Peking, monitored an hour earlier, was speaking of imminent agreement. But so many things remained to be settled. He wrote to Edgar Faure, who was acting premier during his absence from Paris:

I am attempting to put off the date of elections for as long as possible. Needless to say, on this point our adversaries are particularly stiff, and they have substantial aid and support, even among the neutral powers. On the whole, we have been deadlocked for three days and—without really believing it—I sometimes wonder whether we are going to fail in sight of the harbor.

Only forty-eight hours to go.

The next afternoon he was summoned by General Bedell Smith. There appeared to be a new difficulty between Paris and Washington. First of all, Ngo Dinh Diem, head of the Bao Dai government, had just informed the U.S. ambassador in Saigon that, if he received the slightest American support, he was ready to oppose the pending agreements and to renounce all Vietnamese commitments to France. Moreover, informed of the latest proposed agreements, Dulles had just expressed sharp irritation, declaring that they were incompatible with the "seven points" of June 29, and denouncing as particularly inadmissible the proposed "neutralization" of Cambodia and Laos and the participation of a representative from the Socialist camp on the Control Commission overseeing the agreements. "A Communist cannot be a neutral," he grumbled.

The final bargaining took place on the morning of the twentieth. Pham Van Dong had returned, and then Eden and Molotov. The Soviet minister was tired and obviously intent on coming to a conclusion. Mendès France sensed that, with all his force, Molotov would incline toward peace in the final hours, the peace he had glimpsed when he made his wager on June 17. He still had to convince Chou En-lai to work in the same direction, for a favorable settlement. And it was with Chou that he had his last lunch in Geneva, a lunch that lasted past four in the afternoon.

The role of the Chinese minister had, in fact, constantly grown since the day in June when he had saved the conference by declaring that the questions of Laos and Cambodia would be treated separately and differently. A little rigid on his arrival in Geneva at the end of April, he had since then developed increasing ease and authority. He did not have the fire of Pham Van Dong or the formidable immobility of Molotov, but a kind of superior sociability, vigorous charm, and active lucidity. He was not very agitated and intervened only at decisive moments; then he appeared the implacable heir of an ancient diplomatic technique.

In any event, his intentions appeared favorable enough so that the French negotiator tried to persuade him to put further pressure on his Vietminh comrades on the subject of the demarcation line and the date of elections. The Chinese diplomat was thinking especially, and more and more, of avoiding any possibility of the establishment of American bases in one of the kingdoms on his border, Laos or Cambodia. And why not impose their neutralization? Mendès replied that such a formula would be too contrary to the Anglo–American "seven points" and to the objectives of the West. In the end they astutely agreed on a more modest formula: the only alliances forbidden to the states of Indochina would be those considered "contrary to the United Nations Charter."

With this important concession made, Chou En-lai accompanied Mendès France to the seat of the French delegation, where they were to meet with Eden and Molotov in an effort to persuade Pham Van Dong to move the demarcation line one step higher and to delay the date of the elections.

A visitor who had entered unannounced the large common room of the villa a little before five would have recognized with some surprise, shoulder to shoulder, in a scene resembling an improvised country party with chairs in disarray around a large family table, Eden, Molotov, Chou, and Mendès surrounding Pham Van Dong, who was dripping with sweat over a map of Indochina, with a sorrowful, almost haggard face: kilometer by kilometer, Communist Vietnam was shrinking northward. And Molotov, impassive, was still waiting for the moment to interject into the discussion his compromise solution.

It was clearly apparent that he had long believed that he would settle the debate between the Vietminh demand (the thirteenth parallel) and Mendès's (the eighteenth) modified by the Anglo–American "seven points" and the suggestions of General Ely, who envisaged locating the line at the seventeenth parallel, by proposing the sixteenth. The Soviet minister was intent on playing the role of arbitrator and wise man. Chou En-lai had made Pham Van Dong retreat by three parallels: he would ask Ho Chi Minh's representative for only one, but the most important one. And so, on July 20, at around five o'clock, Molotov suddenly said: "Let us agree on the seventeenth parallel."

Eden and Mendès exchanged a rapid glance: the seventeenth parallel was within twenty-five kilometers of what had been proposed in the Anglo–American memorandum of June 29, adopted in the Paris conversation of July 14 as the Western plan of settlement. They were approaching the goal. The head of the French government could hardly find arguments to reject Molotov's offer, especially since Pham Van Dong now had the air of a man from whom nothing more could be extracted, even by a Russian, except his last breath.

But thus crucified on the question of the division, the Vietminh negotiator, as though in an outburst of defiance, became inflexible on the date of elections that were to assure the reunification of his country, which had been torn apart that evening by his own hands. Mendès and his colleagues had tried to avoid fixing a date, while Pham Van Dong had spoken of six months. Now, he demanded a year, or eighteen months.

Molotov: "Suppose we said two years?" Mendès France could only agree, while Eden no longer even attempted to conceal his satisfaction: Molotov was too kind.

It was five-twenty. The rumor spread quickly: agreement had been reached! Then what? It only remained to prepare the formal session in the Palais des Nations. A simple formality? It would be too easy to forget that, although a "Vietnamese" settlement had been reached, peace in Indochina, including Laos and Cambodia, had only been begun—six hours before the deadline.

The journalists were assembled in the press room of the Palais des Nations when it was announced that the final session would be delayed for a few hours. At eight o'clock, the French delegation had received a call from Eden: "Molotov has called and he is furious. Sam Sary, in the name of the Cambodian delegation, has informed the great powers that he will not sign. Cambodia? he said. What has possessed them to put everything in question *now?* And first of all, what on earth is Cambodia?" Eden continued: "Molotov is incensed. He is convinced that it's an American maneuver, either to sabotage the agreements or to extract *in extremis* the Socialist camp's acceptance of the establishment of a U.S. air force base in Cambodia. He has demanded an immediate meeting of the delegation heads. Come to my residence as soon as possible."

A half-hour later, Sam Sary, head of the Phnom Penh delegation, confronted four of the five great powers of world diplomacy. (Bedell Smith was ill and unable to attend).

"I will not sign a text that restricts the freedom of my country. What is the meaning of denying, on the pretext that it might not conform to the UN Charter, the right to establish Western bases in our country? We want to have all means at our disposal to defend ourselves against communism."

"But don't you see that you are calling into question peace in Indochina, in Asia, in the world?"

"I am not like the others, I am not afraid of communism or of the great powers."

The little man remained intractable. Word was sent to Bedell Smith. He was obviously angered and sent an emissary to Sam Sary: "Your country will be defended in all circumstances. We are preparing a Southeast Asian defense pact. And Mr. Dulles has given his agreement to the proposed treaty."

There was nothing to be done, and time was running out. At eleven o'clock, in the hall of the Palais des Nations, illuminated as though for a celebration, the journalists, the experts, and the merely curious were beginning to wonder whether the "wager on peace" had really been won.

Only three-quarters of an hour remained, and none of the delegations had yet arrived. It was past midnight when two or three French diplomats passed through, looking exasperated. "The Cambodian refuses to sign. We are looking for a compromise. We hope to be able to initial the preliminary agreements by two o'clock." But what of the Mendès government? They looked at the clocks: they still registered midnight. Someone had had the idea of stopping them.

In the meanwhile, Sam Sary was in the process of winning the battle. The challenge he had presented to the great powers had finally impressed Molotov, who had understood that the little Khmer was not speaking for anyone else but was fighting as a sensitive nationalist "on his own account."

A formula had to be found to come to a conclusion. What Sam Sary wanted, Molotov was told, was to preserve the freedom to call on a power other than France with a view to establishing bases for the defense of Cambodia. "Bases? Impossible, impossible." Molotov was adamant. "But one might consider certain forms of common defense. Suppose it were said that Cambodia could call for external aid in case of a particular threat, a danger?"

It was a little past two o'clock. Sam Sary, feverishly flipping through his file, said without joking that he had seventeen further demands to present. But the concession that the intractable Molotov had made was such that he could only acquiesce and promise to sign "in the course of the morning." He had won a considerable point. Who could have foreseen that the Russians and the Chinese would accept an American intervention in Cambodia in the event of some unspecified "danger"?

"So," said Molotov, "I hope that everyone is satisfied, now?" Mendès France raised his hand. "I have something to add." "What? More!" "Yes: it is impossible not to grant to Laos what has just been granted to Cambodia. It would be simple justice." The Soviet minister made a sort of heavy grimace. And then brusquely, at the end of his tether: "All right, for Laos as well."

A horseshoe table had been set up in the great hall of the Palais. It was three-twenty. Only the military were called on to sign, since the texts had to do with the cessation of hostilities. The political figures would meet the next day to approve the general agreement. Ta Quang Buu, signatory of the cease-fire agreement for the Vietminh, stood up, glowing, and turned toward his counterpart, General Delteil. "Now, *mon général,* you will agree to take a glass of champagne with us?" The head of the French military commission, livid, rose in turn: "You will understand that I cannot accept."

In the halls and corridors, the atmosphere was effervescent, mingling the seriousness of some with the pleasure of others. The French delegation held an improvised press conference on the conditions under which the cease-fire would enter into force, while the American delegation distributed a brief communiqué which spoke, without ambiguity, of "progress made toward peace."

When everyone, exhausted and feverish, left the Palais des Nations, it was already dawn of July 21. It was now time to set the clocks running again.

The next day there would be no more fighting in the rice paddies. The Indochina war was over.

That evening, although it was not a Saturday, Pierre Mendès France decided to broadcast a message to the French, his voice stern with seriousness:

> Reason and peace have won the day. The cease-fire agreement has been signed. In a few hours, I will present its contents to the National Assembly. But you already know the essential clauses, and you know that there are some that are cruel for the faithful friends of France in Indochina and for ourselves. In my heart and soul, I am certain that these conditions are the best that we could hope for in the current state of affairs.
>
> Let us think together of those who will unfortunately not return, of those who have been wounded in flesh and spirit. I do not need to express the feelings I am experiencing, for they are your own.

If he had had any momentary doubts about the reactions of public opinion, the next day's press reassured him. The readers of *Le Figaro,* not always predisposed in his favor, read the following in the July 21 editorial: "M. Mendès France has labored well for the country in Geneva." No less suspicious of Mendès, *L'Aurore* asserted: "The country will be grateful to Pierre Mendès France for his superior conduct of the negotiations to the conclusion desired by the National Assembly."

It goes without saying that, under the circumstances, nothing was more important to the head of the government than the army's reaction. On his return to Paris on the twenty-second, he found a letter from Marshal Juin that said a great deal in a few sentences:

> Mister President, allow me to tell you how much I rejoice, for the army and the country, over the decisions that have been made in Geneva. We owe them to your tenacity and to your particular tactic of establishing a short time limit for the solution. . . . You may rest assured that the country will be grateful to you.

Even more eloquent was the approval given by General Ely, the man who would be principally responsible for implementing the agreements, who wrote a few days later to his minister, Guy La Chambre:

I have followed, with an interest you will understand, the very difficult and delicate negotiations that Premier Mendès France and you have conducted in Geneva and that have come up with results the value of which I am in a particularly good position to recognize. . . .

This is why I allow myself to express to you, as well as to M. Mendès France, the feelings of gratitude of all those who, understanding the interests of France in Southeast Asia and the role it should play there, and also understanding the difficulties of the negotiations that had to be conducted, have grasped all the meaning and the implications of the agreements that have just been signed.[1]

There remained the parliamentary test. The negotiator faced it on July 22, in a climate of comprehension beyond what he had dared hope. "I would not like anyone to have any illusions about the content of the agreements that have just been signed in Geneva. The text is sometimes cruel, because it registers cruel facts. It was not possible to do otherwise." Thus, Pierre Mendès France, facing the national Assembly, presented the Geneva agreements to the country. With even more vigor than some of his political adversaries, he pointed out what prevented him from considering the agreement as a national success and was content with observing that he was deriving the least unpleasant consequences from a situation that was deplorable in every respect.

Despite the partially pertinent criticisms of Raymond Donne (who had been with General Leclerc during the first attempt at coexistence with the Vietminh in 1946) and of Georges Bidault,[2] who vainly attempted to demonstrate that the Geneva agreements imposed a veritable neutralization on the three associated states of Indochina in opposition to their interests, one of the most massive majorities in the history of the Fourth Republic approved the presentation of July 22 and 23.

The agreements consisted of three cease-fire accords between the Vietminh and the "forces of the French Union," and dealing with Laos, Cambodia, and Vietnam, a final unsigned declaration by the Nine, and an exchange of letters between Pham Van Dong and Mendès France.

The "final declaration" merely registered the contents of the other texts and contained a decision on only one point, but a very important one. It fixed the date of Vietnamese elections in the month of July 1956—consultations were supposed to take place "between the competent representative authorities of the two zones beginning on July 20, 1955."[3]

But the most important text was the one on "the cessation of hostilities" in Vietnam, signed by General Delteil and Ta Quang Buu on July 21, and refined by the French and Vietminh delegates meeting in the field in Trung Gai, which provided that the cease-fire was to take effect on July 27.

To judge this agreement in reasonable terms, we should first be clear about the principle of division. If one is against that division, the text can only appear execrable. But it must be admitted that opponents of partition had become very rare since the end of June 1954. On the twenty-ninth of that month, Dulles himself, a supporter until May of retreat to the two deltas in order to prepare for the resumption of fighting, had counter-signed the "seven-point" memorandum that explicitly recommended it. Several months earlier, the highest-ranking members of the French general staff had rallied to the principle.

There remained those who were principally concerned, the Vietnamese. The attitude of rejection of division adopted by the government of Prince Buu Loc, and then by that of Ngo Dinh Diem (while Bao Dai appeared to have renounced his opposition to this solution on July 4) was certainly worthy of respect and often moving. No Vietnamese worthy of the name, nationalist or Communist, could lightly contemplate even a provisional division of his country.

But no one could have believed, in the event of an intransigent adherence to the principle of the unity of the country, that that unity, in 1954, would not come about in favor of the conquerors of Dien Bien Phu, of those who controlled, throughout the country, experienced troops and fifth columns led by political militants well trained in all the methods of molding public opinion.

If we accept the principle of division, and if we agree that it constituted the best method to attain the three major objectives of the French negotiators—to save the expeditionary force; to stop the killing; and to give a nationalist state the chance to exist and bring together Vietnamese citizens who were hostile to, or discontent under, communism under the (purely relative) shelter of a definite border—then we cannot contest the value of the results obtained by Pierre Mendès France and his colleagues.

On the question of the demarcation line, the Vietminh demanded that it be fixed at the thirteenth parallel, the French at the eighteenth. The latter obtained a compromise, as we have seen, at the seventeenth.[4] With respect to the date of elections, Pham Van Dong wanted a delay of no more than six months; Mendès (more exigent then Bidault) demanded that no date be set: he obtained two years.[5] As for the embarkation of French forces, the enemy demanded an evacuation in three months, the French asked for a year. Agreement was reached on ten months. On each occasion the balance inclined strongly on the side on which the French negotiator placed his weight.

President Eisenhower, asked to comment on the agreements at his weekly press conference on July 21, had simply declared: "I have no criticism to make against what has been done in Geneva, because I had no alternative solution to propose."

And the Vietnamese leaders? When they were asked in October 1980 to characterize Mendès France's actions concerning their country, they provided the following judgment, which cannot be described as evidencing a high degree of benevolence:

Mendès France had clearly realized that France could not in any way continue the Indochina war, and he played a positive role in the reestablishment of peace on the Indochinese peninsula in 1954. On the other hand, he arranged with China to conduct negotiations at the expense of Vietnam. After the Geneva agreements of 1954, the commitments entered into by Mendès France with respect to relations between Vietnam and France were not carried out.

As for Mendès France himself, it is appropriate to revise a legend that has been carefully fostered. If we are to believe his opponents at the time, or more recent ones, the negotiator of Geneva displayed indecent jubilation once his "wager" had been won. Everyone who was with him at the time can on the contrary testify to the harshness with which he attacked those of his friends who congratulated him on his "triumph." At the time, he never failed to retort, as he had done from the rostrum of the Chamber on July 22, that these were "painful" decisions and that it was inappropriate to rejoice at them.

Having put an end to the fighting did not liberate him from Indochinese affairs. Although fighting stopped everywhere in the succeeding days, the exchange of prisoners was carried out at Trung Gia between August 14 and September 9, the International Control Commission[6] representatives began to set themselves up starting on August 10, and the expeditionary force carried out its retreat rationally, the French authorities nevertheless had to square the circle: the dual normalization of their relations with Saigon, which demanded the *exclusivity* of state relations with France, and Hanoi, which called for *equality*.

In this instance, the "man of choice" which Mendès France was above all ("to govern is to choose") found himself involved in a political situation without a resolution, attempting on the one hand to give vigor to relations between Paris and Hanoi, where he had sent a very prominent personality, Jean Sainteny, and subject on the other to American pressure to defend the South at all costs.

An influential force in Saigon was the French representative General Ely, whom Mendès had learned to respect and who became an echo of the bitter calls to order from "nationalist" Vietnam. At the conclusion of the Geneva conference, an exchange of letters between Paris and Saigon had established that France would have diplomatic relations only with South Vietnam: it was on this condition that the Diem government had stopped sabotaging the negotiations. This was the source of the disappointing ambiguities of a policy in which imagination, which encouraged a turn to the North, the almost certain victor in the elections scheduled for 1956, contradicted fidelity to alliances, with the Americans as well as with the South Vietnamese.

All the same, Mendès France wanted to try to build a bridge, as boldly as possible, with Hanoi. On July 24, three days after the conclusion of the Geneva discussions, Jean Sainteny, an old negotiating partner of Ho Chi Minh and Pham Van Dong, signatory of the Franco–Vietminh agreements of 1946 that could have spared the two peoples a war, and a faithful Gaullist, received a telegram summoning him to Paris, where Guy La Chambre, minister in charge of Indochinese affairs, proposed to him on behalf of Mendès France that he become the representative of France in Hanoi. At first refusing to play the role of "liquidator," Sainteny nevertheless went to see De Gaulle to ask his opinion. The general said, "Do you see anyone else who could go to Hanoi?"

With this green light, Sainteny left on August 15. He was to represent, said the head of government, "continuity, not liquidation," and to occupy in Hanoi "a balcony overlooking China."[7] But no sooner had he landed in Saigon than a conversation with General Ely made it clear to him that the South would stand as a screen between Paris and Hanoi and that he would see his mission sabotaged. This is in fact what occurred.

But the pressure placed on Paris from Saigon played a lesser role than that from Washington. Although the negotiating partners of France had been informed of it in Geneva, French adhesion to the Manila pact, which established SEATO (South East Asia Treaty Organization) on September 5, 1954, did nothing to foster the chances of a constructive peace sketched out in Geneva. This was Dulles's revenge on negotiations that he had never at bottom accepted.

With the acceptance, disgruntled but genuine, by Paris and London of "his" anti-Communist pact, the American secretary of state, who, carried along as he was by Mendès France's dynamism and English encouragements, had not been able, or had not wanted, to ruin the Geneva negotiations, thereby cut off the rich political and economic developments in relation to the Communist world that Mendès and Eden had expected as a result.

The admirable negotiator of Geneva could no longer find in himself the resources of boldness that were needed to move from nonwar to peace. The man who had been able to square the circle by transforming a liquidation into a diplomatic success and an element of hope for public opinion allowed himself to be trapped in a situation that was in any event practically inextricable, between new allies who were inaccessible and old allies who were unavoidable. And the politics of Indochina that he had revolutionized seized him in its web again, would not let him go, and pushed him into unwished-for commitments and the transfer of responsibilities to Washington.

13.
BUILDING CARTHAGE

Pierre Mendès France had to some degree been carried into the Indochina conflict by the chances of history. He had found it standing before him as an obsessive obstacle that it was absolutely necessary to overcome as a prerequisite for any other efforts to reestablish the state. He had not chosen to concern himself with a country he did not know, nor with the war, particularly since he considered himself badly informed on military matters. He had simply removed a burden.

In the case of Tunisia, everything was different. This is what he had to say twenty-five years later:

> Tunisia was entirely different. I was fully convinced that what had just taken place in Indochina was the result of years of persistent mistakes, of the desire to preserve at any cost a certain colonialist conception, and I had told myself that we had to do everything to avoid the same thing happening elsewhere. Now, Tunisia was the country about which, because of the chance associations of my past, I was the best informed and the one in which—let us be frank—it was least difficult to succeed, if only because of its dimensions, its size. It was a good testing ground. If we succeeded in Tunisia, it would be a precedent. Not that we should do the same thing in Gabon or Madagascar. But we would demonstrate a spirit of gradual emancipation, a will to put an end to the spirit of domination, to the old colonialism. I knew the Tunisian situation well, I knew exactly what I wanted to do. I knew the men and the

background of the problem. We had interlocutors who spoke the same language that we did. I would say, jokingly of course, that Bourguiba would have been a very good minister in the Third Republic.

Tunisia seemed to him a privileged meeting place of East and West, a Mediterranean forum appropriate for an apprenticeship in democracy. He knew that a party of an almost modern kind, based on the idea of a constitution (Destour), out of which Bourguiba had created the Néo-Destour, was leading the country's movement toward emancipation and that the struggle had not yet taken on extreme forms.

Pierre Mendès France was not, as we have said, a militant in the vanguard of decolonization, like men whom he knew well and respected: Jean Rous, Charles-André Julien, and Claude Bourdet. He was too much the Jacobin, too much an adept of secular education, too much a disciple of Ferry not to recognize some virtues in French or European presence overseas. And his manner of proceeding in this area was always prudent, concerned with progression, stages, and ripening rather than radical breaks. The democrat and the moralist in him questioned colonization. Would he say, with Marx, that "a people that oppresses another is not free"?[1] Yes, but he would not agree with Herriot, and later De Gaulle, that it was important to "liberate France from her colonies."

In any event, in Tunisia there were people, "nationalists," who, following the example of their leader, Habib Bourguiba, were also speaking of "stages" and of "evolution." It seemed that it was in this country, small but important, where the irreparable had not occurred, that it was appropriate to attempt the experiment of contractual and gradual decolonization.

But when Mendès France came to power in June 1954, these considerations might have appeared to be too late. Tunisia was no longer the "first in the class," calmly preparing emancipation by training bilingual leaders. Since the French government, in December 1951, had peremptorily informed Tunisia that there was no question of evolution, even gradual, toward independence, and since Bourguiba had been thrown into prison for the third time on January 18, 1952, Tunisia was gradually drifting toward violence and anarchy.

The Laniel government had accomplished nothing by replacing the governor general. No one could be found among the Tunisian elite who would dare to accept any responsibility from such a compromising colonizer. The degree of statehood that the protectorate had allowed to survive collapsed in a state of inanition aggravated by sabotage. European counterterrorism, using the label of the "Red Hand," ran rampant.[2] And beneath this collapse of order there arose powerful popular anger fostered by the Néo-Destour that was disgusted with its moderation and determined to risk all.

In the countryside, in fact, the nationalist party was outflanked by spontaneously created groups devoted to direct action. Insecurity was covering the entire country, leading to a total paralysis of the government. This was all the more true because the propaganda of the Voice of the Arabs, broadcast from Cairo, mobilized the discontent, and because the most moderate opponents of France could not fail to observe that the United States was developing a policy more and more favorable to Arab emancipation, while the British were preparing to withdraw their last forces from Egypt.

Slipping into chaos and dreaming of other alliances; this was how Mendès France found the Tunisia that he had not long before seen as the pilot country for a French version of decolonization. Nothing could have seemed more necessary to him than to revive in Tunis the movement of reasonable progress the hope for which had been fostered by many official French declarations speaking of the possibility of a movement "toward independence" or of "internal independence." Mendès did not use the word. He held to, and continued to do so, the concept of "autonomy," which he might well have called, like his English friends, "self-government." He believed in union between the two countries and the necessity of very long-term links between them, once Tunisia fully enjoyed the right to govern itself.

Even while the Geneva negotiations were going on, he met twice with Governor General Voizard. From these two conversations, Mendès France drew the following conclusion: In the course of the last two years, Tunisia had fallen into a coma interrupted by more and more violent convulsions. It had to be rescued from this dreadful situation. To be sure, two and a half months earlier, the Laniel government had transferred Habib Bourguiba from a lugubrious prison on an island off the coast of Tunisia to house arrest in a hotel on an island off the coast of Brittany. But for several weeks his living conditions had again deteriorated. He was permitted no visits. The new premier and his interior minister, François Mitterrand, immediately put an end to this idiotic irritation.

But the situation under the regency remained deplorable. While Morocco, after Sultan Sidi Mohammed was deposed in August 1953, had sunk into an even more tragic state of chaos which seemed to be irreparable, Tunisia—with its phantom sovereign forgotten on the throne and its "governments" buffeted by the whims of a colonizer startled by its own tepid audacity—had shut itself up in contemptuous silence. On June 17, 1954, at the moment when the National Assembly was about to grant Mendès France the power to rid France of the Indochinese burden, the last government that Governor General Voizard had managed to form had collapsed, dead of disgust.

After that, nothing remained but a movement to repression for the sake of repression, or else negotiation with those who resisted enough to provide a solid basis on which to stand. As soon as he was invested by the Assembly, the new head of government chose the second option. His speech of candidacy of June 17, 1954, had assumed this as a duty. It would be difficult to be clearer:

> Morocco and Tunisia, to which France has opened the paths of economic, social, and political progress, must not become, on the flanks of our Algerian departments, centers of insecurity and agitation; that I will never accept.
>
> But I add with the same clarity that I will not tolerate either hesitations or reticence in the realization of promises that we have made to populations that have had faith in us.

Mendès could count on the support of the Gaullists in his cabinet, notably Christian Fouchet, the minister chiefly concerned, in part because of the "liberal" evolution De Gaulle had recently begun in this area. But he also knew that he could count on significant external support. In Tunis, first of all, the leader of the Socialist faction, André Cohen-Hadina, was the inspiration of a liberal movement whose influence went beyond the narrow confines of his party and found a rather favorable response among the liberal professions and in the Jewish community. In Paris, the Socialist deputy Alain Savary, one of the very rare French figures to have visited Bourguiba in his Tunisian prison, continued the contact and was preparing to see Bourguiba again. Finally, Roger Stéphane, a writer who was very close to Georges Boris, Mendès's righthand man, also had the confidence of the Néo-Destour and was eager to make himself useful. The communication networks were in place. It only remained to make them means of action.

In the final days of June, between the Bern meeting with Chou En-lai and General Ely's second visit to Paris, Mendès France and his advisers developed their "Tunisian strategy." It can be summed up in three points.

First of all, a restoration of some of the moral authority of the Bey, the only island of power that had survived the disaster, providing limited assurance of the continuity of Tunisian legitimacy. Second, involving the Néo-Destour in negotiations, since it controlled and inspired public opinion. Finally, on the French side, reliance on the military, less shamefully entangled than the civil servants in the intrigues of the decaying protectorate that had led to chaos.

On July 4, Alain Savary met Habib Bourguiba in his Breton hotel. Much more relaxed than he had been in his Tunisian prison, Bourguiba understood that the measures recently taken in his favor presaged other, more significant action, and he clearly saw that what Mendès had undertaken with respect to Indochina was not an isolated expedient but the expression of a new attitude toward the colonized peoples. Savary in fact informed him that important decisions were about to be made, but that they could not possibly bear fruit without the agreement and support of his party, the Néo-Destour. Asked whether he was ready to play the game, the exile gave an encouraging response.

On his return to Geneva on July 15, Mendès France, informed of Savary's impressions of the conversation, decided to set the Tunisian "process" in motion even before being freed from the Indochina burden. He quickly came up with the idea of a psychological shock that could be created by an impromptu visit to Tunis. He spoke about it to one of his advisers: "What would you say if I went directly from Geneva to Tunis?" "Everything would depend on what you brought with you."

Indeed, what should he bring? Mendès thought it essential to supplement the information he had received from Savary by establishing direct contact with the Néo-Destour representative and spokesman in France, Mohammad Masmoudi—more or less in hiding and sought for by the police, but seen often by several of Mendès's friends, like Roger Stéphane.

Stéphane, who was covering the conference for *France-Observateur,* thought that Masmoudi had also come to follow the Indochina conference—an event that was propitious for establishing contacts with the international press, with diplomats, and with political leaders—and he set out in pursuit. He located him by chance and spirited him off to the discreet French Consulate, where the head of the French government was awaiting him in the garden.

Mendès France got directly to the point:

I will sign the agreements here on the night of July 20 or the morning of July 21. I want to be in Tunis on the twenty-second. There I will sketch out the definition of a new French policy, on the basis of internal automony really put into practice. A new government will be formed in which the Néo-Destour will be invited to participate. It will not be a homogeneous cabinet, but you will be well represented in it, if you accept. I am not asking for your approval but for an answer. Is it possible? Will I be well received?

Masmoudi, recovering from his astonishment, replied:

Are you aware of the hostile reactions that will be provoked by what you are accomplishing here? You will have to fight in Paris. And nothing will be ready in Tunis on the twenty-second. But if you are there, we will answer! I do not believe in the possibility of this journey to Tunis, but I will do everything in my power to make it useful. Moreover, I do not have the authority to commit the Néo-Destour. Only our National Council can make a decision.

    How many are you?

    Forty; some are at liberty, others in prison, still others in New York.

    Impossible. It would take too long. Assume your responsibilities.

Then I will have to see Bourguiba. A detail: I came here clandestinely. Can I have papers for the traveling I will have to do and the contacts I will have to make?

Agreed. Maintain contact with Stéphane. The consul here will do what is necessary for your papers. We will meet again very soon.

Four days later, on July 20, at seven in the morning, before moving into the French ambassador's residence to engage the final battle of the Indochinese negotiations, Mendès France again met Mohammed Masmoudi under the trees in the garden of the consul, who had in the meantime taken care of the problem of papers. He handed a blank French passport to the Néo-Destour delegate.

MASMOUDI: You will have your answer. But what you must do is to see Bourguiba, immediately.

MENDÈS: I will not go to Tunis on the date I had hoped, but I will go very soon.

MASMOUDI: See Bourguiba first.

MENDÈS: Bourguiba! What a man, who has made a party out of nothing, a nation out of a party, and out of a nation wants to create a state worthy of the name. And all of that from behind prison bars. It is indeed with a man like that that we must deal. I cannot see him for the moment, but I will quickly establish a dialogue with him. In any event, within a month, real negotiations will be under way. Before that, I want to strike public opinion and show the Tunisians that something has changed, by visiting them myself.

MASMOUDI: On what basis do you intend to negotiate?

MENDÈS: Not on the basis of independence. On that of internal automony.

MASMOUDI: You are making a mistake. But we will discuss that!

On July 16, Habib Bourguiba had been transferred to the Château d'Amilly one hundred kilometers from Paris. He had become accessible to visitors and journalists, and first of all to Mendès France's emissary Alain Savary, who had a significant conversation with him on the seventeenth from which were to flow all the succeeding phases of the "Tunis Operation."

Before changing his mission from a simple sounding out of Bourguiba into a genuine conversation, Savary wanted to have a written document that could serve as a point of reference and a working draft. Mendès at first objected that there was not enough time. "Yes," said Savary. "Give me a week and a working group, and we'll have our text."

In a week, the memorandum was prepared on the basis of which Savary could discuss matters with Bourguiba, laying the foundations for negotiations and for the agreement that was signed the following year. Its broad outlines were: recognition of Tunisian internal autonomy; the principle of stages in the assumption of responsibilities; the formation of a representative government with a strong Néo-Destour participation; and close association of the two countries in the areas of defense and diplomacy.

The next day, Bourguiba received Roger Stéphane, who had received an urgent telephone call from Georges Boris the night before: "You are going to take this as bad news: Mendès is planning to take Marshal Juin to Tunis! What do you think of that?" "Nothing good!" "Feel out Bourguiba on the question."

Masmoudi accompanied the visitor to Amilly. Stéphane admired Bourguiba for not ever mentioning, throughout the two hours of conversation, his personal problems, particularly his unconditional liberation. What did he think of Mendès France? He was both admiring and circumspect:

> I do not know him, but I have great admiration for his intelligence, his realism, and his courage; however, his presence alone is not enough to reassure us. It will not be the first time that men of good will, no matter how full of foresight, were paralyzed by the coalition between the colonists and the administration.[3]

Stéphane then approached the burning question: "Premier Mendès France intends to be accompanied in his journey by Marshal Juin."

Bourguiba was startled: "Juin! Ah, that Mendès, I thought he was sharp, but not as strong as that! It's a stroke of genius that I wish I had thought of myself!"

Before the departure of his guest, the Tunisian leader took Stéphane aside: "Leave for Tunis. And give this letter from me to my comrade Mongi Slim, who has taken the principal responsibilities in my absence."

The letter was written in Arabic, a language that Stéphane did not read. Should he transmit this message, which was perhaps a call for a general uprising? He could consult no one without betraying Bourguiba's extraordinary confidence. He could remember a quotation from Cardinal de Retz: "One is more often deceived by mistrust than by confidence." In short, he put the letter in his pocket, left for Tunis, and turned it over to Mongi Slim, who read it and stood up to embrace him. It was July 29.[4]

The premier had not contented himself with attention to a single constituency, his future Tunisian interlocutors. He knew that they were not the only ones who had to be persuaded to support a policy of gradual emancipation. He also had to consider, in the immediate, the European community that still controlled the essential parts of the governmental apparatus in Tunis and perhaps believed that it still controlled the government in Paris. Christian Fouchet worked on "softening up" the notables of the regency. He soon recognized that the Europeans did not constitute the bloc of benighted conservatives that overly timid or inept civil servants claimed they had to take into account.

Thus, on his arrival in Geneva on July 15, Mendès France received, through his minister for Moroccan and Tunisian affairs, a letter emanating from a group of French inhabitants of Tunisia—teachers, doctors, lawyers, journalists, civil servants—who "coming from different horizons and united only by their anxiety," were eager to "provide testimony devoid of passion" on "a policy that has led to disheartening results." And they explained:

> Insecurity has now spread throughout the country [where] the inaction of public authorities is leading to general disorder.
> The policy of repression and oppression has borne its tragic fruit. Nothing has been resolved through that policy, and everything risks being lost. Many French citizens know it and wish to put an end to police measures and to arrive at a policy of discussion that would substitute the arguments of good sense for the instruments of force."[5]

What did the thoughtful signers of this message represent? Mendès and Fouchet convinced themselves that, by their very appearance, they demonstrated the existence of a local base for an innovative policy. Four days later, he summoned to Geneva the commander-in-chief of French forces in Tunisia, General Boyer de la Tour, whom he had decided to make the pivot of the strange operation which, in his mind, was dramatically to mark the opening of a new era in Tunisia.

For this austere man, this scrupulous jurist, this democrat respectful of the forms, was in the process of inventing, from the "wager" of Geneva to the "coup" of Tunis, a style marked by a spirit of adventure, surprise, and dramatic flair. After situating the Indochinese negotiations in the framework of the astonishing "ultimatum to himself," he was to give the act of reducing the pressure on the Tunisian people the air of a Mediterranean *pronunciamento*.

Mendès France asked General de la Tour to describe for him as lucidly as possible the situation under the regency. The picture painted by the general was as somber as Mendès had imagined. Then he simply offered the general the governor generalship of Tunisia. Did he already know what Mendès expected of him? He was aware of the firm declaration of June 17 and must have sensed that something rather novel was about to occur across the Mediterranean: A former commander of French forces in South Vietnam could not have failed to be struck by the boldness of the new civilian government. In short, given the tone in which the offer was made, he barely resisted. Then, what was his mission?

Mendès France did not yet reveal to him his plan to travel to Tunis. He outlined the essential aspects of his mission in a few sentences: First, with the help of massive reinforcements, to put an end to "local violence" and "external intrusions." And then, to assure that the coming initiatives of the government would be welcomed by his civilian and military subordinates "with neither hesitation nor reticence." He apparently did not pronounce the word *sabotage,* but he thought of it and would use it on later occasions.

On July 21, Mendès was back in Paris, immediately occupied with preparing the Indochina debate, which took place on the following two days. On the twenty-fourth, he was again immersed in the Tunisian problem. To avoid dissipating the surprise that was essential to the success of the operation, he could delay no longer. The thirty-first would be a good day. That left a week. He had still to realize the plan to involve Juin in the adventure.

The marshal was on vacation. Mendès called him on the twenty-eighth. "I need you." "Next week?" "Tomorrow. A plane is coming to get you." Thus Alphonse Juin landed at Villacoublay on July 29.

Legend would have it that he did not know the destination of the journey, or at the very least the meaning of what Mendès France was preparing and in which he too was now involved. Despite a few blunders in the conduct of his public life, the marshal was a thoughtful man, more often cautious then reckless, and very careful about his reputation and the interests of his career. He therefore had the background and conditions of the operation explained to him and agreed to be associated with it in the strongest terms. It is said that his only observations were marked by great simplicity:

> That will mean two nights without sleep. Mister President, do you need me during the day?
> No, Marshal.
> Very well, Mister President, I am going to sleep.[6]

But Mendès France had had to face another test the day before. For several days a rumor had been circulating about a bold initiative by Mendès dealing with Tunisia. Colonial interests were troubled. Antoine Colonna, senator representing the French population of Tunisia, head of the *intégriste* party, had succeeded in getting an appointment with the premier. He was imitated by Henri Bergasse, deputy from Marseille, who had been willing to vote for the Indochina agreements but who wished to be, like his colleagues of the parliamentary right, the preserver of the integrity of the French presence in North Africa.

Late in the morning of the twenty-eighth, Colonna, followed by Bergasse and two representatives of the new group "France-Tunisia," was received at the foreign Office. Mendès France considered it fair to hear him before springing the surprise of July 31. But there was no question of opening a debate. And the various spokesmen of the party of the status quo left in great discomfort, spreading at random the most sinister rumors about the intentions of the "liquidator of the empire." Too late to block the mechanism set in motion with Fouchet, La Tour, and Juin.

It remained for Mendès France to have his plan adopted by the Council of Ministers meeting at the Elysée on July 30, the eve of the operation. Mendès knew that there would be at least one minister whose resistance would have to be overcome, General Koenig, minister of defense. After six hours of debate, at around 10 P.M., a communiqué indicated that "the Council of Ministers has given its full agreement to the president of the Council" so that Franco–Tunisian relations might receive a "new impetus." When the journalists, who sensed that something was in the air, badgered the government spokesman, André Bettencourt, he confined himself to answering, "His Highness the Bey should be the first to hear about the decisions that have been made." And nothing about the Elysée "agreement" came out in the course of the succeeding hours. Remarkable discretion in a period when everything that was said in the Council of Ministers was known to all of Paris.

From the morning of July 30, all air and telephone communications between France and Tunisia had been broken, to avoid outbreaks of panic or emotional "mobilization" at the last minute.

On July 31, at seven o'clock in the morning, in the palace of Carthage, Sidi Lamine, Bey of Tunis, upon whom the duties of his office had seldom imposed such an ordeal, was awaiting the visit of General Boyer de la Tour du Moulin. His highness had some reason to be disturbed. It was rare that generals took such pains so early in the morning to announce good news to a "protégé." The Bey of Tunis thought of his cousin the Sultan of Morocco.[7]

Sidi Lamine suffered nothing but his anxiety. The general had come to present his credentials as governor general and to announce that five hours later he would have to receive the head of the French government, who was coming to tell him important things.

The general returned to his new residence to put the final touches on the operation that he had been preparing like a *Kriegspiel* for a week. Then he settled in at the airport. At nine-thirty, he received a call from the plane that had left Villacoublay at six-thirty carrying, among others, Pierre Mendès France, Alphonse Juin, Christian Fouchet, and Yves Pérussel, leader of the Tunis Gaullists. The pilot: "We are preparing to land." The voice of General Boyer de la Tour, alarmed: "It's a half-hour too soon. My troops do not control the airport." They had to circle before landing.

Was it a putsch? Mendès France did not always contest the word, on condition that it not be taken seriously. In *Choisir,*[8] he agreed that the affair had something of the style of that kind of operation, to the extent that, except for a few dozen people in Paris and Tunis, the world was confronted with a *fait accompli* established by force of arms.

In the palace of Carthage, Mendès, standing in an ill-fitting, slightly rumpled black suit, flanked by a marshal glittering with decorations and by Christian Fouchet, whose North African tribulations had only begun, before Bey Sidi Lamine, read the statement on which he had been working personally for two weeks with the feeling that he was expressing an essential part of himself, a statement that, beneath a benign appearance, would transform the relations between France and her proctectorate, and perhaps do more than that.

> The internal autonomy of the Tunisian state is recognized and proclaimed unequivocally by the French government, which intends both to affirm it in principle and to allow it to achieve success in practice. . . .
>
> From this very moment, if that is your wish, a new government can be established which, besides managing the affairs of the regency, will be charged with negotiating in your name with the French government the agreements that will clearly establish the rights of all parties. . . .
>
> Immediately after these agreements are concluded, internal autonomy will be definitely established, with no restriction or limitation other than those set forth in the agreements themselves. We are certain, knowing the feelings of Your Highness, and the aspirations of his people, that the reforms will mark a progress toward democratic institutions. . . .
>
> In the course of these past weeks, violence has redoubled, as though it wanted to overtake our decisions and create a gulf between populations that are called upon to help one another in a fraternal spirit. Like yourself, I have the right to hope that an end will now be put to this violence. If it were necessary to devote more resources to control it, the French government would not hesitate to send all necessary reinforcements; if it were necessary to resort to draconian measures for public order, regretfully, it would take them. . . .
>
> In any event, terrorism will not reach the goal it is pursuing; it will not block the political decisions we have made. At the very most, it risks delaying their success, while imposing undeserved suffering on your people.
>
> You are not unaware, Your Highness, that you can rely on the complete good will of the French government. That is why I insisted on bringing to you personally the friendly message of the French people.

In material terms, there was nothing new here. The Carthage speech seemed a summary of promises that had been made in Paris for years. There was nothing in it that was not in the final motion of the MRP congress on May 30, 1954, or in the statements of most French leaders of the time. Nothing but the style, the tone, the conviction. Nothing but the personal commitment of a man who created events. Nothing but the art of being taken seriously and having his country taken seriously as well.

As soon as the news of the Carthage meeting was known, it provoked intense emotion in Tunis. On the same deserted avenues that they had hastily traversed in the morning, the visitors were acclaimed in the afternoon. The reaction among Europeans was at first one of stupor. But Marshal Juin delivered a passionate argument in favor of the new policy symbolized by the visit and formulated in the premier's statement. An argument that was strengthened by a favorable reaction in *La Dépêche tunisienne*.

Before leaving Tunis, Pierre Mendès France recorded his weekly talk to the French people:

> This very short message will come to you from Tunis, where an imperious duty has called me for a few hours. In the course of the last few weeks, while I was striving to put an end to an atrocious war, I have been thinking that very near to us, for months and months, blood has been flowing, the blood of the French and the Tunisians, who are nevertheless united by a long past, but now separated by long-lasting misunderstandings.
>
> It was therefore necessary to act, it was necessary to put an end to this bloody disorder, it was necessary to establish the bases for faithful cooperation. I have come to Tunis today to propose these solutions. I have come to persuade all sides that rancor and violence must and can give way to confidence and peaceful order. I hope that I have been heard. The future of Tunisia will say that, in this ancient country, which, in fruitful union with France, is becoming a modern country, today has seen the triumph of reason, progress, and peace.

Facing the Assembly on August 10, Mendès France had to confront more vigorous and pressing objections than those raised about the Indochina agreements. This was all the more true because a violent reaction had taken in place in Morocco. In Fez, the disturbances had resulted in six deaths. And in the large town of Petitjean, on August 4, an incident had led to ten dead and twenty wounded. Mendès France's adversaries made him responsible for these events. The most violent attack was led by Mendès "intimate enemy," Léon Martinaud-Déplat, "administrative president" of his own party, who, after having been Mendès's companion in the Young Turks in their youth, had become the spokesman of the most conservative of the great French interests in North Africa. In particular, he denounced the choice as interlocutors of the representatives of the Néo-Destour, whom he described, reading from the podium from informers' reports, as corrupt bandits. The premier could easily reply:

> M. Martinaud-Déplat has, for a certain number of years, participated in the policies that were carried out in Tunisia. I ask that we look candidly at the results.
>
> M. Christian Fouchet, in sober and stark terms, has just presented an assessment of the situation as we encountered it on June 17.
>
> He also might have spoken, had he wanted to make the debate emo-

tional, of terrorist attacks. He might have spoken of the country daily being shaken in the deepest and most serious manner.

That is the result of the policies that have been followed in the last few years.

Following that, the government's Tunisian policy was approved by 397 votes to 114, with 90 abstentions. Among those in favor, along with the Socialists and Communists, were noted the names of opponents of Mendès (Radicals, of course) like René Mayer and André Morice; those voting against included, this time, the majority of the right; the MRP formed the bulk of the abstentions.

No more than he had been liberated from Indochina by the Geneva agreements was Mendès liberated from Tunisia by the "Carthage Operation." It was, in fact, only a beginning, the opening of a period of negotiations replacing the time of repression. There was first the negotiation over the formation of a government, which, led by a liberal bourgeois, Tahar Ben Amar, was to include four representatives of the Néo-Destour, including Mohammed Masmoudi (Habib Bourguiba remained "in reserve," playing an extremely important role in the background, usually in favor of conciliation); then there was the negotiation on the future status of Tunisia and its association with France, with the latter intent on controlling matters of defense and diplomacy, which was obviously far from a matter of course; and finally, there was the negotiation on the restoration of order, which posed a number of problems as long as the *fellagha* controlled the countryside and sometimes even the major lines of communication.

It took General de la Tour four months to persuade the *fellagha* to surrender their arms; in return they were granted amnesty for their war activities. It was a remarkable political success for the French and Tunisian negotiators, who did not have to deal with a phenomenon that was then considered secondary: the grouping of other guerillas across the western border, in Algeria, where the revolt that had broken out on November 1 was growing. All subsequent researchers have confirmed that "clemency" in Tunisia had no effect on the preparation of the Algerian uprising. What is striking, on the contrary, is the impermeability of the frontier.

Contrary to the predictions, or at least the desires, of Mendès France, the "Carthage policy" could only be a starting point, not a model, for a strategy for North Africa as a whole. This was true because the specific virtues of Tunisia, on which he had decided to base this pilot program, were not those of the two neighboring countries. The visit to Carthage could not, by itself, spare France from a horrible war. It is remarkable that it established between Paris and Tunis relations that a quarter-century of tragic events has not managed to undermine.

In the battle for peace in North Africa, Mendès France did not find the consensus he had achieved from his handling of the Indochina crisis. When it came to the Maghreb, interests were stronger and better represented, the disaster less obvious, and the opposition less disoriented. Just as Léon Blum had been able to ask for everything in June 1936 from a right that was terrified by the May strikes, only to see a powerful class opposition reestablish itself as time went on, so Mendès France saw the opposition restore itself to consolidate stagnation. But before the counterattack, hinted at over Tunisia, stiffened and broadened on the question of Europe, an editorial published by the *New York Herald Tribune* on August 4, 1954, six weeks after the election, can be considered a good diagnosis of the Mendès France government and its leader.

> French Assemblies are notoriously disagreeable and suspicious toward popular men, and the premier is unquestionably the most popular French leader since the heroic days of General de Gaulle. His radio speeches provoke a certain resentment on the part of the Assembly, which, in a perverse way, considers the premier's appeals to the electorate over its head inelegant and politically immoral. Until now, however, M. Mendès France's course has been successful. He may have to undergo an ordeal in the Assembly this week.[9] But it is improbable that he will have to confront more than a slight slowing of his exceptional political impetus.

14.
THE "MENDES SYSTEM"

In the beginning was action. Pierre Mendès France had thrown himself so quickly and so boldly into the critical caldrons, from Geneva to Carthage, that after six weeks of excercising power he had not yet given analysts the time to grasp him. It is impossible to define him otherwise than as a principle of action, a will in movement. He seems to have been inspired by the admirable formulation of François Mauriac, who, astonished by his effervescent ambiguity, wrote in *L'Express* after the Tunisian expedition: "It is this tempo that, for the moment, has made him invulnerable. A government can be shot down when it is fixed. The best shots cannot hit it in full flight."

Let us take a snapshot, between the trip to Carthage, the request for plenary power over economic affairs, and the battle over the CED. *L'Express* had decided to call him PMF, on the model of FDR, and had imposed the fashion. Thus, the accent was placed on dynamism, efficiency, and the sense of timing, virtues attributed to the Americans. Thus was outlined the myth of the imaginative manager, the bold decision maker, the champion with staying power. To act and to choose were the two verbs that recurred most frequently in his speeches. And the rhythm of activity that he imposed on himself did not surprise Mauriac alone.

At forty-seven, he was in excellent physical condition. He had chosen to establish his office at the Foreign Ministry to indicate clearly the priority that he attached to the affairs of Indochina, Tunisia, and the European Community, to signify as well that diplomacy was not a matter for a few specialists, but for the man who had been elected by the people. The majority of his colleagues, and not only the staff of the Ministry of Foreign Affairs, took up residence there as well.

The "PMF system" was, in fact, based on the three principles of choice, action, and communication between the government and the public, made up above all of a group of men. In the government, despite the constant guerrilla warfare conducted against him by *L'Express,* Edgar Faure was essentially Mendès's righthand man, his "vicar." It was he who assumed responsibility for all sectors of the economy and of industry and acted as a liaison between Mendès's "commandos" and the very suspicious, indeed hostile, world of business. And when the head of the government decided to take over economic leadership, he called on Faure to replace him at Foreign Affairs.

To the degree that it was quixotic, the Mendès adventure of 1954 perhaps needed this Sancho. Moreover, Mendès was not a lover of new faces. The old schoolmate who made him laugh, stimulated, instructed, and challenged him, and to whom he remained grateful for his loyalty during the ordeal of the 1941 trial, was a reassuring element that this anxious and bold man needed.

In the light of more recent history, it would be tempting to see in the June 1954 government a troika, with François Mitterrand as the third man: this would be granting him too much. It is not that the young interior minister did not demonstrate at the time the talents, the courage, the cultivation, and the bold dexterity that have marked his subsequent career. But his stature in the French political landscape was not yet comparable to that of his two elders. At thirty-seven, he was as yet only the most brilliant of the "young," the man who, no one doubted, would soon become premier and later president of the Republic. Mendès was astonished by Mitterrand's knowledge of parliamentary circles and put it to good use whom he formed his government. But although he readily confided in Edgar Faure, he continued to feel a little distrust of this too brilliant political animal.

But Mendès's policies were above all developed and shaped in the framework of his staff, his immediate entourage, in what could be called his brain trust. Senior civil servants played their traditional role. But they knew that, although they gave impetus to the management of affairs, the decisions that they executed were prepared elsewhere, that is, in the very informal framework of the brain trust.

At this time, everyone, liberal bankers, innovative journalists, malcontent deputies, heretical officers, rebellious militants, intoxicated technocrats, modernist managers, progressive professors, felt called upon to inspire PMF, to bombard him with suggestions, opinions, warnings, and criticisms. To the extent that Mendésism represented a hope for renewal, more a state of mind than a politics, and as much a state of feeling as a state of mind, the brain trust was in fact made up of a confluence of intelligence and hope. For a few weeks at least, France resembled the Third Estate of 1789. Much that was written in the press at the time was a part of an enormous amount of advice "from below" that offered its unformed, tumultuous, and inconsistent foundations to the new government. An immense amount of mail poured in, clogging the offices of the Ministry of Foreign Affairs. Apparently, one only had to sort through it to find the solution to every problem.

At the summit of this pyramid of advisers, mediators, and executives was, of course, Georges Boris. Of nearly equal importance was the contrasting figure of René de Lacharrière, a professor of law who embodied, perhaps even more than his leader, the spirit of the legislators of the Revolution. Also belonging to the "first circle" of the brain trust was Simon Nora, then an anti-Stalinist Marxist, who admired the Radical leader as the author of the 1938 Plan. Aside from Boris, the new head of government could have relied on no one with more assurance then on Simon Nora, since he had "forgotten" to associate with his team the faithful and enthusiastic Gabriel Ardant. Was this ingratitude toward a man whose research he had shared and some of whose work he had used? Or was it the choice of a more flexible line than the one Ardant would have followed? In fact, Mendès later explained, "I had no position worthy of his stature to offer him."

"One of the virtues of Mendès as a statesman," according to Simon Nora, "was his inability to pay for services rendered. Since he had a highly developed sense of the collective interest, he believed that everyone acted only according to that sense and expected nothing of him, no matter what service he may have performed. Like De Gaulle."

It is today very difficult to arrive at an idea of the exact role played by Jean-Jacques Servan-Schreiber and Françoise Giroud in the final inspiration and execution of Mendès France's policies as premier. One thing cannot be doubted: they helped to encourage him to take healthy risks, beginning with the confirmation battle from June 14 to 18.

The details of particular episodes are of minor importance. The fact is that the two directors of *L'Express*, less directly perhaps than Boris, Lacharrière, Nora, and a few others, but with even more dynamism, were inciters, spurs, motors of the system. And although their agitation against Edgar Faure sometimes took on the air of a ridiculous war against the finance minister, they helped to maintain the imaginative dynamism of the PMF system and to vivify the colors in the popular image of the head of government.

The PMF system also included a network of relations with the press and the various news media. Much more than most of his predecessors, the premier elected on June 18 had an acute sense of the importance of the major news media, perhaps because of his long stays in England and the United States. Hardly had he been nominated when he thought of establishing special links with the two principal news vehicles, and the ones that were closest to the government: radio (television was still in its infancy) and Agence France Presse (AFP). He is even said to have suggested to Servan-Schreiber that he devote himself to the former, and to Pierre Viansson, editor-in-chief of *L'Express,* that he return to the AFP, where he had cut his teeth.[1] Their refusal, at the urging of Françoise Giroud, not only saved *L'Express;* it enabled the new government to avoid assuming an abusive and dangerous ascendancy over the news media.

Of course, one cannot judge the relations between a government and the press as a whole on the basis of a few large Parisian organs. The government set up in June 1954, once the first weeks of euphoria had passed and the relief over Indochina had been absorbed, quickly came up against stiff and varied opposition. The expression "dissipator" of the empire soon became a leitmotif of the provincial press and of the organs of the Parisian right. If we consider the total circulation of French newspapers, we can estimate that by the end of August 1954 Mendès was supported by only a minority of the news media, but by the most prestigious among them.

There is no need to reiterate the support of *L'Express,* which was unfailing, although there was some friction, notably over the CED in late August 1954, and repeatedly over the economic policies of Edgar Faure. More significant was the support of *Le Monde,* which had not departed from its neutrality with regard to any of Mendès's predecessors.

What was more surprising was the at first benevolent neutrality granted to Mendès France by *Le Figaro,* a neutrality that later turned sour and changed to hostility after the Assembly's rejection of the CED. Still more surprising was the approval given to Mendès's first steps by a right-wing daily like *L'Aurore.*

Although *France-Observateur,* the left-wing weekly, thought it appropriate to adopt a protective, readily sarcastic tone toward Mendès, the new head of government could boast of an unprecedented alliance: the one that appeared to have been signed with him by the perennial opposition weekly, *Le Canard enchaîné.* To cover such a reversal, they needed a good headline: "Finally, an Opposition Government!" And the editorialist wrote: "We are, we must admit, thoroughly embarrassed. We have, in fact, become government supporters. And we feel quite foolish applauding PMF. But the truth is out: it is M. Mendès France who is in the opposition."

Not content with being the only head of a French government to be applauded by *Le Monde* and *Le Canard enchaîné*, Pierre Mendès France wanted to establish personal contact with public opinion. This took the form of the Saturday talks, more or less inspired by Roosevelt's fireside chats. From the very first sentences of his first talk on June 26, 1954, PMF clearly defined the objective these conversations were to fulfill:

> My intention is to speak regularly to you, to talk to you with complete simplicity, and to keep you aware of what the government, which is your government, is thinking and doing. I believe that it is one of my tasks to explain to the public the meaning and the scope of our actions.

It was a very judicious choice. Although he was a little too sober an orator, a debater who was sometimes too harsh, and an often obstinate negotiator, he was an incomparable provider of information. He had the gift of clarity combined with that of conviction. His voice, very beautiful, very pure, very calm, worked marvelously over the air. Without slipping into the seductive tone of an intimate conversation, he succeeded in giving the impression that he was speaking for each individual, not as a comrade or an accomplice but as a kind of better informed older brother, responsible but eager for approval and solidarity, unique but helped along by the hope for everyone's support. He later spoke of these talks with affection:

> Hundreds of letters came in every week. We went through them, studied them, classified them. In studying the reaction, we realized that it was a very effective contact with public opinion. Every week, a certain number of friends discussed possible themes for the talk. Boris then came to see me to propose a subject. Except if something seemed more important to me, I accepted his suggestion. He wrote out a preliminary draft, which I corrected extensively. In general, the final text was rather good. Not always.
>
> One day, Boris said to me: "This week is the beginning of the school year; you should talk to the children." I delivered a speech addressed to children, saying they had to be nice to their parents and teachers, and so on. I received some enthuasistic letters, including one from a lady who wrote, "I have not heard anything so beautiful since the speeches of Marshal Pétain!"

Not everyone shared this enthusiasm. Many deputies were offended by a relationship established in that way, independently of the representative system, between the head of the executive and public opinion. One of the leaders of the MRP, François de Menthon, publicly raised the question of the constitutionality of the procedure. The popularity PMF thereby won among the public was certainly harmful to his relations with an

Assembly that was all the more jealous of its prerogatives as it felt the deepest sources of its legitimacy escaping from it.

The PMF system was distinguished not so much by the novelty of its relations with the press and the public as by a kind of reconciliation between the government and the state. Since 1945, with the creation of the Ecole Nationale d'Administration, the Plan, the nationalization of four of the principal depository banks, and the launching of reconstruction, the state was the principal engine of productive activity. In the course of the last ten years, a new type of man had come forward, preparing the future while grumbling against the weakness of the regime, the obstacles of the old bureaucracy, and parliamentary dictatorship. These men were either the top students of the Ecole Nationale d'Administration or those who dreamed of imitating them and becoming their rivals, in the office of the Plan, the large nationalized credit establishments, Renault, or the Caisse des Dépôts. Not all of them had had Mendès France as a teacher at ENA. But they had all heard of him and had all read his critical speeches to the National Assembly. All of them had heard his lessons of vigor. And all of them had more or less expected that he would be given the opportunity to put them into practice. An entire generation was aware that an opportunity had been offered to the country, and more particularly to itself. To be thirty and to have a fragment of responsibility in 1954.

But this wave of hope did not touch only public service. To the extent that, immediately after the Liberation, the ideas of planning, cooperation, and shaping of the economy had been rather arbitrarily embodied by Jean Monnet, while Gruson, Boris, Ardant, and Largentaye had other claims to that paternity, the frontier between the two sectors, at least for the younger generation, remained uncertain. However symbolic he may have appeared of a directed economy, of discipline imposed first on production, then on distribution and consumption, Pierre Mendès France was seen not only as a harsh taskmaster but also as the determined advocate of vigorous management, the enemy of all forms of demagogy, with respect to wages or anything else, and the supporter of a bold policy of investments for the purposes of industrial conversion and growth.

The frontier between Mendès France's supporters and the others did not coincide so much with the rather fuzzy line that separated the public sector (favorable in principle) from the private sector (*a priori* suspicious) as with that dividing the generations on either side of the age of forty. When he called, a little vaguely, on the support of the "young," PMF knew that he was not the representative of poor students and unemployed adolescents but of those who, from the nationalized enterprises to the shoe manufacturers of the Midi and the clothworks of the Nord, were impatiently waiting for reform of their management and renewal—costly or not—of their industrial plant.

We shall see that this expectation was only very partially satisfied. In any event, it was in this broad stratum of producers that the PMF system found its base of support. A country whose economic recovery had taken its first steps two years earlier—at the time of the first Edgar Faure government—was waiting for these creative urgings to manifest themselves in a national effort, and Mendès appeared as the organizer of this attempt, both inspiration and supervisor. He was not given enough time, in this area, to carry out his program. But the human foundations for such an effort now existed.

Although he had invented a new type of relations with public opinion and with the generation of producers, the new premier had nevertheless not isolated himself from all the regime's notables, beginning with the head of state. An old political adversary of Mendès France in Normandy, René Coty had established cordial relations with the premier. He was first of all grateful to Mendès for having so brilliantly resolved the first crisis of his tenure as president, and then for exercising power with such firmness. He disapproved neither of the Indochina peace nor of the Tunisian negotiation, nor even of the burial of the CED. But his support of the first few months was modified in the autumn by some reservations.

"At the beginning," according to Mendès, "he compared me to Waldeck-Rousseau, which was for him a sign of great consideration. Then he spoke of Clemenceau, which indicated for him, a slight falling off. Toward the end he remarked to a friend: "He has the qualities, but also the defects of Clemenceau."

In Parliament and the parties—particularly in the Radical party—knives were soon sharpened. Among the leaders, in any case among the members of what was called the "club of premiers"—René Pleven, Georges Bidault, René Mayer, and Guy Mollet—PMF could only be considered a parenthesis, an accident, a kind of scandal: for one because of Indochina, for a second because of North Africa, for a third over the CED, and for the last for the slight importance he attributed to party leadership by addressing the deputies directly in order to choose his ministers, and the citizens directly in order to govern.

Pierre Mendès France for a long time pretended to scorn this scorn, strengthened as he was by many active sympathizers among the rank and file of the various parties, and even among the leadership.

In short, under his gaze, Parliament had changed from a confederation of principalities into an assembly of persons. And nothing was more in conformity with the deepest thoughts and the temperament of Mendès, who took men one by one, for what they were, believing that each one could be reasoned with and persuaded. But the power of the princes, diminished under his impetus, remained large enough to bring him down.

Apparently little concerned by these vigilant enmities, Mendès

France suffered more from certain reservations expressed toward him by the unions, not only by the CGT, but by FO (Force Ouvrière) and the CFTC (Confédération Française des Travailleurs Chrétiens) as well. In the minds of the spokesmen of the labor movement, he remained the representative of monetary discipline, the minister opposed to the wage increases of autumn 1944, the man who, each time power had been offered to him, had refused any promises with respect to wages before he had made certain of the recovery of production. In his 1954 speech of candidacy, he had remained discreet in this area. And the union representatives noted, to fortify their suspicion that the business confederation (the CNPF) (Confédèration Nationale du Patronat Français) held toward his reputedly "left-wing" government a calm attitude based on the reputation enjoyed in business circles by Edgar Faure. In short, and despite the concessions they were granted in early October without having to formulate threats or exert pressure, the unions were one of the weak links of the PMF system. But the extreme cleverness of the minister of the economy and the nearly full employment enjoyed by French industry in that period of expansion enabled him to avoid excessive tensions.

Mendès France received, with some exceptions, an unusually warm reaction in the international press. We should note in particular the striking response to PMF of a weekly that seldom made such gestures toward French political figures: *Time* magazine made his accession to power its cover story for July 12, 1954. The fourteenth head of government of the Fourth Republic was thus elevated to the rank of international star. Considering French political customs, it was obvious that such a spotlight would consolidate his position. It was fashionable at the time to assert that the new head of government was distinguished not by the novelty of his politics but by the originality of his style. The expression was heard everywhere. But what was understood by style? Without going as far as Buffon, one might suggest that a style original enough to transform stagnation into action, vague impulses into choices, a battle into an armistice, and a conflict into a negotiation, bears a strong resemblance to a politics.

15.
THE EUROPEAN DEFIANCE COMMUNITY

What is happiness in politics if not what Mendès France experienced in early August 1954? Six weeks after his accession to power, he had managed to bring the killing to an end in Indochina; he had opened the path to negotiations in Tunisia; he had received plenary power from Parliament for the purpose of restoring the French economy. Some of the essential clauses of the contract that tied him to the nation from June 18 on had thus already been carried out, and the nation had made him into a kind of hero. Since De Gaulle in August 1944, no other Frenchman had thus mobilized public feeling in his favor. He was perhaps more admired than loved, but he was in any event followed by a vast current of opinion, which expected from him initiatives, drive, impetus.

And then on August 13, at the conclusion of an interminable cabinet session, three of its members left this happy government, three Gaullists, two of whom were of the first rank: General Koenig and Jacques Chaban-Delmas. Why? Because a major obstacle had arisen before the government. The European Defense Community (CED), invented three years earlier by Jean Monnet, Robert Schuman, and René Pleven for the purpose of diluting German rearmament in an integrated group, and which had since then been the subject of a treaty signed by the Pinay government and its five European partners (the Federal Republic of Germany, Italy, Belgium, the Netherlands, and Luxembourg, four of whom had had it ratified by their legislatures; only Italy and France lagged behind).

France's allies, beginning with Washington, pressured Paris to ratify the treaty. But none of Mendès France's predecessors had ventured to take such risks. Signed under the preceding very "European" legislature, the treaty had become since the penetration of Parliament by a strong Gaullist wave in 1951, the target of vigorous attacks. An MRP leader as influential as Georges Bidault spoke of it as a "corpse," the Foreign Affairs and Defense Committees had come out against it, and when he transferred power to his successor on June 20, 1954, Joseph Laniel confided in him: "There is not a majority for this treaty. Do not try to obtain its ratification."

The new head of government considered it unworthy of his country, of the respect he owed to its allies and to its signature, to maintain the ambiguity and to allow the "corpse" to rot in the closet. In his speech of candidacy on June 17, as he had a year earlier, he committed himself to asking the Assembly to declare itself, before the legislative vacation, on "one of the most serious questions of conscience that has ever troubled the country." He knew the risks that he was thereby taking. But he had been able to cut through them in Geneva and Tunis. Decisiveness and boldness based on the promises he had given had paid in both cases.

It turned out that it was impossible to liken the first two debates to the third. Two exceptional forces had inspired Mendès France when he undertook those tasks: intense personal conviction and the awareness that he was carried by the support of a broad fraction of public opinion. In June and July 1954, PMF knew that he had to put an end as quickly as possible, and by paying the price, to the fighting in Asia in which the expeditionary force could be swallowed up and from which could arise a major international conflict, as he knew that in Tunisia hesitations and paralysis were pregnant with a very bloody explosion which would annihilate the chances for peaceful solutions in North Africa. Certain that public opinion was passionately awaiting a cease-fire in Vietnam, he had no doubts either that it would rally to the perspective of an evolution in the Maghreb.

But what did he know with respect to the CED? He knew that in 1954, nine years after the Occupation, half the French were repelled by any prospect of German rearmament, while the other half was resigned to it, within the framework of a European integration, but that that integration, precisely to the extent that it would abolish the military personality of France and its strategic independence, was anathema to what might be called a third half of the citizens. Then, what was to be done?

If he had had at least a particular assurance or will, then his courage, the force of his conviction, and his concern for clarity and decisiveness might have made the difference. But no one could say at the time what this man of choice really *wanted* in this murky area.

Perhaps the most fervent of his opponents at the time, the most vehement advocate for the CED, Pierre-Henri Teitgen, then president of the MRP, put it bluntly: "From the conversation we had on June 18, the evening of his investiture, about the makeup of the new government, I derived the certainty that Mendès France, even more than I had previously believed, was an intractable, irreducible opponent of the construction of Europe."[1] And his colleague Maurice Schumann more subtly: "He was not hostile to it; he was skeptical, which is worse, coming from a man of conviction and commitment like him. Had he been an opponent, we could have tried to persuade him. Since he was neutral, we had no hold over him. [2]

Two of the diplomats who were then among Mendès France's closest colleagues, Jean-Marie Soutou and Philippe de Seynes, allow a refinement and deepening of this "neutrality," which seems in fact to define rather well his attitude at the time and in any event inspired his conduct in Parliament.

Seynes reports a remark Mendès made to him in 1953, more than a year before he became premier, during a trip to the United States:

> The rearmament of Germany seems to me henceforth inevitable, and I am not among those who present it as a catastrophe in itself. Accepting it in principle, I want it to be controlled. But I see no great difference whether or not it takes place within the framework of Europe.[3]

Jean-Marie Soutou went to the heart of the matter:

> With respect to the central problem of French foreign policy, relations with Germany, there were two schools of thought. The first, whose modern theoreticians were Maurras and Bainville—and De Gaulle was for a long time their disciple—aimed only at stifling or dividing Germany. To stand up to the Germans, the Gauls had at any cost to make certain of their alliance with the Slavs, or occasionally with the Turks. It was an implacable strategy of the pincer. Nothing was more foreign to Mendès France than this conception. Of all the French statesmen I have known, he was one of the furthest removed from this approach. For him, as for the supporters of the second school, who were not unaware of German power or of the risks that it might pose for France, the problem was not one of what one might call permanent or preventive reprisal; it was the organization of a balance, not through a reverse alliance, but through an understanding with democratic England. . . .
>
> From that period of debates over the CED in which I was involved night and day for months beside Mendès France, as perhaps the most "European" of his colleagues, I remember him for his totally open mind and desire for compromise, within his government as well as in the National Assembly,

with his European allies as well as with the Anglo-Saxons, and also with the Soviet Union. And he put particular emphasis on the search for close cooperation with London, and was concerned to keep the door open for a broad East–West negotiation that had been sketched out in Geneva with reference to Indochina.[4]

This "neutrality," this openness with reference to the CED, had the disadvantage of depriving Mendès France, for once, of a fundamental motivation related to the solution of the problem, whose urgency he felt. His indecision was further aggravated by the divisions in his entourage and his government, in Parliament, in the parties themselves, and in public opinion.

Reference has often been made, in this connection, to the antagonisms provoked by the Dreyfus affair and those resulting from *"Algérie française."* The lines of division over the CED were perhaps even more complicated and more irrational.

When Mendès France was later questioned about the influences to which he was subjected with respect to the treaty, he answered without hesitation:

> It was Parodi,[5] more than anyone, who warned me against the defects of the CED. Of course, I listened to Boris's arguments, and as usual I paid a great deal of attention to them. But it was Parodi, because he was a technician motivated by no ideology but his patriotism, who then had the most anti-CED influence on me.

The government, the political parties, and the press were all seriously divided over the question. To make certain that nothing was simple, an American lobby openly devoted to the cause of the CED operated in broad daylight, led in Paris by a young diplomat, Tom Tomlinson, and in Brussels by Washington's ambassador to the European Community, David Bruce, a diplomat of great talent who felt invested, in this cause, with a quasi-religious mission. His wife Evangeline, who was closely involved with the campaign, said later: "For us, Europe in every form, among them the CED, was the object of a crusade. We considered ourselves destined to assure to the Europeans a unity necessary for their happiness and their defense."

There were still further complications. The two French parties most directly committed in favor of the CED—the MRP and the SFIO—had, officially or unofficially, close contacts with the Christian Democratic and Social Democratic Parties of the other countries of Western Europe and were sometimes able to bring this kind of influence to bear in the midst of negotiations, over the head of the French representative. Not to mention the encouragements from Moscow to maintain the militant hostility of the PCF.

But, at bottom, what did Mendès think? In January 1981, he said:

The project of the CED, which I didn't like very much, was of French origin, and it was French governments that had gradually persuaded the other countries to rally to it, not without strong opposition, and the various governments had had to fight in their parliaments to convince the legislators to vote in its favor. The time that had passed had been used by French governments continually to assert that they would ratify the CED, so that, if we were not committed juridically and legally, we were committed morally and politically. The rejection of the CED after three years of hesitation risked provoking a major crisis with the rest of the European countries, and it was difficult to foresee all the consequences of this crisis. The worst thing was that the Americans had long before prepared a direct arrangement for German rearmament, organized without our participation in any form, without our having any control, any means of intervening from any perspective. A military arrangement between Washington and Bonn was therefore possible. We would have been confronted with a *fait accompli*. We would have been able to exercise no influence over this veritable military axis between Bonn and Washington. This is what French governments of all kinds had always feared, and it was in fact Washington's deep purpose. And it was especially against this fearful prospect that I struggled.

No terrain was ever more covered with booby traps and mines than the one on which the French negotiator set out during the course of the summer of 1954. He was torn by a thousand contrary influences, less moved by personal conviction than by a few clear, but divergent ideas. "None of the problems that I confronted made me spend so many sleepless nights," he said later. Briefed in particular by Philippe de Seynes, he had understood that his government could not continue to function unless he managed to find a compromise with Parliament and with his allies, and that any decisive solution (rejection of the CED or pure and simple adoption of the treaty) would condemn him to being brought down by one camp or another within three months, while he had given himself a task of much large dimensions. Hence, it followed that the treaty had to be, not destroyed, but modified, in a direction that was both less "supranational," in order not to provoke a Gaullist explosion, and more gradual, more extended in time, in order to leave the door open for discussions with the East.

A single strong conviction inspired him: that the solution to the problem was to be found in London. If he managed to draw the English, if not into the Community, at least onto the territory where it would operate, the risks of German rearmament would be that much the less, as would the hostility that any brake placed on European integration would provoke in Washington. And thinking of the role Anthony Eden had played in Geneva, he thought that the chances of a resumption of a major dialogue with the Socialist camp, not on the peripheral problem of Indochina, but on the central problem of Germany, would thereby be strengthened.

First, he had to attempt to bring about unity within his own government between supporters and opponents of the CED. In the days following the establishment of the cabinet, PMF asked the most notorious representative of each position in the government, the Gaullist Koenig and the Radical Bourgès-Maunoury, to work out the elements of a minimum compromise among members of a team who had discovered elements of convergence in other areas that were strong enough to make them join together in this fighting government exposed to every wind. It was a wasted effort.

In five weeks, the two ministers succeeded only in drawing up a systematic list of their divergences. At the most, one could say that the supporter Bourgès-Maunoury did not exclude all possibility of modification of the most immediately integrationist provisions. But the dialogue did not reach anything resembling a synthesis.

In the meanwhile, immediately after his election, Mendès France had received a kind of call to order from the figure who now embodied the CED, Paul-Henri Spaak, Belgian minister of foreign affairs. Eloquent, warm, eager to play a role beyond the borders of Belgium, and naturally at ease in the framework of a supranationalism that would do justice to his stature as a "great European," Spaak had experienced some displeasure at the interminable delays in ratification of the CED by the French Parliament. But those responsible, Robert Schuman, Guy Mollet, René Mayer, and Georges Bidault, were his friends in the "European Club." Here suddenly was an intruder who was said to be ill disposed toward Europe and more or less "neutralist." The others had been given all the time in the world; he would be given none. No sooner was he in place than the question was put to him: What about the CED?

On June 30, Spaak was at the Foreign Ministry, confronting a Mendès France torn between the Geneva conference and Tunisia. He reminded Spaak that he had to give absolute priority to the negotiations on Indochina, where hundreds of men were dying every day. Spaak pressured him nonetheless: the CED was a French idea.[6] Why was Paris trifling with its partners? Patience was running out in Washington and London; an alternative policy, known as that of the "empty chair"—France's chair, of course—was under consideration. Would France not be distressed to see Germany rearmed without receiving any guarantees in return?

The head of the French government sensed the shape of the threat that was to weigh on him for the following six months. If France were to reject the CED, the others would do without her. He retorted that there was not a majority for the CED in the French Parliament, that an attempt at ratification in current conditions would result in a pure and simple rejection of the treaty, and that, considering that outcome deplorable for the cohesion of the Western alliance, he was preparing modifications in the text of the treaty with a view toward compromise. Spaak pointed out, correctly, that before being submitted to the French legislators these modifications ought to be accepted by the signers of the treaty in the original form. Mendès France agreed, and the two men hoped that a six-party conference to be held in Brussels within the next few weeks would allow the other countries to examine the French "compromise."

On July 13, Mendès was in Paris to meet John Foster Dulles and to attempt to associate the United States with the decisive phase of the Geneva negotiations. Dulles could not refrain from talking about Europe. Mendès replied by warning him against the temptation to link the two problems and thereby to slide toward the notorious "global bargain" that Bidault suspected he was cooking up: a "good" peace in Indochina in exchange for abandoning the CED, a temptation he had resisted three days earlier during his interminable interview with Dulles's counterpart, Vyacheslav Molotov. But since the subject had been broached, Mendès took the opportunity to inform the American diplomat that, given the circumstances, the text of the treaty would not be approved by the French Parliament.

On July 21, with the Indochina negotiation concluded and the "bargain" no longer in question, Mendès France had a final interview with Molotov before leaving Geneva. This time, they discussed Europe. When Molotov spoke of the hostility of his country toward the European Defense Community, which he considered to be directed against the Soviet Union, Mendès pointed out that things could be worse: German rearmament outside any French control, as some English and American figures proposed. Why should not the Soviet Union, with a gesture, a "constructive" initiative, prevent such decisions? For example, why not unblock the question of the Austrian treaty? A solution in Vienna would open so many perspectives for East–West relations.

But three days later, Western diplomats received a note which simply confirmed the fact that the Soviet Union was opposed to German rearmament in any form. The tone of this reminder was not particularly harsh. Mendès had not at all managed to move the stone, but it appeared that, under the impetus of the Geneva conference, Moscow was not seeking to provoke the slightest tension.

In Paris, the experts charged with working out the compromise that was to be submitted before the end of August, to Brussels, and then to the National Assembly, were making progress. By the beginning of August, the "additional protocol" had been drawn up. Its most important clause provided for the suspension of all supranational regulations for eight years. During this "probationary" period, in case of a challenge to a decision by the European Commission by one of the members, the Council of Ministers of the six parties would have to come to a unanimous decision, that is, each state would have veto power.

A second essential modification limited the integration of the armies to the "covering" forces, those stationed in Germany, thereby avoiding the presence of German soldiers in the integrated forces on French territory. Three other provisions appeared more theoretical. But it was not without consequence to provide that the duration of the European treaty would correspond to that of the Atlantic Pact; that the CED would be dissolved if the Atlantic Pact was; and it would also be dissolved if Germany was reunified.

These changes seemed essential. Mendès France believed that they made up the "compromise" upon which a parliamentary majority, followed by France's five partners, could agree. But he had first to persuade his own ministers, from Koenig to Bourgès. According to the narrative of Robert Buron, a loyal "European" and a devoted "Mendésist":

> The cabinet meeting on Friday (August 13), from five-forty-five to twelve-fifteen, with an hour and a half recess just before ten, was extraordinarily passionate. Pathetic appeals from some followed protestations from others of their willingness to make personal sacrifices. The premier himself, ill at ease in this atmosphere, was the victim of a veritable breakdown which required a brief interruption of work. "I am not upset," he repeated, "I am exhausted." I can't go on. It's inhuman." Finally, his proposals were accepted by the cabinet except for the three most Gaullist ministers, who immediately resigned.[7]
>
> I looked at him at the end of the session, slumped in his chair, head forward, his features ravaged by fatigue, with large, dark pouches under his eyes. He made me think of a painting by Rembrandt, and I was filled simultaneously with sympathy, pity, and also anxiety. How would he be able to force a result so obviously distressing to France? Edgar Faure managed to reassure me a little: "That man has such strength of conviction and such strength that with him everything is possible."[8]

Just before leaving to meet the representatives of the five other "European" states waiting for him in Brussels, Mendès France declared over the radio: "Can we hesitate indefinitely? A great country has to choose. For us, the choice today is between a German rearmament that we could still supervise and a rearmament that would escape from all control on our part."

It was an argument with a clearly "European" ring.

On the morning of August 19 in Brussels, before the meeting, Mendès saw prominently displayed on the front pages of *Le Figaro* an article by

Robert Schuman about the new French proposals, an article that could be summed up in one of its sentences: "The right of veto is generalized in such a way that everything would be paralyzed; the treaty is emptied of its substance." This stab in the back of Mendès at the moment when he was about to meet his counterparts had not been premeditated by Schuman. He had written the article ten days earlier in his retreat in Moselle, and it was *Le Figaro* that had chosen the procedure, which Schuman regretted the next day.

But this was not the only blow from France that day against the head of French diplomacy. In *Franc-Tireur,* there was an article in which another European zealot, André Philip, blinded by passion, wrote that "any reduction in supranationality would produce unanimity among the Socialists in opposition to such a truncated text." This was adding stupidity to a bad action: everyone already knew that no group was less unanimous than the Socialists on the question of any form of Europe whatever, supranational or not. That would appear clearly a week later.

It is sad to recall that a man who was so admirable in other respects did something even worse. In his *Combats inachevés* (Unfinished Battles) Spaak published the letter Philip sent him at the time, a letter that had some effect on his behavior toward the spokesman of France:

> The present text of Mendès France is unacceptable to the Socialists and the MRP. If he returns from Brussels with a text accepted by you, we will obviously be obliged to vote for it. If Mendès commits himself and calls for a vote of confidence over any text at all, he has a majority, because his popularity in the country at the present time is immense, and no one will dare to bring him down. It is thus a question not of accepting texts to appease a hypothetical majority, but of personally persuading Mendès who, until very recently, has not been concerned with the question and knows absolutely nothing about it. So, be firm and at the same time sentimental and affectionate, because the man is a bundle of nerves, very touchy, someone who has to be reached through his guts.

This was the climate in which Mendès France confronted what one would barely hesitate to call a trial. The head of the French government was so strongly affected by the climate of this confrontation that, reporting on it a few days later at the podium of the Palais-Bourbon, he committed a quickly corrected slip of the tongue: "The adversaries, I mean, the partners of France."[9]

He opened the conference by declaring himself resolved to have the treaty ratified by the French Parliament, but including the modifications proposed in the "additional protocol" that had been communicated to his interlocutors three days earlier. Beyen, the Dutch representative, interrupted, arguing, not without reason, that these "modifications" changed the text so profoundly, with respect both to supranationality and to equality among the participants, that they made it into a new treaty, obliging the others to return to their respective parliaments to obtain a new ratification: there could be no question of that.

Mendès France defended his "protocol" every step of the way against Beyen (who accused him particularly of submitting Germany to "discriminatory" measures), Spaak, and Adenauer. What concessions did he obtain? According to Spaak's memoirs, the five gave in on two points. With respect to the time during which the participants would have the right to exercise their veto against integrating measures, they proposed to reduce it from eight to three years. As for the rescission clauses proposed by the French delegation, they were, according to Spaak, accepted. Mendès's interlocutors had thus gone part of the way toward compromise, but they remained very far from what he was asking them in order to assure the survival in Paris of "a government with which to negotiate or sign."

There then followed a series of incidents, initiatives, and warnings that brutally aggravated the tension. Spaak's chief of staff informed him that the American ambassador, David Bruce, was waiting for him in the library with an important message. The French delegation was alarmed. Since the day before, according to the very "European" Raymond Cartier in *Paris-Match,* "Bruce had multiplied contacts and interventions, but this was the first time that he presented himself at the Foreign Ministry during a conference session. Mendès understood that a new, sixth, adversary was confronting him and that the American intrusion was going to stiffen further the position of Germany and the Benelux."

The French delegates were not provided immediately with the amazing notes from Dulles, which Spaak was reading in the ministry library and which the four other "partners" of France were to see shortly thereafter:

> If events in Brussels make it seem desirable to you, I have no objection if you inform the ministers in Brussels that you propose immediately to organize a meeting among the Benelux countries, Germany, Italy, the United States, and Great Britain. I think that you should say clearly that the purpose of this meeting would be to consider with great urgency the best way to associate Germany on a footing of complete equality with the West, in order to bring about German rearmament.[10]

Did Dulles want to push France to extremes, to isolate it "as an example," to take revenge for Geneva? One could speculate endlessly about the motives for such a step. Dulles, not content with treating European countries like banana republics, was discriminating outrageously against France as compared to Italy: while the first, attempting to ratify the treaty, was excluded from the "club," the second, which had not even reached that point, remained a member. It is true that the "Reds" (according to Dulles) were not in power in Rome.

Dulles's note must have enchanted Beyen. It probably troubled Adenauer a little, and certainly troubled Spaak, who wrote: "I was not in agreement with the proposed policy: I found it too harsh," and explained that he refused to communicate the note to Mendès in order not to increase his irritation. Had it leaked to the French delegation? Then Mendès received a hastily scribbled note from Parodi:

> You are being subjected to the strongest, the most manifestly concerted, and the most indiscreet pressure that I have ever seen brought to bear on a French government.
>
> The situation in which you find yourself is a test. It indicates what will remain of French independence when we have, to bind us, the mechanism and juridical rules of the treaty. . . .
>
> If you accept, public opinion will clearly realize that you have given in to a maneuver designed to intimidate you. What will remain of the reproach directed against your predecessors for not having been completely independent? And with what bitterness will France take part in the European affair?[11]

The head of the French government then declared that none of the concessions obtained could bring about the adhesion of a sufficient fraction of the French Parliament and that it was therefore necessary to look for "an alternative solution."

Spaak, in his memoirs, after asserting that "the principal French objections were met in a satisfactory manner," adds a few pages later that the very next day, August 24, aware of the disaster provoked by the conference, he proposed to Mendès an addition to the treaty according to which, if a member state considered itself put "in danger" by the Community, it could appeal to the Council, which would in turn consult the Court of Arbitration.[12] This was a purely formal concession, far removed from the right of veto called for by the most moderate French negotiators. And Spaak had had to wait for the breakup of the conference before recognizing this elementary right of protest.

In fact, the Brussels discussions could have led to a "compromise on the compromise." On the one hand, PMF had agreed that each nation's right of veto would last for only two years, and not eight; that the Court of Justice of the CED could oppose this veto; and that the probationary period for the military dispositions would come to an end in eight years. For their part, the five had agreed to the "integration" of the CED into NATO and to the link between membership in the Community and the presence of American and English forces on the continent. Reciprocal concessions had been made. They should have allowed Mendès to bring back from Brussels a compromise that was honorable in his eyes and, considering the immense authority he enjoyed at the time, probably acceptable to a majority of French deputies. But the five insisted that the emphasis be put on the word *supranationality,* which the French negotiator wished to skirt precisely in order not to cut himself off from all his Gaullist allies. This demand pushed Mendès to his limit. Did they want to help him find a way out or to isolate him, to make him bend?

It is possible that the French premier, wounded by the vindictive climate surrounding him and indignant at the American intrusion, was sometimes too abrupt. But it remains true that the Brussels conference was an ambush and that these fervent "Europeans" served Europe badly by forcing into a position of hostility to the CED a statesman who was trying to save whatever there was in the treaty that could be accepted by French public opinion.[13]

Mendès had spoken of "an alternative solution." In his mind, this could only mean an appeal to London. And rather than return to Paris with empty hands, he decided to head for Chartwell, Winston Churchill's summer residence. He met the old prime minister on the morning of the twenty-third, soon joined by Anthony Eden, head of the Foreign Office. The cordiality of their reception could not conceal the fact that there were profound differences of opinion over the CED. With respect to Asia, an immediate understanding had developed between the French and the English, united against American adventurism. But as far as Europe was concerned, London found itself very close to Washington.

In the eyes of a man as single-minded as Churchill, given the fact that the CED was a French idea, why was France now retarding its realization? He repeated to Mendès: "It is the best way out. Its failure would create a dangerous situation, serious for France as well as for the West." And, more friendly than Dulles, but almost as threatening, he warned Mendès that, if the CED were rejected, the British, in agreement with the Americans, would take the initiative of asking France for "an agreement on another form of German contribution to Atlantic defense." The difference with Dulles was that he was not seeking to isolate France. But the blow was nonetheless brutal.

Before returning to Paris, Mendès visited the president of the Republic at a health resort in Normandy. For two hours, he recounted his misadventures in Brussels and, in contrast, what he thought were slightly more positive results in London. Their relations at the time were very cordial, and Mendès found the exchange comforting. The head of state declared himself in agreement with Mendès.

Mendès returned to Paris a little reassured, although he asserted in his radio broadcast of August 24:

> I was unable to accept proposals that risked shocking the conscience of many French citizens and being rejected by their deputies. If I had given in, I would have made commitments in the name of France in the knowledge that they would not be honored. That is the worst of all policies.

To his way of thinking, in the absence of the "protocol" that had been rejected by the five in Brussels, by his English friends, and by the intransigent Europeans, from Schuman to Mollet, the treaty was already doomed. He had made a commitment to open the debate in the National Assembly. He would keep his word, aware of the mortal danger in which his government would be placed by rejection of the CED: neither the MRP, nor the leadership of the SFIO, nor the right wing of the Radical Party would ever forgive him. But was he not the man of choice? Given the fact that he had no settled position on the basic issue, he was at least obliged to allow the "objective" mechanisms of decision making to come rapidly into play.

Suddenly aware of the disaster toward which the rejection of the compromise that offered them a way out was leading them, a compromise to which Mendès would have been committed, the "European" leaders (Pinay, Bidault, René Mayer) attempted in turn to introduce corrections to the text, or to persuade Mendès to call for a vote of confidence, or else to delay the debate.

Against the advice of President Coty, the Council of Ministers decided on August 27 not to call for a vote of confidence. Could the government, should the government, remain neutral? According to P.-H. Teitgen, this attitude was "unworthy" and "unconstitutional."[14] But Jacques Fauvet points out, "If it had not been [neutral], there would have been no debate, for the reason that there would have been no more government."[15]

The death agony of the CED had begun. The debate opened on August 28. PMF's preliminary presentation, which reviewed the history of the negotiations and minutely detailed objections and favorable arguments, seemed to be a discreet encouragement to reject ratification. And this was even more the case for the speech of Jules Moch, reporter of the proposal. Then the supporters of the CED attempted a last maneuver: they presented a "prejudicial motion," with a view toward adjourning the debate. To this the enemies of the CED, sensing the approach of victory, opposed a "preliminary question" (called a "dry guillotine" in parliamentary jargon), which would result in cutting off debate and would automatically bring about rejection of the proposal.

Neither Mendès nor the most conscientious and influential parliamentary leaders wanted this back-alley assassination of a proposal of international scope to which the future of France was linked. They wanted the debate to unfold in broad daylight and each leader to have the opportunity to explain himself. The head of government extracted an agreement in principle from the two camps: the "prejudicial motion" would be given up in return for abandonment of the "preliminary question." But it must be said that the CED was even assailed by the suicidal madness of its friends and that it was destined to die strangled in the shadows. A friend of René Pleven, a certain Chapin, broke the tacit contract and resurrected the "prejudicial motion." The "preliminary question" immediately reappeared; and on August 30, the killing was accomplished, but the matador was not the leader of one of the two groups determined to defeat the CED, the Gaullists and the Communists.

The voice that rose from the center of the Assembly was that of an old European hardly suspect for nationalism, one who had often argued for an understanding with Germany: Edouard Herriot. The former president of the Assembly, now a simple deputy, was so weak that he could not even be carried to the podium. It was from his bench that the famous voice, still astonishingly clear, sprang out of a mountain of tired flesh.

> Germany is taking a bound toward its sovereignty. France is taking a leap backward. It can be said that, in the Paris treaty, there is a discrimination to the detriment of France. If, taking advantage of the freedoms that have been granted it, Germany withdraws from the European Community, what happens to France? Good sense answers: if Germany has the right to withdraw, then France must have the same right. After the Brussels conference, is that the case? I see the premier giving me a negative sign; he has, in fact, explained himself in detail on this point.

The old man evoked the disappointments experienced in his negotiations with German leaders, the necessity of preserving the chances for a dialogue with the East, and concluded:

> There is talk of modifications, amendments, protocols. It is better to speak the truth: the conflict is not a debate about form, it is a fundamental conflict. For us—let me say what I think at the end of my life—the European Community is the end of France.

One can imagine the effect produced on Mendès France, at this solemn moment, by the anathema launched by the man who was at the origin of his political career and who, despite all the later differences, had continued to inspire his diplomatic vision: rejection of any Germanophobia, closeness to London, détente with the Soviet Union. If he had been tempted to reverse the direction of things and to save the CED, the old man's argument would have turned him aside.

The *coup de grâce* had thus been delivered. The voting, precipitated by the expeditious procedure of the "preliminary question" despite the combined efforts of Mendès, Paul Reynaud, and Daniel Mayer, got under way before any of those responsible for the CED (Pleven, Schuman, Pinay) was able to present a defense; and the ratification of the treaty was rejected, in the form of adoption of the "preliminary question," by 319 to 264, in an atmosphere of riot.

This inglorious burial of the CED was not a defeat for the Mendès

France government, but a death sentence. He knew that neither the MRP, nor Guy Mollet, nor René Mayer—nor John Foster Dulles—would ever forgive him for the "crime" of August 30. He was aware of the fact that rejection of the CED would not leave his government long to live. Three ministers who supported the CED—Bourgès-Maunoury, Emile Hughes, and Claudius-Petit—left immediately, while Jacques Chaban-Delmas returned. As for Robert Buron, caught between his loyalty to PMF and his "European" sentiments, he decided to remain in the government.

A quarter-century later, one of Mendès's closest colleagues of the time, and one of the most "European" confided to us:

> The rejection of the CED, which was fatal to the Mendès cabinet, and which I had for my part attempted to avoid, was a historical necessity. The adoption of the CED, the entry of France into the system, would have been the opening of a permanent civil war in France. Imagine the Sunday ceremonies at the war memorial in every village, with the Gaullist and the Communist united behind the tricolor. The RPF–PCF alliance institutionalized from that point on would not only have made France ungovernable, it would have put it in a state of uncontrollable effervescence. It was this mortal danger, which I did not clearly perceive at the time, nor perhaps did Mendès, that we avoided.

But the crisis provoked by the vote of the French Parliament within the Atlantic Alliance took on an extremely violent character. Not content with having ruined in Brussels the last chances for the "compromise" that could have saved something of the CED, on August 31 John Foster Dulles made public a provocative declaration: "We must now restore full sovereignty to Germany. This was promised to it in the proposal for the CED: it cannot be punished, since it has committed no crime." And the American secretary of state concluded by asserting that the United States remained ready to support the European countries that were loyal to the idea of a united Europe and that defection of only one would not prevent them from acting. "Rarely," commented Spaak, "has a more aggressive declaration been made by the representative of a great country to condemn the action of an ally."[16]

While Dulles undertook a journey to Europe, in the course of which he decided not to stop in Paris but only in London and Bonn—where he signed a communiqué with Adenauer specifying that the Federal Republic should, without further delay and on an equal footing, participate in Atlantic defense—Anthony Eden visited Brussels, Bonn, and Paris in turn, with a view to organizing a Euro-Atlantic conference in London. In Paris on September 15, Mendès France presented to him the conditions for French acceptance of such a proposal, which was aimed essentially at organizing and controlling the entry of Germany into the Atlantic defense system: that the future German forces be in proportion to those of the two

Anglo-Saxon powers, that Great Britain participate organically in the new defensive system, that the armaments of the various partners be reciprocally controlled, and finally that there be no atomic armament of Germany.

With these reservations formulated in a way to interfere as little as possible with the reconstruction efforts of the British minister, Mendès in a sense returned to the offensive. On September 19, in Nevers, he delivered a plea for Franco–German reconciliation, the first that had ever been given before a monument to the dead of the Resistance. The next day, September 20, he stepped up to the podium of the European Assembly in Strasbourg, where he finally described the solution that corresponded not only to his deepest wishes but also to the perspectives opened by his conversation with Eden.

Once the proposed community organization had turned out to be impracticable, he said to the Assembly, it was appropriate to return to the formula of an alliance whose structure already existed: the Brussels pact signed immediately after the war by France, England, Belgium, the Netherlands, and Luxembourg. Of course, this pact had the objective of preventing the rebirth of German militarism. But since things were as they were, why not invite Bonn, and of course Rome, to join it?

And the head of the French government then expressed the idea that in a sense linked the future pact to the defunct CED:

> In its current state, the Brussels pact does not include any central authority with the character of an executive. If tomorrow we entrust to the Council of Ministers of this pact executive responsibilities that would be exercised in the military area, we would certainly have to introduce certain elements of authority and, why not say it, a certain dose of supranationality.

The transition had thus been prepared.

On September 28, less than a month after the veto of the French Assembly, the conference of London opened with the aim of replacing the CED with an alliance including Germany. The day before, Eden had sent a note to Churchill specifying that "the success of the conference depended on Great Britain's commitment to maintain its present forces on the continent."

This was the subject of Mendès France's first intervention at the conference table. The French spokesman even insisted that English and American forces be maintained on the continent throughout the duration of the Brussels pact: fifty years. It was asking a good deal of a British government to thus call into question its historic golden rule of free disposition of its forces and to agree to submit London to a form of supranational authority.

Her Majesty's prime minister called a cabinet meeting in the evening which lasted late into the night. The next day, Anthony Eden declared at the conference table, in solemn tones:

> I am authorized by my government to propose to you the following commitment. The United Kingdom will continue to maintain on the European continent, German territory included, troops of a strength equivalent to those now assigned to the supreme command of Allied forces in Europe under the terms of the Atlantic Pact. The United Kingdom commits itself not to withdraw its forces against the wishes of the majority of the Brussels pact powers. I am certain that you will understand, gentlemen, the outstanding step forward that this offer represents for my country, whose history is that of an island.

For Mendès, this was the realization of a long-held hope. It was the acceptance by his English friends of a permanent commitment, of the beginning of a surrender of sovereignty for the benefit of its Western allies. He felt proud to be, along with Anthony Eden, the artisan of this anchoring of England to the continent, a realization of one of his fundamental diplomatic conceptions.

It was nevertheless true that the London agreements signed on October 3 establishing the Western European Union established the principle of German rearmament and full membership of Bonn in NATO. It was this that particularly struck French public opinion, then shocked by the trial of Paris Gestapo chief General Oberg, which recalled the horrors of the Occupation. What Mendès felt as a success—and it was in many respects—was seen by a number of the French only as the acceptance of a *diktat.*

And yet, the French negotiators in London had obtained not only the English guarantee but the limitation of German forces, the control of their armament, Bonn's renunciation of atomic weapons, and, even better, a commitment by the Federal Republic "never to resort to force to achieve German reunification or a modification of its borders," and, "in case such an action was undertaken," the assurance that Washington, London, and Paris would withdraw from Bonn "its rights to any guarantee and any military assistance." This was what, on the insistence of Mendès France, was signed by the governments that, five weeks earlier, had caused his attempted compromise to fail because it contained a shade of "discrimination" against the German Federal Republic.

On October 13, the National Assembly gave the Mendès France government a mandate to continue in Paris the negotiations that had begun in London, concluded by the agreements of October 23, known as the "Paris agreements." The Socialists rallied to it as a bloc, the MRP abstained, the Communists remained irreducibly hostile, and the Gaullists were divided. But he still had to extract from the Assembly the ratification of a treaty that would bring about German rearmament.

Mendès France, who had not been able to avoid playing the role of liquidator of the CED, had still to reach an agreement with Adenauer to liquidate as well the ingenious formula of "Europeanization" of the Sarre put together six months earlier by Pierre-Henri Teitgen (then vice-premier) and the federal chancellor. The progress of German national feeling in the Sarre, encouraged by propaganda from Bonn, as well as by the punctiliousness and delays of French bureaucrats, had made the proposal a dead letter.

However "European" it might proclaim itself to be, the Federal Republic wished to hear no more about that particular "Europeanization." And the spokesmen of Bonn, who in Brussels had so criticized the French "interpretations" of the CED, interpreted in their turn the October 23 agreements on the Sarre (linked with the Paris agreements as a whole) in such a way that the German character of the territory—obvious in any event—was settled even before the projected referendum decided the question. There too, Mendès was obliged to manage a bankruptcy. But the renunciation thereby accepted suddenly opened much more positive perspectives with Bonn. From that moment on, Adenauer forgot to oppose Mendès systematically and stopped considering him a "neutralist" saboteur of Europe.

The "European" debate was closed neither with France's allies nor with its presumed opponents as long as it was not closed in the French Parliament. The treaty was signed on October 23. PMF, all the more determined to go directly to the heart of things since he had been able to measure the disastrous consequences of Paris's hesitations over the CED, decided that it would be submitted for approval by the National Assembly before the end of the year.

16.
THE SUBCONTRACTING OF THE ECONOMY

Since he had left power ten years before, Pierre Mendès France had never thought of returning except to a position of economic and financial responsibility. If he had supposed that the succession to Queuille or Bidault as premier would be offered to him, he had not imagined that it would be for any mission but the restoration of the French economy.

That was the direction he had chosen for his research and his career at the age of twenty; he had devoted himself to the task under both Blum and De Gaulle; he had engaged in international combat on the subject from Bretton Woods to New York; and since 1945, his parliamentary life had been summed up by a merciless annual critique of the budgets of the Fourth Republic's governments—his "Indochinese" indictments were heard for years as little more than an economist's phillipics expressing indignation at the outpouring of "unproductive expenditures."

And yet, when he was catapulted to power by the events of May 1954, he turned away from his chosen area for which he was so well prepared to devote himself to diplomatic battles. Once the burden of Indochina had been set down, one might think that he would return to his vocation, his natural field of action. But Tunisia was waiting for him, and then Europe. He remained at the Foreign Ministry and "subcontracted"[1] the totality of economic responsibilities to a man whose ideas were very different from his own and over whom he had no hold, knowing that he was competent, prestigious, and strengthened by innumerable connections.

It should be noted, however, that although the astounding pragmatism of Edgar Faure was rather distant from Mendès's conceptions, a very subtle blend of realism and interventionist principles, the new premier took account of the fact that Faure as head of government in 1952 had not taken the easy path but had attempted to impose a severe program of budgetary economies and new taxes, regretting perhaps that this courage had slightly retarded his government career.

In his speech of candidacy, Mendès had clearly explained that as soon as the Indochinese settlement had been reached he would ask for special powers to bring about the restoration of the French economy. This operation was planned for the month of August.

From Geneva, on July 18, 1954, only two days before the Indochinese deadline he had imposed on himself, Mendès France sent Faure a note that he characterized as a "working document" which he recognized would be open to modification. And he added: "I have no trouble imagining that, on one point or another, differences of opinion that would be difficult to reconcile will come to light; it would be inappropriate for the final report to present alternative solutions."

It was not on the analysis, which emphasized the low French standard of living, the weakness of productivity, the decline of inflation, the necessity of achieving full employment, and the fundamental requirement of assuring the conversion of unproductive expenditures into productive investments, but on remedies that "Mendèsists" and "Faurists" were to diverge, despite the prudence of the former.

The July 18 note explained:

> One can imagine a brutal conversion:
> —either through a sudden lifting of exchange controls, that is, the confrontation of our economy with more productive and therefore stronger economies;
> —or else through vigorous intervention and adherence to a plan. But these two methods must be discarded, the one because it would impose suffering and would involve intolerable social reactions, the other because it presupposes a political and administrative context that does not exist. Finally, only one procedure is conceivable, which consists in applying both methods, but in a measured and gradual manner.

The most significant proposal in the note had to do with the means for implementing the policy of conversion: "Conversion will speed up the rhythm of elimination of marginal enterprises. It will have to take a form capable of making the process less painful."

He then enumerated, in order, fiscal policy, the direction of appropriations, public investment, and the discriminatory encouragement of internal financing.

> A new character will be given to the policy of conversion by general application of the following principle: reform of the French economy creates innocent victims whom the state will aid by considering them to a certain extent as disaster victims; but this aid will be given only for the purpose of making the victims thereafter productive and capable of being useful to the nation.

It is an understatement to say that Edgar Faure and his colleagues interpreted these directives freely, in relation to a situation that seemed to them less constraining than it did to the experts grouped around the premier. Out of the energetic conversion strategy favored by PMF's entourage and the neoliberalism of the Ministry of Finance, there emerged a hybrid tending to promote a "social market economy," which, instead of *"allowing* economic laws to operate, gave itself the task of *making* them operate."[2]

The government proposal obtained a very large majority, but the Assembly limited the duration of the grant of plenary powers to the end of the year. Moreover, the premier had spoken prudently from the podium of the Assembly:

> We have no intention of giving immediately, by improvisation, and in disorder, a great deal of scope to an action whose objective will be to transform from top to bottom an important part of our national economy. It is a long-term project that we are undertaking; it will have to extend over several years, at the risk of disappointing those who may have developed a slightly puerile idea of our plans.

Those who expected a shock in this area, recalling the initiatives taken by the head of government in other areas, did not hide their disappointment, although they often placed the responsibility on Edgar Faure. They regretted in particular that what had appeared as the foundation of Mendès France's economic strategy, the conversion of marginal industries or enterprises, was given only a very restricted application, with the Conversion Fund receiving a grant of only five billion francs.

The dynamism expected from Mendès France, if not from his economics minister, nevertheless showed itself in some areas, notably with respect to agricultural surpluses, where a program limiting production of sugar beets, among other commodities, ended up dealing with the alcohol problem. This was an old concern for Mendès France, as a rural deputy who had been able to measure the ravages caused by excessive consumption of alcohol in a region like Normandy. The concern was so vigorous, and celebrated, that it had taken on an almost mythic cast and had made the glass of milk he often placed on the podium of the Assembly before beginning to speak a kind of emblem.

A 1954 study of the constellation of problems associated with the production of sugar beets for the purpose of distillation (along with storage) their distribution, and their consumption had led a group of experts under the direction of Georges Boris to the conclusion that it would have been more beneficial to the national community—independently of any problems of health or morality—to pour the alcohol thus produced down the drain, adding a franc for every liter thrown away.

As soon as he came to power, Mendès set up an interdepartmental committee under the direction of Paul Legatte, formerly of the Finance Ministry. The committee came up with various proposals before the beginning of the October Assembly session. While the consumption of milk was encouraged by various procedures for flavoring, long-term storage, and packaging, the government decided on September 25 to transfer two-thirds of beet production from distilleries to sugar plants, without being able to prevent a consequent saturation of the sugar market. The administrative reduction of planting and of producer prices helped to diminish stocks and offered the beginning of a resolution. But the Mendès cabinet was overthrown—with the help of the beet producers—before it had worked out real solutions.

In the mind of Pierre Mendès France, this operation with respect to agricultural surpluses was obviously only a test for the conversion of French production in general. But he considered that, despite the strength of the resistance and the political cost of the operation, the problem was pressing enough, burning enough, the situation absurd enough, for him to obtain from public opinion and from parties like the MRP support equivalent to the risk he was taking, allowing him to create a precedent. He intended to take on next the conversion of energy sources—coal and oil— and the chemical and metallurgical industries.

At the moment of risking an evaluation of the economic policy of the Mendès cabinet, we will give the floor to the two men, one on either side, who tried to make their views prevail. First to the minister in charge, Edgar Faure, who said to us in June 1980:

> In all conscience, I believe that what we accomplished then at the Finance Ministry was very beneficial. If I dared, I would speak, taking account of the data that were available to us, of a masterpiece. Mendès had courageously undertaken the bold work of decolonization and settlement of the European questions. While these surgical operations were under way, we had to protect the patient from any shocks. This is what we did, my colleagues and I. While Mendès was operating, we maintained very close contact with the world of business enterprises, and with wage-earners, to whom we granted important gains. The measures of structural reform were taken flexibly, without provoking disturbances. In sum, we assured for Mendès, launched on his perilous enterprises, economic and social peace. What more could he ask for? In January 1955, he decided to make the revolution in the economic realm as

well, and he moved me from Finance to Foreign Affairs. Mendès is very intelligent, perhaps more intelligent than I, and I admire him a great deal. He is also very courageous. But I have more common sense than he does. And being a good economics minister, you know, is a matter of common sense.

The diagnosis by Simon Nora, formulated in a confidential note prepared for the premier in November 1954, after six months of experiments, was much less optimistic:

From many contacts, official and unofficial, governmental and private, I have developed the very clear feeling that we are in the process of losing credibility every day for everything that has to do with economic policy. Skepticism, and sometimes even anxiety, is growing in management circles, while at the same time we have not avoided disappointment among workers, farmers, and civil servants.

This phenomenon is still very largely masked by the enormous reserve of confidence that you have called forth. But this reserve is being used up. . . . What is the reason for this?

We have done nothing strikingly bad in the economic realm, and we have done some rather good things. But what would have been a success for your predecessors remains far behind the hopes that had been placed in you. . . .

The technique of contact with the public that has succeeed so well for you on general political questions is completely deficient with respect to economic policy. Besides general and necessarily vague speeches, the public does not know where we are going concretely, and you cannot endlessly describe long-term objectives.

With respect to wages, our attitude at the October meeting could be justified only if it were followed by continuous and determined action, backed with sufficient resources to encourage the negotiation of collective bargaining agreements. There is no need to belabor this point; it is enough to say that even this idea is not shared by the majority of those in your government and in the administration, who would have to overcome the real resistance of managment. . . . The economic accounts, contrary to what has been asserted by the Ministry of Finance, do not in any way justify a policy of budgetary austerity. Considering the forecasts concerning resources available in agriculture and industry, they would justify on the contrary a very active policy of investment. Since we have neither carried out large transfers within the budget for the benefit of public investments nor financed those investments through the Treasury, it is all the more necessary to set into motion all the techniques of stimulation and orientation of private investments.

A judgment on the Mendès France government's economic policy as a whole can only come at the close of the experiment, in February 1955, after the brief attempt to impose a bolder stragegy, with Robert Buron replacing Edgar Faure at Finance. But nevertheless, by November 1954, once the broad outlines of the budget were known, one could judge, considering the exceptional powers obtained from the Assembly on August 10, by a premier who was then in possession of a prestige without precedent since De Gaulle, that the use that had been made of those powers was rather modest: the 1955 budget proposed 3,245 billion old francs in appropriations. Military appropriations were reduced by 80 billion compared to 1954, those for education increased by 46 billion, and for investments in general by 160 billion.

This verdict of timidity should be corrected by the following: France in 1954 was a country with only fifty thousand unemployed (officially, hence they were aided), where the wage index climbed by 7.5 percent while the cost of living rose by only 1.3 percent. On this level, we may salute Edgar Faure and recognize that, here, Sancho was useful to Don Quixote.

But it would be tempting to confront Mendès France with the memory of 1945. It was in order to be free to devote himself to "grand designs" that General de Gaulle had at the time chosen to entrust the French economy to the supporter of prudent management, René Pleven, rather than to Mendès, the advocate of harsh therapy. Hadn't Mendès made the same choice in 1954? Entirely turned toward large-scale history, hadn't he let management of the economy stagnate in the same way, delegated a comforting deputy?

The parallel does not hold. The economic and financial situation of the France of 1954 had little do with the tragic conditions of 1945. The drastic procedures called for by Mendès after the Liberation, against inflation and for reconstruction, for the revival of the country, would have been inoperative in 1954. There are times for surgery and times for family medicine.

One may regret that the prestige Mendès France had acquired as head of government was not immediately put at the service of bolder initiatives in that realm. But there is nothing that allows us to assert that the offensive would have been successful on all fronts at once.

17.
A ROPE AND SOME KNIVES

"What a shame," Claude Gruson, economic oracle of the "PMF system," said at the time to a close friend, "that a man like that does not have the time to take care of important things." "Important things," for this specialist, were obviously production, exchange, and the French standard of living. The "October deadline" established by Mendès in his speech of candidacy was approaching. Fighting had ended in Indochina. The Tunisian negotiation was moving along. The London agreements had just been signed.

On October 10, 1954, Pierre Mendès France was in Louviers and, before the pretty façade of "his" city hall—the place in the world where he may have felt most comfortable—he spoke, for once, not to the inhabitants of Louviers, but to the French public as a whole:

> An increase of 5 percent in wages was predicted. Thanks to the possibilities we recognized, the increase will not be 5, but 6.5 percent. This is the case while prices have remained stable for six months. We hope that at the next meeting in April we will be able to present another improvement, concrete and tangible, in the living conditions of the working class.

The unions were not triumphant, if only because of the very personal procedure chosen for the announcement. Mendès was not playing the game of tough negotiations in which the workers' spokesmen extracted

concessions from bourgeois power, what he called, a little contemptu-
ously, "haggling": he decided coolly, he "bestowed," grumbled Benoît
Frachon of the CGT. On this occasion, the head of government was using
the work of the celebrated National Accounts Committee that he had
directed for two years before his election, work which revealed that, in
the autumn of 1954, wages could be increased without affecting prices.[1]

In any event, on October 19, *Le Monde,* which was not in the habit of
bestowing laurels, asserted that "Mendès France is the most popular man
in the country." This evaluation did not help facilitate the negotiations he
was about to undertake to rectify or clarify relations between the government and the various factions of the political class, although not with the
parties themselves, with which he had decided not to deal from the outset.
Now that he thought he had gone through the worst external storms, he
thought, in order to settle economic problems, of broadening the base of
his government with the Socialists, his best supporters, and perhaps with
the MRP, his "best enemies."

But he had not recognized the depth and virulence of the rancor that
had accumulated against him, both among the notables of the Fourth
Republic responsible for the Indochinese disaster and the North African
catastrophes and among the "Europeans," obsessed by the rejection of
the CED, the "crime of August 30." At about this time, with the opening
of the new parliamentary session, there began the war of attrition that the
Assembly, subjugated for a few months, declared against the man it had
chosen at the beginning of the summer in a moment of disarray. Attrition?
Harassment? Guerrilla warfare? A more terrible image was invented by
the most penetrating observer of the period, Jacques Fauvet, who spoke
of the "bathtub torture." It was a matter of gradually suffocating the
government, allowing it to breathe and then pushing it under again.

Why did this torture last so long? The three forces hostile to Mendès—"Europeans," "colonial" Radicals, and the beet lobby (that is, the
MRP, the right wing of the Radical Party, and the extreme right)—in
alliance with the Communists, were in a position to bring him down by
early November. But two important considerations restrained the executioners. First was the fact that until November 22, by virtue of a
strange constitutional provision,[2] if PMF were overthrown by an absolute
majority, he would be able to dissolve the Assembly, which would have
turned into a triumph for him because the public remained very loyal to
him.

There was also the prospect of the ratification of the Paris agreements, which were not very popular. It was important to allow PMF to
carry out this thankless task, which would expose him to some very harsh
attacks, from the extreme right to the extreme left. It was only after the
ratification debate in the Assembly, scheduled for the end of the year, that
the execution would proceed on one pretext or another.

Because this poisoned atmosphere in the Assembly and the various party leaderships was growing thicker, Mendès was able to open his first important political dialogue in an entirely different direction. From the very beginning of his government, as we know, he had maintained cordial relations with the majority of the Gaullists. Although his "appeal" to Colombey at dawn on June 18 had produced only a distant comment, six of the general's most important "companions" had joined his government. And although three of these ministers had left him in August over the CED, Jacques Chaban-Delmas had returned in early September, once the treaty was "buried." It was particularly noteworthy that Christian Fouchet, a Gaullist from June 1940, a "general's man" if there ever was one, had not moved an inch from PMF, serving as a living link between the grandeur of De Gaulle and the effectiveness of Mendès.

Mendès France was nevertheless surprised when, in late September 1954, he was visited by Edmond Michelet, one of the Gaullists most often charged with establishing contact with the left. He had come to set up a meeting that could, of course, remain secret. It was decided that the communiqué from the conversation would be distributed after the meeting was over.

The meting took place on October 13, the day before the publication of De Gaulle's *Mémoires de guerre,* which treated Mendès very well. After approving the "Carthage policy" and the London agreements following the rejection of the CED, the general soon raised fundamental objections having to do not with PMF but with the system. And he objected:[3]

> The regime does not permit you to have a government. It allows you the choice between the front bench and a cabinet that would contain your rivals. The danger will affect you when you decide to undertake structural reforms. No one can act within this system. I myself could do nothing. You were "allowed" to liquidate Indochina, Tunisia, and the CED. But you will not be allowed to pursue a constructive politics, a French politics.
>
> From time to time, people may very well cheer as you pass by, because you are new and attractive, but when you have gotten rid of what troubles the regime, the regime will get rid of you at the first opportunity.

When the premier asked him about the means to impart vigor to the country, the general replied: "I tried to change the regime—you didn't help very much—and I failed."

Since De Gaulle was criticizing him for not "helping" him by joining the RPF, as De Gaulle had proposed, Mendès also had a bone to pick: "You didn't think it necessary to answer the telegram I sent you on June 18."

"You made a mistake," replied De Gaulle, "in not speaking more clearly about the European army, since you were opposed to the proposal. You should have been more energetic, more categorical. The CED would have been rejected by four hundred votes, and you would have been a great man. And you would have been able to speak in London with much more authority."

"It was impossible. The government would have disintegrated before debate opened in Parliament. Another government would have been founded which, like all its predecessors, would have delayed the debate indefinitely. My principal aim was to put an end to a situation that had been paralyzing the country for three years. That has been done."

Observing ironically that "the government has fallen apart even so"—which was neither very accurate nor very equitable, since his own friends had replaced the departing "Europeans"—the general continued in a very cordial, almost paternal tone, offering advice on the search for détente with the East. He was not in favor of a four-power conference, in which everyone would concentrate on taking "spectacular positions," and preferred, he said ordinary methods: "Have a good ambassador in Moscow and use serious diplomatic means—conversations and exchanges of notes."

The last part of the conversation was devoted to a reconsideration of the disagreement of 1945, which led to Mendès France's resignation and to a restatement of the incompatibility between a genuine politics as envisaged by Mendès and the existing system. "You'll see. 'They' will not let you act." As Pierre Rouanet notes,[4] the general seemed to have forgotten (like Mendès, which is even more surprising) that this contemptuous "they" included about a hundred Gaullist deputies, whose support of the government, if he, De Gaulle, were to come out for it, would resolve most of the problems he had called insoluble.

At a Gaullist meeting on December 4, 1954, the general argued without reservation for an international strategy that closely resembled that of Mendès, with an added dash of jingoism.

> The London and Paris agreements are greatly preferable to the rejected treaty. But before implementing a system involving German rearmament, several conditions ought to be fulfilled. The first is that negotiations with the East should clarify whether or not international detente can be brought about. . . . It is incumbent on France above all to undertake such negotiations; France is historically, geographically, and politically qualified to attempt to build a bridge to the Eastern complex.

De Gaulle concluded by saluting "the ardor, the value, the vigor" of Pierre Mendès France, a formulation that seems to come out of the *Mémoires de guerre* and that, coming from the general for PMF, was the moral support that most of the leaders of the Fourth Republic had waited for in vain. De Gaulle did not clearly commit himself in support of his former minister. But he quite obviously found in him, for the first time in the regime, something of what he thought of as a sense for the French state.

He thought, as he had had said, that Mendès France would quickly be defeated by the "system." But he considered that Mendès's efforts would have rectified French policies, put an end to (or rather a brake on) "decadence," and left open the opportunity for renewal for which the absolute prerequisite was a transformation of institutions.

The head of government had at least gotten some favorable words from General de Gaulle. He hardly expected anything more, and all things considered, the episode remained one of the pleasant surprises of that political autumn, a season when he was looking for his second wind.

And then an opportunity arose, in this area, to consolidate a fragile position: the one he occupied in the Radical Party. However peculiar his position in the party, to which he was dispassionately loyal, knowing the feelings toward him harbored by many of its members and especially the heavily conservative tendencies that dominated it, he nevertheless wanted to group the majority of the party behind him and his government before undertaking the parliamentary struggles which promised to be very difficult at the end of the year.

He was fully aware that the majority of the leadership, from the administrative president, Martinaud-Déplat, who controlled the party apparatus under the casual aegis of Herriot, the honorary president, to the professed right wing, had forgiven him neither for Geneva nor for Carthage and would never support him. But it might be possible to seize leadership of the apparatus from Martinaud and thus regain control of the party by isolating the old notables.

When the Radical congress met in Marseille on October 14, it was learned that an old companion in struggle of Mendès, his former "patron" at the time of the Young Turks, Edouard Daladier, had decided to join battle against Martinaud; he was a candidate for the administrative presidency of the party. It was a modest role for such a celebrated figure. But the premier of 1939 thought the young leader, whose talent and courage he admired, worthy of such devotion. The question was whether Daladier had preserved enough authority in the party to do Mendès the service of getting rid of the man that Mauriac described in this way on October 15:

Martinaud-Déplat is bowing and scraping in Marseille before the premier and bathing him in the gentle tears of eternal friendship. But when he took out his handkerchief, perhaps he dropped, on the station platform, the rope he intended for his great friend, the rope he has not yet managed to put around his neck.

Mendès may not have been fully aware of the importance of what was at stake. In the debate, he was almost as neutral as he had been in the Palais-Bourbon on the CED. Although very few of his predecessors had chosen this attitude in such a setting, he considered his governmental functions incompatible with direct involvement in the battle for real power within the party.

> It has often been said that Radicalism is less a party than a state of mind. It is perhaps this flexibility which will allow it today to carry on, through the new requirements of technology, the concern for individual liberty that it has always maintained in the forefront. . . .
>
> Last year I said to you, and I repeat it as I did when I began this speech: make no mistake, we have reached the breaking point of a worn out system, we are in 1788. Well, now look around you. The country has recovered its pride and its hope. The moment has come when old abuses, old privileges long and bitterly defended against the general interest, can and must fall at a single stroke. It now feels possible once again to construct the future.

Martinaud knew he was in danger. The reactionary direction he had given to his activity, his links with the great feudal interests in North Africa, the attacks he had made against the premier in the Assembly in August, had provoked a wave of indignation against him.

But the administrative president knew better than anyone, better even than the old professional Daladier, the mechanisms of the party and how to manipulate a vote. He obtained a vote by representative, not calculated according to the number of members, the overwhelming majority of whom supported Mendès and were thus in favor of Daladier. And he arranged that the majority of representatives would vote for him. He had, just barely, saved his position, and Mendès, who was apparently wary of this little war in Marseille and the "short-lived victory" that would have "crowned a dubious battle,"[5] lost the opportunity to seize, through the intermediary of Daladier, a lever of power. He would later regret it.

One of the sentences of the Marseille speech[6] was, quite obviously, an appeal to the SFIO to participate in his government. When he returned from Marseille, he devoted the time not devoured by negotiating the treaty of Paris to this task, resuming a project developed several months earlier.

If Mendès had not really struggled in June to have the Socialists participate in his government, this was becuase he knew that the SFIO was then too divided over the CED not to fear dealing with the debate Mendès had already announced from within the government. The August 30 vote, splitting the SFIO in two, had confirmed the correctness of this prudence. But when, on October 12, the representatives of the SFIO recovered their unanimity in favor of the London agreements, the time seemed to have arrived for the Socialists to enter a government for which economic and social objectives had become priorities.

On October 19, Mendès France wrote to six Socialist deputies: Augustin Laurent, leader of the Socialist federation of the Nord, Albert Gazier, Robert Lacoste, Gaston Defferre, Marcel David. and Alain Savary. "This government will soon have been in power for five months and, because of the very policies it has followed, you have been its most determined and loyal supporters." He therefore invited them to join the government.

The reaction of Guy Mollet, who was immediately informed, was distinctly unfavorable. First of all because, loyal to his principles, Mendès had addressed the man, not the party, short-circuiting Mollet, the guardian of party orthodoxy. And also because Mendès had called on two men who, in different ways, represented challenges to Mollet: Augustin Laurent, because of his seniority, his prestige, and the influence he exercised from Lille over the neighboring party federations, including Mollet's own more modest one in Pas-de-Calais, and Gaston Defferre, Mollet's young rival for leadership of the party; and also on two "rebels" to the pro-CED line of the SFIO, Savary and Lacoste. Mendès had not shown him enough deference.

In order to approve a decision that everything seemed to favor and that party institutions had made in favor of governments further removed from socialism, Mollet demanded that a special congress be called on November 11. On the eve of the debate, he made known his doctrinaire hostility, although he had been less vigorous in other circumstances, by writing in an internal party bulletin: "If the Socialists enter a government they do so not in order to participate in the management, even the good management, of bourgeois society but in order to transform that society." To this, Edouard Depreux objected that they had participated in governments whose management, bad management, had not transformed society.

At the congress held in Suresnes, three motions were proposed: Lussy's, against participation, received 498 votes; Depreux's, authorizing it, 1,091; and Guy Mollet's, for "constitutional participation," won the day with 1,733 votes. The general secretary, afraid of opposing the prestigious government, had invented the device of posing conditions he knew to be unacceptable: "It was neither a program nor a plan, but a long catalogue, offering immediate satisfaction to different social categories without saying where the corresponding resources were to be found. It was obvious that this constituted a barely camouflaged rejection."[7]

PMF felt that this refusal to join him, coming from the mass party that was, in spirit, closest to his objectives, condemned his government to continue its exhausting voyage without a compass, improvising as it went. Worse: deprived of the structural support of the SFIO, which had nevertheless been nearly unanimous in approving the London agreements and could not fail to support his social policies, cautious as they might be, he would enter the great battle for ratification of the London and Paris agreements at the end of the year alone, confronting the MRP without the "European" credentials of the SFIO. The party of Bidault and Tietgen would feel freer to assault him.

Mendès France had nevertheless not immediately given up the idea of forming an alliance with the MRP. From the outset he had obtained the participation of two of them: Robert Buron and André Monteil. He had rather friendly relationships with others, especially Jacques Fonlupt-Espéraber, his lawyer in the Clermont-Ferrand trial. The MRP had supported him in the battle for "special powers" over the economy and in certain aspects of his North African policy. But then had come August 30 (preceded by Robert Schuman's letter to Le Figaro stabbing Mendès in the back).

The burial of the CED seemed to eliminate hopes for rapprochement. Nevertheless, in October, Mendès began to think of it again. A number of MRP deputies, like Robert Schuman, were planning to support the London agreements. But at the MRP National Council meeting of November 13 and 14, the anti-Mendès faction won out under the leadership of François de Menthon, who would not forgive PMF for his "antidemocratic" radio talks, and P.-H. Teitgen, who oddly alleged that he preferred to support Pinay or Laniel, "who did not raise hopes," rather than Mendès "who had," for "they could only be disappointed." He added, very significantly: "The truth is not always on the side of popular enthusiasm." Thereafter, guerrilla warfare against the government resumed and intensified over the budget, which one of the MRP leaders called a "Laniel budget."

The pivotal party of the Assembly had decided on his defeat. And although some hesitation may have remained in the minds of a few, the premier's institutional proposals, tending toward a very modest strengthening of the executive, and especially his electoral plan for a return to voting by district, definitively alienated from him the MRP, who supported proportional representation.

Deeply devoted to voting by district—because he believed that it was in this framework that could come forth the strength of conviction of public men, the true relationship between voters and elected officials, and the parliamentarian's capacity for accomplishment, and not in the vast machines tinted by ideology that were set in motion by proportional representation—Mendès could not avoid stirring up this hornet's nest, at the risk of intensifying the opposition of the two groups that were hostile by essence to the formula: the Communists and the MRP. He no longer expected anything from the former. And he broke his last ties with the party of Georges Bidault, who sneered: "We have reached the peak of the politics of renewal and hope! Voting by district with two rounds exists nowhere. We are going to be the laughingstock of the universe!"[8]

In short, "the knives were being sharpened," as Mauriac wrote. Brought up inside the party and aware of its internal workings, Robert Buron advised Mendès against making any further attempts with the MRP. "In this movement of passionate men," writes Jacques Julliard, "resentment carried the day."[9] The reprieve granted by the tacticians would not last. Others were preparing to place the rope that Martinaud-Déplat had not dropped in Marseille around the neck of the man of Geneva, Carthage, and the rejection of the CED.

On August 30, John Foster Dulles had suddenly taken Mendès aside: "I have been told some dirty things about you. But our experts have determined that the 'information' was counterfeit." "I hope," retorted the head of the French government, "that you didn't pay too much for it."[10]

These "dirty things" had been floating around for a long time, long before Mendès was voted into power by the National Assembly and he undertook negotiations with Asian Communists and Tunisian nationalists that were to make him, in the eyes of the right, the "dissipator of the empire." Anti-Semitism naturally served as a backdrop to a campaign focused on the "progressivism" or the "neutralism" of PMF, on his more or less active collusion with communism.

"Early in the summer," writes Jacques Fauvet in his *IVe République* (Fourth Republic),

> some members of Parliament, one of them in good faith, carried around to editoral offices and restaurants, with photocopies in support, the "proof" that M. Mendès France was really named Cerf[11] and that his government contained a traitor in the person of M. Mitterrand. The two accusations supported one another: a man capable of changing his identity was just as capable of revealing national defense secrets.

Thus was created the atmosphere for "the affair of the leaks."

Leaks had in fact occurred, well before Mendès France came to power flanked by Edgar Faure and Mitterrand. But it was not until early July 1954, immediately after PMF formed his cabinet, that those who had evidence of them—the most authentic and the least—decided to make the scandal public. Some were mere henchmen, and others were political figures. The most active of the former was a policeman named Jean Dides, who, associated with a man named Delarue, a former collaborator with the Gestapo known as "M. Charles," and possessor of a precious list, had devoted himself to the struggle against communism, with the encouragement and protection of the interior minister of the Laniel cabinet, Léon Martinaud-Déplat, and of the prefect of police, Jean Baylot.

It happened that the former had been eliminated on June 13 and replaced on the nineteenth by François Mitterrand, who had, a month later, "chewed the ear off" the latter. That the rancor of Martinaud and Baylot played a role in the explosion and developments of the affair, intensifying and embittering their political convictions, is obvious. In power, they were silent; in opposition, they accused. Through the intermediary of Dides, they were aiming at the two ministers closest to Mendès: Mitterrand and Edgar Faure.

It was Christian Fouchet, "companion" of Dides during his days with the RPF, who alerted Mendès France in early July: Dides had just shown him documents provided by "his" informant in the Communist Party that referred to a meeting of the Politburo of the PCF. But the most remarkable thing was not that Jacques Duclos denounced the "lying" policies of the government, but that in support of this accusation he quoted word for word from the minutes of a session of the Committee of National Defense that had taken place on June 28, a week earlier: the session, chaired by René Coty, and attended by Mendès, the principal ministers—including Mitterrand, Edgar Faure, and Koenig—and several generals, in which there had been discussion of the possibility of sending draftees to Indochina.

Fouchet had immediately asked Dides on whom his suspicions fell. "My informant thinks it's Edgar Faure. But I think it's Mitterrand. That is why I did not bring this document to the Interior Ministry." Mendès chose not to turn the matter over to the interior minister, who had been called into question, but to his chief of staff, Pélabon, who a few weeks later put Roger Wybot, head of the DST (Défense de la Sécurité du Territoire) in charge of the investigation. The fact that he was informed only two months later, on September 8, of the affair of which he was the principal target, always remained a source of bitterness for François Mitterrand. The shadow this cast between Mendès and him was never totally removed.

Pierre Mendès France provided the following explanation:

It may be difficult to believe, but I really did not know that an affair of this kind was within the competence of the Interior Ministry. I thought that it had above all a military character and that it was the responsibility of the Defense Ministry. I obviously had no suspicions of General Koenig either. But he was part of the political personnel whom I wanted to keep as much as possible away from the development of events for the time that was necessary. That is the reason why I asked Pélabon to deal with the matter himself, especially when I was away from Paris (notably in London in the following weeks), and to speak to no one about it, that is, in particular, to no member of the government. That does not mean that I distrusted them. That is why Mitterrand, like all the members of the government, was not immediately informed.

I know he has always held it against me. It is not true that, in my mind, that implied in any way a suspicion that fell on him personally!

Pélabon, and later Wybot, thought that the source of the leaks should be looked for not in one of the ministers but in the Permanent General Secretariat of National Defense (SGPDN). The precision of the leaks led to the conclusion that the informant or informants had had a written text in hand. Now, the preparation of the minutes was the duty of the SGPDN, whose director was Jean Mons, a union militant and a Socialist who was greatly admired by Blum, a companion of Jean Moulin, and former resident general in Tunisia.

Mendès France continued:

I immediately[12] summoned Mons and asked him a certain number of questions: "What kind of papers do you prepare? Where do you store your notes? Who is entrusted with them? Who types them?" After a few minutes, Mons interrupted me: "You are asking me exactly the questions that M. Pleven, then minister of defense, asked me a month ago." As I expressed surprise, he continued: "Yes, a month ago, there were leaks."

Then I telephoned Pleven, with whom I was direct, even though our relations had always been "peculiar." He was in his district in Brittany. I asked him to come to see me. He knew that if I was calling him, given the nature of our relations, it was serious. "When do you want to see me?" "Immediately." "I'm on my way."

I questioned him: "Mons told me that you had grilled him a month ago about leaks from National Defense." He answered: "Well, one day, the minister of the interior, Martinaud-Déplat, comes and tells me that there have been leaks from the Committee of National Defense, that we have to have an investigation, that he had had before his eyes a kind of analysis of committee discussions, and so on."

I verified with Pleven that Martinaud-Déplat had not shown him a document but that he himself had gotten the information from Baylot, who had gotten it from a policeman, who had gotten it from an informant with the duty of keeping him posted on the internal life of the Communist Party—the policeman and the informant in question (their names were revealed later) were Dides and Baranès. My impression was that at that moment it was hardly anything more than a quarrel between the Baylot "shop"—specialists in anticommunism—and the Mons "shop," who had friends on the left. But when the new government was set up, political concerns were grafted onto the affair.

What is striking is that, at least a month earlier, leaks had been discovered in the Defense Ministry, whose permanent secretary was notified. But when Mendès France came to power, in dramatic circumstances, in the heat of war and international negotiations, no one thought or decided to inform him! A strange conception of the continuity of the state. Laniel had found the time to advise Mendès France to leave the

CED alone but not the opportunity to warn him about what was transpiring in the offices of the Defense Ministry.

Mendès France continued:

> The target of the Baylot–Dides group was first Mitterrand, who was criticized for having negotiated with Houphouet's party in Africa, while he had in reality detached it from the Communists! They realized rather quickly that they were on the wrong track. Then they looked for someone else, along with Tixier-Vignancour, who said to himself: "Why not Mendès?" Besides, he said it explicitly to Mitterrand during the trial two years later, when the hearing was adjourned: "You know very well that you are not the one we are after, but someone higher than you. Help us and you'll get out of this business." Naturally, Mitterrand sent him packing, before being found totally innocent. The affair was not "invented" against us; but circumstances allowed the exploitation of a dark episode, first against Mitterrand, then against me.

Leaks had taken place after sessions of the Committee of National Defense in May and July 1953 (thirteen and eleven months before Mendès took power), in May 1954 (three weeks before his election, while Mitterrand had resigned from the Laniel cabinet several months earlier), and the following June 28—with respect, as we have seen, to military precautions taken during the Geneva negotiations. The first series of supposedly secret revelations appeared in *France-Observateur,* emphasizing the weakness of certain French installations in Indochina. *L'Express* picked up a few scraps of the second (incidentally less enlightening than the confidences revealed in person to the editor-in-chief, Pierre Viansson-Ponté, by General Salan, which led to a seizure of the weekly at the request of René Pleven). The third series of leaks had to do with information known to everyone, since the head of government had already publicly anticipated sending draftees to Indochina in case the Geneva negotiations failed. But what was striking at the time was less the importance of the revelations than the literal precision of the minutes that the Communist Party was supposed to have received.

Therefore, the next session of the Committee on September 10 was provided with extra security precautions. Questioning Dides a few days later, Christian Fouchet was nevertheless told that leaks had again taken place and that Dides had proof. Asked to transmit the evidence to the government, Dides refused (his first revelations had ended up by "blowing the cover" of his informant, André Baranès). Then Mitterrand, who had in the interim been informed and had hastily returned from his vacation, decided to arrest this policeman who dared to keep for himself files that concerned the Ministry of Defense.

Dides's arrest was followed by a search of Baranès's home, which uncovered, transcribed in his handwriting, minutes of the meetings of

May 26, June 28, and September 10. It soon became clear that, although these documents were dressed up and filled with embellishments designed to cast suspicion on various ministers, they were a rather accurate reflection of the notes taken at the meetings by Jean Mons.

Roger Wybot was then able to reveal those responsible: two colleagues of Jean Mons: Turpin, his secretary; and Labrusse, director of civil protection. Turpin had been seen by a Secretariat official copying notes on Mons's desk. He confessed. And Labrusse soon admitted to circulating the stolen information among his friends on the left, to "serve the cause of peace." As a result, Dides and Baranès were released, since they had only been doing their jobs, and Mons, Turpin, and Labrusse were arrested.[13]

Mendès France, Mitterrand, and Wybot had unmasked the guilty. But already in Dreyfus's time the revelation of the guilty had not been enough to silence a calumny. During all the days of September in London and Paris, when he was trying with Eden to set up an alternative to the CED, the sinister accusatory rumors continued to weigh on the French negotiator. How far did his collusion with the Communists go? What confidence could be placed in a man and an administration that allowed such leaks of defense secrets?

Thus one could read in *Le Figaro* of September 27, under the signature of Louis-Gabriel Robinet:

> A question comes to mind to which there will sooner or later have to be an answer. Why, when the investigation to recover the missing documents was directed toward the Communist Party, why do we suddenly learn that the intelligence agents charged with surveillance of the antinational activities of the Communist Party have had their cover "blown"?[14]

But another hypothesis came to light through later statements from Baranès: a maneuver of intoxication conducted by the PCF against the Mendès cabinet and its attempts to reorganize Western defense: the credibility and the efforts of Mendès in London and Paris would be weakened by the knowledge his adversaries had of his most secret plans. Wouldn't his allies avoid such an uncertain partner? This is one explanation.

The one proposed by Mendès France many years later was very different. He thought that, in fact, the PCF had not received any of the documents created by Baranès on the basis of "leaks" from the SGPDN and turned over by him to anti-Communist groups as though he had gotten them from the Communists.

On December 3, the National Assembly debated the "affair of the leaks." To a wide sector of public opinion, it almost represented a treason trial for Mitterrand. A prosecutor stepped forward, Jean Legendre, deputy from Oise, spokesman for the beet growers and other alcohol producers. He spoke in a formidable voice, thundering like a tribune of the people. And he very quickly lost all sense of proportion. He imputed the Indochinese disasters to the interior minister; he accused him of sabotaging, by destroying an anti-Communist network, national security and the search for truth. As for the RPF deputy Dronne, to bring down Mitterrand and Mendès, he attacked the homosexuals.

Then Mendès mounted the podium:

> Never, not for a day or an hour, have I regretted entrusting a position of responsibility and courage to M. Mitterrand. I am proud to have such a colleague in my government. But I felt an immense humiliation in the course of negotiations, when I saw my own compatriots warn my foreign interlocutors against me with the help of files fabricated in France. I am not certain whether our efforts toward greater common security would have borne fruit if, thanks to the courageous activity of the interior minister, the discovery of the origin of the leaks had not put an end to the frightful suspicion that some Frenchmen caused to weigh on the government.

But at the conclusion of a debate in which Mitterrand, with irresistible talent and passion, had confronted the accusations made against him, the Mendès France cabinet won a vote of confidence by only 278 to 240, with 71 abstentions.

The affair of the leaks, which was a personal tragedy for Mitterrand, does not seem to have affected Mendès France to the same extent. His younger colleague was now undergoing an ordeal like the one that he experienced during the Clermont-Ferrand trial. He did not feel touched by the mud. As a man, in any case. For it is obvious that as a negotiator—he spoke of it in his defense of Mitterrand—the campaign prejudiced him very seriously.

But the very excess of the defamation seems to have had no effect on him. He later spoke of parliamentry mud-slinging and did not believe that public opinion could have believed for a moment in "treason." He nevertheless felt stung by hatred in the course of the trial in March 1956.

In the course of the hearings, closed because they concerned a matter of national defense, Tixier-Vignancour, lawyer for the informant Baranès, took advantage of the situation to make serious accusations against several of his colleagues: Boris, Léone Georges-Picot, and Simon Nora. Mendès stepped to the bar to hurl this challenge at the lawyer:

> I came to make myself available for an adversarial explanation, if anyone wishes it, and if anyone has anything to say to me. But when I have left this bar, I think it would be a cowardly action to dare, in my absence, to say things that one would not have dared to say to my face.

Tixier-Vignancour retorted:

In my argument, I will take account of all the testimony that has been offered to the court. M. Mendès France will no longer be present, but I hope he will allow me to tell him courteously, in the loyal opposition to him that has always been the rule of my life, that I will use that testimony, to the full extent that I can, against him. He knows very well that I consider that his politics are the origin of the ruin and the misfortunes of my country.

But this kind of aggression had little effect on him.

Questioned twenty-five years later about "the affair of the leaks," one of his closest colleagues of the period observed. "He probably spent no more than an hour on it in the course of his seven months in power." But who can tell how heavily such a campaign weighed, how great was the psychological erosion that it provoked?

18.
ALGERIA IS FRANCE

On November 1, 1954, at 9 A.M. Mendès France received a telephone call from François Mitterrand, minister of the interior. This time, it was not a matter of obscure conspiracies: several dozen terrorist attacks had taken place in Algeria the night before. The distribution of attacks throughout the territory of the three Algerian departments, their simultaneity, and the choice of targets like police stations showed that an ambitious plan was being carried out. If it was not a general uprising, it was at least a concerted action.

Driven by his desire to work out a political solution in Tunisia, to the point of seeming to forget that the crisis in Morocco was daily becoming more poisonous, Mendès had paid little attention to Algeria in the preceding five months. In August, he nevertheless agreed, on the insistence of his friend Gaston Monnerville, to meet three figures who were considered most representative of Algerian public opinion, among them Ferhat Abbas and Ahmed Francis. They had asked him, almost begged him, to pay attention to developments in Algeria that would sooner or later, according to them, lead to violence if, at the least, "equality" was not granted to the Algerian people.

The head of government, whose attention was monopolized by the Tunisian affair and preparation for the Brussels confrontation over the

CED, had clearly registered this touching appeal. Ferhat Abbas had been moving and convincing. After all, he did not speak of independence. PMF had promised that he would study the question once the European debate was over, in the autumn.

He appeared to have taken significant risks by receiving at the Foreign Ministry a figure as "troubling" as Ferhat Abbas, a man whom Mendès's friend General Catroux had deported to the Sahara region in 1943. Which of his predecessors would have dared take such a risk? He had promised his interlocutors that he would "disinter" the Algerian question, do everything possible to revive democracy in the country, and no longer tolerate the permanent denial of justice. This was a great deal. Was it not, until a new order was established, enough?

No, said a troubled voice in his ear, the voice of François Mitterrand. Because of his position, the interior minister had complete control over Algeria. When the government was established and Mitterrand asked Mendès to "give" him Interior, the new premier, a little surprised, asked why. Mitterrand had replied: "I think we should concern ourselves with Algeria immediately if we want to avoid an explosion."[1]

At a time, said Mendès France many years later, when "I did not think it was urgent or that it would explode, Mitterrand 'sensed' it. In spite of official intelligence, all of which was reassuring, he had very quickly grasped that 'things were happening in Algeria and that there was a risk of everything turning out badly.' "

The response, for Mendès, as for his staff director Andre Pélabon, former general secretary for Algeria (not a certificate of lucidity), and for Mitterrand, was first of all military. Blood had been spilled. A primary school teacher and his wife had been killed in one of the ambushes. Several dozen people had been wounded. Police headquarters had been attacked. It seemed necessary to react first of all by reaffirming the force of law. In Tunisia, by sending substantial numbers of troops at the moment negotiations began, PMF had the sense that he had prevented an outbreak of violence. But, in Tunisia he had been negotiating at the same time.

In brief, at the very moment that he heard the shocking news, Mendès France learned from his interior minister that three companies of CRS (Compagnies Républicaines de Sécurité) were already in a state of alert; they were to land at Oran, Algiers, and Constantine during the evening and night of the first. A battalion of parachute troops was to join them the next day, although General Cherrière, commander of the tenth region—the region of Algiers, which made him the chief military offier for Algeria as a whole—had immediately let it be known that the CRS was enough.

Early in the morning of November 2, the premier sent this eloquent note to André Pélabon:

First: we must make sure that the troop movements have been carried out.

Second: we must at least triple the number of troops and CRS sent to Algeria.

Remember the massive effort we made for Tunisia and the reticence we encountered among the military. We must act on them in the most energetic way so that they do not lose a moment.[2]

The press, however, remained calm. *Le Monde* noted an "outbreak of terrorism" in Algeria in a two-column article on the first page, but it did not give prominence to the story. *L'Humanité* at first reacted by condemning both the adventurism of the attackers and the colonization policies of the government.[3] And Pierre Mendès France himself, preoccupied as he might be, did not devote his next radio broadcast to the nascent insurrection but to the struggle against alcoholism.

It was François Mauriac, in his column of the next day, who was most sensitive to the dimensions of the event:

I did not believe that the worst was so close. But my friends know that I am overwhelmed by it. The immediate responsibility of the *fellaghas* does not in any way attenuate the responsibility that has weighed on us for the last 120 years, a burden that has increased in each generation. The horror of what is about to break out must be completely softened by a concerted offensive against low salaries, unemployment, ignorance, and misery, and by the structural reforms the Algerian people are calling for. And, at any cost, the police must be prevented from torturing.[4]

The Assembly took up the problem on November 9. Four days earlier, before the Interior Committee, Mitterrand had rejected an idea of negotiating with the "rebels" and asserted that if war was forced on France, the challenge would be taken up without weakness. And he had secured approval from the Council of Ministers for dissolution of the MTLD (Movement for the Triumph of Democratic Liberties), the most "advanced" of the Algerian parties (apparently unaware that this organization had so far been unconnected with the movement that had been set in motion by dissidents). Thus, when the parliamentary debate opened, the head of government and his minister found themselves bringing praise "for the promptness and vigor" of their response by René Mayer, spokesman for the great colonial interests. Were they pleased by this praise?

In any event, they found similar words to describe the situation and define the government's attitude. A sentence by PMF summed things up. "Algeria is France, not a foreign country. One does not compromise when it is a matter of defending the domestic peace of the union, the unity and integrity of the Republic."

Typically Jacobin remarks, which are nevertheless strange to quote twenty-six years later. In 1980, Mendés pointed out:

Unlike what had happened in Tunisia and Morocco, French colonization in Algeria had destroyed the indigenous elites. There was thus no one to negotiate with.[5] What I tried to make people understand was that we had to begin with a procedure that would allow the Algerians to designate spokesmen with whom we could carry on a dialogue. We had to begin with acts under French law: judicially, Algeria was France. We could do nothing but consider it as part of France with which it is necessary to carry on a debate.

But a debate with whom? The 1947 statute, never applied, had created the Algerian Assembly. God knows that it was open to criticism, but it existed. The statute provided for the creation of a sort of government, the Executive Council, made up of three Europeans and three Algerians, and never set up. Starting with this 1947 statute, imperfact as it may have been, and finally putting it into effect in good faith, without electoral fraud, without cheating, would havc been a beginning, allowing us to have people to talk to. We could not fail to begin by finally imposing respect for French law, which had been cast aside by the colonial powers. And they were not mistaken about the meaning of my remarks that called their hegemony into question.

Moreover, I also had to keep in mind the political context. I was involved in the Tunisian negotiation, which was already very difficult to make people swallow. I could not risk an overload, making my position even worse. Speaking of French legality, that is, the statute that, however imperfect, opened the way for equality of the two populations and Algerian emancipation, was a way both of giving hope to the Moslems and, to a certain extent, of reassuring the Europeans.

Before an agitated, nervous Chamber, on November 12, Mendès France also delivered some remarks that raised the eyebrows of those who had praised the "virile measures" he had taken:

> We must attack the deep roots of the problems. Measures are being studied. A significant effort is going to be made to improve uncultivated land and to develop industry. Through the exercise of democratic rights, through the generous cooperation of metropolitan France, we will be able to create in Algeria the better life that the nation wants to provide to all its citizens.

In reaction, the spokemen for colonial interests launched a violent attack on the Mendès cabinet. One proclaimed that "liberties are not appropriate for insufficiently evolved peoples," a second that "repression comes first," a third that "the *fellahs* want bread, not political rights," a fourth that this was a government of "national surrender." And they all agreed that it was the policy of "concessions" in Tunisia that had "provoked the troubles" and "shattered harmony" in Algeria.

These criticisms very soon turned into indictments, when Mendès and Mitterrand, alerted by articles by Mauriac, Bourdet, and in *L'Humanité* denouncing the tortures inflicted on Algerian suspects, transferred nine policemen reputed to be torturers to the mainland and prepared a measure that infuriated the "ultras": fusion between Algerian and French police. However untender the men of the Sûreté Nationale might be in France, they nevertheless applied the Code of Criminal Procedure. While the police in Algiers . . .

The reforms announced by Mitterrand at the cabinet meeting on January 5, which ranged from equalization of wages between Algeria and France to granting voting rights to Algerian women, and from local government reform to an outline for agrarian reform, further stimulated the anger and anxiety of representatives from Algiers and Oran. To the point that, on the eve of the great "North African" debate scheduled for February 2 in the National Assembly, the leader of the Algerian lobby, the Radical senator Henri Borgeaud, moving force behind Martinaud-Déplat and René Mayer, informed Mendès that if these proposals were submitted his friends would vote against the government.

PMF was not unaware that the death of his government had just been announced to him. But he also knew that surrender on these timid reforms in Algeria would be surrender on the essentials. Whether or not he saw it as a caricature of the bitter reality, whether or not he saw the title as a provocation, he had been stricken by the article Claude Bourdet published in *France-Observateur* on January 13, 1955: "Votre Gestapo algérien" (Your Algerian Gestapo), which described in particular the tortures inflicted on a leader of the MTLD and the frightful conditions in the prison of Tizi-Ouzou. Bourdet's conclusion was a slap in the face:

> Can our statesmen . . . calmly stand for what is happening? It is the great colonial interests that are giving the orders, but it is MM. Mendès France and Mitterrand who are responsible before public opinion and before history.
>
> When you allow such crimes to be committed, you do not save yourself by saying: "Others would do worse."

It was in this atmosphere of challenge and hyperbole, and of denunciations from opposite poles of opinion that the great debate on the Maghreb was to open on February 2, a debate that would lead to the downfall of the cabinet of the first statesman of the Fourth Republic who had attempted to challenge colonial hegemony in Asia and Africa.

With respect to Tunisia, in fact, the "policy of Carthage" was working through its logical consequences on two levels: a return to civil peace, and negotiations toward a definition of the Tunisian system of "internal autonomy." A week after Mendès France's visit to Carthage, on August 8, a government had been formed under the leadership of a moderate notable who then enjoyed the confidence of the nationalists. Four of the eight members of the government belonged to the Néo-Destour, among them Bourguiba's lieutenant Mongi Slim.

Four members of the Tunisian government, two from the Néo-Destour and two others were given the task of negotiating with the French delegation led by Christian Fouchet. The talks opened in Paris on September 13. They were difficult: the Tunisians wanted to push their advantages as far as possible, notably by trying to impose recognition of their right to raise an army and set up a diplomatic corps, the French insisting that they stick to the "Carthage framework," which provided, as we have seen, for only "internal" autonomy.

Now the Tunisian negotiators, although they enjoyed the support of the majority Bourguiba wing of the Néo-Destour and of public opinion, were subject to pressure from two sides: from the radical wing of the party led by Bourguiba's rival Salah Ben Youssef, and from the *fellaghas,* guerrilla fighters who conducted sporadic military actions in the southern part of the country. The French negotiators called on their Tunisian counterparts to dissociate themselves from the *fellaghas* and to condemn that form of action. Mongi Slim and his comrades refused: by doing so they would weaken their credit as nationalists and would lose a means of pressure.

Then a few intelligent French officers invented a direct means to "co-opt" the *fellaghas.* Toward the end of October, they prepared an offer "from soldier to soldier" to surrender their arms and return home peacefully, with "the honors of war." The operation was scheduled for late October or early November. The Algerian uprising delayed it. It was set in motion beginning on November 22, with the cooperation of the Tunisian government—and of Bourguiba—and concluded around December 10, returning 2,700 guerrillas to their homes and restoring peace[6] to the whole country.

In the meantime, these transaction with "rebels," and certain declarations by Tunisian personalities like Bourguiba recalling that their real objective was not internal autonomy but independence, had alerted Parisian conservative circles and provoked heated debate in Parliament that was all the more vigorous because the head of government was on a trip to the United States. Hence this exchange of messages between Mendès and his minister of Tunisian affairs on November 18:

From Fouchet to PMF:

> You must know that the dogs are loose and that the big bloodhounds are leading the pack. Since a warm trail is available for their keen scent, "forward" to North Africa! And I swear to you that they're barking in the corridors, the party offices, and the newspapers.

From PMF to Fouchet:

> I know that it is a hard fight, both with respect to our relations with the Tunisians and with respect to the shameless exploitation that has been made of them in Parliament. I am grateful to you for the courage with which you have stood fast. I remain convinced that nothing is more important than the

negotiations themselves. That is what has to be thought of before anything else. For, from now on, time will work against us. Affectionately yours.[7]

A month after Mendès France's return from the United States, at the moment when the great debate on ratification of the Paris agreements was about to open in the Chamber, the Franco–Tunisian negotiations were still stalled on a few points—notably French participation in municipal government and the powers of the autonomous Tunisian police. To attempt to extract agreement from Mongi Slim and his comrades, Mendès France participated in several working sessions in January. He did not completely succeed in removing the reservations of his interlocutors, who found him a "particularly tough" negotiator.[8] When the February 2 debate began, differences remained preventing the head of government from claiming a significant success.[9]

Would he have achieved it if he had agreed, on the question of police forces or the Tunisian army, to go outside the "Carthage framework"? He did not consider it, struck as he had been by Bourguiba's remark: "It will take us fifteen years to assimilate what has been conceded to us. It is only afterward that we will move to the stage of independence."

The acceleration of history in Morocco and Algeria soon made the Tunisian leader's prognosis absurd. But it is a fact that the negotiators of both camps were working in this perspective, inspired by what remained the very vital "spirit of Carthage!"

On August 27, 1954, François Mauriac, who had been struggling for twenty months to reestablish understanding between the Moroccans and the French, having denounced a year earlier the overthrow and exile of Sultan Sihi Mohammed Ben Youssef as "a crime and a mistake," and who obviously expected the new premier to exercise his passion for justice in Morocco, described a "lugubrious afternoon" in the National Assembly in his *Bloc Notes* (Notebooks) in these terms:

> Finally, the premier entered the Chamber. He had just left, highly excited, a dramatic cabinet meeting, full of the CED, preoccupied with another drama, like an actor in the wrong play. In a neutral voice, he pronounced the fateful sentence: "Although the government intends to improve the situation of the ex-Sultan and his family, it will not restore him to the throne." He must not have been aware of what he was doing; he did not know that at that moment he was at one blow killing all hope in millions of hearts.

It might be said that, however harsh his criticism of those responsible for kidnapping the Moroccan sovereign, and however convinced he was of the rights of the Moroccans, Mendès felt more ill at ease in this debate over a throne, this dynastic affair, than he did with the Tunisians, their leaders, their party, and their arguments. He had thus remained aloof from the France–Maghreb Association (established in 1953 under the leadership of Mauriac; Mitterrand was a member), which concentrated its efforts on the Moroccan dynastic question and tended to neglect the Tunisian, and later the Algerian crisis.

The intervention of the Mendès government in the Moroccan tragedy—which was at the time growing constantly deeper and taking on the form of bloodier and bloodier terroism—was limited to humanitarian measures. On his personal initiative, an investigating commission was established to prepare a report for the government on conditions in Moroccan prisons.

From the report, Mendès France warned that arbitrariness and brutality were as prevalent in the jails of Casablanca and Marrakesh as in those of Algiers and Tunis. He brought about the liberation of several hundred detainees, among them dozens of children.

A few weeks later, Mendès France was fighting his last battle against the Assembly. Two spokesmen for the MRP charged that the prisons of Algeria were full. He retorted by recalling the conditions that his envoys to Casablanca had found in the Moroccan prisons and the children they had been able to free. Jean Daniel tells the story that, listening to an account of the debate that evening, Albert Camus asked him what he could do to help a political figure who was capable, at the moment when his public life was at stake, of speaking of the fate of a few imprisoned children.

19.
AMERICA WITHOUT DOLLARS
AND EUROPE WITHOUT JOY

Since the dramatic crossing of 1942 that had taken Lieutenant Mendès France to the New World, past icebergs and Nazi submarines, there had hardly been a year when he had not visited the United States. But his trip that autumn was of much greater importance.

What he had undertaken in Geneva, London, Carthage, and Bonn called for frank explanation with the Americans, all the more so because each one of his initiatives had caused a scandal. When one creates such disturbance, it is appropriate to speak clearly, and there was no one in France, aside from Jean Monnet, better suited to make himself understood by the Americans than Mendès—decolonizer, economist intent on increasing productivity, cofounder of the World Bank and the International Monetary Fund, a wartime ally who was already familiar with New York, Washington, and Bretton Woods and who handled English quite well.

Mendès attached extreme importance to the trip, firmly determined not to beg for financial aid like his predecessors but to seize the opportunity of a visit to Washington and his reception at the United Nations to explain to American leaders and to world opinion his past initiatives and especially his immediate intentions. We have seen him as a man of conviction, argument, persuasion, and debate. Pragmatists like him, the Americans represented for him desirable interlocutors. He felt capable of convincing them with the evidence, of interesting them, of drawing them into his great enterprise of East–West détente.

But he had had the idea, in order to indicate clearly the psychological and political (as opposed to financial) character of his trip, to begin it with a visit to Canada. This was a way of indicating that France was still a presence in the world, of emphasizing continuity. And Canada, on this occasion, would be not only Ottawa, but first Quebec and then Montreal, before the federal capital.

The entourage left Paris on November 14, 1954. In addition to Mendès France and his wife, there were four particularly competent advisers—Georges Boris, Jean-Marie Soutou, Phillippe de Seynes, and Claude Cheysson—the press secretary of the Foreign Ministry and his assistant, an interpreter, and Léone Georges-Picot.

He was greeted in Quebec with unexpected warmth. Mendès was the first head of a French government to visit the old capital. He was astonished by the outpouring of sympathy. It was true that his arrival had been prepared by unprecedented press coverage. In the most prestigious daily, *Le Devoir,* Gerard Filion wrote:

> On this side of the Atlantic, Mendès France is seen as the man who got France moving. His accomplishment of this Herculean task has earned him immense popularity. The man has done more in five months than his predecessors in five years. He has reduced the commitments of France to the level of its capacities. He has liquidated the Indochina adventure, he has buried the CED, he has concluded the London and Paris agreements. All that represents more problems resolved or in the process of being resolved than what has been done since the end of the war. Mendès France is in the process of cleansing the French mind from the "Maginot Line" mentality.

Less certain of the durability of the work Mendès had undertaken, Maurice Duplessis, the old prime minister, who managed the province like a family business, greeted him at his office door with these disconcerting words: "I salute you with the title of premier. But are you sure that you still are premier, right now?" The visitor had the good taste to take as a joke "between colleagues" what was perhaps the expression of a very significant suspicion toward the political system, the fantasies, and the congenital instability of those "damned Frenchmen." But everywhere else he received nothing but marks of sympathy, warm-hearted expectations, and calls for lasting attachment.

The atmosphere was more reserved in Ottawa, where the French visitors had to share the limelight with Queen Mother Elizabeth. Mendès France, very cordially received by Prime Minister Louis Saint-Laurent, was able to prepare at leisure for his visit to Washington with the federal minister of foreign affairs, Lester Pearson, a competent expert in trans-Atlantic relations. The meeting with Pearson, to prepare those in Washington, was one of the purposes of the Canadian trip. When PMF flew to Washington on the seventeenth, Pearson telegraphed Dulles to guarantee the visitor's loyalty to the Atlantic Alliance. Moreover, before leaving Ottawa, Mendès France had held a press conference in the course of which he had declared himself in favor of rejecting the offer the Soviets had just made of holding a four-power conference before any ratification of the Paris agreements.

In the favorable atmosphere thereby created, Mendès landed in Washington on the seventeenth. There was still some suspiciousness in the greeting offered to this "troubling" figure who had come to power in June with the help (even though he had not counted them) of Communist votes; who had immediately hastened to meet Chou En-lai, and then to negotiate with Molotov and Pham Van Dong; and who was denounced as a crypto-Communist by the experts of the American Embassy in Paris. To be sure, on July 13, during their first meeting in Paris, Dulles had exclaimed after a conversation on Indochina: "This guy is terrific!" But there was perhaps some ambiguity in the remark. And throughout the "European" negotiations, Dulles had constantly acted as an opponent of Mendès France.

Mendès had declared on his arrival that he had "twenty important questions of international concern" to discuss with his hosts, specifying that he would refuse to approach financial problems in order to indicate clearly that he was not coming as a beggar but as a negotiator. When the *New York Times,* which was rather favorable to him, wrote on November 19 that "Premier Mendès France asked the United States today to increase its financial aid to help save South Vietnam from communism," Mendès sent a very dry correction. No, he had not evoked the financial aspect of the problem, in order to emphasize that any policy—that of the United States like that of France—is a function of the resources it involves.

The conversations with Eisenhower and Dulles on November 18 were devoted to Indochinese questions. Mendès France had just learned that the recently appointed "special representative of the United States in South Vietnam," General Lawton Collins, had informed General Ely that he considered himself empowered to treat the entirety of the country's defense problems independently of his French colleague, in direct consultation with the Vietnamese. Moreover, he had explained that, instead of going through the French, U.S. aid would henceforth be provided directly to the Saigon authorities.

The head of the French government firmly warned his conterparts against this violation of the Geneva agreements, which might provoke the most vigorous reactions from Hanoi, if not from its Chinese allies. It was clear that the Chinese had put so much pressure on their Vietnamese comrades to gain concessions leading to a rapid solution in order to avoid a prolongation of the war bringing American military might onto the continent. Wouldn't they consider themselves deceived if, taking advantage of peace, Washington carried out the operation that the war had not allowed it to accomplish? Wasn't there a risk of resumption of hostilities?

Dulles said that he was sensitive to what he thought was, for the French visitor, a question of prestige: no, the United States did not want to take the place of France. It simply intended to assure the survival of South Vietnam. Would this be accomplished, objected Mendès, by risking, through initiatives contrary to the spirit and the letter of the Geneva agreements,[1] the provocation of a renewal of the conflict against the powerful Hanoi army? It seemed clear to PMF that the July agreements counted little for Dulles: the Manila pact that had created SEATO on September 8 took care of everything. In the end, the communiqué issued on November 20 gave assurances of "the identity of views" of the two parties and their desire for "cooperation." This would allow Dulles and Collins to remove the final French obstacles.

Why had Mendès France thereby opened the way for the American presence in Indochina that would lead to the later disasters? First, because he no longer had the means to do otherwise. His American interlocutors, pressed by congressional leaders[2] who demanded the rapid elimination of all French presence in Saigon, constantly confronted him with *faits accomplis,* while French public opinion was becoming less and less concerned with Indochina ("What are we still doing there?"). Two months earlier, his ministers Edgar Faure and Guy La Chambre had opened the way for the substitution by suggesting that U.S. aid be continued. A few weeks later, General Ely was to sign an agreement with Lawton Collins officially associating Washington with the training of the South Vietnamese army.

Moreover, all the information he received from Jean Sainteny in Hanoi led Mendès to conclude that the Communist power of the North did not really wish to cooperate with France. The great policy of which he had dreamed was getting lost in petty disputes, remonstrances, and annoyances. As always, the responsibilities were shared, with French enterprises in Hanoi thinking above all about repatriation and indemnities and metropolitan French industry balking at the risks of serious investments in North Vietnam. In short, from that angle, the perspectives were blocked.

Much more than the mishaps on one side and the pressures from another, another factor dissuaded Mendès France from fighting against

American intrusion into Indochina: the mission he had assumed of drawing the Americans into a real strategy of détente with the East. For him, the key was not in Asia, where the West had lost its bargaining chips, but in Europe. And this was the objective that he attempted to have Dulles adopt, although he had agreed not to propose a general negotiation with Moscow until after the European parliaments had ratified the Paris agreements.

Quite obviously the American secretary of state was hardly enchanted by his visitor's suggestion. But this did not keep him from covering Mendès with extravagant praise.

> I would like to say that the unusual qualities of Mr. Mendès France have struck our people's imagination. He is a superman to be able to carry out successfully his duties as premier and as minister of foreign affairs. We knew of your abilities. Since I had the opportunity to meet you last July 14, I have developed the strongest admiration for you, and I consider it a privilege to work with you. Mendès France possesses a quality that many American politicians claim for themselves: he is a doer.

For PMF, the real objective of the trip was the platform of the United Nations. It was there that he wanted to strike a great blow for the détente that was now his principal aim. To the draft prepared primarily by Jean-Jacques Servan-Schreiber, who now joined the group in New York, he had in the course of the trip constantly been making changes, additions, and cuts, as a result of the conversations with Eisenhower and Dulles, with Henri Bonnet and his colleagues at the French Embassy in Washington, and with Henri Hoppenot, French representative to the United Nations.

The draft of the speech was submitted to Ambassador Hoppenot, who was disturbed, and to American friends of Charles Gombault, who asked Mendès: "Have you informed Dulles and Churchill?" "No." "With this speech you would be elected president of the United States. But you risk bringing down the anger of your allies on your head."

What was this all about, and why was there so much emotion? Because, in this appeal to international opinion, Pierre Mendès France was not content with proposing to the Soviet Union a four power conference in Paris, but also the rapid conclusion of the Austrian peace treaty, on the basis of neutralization of the country, and further, the symmetrical organization of the two ideologically opposed Europes, all the more apt to negotiate if they were constructed according to the same strategic model. And finally—and this is where the problem really lay—the interruption, at the end of two years, of the nuclear experiments of the two superpowers.

The nuclear question was one of the problems that most vividly preoccupied Mendès France, like everything that concerned scientific research on the one hand or national independence on the other.

The problem was not whether mastery over fission of the atom was to be boldly pursued but to define the application that was to be made of that energy. Military or civilian? PMF declared himself strongly opposed to French use of atomic weapons. But it happened that the military leaders were exerting pressure to prevent French strategy from being entirely dependent on that of the United States in this essential area and that French research had already progressed far enough for military application to have been a reasonable prospect in the medium term.

On the second Sunday in October, while he was preparing for his trip to the United States and already thinking of his Manhattan speech, the head of government had called a cabinet meeting at the Foreign Ministry devoted to the French atomic bomb. Present were Edgar Faure, minister of finance and economic affairs; Emmanuel Temple, minister of defense, Jacques Chevallier, Henri Caillavet, and Diomède Catroux, secretaries of war, navy, and air force; Henri Longchambon, secretary of scientific research; Jules Moch, French representative to the United Nations Commission on problems of disarmament; Francis Perrin, high commissioner of atomic energy; and Etienne Hirsch, general director of the Plan.

Very quickly the debate opposed those like Faure, Temple, and Chevallier who emphasized the strengthening of French diplomacy that would be brought about by the possession of atomic weapons against those like Perrin, Hirsch, and Moch who maintained that peaceful use would be profitable. Mendès intervened in the debate on several occasions, indicating that he was affected by both arguments. At the height of the discussion, he asked Francis Perrin whether research might not be continued before coming to the "crossroads," the point at which a choice would of necessity have to be made between civilian and military uses. It seemed that the "crossroads" was near.

"I wanted," Mendès said later, "to put some kind of pressure on the Russians and the Americans with a view toward possible negotiations on the prohibition of all experimental explosions, an idea which was among the proposals I wanted to make, first in Washington, and then at the UN."

Then Mendès had a decree prepared that established a commission for military applications of nuclear energy, which is at the origin of the considerable developments in that field of research, first under the Edgar Faure government the following year, and then under General de Gaulle. When he was later asked about his decision, Mendès constantly emphasized the idea that he had not gone beyond the "crossroads" and that he was entitled to say that his actions with respect to the nuclear question had not deliberately left the peaceful area. It is a point of view that others who are not hostile to him have challenged.

On the evening of the twenty-first, Ambassador Hoppenot hosted a dinner in honor of the head of the French government to which were invited the representatives of the three other great powers: Henry Cabot Lodge of the United States, Vyshinsky of the Soviet Union, and Anthony Nutting of Great Britain. At the end of the meal, Hoppenot drew Mendès into a private conversation with Vyshinsky, whom he had known for a long time. In the course of a long conversation, Mendès informed the Soviet representative of the principal subjects of his speech. Vyshinsky seemed interested, surprised by so much boldness, and charmed. He promised to telegraph Moscow immediately.

On November 22, at three in the afternoon, Mendès France waited to be summoned by the president's bell to enter the Assembly hall. It seemed that it was the Russians for once who were late.

Could he deliver his speech in their absence when everyone knew that it was largely an appeal to their understanding? Finally, two low-level diplomats took their seats at the Soviet delegation's bench. PMF mounted the podium with a feeling of some bitterness: once again the Russians had rejected an outstretched hand, and had done so with ponderous affectation. It would be said that his creative imagination had come up, on their side, against a kind of theatrical and premeditated sabotage. Vyshinsky had not even bothered to appear.

It was not until the end of Mendès France's speech that the news ran through the Assembly: "Vyshinsky is dead!" The morning after the conversation with Mendès, Stalin's former prosecutor, the virulent and immovable Soviet spokesman in New York, had been stricken by an embolism while he was working in his Park Avenue study.

Mendès's voice was as clear as ever, his delivery as didactic, the flow of language as courteous and balanced. But a feeling of passionate conviction lurked in the background when he spoke of disarmament, of the struggle against hunger and underdevelopment—even when he pointed to the necessity for a method and the respect for priorities. And then he came to the heart of his speech: East–West relations. He spoke of them with a frankness that could only, at first, charm his allies: the latest Soviet proposals were, he said, "neither realistic nor reasonable." And he explained:

> To ask on November 13 that twenty-five countries meet two weeks later to discuss a nonexistent agenda, I say unhesitatingly to our Soviet colleagues, is not serious. But did they believe for a single moment that we would accept the invitation? It is all the easier to doubt that because, only two days ago, Mr. Molotov proposed, with the same suddenness, to postpone the conference scheduled for the twenty-ninth.
>
> He added, however, that the Western nations should in return delay the ratification of the agreements they have worked out in London and Paris.

There will be no objective and effective discussion in a four-power conference until after the Western European countries directly concerned have ratified the Paris agreement. To act otherwise would be adventurism.

Asserting that the parliaments of France and the other Western countries would ratify the agreements by the month of April, Mendès France came to the formulation of his offer: "Why not then decide that a four-power conference will be held, for example, in the month of May, in Paris?" And to give more substance to this overture, he had come up with the idea of linking it to a resolution of the Austrian treaty. He recalled that since the Western powers had accepted the Soviet proposals, "the agreement is practically concluded." Why not sign very quickly in order to "create a climate of confidence," even if it might be necessary to extend the scheduled deadline for evacuation of the four occupying armies?

And it was then that he launched his idea of "symmetry" between the two Europes:

At the risk of surprising my colleagues who represent those countries here, I affirm, for my part, that I would be happy to see the creation, on the model of the Western European Union, of an Eastern European association, provided that it adopt the methods we have established in the West for publicity, limitation, and control of armaments. Later, exchanges of information might possibly be established between the two systems. And it is even possible that those limitations, and even control, could take on a contractual form.

Wasn't this to consider that the problem had been resolved, that is, the basic hermeticism of Communist societies, particularly in matters of defense? In any event, this attractive idea, like the speech as a whole, was greeted favorably by the great majority of the Assembly, which gave the speaker an ovation. But the American delegation remained icy and appeared to feel no gratitude toward Mendès France for having affirmed that France would take no part in negotiations that excluded its "American and English friends," and especially for having kept to himself the suggestion of prohibiting nuclear tests, softening the aspects of his speech that cut most boldly through ordinary procedures.

In the plane returning him the next day to Paris and harsh French realities, PMF drew up a balance sheet for the American trip. On the personal level, it was an obvious success. But although he made a strong personal impression, the ideas that he advocated had not pierced the wall of suspicion erected at the State Department and, to a lesser degree, the Senate. With respect to Indochina, his warnings about the Diem regime and the establishment of a U.S. military presence in contravention of the Geneva agreement had not managed to budge Dulles. With respect to East–West relations, his firmness in the face of Soviet maneuvers, which was strongly appreciated, had not been enough to gain support for his ingenious negotiating proposals. Washington admired the lucid progressive confronting Moscow's advances, not the French statesman who was eager to give his country an original role in the search for détente.

When Mendès France and his group landed at Orly on November 24, Reuters distributed the following dispatch: "The general impression here is that his visit to the United States was extremely fruitful, but that the local political situation has, during his absence, taken a turn against him." The press in general considered that the trip had opportunely increased the international prestige of France. But *Combat* noted, "Mendès France is too intelligent not to be aware of the difference between the current political situation in France and the one that existed before his departure. His opponents are far from being disarmed, and his supporters are troubled."

The battle for ratification of the Paris agreements, which Mendès had made a prerequisite for the great conversation with the East, remained to be fought. Thus, when he addressed the nation four days later, in his radio broadcast, he particularly emphasized the "desire for peace" of his American interlocutors, and he very cleverly linked the ratification of the agreements—an unpopular subject—to the future four-power conference—a much more attractive one.

The debate that opened on December 22, 1954, and ended five days later was the fifth act, the most turbulent, rich in episodes, reversals, arguments, and rhetorical effects, of the "tragedy of Europe" whose first act had taken place at the Elysée Palace on August 13, the second in Brussels from the nineteenth to the twenty-second of August, the third in the National Assembly on August 30, and the fourth from September 28 to October 23 in London and from October 20 to 23 at the French Foreign Ministry.

In the meantime, the prestigious government of early summer, riding on the success of Geneva and Tunis, had suffered harsh attacks, alienated the MRP, the PCF, and the "colonial" wing of the Radical Party, and had lost some of its reputation in the intellectual left that expected from more boldness in economic affairs, more resistance in the Atlantic Pact and German rearmament, and more openness in the colonial realm. And it had seen the outbreak of the Algerian troubles, still hard to judge, but dangerous. On the other hand, his trip to the United States and especially his United Nations speech had made him a pioneer of international détente.

Placed on the defensive in certain areas, in a false position in others, isolated at times, but still considered by the majority of the country as the only head of government worthy of the name that France had known since De Gaulle's withdrawal, he confronted the decisive test, weakened but still vigorous, while the impression created in public opinion and in political circles had only deteriorated. A first reading of the text had brought out the concessions and the guarantees that the French had extracted from their partners, notably the right of control over German armament. But subsequent readings emphasized only a single obsessive idea: the Federal Republic of Germany was going to be rearmed, and sovereign. The possibility, considered inevitable, accepted by everyone, at least in private, was becoming a reality after having become a reality in East Germany, which everyone tended to forget. In any event, French sensitivity was in a state of alert.

At this point, on December 18, 1954, he received from one of his closest colleagues, a very curious note:

> The ratification of the agreements, if I have understood correctly, is not a good in itself, but:
>
> a. the way out of a diplomatic impasse into which your predecessors have placed France;
>
> b. a detour to bring our Western allies to accept the "four-power confrontation" from which should come one of two solutions that can command broad national acceptance:
>
> —four-power agreements on Germany, international détente, and arms control;
>
> —clearly demonstrated disagreement, leading to acceptance of definitive rearmament of Germany.
>
> Now, even considering:
>
> —the fact that present Soviet reactions (before ratification) can be interpreted as tactical maneuvers in a war of nerves;
>
> —the miracles you can carry off in Parliament, it seems to me more and more improbable:
>
> —that a conference can be held in May on the initiative of France, which by ratifying the London agreements, will deprive itself of a substantial means of pressuring the United States and of its most important tool for negotiating with the Soviets;
>
> —that you can hold onto power until this hypothetical conference.
>
> Given the extreme weakness of the majority that can be predicted in favor of ratification, it should be possible to create a parliamentary situation in which you will be led to *agree to attach a conditional clause to the agreements,* suspending their execution until after the failure of a "four-power conference. . . . By establishing a deadline for this suspension, you will place the Soviets in the Geneva situation.

But Mendès rejected this kind of maneuver. He would fight without reservation, as though it were a policy that fully expressed him.

The debate, even more than that devoted to the CED, was dominated by three themes: the dangers involved in German rearmament, the increase in hegemony that would be granted to the English and the Americans by ratification of the October agreements, and the threat that that ratification would pose to any attempt at reconciliation with the Soviet Union, notably in the form of the four-power conference that Mendès had proposed in his UN speech. A note that was then sent to France by the Soviet government, warning it against any approval of German rearmament, and threatening it with a rupture of the Franco–Soviet pact, weakened, by its very harshness, the argument of those who favored conciliation.

On December 23, late in the afternoon, Pierre Mendès France mounted the rostrum, even paler than usual. A prestigious ally had just abandoned him: *Le Monde* had indicated that day its hostility to the agreements. There was more and more talk of massive abstentions, and even of a rejection of ratification. He spoke in a harsh voice, often striking the podium with his fist.

> What credibility will we have to influence decisions of our allies if we have been incapable of making our own? Do not forget, either, that our vote will have its repercussions on the other side of the iron curtain. We would encourage those who speculate about our decisions, if we did not make a vigorous and clear decision. A four-power conference will be fruitful only if our representatives are able to speak in the name of a united country. I appeal to your patriotism and your courage. Those who want France to play a major role in the alliance will vote for the agreements. Those who want to be able to convince our allies in case of later disputes will vote for the agreements. Those who want an international conference to be organized on our initiative and who want our country to be able to force a decision for peace will also vote for the agreements.

But six hours later, at dawn on December 24, article 1 of the bill proposed by the government, the one that involved the acceptance of German rearmament, was rejected by 280 votes to 259. Mendès France had been placed in the minority on a fundamental question on which he had commited his prestige and the prestige of his country. The sensation was extraordinary. His reaction was immediate: he called for a vote of confidence on the other articles of the bill, without asking for a second reading of article 1. The fate of the government presided over by the escaped prisoner of Clermont-Ferrand, the aviator of the Lorraine group, the minister of De Gaulle, was irrevocably tied to the rearmament of Germany.

It was Saturday, Christmas Eve. The principal leaders agreed to adjourn the continuation of the debate until Monday. But throughout the weekend shock waves even stronger than those following the rejection of the CED went around the world: for this time considering his commitment, Mendès authority over Parliament seemed solid. The surprise aggravated anger in Washington, Bonn, Brussels, and London. President Eisenhower immediately expressed his "worry," while the *New York Times* denounced "the atmosphere of personal rancor, cynicism, defeatism, and individual irresponsibility" which had led to the "assassination" of the Paris agreements. But it was London, on this occasion, that arrogated to itself the right to belabor Paris with the most intense scorn. Disappointed by the sabotage of his efforts, Eden assumed the tone of a policeman. "The consent of France to an enterprise with which it is directly involved is in the end without any importance; whether it likes it or not, the German Federal Republic will rearm."

But the reaction of the British cabinet to the French Assembly's vote was not limited to these hostile remarks. On the twenty-fifth, the Washington correspondent of *France-Soir* informed two members of the French Embassy staff that he had just heard some disturbing news: As a result of contacts that had just taken place between the State Department and the British ambassador, the two capitals were preparing to sign an agreement excluding France if the Paris agreements were not ratified.

The two French diplomats located the British ambassador at a Washington party and received grudging confirmation of the existence of the proposal. A cable was immediately sent from the French Embassy to Mendès France, who might be able to use it with deputies who were hesitating between their hostility to German rearmament and their fear of seeing a dissolution of the Atlantic Alliance. And the shadow of this "Washington agreement" excluding France did in fact play a role in the feverish deliberations before the resumption of debate in the Palais-Bourbon on Monday.

That Monday morning, he could only have read with a kind of bitter laughter the cruel article by Jean Fabiani in *Combat:*

> It is possible, even probable, that M. Mendès France will be able to return to the Assembly on Monday.
>
> It will nevertheless be true that M. Mendès France will be able to include among his personal successes, and in the first rank, the acceptance by the French Parliament of a reconstituted *Wehrmacht.* This is to indicate the bitterness with which those who have for months placed their confidence in this intelligent and courageous man will be obligated to recognize that it was precisely that man who was able to bring about a decision that they see as fatal for the future of their country and the future of peace. . . .
>
> The irony of the political fate of a man who was brought to power to carry out economic, financial, and foreign policies based on national sovereignty and independence, and who found himself, from the very moment of his rise to a position of responsibility, entrusted with concluding what had been begun by those he condemned. . . .
>
> M. Mendès France will thus, with verve, have kept other men's promises. We hope that he may one day keep his own. But will he be given the time?

The debate was for Mendès France nothing but a long and cruel ordeal. Many men whom he respected, like Herriot and Daniel Mayer, or who had supported him even though they were members of opposing groups, like Palewski, Soustelle, Pierre Cot, and Jacques Bardoux, followed one another in opposing his arguments or calling for significant amendments, less often based on the fear of German rearmament than on that of seeing the chances for East–West negotiations destroyed.

When he returned to the podium on the thirtieth to extract at last the vote of confidence on all the articles of the bill, the first of which had been rejected by the Assembly on the twenty-fourth, and again on the twenty-ninth by the Foreign Affairs Committee, he threw his last strength into the battle. For the men confronting him, skeptical, hostile, or mocking, he was no longer anything but the defender of a questionable bill and an unpopular treaty. But he felt himself in his depths to be the spokesman of French continuity. He felt concentrated on him the eyes of Churchill and Eisenhower, of the Soviet leaders and Adenauer, of De Gaulle and a hundred nations.

Had he chosen the wrong battle? After all the hesitations and cowardice of his predecessors, he believed, he knew that nothing would be worse than another rejection.

> To bring about a four-power conference, we needed the agreement of the four partners. As for the Soviets, had they wanted to take a step forward, they have had many opportunities to do so in recent months. They saw France hesitate, reject the CED. That was the moment to talk. Time went by: instead of making a few concessions on Germany or Austria, they chose to make threats. If we had suspended our program at that time, we would have been acceding not to hope but to fear.
>
> To reject the Paris agreements would be to make it more difficult to convene the four-power conference that must meet one day. There would perhaps be a three-power or a two-power conference. We would not even be invited, because we would have left the Atlantic Alliance.
>
> But if the agreements are rejected, what credibility will we have in international discussions: vis-à-vis our American and English allies, it will be reduced to nothing. As for the Soviets, what position can a country take that has broken with its allies and chosen isolation?
>
> Our colleagues should reflect on this: to what extent are we of interest to the Soviet government? Either its objective is to detach us from the Atlantic Alliance, and we must resist every pressure, or else it is seeking genuine détente; in that case, we may be able to encourage rapprochement, but we can only do so within the alliance. If we leave it, there remains only one posture for us: a reversal of alliances. It is on this question that the Assembly must declare itself.

Things had come full circle: the man whom "Atlanticists" and "Europeans" had suspected of favoring appeasement of Moscow at any price, whom they had constantly harassed and whose positions they had undermined, was now staking the fate of his government by opposing a reversal of alliances and supporting the strengthening of ties with the Western alliance in order to promote an equal bargaining position for negotiations with the Socialist camp.

The strong majority of June was reduced to 287 in favor as opposed to 260 against. It was a bitter, narrow, melancholy victory, carried off in a domain where his real friends were less numerous than were suspect allies. He had once again demonstrated the strength of his conviction, his parliamentary mastery, and his talent as a debater. He had fostered the triumph of the feeling of Western solidarity over French nationalism, and the diplomacy of the balance of power over that of unconditional openness. But he had sometimes given the impression of being engaged "in dubious battle," wearing the disguise of an absent predecessor.

Five days after extracting the vote from the Assembly, PMF wrote to the American leaders and at the same time to the man he most admired and whom the agreements made into something like the lord protector of the Western European Union: Winston Churchill. After reminding him of the "the efforts that had been made to assure the cohesion of the Western powers," Mendès France suggested either that France propose to the Soviet Union that negotiations be opened with a view toward organizing a four-power conference or else that the three powers make the invitation together.

Dulles's negative response was not especially surprising to the head of the French government, nor was the warning that was once again made: if France acted alone, it would isolate itself, and its allies would draw the appropriate conclusions. But Churchill's response was of an entirely different significance.

It might have been expected that the British prime minister would temper the dynamism of his French colleague by encouraging him to wait until the Senate had voted; or that he politely point out that Paris was being quite presumptuous by shifting so suddenly from the role of laggard to that of pioneer. But Churchill took an entirely different tone, or rather two: flattery and threat, a threat that was even more shocking than the one Dulles had made in Brussels.

> I repeat my congratulations for your success in the Chamber. I sense the enormity of your difficulties with those vehement and egotistical groups. Your courage and your energy have given me an impression of French authority that I have not experienced since Clemenceau.
>
> For some time now, I have felt a strong wish to establish direct personal contact with the new Soviet leaders that might lead to a fruitful quadripartite conference. However, my thoughts were badly shaken when the Soviets requested a meeting of the four foreign ministers, apparently with the aim of stimulating opposition within the French Parliament to ratification of the CED. . . .

I nevertheless do not think that in the current situation negotiations with the Soviets about a four-power meeting, even on the condition of previous ratification of precise agreements, would help our common cause. The Soviets have no respect for weakness.

However great our sympathy in the difficulties you are experiencing and our admiration for your efforts, it must be recognized that myself and my colleagues are heartily determined to oppose any meetings or invitations . . . among the four powers, either at the level of foreign ministers, or at that of heads of government, before the London and Paris agreements have been ratified by all the signatories. In this, we are in complete agreement with the United States. I do not think there is the slightest chance of a change of attitude on this point in either of our two countries. In fact, I am afraid that a process of indefinite postponement will lead to the adoption of other solutions which are certainly under study on both sides of the Atlantic.

Personally, I am strongly opposed to the withdrawal of all American and British troops from the continent. You may count on me to oppose to the best of my ability the so-called peripheral strategy. But, on the other hand, I feel obliged, as prime minister and member of the Privy Council, to support the policy of the "empty chair," even though that risks bringing about great changes in the infrastructure of NATO, from the military as well as the political point of view.

I think that the United States, thanks to their immense superiority in nuclear weapons and acting in association with Great Britain, the British Commonwealth, and the German Federal Republic, will be strong enough, at least during the next few years, to offer to the Benelux countries, and to our allies for whom we have great consideration, and also to the German Federal Republic, to which we feel bound by honor, real and substantial security based on a physical and psychological "deterrent" force.

A good deal can be accomplished in this short period of time. But having worked and fought since 1910 with and for France, for whose people I have deep affection, I would be distressed to see it isolated and losing its influence in the rest of the world. I hope that you will have the opportunity to save your country from this unfortunate situation.

The Americans had never been so precise in their threats, one might almost say blackmail. They had never dared go so far toward the possibility of the "empty chair," the isolation of France, and the alternative solution based on Germany.

General de Gaulle said one day to Couve de Murville that "a state worthy of the name has no friends." Should the remarks be extended to include statesmen, including De Gaulle and his English counterpart?

Thus concluded, on this cruel note, the exhausting battle Mendès France had conducted to resolve the European problem, particularly the problem of German rearmament, in close agreement with London and without cutting off bridges to Moscow. From the Americans he had received little but warnings. From the Soviets he had gotten little but rebuffs. And now from London, his closest allies, he felt the most precise threat directed at him.

Speaking to the French on January 1, 1955, Mendès France could not conceal the extent to which the victory he had just won had cost him dearly, or the bitter taste it left in his mouth.

> A week has come to an end, perhaps the most painful week since the government was formed. Following an around-the-clock debate whose subject deeply troubled everyone's mind, the National Assembly has approved the Paris agreements. The choice was between that solution or an adventure.

But he did not want to stop with this observation. He counter-attacked:

> For too long, France has marked time, indecisive, hesitant, lacking energy in the face of the difficult and weighty obstacles blocking the way. What we have done in 1954 consists first of all in having made our resolutions and then in having picked up and removed the obstacles, cleared the path. And, finally, in having begun the march forward.

Would he be given the time? It was clear, now that he had, in Indochina, North Africa, and Europe, staunched the wounds, filled in the gaps, and opened new perspectives, that the parliamentary notables thought he had no further purpose. The two great tasks he had given himself—conversion of the French economy and the opening to the East—were too bold. He had been allowed to clear away the past. There was no question of allowing him to set out on the paths of the future. The conspiracy to bring him down was at work.

20.
"TONIGHT OR NEVER!"

What is most surprising in conspiracies is not the boldness but the timidity of the conspirators. Julius Caesar, Robespierre, and Mendès France were all men whom a group of conspirators, who had them at their mercy, had decided to destroy. Except for the Thermidorians, themselves threatened with imminent death, each group hesitated, temporized, invented pretexts for not acting. In one case, the people might not follow the "liberators" and might be swayed by Marc Anthony; in the second, overthrowing the leader would mean accepting the burden of office too soon; and in the third, there were too many unpopular tasks that remained to be accomplished not to let him take them on.

From the parliamentary point of view, by early January 1955, Mendès France was at the end of his rope. During his trip to the United States, and again during the Assembly debate at the end of the year, his enemies had continued to tighten the net. The weakness of the majority vote pulled off on December 30 was evidence of the terrible erosion the government had suffered. Of the three groups that were more or less favorable to him—Radicals, Socialists, and Gaullists—the first had moved away from him over North Africa; the second, by refusing to join the government had shown the limits of its loyalty; and the third was fragmenting and dividing, with regard to him, between violent anti-Europeans and intransigent defenders of the "empire."

Even worse, after November 22, and even more after December 30, PMF was what the English call expendable. After November 22, in fact, the deputies who might overthrow him no longer risked the reprisal of a dissolution of the Assembly. And on December 30, he had cut the Gordian knot of Europe. With this service rendered, nothing more was expected of him. He was deprived of the weapon of dissolution, and he had accomplished the task for which he had been spared.

On January 5, on the eve of a trip to Italy in the course of which he was to have an audience with Pius XII, the cabinet made two decisions that strongly contributed to his defeat: it adopted the system of voting by district that had been talked about for months, with fear and trembling, among the MRP and the Communists; and François Mitterrand announced to his colleagues the fusion of Algerian and metropolitan police forces, a step that Henri Borgeaud and the large landowners in Algeria had been attempting to prevent. In a few hours, PMF had just filled the cup of anger against him to overflowing. His trip to Italy and Germany, from January 6 to 15, gave the conspirators the opportunity to organize. During a "little Radical congress" on the twenty-sixth, René Mayer, who had been sharpening his weapons since the rejection of the CED and the Algerian uprising, threw down a kind of challenge. Mendès knew from then on that the hardest blows would come from within his own party.

What had so strongly irritated René Mayer and stirred his anger to the point of imprudence? The day before, Mendès France had decided to name a new governor general for Algeria. In place of the dim Roger Léonard, who had taken the November uprising for a wave of banditry, he had named Jacques Soustelle. If Mayer knew what was to come . . . But he did not know, nor did anyone, not even Soustelle, what the new proconsul's policies would be.

In calling on the former general secretary of the RPF, Mendès had chosen first of all a Gaullist, both because of his past as a lieutenant of the leader of Free France in London and because of the evolution of the general's positions in overseas matters. He had had nothing but praise for Christian Fouchet's conduct with respect to Tunisia; why not repeat the same operation in Algeria, with another of those French nationalists who were capable of recognizing the nationalism of others?

A former left-wing activist, a famous ethnologist, and as such presumed to be respectful of different civilizations, Soustelle ought to have been the man to carry out the egalitarian, and then federalist, solution envisaged by Mendès. In any event, his appointment was very badly received on the right, where the new governor was called a "progressive," which would provoke a negative reaction from the European community of Algiers. It was admitted that his position and intentions were ambiguous. But the conservatives of Algiers soon noticed the presence on his staff of two figures whose ideas and whose past were not ambiguous: Germaine Tillion and Vincent Monteil were enough to symbolize a fraternal and innovative policy. The apprehensions of René Mayer and the colonial right were not as absurd as they may appear today.

The colonial party was thus on the warpath, along with the party of alcohol. In November and January, the steps taken to convert and then to limit beet production and to control alcohol consumption in the school population were seen as so many declarations of war. A third lobby would complete the coalition: construction interests.

On January 20, in fact, Mendès France revealed the cabinet reshuffle that had been in preparation for months in order to allow him at last to devote a large part of his time to the conversion of the French economy. Since there was no question of punishing or devaluing Edgar Faure, his grand vizier, he offered him the Foreign Ministry, installing at Finance the "heretical" MRP Robert Buron, whom he respected for his lighthearted courage, his independence from powerful interest groups, and his loyalty, which had been demonstrated during the great CED crisis.

In any event, Mendès France's assumption of control over economic and financial matters stirred anxiety among the wealthy. No one had entirely forgotten the "minister of rigor" of 1945. Everyone knew that this supporter of planning had been born to disturb. No one had any illusions about what the word *conversion* meant for him, Georges Boris, Simon Nora, and Claude Gruson. Least of all those who controlled the construction industry.

It was known that this would be the government's emphasis: in the eyes of Mendès and his brain trust, low-cost housing, for economic as well as social reasons, had to be the focal point of conversion and "dynamization." The protected domain of construction was thus going to experience the sudden arrival of new forces. Prices were going to be drastically reduced and profitable arrangements called into question. Although it was much less powerful than that of the beet growers, the construction lobby attempted to mobilize—without much effect.

There was thus established in broad sectors of economic activity what was at first a parliamentary Fronde. To be sure, it was not the alcohol producers or the promoters of large construction projects that set the leaders of the MRP against Mendès: Pierre-Henri Teitgen and François de Menthon had only to think of the "crime of August 30," or to hear Mendès speak of the cordial reception he had been given by the Pope on January 12, or of the friendly conversation he had had with Adenauer in Baden-Baden on the fourteenth, to lose all control over their anger. Nor was it the great Algerian wine producers or the beet growers who stimulated the hostility of the Communist Party against PMF. There was an ideological opposition, which expressed the rejection of the Mendès government by broad sectors of the population, haunted by a supra-national Europe, allergic to German rearmament, or exasperated by the successes (or the timidity) of its virtuous reformism.

But this "resistance" would not have been able to overthrow a government that had withstood the storms of August, October, and December without the reinforcement of circumstantial allies coming from all sides—even from the SFIO, whose votes in the Assembly did not reveal all—to bring down the man who negotiated in North Africa, recalled police torturers from Algiers, limited the consumption of alcohol, was preparing to control the construction of low-cost housing, and intended to work for détente with the East and to begin the process of "converting" the French economy.

A debate on North Africa was scheduled for February 2. It was thus "on Algeria" that the death blow would be struck.

"It might have been almost anything else," Mendès said many years later.

> Beginning with the new parliamentary session in November, I was attacked on everything: once it was agriculture, another time the leaks, a third Indochina: every opportunity was seized. It is obvious that Algeria was a sensitive point; there were people there who had substantial means, there was the army, and so on. But if it hadn't been Algeria, it would have been something else. If I hadn't been defeated on that day, it would have been a week later over something else. I really believe that it was only a pretext. The Assembly majority that voted me down was not in bad faith. It really believed that a policy different from the one, let's say, of dialogue had to be followed. The Assembly did not vote against its conscience: it quite simply wanted to overthrow me.

We should add that, although the conspiracy, within and outside the Assembly, had its axis on the right, Mendès was far from being able to count on coherent support from the left. Not only had the Communists made him the man who had to be politically defeated, not only was the SFIO quietly undermining his positions and part of the "liberal" wing of the MRP moving away from him, but even what was rather vaguely known as the "non-Communist left" provided little support.

While Sartre's monthly Les Temps modernes published an article that defined Mendès's Algerian policy as a choice of evolutionary capitalism over blinkered colonialism, in France-Observateur, Claude Bourdet attacked the plan attributed to friends of Mendès of creating a "new left" around PMF, François Mauriac, André Malraux, and the modernist wing of French Catholicism. "It would be nothing but a new right," scornfully concluded Bourdet, who was himself in the process of setting up a parallel operation with a much more "progressive" axis.

And even L'Express caused some concern to the harried Mendès.

When he took over the Finance Ministry, Robert Buron found a proposed regulation on horseracing that appeared to favor wealthy owners like Marcel Boussac, who was thought to be a friend of Edgar Faure's. The director of *L'Express,* who had never resigned himself to Faure's presence in the reforming government, saw the opportunity for a cruel attack calling his honesty into question. Faure's reaction was astounding: he challenged the journalist to a duel, which was accepted. Here was the head of government, at the edge of the abyss, caught up in a cloak-and-dagger affair, which he managed to defuse, but not before public opinion had been shaken by an enormous burst of laughter: PMF or d'Artagnan?

Thus, on February 2, the Palais-Bourbon brought to mind the Convention on the morning of 8 Thermidor. The conspirators had no fear for their lives. But like their ancestors, they had "decided on the death of the tyrant." And the president of the MRP, in the course of those feverish days, spoke some astonishing words that seemed to come straight from a nineteenth-century historical romance: "It is tonight or never!"

Two days earlier, the conspirators had already taken the measure of their adversary's fragility and demonstrated their own strength. By a vote of 325 to 288, they had rejected a very banal request for an advance on the budget which Mendès had asked to be granted, like all his predecessors, until the finance bill could be voted on. Mendès had been warned. However unsurprised he may have been to see the circle of executioners close in on him, he was furious at the device. The man who had presented himself as the voice of rigor and sound management, the Poincaré of the left, had been forced to suspend payments simply because they wanted to make him stumble before bringing him down, psychologically push him to the limit.

It was in this dramatic and poisonous atmosphere that on the second day, February 3, René Mayer, deputy from Constantine, mounted the podium. His speech was indeed the anticipated indictment, brilliant and wounding. The Algerian wine interests and the party of racial discrimination had found a voice of high quality.

> Successive contradictions do not make up a policy. The politics of the wager has given way to that of diversion.
>
> If, Mister Prime Minister, you ask us again for a vote of confidence, I regret that I will not be able to renew mine for you, for a reason which relates not only to the subject we are discussing but which affects your politics as a whole, particularly in the international realm.
>
> I do not know where you are going, and I cannot believe that a politics of movement is unable to find a middle term between immobility and adventurism.

The cruelty of the attack and the jubilant response it provoked on many benches showed that the execution had begun. But however affected he may have been by the very personalized attack, one can imagine that Mendès France suffered even more cruelly in listening to the other deputy from Constantine, the Moslem and Socialist Mostefa Benbahmed. For what he said, despite his intentions, went further than the sarcasms of René Mayer.

> Tortures have been inflicted on those of my coreligionists who have remained deaf to calls to adventurism. . . . They are no longer unaware of the bathtub torture. They are acquainted with what they call the water tube: the device by means of which people are forced to swallow water, and not even guilty people, but simply those who have been denounced, sometimes anonymously. The Moslems in the countryside now know what electricity is!

François Mitterrand did not fail to join Benbahmed's protest and to assert that orders had been given to put an end to these practices. The blow had nevertheless been struck. Given the nature of the debate, this terrible evocation had more immediate effect on the "reformists" of the government than on the repressive conservatives whose position was supported by René Mayer. It was useless for Benbahmed subsequently to declare to the Assembly: "The Moslem population would see a vote against the government as a condemnation of the policy of reforms. I adjure you to master your bitterness and your complaints. If you were to overthrow the government, you would dig a valley of tears and of blood."

Mendès was tense and febrile when he mounted the podium.

> This afternoon, M. René Mayer has spoken of our mistakes and their catastrophic consequences. I would point out to him that he has shared and still shares these responsibilities, since he has always supported them with his votes. If the Assembly were to condemn us, it would condemn M. René Mayer as well, who, six months late, has noticed that the government is betraying the country, is liquidating North Africa, and is unworthy of the confidence of the French.

Then, having expressed his fury and recovered his serenity, he broadened the debate.

> Some may think that a head of government whose position has been eaten away in all the debates and who—an unprecedented event—has even been refused a budget advance, has the right to abandon the fight in conditions that are honorable, even favorable for him. Well, precisely in the present instance, the public interest prohibits such a calculation.
>
> I have pursued a policy in North Africa for which only one other policy can be substituted, the one that I believe to be injurious to the interests of the country. Either we have a policy of understanding, or else a policy of repression and force, with all its horrible consequences.
>
> I cannot today allow the condemnation of the policy that I believe to be

salutary and necessary. I will defend it to the end, with scorn for all clever maneuvers.

The next morning, observers saw practically no chances for the government's survival. According to Jacques Fauvet in *Le Monde:*

> The premier . . . remains guilty of having interrupted the continuity of a system, of being a kind of usurper. Having confronted his predecessors, and often Parliament as a whole, with harshness, sometimes with excess, he is loved by neither; he is even hated by many. The vote of confidence or, if he miraculously survives, the succeeding votes will constitute a vast settling of scores.

On the fourth, it was up to Mendès France to deliver his final argument before the decision. He had recovered his equilibrium and his strength, and he made a powerful impression. One could see, beneath the exhausted champion, signs of the radiant leader of June.

> When you are asked why you overthrew the government on African policy, oh, I know, you will say that you overthrew it not for its actions in North Africa, but for other reasons and because of the chance offered by a propitious debate! . . . I ask those who do not condemn our policy of reforms: Why take this pretext to overthrow us? What strange majority do you wish to see come out of the vote? On the one hand, men who want reforms but vote against the government that applies them; on the other, men who want to return to a policy of repression.
>
> What is at stake in the vote is not the fate of a premier. You must make a choice in North Africa. For our part, we have chosen. . . . This choice is perhaps the most serious that you have had to make for months, perhaps for years, for it involves the future of France. As an MRP deputy said, will we be capable, through a bold effort, of building with the Moslem peoples a common edifice, or else will the legacy of a century of history crumble in hatred and bloodshed?
>
> Your responsibilities have never been weightier. The government has never betrayed its own.

It was 2:40 A.M. when PMF returned to the government bench. The session did not resume until 4:50. The president of the Assembly announced the result of the vote:

For confidence	273 votes,
Against	319 votes,
Abstentions	22 votes

The government has lost the vote of confidence.

Finished. This was indeed the night. The silence was total. There were no demonstrations. But what was happening? Ordinarily, the defeated premier left the chamber as soon as the vote was known, followed by the ministers present, to transmit his resignation to the head of state.

Mendès, decidedly nonconformist, walked toward the podium, mounted it, and took a paper out of his pocket. The president of the Assembly seemed to find this step quite natural and gave him the floor. The deputies who had not left the Chamber, around two-thirds, stared, dumbfounded. And Mendès read in a tense voice:

It is not the custom for a premier who has lost the confidence of a majority of the Assembly to ask to speak again. If before going to present the government's resignation to the president of the Republic, I have mounted this podium, it is not, you may be sure, to recriminate against the sovereign decision made by the Assembly after it heard the explanations and the warnings of the government.

On North Africa, subject of this debate, I will refrain from saying a word that might interfere with our successors, in a task whose difficulties we have experienced. My most ardent wish, the wish of all patriots, is that the solution to the Tunisian problem, now within reach, will be neither blocked nor delayed. A matter of such high interest, our African future, should not depend on the fate of a government. I say that so that it may be heard, not only here, but outside.

Up to that point, caught short, the Assembly had not reacted. But murmurs were beginning to rise among the Communists and the right.

No, the work that has been accomplished will not be erased, neither in this area nor in any of the others in which, during these last months, we have had to struggle without interruption to confront accumulated dilemmas and daily events, and especially to obey the desire for renovation and peace of the entire country. What has been done in these seven or eight months, what has been set in motion in this country will not stop. Men pass, national necessities remain.

At that point, the Assembly grumbled. There was an uproar among the Communists, the MRP, and the right. In a voice beginning to grow hoarse, Mendès declared: "How could the nation forget the hopes that we have revived?"

From that moment on, he could only speak a few words in brief moments of calm, like so many bottles in the ocean.

"How can we think that the nation will lose the taste for truth, now that it knows its flavor that is bitter but always healthy?"

FRANÇOIS DE MENTHON (MRP): I demand the floor for a point of order.
PRESIDENT OF THE ASSEMBLY: I give you the floor with the speaker's consent.
FRANÇOIS DE MENTHON: The agenda of the session has been completed by the proclamation of the vote, and it is normal that the session be adjourned.
ROBERT BICHET: The Constitution is violated! This is fascism.
PRESIDENT: I thought it was possible, in an atmosphere of courtesy, to au-

thorize the outgoing premier to say a few words. None of the regulations forbids it. I ask you, in the national interest . . . to show some courtesy.
FERNAND BOUXOM (MRP): The podium is not made for personal propaganda.
FRANÇOIS DE MENTHON: The vote is completed and proclaimed. We should, especially in so serious a matter, hold to formal observation of the regulations. It is inadmissible that a kind of appeal to public opinion against the Parliament should be made under the protection of your courtesy, Mr. President.

In the uproar, the stenographers managed to transcribe Mendès France's final words:

At the moment when it has just overthrown the government, the Assembly is not showing itself worthy of its responsibilities. I hope that tomorrow, in a better climate and in mutual understanding among patriots, we will be able to give this country reasons to hope and to overcome the hatred which we have too often made into a spectacle. *Vive la France!*

Then Mendès came down from the podium again, returned to the government bench, picked up the briefcase containing his files, and followed by the ministers, who had been willing to share the ordeal to the end, left the Assembly, applauded by the Socialists on their feet and booed by the MRP, the right, and the Communists. It was 5 A.M., February 5, 1955.

This strange episode has given rise to untold commentaries on the personality, the democratic ideas, the character, and the cleverness of Mendès. In the corridors of the Assembly, first of all, reactions ranged from barely concealed racism to finally unmasked hatred. A privileged witness, Robert Buron, gives this version of the affair:

He had carefully prepared a declaration, convinced that the government would be beaten without there being a constitutional majority against it.[1] From the moment when that opposition showed itself against us, the legal justification for this final appeal was lacking. François Mitterrand and I tried in vain to make the premier understand it. Simultaneously exhausted and tense, he was in a sort of an exalted state and was thinking of only one thing: reading the text he had prepared.[2]

And what did Mendès France think twenty-five years later?

I made a blunder. I could very well have delivered the same speech—which was very sober, very serene—on the radio. I had not realized that there was so much bile. The Parliament could no longer stomach me, that was the fact. So it decided to consider as an appeal to the people over its head, what was simultaneously a sketch for a balance sheet, a call for unity, and a reminder addressed to the people of North Africa that France's commitments would be honored.

There remained to carry out the final formalities, the trip to the

Elysée Palace in the cold night, President Coty's regrets expressed with a ceremony that let his feelings through, and, disconcertingly, iced champagne, served in the circumstances to the members of a government struggling against alcohol. Mendès chose to gulp down a steaming cup of coffee. Coty continued a private conversation with Mendès for another twenty minutes. Then, on the steps of the Elysée, at dawn, Mendès declared to the press:

> I will not hide my emotions or my pain, not for me, but for the country. I regret that the work undertaken by my government has not been able to be carried on. I hope that it will not be interrupted, because what has been done has been done for the good of the country.
>
> In many areas, what has been begun must be continued. I hope with all my heart that the government that succeeds me, whatever its makeup, will continue my work. I hope that it succeeds for the greater good of the country.

Was Mendès France deeply wounded by this tumultuous dismissal, with a wound as incurable as those inflicted at the trial "for desertion" in Clermont-Ferrand? "No," he said years later.

> The 1941 trial scared me much more. I was young then, less experienced. Naturally, in February 1955, I was very hurt that I was overthrown, because many things remained to be done. But I don't really think that I was as traumatized as I had been in Clermont-Ferrand. It was of a different character. A risk of the profession, in sum. Even if certain shouts, certain threats, reminded me of what I had lived through in 1941.

Did he think he would quickly return to power? Probably, according to most of those who were close to him at the time. Just as, before June 18, 1954, he had been skeptical about his chances, so the awareness of what he had accomplished in seven and a half months fostered his hope after February 5. Elections were scheduled for 1956. Who did not believe that a wave of support for Mendès would arise at that point?

This prognosis, which might have been contradicted in January by the twilight of the government, over which the difficult debate on ratification of the Paris agreements in December and the successive cabinet shuffles of the final weeks had cast a shadow, had been revived by the spectacle of the "execution" in February.

But the time to withdraw had not yet come for Mendès France. Overthrown, he had to take care of routine business while the merry-go-round of possible successors was set in motion. This opened an eighteen-day reprieve, which he remembered with enchantment.

> During those two interim weeks, I made the unexpected discovery that I had all the powers of a government, but not the risk of being overthrown. It was magnificent! It was at that point that a very curious thing happened to me. One of the problems that remained in suspension was the problem of Tunisia.

The negotiations were moving toward their conclusion, but the situation remained tense in southern Tunisia. In Paris, the high command formulated unreasonable demands. One day, during this interim, into my office came a colonel I did not yet know who commanded the most difficult sector. He explained what had to be done, in a manner that seemed to me very reasonable and acceptable for the Tunisians. Men in the field like him understood much better than their superiors in Paris the need to take account of evolution. So he gave me his report. I accompanied him to the door, shook his hand, and suddenly he started to stammer and said to me: "Mister Prime Minister, I am distressed that you have been overthrown; it is the first time since I have been a soldier that I have been proud of the government of my country." Thereupon, astonished that he dared violate protocol—to such a degree—he clicked his heels and ran off at top speed. He was already at the outer door before I had the time to answer. That was how I met him. It's rather moving, isn't it?

On February 23, at the Hôtel Matignon, Mendès France gave way to his minister of foreign affairs, Edgar Faure, 245 days after his investiture by the National Assembly.

Unlike many public men who are highly educated, admirable for competence and lucidity in planning or criticizing, but whose fragility or limits are revealed by the exercise of power, like Paul Reynaud, Mendès France, often stiff and abstract in opposition, "found" himself in the exercise of power, fulfilled himself, made fruitful his gifts for courage and lucidity, for concentration, and especially for decisiveness.

It is at the conclusion of this trying ordeal of eight months that we should consider Pierre Mendès France as a public man. A long career was still open to him. But it is in the shadows of this kind of sunset of February 1955 that can be most clearly seen the features of the man of government, his historical significance, and his presence in the collective consciousness of the French.

He was first of all a character, expressed through his will. Not that he was not capable of hesitation. But when he had made a decision and built a plan, he moved forward with it.

His "character" could be one of redoubtable harshness. One could cite instances when his manner of expression put off possible friends or well-disposed partners.

He often seemed eager for solitude, seeming to take Alceste for a model.

The difficulty of approaching him came, of course, from his passion to be right, which could reach the level of obstinacy and stubbornness. Whether flying over England with Romain Gary, or examining an economic problem with Gabriel Ardant, or debating the Algerian policy of

Charles de Gaulle, he was sometimes so intent on persuading others that he would occasionally deny the obvious. But he was nevertheless capable, on serious questions, of recognizing a mistake.

In a fine article in *L'Express* in March 1967, Françoise Giroud described him as saving

> for those who loved him his tyranny, his sarcasms, his complaints, and a permanent questioning of their loyalty. Who would betray him before cockcrow? The slightest sign of affection moved him deeply, the slightest reservation provided him with a structure of suppositions about the reasons for which "he doesn't like me, I assure you, he doesn't like me." "He" would throw himself into the fire for Mendès. "All that is very well," declares Mendès France, "but in 1947 . . ." There follows an enumeration of the crimes of *lèse*-Mendès France accumulated in his memory, so that he can say, as touching as though he believed it: "You see. I am not liked." In fact, a man among men, enormously good and attentive to others, superior without arrogance, demanding less of others than he demands from himself, he has provoked without ever looking for them the deepest devotion and most constant admiration.

Françoise Giroud knows what she is talking about. Four years earlier, after publishing an article for the tenth anniversary of *L'Express,* she received a letter from PMF written in a style that is apparently little used by statesmen, people who are reputed to be severe and without heart: "You must have felt, at moments, some emotion in recalling those episodes, those struggles, those disappointments, but also that success that owes so much to you. I share your feeling at this moment, as we shared, week by week, so many feelings, hopes, and angers."

Feelings, hopes, angers: from what other professional politicians could one expect such language?

A sneer in this instance would be a judgment on whoever surrendered to it. Whoever does not involve his whole being in public action, whoever does not experience it in the depths of his sensibility, is nothing but the head of an office.

And yet, he was an intellectual, that is, a man whose ideas directed his behavior and who dreamed of shaping the world according to his thought; who tended to conceptualize history; and who formulated his concepts in terms understood by other intellectuals, from Princeton to Florence, better than by the railroad workers on the Paris–Louviers line. But this last point has to be qualified.

First of all because, by the end of his adolescence, Mendès chose between the two political movements that could claim his adherence—the party of Herriot and the "house" of Blum—the first, which emphasized reality, rather than the second, which placed the accent on ideas. It was again the passion for reality that led him to devote his entire being to his duties as mayor of Louviers. And it was also the concern for the concrete that drew him to the study of economics and made him a master of vigorous accounting.

Second because the head of the 1954 government might very well be the author of a book, *La Science économique et l'action* (Economic Science and [Political] Action) which was very austere and written in technical language, but it must also be recognized that the representative of the Eure peasants was a vital enough part of him that he could address the French with the most authentic simplicity.

The best definition he could give of his politics was "revolution through law." And he was too imbued with law to believe that the world he was designing contained frontiers and a margin of relativity. It was not an accident that the young Mendès received his highest grade in constitutional law, and that his arguments in the European negotiations constantly relied on juridical references and appeals to legitimacy.

All the same, it was the teacher in him that dominated. In search of ancestors, one thinks of Gambetta the republican, Poincaré the accountant (since he encouraged us to do so) and Caillaux the imaginative economist who was so successful in making himself hated. All things considered, Jules Ferry provides the best model. Let us forget the ironic link created between them by Indochina—Ferry ruined himself in conquering it, and Mendès later disengaged France. What is more important is the passion to instruct, to persuade.

Ferry wanted to establish the Republic in the hearts and minds of the French. Mendès wanted to persuade them to conquer freedom and prosperity through productive investment. Both believed in the virtues of didacticism. Ferry chose the school as a weapon, Mendès the radio. Both were harassed, attacked, overthrown in anger, but without losing their faith.

At the heart of power as in opposition, and later in retirement, he devoted all his time not taken up by action to reading. Professional reading to begin with: everything that was published on contemporary history, economics, and the social sciences. He harassed his colleagues to learn more, to find out about a detail, to discover a contradiction.

Although he may have appreciated the relative comfort of the small official residence in Marly where he spent most of his weekends as head of government, he never made his house in Louviers anything more than a small Norman landowner's residence. In any event, completely indifferent to money and almost never carrying any with him, this economist passionately concerned with the nation's accounts never knew anything about his own, ignorant of the price of a pound of butter, a pair of socks, or a ticket to the movies.

He was a democrat, but in the style of Clemenceau or Caillaux, a leader and not very collegial. Robert Buron remembered the 1954 government, in which he had been a prominent and active member, as a one-man show. In a scintillating but venomous portrait of PMF, Pierre-Olivier Lapie,[3] who was also a colleague of Leon Blum's, writes: "He considered his ministers as his subordinates, among whom his role was not to arbitrate, alone or in cabinet meetings, but to command." Very careful to surround himself with competent men with diverse opinions, very far from believing in his own omniscience, even modest on occasion, Pierre Mendès France was not entirely a man of dialogue like Léon Blum.

He placed himself in the center of the debate, breathing in and concentrating everything, and deciding. A magnetic pole rather than an arbitrator, less the catalyst of a group than the head of a brain trust, insisting on his own responsibilities as though he was afraid of not taking enough risks, of exposing himself too little to attacks, constantly posing problems as though they were absolutes, and often playing on his personal relations with his interlocutor, injecting passion into debates, he was truly "his" government all by himself.

He was called PMF. In a political society that was eager to cover itself, clever in diluting personal responsibilities, he did not create a scandal, he was a scandal. He was made to pay for it on February 5, 1955.

But which of his executioners that morning could not have subscribed to this statement from one of Mendès France's most penetrating friends: "I have known him to be abrupt, disagreeable, unjust, sometimes even ungrateful. I have never seen him low"?

THE PASSION TO BE RIGHT

21.
RADICALLY YOURS, OR THE VERY YOUNG TURKS

PMF spent a few days relaxing in Mégève, in the snow, far from René Mayer and Fernand Bouxom. But even those few days seemed long to him.

I kept quiet for a few weeks. I had things to put in order. But very soon, friends started to say to me: "We have to create a party. We have to give form to the movement of public opinion that has just surfaced around you." I thought about it. I remembered the experience of De Gaulle's RPF, that personalization of politics that brought right and left together merely in the name of one man. I was perfectly willing to admit that there were Gaullists. I hated any talk of "Mendésists." Did I ever ask, in my name, for unconditional commitment?

So I said to myself that it was better to restore and renovate the Radical Party. By staying on the Radical track (with the hope of influencing the party), it seemed to me that I would remain all the more clearly on the left because my first priority would be an alliance with the Socialists and a break with the right. Furthermore, the tradition, the past of the old Radical Party was after all republican: against the forces of wealth, against what were called the economic combines, for the abolition of wage slavery. The leaders had been perverted, or in any case were drifting toward the right; the masses,

345

the rank and file, the "foot soldiers," as Herriot called them, remained un-
contestably on the left.

This choice was not an improvisation. A year earlier, in May 1954,
L'Express gave a party to celebrate its first year of publication. From a
group of young people around Mendès came a question: "What can we do
to help you?" "Join the Radical Party!" And thus began for several dozen
adolescents, who were to become thousands, a strange archeological expedition.

French Radicalism could and can be defined in many ways. One
would be to quote the aphorisms of two of its tutelary spirits: Herriot,
"No enemies on the left!"; Sarraut, "Communism, that's the enemy!"
Another would be to picture simultaneously a party meeting of bearded,
overweight, and perspiring men, and the death by torture of Jean Moulin,
Radical militant. And a third would be to read in alternation a page from
Alain the philosopher and a page from a speech by André Morice, a
minister from the same party. Vice and virtue. Being and nothingness.
Having made the Republic, from secular education to the income tax, the
party seemed to consider itself entitled to unmake it.

French Radicalism was (paradoxically) the party of Dr. Queuille,
twenty-seven times a minister, whose political philosophy could be
summed up in a precept: "If a problem is hard to solve, it is best not to
raise it." But it had also been the party of Clemenceau, Caillaux, and the
Young Turks. If, in the late 1920s, in the wake of Daladier, young men like
Bergery, Kayser, and Cot had imposed the Young Turk movement, why,
in 1955, could a leader of international stature not revive the party on the
basis of a comparable movement, inspiring it with his prestige and effectiveness?

The problem was perhaps less the renovation of the dilapidated structure than the question of whether the presumed reformer belonged to the
"church." Alain asserted that Blum was not a real Socialist but a "Parisian
Radical." What would he have said of Mendès? That he was a Normandy
Socialist? As with Blum, who was a true Socialist, he would have been
wrong: Mendès, at least until the late 1950s—and perhaps thereafter—
was a true Radical, profoundly attached to some articles of the
"dogma"—pacifism, secularism, opening to the left—as well as to the
eminently "reasonable" character of his original party.

An "extraordinary Congress" was called for May 4 (the regular Congress having taken place, as we have seen, in October in Marseille) at the
Salle Wagram in Paris, where the structures of the oldest party in France
would be subjected to the assaults of the youngest militants in Paris.

Everything began in the morning in the Salle Wagram in a feverish
atmosphere and ended in the evening at the Mutualité in an uproar. Called

to put some mustaches on the statues and to clear out the "traitor" Léon Martinaud-Déplat—the administrative president who, having survived PMF's Marseille triumph, had, with René Mayer, organized the execution of Mendès in the Chamber—the Jacobins and very young Radicals, mostly Parisian and often subscribers to *L'Express,* transformed the Congress into a reply to the night of February 5. The seizure of the Radical Party did not have the elegant style of the June 18 investiture.

In short, Martinaud was thrown out, and the Radical Party, led by the Jacobins, proceeded to elect an "action committee" to replace the administrative president, known as the group of seven, charged with rewriting the party statutes.

This movement, which shook the very old house of the place de Valois, was inspired by three central ideas. First was the certainty that politics was less based on ideology than created by action. These young men were contemporaries of the first phase of the vast movement of rejection or calling into question that accelerated after the Twentieth Congress of the Soviet Communist Party in 1956. Marxism, which had been the ideology of reference for ten years, from the Ecole Normale Supérieure to economic research circles, had ceased to reign, although it had not yet been replaced. The young men gathered around PMF did not expect him to substitute another doctrine for Leninism but to call them to renovate society through action. In this sense, Mendésist neoradicalism was faithful to the tradition that had attracted the student of 1925: pragmatism in the style of Clemenceau.

A second idea of Mendès's young supporters was that the movement could rely only on alliances with the left. It was the old spirit of the Cartel des Gauches of 1924, the time of Mendès's adolescence. There was even in the speeches of these Jacobins a hint of the Popular Front,[1] or, to remain within party history, an echo of the Young Turks of 1930. Here, too, there was an easy connection to the past. It was the "no enemies on the left" of Herriot, except that secularism was no longer the motivating force: among these young Radicals there were soon to be found militant Catholics. Readers of Mauriac or Domenach, one current in Mendésism did not stay away from mass.

The third element in the 1955 movement might appear more novel in the history of French Radicalism: the one that emphasized economic research, planning, industrial conversion, and development. This was what might be called Keynesian Radicalism. This primacy of economics might seem a break with the tradition of the party of Herriot and Daladier. But this would be to forget Caillaux, the man of his time who was most concerned with monetary and fiscal questions, the ancestor of this calculating Radicalism.

In short, this movement under the banner of PMF and the sign of youth could surprise only those who did not know the history of the Radical Party: it was the heir of Clemenceau, of the founders of the Cartel des Gauches, and of Joseph Caillaux, inventor of the income tax. It was a new avatar of the Young Turks. But this time the leader was not distant and prudent like Daladier, ambiguous like Bergery, or too young like Pierre Cot. He had been for the past year the most vigorous figure in the French political world.

And yet, the movement came to nothing. Two years later, Mendès France withdrew from the leadership of the party. Four years later, breaking with the Radical Party because young people were drifting away from it, he began his movement toward organizations that called themselves Socialist.

The operation of converting the Radical Party in order to provide the man of change with a political base that would enable him to avoid being, as he had been for seven months, the hostage of shifting alliances and unstable cabinets, had nevertheless developed at a rapid pace. In November 1955, the regular party congress had endorsed and deepened the gains of the extraordinary congress of the Salle Wagram. Mendès France, in opposition to his successor Edgar Faure, who argued for his conception of a "party of management," had imposed the idea of a "party of opposition and renewal." On this platform, he was elected first vice-president of the party, which made him de facto president, considering the age and condition of the "president for life," Edouard Herriot. And at his request, the party adopted a motion calling for a "decisive modification" of the government's Algerian policy.

Everything seemed permitted. Finally master of the movement, whose membership had increased in six months from less than 30,000 to more than 100,000 (and in the Paris region from nothing to 15,000), Mendès was in a position to prepare, with real chances of success, for the elections scheduled for seven or eight months later. He could count on a party with 200,000 members capable of drawing in and uniting the numberless sympathizers of the Geneva negotiator. He seemed to be able to hope for three million voters and a hundred deputies. Many observers made this prognosis in November 1955.

It was then that a dramatic series of events occurred that suddenly interfered with what many observers saw as the rise of "organic" Mendésism. Voted down by the Chamber, Edgar Faure decided to dissolve the Assembly and call for early elections. In the name of the "business Radicals" for whom he had argued at the November congress, Faure had just stifled the grand design of Mendès and his friends. To advance the elections by six or seven months was to prevent the new party from consolidating, from extending its support in the provinces, and from carrying out its electoral reform. A hope aimed at June 1956, twentieth anniversary of the Popular Front victory, could not be realized in December 1955.

The reaction of the Mendès group was brutal. Edgard Faure, who Mendès later thought was at the time the instrument of a maneuver invented or imposed by the leadership of the MRP, was expelled from the party on December 1. And a week later the extreme right of the party was also drummed out. But the blow from which Mendès's brand of Radicalism would not recover had been struck. Early elections had cut the ground from under it. And later, the exacerbation of the Algerian war and the explosion of French nationalism it provoked from spring 1956 on made Mendès a marginal figure.

To be sure, by functioning as a catalyst for the Republican Front formed for purposes of the election, the Radical Party had apparently reconquered an essential strategic position as arbiter of French political life. In fact, the exclusions of the previous weeks had reduced its parliamentary representation, while PMF himself was confined to the abstract functions of a minister without portfolio. And beginning in April 1956, those who had been defeated in the two congresses of 1955 gradually reversed the opinion of party members, first with an argument against the coup of which they had been the victims, and later, and especially, over the Algerian war. The colonial old guard unleashed a counterattack by calling for collective leadership of the party.

At first, Mendès France and his friends resisted this attempt: the Lyon congress, from October 11 to 13, 1956, reelected him as first vice-president, confirmed the expulsion of Edgar Faure, and accepted the resignation of colonial spokesman André Morice. But the spirit was already broken, and by resigning from the government in May, PMF weakened his position in the party. The events of the Algerian conflict, which mobilized the passions of Radical voters, to whom a number of their representatives accused Mendès of being a "traitor," did their work, isolating Mendès and forcing him to resign the vice-presidency on May 23, 1957.

The attempted conquest and renewal of the Radical Party had failed for very diverse reasons. The first had to do with the very character of the "conqueror." A good description of his behavior as the dauphin of Radicalism is provided by Alain Gourdon, who was closely involved with the 1955 events in the ranks of the Jacobins:

> Mendès France, who has a better grasp on international problems than on the organization of the Radical Party, has in addition made the mistake of preserving the old patterns of government by the Assembly and of wanting to restore to the executive committees their presumed past vigor. By multiplying minor congresses, he multiplies opportunities for intrigue and the

chances for proliferating demagoguery; he erodes his prestige and wastes his talent.[2]

A member of the party for more than thirty years, Pierre Mendès France remained, according to Francis de Tarr, "the most Radical of the Mendésist Radicals."[3] But his very personal Radicalism, politically connected to the history of the Young Turks, economically based on a conception of democratic planning shared by very few of his colleagues, and more and more marked by determined anticolonialism, could be that of an eminent militant, not that of the party leader. The Mendésism of 1955–1956 was an ideology as difficult to assimilate by the Radical machinery as Gaullism was by the old right.

Called on early in 1955 to take the leadership of a broad movement, Mendès France had preferred to attempt to regenerate the old party of Herriot rather than to create an RPF of the left. Although the popular Radicalism of the Midi had gone along, the modernist graft had not really taken. Because it had been carried out with too much haste? Because the opening to the left had deprived the one-third of the deputies leaning to the right of their seats, without the immediate prospect of their replacement by more left-wing deputies? Because the dissolution carried out by Edgar Faure had deprived Mendès of the parliamentary majority anticipated in June 1956, which would have allowed him, at a second stage, to assure his control over the party? Or because the dramatization of the Algerian war imbued the rejection by the old guard with an intractable violence against the "dissipator" of the empire?

Even more than all this, the rejection appears to have been a sociological or socioeconomic phenomenon. The old party had been rooted in a retrograde economy, that of the Southwest and the Midi as a whole, based on a system of ownership and exchange that was resistant to change. How could it have chosen as a leader, once the moment of collective excitement had passed, the man who represented economic transformation?

Reflecting on his enterprise many years later, Mendès France offered a more nuanced description:

> The Radical Party was "on the left," not only in a historical sense. The rank and file, the "foot soldiers," the citizen—voters in 1955 and 1956—still had, as they say "their hearts on the left." The difficulties we had were always at the top among the important people, generally the elected officials, former ministers, former premiers, and so on. Besides, they were all recent Radicals, who had no real contact with the Radical rank and file. These men, Felix Gaillard, Bourgès-Maunoury, René Mayer, Edgar Faure, were brilliant but recent Radicals, and had no contacts with the party rank and file.
>
> The party in itself never disowned me. The battles we had to fight were at the top. The expulsions you talk about were all expulsions of leaders. We

had no discipline difficulties in the provincial federations or the sections. The party, as such, reacted well.

At a certain point, it happened that the recent recruits, particularly the young ones, became discouraged and thought there was decidedly nothing that could be done. It was their discouragement, the fact that some of them no longer came to meetings or had even left the party, that was the decisive element for me. Otherwise, I would not have hesitated to continue to lead the battle, even if that were to force us into periodic amputations in the form of breaks with important, brilliant, and spectacular men, but who were not real forces in the party and had no roots in it.

22.
UNDER THE PHRYGIAN CAP

With the dissolution of the Assembly on December 1, 1955, less than a month remained before the elections. Less than a month, while the hatred of the right had become even more vigorous with an explosion of openly racist Poujadism, the MRP had just expressed its unmitigated rancor by inspiring the dissolution, and the hostility of the PCF was so vigilant that Maurice Thorez had declared in May that the renovation of the Radical Party was nothing but "a political maneuver aimed at capturing and diverting for the benefit of the *grande bourgeoisie* the movement in favor of the union of popular forces and at setting up a political and electoral formation essentially directed against our party."

What electoral hopes could there be for a Radical Party that was bleeding from the surgical operation that had eliminated Edgar Faure, René Mayer, and Martinaud-Déplat and provoked the furious hostility of powerful bosses of the party? Prophets had already come up with figures: forty to fifty seats, with the "Faurists" reduced to fewer than thirty.

The whole problem was thus one of electoral alliances. The idea of a popular front with the Communists, favored by certain Jacobins, was not acceptable. Despite the step toward international détente manifested by the four-power conference with the Soviets in Geneva in July, the "nationalist," "European," and "Algerian" discontents still seemed too vigorous to permit a 1936-style alliance. For the leaders of the PCF, Mendès remained the man who had rejected Communist votes on June 17, 1954, who had favored German rearmament, and above all the man who was in the process of creating a deeply troubling movement of public opinion: on the basis of themes of renewal and peace, he was burning away a fraction of the PCF's electoral "clientele," the young intellectuals.

For Pierre Mendès France, the privileged allies were the Socialists. In the eyes of this man who was so strongly attached to his youth, the salutary strategy, the "good alliance," was the Cartel des Gauches, the coalition of Radicals and Socialists, Herriot and Blum. The head of the 1954 government, although he had unfortunately been unable to obtain the participation of Guy Mollet's comrades, had constantly benefited from their support, even in the bitterest debates over the ratification of the Paris agreements. As soon as the electoral contest became known, the head of the new Radical Party thought first of forming an alliance with the SFIO.

The dissolution became known on Thursday, December 1. Contacts were immediately established between PMF and his closest Socialist friend, Gaston Defferre, who was also involved with *L'Express.*It was there, on Friday the second, that Jean-Jacques Servan-Schreiber improvised the formula of the Republican Front, to replace the Popular Front that everyone thought premature. Defferre was confident that he could quickly persuade Guy Mollet: however suspicious the general secretary of the SFIO might be of PMF, he could not possibly block a movement of convergence which had proved fruitful and popular at the time of the 1954 government. Within a few hours, Guy Mollet gave his consent to the establishment of the Republican Front.

The creators of the coalition immediately thought of broadening it. They turned to the UDSR, whose leader was Mitterrand, despite the challenge to his leadership of this little party posed by his rival René Pleven. The former interior minister immediately agreed to bring the majority of his friends into the coalition. The "conspirators" of *L'Express* also called on Jacques Chaban-Delmas, the leader of the Social Republicans, a rather leafless branch of the Gaullist tree.

The whole operation was organized around and in the name of Pierre Mendès France. He was the symbol and the common denominator of the coalition. It was on themes that he had proclaimed and popularized as head of government that battle would be joined. And this was how public opinion reacted, alerted by a manifesto published in *L'Express* on December 5 and signed by the four leaders of the Republican Front, which was both a protest against the "December 2 coup" (the dissolution) and a call to struggle "for the defense of the Republic."

It very soon turned out that everyone attempted to confiscate the label PMF for his own benefit. Republican or not, every candidate wanted to be part of the Front, which was, without any play on words, popular. How could a secretly Faurist Radical be prevented from using the name that he privately execrated in order to steal votes? It was again Jean-Jacques Servan-Schreiber who came up with the idea of putting a Phrygian cap, a republican emblem if there ever was one, on the heads of the *good* candidates, the *real* Mendésists. "We are about to sink into the ridiculous," objected some Mendésists as enlightened as Pierre Viansson-Ponté, editor-in-chief of *L'Express*.

> The publication of lists of candidates with a Phrygian cap nevertheless began on December 19. Political leaders pretended to laugh at it. But they quickly revised themselves and picked up the telephone to ask for a cap! Pleading or threatening letters with "supporting documents" arrived at *L'Express,* where one could see lines of gentlemen with the *Légion d'honneur* quietly waiting to be received by the two young women who were responsible for making selections.[1]

How could a *good* candidate be recognized? From his offers of service, his declarations of love, his hastily improvised program? No, of course not. Why not from his votes in Parliament? Thus, one could consider as Mendésists worthy of the cap only those who had not voted against the government on February 5, 1955. But had not Edgar Faure supported the cabinet of which he was an eminent member? Then, PMF's staff invented a series of criteria: votes on the anti-alcohol bills, on Edgar Faure's early elections, and so on. And then there were the nonparliamentarian candidates. Their claims to the Phrygian cap were seriously studied by Léone Nora and Servan-Schreiber's sister, Brigitte Gros.

Choices were often difficult, especially between Radical and Socialist candidates, not in regions where one or the other party was very strongly established and better placed than its neighbor—the Radicals in the Southwest, the Socialists in the Nord—but in the Paris region, the Rhône Valley, and the Pas-de-Calais.

The choices were painful. As a rule, Mendès France threw his influence, which was decisive, toward withdrawal of Radicals in favor of their Socialist comrades, to the great chagrin of his party comrades, and against the advice, and sometimes friends, of François Mitterrand ("In most cases, it was Mitterrand who was right," according to Simon Nora). Mendès France himself spoke of the episode with a great deal of circumspection: "Everything was really cobbled together. We improvised nominations about which, after the fact, I am not very proud. Everything was done so quickly, in such chaotic conditions."

But is it necessarily the case that on this occasion "Mendès France did not go all out," as Alain Gourdon suggests? He adds: "Not very confident in his legend, he went into battle without much faith and, not seeing himself as strong enough to oppose compromise, he acquiesced to the nomination of his worst enemies."[2] This last assertion is not excessive. The first is contested by those who joined the battle with PMF at the time. However pessimistic he may have been by nature, loyalty dominated every other habit of mind. Once he had drawn into the adventure not only his friends but other groups, he was duty bound to commit himself thoroughly, and he did.

Although they were the generous leaders of the new alliances, PMF's Radicals nevertheless conducted their own battle, defending their specific program summed up in a widely distributed tract that read as follows:

The Platform of the Radical Party
—create effective institutions, a government capable of acting, and reestablish voting by district,
—restore France to its role as a great power,
—make peace in Algeria,
—guarantee social progress,
—give opportunities to all young people,
—defend the middle classes,
—modernize agriculture,
—construct 350,000 dwellings each year.

This catalogue, which was rather banal as the genre required, and of which only the third and final elements were a little original, was completed by a sentence in Mendès's handwriting: "For the complete application of this program of renewal, and to turn the December 2 coup against its authors, vote Radical-Socialist because *the Radical Party will keep its word.* Pierre Mendès France."

Algeria very quickly moved to the center of the debate, especially in the columns of *L'Express,* where the articles of Jean Daniel denounced the extension and deepening of the conflict, and where Albert Camus launched an appeal for an "end to bloodshed" and proposed the organization of a roundtable where all tendencies would be represented, including the FLN (Front de Libération Nationale) that had been confirmed as organizer of the Algerian national uprising.

Mendès France's positions on Algeria were then close to those of Camus. In Marseille on December 26, he asserted,

We will not maintain ourselves, no more in Algeria than in any other country of North Africa or the French Union, by force, violence, and repression, but by searching for an agreement with those peoples and among the peoples who live there. We must seek conciliation, and it can be found."

And then he made, in the style of the "wager of Geneva," a sort of commitment that created a sensation: if elected head of government, he would first establish himself in Algiers to devote himself to the solution of the problem and "to master all varieties of opposition."

Guy Mollet was less precise, but more vehement. He devoted a number of his election speeches to denouncing "this stupid war that was leading nowhere." In some of his speeches he even considered the possibility of independence, putting his friends in the Republican Front who had not reached that point—particularly Jacques Chaban-Delmas—on alert. Thus the Republican Front went into battle in some disarray: its views on Algeria were thoroughly diverse, and the rather demagogic economic proposals of the SFIO differed substantially from the recommendations, based on his customary rigor, of Pierre Mendès France.

The people's verdict was delivered on the night of January 2. Mendès was too lucid not to recognize—alone of his group—that the success of the Republican Front lists, difficult to measure because of the originality of the situation compared to that of 1951, but which could be evaluated at 31 percent of the vote and 185 seats in the Assembly, thanks to the cruel defeat of the "majority of Dien Bien Phu," was darkened by the brutal rise of the Poujade movement. By means of antistate and chauvinistic slogans, this incarnation of the old French antiparliamentarianism had won two and a half million votes. It had thereby won 52 seats in the Chamber, helping all the more to complicate the discovery of a majority because the Communists returned with 151 seats. Edgar Faure and the MRP, the man of the "December 2 coup" and the "majority of Dien Bien Phu" were the great losers, but also the Social Republicans of Chaban, founding member of the Republican Front.

The fact remained that the Radicals who supported Mendès had made great progress, especially in Seine, where the majority of their young leaders were elected, providing the party with its largest Parisian representation in the history of the Republic, although they had retreated in the Midi and the Southwest. Thus, the arrival of the deputy from Louviers at the head of the party of Herriot had ended by urbanizing and modernizing it, both in its ideas and in the bases of its support—briefly, as we shall see. The fact also remained that the SFIO had greatly profited from the establishment of the Republican Front. It had constantly lost votes since 1945 and had now gained, and not at the expense of the PCF. It had consolidated its positions throughout the country.

All things considered, on January 3, conditions seemed ripe for a change in the majority, or rather for a change of direction. Taking into account the Poujade factor, which complicated all calculations, what might be projected was a majority modeled on the one that, in dramatic circumstances, had brought PMF to power in June 1954. To be sure, many moderate and Gaullist votes would be lacking: Poujade had confiscated voters from the right and the Social Republicans. But the Radical and Socialist axis of the alliance remained about the same. And this time there would be no rejection of the Communist votes that would again be offered.

A majority of the right including the Poujadists was impossible. A majority of the left including the Communists seemed premature. In fact, the January 2 election had outlined a center-left movement, even if the Poujade "mishap" were considered. The Republican Front, which might have carried off a triumph in June 1956, had obtained only a success. But it was large enough to appear as a mandate given to its founders, or rather its founder.

In the public mind it was obvious that the Republican Front was Mendès. Not only had almost all the Radicals been elected in his name, but also a substantial number of the Socialists and the Gaullists who entered the Palais-Bourbon in January 1956. He was the one who wore the Phrygian cap. To the extent that the January 2 election was a referendum before the fact, he was the man it named.

Nothing had been signed on December 3, 1955, by the "founding fathers," Mendès, Mollet, Mitterrand, and Chaban. Nothing but a few sentences outlining a vague electoral strategy: barely an agreement of alliance and for stepping aside in favor of the best-placed candidates. In the event of a victory, the moral preeminence of Mendès was obviously accepted. But it is well known that that is not the determining factor in political choices. And the results of the January 2 election did not make it necessary that Mendès, moral leader, be the political leader of the very relative majority that had come out of the vote: elected in his name or not, the SFIO held ninety-five seats in the Assembly, the Mendésist Radicals along with Mitterrand's UDSR about eighty. The rule was that leadership of the government fell to the head of the largest party in the Assembly.

On January 5, 1956, at noon, in their minuscule Paris apartment, Gaston Defferre and his wife greeted three guests: Guy Mollet, Pierre Mendès France, and Jean-Jacques Servan-Schreiber. The atmosphere was relaxed and the food and wine excellent.

Of course, Mollet and Mendès did not like each other. Mollet could not forgive PMF for his intellectual superiority, his brilliant connections, his press, the movement that supported his efforts, and the lack of consideration he showed for party mechanisms. And he attributed the failure of the CED to Mendès. As for Mendès France, he retained an unpleasant memory of the episodes of 1954, the rejections by Mollet of the offers of participation he had made to the SFIO. In short, mediation was required. Defferre was warm and Servan-Schreiber full of ideas.

According to Mendès France,

Guy Mollet was very hesitant. He used a strange argument: "If I form a government and fail, it's dramatic, it's the end of the Socialist Party; if it's you, the party remains! But if I withdraw, I don't know whether my comrades will understand." In fact, it must be said that the Constitution was what it was, it was not really up to us to discuss it! The choice was the responsibility of the president of the Republic, and we didn't really know what he thought. We beat around the bush, we hesitated a great deal. I was ready to be a candidate, but I didn't want to impose myself.

In the end, I didn't dislike a man like Guy Mollet. On Algeria, of course, he had been imprudent, he had spoken of immediate independence, which was going a little too fast. But, in the end, the experience of power would teach him many things. That day, in any event, we behaved like "good comrades," but without making a decision.

According to Defferre and Servan-Schreiber, however, the two men had come to agreement on an important point: whichever of the two leaders was not chosen by the head of the state as premier would obtain the ministry of his choice, implicitly Foreign Affairs, because, with respect to Finance, they knew that there remained too serious divergences between Mendès's austerity and the distributionist ideas of the SFIO to allow those responsibilities to be exercised by anyone but a member of the same party as that of the head of government.

After the lunch in his apartment, Gaston Defferre considered the situation carefully. By the twentieth, he could no longer hold back and went to see Guy Mollet at party headquarters. "You must not accept the premiership. It is not a role for you. You'll come to grief over the Algerian affair, and the party will suffer with you. Let Mendès be premier, he has more experience in world affairs and in North Africa."

Mollet seemed to agree. "If you approve," continued Defferre, "arrange it so that Coty does not call on you. Seize the initiative from him. Let's call his office right away." Since Mollet said nothing, Defferre called the president's chief of staff, whom he knew well. He wasn't in. The mayor of Marseille pressed Mollet: "Promise me that you will do it yourself." Mollet did not say no.

Defferre then turned to Mendès France. "You have to ask René Coty for an audience. Mollet is standing aside. You have to push the president a little."[3] The head of state had probably made his choice by that point. But out of sympathy, or courtesy, or to complete his file, he made an appointment with Mendès France.

There then occurred a twist even more surprising than the others. We know that in December 1954 Mendès France had pushed through a small constitutional reform which tended to consolidate the powers of the executive. This bill provided that in the event the Assembly was dissolved, the head of government would not surrender his powers to the president of the Assembly but would head a caretaker government, a provision of which Edgar Faure was the first beneficiary. Defeated though he had been on January 2, he remained at Matignon and met with René Coty every day.

As he told Defferre a few years later, learning that the president had granted Mendès France an audience, he hurried to the Elysée: "Mister President, if you receive Mendès, you will not resist his charm, his power. Before he comes, create the irreparable. Put yourself in front of a *fait accompli*. Summon Guy Mollet. Then the mechanism will be set in motion, and your dialogue with Mendès will be only for informational purposes." This is what was done. And thus the provision inserted into the Constitution on Mendès France's initiative in 1954 allowed Edgar Faure in 1956 to block the path of his return to power.[4]

It was on January 25, apparently, that René Coty made his decision. In any event, that was when he informed parliamentary leaders. "I was received by President Coty on January 25," wrote Edouard Depreux, president of the Socialist group. "He began by saying: 'My decision has been made: I am going to call on Guy Mollet. My choice has been dictated by the gravity of the situation.' In other circumstances, he might have chosen Pierre Mendès France, but he frightened many people whereas Guy Mollet was reassuring."[5]

Kept from the premiership, Mendès France seemed destined, by the January 5 agreement, to return to the Foreign Ministry that he had left exactly a year before. But a real cabal was organized around Guy Mollet. Given the fact that the government did not hold a clear majority in the Assembly, it had to rely either on the cooperation of the MRP or on that of the Communists. It was not done to consult the leaders of the PCF. But Teitgen and his friends were explicit: they would never vote for a government in which Mendès, the "man of August 30," held the Foreign Ministry. Various moderate spokesmen made the same point, emphasizing the progressivism of the Radical leader. In short, Guy Mollet, forgetting the commitments he had made at the beginning of the month, gave in. Mendès would be neither premier nor foreign minister.

Why not Finance and Economic Affairs? suggested the premier-designate. But he knew, since Mendès had clearly informed him, that on this point the differences between them were too great. Finance, according to Mendès, should go to a man who was in agreement with the premier. Why repeat the conflict that he had had with Pleven in 1945?

Many of his friends urged PMF to distance himself from a government that intended to place him in a minor role, even though it was he who had won the elections. Mendès—because he believed that he had played too important a role in setting up the majority not to take on some responsibilities, and because the Algerian question was too urgent for him not to play a role in dealing with it inside the government—accepted a ministry without portfolio, which allowed him to sit in the cabinet only to experience more directly, and observe more sadly, a policy almost all of whose manifestations he disavowed.

The Radical leader refused to open a public debate, but he did not allow himself to be despoiled without letting his friends know what he thought of the operation. In a letter sent to the militants of the Radical federations on January 30, under the title, "Why and How We Are Participating," he wrote that "in his desire to conciliate the MRP and the moderates, M. Guy Mollet has inflicted on the Radical Party and on one of its leaders a painful disavowal . . . which cannot fail to undermine the solidarity of the Republican Front." Less than a month after the electoral victory, and in order to conciliate the "majority of Dien Bien Phu," Guy Mollet had thus broken the December pact and alienated the man to whom he owed the consolidation of his party and the success of the Front of which he was one of the founders.

Many have severely criticized Mendès France for not having fought harder to extract, to demand the leadership implicit in his major role in the January 2 success. Shouldn't the man who had been designated by a substantial portion of the people be invested with power? Otherwise, what did democracy mean? By not demanding what was "owed" to him, hadn't Mendès become an accomplice to an evasion of the rules and, more important, the spirit, of popular election?

It happened that one of the few powers of the president under the Fourth Republic was to designate the head of the government of his choice, and his choice depended on a number of considerations. For acting as he did, paying more attention to numerical forces than to the "spirit" of the situation, Coty is open to criticism. But it is difficult to argue that Mendès France could have done anything but accept the choice.

In 1954, confronting the Indochina tragedy, he was the man people were waiting for, the one best prepared to reach a resolution, who knew it, and to whom Parliament gave the means to act. In 1956, the electoral victory was not decisive, and the problems to be resolved were uncertain. And Mendès France did not have the same mastery over the Algerian problem, which he knew and declared to be major and to which he would devote himself, that he had had over Indochina two years earlier. This is why, although he was determined to respond to an appeal, he was not ready to disturb everything in order to impose himself.

Meditating on Mendès France's eviction, twenty-five years later, Gaston Defferre considered it a disaster:

> It was a decisive turning point. With Mendès in power, our history would have taken a different direction. He would not have let himself fall into the trap in Algiers on February 6, where Guy Mollet sank along with the authority of the republican state, and when the army became aware of its power of political pressure. Without February 6, there would have been neither the later sedition nor De Gaulle. Only Mendès had the character and the moral

authority which would have prevented the collapse of the Republic and simultaneously brought about peace in Algeria.

This perhaps underestimates the hatred that had accumulated around Mendès France since his campaign against the Indochina War. Many of the rebel officers in Algeria were nostalgic for, frustrated over Indochina. But in any event, history turned out otherwise. As it happened, René Coty, Edgar Faure, and Guy Mollet were more important actors than the man of Geneva.

From then on, the Republican Front was nothing but one of the empty signs that clutters the history of the Republic. Edouard Depreux entitled the chapter of his memoirs on the subject: "My Cruelest Disappointment: The Republican Front."

February 6, 1956, represented the definitive collapse of the hopes forged in the heat of the December 1955 campaign. Republican Front voters had had to resign themselves to the elimination of the leader for whom they had voted. But there remained at least the hope of seeing the government under Socialist leadership apply the principal ideas of its campaign, above all with respect to Algeria.

The choice of the minister for Algeria argued well for Mollet's intentions. Curiously, the idea of calling on General Catroux did not come from Mendès, who had admired his conduct in Algeria at the time of the provisional government. The general, who had been capable of breaking with the RPF, whose colonial policy in Indochina he condemned, and who had very courageously opposed the dethronement of the Sultan of Morocco, had the confidence of the Moslems.

In the course of the campaign, Mendès had indicated his intention, if elected premier, to reside for a time in Algiers in order to manifest the authority of the state in aid of a peaceful solution. The idea had struck Guy Mollet, and he therefore decided to adopt it himself, at least for a short visit to install General Catroux in his post.

In the meantime, Mendès France and his friends had received reports on the rapid evolution of thinking and of passions in Algeria: The nationalists were favorably disposed toward the new government and its representative, but conservative European circles had reacted very badly to Mollet's campaign proposals and to the nomination of Catroux.

André Mandouze, an eminent specialist in Saint Augustine and a militant supporter of Algerian emancipation, had come to warn Mendès against an improvised official visit to Algiers: the patriotic organizations would organize demonstrations like the one saluting the departure of Soustelle. The governor general appointed a year earlier by PMF, who had at first been greeted with suspicion, had since then, because of the positions he had adopted, become a hero of "French Algeria." Mandouze knew from a reliable source that Jacques Chevallier, even though he had been a member of the Mendès cabinet, would refuse to receive the new premier and that broad sectors of the police and the administration were joining forces with the organizers of "ultra" demonstrations. No one could guarantee the maintenance of public order during an official visit to Algiers.

During the first cabinet meeting of the new government on February 3, Guy Mollet informed his colleagues of his intention to go to Algiers the following Monday, February 6. Mendès intervened to try to dissuade him: "If you go, considering the current climate, you must do so by catching the Algiers organizations off guard—immediately. Leave right away, get there before anyone can react. Play on the advantage of surprise." Guy Mollet was unmoved by these arguments. At the end of the meeting the press was informed of the departure of the head of government for Algiers on February 6. The die was cast.

On February 6, at 2 P.M., the plane carrying the premier, who had come, he said, to "learn of everyone's aspirations," landed at the Algiers airport. Until it reached the center of the city, the cortege passed between two rows of CRS in a deathlike silence. But no sooner had the cars stopped in front of the war memorial, where Mollet planned to lay a wreath, than a demonstration whose violence approached that of a riot broke out. For nearly two hours, the head of government was surrounded, pressed, vilified: "Death to Mollet! Send Mendès to Egypt!"

The uproar constantly grew, fists were flourished, and all sorts of projectiles rained down on the little group of officials. There has been much talk of the symbolic tomatoes. There were also rotten oranges, garbage, and stones. In any event, Max Lejeune, secretary of state, was hit in the face with a tomato; so much red led people to think he was wounded, and the fear of the officials and the fury of the mob grew greater. Mollet and Lejeune, pressed from all sides, were rescued only by the intervention of General Massu's parachute troops, who escorted them to the GG, the governor general's building.

But the riot went on for hours; the GG was besieged. And what struck Guy Mollet above all was the fact that the rioters were not "big colonists," as Socialist rallies would have it, but little people, mailmen, trolley workers, shopkeepers—his constituents in Arras, the militants whose mandate he had received as head of the SFIO. Morally shattered, physically exhausted, he called Paris while the crowd rumbled around him. In a few sentences, he described the situation to President Coty, who had several ministers, including Mendès, in his office. "I have to be able to announce that I have accepted the resignation of General Catroux."

Catroux had not submitted his resignation, but informed of the situation and the wish of the floundering premier, he agreed.[6]

The news, communicated to the Algiers crowd, lowered the tension a little, and enough calm returned in the course of the night to restore freedom of movement to the head of government. Before leaving for Paris, he had the time to meet with many union organizations and left-wing political groups, who confirmed what he had glimpsed at the height of the riot: that the spirit of "French Algeria" was as strong, if not more so, among the lower-middle classes as it was among the privileged. Did he also realize that he had presided over a humiliation of state authority by the rioters and that the officers who had rescued him from the crowd had thereby become aware of the weakness of civilian power and the strength of military power?

After futile attempts to persuade Defferre to accept the position, Catroux was finally replaced by Robert Lacoste, minister of finance: the direction had shifted. Mendès was isolated in his phantom ministry, when his real concern was with Algeria. Even before taking up his government post he had met with Algerian militants, particularly a key man, Ben Khedda. As Mendès said later,

> I had always thought discussion with people who were fighting was finally more serious than with men who were in Cairo or elsewhere, all the more intransigent the farther they were from the battle. The idea of talking with fighters from the Casbah seemed like a good one. . . . In any event, their proposals were interesting: "We don't know what you are going to do, but really, a left-wing government must attempt something. What you did in Tunisia indicates your state of mind. That way may not fully satisfy us, but we will discuss it. Only, what guarantee do we have that the promises you make us will be kept? It won't be the first time that a Paris government has made us promises and not kept them, or been overthrown before being able to keep them. Nor will it be the first time a Paris government had made good decisions that the Algiers government has not followed. What guarantees do we have?"
>
> On substantive matters, they said rather little: "You know very well that we want independence but that we are not ready." They were very realistic. They insisted above all on guarantees, and they were looking for solutions: the UN or some kind of supreme arbitrational tribunal. "We will nominate people," they said, "but you will have to name trustworthy Frenchmen whom we will have no reasons to doubt." They even suggested two or three names, Mauriac among others.
>
> When the government was set up, I spoke about it to Guy Mollet, who told me: "Keep up the contact, say that the government has not yet had the time to deal with all that." A little later, he confided to me: "I have to talk to Lacoste about it." There was an explosion. Lacoste let out a howl, and

everything was broken off. Then it was decided to speak with the people in Cairo instead. It was like Indochina in Bidault's time: better to go through Peking, or a major power conference, than to negotiate with the combatants. Christian Pineau, who had been named foreign minister by Mollet, cooked up a trip to India so that he would be able to stop in Cairo on the way back and meet Colonel Nasser, who told him whatever he wanted to.

With real negotiations thus becoming remote, Mendès France looked on with despair as the war deepened and repression grew harsher. By the end of February, a problem arose in the cabinet that was as serious as that of torture: capital punishment inflicted on convicted Algerian militants. The guillotining of men who, however atrocious their actions, were fighting for the emancipation of their country was a gesture that could only increase hatred. President Coty's occasional exercise of his pardoning power was inadequate to counteract this effect.

Every passing week placed more distance between the government, with Mollet simply responding to pressure imposed by Algiers through Lacoste, and the promises Mendès and Mollet had made during the campaign. Prohibited from negotiating, Mendès attempted at least to promote something besides repression. In early April, he sent a "note on Algeria" to the premier, a group effort which, in parallel with Albert Camus's effort toward a "civil truce," was the most serious effort made to prevent a slide into total war.

At the conclusion of an analysis demonstrating that repression could not possibly overcome the uprising and that the real solutions were political ones, Mendès, as a working proposal and to create a favorable climate for negotiations, called for a group of seven measures ranging from the liberation of unindicted political prisoners to the restoration of freedom of the press, the dismissal of bureaucrats responsible for denial of justice, the dissolution of municipal governments that had abused their powers and the promulgation of a new municipal law, and the effective expropriation of great landed estates.

There was, of course, nothing revolutionary in this program of decent reforms. But in the spring of 1956, such a proposal, adopted and applied with vigor, might have been able to change the climate and prepare the way for the "dialogue" that was so insistently called for by the Radical leader. Guy Mollet simply acknowledged receipt and indicated to Mendès that he was sending it on to Lacoste, who must have shrugged his shoulders.

In the cabinet, relations between Mendès and the minister for Algeria were becoming explosive. According to Mendès,

Lacoste resorted to the most vulgar vocabulary in the presence of the president of the Republic. Since Guy Mollet did not intervene, I was the one who had to apologize for him to the head of state. We claimed to be making reforms; but when you looked closely, it was all a bluff. My chief of staff, André Pélabon, who knew Algerian affairs well, had very good contacts with Algerians in Paris and Algiers. Every time an apparently reasonable bill was proposed, he would say to me, "Look at what lies behind it." And when we examined the proposal, we realized that it was a falsification.

In the month of April 1956, everything moved rapidly to a new stage of bitterness. While the Mollet government imprisoned one of the most distinguished French journalists, Claude Bourdet, because his paper *France-Observateur* had published terrible reports on torture in Algeria, it was learned that Ferhat Abbas, symbol of moderate nationalism and of the possibilities of dialogue between the Algerians and the French, had joined the FLN in Cairo and openly placed himself under the banner of the most determined fighters.

On April 20, the new president of the Radical federation of Seine, Jacques Périer, begged Mendès to justify his presence in the government and defined him as a "prisoner." Then, on May 10, Robert Buron, companion of the struggles of 1954 and 1955, met in the Palais-Bourbon a Pierre Mendès France "in complete disarray," who confessed to him: "I don't know where I am. It will be this way as long as, out of perhaps excessive loyalty, I stay in a government that is pursuing a policy that is not mine."[7]

Finally, on May 23, Mendès France, after meeting with his Radical colleagues to ask them to remain in the government, went with them to the cabinet meeting and submitted his resignation to Guy Mollet.

Unlike the one he had sent to De Gaulle in 1945, his farewell letter to the premier was immediately made public. It did not fail to impress public opinion:

My dear Premier,

I have come to give you my resignation, which is motivated by your policy in Algeria. . . .

Resort to arms was, unfortunately, necessary for us. I would even have preferred, as you know, sending more troops more quickly. But I have also maintained that resort to arms could not possibly be enough. By allowing only them to speak we risk creating a definitive divorce with the Moslem masses. . . .

Now, any policy that pays no attention to the feelings and the sufferings of the indigenous population leads, little by little, from the loss of the Algerian people to the loss of Algeria, and then, unfailingly, to the loss of all of our Africa. It is a politics of abandonment.

I implored the government to follow another path and to adopt resolutely—against the opposition of those who do not see the precipice toward which they are racing and drawing us with them—another policy, often badly understood and sometimes even characterized in shocking terms. . . .

It was thus indispensable, in my eyes, to bring about by actions, which would have been the equivalent of pledges, the rebirth of confidence and hope, in the absence of which our expulsion from Algeria is only a matter of time, that expulsion that it is our duty to prevent at any price.

Unfortunately, the moderate elements among the Moslems of Algeria, those whom we ought to have supported, continue to be harassed daily by an administration, municipal governments, and press that are too often animated by a state of mind that causes us terrible harm. Thus men have been subjected to torture, thrown into internment camps, deprived of all means of expression, driven far away from us, and we have in fact thrown them into the arms of our worst enemies.

In a letter that I sent to you more than a month ago, I enumerated, as a working proposal, measures that would have produced a salutary effect from this point of view. None was adopted, and I have watched with growing anxiety as the chances of pointing the government toward the only path to salvation have vanished.

I know, however, my dear premier, that you understand my feelings. Thus it is with deepest emotion that I leave you and leave this government, upon which so many Frenchmen like you and like me have based great hopes. I would at least like my resignation to have the sense of a new and anguished appeal that the government make the necessary decisions, however difficult they may be.

Mendès now had freedom of movement. He was free to use all his influence in favor of negotiations in Algeria. He was also free to attempt to recover control over a Radical Party torn between its progressive and reactionary wings.

On June 8, 1956, Mendès delivered a speech to the executive committee of the Radical Party in which he summed up what could be called his Algerian "doctrine." The key word was "dialogue," and a dialogue "on the scene, even if it is difficult." Otherwise, he asserted, if there were no "compromise solutions," Algeria was condemned to the "Indochinese solution." To the question of the basis for negotiations, he answered prudently:

There are in such matters things that cannot be announced in advance, concessions that may be considered but that must not be formulated explicitly, or else what is a maximum, a point of arrival, inevitably becomes, in the debate, a point of departure. What counts is to create the psychological shock that is indispensable to restore the interrupted dialogue.

He was obviously thinking of the Tunisian experience, of the "internal autonomy" he had proclaimed in Carthage that his interlocutors—or rather those of his successor—had used as a point of departure.

We are accused of undermining the country's morale. What affects the country's morale is the constantly repeated assertion that, in the Assembly and the government, there are "traitors" who are deliberately preparing new defeats for the country. Their false argument, beyond individual targets, is really aimed at the left as a whole, and they are preparing to put the Republic itself on trial. We are witnessing a maneuver on a large scale to place blame in the future on republican principles for all the disappointments, all the reversals suffered overseas, and all those with which we are threatened.[8]

PMF's warning was launched at the beginning of a summer that was to thrust France from the jealous nationalism into which the Algerian war had plunged it to the feverish chauvinistic excitement expressed by the Suez expedition. On July 26, in Alexandria, Nasser announced the nationalization of the Compagnie de Suez, located on Egyptian territory, a measure which would have been quite justifiable had he not immediately proceeded to conduct military occupation of their holdings and had he immediately proclaimed universal freedom of navigation through the canal. The reaction in Paris was nearly delirious. Although he severely criticized Nasser's action, Mendès France remained calm. He simply stated to Françoise Giroud that Nasser would be embarrassed by his seizure and that he would not be able to maintain operations on the canal that was one of poor Egypt's principal sources of revenue.

But Guy Mollet and his colleagues were not content with harsh judgments, pessimistic prognoses, or appropriate retaliatory measures. They prepared to punish the "insolent dictator." After circulating a falsified version of his *Philosophy of Revolution* that transformed his simple nationalism into racism, in order to make public opinion equate this naïve and brutal pamphlet with *Mein Kampf,* launching the slogan Nasser = Hitler, and evoking Munich, these elected officials of the "Republican Front" that had been formed to make peace in Algeria prepared a new joint expedition to Egypt. And they associated with their adventurous enterprise not only a surprised England but also Israel, which had good reasons to feel threatened by the pan-Arab nationalism that had been exacerbated by the crisis, and which found this to be a good opportunity to strike at the head of the coalition that was besieging it.

This mad operation, about which anyone with any common sense today wonders how responsible men could have dreamed it up, then planned it, then carried it out (without even having seriously investigated the intentions of the two superpowers), had been preceded on October 22 by the kidnapping in flight, between Rabat and Tunis, outside the territory and the territorial waters of France, of the leaders of the FLN. Even though, in this instance, it had been confronted by a *fait accompli,* the fact is that the government of the Republic accepted this act of piracy, which Mendès saw as "banditry."

Did he regret that he had already resigned, thus losing the possibility of giving it, on that day, a more solemn character? From then on, it was less a matter of symbolic gestures than of facts. And the facts were the ruin of an attempt at negotiation that was to begin in Tunis with Bourguiba's "good offices" and the definitive confiscation of Algerian policy by the military officers of Algiers and their stand-ins, Lacoste and Lejeune.

Five days later, in an atmosphere of exaltation, came the departure for the Suez crusade. Mendès France related his reactions to the enterprise a month later:

> In the afternoon of Monday, October 29, I learned first that an imminent military action was planned; then, around eight o'clock, that Israel's troops had entered the Sinai region.
>
> It immediately appeared to me that, in order to attempt to prevent fearful events, a speech from the Assembly rostrum would be belated and useless; it might even be exploited against France, while the die had already been cast in an irreversible way. Only a direct approach to the premier had a chance of having any effect.
>
> I asked to see M. Guy Mollet. He received me at nine-thirty. I questioned him; he neither confirmed nor denied the rumors that were beginning to circulate, and he didn't breathe a word about the Anglo–French ultimatum that was to be delivered a few hours later.
>
> I warned him against the risks of an armed action on our part. I argued that it was improbable, if not impossible, that a conflict could be localized, and spoke of the danger of spreading warfare. He did nothing but answer that he did not want war and that he didn't believe it would come.
>
> A few hours later, I published a declaration confessing my fear for world peace and asserting that a four-power conference was, in my eyes, the best solution. "Don't expect me to do anything that might introduce the Soviet Union into the Middle East," replied Mollet. On the thirtieth, speaking to the Radical group, I implored our ministers to consider the gravity of the action in which they were about to participate. They answered that, in the opinion of the government, all precautions had been taken, on the military and diplomatic levels, so that we would thenceforth be able to "speak from a position of strength."
>
> I believe, in my heart and soul, that I used all the authority I may have had as former premier, as member of the Assembly, as vice-president of a great party, to oppose the country's entry into an adventure whose consequences we have not begun to measure.

A reliable witness, Françoise Giroud, recalls his attitude: "He totally disapproved of [the operation]. I can still hear him at the moment he learned of it, picking up his phone and calling Guy Mollet, icy, terrifying." It was he, and he alone, who, refusing to surrender to mass hysteria, dissuaded *L'Express* from (for once) approving Guy Mollet. Never perhaps had his independence of mind and his courage been asserted with more tranquil strength.

On November 10, while Soviet tanks and artillery were continuing an operation against the people of Budapest, made easier, if not justified, by the Suez adventure, the National Assembly listened to speeches on the Middle East affair.

It is hardly possible to imagine the atmosphere of chauvinistic passion in which this debate took place. The word *passion* is weak: it would be better to speak of exaltation, of delirium. Mendès France, recalling these trancelike hours, suggested that they were even more excessive than the outpourings of August 1914, and certainly than the emotions of September 1939. Whoever appeared to reject approval of the adventure drew upon himself an angry outburst: "The flag is committed, you do not vote against the flag!"

> Most of my friends among the deputies who declared themselves in favor of the expedition and the landing were drawn along by the general movement; according to them, it was impossible to be against, and in any event to vote against. Of about fifteen deputies in the Radical group on whom I thought I could count, more than half were determined to vote in favor. In the end, there were only four deputies who agreed to vote against. Three or four others resigned themselves to voting for the government, although with some hesitation. Finally, after interminable bargaining, it was possible to bring them around and to get them to abstain; but they had set a condition, that the deputies who were opposed abstain as well.
>
> In the end, we had to choose for a final result between four negative votes and eight abstentions. It seemed to us that we would emphasize our rejection more effectively by uniting eight deputies rather than four, and that's the reason why the deputies who were opposed finally agreed to abstain.
>
> In the corridors, I met Paul Reynaud, who was furious and who said to me aggressively: "How can you vote for that?" I reassured him and told him that in no event would I vote for "that." Then I asked him how he himself would vote. He didn't say a word, but he made a gesture of despairing discouragement.

Because he dissociated himself from an action that, in his eyes, had placed the world on the brink of war, an action for which France was responsible, Mendès France was more cruelly vilified than ever. He was insulted, threatened with death, and told to go to Moscow (it is true that, when Tixier-Vignancour was arguing in favor of the expedition, a voice from the far left cried out: "To Tel Aviv!").

The members of a democratic party like the MRP or those who were decently republican, who might have been brought closer to Mendès France by such outbursts, remained exasperated by most of his positions, if not on Algeria, at least on Europe. Many held against him his negative vote on the Treaty of Rome establishing the Common Market on July 7, 1957, even though the treaty had been presented to Parliament with Mendès-like rigor by his friend Alain Savary, who recommended acceptance.

Mendès France, a convinced but not uncritical "European," had for-mulated several interesting criticisms of the treaty. Two of them were not surprising: they had to do with the absence of England, which PMF always considered a key element in the European balance and even in its dynamism, and with the excessive role to be played, at least with the current economic and social power relationships, by large capitalist enter-prises. A third argument was more surprising. It revealed the absolute priority he accorded at the time to the question of North Africa, more precisely, Algeria.

> The provisions [of the treaty] have as a consequence the opening of the whole of Algerian territory to the products of the five countries who are joining with us. It would have been normal, in exchange, that the European countries consent to greater use of Algerian labor. A difference is established between the metropolitan French and the Moslem French of Algeria; French workers will enjoy new rights . . . that the provisions which have been signed do not grant to Moslem workers. . . . Once again, you are giving Algerian Moslems the impression that no account is being taken of their interests and that you have not looked for a solution to their unemployment and their poverty.

From the end of 1956 on, Mendès had to confront two varieties of hatred, purely political from some, openly racial from others. I will never forget a rally held in early 1957 at the Mutualité. Mendès was on the platform. Sympathizers made up a majority of the audience, but toward the back a crowd, including many military officers, was spewing forth its fury. There were cries of "Death!" "Dirty Jew!" "Sell-out!" "Red!"

> One of the last statesmen of his generation who does not belong to the inevitable group, Pierre Mendès France for that very reason provokes the most furious hatred inspired by a French deputy since Clemenceau. When almost everyone is guilty, it is the innocent man who becomes the outlaw,

Mauriac wrote at the time. And a few months later, in an interview with Philip Toynbee of the *Observer*,[9] he put his finger on the festering wound: "He is Jewish, as you know, and that has caused him terrible harm. No one wants to admit it, but racism is what is attacking him, in reality."

Mendès France later recalled the vicious attacks made against him with serenity:

> There were two very distinct periods. Before my resignation, the extreme right was violently opposed to me: *L'Aurore* and *Le Journal du Parlement* criticized me harshly. But I was not alone, and the Radical Party stood up to the attack. In short, it was normal political combat. And then there was a second period. A kind of spasm of anger and incredible hatred, going as far as attempts at or plans for assassination, two in Morocco and one in Paris.
>
> One day, a guy who was apparently a little crazy came to see Françoise

Giroud and told her: "I've been offered millions to kill Mendès. I've killed wogs, but never a Frenchman, that's something I won't do. Warn him, tell him to be careful!" Françoise Giroud warned me and added: "Be careful: if the people who set him off learn what he has done, he is in danger of being killed." So, for a few weeks, I was very careful. The guy wanted a little money, and I gave it to him.

There were two affairs in Morocco. The first took place after the assassination of Lemaigre-Dubreuil,[10] in April 1955. I hardly knew him, but his assassination had a very political meaning: he was one of the leaders of the "liberal French" of Morocco. After hesitating for a long time, I decided to attend the funeral in Casablanca. Jacques Duhamel was sent by Edgar Faure, then premier, to tell me: "For the love of heaven, don't go!" I went anyway.

During the investigation of Lemaigre-Dubreuil's assassination, one of the people arrested told a rather curious story: "We took the presence of Mendès for a real provocation, and we decided to kill him on his way out of the burial mass, in the crowd. But the killer who was chosen finally backed down and ran away." Now, there was a French photographer in Casablanca who was working for *Paris-Match,* among other publications. On the way out of the mass, he took a photograph of me and the people around me, including the man who was supposed to assassinate me. Since nothing had happened, since there was no corpse of Mendès on the pavement, his photographs were of no interest to *Paris-Match* or anyone else. So he put them in his store. Morocco became independent and the photographer in question sold his business to a Moroccan, who found a stock of old film in the closet. He told me about this shot of the funeral. I bought it: you can see the man approaching me.

The second attempt, a much more serious one, took place in Rabat in 1957. I was staying at the official residence, and four men decided to do me in during the night. They arrived. They may not have been very well prepared for this kind of operation, and they came upon a police patrol. One of them lost his head and shot, and a policeman was struck by a machine-gun blast, suffering seventeen intestinal perforations. The second policeman shot back, seriously wounding the gunman, who was taken to the hospital and confessed. His accomplices were arrested, denied everything, and were immediately released; but they had to keep him in custody. He appeared before a military tribunal a year later.

The chief judge said he didn't want to know anything about the political aspects of the affair ("the question will not be raised!"), but that there had been an assault. The man was sentenced to a year in prison. Since he had served his time in the hospital, he was released the same evening, expelled from Morocco, and sent to France, where his friends welcomed him as a hero. This was in 1958. I saw him again ten years later in Grenoble: he was one of my opponent's bodyguards during the election campaign.

Among the campaigns conducted against him at the time, the ones that affected Mendès France more than others were those carried out within the Radical Party. This was particularly the case for the one led by

André Morice, whose name was to be involved with the most somber aspects of the Algerian war. Supported from outside by those who had been excluded in 1955 (René Mayer, J.-P. David, and Martinaud-Déplat) and from within by Henri Queuille, symbol of the radicalism of immobility, André Morice, elected in January 1956 under the banner of the Republican Front, attempted to bring together all the anti-Mendès forces to make the Radical congress of Lyon in November 1956 into the great revenge of the past.

As nearly his final act as president of the party, Edouard Herriot finally threw his support behind Mendès. Defeated, Queuille and Morice set in motion a split that gradually detached from the Mendès majority a good third of the party. Mendès France's program of renewal would not resist. From that moment on, the deputy from Eure understood that the graft had taken in only the most superficial way. His prestige in the depths of the party maintained a solid cohort around him. But the parliamentary group was dissolving, carried off by the neonationalism that was then stirring the Radical Party: Maurice Bourgès-Maunoury, minister of defense responsible for the Suez expedition, replaced Guy Mollet at the head of the government and gave his place at the head of the armed forces to André Morice.

There was simultaneously a regression to the comforting rural past of a certain radicalism embodied by Henri Queuille and a flight forward into the chauvinism of "French Algeria," that forced Mendès France to resign from the vice-presidency of the Radical Party and to give up the enterprise, at least on the level of a strictly political strategy.

There is however a survival of the attempt to renew the Radical Party from 1955 to 1957: the *Cahiers de la République.* Established by Mendès France in the spring of 1956, when he was still in the government, with a group of loyal friends, this "bimonthly review of politics," which featured the Phrygian cap—again—on its cover, claimed not to be "the platform of a faction but the expression of a party, of the broad party that brings together all citizens who are devoted to reason and freedom. They do not provide a doctrine but the stimulus for a doctrine," far, in any event, "from every orthodoxy."

Mendès agreed to preside over the editorial committee, recognizing only later all the servitudes the position involved. He tried on numerous occasions to establish some distance, but his colleagues clearly pointed out that without him everything would fall apart. He therefore remained for five years in the position that assured the publication's existence and prestige.

The *Cahiers de la République* nevertheless did not fulfill the promises of the first issue. But it continued to publish good articles and to demonstrate a thoroughly "Mendésian" desire for openness.

The political and moral image of the former head of government was not weakened by the enterprise. But the intellectual hypothesis for which it was an underpinning, the promotion of political and economic rationalism, based on democratic planning and connected to the new forces of the Third World, did not find in the publication the impulse and the enlightenment that its founders had hoped for.

Confronted with the central problem of renewal of the state at the moment when the forces of colonial conservatism and nationalism, which found their greatest support in his own party, were ranged against him, Mendès France had not become again a man alone, but he remained a man who could count on only a few friendships, a few loyalties, a few enthusiasms, and his own energy to attempt to recover the political initiative.

At the height of the Algerian conflagration, the decisive acts would come from another quarter.

23.
NO TO DE GAULLE

Pierre Mendès France was one of those who denounced the stench of the swamp and of coagulated blood rising from both the Palais-Bourbon and Algiers in the spring of 1958, sensing it as a warning sign of the death of the regime. In 1953, he had announced to the French that they were "in 1788." At a conference in Dijon on the decline of individual liberties in October 1957, he denounced "the frightful danger of the poisons threatening [our] youth and its future." Several weeks later, at the end of January 1958, he noted that there was "a fascist danger" because of "the weakness of the regime."

On the crucial subject of torture in Algeria, he had a good source of information. At the end of August 1956, after he had left the government, he was invited to a conversation with Robert Lacoste. What did the proconsul of Algeria want from him? "This is it. The UN session that is about to open is going to be hard. Ask your friends on *L'Express* not to join the chorus of those who are going to pillory France over torture." "All right," said Mendès, "but to cut the ground from under the feet of the accusers, why not take energetic measures and proclaim your reprobation?" Then, according to PMF, "I saw him turn green and fall apart before my eyes. Visibly, I was asking him to do the only thing he could not do. From that day on, I knew that he was complicit in all of it."

A handful of colonels who took themselves for Mao, or Nasser, or

Franco, had swallowed up Robert Lacoste's staff and were already the dominant power in Algiers, with the likelihood of being in turn succeeded by civilian and military activist factions. The rise in the power of the FLN, which, especially in the Constantine region near the Tunisian border, was inflicting heavy losses on the paratroopers, destroyed the calm of leaders who were incapable of raising themselves to a genuinely strategic vision of the affair.

There was then a proliferation of aberrant reactions on their part, on the model of the Suez expedition, culminating in February 1958 with the bombardment of the Tunisian village of Sakhiet-Sidi-Youssef, the site of an FLN camp: there were dozens killed, among them children coming out of school. The internationalization of the conflict that was thereby made certain would remove control from the colonels unless they seized full power in Algiers, and then in Paris.

At the same time, if not for the same reasons, rumors began to be heard from Colombey-les-Deux-Eglises, where General de Gaulle had been locked up for three years in haughty silence.

Mendès France, who had never severed contact with the former leader of Free France and who still felt a certain gratitude for the public praise he had received as premier in 1954, was not the last to think that General de Gaulle was perhaps the only man of enough stature to deal with the Algerian tragedy, especially considering the military factors involved. Whether it was a matter of making the voice of the French nation heard by an armed liberation movement or of restoring the authority of the state over a military society that was in ferment but not yet in rebellion, Charles de Gaulle had unrivaled stature and credibility.

At the end of March, a conversation among Mendès and a number of friends led to the conclusion that it was only a matter of time before De Gaulle returned to power. Mendès calmly told Jean Daniel: "The question is not whether General de Gaulle will return, but when and in favor of what he will return."[1]

It was also in March 1958 that Mendès received a visit that surprised him a little, from Michel Debré. This Radical senator, who was known at the time for his fanatical devotion to French Algeria as well as to General de Gaulle, had come to ask for his help in promoting a solution for Algeria: the former leader of Free France would be recalled "for an extraordinary mission," given exceptional powers, a veritable blank check for a period of six months, in order to restore peace in Algeria (Debré did not specify the means or the nature of the ultimate solution). Mendès listened to him politely, reminded him of the admiration he felt for the general and how eager he was to see Algeria at peace, and concluded: "All the same, I prefer the Republic."

In fact, what did De Gaulle think about Algeria? Everything and all at once. To Soustelle and Debré he asserted: "We will remain." To Jean Amrouche, André Philip, Maurice Schumann, and a little later to Georges Boris, he declared: "Algeria will be independent" or "must be free to determine itself." In any event, he had shown his sympathy for the exiled Sultan of Morocco three years earlier. And in February 1958, he had cordially received the Tunisian Ambassador Mohammed Masmoudi, who had been recalled by his government after the sinister episode of Sakhiet-Sidi-Youssef. There was a De Gaulle for everyone; he was no longer a general, he was a battlefield.

For Mendès France, in the feverish spring of 1958, his name evoked a possible way out rather than a threat. And when he invited François Mauriac to lunch on May 14, Mendès knew that there would be talk of De Gaulle, in a rather favorable sense: in his column in *L'Express,* Mauriac had recently associated, in praise and nostalgia, the name of De Gaulle with that of Mendès, who had not been troubled by it.

But in the meantime, on the thirteenth, the activists had seized power in Algiers and created a "committee of public safety," among whom were Gaullists and some officers, including the holder of real power, General Massu, commander of the Algiers garrison and loyal to De Gaulle. This seemed to condemn the regime which was once again in search of a government, since that of Félix Gaillard had been overthrown. But not at first: in the course of the following night, the MRP leader Pierre Pflimlin was named premier. This reply by the Assembly seemed to strike a decisive blow against the Algiers sedition. In Paris, Soustelle, who was one of the instigators of the decision, and, in Algiers, Massu, who was its apparent beneficiary, each had the same reaction expressed by the same word: "Screwed!"

The next day, Wednesday the fourteenth, François Mauriac met for lunch with Mendès and a few friends, Françoise Giroud, Jean-Jacques Servan-Schreiber, and Lucien Rachet, administrator of *L'Express* and a fervent Gaullist.

According to Mendès:

> Very troubled by what had happened the day before in Algiers, we said to ourselves: in the end, why not De Gaulle? But he must not compromise with those people in Algiers. He has to return through legal means. Everyone placed that condition on the general's return, Mauriac first of all. Rachet said a good deal in the same sense: "It's obvious. De Gaulle can only condemn the behavior of the Algiers troublemakers. Besides, he is in Paris every Wednesday; I'll go to see him right now and I'll get a statement from him in this sense which will put forth his candidacy." He left before dessert to bring us this manifesto more quickly, and he has not yet returned.

The next day at noon, invested with full powers in Algiers by the new Pflimlin government, General Salan, prompted by a Gaullist emissary, launched the cry: *"Vive De Gaulle!"* which set in motion a mechanism that was well enough prepared so that six hours later, in Paris, De Gaulle distributed to the press a statement indicating that he held himself "in readiness to take on the powers of the Republic." Not a word about the rioters, not a call to discipline, not a reminder of their dignity to the military leaders who were associated with street-corner agitators in the Algiers committees. Quite obviously, whatever his opinion of the procedures, De Gaulle was using the Algiers uprising as a means to be projected into power.

Four days later, May 19, the general called a press conference. It was suggested that he take a position against the civilian and military rioters. "The government has not condemned them. Why should I?" Then, justly alarmed, Maurice Duverger asked the question on everyone's tongue: "Will you respect republican freedoms?" And De Gaulle stiffened, his voice suddenly strident: "I restored the Republic! Why will I begin, at the age of sixty-seven, a career as a dictator?"

Some of Mendès's friends who had been rather favorably inclined toward the general left this confrontation very troubled, others rather reassured. The reading of the text led Mendès France to join the ranks of the pessimists, all the more so because Georges Boris had returned from a visit to the general with the impression that, without feeling authorized to violate the Constitution, he would continue to play on the pressure the officers in Algiers were exercising on Parliament in order to increase the suspense, impose the necessity of an arbiter, a savior, and obtain the most "legal" of investitures.

On May 20, the deputy from Eure mounted the rostrum of the Assembly. In a solemn voice, he read a solemn text:

> I am among those who followed General de Gaulle during the war and who have preserved some pride from that. I am also among those . . . who think that De Gaulle could be the best instrument for national reconciliation. The voice of June 18 has raised itself again but, unfortunately . . . to reinvigorate, whether he likes it or not, a movement that was weakening. That voice has offered to the Algiers insurrection an echo in metropolitan France. General de Gaulle cannot have wanted the new convulsions that this country is experiencing, and yet he has just aggravated an already dramatic situation by what he has said and also by what he has not said. This is why men who joined him, followed him, listened to him, and admired and loved him, implore him, if there is still time, to dissipate the ambiguity.

And Mendès concluded with a very urgent appeal to Pierre Pflimlin, the premier: "We entrusted you with the Republic and the nation. Their fate depends on you!"

It was no longer up to Pflimlin, already dispossessed of the reality of power, to make use of it. Moreover, a week later, he hastened to place what remained in the hands of President Coty, who transferred it, multiplied many times over, to the "most illustrious Frenchman," following a parliamentary procedure in which the forms were barely disturbed. But the general, on the eve of appearing before the Assembly, thought it appropriate to telegraph Salan, the man who had opened the gates of power for him: "What the army has done, it has done well!" That was clear. Solidarity between the men of May 13 and De Gaulle, however provisional it may already have appeared to the most lucid, had been proclaimed. For Mendès France, it was the decisive sign.

On June 1, the National Assembly was asked to declare itself. Alone on the government bench sat Charles de Gaulle, dressed in dark gray, impassive, with a distant air. Mendès France was at the podium:

> The Fourth Republic is perishing from its own mistakes, This regime is disappearing because it has been unable to resolve the problems that it confronted. . . . The "system" that General de Gaulle has so often criticized and that deserved, in fact, many criticisms, has failed. But it is not democracy that has failed, for it is because we have not respected its principles that we find ourselves in our present position. . . .
>
> Whatever the cost to my feelings for the person and the past of General de Gaulle, I will not vote in favor of his investiture; and he will be neither surprised nor offended. . . . I cannot accept giving a vote constrained by insurrection and the threat of a military coup. For the decision the Assembly is going to make—everyone here knows it—is not a free decision, the consent that is going to be given is corrupted. I am not alluding at this moment to the individual, almost official, threats that have been made against a certain number of us by name which the censor prohibits me from repeating; I am referring to the blackmail of civil war, the announcement of a coup organized against the representatives of the people in the event their decision is not the one that is being forced upon them. The government is aware of these preparations, the foreign press has reported them, and we talk about them constantly even in the corridors of this Assembly. The French people believe that we are free; we are so no longer. . . .
>
> Who is imposing this government on us? Unfortunately, it is the same men who have in the past caused the defeat of all attempts at a reasonable and humane settlement in North Africa, who have made war inevitable, have directed it toward repression without a political solution, have played on the nerves of a terrified European population, and are exultant at this moment because they flatter themselves that they have brought General de Gaulle to power. Oh, let them be disappointed! I would like to hope so for France and for the glory of General de Gaulle himself.
>
> Of course, he has revealed nothing about the solutions he is contemplating to put an end to the Algerian war. This is understandable. Perhaps it is inappropriate to reveal a precise plan before one is in a position to put it into action, considering the circumstances in which that action must operate. One cannot, in these conditions, discuss one intention or another that is attributed

to the head of government; but we know enough of his understanding of the great movements of history to be confident that he will wish to direct them in the paths of freedom and association. . . .

The pressure that General de Gaulle will experience from some of his strongest, most recent supporters, from those from whom he has insufficiently separated himself, from those who, nevertheless, without even concealing it, intend to establish a fascist dictatorship . . . that pressure will very soon become formidable. Will De Gaulle wish to resist it? I hope so. . . .

Can he do it? Hasn't he, from the outset, put himself in a subordinate position, speaking as he will tomorrow in the name of the state and allowing his name to be exploited in Algiers, in Ajaccio,[2] as in Paris, by allowing his investiture to be extorted from the Assembly by the threat of sedition? . . .

Let him break starting tomorrow with those who constantly use his name, let him restore independence and dignity to the state he is going to personify. On that day, we will help him without reservation and with all our strength. Our attitude toward him will never be one of sterile and destructive opposition; it will be one of vigilant criticism, constructive and useful to the country. But De Gaulle should not delay in the effort that is required, that effort which will daily be made more difficult by the increased demands of those who are already crying victory.

May history say one day that De Gaulle eliminated the fascist peril, that he maintained and restored freedom, that he reestablished discipline in the administration and the army, that he exterminated the torture that dishonors the state, in a word, that he consolidated and strengthened the Republic. Then, but only then, General de Gaulle will represent legitimacy.

Two or three days later he received me in Louviers. An article I had published in *Le Monde,* in which I thought I had shown that the general would be prevented by his current supporters from making peace in Algeria, had brought me so much criticism that I wanted to confirm my arguments by contact with his, or else deepen my doubts about my own lucidity.

It is impossible to forget this walk by his side, on the hills overlooking Louviers, near his house at Monts. There was a strong wind. PMF had thrown a coat over his shoulders, and leaving the large dog who was then indeed a "watchdog" under the care of Lily Mendès France, we set off at a brisk pace, as he liked to do.

De Gaulle? How can you agree that a coup can be the basis for legality? We are not against the general, the man, the leader, but against a strategy which has not only been one of intimidation but which also implied a Brumaire coup. Because the Chamber lay down, we did not have a *coup d'état,* only some raised eyebrows. The men of the Fourth Republic allowed him not to dirty his hands. Fine. But there are a certain number of us who will not march.

In July 1940, there was no bloodshed either. The representatives of the people had already rushed into servitude. Of course, De Gaulle is not Pétain. And you heard the tone in which I spoke, leaving all doors open. But as long as law has not been restored in Algiers, the rioters put down, the colonels made to obey, the democrats assured of safety, we will remain inflexible. And make no mistake. A regime born in illegality like this will fall only in the streets. Those people will never legally surrender power that has been conquered by fraud and threats.

How can I describe the impression that Mendès made in such circumstances: irrefutable strength and certainty, passionate solidity. One could discuss his reasons, find them accented with a strange passion. That *passion* to be *right*. But the thread of his argument, a mixture of legalism and a deep love of liberty, was extremely persuasive.

For PMF, the new regime was diseased to the marrow, by its origin. Behind each word, each act of the general-president, he would thenceforth see a rioter of May, a paratrooper of June, an agitator of July.

But something like an expectation, a question (perhaps a hope), still appeared on June 21 in a letter to François Mauriac after he had read a column in which Mauriac spoke of the "somber loyalty" of the leaders of the left to the Fourth Republic and of the "horrible charm" that the former heads of government found in its games—remarks that were not directed at Mendès but did not explicitly exclude him.

You have spoken of me in your column so often and in such laudatory and unforgettable terms, that I cannot resist the need to tell you, in all frankness, that I was hurt by the column of June 19.

I am not speaking, of course, of the position you reaffirm in favor of General de Gaulle's government. I understand that position; it is based on feelings and hopes that I share—even though, for me, other considerations in the opposite direction tip the scale that determines our judgments and decisions on the other side. Among those considerations is not included, believe me, that "somber loyalty" to the Fourth Republic and its defects which, according to you, would explain my attitude and that of my friends. No, I never "accepted" or found a "horrible charm" in the "game" that has cost the country so dearly. Like you, I have felt contempt for that game in which a premier could participate "only with painkillers," and I suffered from it like you, and more than you. No doubt, I participated in it—but only because untold number of men, like you, asked me to. . . .

Political cleansing, a return to honesty and uprightness in public life, the restoration of genuine authority, revelation to the country of the truth about the way its affairs have been managed in the past and the chances that they will be better handled in the future—all of that now depends on General de Gaulle. But he should not adopt from the old regime the most blameworthy habits, nor disappoint those who have constantly combatted demagoguery, weakness, and narrow and egotistical interests. Shouldn't voices like yours remind him of this? You can have no doubt of the importance I have always attached to your opinions and your judgments. But today they can exercise a decisive influence on the man who will save what remains to us or who will lose it without hope of return.

He would recognize not the legitimacy of this consular Republic, but its raison d'être, if the general were immediately to apply in Algeria the program that Mendès had suggested on June 1, leading to "freedom and association." They could come together, or at least understand one another, on this level. And however violent the criticisms he directed, unceasingly, against the system, government practice, the government itself, and the Constitution (the fragile "cartel of opposition" that he set up with Mitterrand and the PCF against the Constitution suffered a stinging defeat on September 28, 1958), he found on the Algerian question a reason to show his understanding and to demonstrate that his June 1 remarks on "constructive opposition" were not empty words.

On October 14, 1958, in a letter to General Salan, who was to be commander-in-chief in Algiers for a few weeks longer, De Gaulle had made public the direction he intended to give to his policy, against the de facto powers that had come out of the May movement, and toward a free consultation of the Algerian people. Mendès reacted immediately:

> The instructions of General de Gaulle, as we read them in the press, constitute a new fact, whose consequences may be very important . . . the apparent intentions, the decisions of principle that have been announced point in the right direction. . . . If these intentions are faithfully put into practice, if indisputable actions follow, a way may be opened to détente and peace.[3]

Nine days later, in the course of an impatiently awaited press conference, General de Gaulle launched an appeal to the FLN fighters, proposing that they use the "white flag of parliamentarians" to reach with him a "peace of the brave." Some observers, including those who were not locked into opposition, saw in this initiative a demand for "surrender."[4] Not Mendès. His reaction, on the contrary, was very positive:

> I hope with all my heart that the representatives of the FLN will answer the invitation addressed to them and that they will come to Paris to negotiate with General de Gaulle. A serious opportunity to restore peace has presented itself. No one has the right to neglect it.

It would be difficult to commit oneself more totally on the side of the general. Mendès France was using the considerable credibility that he had obtained with the peoples of the Maghreb to support an offer that was in the end rather ambiguous, perhaps to broaden its meaning, to go beyond the "white flag." Thus was formed, suddenly and fleetingly, a De Gaulle–Mendès association, with the latter modifying, deepening, and balancing the former, an association that made many French citizens cheer. But the

FLN said no, a no to De Gaulle that was also a no to Mendès. And the provisional convergence was thereby broken.

Why did Mendès, who had so boldly put his credibility at the service of the general's initiative, suddenly turn away? Because, according to him,

> De Gaulle had just demonstrated how ambiguous his offer was by allowing the press and the radio of Algiers to sabotage it cynically. Now, if the FLN leaders in Cairo had the authentic version of the appeal, the Algerians in the Casbah and the countryside had *L'Echo d'Alger*, and what they saw there was a demand for surrender. If Ben Bella and his comrades had agreed to negotiate on this basis, would they have been followed by the masses? Did De Gaulle really want to reach a conclusion? Then he had to put an end to the interpretations in Algiers and specify his intentions. He did not do so. That seemed revealing to me.

One may wonder what his relations would have been with the Fifth Republic if the FLN had agreed to open negotiations. The fact is that, FLN or not, he was set in a position of absolute rejection. He was often heard to say that "this regime has only six months to go." In an editorial in the *Cahiers de la République,* he wrote, "There are no institutions, because there is no national adhesion to a permanent body of principles and rules. There is a provisional abandonment of the national destiny to a prestigious man."

The better to fight him, Mendès joined the Union of Democratic Forces (UFD), grouped around François Mitterrand, which attempted to institutionalize the "opposition cartel" of September. This gave his Radical adversaries, like Félix Gaillard, the opportunity to declare that Mendès had thereby placed himself "outside the party." Thus, in early 1959, Pierre Mendès France was excluded from a movement to which he had belonged for thirty-five years, whose glory he was, and to which he had attempted to restore life four years earlier.

PMF's rejection of the regime not only placed him in an almost solitary position in the face of petty maneuvers of a party in whose future he no longer believed. It also led to the loss of a significant portion of his electorate in Louviers, which, like the great majority of the French, had rallied to General de Gaulle, executioner of the Fourth Republic, restorer of order, savior of the franc, preserver of "French grandeur," father.

For many long months, since his resignation from the 1956 government, Mendès France had felt the atmosphere around him become more rarefied. Faithful friendships continued, of course. None of his companions of 1954 had dropped him. But in Parliament, in his party, in the press, he was made to pay dearly for the lessons he had given, the warnings that had not been heeded, and for what the behavior of his supporters had often had of the triumphant and self-satisfied.

He still had his city, Louviers, where he had spent so many beneficial hours as mayor, the constituency he had criss-crossed for nearly thirty years. There in January 1956, at the time of the Republican Front, he had won the greatest electoral success of his career.

Everything indicated that his position, despite the efforts of *Eure-Eclair,* which had replaced *L'Industriel de Louviers* as the organ of the most militant right, remained solid on the eve of the legislative elections scheduled for November 1958 to replace the Chamber elected in 1956: even though it had unrolled the red carpet beneath the feet of General de Gaulle, the Assembly no longer reflected the political society transformed by the "events" of May.

He nevertheless received a serious warning in September. For the referendum on the Constitution, he favored a no vote. A little bit more than 79 percent of his electors had voted in favor of it. Of course, this vote on principles could not be compared to the choice of a deputy. But Mendès was precisely too much a man of principle, he based his political life too much on ideas, not to take this minority position as a very cruel disavowal.

The ordeal would be all the more personal because the Constitution had just restored the district voting system he was so attached to but which he had not favored without recognizing the great risks to himself, since the electorate of Eure was the way it was. The risks were all the greater because, for the last few years, Mendès had encountered in the territory Rémy Montagne, former president of Catholic Youth, former MRP leader (although he had declared himself a Mendésist in 1954, as long as Europe was not at issue). It was this forty-year-old lawyer, with a rather "liberal" profile, that the regime, determined to bring down this major opponent by depriving him of his local base, had chosen to put up against the deputy from the second district of Eure.

As soon as PMF's opposition seemed to it to be permanent and unchangeable, the government mobilized all its forces against him. According to Mendès,

> One might say that they went all the way. It was extraordinary: in a few weeks, the prefect, the general secretary, the prefect's chief of staff, the two subprefects, the director of the intelligence service, the local finance director, everybody was "purged." Even though I was a figure in the department, the new prefect didn't even pay me a courtesy visit.

Mendès, who could have tried to campaign on the theme of services rendered, local accomplishments, and personal loyalties, a campaign that would have certainly paid off, chose instead to speak only of the burning subject, Algeria. Knowing the extent to which the May movement had helped to make him one of the targets of French nationalism as "dissipator" of the empire, he insisted on justifying his no in the referendum and his suspicion, if not of De Gaulle, at least of the new "system." This is from a speech to his constituents in Louviers:

> I expected the instructions given to General Salan on October 9 by General de Gaulle. I was pleased with them, but I must observe today that they had no effect in the field. It is an intolerable situation that the policy defined by Paris is not carried out in Algiers, when it is metropolitan France that has accepted all the sacrifices.

Montagne's equivocal campaign, which did not fully disavow the May rioters and contained hints of anti-Semitism, left a disheartening memory in the minds of many Louviers voters; Mendès spoke of it soberly:

> I cannot attribute to Montagne any specific detail for which he was directly responsible. But he could not have been unaware of the anti-Semitic arguments of the filthy little broadsheets, the anonymous tracts, and a certain number of scurrilous things that circulated. He made a pretense of not seeing them or of saying that he had nothing to do with them. The fact is that he had allies who were not free from reproach on their choice of methods.

In short, on November 23, 1958, Pierre Mendès France suffered a cruel defeat. Rémy Montagne, profiting from the Gaullist landslide and capturing the yes votes of the referendum, was elected on the first round. Immediately drawing the conclusions from this electoral verdict, Mendès resigned from all his elected positions—as mayor of Louviers and as general counsellor of Eure. Twenty-six years after his election as the youngest deputy in France, eighteen years after being removed from office by Vichy, two years after winning his greatest electoral success in Louviers, he was now nothing but citizen Mendès France, head of the opposition without a mandate.

> Louviers. I had been settled there for a very long time, my house was there. Reelection seemed normal to me. I was not psychologically prepared to be beaten. It was even worse because I was in the minority not only in the district as a whole but also in the city, which was mortifying to me as its happy mayor. The voters had the right to get rid of me if they did not agree with me. But I experienced, I confess, real hurt, a great sadness. I handed in my resignation for all the positions I occupied, and from that moment on, I remained completely apart from local political life.
>
> In 1967, when friends suggested that I run for deputy again, or else when certain municipal events led many citizens of Louviers to suggest that I run for mayor again, letting me understand that other posts would follow, I did not attempt to do it. The wound of 1958 remained stinging.

Mendès France did not leave the podium of Parliament without reaction from public opinion. Frightened by the makeup of this reactionary Chamber, which had found no place for the head of the 1954 government, Mauriac wrote that "between the paratroop commandos and the Republic, there remains only Charles de Gaulle." And he added an homage to Mendès that few defeated men have received:

> Pierre Mendès France is leaving a Chamber whose political role will be severely reduced, at a moment when it is now important to address oneself directly to the country, in speech or in writing; and that will be his way, he who voted no, to defend De Gaulle against those who voted yes, and who are secretly fighting against him. Our Pierre Mendès France does not need the parliamentary platform in order to tell us the truth: his noble destiny continues. I salute him here with admiration, affection, and respect.

24.
FOR A CONCRETE SOCIALISM

What is a Socialist? One who believes in the possibility of human happiness; who thinks that that happiness should be based on justice and freedom; who is persuaded that only reason can organize that justice and that freedom, material things first of all, expressed in rights and in goods that are limited and controlled by neither frontiers nor ethnic differences, and that only reason can assure that there is no contradiction between those two fundamental values?

If these are the criteria by which one recognizes a Socialist, we can agree that few French citizens of the twentieth century were more inclined toward socialism than Pierre Mendès France. What is surprising is that this militant for justice, this fighter for freedom, this planner and rationalist, this pioneer of aid to the Third World, waited until he was fifty-two to declare his allegiance to that spiritual family.

He was a Radical in his bones. But what a strange Radical. Wanting to be free, autonomous in his activities, even if they were clearly articulated, Mendès France could not be put off by what French Radicalism involved in the way of doctrinal vagueness and lax organization. He found his dual pattern of behavior in this soft environment in which his powerful personality could comfortably express itself and in his adhesion to the very dynamic group of the Young Turks. Having entered politics at the time of the Cartel des Gauches, and governmental life at the time of the

Popular Front, which was an enlarged Cartel, he had seen the operations of the two great apparatuses of the non-Communist left. And however attracted he was by Blum's doctrine, he considered the discipline that Paul Faure imposed on the SFIO too constricting and preferred to practice socialism as a guerrilla fighter.

He might have been tempted to join Blum's party after the liberation if the old leader and Daniel Mayer had not been forced out of the leadership by Guy Mollet and his doctrinaire friends, and if the majority of SFIO leaders had not misunderstood and failed to support his 1945 austerity program. While he discreetly broke with the Masons, he rejoined the old Radical group, in part because it was open to all currents. But his friends of the left-wing faction had been dispersed. So, for nearly ten years, he would be the Young Turks all by himself.

The experience of government, the attempt to renew the Radical Party, and the collapse of the regime when confronted by De Gaulle, taught him that it was difficult to be alone. As head of government, he had had only one loyal parliamentary support: the Socialist Party. Attempting to renew the Radical Party, Mendès observed that the rheumatism attacking the old organism was all the more painful because the party had no project and was constricted by its traditions. And in opposing Gaullist power he discovered the terrible fragmentation of the left.

So this political orphan set out in search of a family.

In September 1958, the Socialist congress at Issy-les-Moulineaux resulted in a dislocation of the SFIO. Against the acceptance by the majority of the Gaullist regime, and even more against its decisive participation in the horrors of the Algerian war, a minority led by Depreux, Verdier, and Savary first protested and then separated itself from the party which, having been the party of Blum, had become the party of Mollet, Lacoste, and Lejeune, to form the Autonomous Socialist Party (PSA).

At its first conference in May 1959, a message from Mendès to the militants was read from the platform, evoking the "common struggles" and his desire to pursue them "to realize the Socialist ideal." He made his attitude more specific a few weeks later, on June 20, 1959, when he delivered a speech for the centenary of the birth of Jean Jaurès in praise of "open socialism."

One would not have to strain very much to find in this speech the signs of his rallying to the party, if only in these two formulations: "Whoever associates himself with the 1789 Revolution, who wishes to carry out all of its consequences, is already a Socialist," and "Republican politics can and must gradually broaden into Socialist politics."

On September 22, 1959, Georges Boris brought to Edouard Depreux a message of adhesion from PMF, formulated in these terms:

I turn toward those who are not afraid of considering and advocating deep structural reforms of our society. I feel, in fact, more and more strongly that the demands of economic progress, a condition for social progress, the necessity for planning which alone can provide both forms of progress with an adequate impetus, are directing our efforts in the paths of socialism, a socialism which, to triumph in France, must take its inspiration from the humanist tradition of Jean Jaurès and Léon Blum. . . . I am convinced that our future, our country's future, and the future of the whole world, lies in socialism.

The name of Pierre Mendès France had so long and so brilliantly been associated with the history of the Radical Party that his adhesion to an organization based not on some vague laborism or Socialist-leaning planning, but on "scientific socialism," was not a matter of course. To take this step, Mendès had had to experience the shock of May–June 1958, the defeat of Louviers, the cruel divorce from the Radical Party, and the feeling of solitude into which he was plunged by all these ordeals.

His adhesion to the PSA gave a vigorous impulse to the new party. "Never," wrote Depreux, "did the PSA recruit as much as in the wake of Pierre Mendès France. Young people in particular, who had never belonged to any organization, joined PSA sections by the hundreds throughout France. Our penetration in student circles, already substantial, increased significantly."[1]

On October 14, 1959, Mendès France's adhesion to the PSA took a public and, in a sense, doctrinal form. The Mutualité was full and the atmosphere stormy: an extreme right-wing commando unit had come equipped with tear gas grenades that it threw at Depreux, although Mendès was the intended target—the two speakers had changed their order of appearance. Never before had the former head of government so clearly and firmly articulated the reasons for his passage from radicalism to socialism:

> For years now, without having made a contract, I have been in agreement with those who are here against the tyranny of pressure groups, colonialism, racism, torture, political lying, and its clever devices. However, my friends and I would not have asked to join had we not been aware of a similarity of judgment on the structure of the economic system in which we are living. We do not have to reject, but to extend our earlier thinking. For a long time, democracy has been able to realize significant progress through piecemeal reforms. But now that the outposts have been conquered, we are in front of the Bastille. We can no longer usefully confront problems one by one: it is the whole system that calls for global reform, as in 1789, and for the same reasons.

"He did not mention the word *revolution!*" groaned a few doctrinaire members. What is interesting in this speech is the abandonment of a procedure that had until then summed up Mendès France's method: that of the "point by point," "one problem at a time." It was perhaps by moving from the specific to the general that the former Radical leader had become a Socialist militant.

But the PSA was only a stage. Between Guy Mollet and Jacques Duclos the "space of socialism" was ample, and there were many currents. Other groups of the left independent of the PCF—the UGS (Union de la Gauche Socialiste) of Bourdet and Martinet, the MLP (People's Liberation Movement) led by Alverguat, the Tribune du communisme of Jean Poperen—wished for unification. But the narrower a sect, the more exacting the demands of its sectarians. Suspicions were expressed particularly toward those who were known in the UGS as the "*ci-devant* Radicals." But the cleverness of Gilles Martinet managed to bring about unity.

Finally, on April 3, 1960, at the conclusion of a unity congress presided over by Laurent Schwartz, the PSU (Unified Socialist Party) was established, claiming from the outset fifteen thousand members, one-third of them workers. The party program proposed a "radical break" with capitalism without excluding a "transition phase." Mendès had made no objection, but he kept away from the founding conference of Issy-les-Moulineaux and from the following one.

Absent, but the principal character in the play "like God in *Athalie*," he called on his allies to "stir up the thick soup of the new socialism'" and to maintain contact with the militants. In fact, he had never been a man for congresses: until 1955 in the Radical Party he had shown so much reserve in such circumstances that there had been gossip. But in the PSU, Mendès France really cut a strange figure.

Etienne Burin des Roziers, a very close collaborator of General de Gaulle, one day expressed regret that Mendès had not wanted to be "the Colbert of the Fifth Republic." He did not have the opportunity to refuse, since no one made him the offer, except for Mauriac, who constantly repeated that an alliance between De Gaulle and Mendès would be "the best thing that could happen to France." Removed from Parliament and his mayoralty, he had himself burned his bridges, but without isolating himself since he had joined one of the currents of socialism. In any event, he did not sink into silence, notably not on the key question of Algeria.

On September 16, 1959, after testing the waters in very diverse and contradictory ways, General de Gaulle had recognized the right of the Algerians to "self-determination." Pierre Mendès France, who a year earlier had tried to find in the "peace of the brave" a real opening toward peace, this time refused to believe in the prospects that could be opened up by this new proposal. Because the general had referred to the independence of Algeria as a possibility as catastrophic as its "Frenchification," seeing the future only in "association," and especially because he had thereafter, in the course of an inspection tour of the troops in Algeria, assured the officers that in any event the solution would come through a military victory over the FLN, the man who had made the Carthage declaration exhibited a skepticism that surprised a number of his friends.

He was skeptical too of the June 14 speech in which De Gaulle, comparing it to "oil lamps" and "a navy of sailing ships," declared that colonization was a thing of the past. And he was still skeptical of the Melun talks, which were organized in such a way that one had the impression that the head of state hoped for failure. And he was finally skeptical on the eve of the opening of the first serious talks in Evian, in March 1961.

It is true that De Gaulle's march toward peace in Algeria was long, tortuous, and ambiguous. It is true that this great strategist made a strange use of the immense powers he had arrogated to himself in order to reach that goal. If the Parliament of the Fourth Republic had given him, Mendès, such a formidable lever . . . But wasn't the general's double or triple game, by ruse, ulterior motive, and deception, leading to a political settlement based on the emancipation of Algeria?

At a press conference on April 5, 1961, refusing to "substitute for the negotiators" in order to "tell them what has to be done," Mendès was not content with criticizing the delays and ruses of Paris: he encouraged the FLN, like De Gaulle, to throw itself more boldly into the negotiations.

> I call upon the responsible men in both camps to put an end to the petty diplomatic guerrilla warfare which is prolonging the real war, with its increasingly useless human sacrifices and its innumerable sufferings. Nothing justifies new delays and new adjournments. Everyone knows very well, now, what the final solutions will be.
> But I call especially on the men and women of these two countries not to abandon their fate to the marches and countermarches of their leaders, to exert pressure on them, to force them to make peace! . . . Those who want peace must struggle tenaciously, without respite, as those who want the war to continue are struggling tenaciously and without respite. There are men in France who have confidence in the government and in its willingness to negotiate and other men who are suspicious of it. All of them have the same duty: not to relax their effort and their pressure.

Three weeks later, four generals seized power in Algiers, trying to turn the May 13 coup against De Gaulle. For two nights all Paris, with its nose in the air, waited for a paratroop landing that presented a serious risk of leading the French left, with Mendès France at its head, to the slaughterhouse. But the refusal of intermediate officers and draftees to support the military coup, even to defend "French Algeria," led to the failure of the putsch. What did PMF think of the attitude of the state toward those De Gaulle had scornfully called a "quartet of retired generals"?

Asked the question by a journalist from *L'Express,* PMF answered on May 4, 1961.

Civil war was avoided, everything ended with unexpected, almost miraculous speed. Everyone is delighted that the worst dangers were staved off. And the majority of the French give the credit for this to the head of state. . . . De Gaulle and Debré[3] have energetically demonstrated their will to resist— during the crisis. They must be given credit for that.

But the former head of government did not really believe that, even though it had stood up to military fascism, the regime that had come out of May 13 would change in depth: "Nothing indicates that the government has the intention of establishing closer contact with what used to be called the party of movement: the working class, young people, intellectuals, young farmers, and so on."

The Evian talks stalled first over the general's claim to keep the Sahara outside "self-determination." Mendès did not simply say: "I told you so." He waited for a few months, and since no sign of progress appeared on the Algerian horizon, he called a press conference in September to proclaim that, since the regime was doomed in the short term and metropolitan France was threatened with "Algerianization" by the OAS (Organisation de l'Armée Secrète) rebels, he proposed the "establishment of an interim government" whose mandate would be limited to two months. There was widespread surprise. Of course, the regime, caught up in its contradictions and the general's clever maneuvers on Algeria, was losing its spirit and its credibility. But it was going too far to say it was on its death bed and to open the will. Besides, he was asked, how did he envisage the general's departure? "The procedures are secondary," he replied, relying on the "circumstances." This did not fail to surprise the skeptics, coming from a man of rigor so passionately attached to the realities.

Mendès France then undertook a tour throughout France on the theme of the death agony of the regime that was unable to make peace. For nine months he spoke in cities and hamlets, to unions and universities, preaching a democratic succession to the collapsing Fifth Republic. Cassandra had never been in better form; his arguments had never seemed more striking; and the facts had never managed so wickedly to contradict him.

On March 20, 1962, while the murderous bombs of the OAS were exploding almost everywhere, the Evian agreements were finally signed. They recognized the right of the Algerians to proclaim their independence, in the form of a vote on "self-determination" whose result was not in doubt. Well, hadn't De Gaulle made peace? For Mendès France, this conclusion demonstrated that General de Gaulle, content to wait for the moment to "grant" independence, had never really negotiated. Had he negotiated step by step, and earlier, wouldn't he have been able to obtain more serious guarantees for the Europeans of Algeria, French economic and cultural interests, and the cooperation that ought to be established between the two states?

In the referendum De Gaulle called to ratify the agreements, Mendès called on voters to spoil their ballots. But three weeks later, when De Gaulle, without having fulfilled all the conditions imposed by his own Constitution, called another referendum to establish election of the president of the Republic by popular vote, Mendès advocated a clear and decisive no vote.

In the wake of the referendum, which was a triumph for the general, legislative elections offered the Fifth Republic the opportunity to purge its reactionary elements that had been given prominence by the May 13 crisis and to bring together the mass of those voters who were looking only for a father.

The former deputy from Eure saw the approach of this new electoral ordeal without enthusiasm. The Gaullist wave, swollen by the referendum, remained powerful in his district. He had been able to verify by 1958 that the restoration of voting by district, which he had so strongly advocated, worked against him in such a conservative region. Most of his Norman friends advised him to run again in Louviers, arguing that most of his former constituents had, immediately after the 1958 vote, begun to regret the loss of the man who had long been their deputy and their mayor. But PMF had too painful a memory of the episode. Moreover, it happened that Rémy Montagne, who had been elected in 1958, had shifted from the majority to the opposition. A campaign against him would have no specifically political meaning. But in the neighboring district of Evreux the sitting deputy was Prince Jean de Broglie, member of the government. He was the man to defeat.

Jean de Broglie was one of the Evian negotiators. In this battle it was he, so long an advocate for French Algeria, who presented himself as a man of peace, who described himself to mothers as the savior keeping their sons from having to go to war in the Algerian countryside. It was almost as though Mendès were being treated as a warmonger and a conservative. Moreover, the campaign was conducted by de Broglie's staff with arguments that were even more venomous than those used by Montagne's supporters four years earlier.

PMF conducted a strong campaign, and the prognosis was very favorable. But he was beaten in the first round by the Giscardian prince and deputy.

For several years, Mendès had been working on a programmatic book based on conversations with Georges Boris. After the death of his friend in 1960, for which he was inconsolable, as a sort of homage to their friendship, he began to put into shape this attempt at clarification of his thought and his experiences. He had the help of Colette Audry, philosophy teacher, friend of Sartre, PSU militant, and author of an acid and penetrating essay on Léon Blum. The book was dedicated to Boris, "irreplaceable friend."

La République moderne (The Modern Republic) was published in October 1962. From the very first pages, the author asserted that he "claimed no originality" and that the ideas "summed up" in his work "were in the air." Indeed. But the originality of the treatise lies in the rigorous connection it establishes between a society's model of economic development and its institutions. The link may seem obvious, but no one before him had so carefully articulated it.

The richest and most novel part of the book tended to place at the center of the system, as its cornerstone, "democratic planning." This was the primary objective, the raison d'être of La République moderne, which was structured around the Plan, that effort of reason to organize a future based on productive investment. The Republic that PMF called modern was one that tended to take the Plan as the basis of the "social democracy" that Jaurès had dreamed of.

But the problem was not only to organize rationally. It was also to control the formidable power of the planner, to prevent the Plan from becoming the all-consuming idol that the totalitarian systems had made of it. The modern Republic was one that organized collective development of and democratic control over the Plan, that made the Plan the central element in the social contract.

In order that planning not be the iron corset that was suffocating totalitarian societies, Mendès France formulated a series of suggestions drawn from his experience as a statesman who had had significant responsibilities. Because it was important that the executive be stable, he proposed a government lasting the length of a legislature, which, on the basis of the "contract" represented by the Plan, would link the fate of the head of government to that of the Assembly. The latter could vote down the former, who could in turn dissolve it. But they would confront the popular vote together.

To restore real significance to Parliament, Mendès proposed that the National Assembly be associated not with a Senate but with an "Economic Chamber," where the Plan would be elaborated, and whose work would be supplemented by that of regional economic assemblies. This would bring into a public forum the debates on the Plan which had until then been confined to specialists, technocrats, and lobbyists. There would thus be established a convergence between organization and debate, and among the fundamental values of socialism: the development of wealth, the demand for justice, and the rights of freedom.

What was a little surprising in this programmatic book written by a man who had joined the Socialist movement three years before and who was at the time an eminent member of the PSU was the infrequency of his references to the classics of socialism. The epigraph for the conclusion was a sentence borrowed from the American astronaut John Glenn; the concluding quotation was taken from a manifesto of the Jeunes Patrons. And the term that he used at the end of the central argument was neither collectivization, socialization, or even planning, but "solidarity."[4]

Pierre Mendès France was not easy to classify. As a Radical, he carried out a kind of independent socialism. As a Socialist, he produced an elegant treatise on "democratic planning" which, although imbued with a Socialist spirit, posed a challenge to the clichés and rituals of socialism and would certainly have surprised Jules Guesde, if not Jean Jaurès and Léon Blum.

With the end of the Algerian war and the stabilization of Gaullist power in the electoral victory of the autumn of 1962, and his own program formulated in *La République moderne,* what perspectives were open to Mendès France? His defeats in Normandy had not ruined his standing on the national level, and his exile from Parliament weakened his role only to the extent that the Assembly retained any importance in the life of the Fifth Republic, which it hardly did. He remained the inescapable recourse of the non-Communist left. Against the Algerian uprising, the country called on De Gaulle. To De Gaulle, the answer was Mendès.

By 1963, the political class had begun to think of what was to happen in 1965: the first election of the president of the Republic by popular vote. If De Gaulle were to run again, there was little chance of blocking his reelection. But would he run at the age of seventy-five? In any event, it was necessary to be prepared. And the name that came first to everyone's mind was that of Mendès France. There were numerous consultations among left-wing civil servants, committed intellectuals, and progressive journalists as well as a testing of Communist Party opinion.

But the PMF candidacy very quickly evaporated, for the very simple reason that the man principally concerned rejected it. He was to begin with hostile to a Constitution modeled on the Consulate and hostile as well to a presidential regime and to popular election of the head of state. It was impossible to imagine that such a principled man could compromise on so many fundamental questions. To everyone who saw him at the time to sound him out or to encourage his candidacy, Mendès France gave the same answer. And all the arguments that were offered (hadn't he exercised power in the framework of the Fourth Republic, whose Constitution he had fought, whose morals he had attacked, and whose weakness and compromises he had condemned?) came up against an unambiguous veto, "Out of the question. I am not your man."

The effort was finally abandoned in favor of an effort to launch the candidacy of Gaston Defferre, a campaign that fizzled, as did the attempt to establish a broad center-left coalition. But in the following year, François Mitterrand set up the Convention des Institutions Républicaines, which was the basis of his vigorous campaign against De Gaulle, who, against all predictions, was forced into a runoff election.

Mendès France supported Mitterrand's campaign without reservation. On October 25, he declared in an interview:

> Mitterrand has done us all a great service. I may mention here one thing that was decisive for me: in all the serious affairs of the last twenty-five years, I have found him on the right side of the barricades. I will vote for him, and I ask all those who have confidence in me to vote for him.

And then, in early December, PMF confronted Michel Debré, De Gaulle's former premier, for three radio debates of two hours each. In the first of the three broadcasts, in which he delivered a mordant indictment of the Fifth Republic's economic strategy, based on a Fifth Plan that was "retrograde, characteristic of a class politics," and institutionalized the unemployment of 600,000 workers euphemistically characterized as a "phalanx of available manpower," the head of the 1954 government convinced millions of French, and especially a young student public that hardly knew him, of the rational power of his arguments, now reinforced by obvious Socialist convictions. De Gaulle asserted that a victory of the left would mean "chaos." Mendès demonstrated that there was no intellectual chaos.

As for his general attitude toward the regime, called into question by Michel Debré ("When it's a question of the Fifth Republic and its leader, Mendès France, you indulge in a permanent and systematic critique, and I have never heard you admit that, on one point or another, De Gaulle was right"), Mendès retorted by recalling his appeal to the FLN to respond favorably to the offer of a "peace of the brave" thus "certified" by him. He also recalled his public approval of diplomatic recognition of China and of General de Gaulle's positions in favor of revaluations of commodity prices and aid to the Third World.

François Mitterrand managed to mount a serious campaign against the general. The 45 percent of the vote that Mendès's former interior minister obtained in the second round rescued the left from the abyss and restored its political credibility. The possibility of a victory was henceforth plausible. In this perspective, Mendès assigned himself a primarily doctrinal role. Since socialism was the framework within which the strategy of "democratic planning" was located, the question was what real content was to be given to the magic word that French social democracy, by evasion, and Soviet bolshevism, through abuse, had denatured.

This was the question that was addressed at a conference held in Grenoble in late April and early May 1966. The statement calling for the conference provides an excellent summary of the spirit of the work to which Mendès France lent his authority, in an atmosphere that enabled him freely to express his vision of socialism:

> Something has changed in French politics. The post-Gaullist era has, in fact, clearly begun, and the contradictions of the regime will soon express themselves in terms of political divisions. A broad sector of public opinion, "frozen" until now within the heterogeneous Gaullist electorate, will soon become available. The future direction of the country depends to a large extent on its choices. . . . The Socialist left can and must become the majority. To transform into an actual majority the possibilities that economic and social analysis has revealed, the left—and particularly the Socialist movement—must undertake a profound effort of renewal and adaptation. It must stop posing the problems of the transition to socialism in general terms that have been outdated by its own evolution. It must give up disguising the worst opportunistic practices beneath revolutionary phraseology. It must formulate in clear terms what it intends to do if it attains power, according to what social model it intends to direct the country, and by what means it intends to reach its goals.

A program rather than a doctrine, means given as much attention as ends, and a link established between economic analysis of concrete realities and political strategy; Mendès was completely at home.

Reporting in *L'Evénement* of June 1966 on the remarkable efforts carried out in Grenoble with a view toward a renewal and rerooting of socialism in reality, Roland Cayrol wrote: "Pierre Mendès France was among the speakers. His speech dominated the debates: there was talk of a 'political comeback,' and some even claimed to see PMF as the future leader of a modern socialism." What is certain is that he found, at this Grenoble meeting, the studious and scientific atmosphere of deep analysis, exact evaluation, and free debate that he had anticipated when he joined the Socialist Party. If he ever thought of himself as a Socialist, it was certainly during those days in Grenoble, and particularly on the basis of that meeting.

25.
THE YOUNGEST ELECTORATE
IN FRANCE

When the question of running for office came up in the following year, it was suggested either that Mendès France return to Louviers, where his friends assured him of victory, or that he run in Brive, where prospects were good for a candidate of the united left, or else in Paris, in the third *arrondissement*, where he had been born. But he decided to conduct his campaign in Grenoble. Why?

What led me to Grenoble was first of all the youth of the electorate, and then the kind of political and economic problems that were raised, and the level at which they were treated. I will sum it up with an illustration. When the problem of a substitute[1] was raised in Louviers: "You should choose a country mayor, slightly illiterate if possible, a peasant whose wife goes to mass." In Grenoble, I was asked: "Whom do you want as a substitute? There is the dean of the faculty of science, who would like nothing better; unless you prefer the dean of the law school." And then there was an appeal from three men: Dubedout, the mayor; Verlhac, his deputy; and Weil, dean of the faculty of science.

Verlhac belonged to the PSU, where I had known him long before my candidacy in Grenoble came up. He had been wounded at the great demonstration against the Algerian war at the Charonne metro station. He had been sent for treatment to Grenoble, where he was teaching in the faculty of

397

letters. The second district of Isère was traditionally represented in the Assembly by a Socialist. The Gaullist who had been elected in 1958 and 1962 could be beaten. To establish the unity of the left, Verlhac wanted a PSU candidate. But no local PSU member had enough stature, so that, although he was not passionately in my favor, Verlhac had arrived at the idea that I would be the best possible candidate. His proposal impressed me, for it didn't come from the PSU alone: he had obtained the agreement in principle of all the other groups of the left, except the PCF.

The problem was obviously to come in ahead of the Communist candidate, in order to benefit from his votes in the second round. And for this to succeed there had to be only one candidate for the non-Communist left. Verlhac set about creating agreement on this point with extraordinary diplomacy.

Before beginning his campaign (legislative elections were set for March 5 and 12, 1967), Mendès France saw the opportunity of appearing on television, and thereby reaching a large public, in a debate with Maurice Schumann. While the head of the Federation of the Democratic and Socialist Left, François Mitterrand, had become the leader of the parliamentary and strictly political opposition, Mendès France once again appeared, through the medium of television, as the ideological opposition.

This appearance on television also had a very political character. For several months, circles close to the government had once again been suggesting that, on the basis of national independence and economic efficiency, Mendès could come closer to the majority and even participate in a government. But his preliminary statement in response to that of Maurice Schumann was a manifesto of fundamental opposition. Asked to "define himself in relation to General de Gaulle," he replied:

> I find it significant and almost symbolic that such a question is asked to open the debate. It proves the extent to which we have developed the habit in the course of the last few years, distressingly in my opinion, of subsuming politics within the relations, the judgments, or the feelings each of us may have with respect to one man. As for me, I do not forget what all of the French owe to General de Gaulle. I will never forget it. But that should not lead me in every circumstance to be in agreement with the policy he carries out, the decisions he makes. When De Gaulle was fighting for liberation of the territory, our duty was to be behind him. With De Gaulle as a political man, the head of a party, each of us has the right to judge him and to express his complete disagreement, I am in complete disagreement, particularly on his conception of the conduct of a country like ours.

No candidate had ever had such glittering and diverse endorsements. Four Nobel Prize winners (François Jacob, Jacques Monod, André Lwoff, and Alfred Kastler), and Jean Rostand, Jean Vilar, Daniel Mayer, Maurice Duverger, Jacques Brel, Serge Reggiani, Marie Dubois, Jacques

Martin. Several of them came to speak or to sing in Grenoble, and Mendès, who was not an habitué of the Olympia, discovered Brel with delight. And Jacques Monod declared: "I support the man who symbolizes for me the only regime that is acceptable for a country of high culture, that is, social democracy."

PMF's headquarters in the center of town, above an antique shop, was a kind of factory. He had brought with him people who had helped lead the battle of Evreux with much weaker resources. Here, there was not only the impression that it was impossible to lose, but also that one was the center of an immense debate, and that the heart of the French left, victorious or vanquished, was beating in those three overheated rooms buzzing with excitement.

It was nevertheless a hard campaign. Claude Glaymann, who covered it step by step for *Combat,* described a meeting in a Communist stronghold:

> The young voice of Mendès rang out, argumentative and with a hint of underlying humor. One felt him seizing the audience. There were two hundred people present, a good deal for a Communist stronghold. There was also a substantial number of supporters. They applauded, but it was clear that both sides would have to explain themselves. The central theme, he said, was "the unity of the left, among our three organizations. Tomorrow, this can be a new majority. For the moment, it is still insufficient. The party I belong to has for months and months been calling for a common program."
>
> A Communist heckler shouted out the argument that keeps the campaign against PMF going: hadn't he negotiated and obtained—in exchange for what?—the withdrawal of one of Lecanuet's candidates, to have a free hand with respect to the center? He retorted:
>
> "The men from the Democratic Center of Grenoble came to see me. They were divided on the question of running a candidate. I said to them: in any event, you will not win. If you agree with the regime, vote for the incumbent, if not, vote for one of the representatives of the opposition. That's it. You claim that I negotiated. What did I offer in return?" Shaking his finger at the audience, he repeated in ringing tones: "What did I bargain with? Nothing. Who can say otherwise?"

But the great test was on February 27. Mendès's opponent, Jean Vanier, had invited him to a debate with the premier, Georges Pompidou, to be held in an immense auditorium with seven thousand seats. There was a crowd at the doors two hours before opening time, and journalists from around the world were present.

It was an extraordinary evening. The incumbent opened hostilities, unleashing an uproar in the grand manner. As he persisted in speaking of "M. Mendès," half the audience yelled "France," drowning out the rest of his speech. Georges Pompidou, speaking before Mendès France, delivered such a technical speech full of statistics that the excitement subsided. But when PMF mounted the platform, the uproar was so loud that he could not be heard for three or four minutes.

Impassive, Mendès France reiterated an indictment that had often been heard against the antidemocratic character of the regime. And he went directly to the heart of the matter. Did this Republic still recognize the law of popular election?

> You yourself present the president of the Republic as the source of all power. From that point on, you can abolish elections: it would be simpler and clearer! And if the left wins, if the majority is defeated, won't you maintain a minority government?
> POMPIDOU: I do not know what the president of the Republic would do. I deliberately choose not to know. We shall see!
> MENDÈS: There's your monarchical conception of abdication before the sovereign!
> POMPIDOU: You have remained a man of the Third Republic!
> MENDÈS: And you, you have become a man of the Second Empire!

A week later, the incumbent Jean Vanier was forced into a runoff. Giard, the Communist candidate, stood aside for Mendès. And on March 12, 1967, the former deputy from Eure became a deputy from Isère. For fifteen months, he was a very attentive deputy, particularly for the preparations for the Winter Olympics, held in Grenoble in February 1968. Whatever one's judgment about the Olympic celebration, the important thing was that the enormous expenditures it required on the part of the city be integrated into a program of development. The housing built for athletes, journalists, and spectators had to be made available to the citizens of Grenoble, particularly young families in search of a roof over their heads: this was largely accomplished.

This grand political comeback, and the very active joy he experienced from it, was deeply darkened by the illness and death of his wife Lily, who died on November 24, 1967. Mendès France was so affected by her illness that a few weeks earlier, while his wife was still struggling against death, he had suffered a heart attack.

But his electoral success of March 1967, which was part of a rising movement of a united left in the second round, which fell short by only three seats of a reversal of the majority, also restored to Mendès France the full extent of his representative character on the national political scene. Both at the podium of the Assembly, where he represented one of the most advanced constituencies in the nation, and in the Finance Committee, where he resumed an authority that no one challenged, the former head of government was restored, reintegrated, returned from exile, deputy of a minuscule party (that did have four deputies), who was listened to with more attention than those who spoke in the name of millions of voters.

On May 18, 1967, for example, arguing against Pompidou's request for exceptional powers, PMF harshly and bluntly declared: "Your planning is secret, without supervision. You meet only with business groups, for their benefit. You refuse to inform, to carry on a dialogue."

Deputy from Grenoble. All the myths gathered around him—advanced industries, the modern university, the "practical" left, the Olympic games—to solidify and broaden his audience. He no longer represented apple pickers but an urban society in which, as in a model laboratory, the new society was being developed that he wanted to make into a "social democracy."

But even as the Olympic games were opening, rather strange celebrations were in preparation. From the beginning of the year, there had appeared some signs of agitation not only on the surface of the university community but also in the working-class world, where there were manifestations of spontaneous protest indicative of deeper movements. In January, a minister had been manhandled by a group of students at Nanterre. In Strasbourg, the situationist movement was asserting itself. Still more significant, in February, in Caen, a strike at the Saviem factory had given rise to union demonstrations in which student organizations had participated.

This was something new, and it meant a great deal to the very few careful observers. If working-class bitterness provoked by conservative social policies overlapped with the anger stimulated among young intellectuals, students and teachers, by the constricting structures of the French university system, their archaism in relation to economic developments, the troubles that had already been observed could expand dangerously.

These were questions that Mendès France asked himself in early 1968, as did many of his countrymen. More clearly than many others, for he saw in these developments the answers to questions that he had been asking for a long time.

26.
CHARLETY: A REFORMIST IN THE REVOLUTION

On the Pont Saint-Michel, the march grew to formidable size, as though to challenge more strongly the nearby police headquarters. The March 22 Group[1] had already passed, and the Maoists, and the Trotskyites of the JCR (Revolutionary Communist Youth). "Ten years is enough!" chanted the marchers with long hair, and the marchers in factory clothes, and the marchers with raised fists. And there was the PSU and, surrounded by fraternal students, Mendès France, walking vigorously, a little surprised but above all delighted to be there, in this company, and no longer with Daladier, Depreux, Bourdet, and Duclos, as in "ordinary" marches. It was May 13, 1968. "Ten years is enough!"

How could Mendès not be seized by a certain jubilation on this May afternoon when, as he had so often predicted, the streets were in the process of challenging a system that had itself sprung out of a riot? He had, of course, not foreseen this kind of uprising. No one had quite predicted it, not even the most penetrating sociologists, Henri Lefebvre and Alain Touraine. But whatever form subversion had assumed, it seemed that the regime was in the process of paying for its "original sin."

That this type of radical challenge to the Fifth Republic was coming first from the mass of students was perhaps less surprising to Mendès than to anyone else in the political world. As head of the University Antifascist League in the late 1920s, he had been able to link intellectual and political struggles, and since then he had never stopped emphasizing the problems of young people. In 1954, he had created a Ministry of Youth, and one of his staff members had been given, as an essential mission, the task of studying educational reform. In 1955, he had attempted to take in hand and regenerate the oldest party in France with the help of a cohort of young people. And the various publications with which he had been associated constantly emphasized questions of youth and education.

In 1966, he had opened a conference in Caen devoted to the study of the crisis in French education, and two years later, a few weeks before the May explosion, he had done the same at an Amiens conference. As soon as university people and specialists decided to broaden their debates about the future of the educational system, they immediately thought of PMF, even though he had never been the minister in charge. Called upon to do so, he had worked on these questions sufficiently to be aware that he should emphasize in such circumstances the problems of secondary education, which, correctly, appeared to him more significant than the more spectacular problems posed by higher education.

In short, when the effervescence of May came to the fore, and when it became large and violent enough to change into a matter of national interest demanding a political interpretation, Mendès seemed to be the man of the hour, as he had been fourteen years before on Indochina, and then on Algeria and on the recasting of institutions. Mendésism was a movement focused on the young. Three-quarters of the membership of the PSU, his party, was under thirty; and he escaped from the curse, especially among the demonstrators of Nanterre and the Sorbonne, that lay upon the parties and their leaders.

The explosion of May 3 surprised him in Grenoble. That day, the government, phlegmatic until then, decided to have the police enter the Sorbonne and arrest 580 students, who were judged according to the summary procedure of *flagrants délits:* four of them were sentenced to prison terms. Mendès, who returned to Paris the next day, was indignant, and even more indignant at the violence of police reactions on May 6. The CRS assault waves to clear away from the Latin Quarter the students who were fighting under the slogans "Free our comrades!" seemed to him to be acts of civil war against which he protested.

But on May 10, while negotiations between Vietnamese and Americans (how many memories for Mendès) were opening at the conference center on the avenue Kléber, the situation did not seem serious enough to keep him from returning to Grenoble: nervousness was growing there, too, and his friends had called on him as deputy and as leader of the PSU. Hardly had he arrived in his constituency on the morning of the eleventh when he received two phone calls from his friends Michel Rocard and Georges Kiejman describing in a few sentences the terrible night of rioting on the tenth—the appearance of barricades, built at five in the afternoon and conquered by the CRS at three in the morning after extremely violent confrontations. They begged him to return urgently to Paris, "within the hour!"

He returned to Paris the next day. Permanent contact had to be established with party militants, which was not easy. However young and intelligent it may have been, PMF's entourage did not clearly realize the extent to which the situation that was in process of being created was a break with the past, the extent to which everything was rising up against the "institution": Was Mendès France, in the eyes of the young, not himself also an institution?

PMF was thus "in the soup." However disconcerting it may have been—the Sorbonne as a fortified camp, a forum, and a fair of ideas, the streets of the Left Bank bristling with barricades, French political society in a state of frightened contrition—the event did not entirely disconcert him. It was in a certain sense along the lines of what he had predicted: that the regime would collapse in an uproar. For a time, he could believe that his predictions were being fulfilled. And if he entered so well into the situation, this was because it was created by the young people in whom he was more interested than were other political figures and whom he observed while feeling his way. As a university woman who was very involved in the movement said sharply to Georges Kiejman: "Your boss isn't as dumb as you. He sensed immediately that what counts from now on is to listen!"

Mendès joined the tacit committee of mediators or intercessors inspired by several distinguished professors with several lawyers as active participants. The principal objective: no shooting! They had to persuade the authorities, that is, Louis Joxe, interim head of government,[2] Christian Fouchet, minister of the interior, and Maurice Grimaud, prefect of police, to prohibit the police forces from using firearms. These three men, moreover, hardly needed persuading. They also had to persuade the student leaders not to engage in provocation.

Did General de Gaulle, in the course of the night of May 10, consider having the army intervene? Pierre Viansson-Ponté says that he did.[3] Cutting short his trip to Afghanistan, Georges Pompidou landed in Paris and extracted from De Gaulle the authorization to negotiate by making a first concession: the reopening of the Sorbonne. It was immediately occupied by the students. There was a slight lowering of tension, recognized as such by Mendès and his friends. Above all, no shooting!

And then there was the tumultuous and cheerful May 13, a half-million enthusiastic marchers. Since May 13, 1958, those who had

405 CHARLETY: A REFORMIST IN THE REVOLUTION

marched from Nation to République had grown. A smiling PMF said to his young neighbors: "There were less than 200,000 of us; now we are more than 500,000, and all the young people together." On occasion, the atmosphere grew tense: when the black flags of the anarchists went by, the PCF marshals were furious. But they let them through, for the first time in their lives.

This exalted and disordered movement, lyrical and lawless, spontaneous and provocative, was not PMF's style. So many words, so many gestures, and so little of a program. It lacked a "positive" will, a "constructive" view, he thought. But there was a warmth emanating from all that that moved the austere deputy from Grenoble.

On the fourteenth, a debate on the situation opened in the Chamber. Mendès France, pressed by some to intervene to present in broad terms the demands of the students as they had been formulated by his PSU comrades Michel Rocard and Marc Heurgon, refused. He did not think he had the right to speak in the name of the young. He was merely "listening." But a phone conversation that day with Jacques Sauvageot, leader of UNEF (Union Nationale des Etudiants Français), the principal student organization, led him to denounce police brutality from the podium of the Assembly. Faithful to a principle he had always held, Mendès refused to play a purely negative role. He spoke only if he had proposals to formulate.

But Sauvageot and his comrades had already lost their monopoly of the movement. That very day, in fact, at the Sud-Aviation factory in a Nantes suburb, there began the factory occupation movement, which posed a much more serious long-term problem than student effervescence: all of French industrial production was at stake. Ten million strikers.

Only five days later, on May 19, did Mendès France intervene, after several consultations between his friends and advisers and those of François Mitterrand that had led to nothing. The two men were not on the same wavelength. Mitterrand, president of the FGDS (Fédération de la Gauche Démocrate et Socialiste), asserted that political leaders had nothing to do with this adolescent explosion; Mendès, on the contrary, emphasized their responsibilities, especially if the signs of increasing bankruptcy of the government were to become clearer.

His declaration, according to Alain Gourdon, seemed to be a distant echo of the one Charles de Gaulle had published ten years earlier, on May 15, 1958—with the difference that Mendès had done nothing to encourage the violent challenge and that angry students were not rebellious paratroopers: "The government can now render only one more service to the country: withdraw." Having spoken, he remained silent in the parliamentary debate on the twenty-second, although he voted for the censure motion against Pompidou. This was the day when De Gaulle, returning hastily from a trip to Romania, thundered to his petrified ministers: "Enough games: reforms yes, chaos no!" What means did he envisage to sweep away the "chaos"? Perhaps because this kind of reaction gave rise to fears of the worst and stimulated the idea of a third solution, an association of support of Pierre Mendès France was created on May 21, including a large number of university people. He had done nothing to encourage it. It did not facilitate his relations with the Communists in the succeeding days: *L'Humanité* was already making ironic references to "the providential man."

Nor did it make things easier with François Mitterrand. On the evening of May 23, the two men met at Mitterrand's apartment. According to Mendès:

> I had gone to the Latin Quarter once or twice, not to speak but to indicate my solidarity with a certain number of the demonstrators. I saw Mitterrand from time to time. On the evening of the twenty-third, we talked about the situation. There were friends there who wanted Mitterrand and me to go out and meet the demonstrators. As for me, I didn't want to take an initiative of this kind. I had accepted invitations in very precise particular cases, but I didn't want to seem to impose myself. And I wondered how Mitterrand would be received. There were people who would have welcomed him, others who would not have received him at all and who might have reproached me for bringing him along. As a result, I was hesitant. I couldn't see us arriving at a barricade, introducing ourselves, and saying: "Here we are, we've come to help you." In short, after a discussion between Hernu, who wanted to go, and Kiejman, who was against it, we decided to abstain, and promised to keep in contact.

But on the evening on the twenty-fourth, Mendès France, his future wife Marie-Claire, and a few friends, including Georges Kiejman, who had left Mitterrand on the twenty-third with a decision to maintain reserve toward the students, found themselves on rue Soufflot, at the heart of the movement. Some observers, including those sympathetic to Mendès, have seen this as a Machiavellian gesture. Thus, in his *Lettre ouverte aux hommes politiques* (Open Letter to the Politicians),[4] Pierre Viansson-Ponté addressed Mendès in these terms:

> You go to the Latin Quarter, you appear in person at the heart of the riot, you speak, heard more than acclaimed. That evening, not only did you maneuver to eliminate a rival, you lost the game at one stroke by betting on red and black at the same time.

This version of the event presents a rather short-sighted ruse, ill-suited to the figure of Mendès.

On such an occasion, it is tempting to attribute great influence to what we will call neither chance nor destiny, but the weight of the event. According to Georges Kiejman:

> The evening of May 23, Mendès and Marie-Claire are at Mitterrand's on rue Guynemer. Mitterrand's lieutenants want to take the two of them inside the perimeter of the barricades; neither one is particularly enthusiastic. Marie-Claire telephones me to come and join Mendès. I live nearby and come immediately. We talk. I am against the expedition. Finally, a little commando group is sent to explore the situation, made up of Mitterrand's lieutenants, with Hernu in the lead.
>
> They return, insisting that the two leaders go to the Latin Quarter. I continue to be opposed. In comes Pierre Soudet, a great friend of Mitterrand's, who shares my point of view: it's inopportune. Since he's an adviser to Mitterrand, he is listened to more than I. We decide not to go out.
>
> The next day, May 24, is the day of De Gaulle's failed speech. Mendès, who has set up a meeting with journalists at Marie-Claire's apartment on avenue Montaigne to comment on the speech, doesn't feel like talking. "There is nothing in the speech," he objects. "What can I say about it?" But since he has inconvenienced people, he resigns himself to answering them. And since he is forcing himself, he goes further than he wanted to and makes violent remarks like: "The streets have answered!" And since he has made these revolutionary remarks, he finds himself caught up in the atmosphere and, in fact, goes down into the street. Professor Marcel-Francis Kahn is waiting for us with his car, and there we are on our way toward the demonstrators, who, that evening, are on the Right Bank. Activist groups have just tried to set the Bourse on fire, we are told, but the fire is out when we get there, without reaching the Bourse itself.
>
> Rue de Richelieu, we join a movement going toward the Comédie-Française, and we glimpse Geismar at the head of a group of anarchists, who have no desire to associate with Mendès. So we form a little group of independent Mendésists. People recognize him and join us. We easily cross one of the bridges—at the Ile Saint-Louis—which are, however, carefully guarded by the police, and there we are on boulevard Saint-Germain, then boulevard Saint-Michel, then rue Monsieur-le-Prince, and we find ourselves somehow carried by the crowd toward the Sorbonne, which has been evacuated and is now little more than an infirmary. Obviously, many people gather around Mendès, and we have to explain that he has no intention of speaking, that he is there only as a witness, an observer, and we have to set up a kind of barrier around him.
>
> Then we're in the UNEF offices on the rue Soufflot, where the atmosphere isn't very good. People are snubbing each other. No leader is present. The night is dragging on, tear gas grenades explode in the rue Soufflot. What are we doing there?
>
> We withdraw, I think, along the rue Gay-Lussac. We have to cross various police blockades, where some are mocking, others respectful, according to whether the officers, says Mendès, are "well behaved" or not. Thus, in front of the Odéon, there was a discussion about a kind of truce,

between the demonstrators and the CRS blockade, to let Mendès through, followed by Marie-Claire, her daughter Nathalie, and me. In any event, wherever he made contact with young people that night, Mendès France was greeted with sympathy, even with warmth.

Nothing happened or was said that was of any importance in the course of the night of May 24, but François Mitterrand and his friends have always believed that our expedition had been premeditated and that it was the better to prepare it and inflate the personal role of Mendès that I had opposed an initiative in common on the twenty-third. But I was certainly not alone in having taken that position. And who could have foreseen the extraordinary sequence of events on the twenty-fourth?

The incident cannot be treated lightly because it weighed heavily on relations between the two men. Influenced or not by his entourage, Mitterrand always believed that Mendès, whom he already resented for not having informed him soon enough about the "affair of the leaks," had tried to outflank him that night. And his attitude during the succeeding days was affected by that feeling.

On May 24, the crisis was approaching its paroxysm. While factory occupations were proliferating throughout the country, in Paris the uprising was overflowing the boundaries of the Latin Quarter and reaching the Right Bank. The original demonstration organized in front of the Gare de Lyon quickly became boisterous. At eight o'clock, General de Gaulle appeared on television: this speech, which was eagerly anticipated and loudly announced by all the government spokesmen, is the worst that he ever delivered. The man with the lightning bolt of 1961, the sarcastic genius of the 1965 campaign, the uncontested champion of the galaxy of images and words, was nothing more than an old man who was angry because his house had been dirtied and his legend had been attacked. As a supreme weapon, he brandished a referendum, and as an absolute threat, his retirement. A wounding outburst of laughter greeted his harangue, from the Gare de Lyon to the Left Bank: "Great!"

It was then that Mendès came up with the famous formulation: "You do not discuss a plebiscite, you fight against it!" The day after this night of errors, violence, and failures, François Mitterrand held a meeting of the leadership of the FGDS. The Radical leader René Billières proposed that, given the circumstances, the federation should move closer to Mendès, "who has the ear of the students." Mitterrand's reaction was very dry and very bitter. "If you wish to replace me at the head of the federation, you should say so right away! . . . That will be better for Mendès and for me."[5]

On these painful misunderstandings with Mitterrand, it is worth hearing Mendès again:

At bottom, there was between us a difference of interpretation of the phenomenon. I cannot say that mine was very precise. But all the same, I realized that it was something very serious, very profound, very significant, that revealed convulsions, a resistance, a deep challenge. De Gaulle himself has said on several occasions that throughout this period the situation and states of mind were "ungraspable." In the opposition, things were the same. I understood a little better the profundity of things, but I didn't see exactly where that would lead.

There was another point on which I was inadequately informed about the situation: I didn't see the extent to which the Communists were determined, whatever happened, to help the government. Their conflict with the *gauchistes* was much more important for them than their opposition to De Gaulle. I didn't think, as I do today, that they would go so far as to hope that the regime would be saved.

The wage demands formulated at the Grenoble negotiations were used only to detour the workers' movement. When there is a strike and one wants to calm or channel a workers' movement, one talks of wages. But at the origin, there was an enormous ferment among the workers, and the PCF had to take control over it. The CGT literally conducted a war against the spontaneous workers' movement at Renault, where it had powerful resources: but elsewhere it was overwhelmed.

I committed a second mistake with respect to the Communists. I knew very well that they didn't like me. Now, the question was to present a solution that would receive support from the entire left. Because Mitterrand had personified the union of the left since the elections of 1965, and because he considered himself responsible for dialogue with the Communists, it seemed normal to me that he be the intermediary between them and me. I did not realize that, even then, the Communists mistrusted him and that he was perhaps not the best intermediary. Could I have tried to contact the Communists, to influence them, to persuade them? I don't think so. In fact, Mitterrand was at the center of the spider web and thought, as a consequence, that it was up to him to spin. That's normal.

On Sunday the twenty-sixth, while the "Grenelle" negotiations were taking place at the Hôtel Matignon, through which Pompidou was attempting to halt subversion by filling the bellies, at least of the working-class fraction of the movement, in order later to turn against the students, there were feverish consultations around and about Mendès France. His friend Charles Gombault called him in the morning. He had just been told of threatening remarks by Georges Pompidou against the *gauchistes*. A large rally organized by the UNEF was scheduled for the next day. The students were said to be "on the rampage."

Charles Gombault telephoned Maurice Schumann, a member of the government, and asserted that, if they wanted to reason with the students, the only man who had the stature to do so was Jacques Monod. Mendès spoke to Monod and then called Monseigneur Marty, asking him to intercede for the same purpose. It was agreed with Christian Fouchet and the prefect of police, Maurice Grimaud, who was very intent on avoiding the worst, that if the next day's rally was held in an enclosed space the police would remain at a distance in order to avoid confrontations.[6]

But a communiqué from the premier published in the afternoon, encouraging the police to disperse all gatherings, revived his fears. The rally set for the following evening, May 27, for which the UNEF leaders had chosen Charléty stadium—near the Cité Universitaire but also close to an occupied and very politically active factory—posed risks of disorder. Since the Communists were opposed to the celebration of what seemed to them a high mass of *gauchisme* where they were in danger of being attacked "by anarchists," one could not count on CGT marshals to keep order, as on May 13. There was doubt as to whether the UNEF marshals could channel the passions.

On the evening of the twenty-sixth, there was a meeting of the national council of the PSU, with the participation of several CFDT (Confédération Française Démocratique du Travail) leaders. Various opinions were expressed. Mendès was perplexed. And one of the union leaders observed: "In short, you are all agreed to urge Mendès to power, and all agreed to prevent him, perhaps tomorrow, from doing something to help that along, and you are all agreed to make his life impossible."

Simultaneously, there was a meeting between a government official and a group representing the UNEF and the PSU. It was agreed that the rally at Charléty stadium would not overflow the gates of the arena and that dispersion at the exits would be immediate. In return, no police force would show itself. In the course of the next day's cabinet meeting, Fouchet supported this arrangement, which Grimaud had promised to respect. The general, although he was hostile to authorization of the rally, finally accepted the advice of the prudent, all the more readily because the conclusion of the Grenelle agreements had not reduced tension among the workers: in its dilapidated state, the government could hardly fight on two fronts.[7]

All things considered, Mendès France decided to go to Charléty. It would be first of all a means of informing himself. What was the students' position? In their heart of hearts, what did they want? It would also be a gesture of solidarity, of sympathy toward a movement in which he saw a "force of renewal." "I wanted," he said, to show "what side of the barricades I was on." It would finally be a protective measure. Of course, he knew that by himself he was not capable of cutting off violence. But if he were present, the orders for tolerance that Grimaud wanted to put into effect would be better respected by the police. He thought he could play a pacifying role, all the more useful in his eyes because the most recent remarks attributed to Georges Pompidou were not reassuring. He was especially afraid of the dispersal at the end of the rally.

The crowd had occupied the space of the stadium; the green of the grass had disappeared. This sort of picnic on the grass had finally taken on its meaning. With the help of the CFDT, FEN (Fédération de l'Education Nationale), and the PSU, the UNEF had won its bet, had filled the stadium with thirty thousand young people, and especially had brought together young workers and students. But in the crowd could also be seen a number of "ordinary" people, middle managers, and bourgeois from the neighborhood who had come out of curiosity. Mendès France arrived toward eight o'clock, after the first speeches had been delivered. He was warmly greeted by the many people who recognized him. One sensed that he was moved and a little anxious. The atmosphere of the rally was not too vehement. But why were there so many attacks against the CGT and the Communists? Why was there so much incoherence?

Did he have in his pocket, as some have asserted,[8] a prepared speech that he finally kept to himself, feeling that it was not consonant with the atmosphere that prevailed at Charléty? PMF forcefully denied it: "I had always refused to speak at these demonstrations, and I did not have the intention of changing my mind that day."

After Sauvageot, Labi from the FO clerical union, and Geismar, who all fiercely criticized the CGT and the Communist Party, and after a CGT speaker who stoically argued for his union and was also applauded by part of the audience, the union leader André Barjonet stepped to the microphone. His speech provoked a wave of enthusiasm.

> I have left the CGT above all because the leaders could not or perhaps did not want to recognize that the situation we are in is truly revolutionary. Today everything is possible. But we have to organize ourselves quickly, very quickly, in an atmosphere of free discussion. The revolution demands the proliferation and the diversity of ideas.

Then Sauvageot handed the microphone to Mendès, who refused it, pointing out that he had no place speaking at a "union meeting." A bizarre argument, but a judicious decision. However capable he was of communicating with crowds, of grasping their feelings, and of confronting storms of opposition, that night his voice would probably have struck a false note. But his mere presence was enough to excite bitter feelings against him in the PCF, who saw the Charléty rally as a challenge. The next day, L'Humanité asserted that "the CGT seemed to be the favorite target of the demonstration."

With committees of support designed to promote his return to the government proliferating, Mendès France's apartment was constantly full. He was to such an extent the "providential man" that even on the right and the extreme right there were those who implored his intervention. On May 29, in *Le Monde,* there was an article by Alfred Fabre-Luce, who fifteen years earlier had published a book attacking Mendès and supporting Pinay:

> Mendès has the necessary international stature and authority. One grandeur is coming to an end, another must begin. . . . Ten years ago, an obscure conspiracy . . . brought General de Gaulle to power. The "strong" state that resulted is disappearing in the same way that it was born: in a riot. In 1958, we went to Colombey to find a "hermit." I propose an open conspiracy to find in the midst of the National Assembly another solitary man. He is respectful of the community. He will not plot to arrive at the summit of the state. It is therefore up to all of us to make him accede to that position by repeating, constantly and fraternally, during the brief time we have: Mendès to the Elysée.

Everything moved very rapidly at the time. A few hours after the Charléty rally, François Mitterrand, as though suddenly seized by irrepressible haste, declared at a press conference,

> There is no more state, and what is standing in for it does not even have the appearances of power. What De Gaulle is proposing to the French is a plebiscite. If he does not get the "yes" he demands, he will leave. What allows me to contemplate such a departure is the fact that after all General de Gaulle might understand his duty. We must prepare for this vacuum of power by considering the establishment of a "provisional caretaker government" made up of ten men chosen without excluding any group and not according to outdated balances. To form it, I think first of Pierre Mendès France. And as for the presidency of the Republic, the popular vote will decide. But I will announce it to you now: I am a candidate.

Had Mendès been informed in advance? In any event, he considered that he had been "confronted with a *fait accompli.*" He had no memory of any contact from a friend of Mitterrand's and learned of the declaration, he said, only by listening to the radio.

Like PMF's participation in the Charléty rally, this intervention has given rise to the most severe judgments. In *Le Monde* on May 30, Raymond Barrillon summed up the opinion of the majority of observers in a short article entitled "Le Tandem de demain" (Tomorrow's Tandem).

> The hypothesis of an effective vacuum of power . . . is not at all excessive. M. Daniel Cohn-Bendit, who has been expelled, is at the Sorbonne, and the workers with whose representatives a dialogue is going on are still occupying the factories. By his presence at Charléty stadium Monday evening, M. Pierre Mendès France may have given the impression to the Communist Party that he was joining an enterprise aimed at outflanking them on the left . . . but the former premier does not intend to lend his assistance to any attempt not based first of all on understanding and collaboration among all

forces of the left without exceptions. . . . Everything is, of course, not yet settled: but it is possible to foresee in such conditions the establishment of a formula and the setting up of a team that would permit both the avoidance of disaster and the assumption of leadership over the current revolutionary movement, at least those of its fractions that can be assimilated.

Mendès was more struck by the support of militant workers than by that of political personalities or a major newspaper. On the afternoon of the twenty-ninth, Eugène Descamps, general secretary of the CFDT, declared: "Mendès France is the man capable of taking on, with the parties of the left and the new forces, the responsibilities of power." Then PMF called a press conference for the evening of the twenty-ninth in the room of the Committee on Laws of the National Assembly (a significant location) to read a declaration. It was a kind of acceptance of the "Mitterrand plan."

The creation of a government of transition . . . is what the opposition of the left should put forward. . . . This government would have no meaning if it did not obtain the confidence of all those who have demonstrated their opposition to the regime, and it is obvious that the vital forces of the nation must all be brought together tomorrow to reconstruct, as M. Mitterrand has said, "without exclusions and without political balancing," within an activist government. For my part, I was touched that M. Mitterrand put my name forward. It is obvious that my cooperation is guaranteed to the men of the left and that I will not refuse the responsibilities which may be entrusted to me by the left, by the entire united left.

Did he already know that the PCF had in fact excluded him as a possibility? The condition he placed on the exercise of responsibilities— that they be "granted by the entire united left"—allowed for a way out. In any event, the Politburo of the Communist Party published that evening a declaration denouncing the "illusions of a new 'miracle man' who would be only a variant of the regime which, in ten years, has led our country to the current collapse."

This was clear. In fact, the strong men of the party, beginning with Jacques Duclos, had made their choice between Mendès and De Gaulle: for De Gaulle, against Mendès.

But there was already unfolding the extraordinary turn of events that had more effect than anything else: Mendès's actions and the decisions of the Communists included: the disappearance of General de Gaulle.

Whether it was a lucidly prepared operation, ingeniously carried out by a tactician dominating and controlling events from above and deceiving those close to him even more than his enemies, or whether the strategist's ruses were only a disguise for an immense disarray in which professional genius found the fodder for his plotting, the fact is that on the afternoon of May 29, a few hours after his "comeback" declaration, Mendès France learned, along with the rest of France, of the delay of the cabinet meeting, the departure of the general (for Colombey, it was at first rumored), and then the actual "disappearance" of the head of state late in the afternoon. The general had indeed disappeared. He was not in Colombey; he was nowhere. The state had no head and France no master. It was a void, and it was from this void that in a few hours De Gaulle would make the weapon of his resurrection. But in the meanwhile, on May 29, 1968, in the middle of the afternoon, while De Gaulle was the guest of General Massu in Baden-Baden, the "hypothesis" formulated the day before by Mitterrand and Barrillon had been realized. A power vacuum.

We must try to imagine Pierre Mendès France that evening, surrounded by his friends, encouraged to grasp the power that was there to be recreated. For ten years, he had been asserting that the government was a deception, a defiance of reason and law, an improvised construct that would collapse at one blow, that born from a riot, it would perish in a riot. Because he persisted in saying this when all the signs belied him and when to all appearances the regime was established with the solidity of a dynasty of the classical era, he had been mocked and derided. And now his prediction was realized, the old king had fled to Varennes, and, not without a wrenching feeling, he could triumph. He had been right. And he liked to be right.

Jean Daniel describes him, during that night of destiny, as having for the "first time, the feeling that history was being made." Mendès returned from a visit to Cardinal Marty, whom he had asked to do everything to avoid the police attempting to retake the Sorbonne—as before Charléty, the fear of a "bloodbath." He was, writes Daniel, "impressively calm and determined. History, which he willingly called democracy, was finally giving him the role that was his and that could only be the primary role. He believed that justice was inherent in democracy. . . . He had identified himself with democracy to the point of thinking that immanent justice, by means of the brusque end of Gaullism, would bring him back to power and consecrate him as the best of democrats."[9]

That evening, May 29, he had another meeting with Mitterrand. Despite a warm handshake, the atmosphere between the two heirs apparent was no better than it had been during the last few days. Mendès expected a discreet meeting to prepare the new government: he was exasperated to see the other leaders of the FGDS, who were out of touch with the events in progress. In any event, PMF suddenly felt far from Charléty. Mitterrand, obviously exasperated, was harsh.

"The Communists do not want you as premier. But they would agree to your having a portfolio, perhaps Education." When Mendès France retorted that the new forces—unions, students, peasants—had to be represented in the government, Mitterrand protested with respect to the students: "It's a provocation. You are going to make everything fail. You want a portfolio for Geismar." In reality, Mendès France was thinking of a representative of the CFDT. Moreover, he suggested among others the name of Jacques Monod for Education.[10]

The next day, May 30, at two in the afternoon, still smarting from this disappointing meeting, PMF paid a visit to his old friend Gaston Monnerville, who, as president of the Senate, was supposed to step in in the event of a power vacuum (which seemed to be the case with De Gaulle's disappearance). The deputy from Grenoble, observed Monnerville, was "the only one, in this stew of ambitions" who reacted in that way, respectful of legality. "With that lucidity and that clear intelligence that made his analyses so forceful, he presented a not very optimistic summary of the situation and of the difficulties that would arise for any new government."[11]

The two men were still talking at around three o'clock when a motorcyclist brought the president of the Senate a message from the Elysée which spoke of a dissolution of the National Assembly.

Less than two hours later, in fact, came the *coup de théâtre* that, in midafternoon of May 30, reversed the balance of forces. The vanished general reappeared, masked but all the more formidable at the radio microphone, launching an anathema against the "worn out politicians." And the Gaullist ranks, resurrected and reunited, fell in behind him, restoring the Fifth Republic in a few hours.

For Mendès, from this month when history had seemed to point its finger at him more imperiously than ever, there remained only a new battle to fight and some letters from notables of the Fifth Republic calling on him to take up the succession. But since the mails were barely functioning during those fevered days, these appeals from Gaullist ministers and deputies, written in the storms of May 25, 27, or 29, on the evening of Charléty or the morning of De Gaulle's disappearance, were received by Mendès only on June 3, 5, or 10, when their authors had blithely resumed their posts and forgotten the appeal made to the alternative "providential man."

PMF did not publish these letters.

27.
THE SHOCKING BEHAVIOR OF GRENOBLE

Could Mendès France have made of May 1968 what De Gaulle had made of May 1958? The state was teetering. The masses were awaiting a savior. Mendès could have used Charléty as De Gaulle had used the Forum of Algiers ten years earlier, a conspirator disguised as a mediator. "You are waiting for an arbiter, a recourse," De Gaulle had said. "To rescue you from the rebels, accept my person and my law." "To protect yourselves from the *gauchistes* and the black flag of anarchy, wear my colors and I will restore order at the cost of a drastic reform of the state and of social hierarchies," Mendès could have proposed.

He did not, because he was a legalistic democrat and because, although he had immersed himself for a few hours in the revolutionary ferment, he was not the type to storm the Winter Palace. Revolution through law—that was his rule, and he held to it. Even if there had been a René Coty or a Pflimlin to open the door for him with legalistic alibis, he would not have acted otherwise.

In short, outflanked in 1956 by an indecisive Guy Mollet, and thereby deprived of the victory of the Republican Front that was his work, Mendès France, because he had waited to be designated by law in a situation where legality was absent, found himself in June 1968 the moral leader of an abortive prerevolution.

On May 30, De Gaulle dissolved the Assembly, as Pompidou had urgently advised him to do. Elections were scheduled for June 23 and 30. From the outset, Mendès adopted a style that could be characterized as fortified by the graffiti of the student commune:

> When De Gaulle claimed he would resolve the French political crisis with a referendum which was in fact a plebiscite, I said: "One fights against a plebiscite." All the forces of the left adopted that attitude, and the government was forced to capitulate.
>
> Today we are faced not with a plebiscite but with elections. Today I say: "One wins elections." And we must win them.[1]

He knew that it would be hard, harder than in 1967, because of the circumstances, because of the evolution of the silent and acquiescent majority, and because of the opponent he had to confront.

To the pale M. Vanier, the UNR (Union pour la Nouvelle République) candidate he had swallowed whole fifteen months earlier, succeeded, as spokesman of the majority, Jean-Marcel Jeanneny, son of the former president of the Senate, who had for decades, as much as Herriot, embodied the Republic and had been in his last years a fervent supporter of the PMF of 1954. Former dean of the Grenoble Faculty of Law, former minister of social affairs for General de Gaulle, first French ambassador to Algeria, president of a commission charged with establishing serious cooperation between France and the recently emancipated colonies, this internationally renowned economist had, at bottom, a more or less Mendésist profile. In 1945, he had approved the Mendès France plan.

The major theme of his campaign would be to demonstrate that, although he admired the minister of De Gaulle, the head of the 1954 government, the planner, the decolonizer, he was now standing up, as a scrupulous republican, against the ally of the *gauchistes,* the man of the barricades who had spoken of "creating the irreversible." For a campaign based on the fears of the well-to-do, it was a weighty argument in the hands of an effective competitor.

However attenuated it may have been in the city of the Olympic games, where the climate in the university was very different from that of Paris and the social atmosphere was kept calm by the mayor's skill and the unions' prudence, the May movement had an impact on the elections. Violence had been rare, the police forces almost invisible, the demonstrations moderate. But the local bourgeoisie was no less haunted than bourgeoisies elsewhere by the angels of disorder and the black flags of anarchy.

It had been spared the barricades, but not economic anxiety. Grenoble, whose past was not so calm, had not relived earlier disorders. But the post-Olympic recession had created a climate where the smallest business failure appeared to be a disaster and where every strike seemed to announce an increase in unemployment.

Mendès France was aware of all this. And this is why his campaign was essentially directed toward showing that "Gaullist authoritarianism" was not the remedy, but the evil; not the shield, but the source of disorder. But what opponent is more difficult to combat than anxiety? What argument more difficult than one tending to prove to someone that you do not frighten him? This was all the more the case because Mendès refused to play the hypocrite. Speaking to voters of every variety, he did not attempt to dissociate himself from the students and the young people, to make them forget his visits to the Latin Quarter and his appearance at Charléty.

The relations between Mendès and Grenoble had become ambiguous since the crisis had radicalized his positions. This city of liberal traditions, which had experienced an expansion in the course of the preceding five years that was unprecedented and therefore fragile, contained simultaneously an old bourgeoisie that was hidebound and suspicious, a population of technologically sophisticated managers practically without rival in France, and a proletariat that was threatened, because of industrial mergers, with increased unemployment.

A match had been made between Grenoble and PMF in 1967, but a rather long absence[2] and his adoption of polemical positions had weakened the links established since the previous election. A substantial part of the local bourgeoisie was inalterably opposed to a Socialist leader. As for the proletariat, it was generally loyal to the PCF.

But in 1968, PMF was nonetheless the title holder and not a mere challenger. He had the more and more explicit support of the municipality and of the mayor, Dubedout, who was prodigal in his praise of their collaboration and was a popular and weighty ally. Mendès could count on very broad support among industrial managers, militants of the CFDT, and the local PSU, which held key positions in municipal government and in intellectual circles.

Given the climate in which the debate took place and the fear of a substantial number of the voters of Dauphiné, PMF's chances seemed linked to the restoration of social peace. If troubles were to recur, they would fall upon him, costing him votes of the "party of the frightened," as De Gaulle said; if they stopped, the shadow of the statesman would cover that of the friend of the insurgents, restoring to him the few hundred votes of the center that would decide the result of the election.

The competition between Mendès and Jeanneny took the form of two confrontations: a radio debate, sober and dignified; and a meeting in the same auditorium where he had debated Pompidou the year before, whose tone was so vehement that it certainly cost Mendès some votes—the votes of fear.

In the radio debate, Jeanneny argued: "It seemed to me that you placed yourself outside the Republic and outside democracy, that is, beyond respect for the laws and for universal suffrage. By your presence at the Charléty rally, you demonstrated that you were a different kind of political man from the one I had known."

PMF retorted:

For my entire life, I have been attached to the forces of renewal, for my entire life I have believed that we must have confidence in the young to assure a politics of movement and progress. I do not regret my presence at the Charléty rally, even though I do not agree with everything that was said there. . . . You have chosen authority, command, repression. For the last ten years, no one has had the feeling that they are even consulted. I have chosen dialogue: I did not believe that by doing so I was violating the rules of the Republic or of democracy.

The meeting in the auditorium in the second week of the campaign was much more violent. As during the Louviers campaign of 1958, attacks were launched against Mendès and an anti-Semitic caricature printed in a majority pamphlet, which were not worthy of his opponent. "Just as I had not personally accused Rémy Montagne ten years earlier," observed Mendès, "I did not consider Jeanneny directly responsible for the tone of the campaign in its last days. But he covered these excesses with his name."

Mendès France did not believe he was likely to win. He wrote to Marie-Claire, his confidante, what he obviously would say to no one else:

The first round comes a week from now. There is no doubt for me (I have known this for two weeks) that it will be bad and that I will be beaten in the second round. I don't want you to talk to me about it on the phone, but you have to know that this is the way things look.

This campaign reminded me from the beginning of the campaign of 1958. The cowardice of one part of the electorate, discontent with Gaullism but lacking character and courage, the accumulated foolishness of the left, and so on.

Do not think that I am sad. Of course, for years, I have been fighting for something else. But since events have turned out this way, it is better, I say it with complete serenity, that circumstances allow me to detach myself and to lead from now on a personal life, of which I have been so long deprived.

I write you all this with a good deal of cool-headedness. But it would have been better if things had turned out otherwise; but, "things being what they are," I cannot regret, at bottom, that I am now liberated.

It is probable that you will take this harder than I. Perhaps because you are younger. I am perfectly calm and I appreciate the opportunity that allows me to turn the page today, while I still have a certain number of years left to live.

The two minor candidates of the right were eliminated in the first round, and the Communist candidate, unenthusiastically, stood aside in favor of Mendès. There was a movement among the Grenoble voters to avoid the error of their Louviers counterparts in 1958 and to maintain Mendès in Parliament. But the effort came to nothing. Mendès lost, on June 30, by 132 votes. Georges Kiejman narrates the events:

> Sunday, late in the afternoon after the second round, with nothing left to do. The campaign is over, we have only to wait for the results. So we went to dinner with Marie-Hélène Estienne in a restaurant a few miles from Grenoble. I got up every ten minutes to call our headquarters to hear the results of the count; Mendès pretended to make fun of me and not to pay very much attention, but at one point he did take in what I was saying: it turned out that we were going to be beaten by a very small margin. Twice in my life I saw Mendès's face when he heard the news of an election defeat, in Evreux in 1962 and in Grenoble in 1968. Very pale, his features drawn, he always remained extremely dignified. In Evreux, in 1962, he immediately comforted the young women who were there, who had helped the campaign a great deal, and who burst into tears. In 1968, we hastily returned to headquarters to console the campaign workers.
>
> What is even more interesting for an understanding of his character is that before we had the results, while we were driving the few miles on the highway to the restaurant, Mendès had been seized by the melancholy that I had seen in him one day when he recalled the moment when, after escaping from the Clermont-Ferrand prison, he had felt a sense of vertigo at the idea of presenting himself under his false identity as a notary's clerk from Abbeville never to reappear again, so that he would lead the life of a little provincial office worker, breaking with the political battle, his family, everything—one of those fantasies to which, of course, one does not surrender, but which it is significant that one experiences. There, with a kind of thoroughly moralistic melancholy, on the outskirts of Grenoble, he murmured: "Suppose we kept going? In the end, are we really interested in all that? Suppose we don't come back?" It is rather moving to think that this solid man had a touch of Fitzgerald's novelistic evasion, melancholy, and childishness. Since, no matter what, I'm going to get bad grades, there's no point in knowing the results. Let's leave.

One hundred thirty-two votes. There was much commentary on the results of the vote. In *Le Nouvel Observateur* of July 3, René Backmann wrote:

> The initiates don't have to go to the end of the count to understand. Three names—those of the three "red" districts—and a few figures explain Mendès France's defeat. . . . He lacked 132 votes, and in those districts at least 160 Communist votes did not answer the call. That was enough.

The Machiavellianism of the PCF strategists, eager to make Mendès pay for the Charléty rally and the attacks on the CGT that were made there, obviously played a role in this distressing defeat. But, in the event, PMF seems above all to have been the victim of the party of fear. Because he was at no time willing to dissociate himself from the student movement, from the sympathy shown toward him by young people who despised the political class as a whole, because he had not wanted to make public his resignation from the PSU, whose extravagances he had disapproved for weeks, a resignation that would have won him more votes from the center (if not more transfers of Communists votes) than it would have lost on the left, he was swept away in the formidable Gaullist tidal wave and once again exiled from Parliament.

He had resisted better than almost all the others.[3] Against a substantial opponent, and in an atmosphere corrupted by rancor and fear, he had preserved the essentials of what had been won fifteen months earlier in an election conducted in a euphoric atmosphere. But the raw result was there. Whatever the value of the man who was elected, for 132 votes Grenoble had deprived itself, and deprived the Assembly and French democracy, of a brilliant representative. The city that had appeared for years as a pilot city, a laboratory for the future, a paradise for researchers, the society of tomorrow, took on some wrinkles in a few hours. Many of us, that night, cursed the shocking behavior of Grenoble.

But not François Mauriac, who was for once not very generous toward the man of Carthage. Some time later he declared to *Le Figaro littéraire:*

> God knows that I have fought for Mendès France and that I have . . . been a fervent Mendésist. But I found him unjust during the campaign that has just ended. I thought that he wasn't playing the game honestly. It is too easy to hold Pompidou responsible for the fragility of the franc.[4]

PMF responded with a long and passionate letter in which, with ten pages filled with statistics, the former premier asserted that he could not fail to respond to the accusation that he had "distorted the figures for electoral purposes," nor accept that a man like Mauriac could be "deceived by official propaganda to the extent that he endorsed its arguments and . . . turned the French away from the necessary realizations."[5]

28.
THE STONES OF SISYPHUS

Ten years earlier, Mendès France had suffered from the defeat in Louviers, administered by people who had voted for him for twenty-five years, his administrative charges, his neighbors. It was a wrenching conclusion. In Grenoble, he had just lost a battle. But his connection with the city had been too brief for him to feel personally affected. He saw himself as the victim of a political wave of national dimensions, a victim of fear, but he was ready for new battles, in Grenoble or elsewhere.

Ten months later, on April 22, 1969, in one of those self-destructive gestures which suggested a certain resemblance to Mendès France, General de Gaulle invented the most ambiguous of referendums, which destroyed his power. His resurrection on May 30, 1968, had exhausted his stupefying resources as a strategist and a fighter. Premeditated or not, suicidal or merely adventurous, he acted to take his leave of history. And he left a power vacuum.

And once again, the "other," the antithetical double, the ultimate recourse, felt all eyes turned on him. The period from May 30, 1968, to April 22, 1969, appeared to have been a reprieve or a parenthesis. Mendes's credibility was not altogether undermined either by the fever of May 1968 or by his defeat in Grenoble; the latter, in fact, seemed to have recreated around him the powerful nostalgia based on sympathy that was

422

an essential component of Mendésism. Polls at the end of 1968 showed that a majority of public opinion was still favorable to him.

On this occasion, there was no question of "killing the father," as in 1965, nor of skirting illegality as in 1968. The succession was opened according to normal procedures. De Gaulle had given way, and what remained, Gaullism without De Gaulle, was exactly what Mendès, as a fighter of Free France and a Socialist, felt most eager to combat. Did he consider reversing himself, finally agreeing to enter the contest within the constitutional framework, though he would call for its amendment from the outset?

He remained firmly opposed to the principles on which the Fifth Republic was founded and to the mechanisms by which it functioned, and he restated this position in a letter to a friend:

> The Fifth Republic has invented an extremely perfidious weapon—bipolarization. Is there a referendum? We have to vote yes or no. Is there a presidential election? There are in the end only two candidates. Is there a legislative election? There are only two broad coalitions. The system finds it advantageous to foster such a conditioning of political life. But by the same token, it prevents any serious and objective debate on the real problems; it reduces everything to a confrontation between the good and the evil and uses the Communist Party (which it never fails to assist every chance it gets) as a useful scarecrow. I have no intention of praising the previous regimes; I can nevertheless say that they were as a whole more pedagogical, that is, in the last analysis, much more democratic than the present regime.[1]

But even though, in Grenoble on April 23, he excluded his candidacy, in early May 1969, the name of Mendès France was circulating once again. The left had never been so divided. A victim of the storms of May and the wounds they had inflicted on its leader, François Mitterrand's federation had been dissolved. Guy Mollet was looking only toward the center: he was considering sponsoring Antoine Pinay. Other fractions of the left put forth the names of Alain Savary and Gaston Defferre. Never was a unifier more necessary.

A consensus began to develop in the left around PMF's candidacy, with some indication that even the Communists would support it. But on May 7, things became very clear. In a radio interview, Georges Marchais formulated the Communist veto: "Mendès France a candidate? In the name of what party, what political forces? Are we to be presented with him again as a kind of providential man? Besides, there is the past, there is Charléty. There was his own attempt to establish a Mendès France government."

Once the PCF had indicated its veto, it become impossible for Mendès or anyone else to prevent a fragmentation of the former federation.

The PSU presented Michel Rocard, who offered new ideas with an often Mendésist flavor. The PCF found the ideal candidate in Jacques Duclos, who was able to conceal his past as a Stalinist *apparatchik* behind the genial mask of a *méridional*. And what was left of the FGDS, which was laboriously preparing the birth of the new Socialist Party, finally designated Gaston Defferre.

The mayor of Marseille knew very well that the battle was hopeless, that he was swimming against the current, and that he was heading toward a rather cruel defeat. But he had no ambition to succeed De Gaulle: his aim was to rid French socialism of Guy Mollet. "I knew," he said later,

> that as candidate of the SFIO, I would automatically become leader of the party. I was no more eager to succeed Guy Mollet than I was to succeed De Gaulle. I simply wanted to dislodge him from the position of command he had occupied for twenty-five years, to provide the opportunity for a renewal.[2]

Pierre Mendès France, for his part, seeing the disarray, the anger, the "nausea" of those who had been his companions for so many years and had so often called on him, looked for a way to intervene in this confusion, if only, he said, "to broaden the movement of the non-Communist left, make a better showing, and prepare for future negotiations with the PCF."

Thus was established an alliance in which Mendès France heard something of an echo of the battles of 1954 and 1956: Wasn't it the Socialist faction embodied by Defferre, despite the mistrust and secret sabotage of Mollet, that had first allowed him to govern and then to obtain the successes of the Republican Front? But in PMF's mind the alliance very soon took on a meaning less tied to the past, turned more toward the future. Defferre let it be known that, if he were elected, Mendès would be his premier. By voting for one, one would choose the other. Thus PMF, without being a candidate for a position the structure and extent of whose power he rejected, entered the system by the back door. But he did so in order to transform it.

The intention of this bizarre candidacy was to restore the power of the premier, that is, the office that was responsible to popularly elected representatives, in relation to the power without responsibility held by the head of state. It was the reverse of what had happened in 1962. It was at least a return to the Constitution of 1958, before the general had reshaped it to his advantage by establishing the mystifying "reserved domain," which assured him absolute power in military and diplomatic affairs. These institutions and structures may very well have been established in time of war. But once the war was over, De Gaulle had hastened to broaden and personalize the powers of the president by establishing popular election to the office. It was against that evolution toward monarchy that the combined candidacy of Defferre and Mendès intended to set itself.

In theory, the project was salutary. But all indications were that it was suicidal. Many of PMF's friends urged him not to join the enterprise. His supporters in Grenoble, and his son Bernard, who did not usually get involved with his father's plans, for once tried to warn him.[3] Mendès listened a great deal, but he did not give in. He would go through with this impossible, lost campaign.

Defferre and Mendès presented their program in a manifesto on May 14. It emphasized modernization of the industrial apparatus and of education and investment in public resources—especially in housing. It naturally contained echoes of the last campaign in Grenoble and of *La République moderne.*

Their rather lugubrious campaign confronted the obvious dilemma of convincing the voters to elect them only so that they might reduce the powers they appeared to be seeking. Of course, objected Mendès France, it was not a question of men but of a program; that was even, he insisted,

> the basis of the affair. De Gaulle said: me or chaos. Pompidou repeated: me or a void. We called on the French to declare themselves on a policy. What did the candidates matter? It was on ideas, programs, a contract, that it was finally important that the voters declare themselves. We wanted to depersonalize and thereby democratize the political patterns of the country. Well, we failed, not only because we won few votes, but because we were not even able to make our position understood.

Defferre had only one objective: to eliminate Guy Mollet by occupying center stage. Mendès aimed only to abolish personal power in order to attain pluralistic and responsible democracy. These were admirable aims. But far from complementing one another, the two battles canceled each other out.

Gaston Defferre later had the grace to assume responsibility for the failure: "I was very bad," he asserted. Mendès France, for his part, agreed that he made an "error of judgment" on the chances for the enterprise. But he maintained that the theoretical objective remained valid.

In short, it was his worst defeat, even though it was shared with another. But it was a failure that could not call into question the PMF myth, the certainty that many citizens of the country had that somewhere in the French political landscape there existed an exceptional figure who could and must be called upon, a different man, who embodied a sense of the state, financial rigor, the desire for full employment, a spirit of egalitarian development, international détente, and the establishment of relations based on mutual respect with the Third World. That indeed appeared indestructible. But something that might be called the tactical credibility of the public man had been undermined.

It has often been said that De Gaulle was afflicted with farsightedness in politics, that he saw distant objectives more clearly than nearby obstacles—a great strategist but a clumsy tactician. The observation seems to apply better to Mendès France. De Gaulle often demonstrated his tactical dexterity, from the plots in Algiers in 1943 to the two "resurrection" operations in 1958 and 1968. It was rather with Mendès that the long view took precedence over the vision of the immediate, the strategist over the tactician.

The recurring parallel between De Gaulle and Mendès France, which the latter considered both "flattering" and "absurd," came up again at the general's death on November 9, 1970, on the eve of his eightieth birthday. Mendès published a long article on De Gaulle in *Le Monde* on November 12.

Rather than noting the homage from an opponent to the general's past services, people were surprised that the bitterness of Mendès's refusal of 1958 had not been softened by time or the circumstances. PMF continued to maintain that the peace in Algeria had been "the worst" imaginable, that the institutions would not hold up "without very broad modifications," and that, in foreign policy itself, the general's glory, "the well-understood interest of France should have had more place than susceptibility, pride, and authoritarianism."

The conclusion to this apparently bitter funeral oration was in an entirely different tone, returning to the great days of Free France. Then, wrote Mendès:

> De Gaulle was the interpreter and the instrument of the nation in its true destiny. Because of that epic adventure, still living in our memories and our hearts, and with an emotion that later divergences in no way change, we enter into mourning today. Such as eternity now has made him, we salute the man who, in the storm in which they almost perished, led the struggle for honor and for freedom.

In the months of 1971 and 1972, when the fragments of the Socialist puzzle were coming together and the Common Program was being forged, Pierre Mendès France was no longer called on by the actors of the drama. He was the great forgotten man. Was it only because he was often traveling? He took a long journey through Asia with Marie-Claire, whom he married in 1971.

From his notes, he derived a book, *Dialogues avec l'Asie d'aujourd'hui* (Dialogues with Today's Asia), which concludes with these words:

Suppose the small and medium-sized nations one day decided to extricate themselves from outside interventions, to take their own interests in hand, to settle by themselves their affairs and their conflicts?

It is only a dream, of course. But I believe in the virtue of those dreams that, from generation to generation, although they have rocked human misery to sleep, have also engendered its progress. History has shown that resolute small nations, demonstrating to the world their will to determine themselves freely, imposing on themselves the discipline, and if necessary, the sacrifices they must, in the end hold irresistible cards, and also that it is possible for them to increase their resources by coming together in precise agreements.

He was preparing to run in the 1973 legislative elections in Grenoble when, in September 1972, he suffered a second heart attack. For weeks, there was fear for his life. This second attack was much more serious than the one he had suffered at the death of Lily. Could he recover in time, be ready for March 5, 1973? Week by week, he recovered slowly. Friends and emissaries arrived from Grenoble: "A campaign is not necessary for success. A simple appearance will be enough. Grenoble knows you, has confidence in you. Say yes, and you will be elected."

He said no. He was enough of a democrat not to accept an office, even offered quite legally by popular vote, if he was not certain that he could assume all its obligations. Could he impose on the voters a part-time deputy who could not present his program to them in debate with his opponents, a man who risked being prevented for a while from representing them in Parliament?

"I had no luck," he said later. "Within a very few weeks I would have been able to appear properly before the voters of Grenoble. I would have been overjoyed to represent them again. But not by half-measures."

By making this decision, inspired by the very acute sense of responsibility that symbolizes and, in a sense, sums up his concept of public life, Pierre Mendès France was aware that he was putting an end to his political career. Whatever the future turns of history and the emergencies France would have to confront, the man of June 1954 had chosen to go into retirement. He no longer considered himself as a "professional" of politics, as an integral part of that "class" among whom the Republic, by means of popular voting and the functioning of the parties, chose those responsible for its management.

Mendès France did not think it necessary to mark this important decision for French democracy with a solemn declaration or a colorful farewell. He was content to draw the lesson from a situation—the state of his health—which, at sixty-five, he thought, made impossible for him the "full use" of his faculties, his competence, and his devotion to the public welfare.

Exiled from the highest positions in the Fifth Republic by his principles and by many enmities, and from representing Grenoble by his illness,
was all that was left to Mendès France the function of oracle and adviser?
Would he thereafter have to be content with the role of writer or
memorialist—a role he admirably fulfilled by publishing, in collaboration
with Jean Botherel, *Choisir* (To Choose) an autobiography in the form of
dialogues? This was not certain. But in 1975 his health was again to
deteriorate.

In April 1974, when the sudden death of Georges Pompidou opened
the succession again, PMF was in Geneva presenting *Choisir,* which was
very successful. The Swiss journalists bombarded him with questions.
Would he intervene? Would he run? Support a candidate? "I will no doubt
be asked to take on responsibilities and to declare in favor of one candidate or another." (He did not say which one, but everyone knew that,
since François Mitterrand was a candidate, he would receive Mendès's
support.) In any event, he pointed out, the campaign "should not be an
affair of persons, but of fundamental choices."

In fact, he supported Mitterrand with more dynamism than he had in
1965. Moreover, this campaign was much more geared toward "fundamental choices" than the one that had pitted the most brilliant representative of the opposition against personal power. This time, his former
interior minister was the leader of the Socialist Party, with which PMF
recognized his connection. Mitterrand's arguments were based on a fundamental social choice. How could he not demonstrate his solidarity, his
support, and his good will?

Mendès France was generous with his support, emphasizing on sev-
eral occasions the "renewal" of French socialism due to the efforts of
François Mitterrand. The latter, according to his biographer Franz-Olivier
Giesbert, drawing up the list of the "united left" government in May 1974
in case of a victory against Valéry Giscard d'Estaing, had decided to ask
Mendès to take on Foreign Affairs.

He held five or six meetings in support of Mitterrand, presuming on
his strength. His doctor put him on guard, and immediately after the
unsuccessful campaign he had to be hastily hospitalized for a two-month
stay.

He was thus forced into retirement by fragile health, a retirement that
affected this man of action more than it would have others. He worked, of
course, read a lot, and maintained contacts. And the opportunity would
again arise to carry out important tasks.

He felt it incumbent on him, above all, to work for peace in Palestine.
Was Mendès France a Zionist or an anti-Zionist? This is an idle
question about a man who had so thoroughly invested himself in the

national fate of France and become so identified with it that he had appeared for more than thirty-five years as an embodiment of French democracy. As Léon Blum so sharply recalled with reference to his own history, he was a Jew who had found his fatherland in the country of Descartes and Hugo.

Profoundly integrated into the secular and republican civilization of France, PMF found his cultural universe defined if not delimited by Jules Ferry and Jean Jaurès, Zola and Herriot, Blum and De Gaulle. However unworthy and revolting the treatment he had received from the Vichy tribunals which had attempted to exclude him from the national community, he had found in that no reason to question the very old French roots of the Mendès France family. But he joyfully greeted the creation of the state of Israel, the accomplishment of a historical hope, and the forge for a Jewish future.

Quoting him, we have already given a Sartrian definition of his Jewish consciousness and described his Judaism as a reverse image of anti-Semitism. The ordeals he had gone through and the flourishing of a Jewish renaissance in the diaspora, notably in France, may have reshaped this basic consciousness in a more positive direction. Similarly, his feeling of solidarity toward Israel could only have been intensified by the terrorism that assailed it and by the suicidal policies of a government like that of Begin. His sympathy was quite obviously of a rather different kind from that he felt, however strongly, for Vietnam in crisis or Tunisia in its ordeal.

From 1948 to 1956, from the proclamation of the Jewish state to the Suez war, there were no divergences between Mendès France and the state of Israel. Several of the founders were his friends. He took every opportunity to proclaim his admiration for David Ben-Gurion or Golda Meir. It was known that he favored the emancipation of the Arabs, and he had demonstrated this, when he was in power, in Tunisia. But this could not be at the expense of Israel, and his praise of Bourguiba owed a good deal to the very particular attitude of the Tunisian leader in this area, to the distrust displayed in Tunis toward a certain form of bellicose pan-Arabism.

In 1956, a dissonance appeared over Suez. PMF did not doubt Israel's right to fight, in view of the open threats from Nasser's Egypt, the blocking of free navigation of its ships through the Suez Canal, and the fact that Egypt was free to act after the British evacuation. But in attacking as he had the strategy of Guy Mollet and Anthony Eden, Mendès France was indirectly criticizing Ben-Gurion and his government, who, for very specific reasons, and encouraged to do so by French leaders, had joined the suicidal spasm of the two ebbing empires.

By abstaining in the vote on the Suez expedition (he had intended to

vote against but refused in order to avoid provoking too great a disturbance in the Radical Party), PMF opened a breach. He was one of the
very few non-Communist French public men not to approve the operation
that concluded with an Israeli triumph, even though Nasser remained in
place. He very clearly detected the links that had just been forged between French nationalism and the Jewish state. The most vociferous pro-
Israeli forces in France were thenceforth recruited, in Algiers as in Paris,
in traditionally anti-Semitic circles. This was an alarming development,
for they would be allies only as long as the Algerian War lasted. In the
meanwhile, they would drive away real friends of Israel and trouble the
indestructible sympathy of others.

He very early made the decisive remark that the reason for the success of Israel "must be looked for in the level of culture and of general
education of the population . . . a specific element of Israeli reality."
Although one may find hardly convincing the traveler's arguments that
Israel could one day do without external aid, his forceful affirmation of
the permanence of Israel carries conviction: "The Israeli political fact is
now encrusted in geography and history; it has imposed itself, it has
planted deep roots in the soil, it has brought together a million newcomers, and it will not be extirpated." This was the heart of the matter and the
heart of Mendès's thinking. And on this point he never varied.

Interviewed by *Paris-Presse* a few months after the Six Day War of
1967,[4] Mendès France declared:

> Because it has won, the Israeli government must be more active diplo-
> matically. It must not give its opponents any pretext to accuse it of wanting to
> annex territories and integrate non-Israeli populations.
>
> The Israeli government would be well advised, as rapidly as possible, to
> publish a peace program, showing its territorial disinterestedness, and also
> bringing into the light the need to remove this zone of the world from the
> intrigues of the great powers. This would be a way, over the heads of govern-
> ments, to establish a dialogue with the peoples.

And he added this observation: "France could have exercised its
influence in Jerusalem in this sense, if it had not, in the course of the last
six months, adopted such a systematically anti-Israeli attitude."

From then on, Mendès would fight on two fronts. Denouncing the
harshness of Gaullist diplomacy toward Israel, he also fought as a loyal
friend to urge Israel toward more boldness in seeking an accommodation
with the Arab world.

He used his influence in two major areas. Just as, between 1950 and
1954, he had argued for a direct understanding between France and the
Vietminh without going through any international procedure involving the
great powers, he urged that direct contacts be established among the

states of the region. The superpowers could serve no purpose but incidentally to promote their interests and to swallow up those of the small nations in the play of their giant intrigue.

Secondly, the Palestinians were now at the center of the debate. From 1967 on, it appeared that no solution would be durable unless it gave this original people a territory. This never led PMF to approve or even to understand the kind of combat that for years made up the visible activity of Yasser Arafat and his friends. But even though they demonstrated it by horrible means, these men had rights. After responding to the challenge and fighting against terrorism, only by recognition of those rights could violence be stopped in the long run.

Pierre Mendès France had no prefabricated solution to propose. In what form could Palestinian aspirations be realized without putting the survival of Israel in danger? It was only by consultation, conversation, debate, followed by negotiation, that this question could be answered. On this point, as on many others, he shared the views of his friend Nahum Goldmann, then president of the Jewish World Congress.

In 1976, after a two-week stay in Israel, Mendès launched in *Le Nouvel Observateur* a kind of appeal to the Jewish state:

Israel must create a new situation, and to do that make a significant gesture, remove the obstacle that is blocking everything. You know what that gesture should be: say to the Palestinians that you intend to place no obstacles in the way of their freedom and their rights. . . . With all my heart, I would prefer that Israel take the first step. To avoid a new Munich. An offer from Israel, in any event, is worth more than a forced solution, even if it is almost the same.

And a few days later, during the "Twelve Hours for Israel" demonstration, before tens of thousands of listeners who were unreservedly attached to the Jewish state, he added:

We share the desire to make known or support for the survival of a nation to which all democrats are attached. . . . One can be a friend of Israel and still criticize certain aspects of Israeli policy. We are not always in agreement with certain actions, or failures to act, on the part of Israel, and the men who lead Israel are fallible like all others.

Not everyone liked this firmness, but it soon led to his being recognized by the Palestinians as an intermediary and an arbiter for essential conversations.

On September 24, 1976, the Israeli daily, *Yedioth Ahronoth,* published the following dispatch:

Pierre Mendès France has organized meetings in Paris between Israeli figures of the left and Palestinian figures close to the PLO. The most recent of these meetings took place, it is believed, on September 11. The deputy "Lyova" Eliav met with a Palestinian whose name cannot be revealed for security reasons. . . . Two other similar meetings organized by Mendès France had taken place in the spring and in early summer. M. Mendès France has refused to confirm or deny this report. "The less talk there is about these meetings, the better it will be," he said.

A few weeks later in *Le Monde,* one of the best spokesmen of the Israeli left, Ammon Kapeliouk, presented, with some variants, the history of these mysterious meetings:

In the spring of 1976, an emissary from Paris met Reserve General Matti Peled, president of the [Israeli] Council [for Israeli-Palestinian Peace] and professor of modern Arab literature at Tel Aviv University, at his home near Jerusalem, and announced to him that members of the leadership of the PLO wanted to meet him and his comrades to begin discussions. General Peled agreed, even though he knew that contacts with the PLO were considered by the majority of Israeli public opinion as "anti-Israeli" acts.

The first meeting did not take place until some months had passed. On July 21, General Peled left for Paris to meet members of the PLO. The conversations lasted for two days. They discussed ways of attaining peace on the basis of the existence of two states in Palestine. . . .

The conversations took place in Paris or its suburbs, and once in the south of France, in Pierre Mendès France's summer home. The two sides had come to ask his advice. He encouraged them, while advocating a great deal of prudence. The PLO representative in all the meetings was Doctor Sertawi, a member of the central committee who was close to Arafat. He was accompanied by another representative, sometimes two, who were also accredited by the PLO leadership. Unlike the PLO members, who were official figures, the Israelis came from the opposition, at least as far as the Palestinian problem was concerned. General Peled, one of the heroes of the Six Day War, participated in four of the five meetings.[5]

He was the only Israeli representative in two of the meetings. In another, the only Israeli representative was deputy Eliav. All the Israelis were Zionists, and almost all men of the left.

According to Mendès himself, his role, although less central than *Yedioth Ahronoth* asserted, was more important than Kapeliouk suggested:

I had always had contacts with a certain number of people in the Arab countries and in militant Arab circles. Without any intimacy or permanent relations, the prevailing idea was that I was an interlocutor who was not a priori antagonistic or hostile toward them. On the Israeli side, I had many friends, especially on the left. At one point, a certain number of Israeli peace activists established, I don't really know how, contact with Palestinian elements who were also looking for dialogue: Sertawi personified this orientation fairly well. Arafat was in favor of such an attempt. Rather quickly, both sides arrived at the notion that it wouldn't be a bad idea to have a "moderator," and both sides asked me if I would agree to play that role. That was how I found myself involved in a whole series of conversations, some of which took place in my living room.

These meetings were surrounded with great precautions, which I encouraged the participants to take. The atmosphere was relatively calm. The conversations were rather curious. On both sides, they said: "We are here in a private capacity, we represent no one. Therefore, we are speaking completely freely."

The fact remains that Sertawi would have done nothing if he had not had a green light from Arafat. At certain points, he asked his Israeli partners for time to "consult"—he was not asked whom. As for Rabin, who was then head of the Israeli government, he regularly received reports of what was said, and he sometimes added: "Keep me posted." There were even times when some kind of understanding was reached at the summit, even though both sides pretended to ignore one another.

With reference to conversations like these, one can obviously not speak of negotiations, since the two governments, if I can use that word, did not recognize one another. At one point, an extraordinary thing happened: Begin demanded that Peled, Eliav, and the others be indicted for contact with the enemy, and there was a very dramatic debate in the Knesset. Begin's proposal was rejected. Then Eliav mounted the rostrum and declared: "Absolutely, we did it, and we'll do it again!" The fact that the Knesset, without approving Eliav and Peled, refused to condemn them, was after all rather encouraging.

Plans were drawn up. Senghor, seeing alternately the Israelis and the Palestinians, had taken the initiative of organizing a meeting in Dakar. Then there was a proposal for a meeting of intellectuals in Paris, and so on.

Unfortunately, none of this really took shape, and in spite of many efforts and much expenditure of time, none of the initiatives of this period amounted to anything.

I continued to see both sides, and the very fact that they wished to do so was itself significant. But the conversations as such were suspended. Not broken off, suspended. Then came Sadat's *coup de théâtre.*

Mendès France was a privileged witness to Sadat's celebrated visit to Jerusalem in November 1977. A few days later I had the opportunity to record his impressions for *Le Nouvel Observateur.* He was in very high spirits, rather unusual for him:

Contrary to what has been said, I had nothing to do with the event that Sadat's visit represents. . . .

When I went to Tel Aviv, it was only to participate in a symposium organized by an Israeli journal of the left, *New Outlook,* for an Arab–Israeli dialogue. [There were] Palestinians . . . of rather diverse tendencies. Some of them were openly (and sometimes aggressively) nationalistic, and did not at all hide their sympathies for the PLO, even if they did not represent it officially. And they spoke about Palestinian self-determination, the Palestine Liberation Organization, and the evacuation of Israeli forces. . . .

I saw Sadat's arrival at the airport on television; the plane advanced slowly, slowly, it was overwhelming! No one had been seen yet, the plane door wasn't even open, but that plane gently moving forward, and then the hymns! Many people told me: "We wept." We knew that we owed that feeling to Sadat. Later, he was able to remain the man who made the end of the nightmare possible. . . . I have never seen such feeling, such enthusiasm. People were dancing in the streets. I really think that everyone was impressed and moved and that public opinion was suddenly seized by an immense hope for peace. . . .

The establishment is obviously more reserved. What has changed especially is the people, I would even say the little people, that is, the Sephardim, the poor ones, victims of racist slurs. . . . If Begin proposes concessions tomorrow, even substantial ones, he will have 90 percent of the votes. . . . You would now find in Israel a majority that would say: "We must, of course, take security precautions, perhaps install electronic devices near the borders (as there are in the Sinai) which will allow us to conduct surveillance of the other side; there will have to be transitions, methods to discuss. There remains a basic question: allowing the Palestinians to set their own destiny." . . .

If everyone agrees that X, Y, or Z, member or not, sympathizer or not of the PLO, elected or not, should participate in a negotiation and be considered as a representative of the Palestinians, I would be very happy. But the way things have developed over the years has had as a result the fact that the PLO has more and more taken on the appearance of a spokesman. I am not saying that it is "representative," since its leaders have not been elected; but, they have assumed a prominence and a political stature that are undeniable.

I do not think that the PLO by itself represents the whole of the Palestinian population. There are people who are not pro-PLO. King Hussein . . . asserts that, if there were an absolutely free and impartial popular consultation, there would be a majority for him. . . . The people have to declare themselves.

Begin? [He] is a very peculiar figure. He is a fanatic. What he has been saying for forty years he thinks viscerally, which is very respectable, but has perhaps not prepared him for compromises. Is he capable today of making the necessary decisions? I am a little afraid of his convictions because they are deeply sincere. . . .

I think that the Palestinians—especially the political strategists of the PLO—made a great mistake when they believed that their grand designs would be realized thanks to the aid of the Arab governments alone. On the diplomatic front, they have made some gains—Rabat, the UN—but there is an interlocutor they have never taken into account—the state of Israel. One can cause Israel a great deal of harm, but one cannot really extirpate it. There will have to come, in one way or another, a kind of coexistence, and the Palestinians have not paid enough attention to that future. . . .

Whatever the word and the techniques that will be used . . . it is the principle of self-determination that can save face for everyone. It is difficult for the Israelis to recognize the PLO; but they can agree to have the Palestinian population freely express its aspirations. When the Israelis, in the midst of the worst threats, desperately asked to survive, that meant: we want to be free citizens. They cannot refuse that to others.

If tomorrow Sadat can say to the Palestinians and to the Arab world as a whole: "I am the one who brought you that," most of the recriminations against him, from the Syrians or the Palestinians, will become attenuated or will quickly cease. It will have been proven that he was right in his undertaking.

Three years later, Mendès France, considering the same realities, added something to these remarks made in an atmosphere of euphoria. Neither Sadat's Israeli hosts nor the Arabs of the Rejection Front had agreed to modify their intransigence on the Palestinian question. From the great universal hope of November 1977, there survived only the "politics of Camp David," the separate peace between Israel and Egypt, an important gain, but also a deviation, a fragmentation of the great hope that had been provoked by Anwar El-Sadat:

I said to myself at that moment[6] that, although the principal problem was not between Israel and Egypt, it was nevertheless impossible that everything, including the most difficult, the Palestinian problem, would not be changed by it. I must say that this was also the sense of a large number of Palestinians I saw at the time—practically all the mayors of the occupied territories on the West Bank. And I think that Arafat himself, at the beginning, hoped for something.

But there is on the one hand the Rejection Front, which has been very violent; and on the other there is the fact that Sadat did not name the PLO from the podium of the Knesset, which may have been a mistake: he could have spoken its name without making too precise a commitment. And there is the fact that Begin has been even more blinkered and negative than I feared.

In any event, the most sectarian and hard-line elements have taken the lead, and today everything is at a standstill. After an initiative as extraordinary as Sadat's! It is really one of the great missed opportunities of our time.

Mendès was determined to make new contributions to the Israeli–Arab peace that he might embody as the heir of a Semitism imbued with coexistence.

He was not the kind of man who would give up. He had other visitors to the austere living room of his apartment. If he thought himself entrusted with a mission that would crown his career as a negotiator, a promoter of development, and a democrat, it was with the mission of helping to make peace in Palestine.

He knew very well that peace is always made by the combatants. But he had seen, from Geneva to kilometer 101 of the Cairo–Jerusalem road, that between one hand and another the gesture of a third could be helpful.

29.
MAKING REALITY RATIONAL

No other French statesman had ever prepared himself so thoroughly to manage, reshape, or, if necessary, revolutionize the economy. Neither Poincaré, nor Caillaux, nor Reynaud had plowed that field so precociously or with such determination. At twenty-one, Mendès France published a refutation of Poincaré's prestigious stabilization program. He was twenty-seven when he demolished the fiscal reform of his former teacher Germain-Martin on the floor of the Chamber of Deputies, and thirty-one when he coauthorized the first French planning program with Georges Boris. Finally, at thirty-eight, he was called by De Gaulle to reinvent the French economy that had just been wrested from the occupation forces.

Would he become a Colbert or a Turgot, a Guizot or a Baron Louis? Circumstances and people together urged on him the role of thoughtful economic manager. And this was his natural vocation. The young Mendès did not need to meet Georges Boris, to read Keynes, or to be chosen for this purpose by Blum and then De Gaulle in order to devote his life to the organization of production and exchange in the French community. The only "business" that interested him was the business of the state. Devoting himself from the outset to public service, despite his legal training, he served above all the public wealth.

History did its best to tear him away from this dominant vocation and to impose other tasks on him. Out of the 245 days he was granted to exercise power, fewer than 30 were given over to what the coauthor of *La Science économique et l'action* had been preparing himself for during the preceding twenty-five years. In a sense, the storms of the time not only cut off his mission but they deprived PMF of Mendès France.

Of course the public man had come into being before June 17, 1954, and he outlived February 5, 1955. As minister from 1943 to 1945, governor of the World Bank, French representative to the United Nations Social and Economic Council, interlocutor of Lord Keynes at Bretton Woods, and parliamentary prosecutor who, for nine long years, predicted the disaster that was to swallow up the Fourth Republic because it favored unproductive over productive expenditures, by his actions and his words, Mendès France brought to fruition the extraordinary intellectual baggage he had developed since adolescence and imposed his authority.

Because that authority was for many years exercised in opposition, his activity in this area has often been characterized as that of a Cassandra. This amounts to attributing a vast background in economics to the Trojan heroine with the piercing gaze. Mendès did not present himself as a prophet. He was satisfied with keeping accounts, studying trends and production statistics, and comparing election promises to government actions. Like artistic genius, political lucidity is made up primarily of attentiveness. This Cassandra did not listen to voices: he read reports and statistics, but with a system of interpretation.

Mendès's system was made up of three or four principles, linked first of all to those aspects of his nature that were rooted in reality; second, to the exuberance of his voluntarist imagination; and finally to what he had learned from long acquaintance with classical and modern economists, from Smith to Ricardo, from Say to Keynes, from Veblen to Leontieff, and from Galbraith to Perroux.

He had one fundamental principle: scrupulous attention to facts and figures. This has been characterized as "rigor," but it is merely respect for reality. And he had one essential idea: everything in the economy is in a state of flux. On the basis of these accounting principles, what is important is not equilibrium, but the dynamism linked to a certain form of disequilibrium; not stability, but flux; not wealth, but the production of resources; not stasis, but movement. (This might be called Darwinism or existentialist economics. In any case, it was a condemnation of monetarist essentialism, of the received religion of "balanced budgets," nest eggs, and the gold standard.) There was one important theme: the need constantly to distinguish between particular interests and the common interest—the celebrated "general interest" of the Jacobins—which does not flow automatically from the sum of particular interests; hence the necessity of the Plan, around which democracy would function and which would lead to full employment, a basic prerequisite to the harmonious creation of wealth in view of a just system of distribution. Finally, he had a strategy: as far as public wealth was concerned, the monetary had to be subordinate to the economic, which was in turn subordinate to social considerations, everything in the end being a question of politics.

On the basis of these few principles, we can see a strong continuity in the policies of Mendès France the economist—from the 1934 debate on fiscal reform (where the accent was placed on a more *just* distribution of burdens), to the program for the 1938 Plan (where the emphasis was placed on the state's stimulation of *full employment* through arms production), and to the financial stabilization effort of 1944 (focused on principles of action and a return to *reality*, in order to establish the foundations of the liberated nation's economy on precise data and a correct relationship between production and expenditures).

It is worth pausing for a moment over the great conflict of 1944–1945, which has a little hastily been summed up as a dialogue between Mendès and Pleven, while it was also a debate between Pierre Mendès France and General de Gaulle, between PMF and the great majority of the SFIO, between Mendès and the entirety of the Communist Party and the CGT, that is, all those who wanted to distribute without possessing, to gain political credit without controlling financial resources. There are few texts in which this advocate of the general welfare expressed himself better than in his January 1945 letter of resignation to Charles de Gaulle.

This exemplary lesson in political pedagogy, which remained buried for years in the general's files (although its recipient admirably published it nearly ten years later), expressed the essentials of its author's thought: voluntaristic justice supported by accounting realities. This is the dual message whose terms, for many years, established the confines of Mendès's teaching considered in its defensive aspects: calling attention to the realities of the situation, and opposition to the surrender to inflation and unproductive expenditures. But this view neglected to some extent the third facet of the analysis: dynamism, movement, productive investment, and expansion through the Plan.

Since the French political elite denied him the opportunity to put these ideas into practice, confining him to the role of the slightly dyspeptic "reasoner" of Molière's plays, he expressed himself in a book, *La Science économique et l'action,* written in collaboration with his friend Gabriel Ardant and published by UNESCO in early 1954 (a few months before his investiture as premier by the National Assembly). The London *Sunday Times* published a very important review of the work on June 13, 1955.

The British reviewer, Ray Harrod, expressing surprise that a prime minister (and a French one to boot) demonstrated such extensive background in an area for which the French were not particularly noted, wrote:

Keynes is the hero of this book. This presentation of his ideas shows that the authors have a deep understanding of them, and one wonders what British statesman could pass such an examination. . . . The critique of the mistakes committed before the intervention of Keynes is so remarkable that I know of no British or American work that can be compared to this one for the lucidity and accuracy of its perspectives.

Admiring without reservation the interpretation of Keynesianism offered by Mendès and Ardant, the *Sunday Times* reviewer expressed only one regret: that they had almost nothing to say about one of its implications, the welfare state created by the Labour Party disciples of the author of *The General Theory*. The concept and the program were nonetheless in profound consonance with the thought of Pierre Mendès France. What is "democratic planning" but the means of guaranteeing a similar form of government and a similar future to the national community?

It has been said that, granted power in 1954—power that was hardly more than a mandate from Parliament to rid it of Indochina and, incidentally, to lance the European boil—Pierre Mendès France did not find the time to put his economic thought into effect. Delegating control over the French economy in a period of relative stability to a clever manager, in order to be able to devote himself fully to the dramatic negotiations over Indochina, Tunisia, and Europe, he was able merely to initiate the execution of his grand design: the redirection of the French productive apparatus, agricultural as well as industrial, toward the ends of productivity and justice. And justice could take the form of public health, which is why the first reform had to do with sugar beet cultivation, that is, with overproduction of alcohol (which might be less counterindicated today in a period of oil shortage), that is, with the struggle against alcoholism, a plague which, in the final analysis, particularly affected the underprivileged classes. Thus, as was often the case with him, moralism became involved with a plan originating in considerations of production, giving it its real meaning.

The most interesting economic program of his 245-day government was nevertheless the one dealing with low-cost housing construction. As deputy from Eure, he had carried on a long correspondence with an expert in the area, Paul Grunebaum-Ballin, who, after having been Briand's righthand man, then one of Léon Blum's advisers, and then a close associate of Colonel de Gaulle, had, as a colleague of Minister Sellier, established himself as a proponent of the development of low-rent housing during the Popular Front.

From the moment his government was installed, PMF oriented the committee of nine experts presided over by Claude Gruson in this direction. It was agreed that a bold plan for low-cost housing construction, like rearmament in 1938, ought to be the stimulus for the expansion the government was looking for through full employment and productive invest-ment. The budgetary resources made available for the program nevertheless remained too far below what Mendès's brain trust had antici-pated to enable what was accomplished to correspond at all to what had been imagined. And so, his eight months of power did not grant the interventionist Mendès France the opportunity to make his mark on the French economy.

Speaking at the April 1958 seminar of the Institut d'Etudes Politiques devoted to the 1954 government, Jean-Marcel Jeanneny expressed this judgment:

> Mendès France's politics was based on the long term. Obviously, he could not have thought that he would achieve spectacular results in six months or a year. He did not hesitate to make unpopular decisions, convinced as he was that they would produce results ten years later. But for this he received no political rewards.
>
> In sum, the balance sheet of these economic policies is rather thin, although he cannot really be criticized for this fact, not only because he did not have time to deal with them, but above all because the process had begun before his election through the application of his ideas, ideas to which he had given a striking and official expression in his inaugural speech.

Five years later, Pierre Mendès France joined the Socialist move-ment. This move involved no substantial change in his economic vision, except by universalizing it, making clearer to him the urgency of struc-tural reforms. In two 1970 letters to his young colleague and friend, Claude Nicolet, he explained this point clearly:

> I have never considered myself a Marxist, and although I have always, even when I belonged to the Radical party, anticipated evolution toward socialism, that does not imply that I accepted theories and doctrines that go back a hundred years and which, in any case, cannot be adapted to the present situation.
>
> Without being a Marxist, I believe very strongly that there are very close relations between economic structures and political forms. If one were to believe that economic, agricultural, social, and monetary structures could be changed without dealing with the problems connected with the structure of society itself and the actions and interactions of social classes with one another, one would be sadly mistaken.

This thinking and this terminology are typical. The formulation "ac-tions and interactions" replaces "class struggle" to indicate clearly the complexity of modern social mechanisms where interpenetration is as strongly evident as confrontation, and where structures shift and rear-range themselves in response to crises, expansions, wars, and cultural and technological revolutions.

The complexity and mobility of contemporary society seemed so basic to him that he often stressed the elements that capitalism and social-ism should borrow from one another. Whatever his ideological choices might have been, clearly asserted from 1959 on, one could almost formu-late "Mendès's theorem" in these terms: just as a capitalist program has no chance of success except insofar as it borrows procedures and methods from socialism, so a Socialist plan will succeed only insofar as it assimilates the techniques and the dynamism of capitalism. The idea ap-pears on several occasions in the second version of *La Science écono-mique et l'action,* thoroughly revised in 1973 (again in collaboration with Gabriel Ardant), and published under the title *Science économique et lucidité politique* (Economic Science and Political Lucidity).

Before setting out multiple arguments in favor of socialism, toward which the lives of both authors had long been tending, concluding with the hope for "a civilization which would finally recognize the primacy of the needs and interests of the greatest number, that is, a civilization of the Socialist variety," Mendès and Ardant emphasized the growing complex-ity of contemporary societies and the consequent complexity of the solu-tions that should be favored:

> Because of this . . . complexity . . . we cannot be satisfied with some sort of general, indiscriminate, or blind activity. [At this point] we can recognize the usefulness of mechanisms whose importance has not always been clearly grasped by the most modern economists. One of the great problems of the present, for example, involves harmonizing the play of market forces with effective planning. The market allows consumers to express choices, allows users to make their needs known, and the governments of the Socialist countries have become aware of this fact. It is nevertheless true that, when profound reforms are required, when organic transformations have become necessary, when it is a question of overcoming egotistical interests (even if they are neither illegal nor illegitimate), planning must take control.

Take control? If there is one constant with PMF, it is the notion that the Plan, kernel or source of economic activity, is also the kernel and source of democratic life. It is the focus of the debate, the basis on which the government must be organized, the subject with which Parliament must concern itself. Developed by citizens at the regional, then at the national level, authenticated and then criticized by elected officials, the Plan should be the legislative contract between the head of government and the Parliament. This is the primary emphasis of *La République mo-derne.*

Even though it might be categorized by ideologues as a Scandina-vian-style reformism giving rather substantial place to the laws of the market, tending toward the dominance of a rationalism of the plan with a view to channeling savings in the direction of the general interest before reshaping the structures of society, and placing the emphasis on control over the decision-making powers of producers rather than on the suppression of private property, Mendès's socialism had an international dimension that gave it a measure of grandeur.

No one in France sensed sooner or more strongly the emergence of traditional societies or foresaw the necessary consequences for Europe and the West more clearly than this patriotic Jacobin. As early as 1946, along with his friend Boris at the UN Economic and Social Council, he became aware of this immense flowering of civilizations and of hopes. He saw in this, as he often reiterated, the primary phenomenon of our time.

And he acted accordingly. Not only did he draw the conclusion that it was necessary to modify profoundly the political relationships between dominant states and provisionally dominated nations, but also that economic relations between the two systems, industrialized and underdeveloped, had to be reinvented. The notion that the real problems of the contemporary world have less to do with East–West than with North–South relations has become a banality. He had been thinking and saying as much for thirty years.

The boldest conclusion that he drew from these considerations was the support he gave to the idea of a currency based on raw materials. Not that this proposal had as its principal motive the encouragement of dependent or "peripheral" economies; it was first of all a homage to reality. But it is a fact that, once established, it would favor countries producing raw materials with unstable prices, like copper, vanilla, and coffee. He has often been called the father of the idea, but he declined the honor, pointing out that it was invented by the American Graham and the Australian Goudrian, promoted by Nicholas Kaldor and Jan Tiberghen, and popularized by Raul Prebitsch and John Kenneth Galbraith. But in *Choisir* he explained this form of economy with a genuinely paternal warmth:

> It is easy to ridicule "rubber currency" and "chocolate currency"; but this amounts to an impartial, objective, and neutral solution which can, for this reason, be accepted by everyone. . . . It consists in monetizing stocks of raw materials, mineral or agricultural. Instead of basing the world financial system on a single commodity, gold, it is necessary to establish "cash" reserves of diversified stocks of commodities required by world consumption.

Explaining that the International Monetary Fund would naturally be the regulatory organ for the system, Mendès France observed that what was important was that the international currency defined in this way, a kind of reserve currency, "should always correspond to stabilizing stocks, whose composition would be public and verifiable." Thus, he concluded, "everything rests upon the most concrete reality."

Pierre Mendès France presented this suggestion to the Socialist conference of Grenoble in 1966, without convincing all his listeners. Michel Rocard and Robert Fossaert, in particular, pointed out that if, tactically, his thesis were to serve as a basis for an indispensable international renegotiation with a view toward "triangulating" the relationships among Europe, the United States, and the Southern hemisphere, economically it did not stand up, because the arrangement of a monetary system, domestic or international, is a problem of political power rather than of risk.

More recently, Mendès France emphasized the necessary correlation between economic life and currency:

> When I supported the principle of a currency based on commodities, I hoped that an effort would be made to revalue raw materials and energy sources. The creation of a stock of such commodities established as monetary reserves would have led to a better equilibrium, and we would not have experienced the economic difficulties we have been suffering from for the last fifteen years. The prices of raw materials would have been revalued, which would have been advantageous to the underdeveloped countries. There would have been an organic and structural link between international currency and the economic situation. As in 1944, my basic idea was the search for an effective connection between production and distribution (national in 1944, international fifteen or twenty years later) and the currency placed at their service. This has become much more difficult to accomplish today.

Mendès France at twenty denounced Poincaré as the man who made the poor pay for stability; as an undersecretary of thirty, he intended to give to France a Plan based on full employment. As a minister of thirty-eight, he reminded Charles de Gaulle that one could not build the pure and lasting republic of which they both dreamed without basing oneself on economic and monetary realities. The most respected member of the Chamber became the president of the legislative commission on the national economy. The premier-designate of 1953 proclaimed, with enough harshness to lose the thirteen votes he needed for investiture, that France would save itself only by establishing the primacy of productive over unproductive expenditures—above all military expenditures.

In this way he argued for an economy of movement, and although he demanded truthful accounts, he was careful, unlike others, not to make that an end; this economic system tended to transform basic rigor into creative energy ("Control the currency to stimulate development," said PMF) and aimed for an organization of production by the Plan. But in searching for a formula to define Mendès France the economist—rationalist voluntarism? passion for the general interest? concern for democratization of the Plan?—we come to another term, which serves as a conclusion to *Science économique et lucidité politique* and gives full expression to his enthusiasm as a teacher:

The science of economics must be accompanied by attention to the science of *communication*. . . . The most difficult thing is to bring men to realize that no one can think for them, that they can and must demand complete information, constantly subject to the control of public opinion and to public debate. Everyone must judge for himself both data and decisions. . . . Everyone knows that any particular measure—a credit restriction, a freeze on prices, wages, or dividends, exchange controls—affects him directly. But few men know how to situate these decisions within the general framework which would enable them to be understood . . . with a view toward bringing out and progressively accomplishing what is *simultaneously* the *particular interest* of each individual and the *common interest*—even if it happens that the majority is wrong for a time, which is the normal, but finally salutary risk of democracy. . . .

For what is important in the end is to *help men choose their fate themselves*.

Before formulating an appreciation of Pierre Mendès France as critic and architect of the French economy, promoter of and advocate for a system of production tending toward justice and efficiency in which the state would play the role of stimulus and arbiter, it seemed prudent to ask the opinion of one of the men who, without having been an actual colleague of PMF, is an archetype of those public servants of the republican state for whom he was and remains the point of reference: François Bloch-Lainé.

The thought and the attitude of Pierre Mendès France remain exemplary and are the basis for the most persistent nostalgia of the half-century, for that which never happened.

Could it ever have happened? That question necessarily arises as a consequence of another one: Wasn't the behavior of PMF more impressive, more determinative than his doctrine, and thus more important for an analysis of his history, in the positive as well as the negative sense? What will occupy the attention of historians, form or substance? His doctrine was pure, hard, true, what must be aimed for in the absolute, what is difficult to deny in principle; it prescribed virtues almost as though they were self-evident. His behavior was more extraordinary; it provides a better explanation for his attractiveness, his influence, the respect he inspired, and his failure. His historic pronouncements are more explicit and convincing on the duty to choose and the nature of the choices than on the manner of carrying them out. And, in action, his procedure dazzled for a moment, but more often, unfortunately, disappointed.

His intelligence, rigor, and scrupulous reasoning produced agreement. But, outside a few noneconomic exceptions (Vietnam, Tunisia, the European Defense Community), the rejection of all useful ruses expressed, or so it seems, a taste for being right that was stronger than the desire for accomplishment, an art of debate for the good cause stronger than the art of winning the battle. Wasn't the optimism of his proposals constantly counterbalanced by a fundamental pessimism about "feasibility"? Was Dr. PMF characterized more accurately by the hopefulness of his program or the resignation of his prognosis?

The lesson for the future provided by this strange fate is not easy to draw, because his case is so peculiar—luckily or unluckily, he created the impression of being a statesman before he governed, and even without having really governed at all. This is an odd status for a leader of men, consecrated independently of the opportunities he had to legislate. He was a *commendatore* permanently present on the political stage, connected with the administration (closely acquainted with his thought and eager to consult him), but always outside the action of the players on the stage. . . .

In the eyes of senior civil servants, what constituted the pleasant particularity of PMF was also, and perhaps above all, the quality of his grasp of problems, the seriousness and conscientiousness with which he read, listened, and discussed. We have known very few—hardly any—other political men who moved so lucidly toward the substance of questions and so clearly toward the formulation of solutions. . . . There are a number of us who, as well as we were able, have carried out Mendès-like policies for thirty years, more or less in liaison with this solitary keeper of the flame.

History, according to Pierre Mendès France, has a meaning. We should not pretend to say, in his name, that it is ineluctably tending toward the advent of justice through development. Let us say that history is for him neither tragic, as Malraux asserted, nor absurd, as Camus thought. It is made up of a series of problems, and it is incumbent on man to resolve them. These problems, if they are well formulated and carefully studied, should call forth equitable solutions. If history is a Sphinx, man as Oedipus must know how to answer her. In agreement with Marx on this point, Mendès thought that history poses only those problems that humanity is in a position to resolve.

But suppose the Sphinx were mad or perverse and her riddles had no solution. No, with an irritated movement of the head and a brief shrug of the shoulders, Mendès would dismiss the objection. For man has an absolute weapon at his disposal: reason. With all his passion, and without feeling the slightest contradiction in doing so, Mendès France established reason, not as a goddess, like some of his illustrious Jacobin ancestors, but as an adviser and infallible friend.

Isn't the world in which the statesman's mission is to act in the name of the community unreasonable, harsh, and cruel? Isn't the world Auschwitz, apartheid, and the Gulag? Isn't that reality, the reality to which the man of Geneva and Carthage was so attached? Yes, of course. But the great thing is to make reality conform to reason, to draw out of that clay human form and a reasonable structure. However frightful the immediate data, the reality that first strikes us, may be, the only aim worthy of man is to organize it, harmonize it by an effort of reason—republic, democracy, planning, socialism.

Is reason the supreme law, the rule of the game? A man PMF admired, John Maynard Keynes, formulated a serious objection which applies also to Mendès France: "All my life, I have suffered from the fault of attributing to others my own rational ways of thinking and acting." As long as one is concerned with the administration of things, rationalism is certainly of great usefulness. But what if the question is governing men? The problem with the Plan is that, intending to control steel production, it has to deal with factory owners whose "reasons" may be recalcitrant to the arguments of reason.

For Pierre Mendès France, as for Léon Blum, the best procedure to bring about a conformity of reality with reason is to extend the notion of contract to the entirety of political life. Freely debated but, once signed, binding, the contract between the government and the governed (or the elected representatives of the governed) must be maintained as the framework for political activity. This is the concept he referred to when he presented himself before the Assembly in 1953, and again in 1954, and then when he undertook the Geneva negotiations or extended those of Carthage.

In speaking of him, people have often used the phrase "revolution through law." But the concept of law is inappropriate here because of its rigidity. "Revolution through contract" would better describe his vision of politics, as it would that of Blum. A contract can be discussed and renegotiated. It is a concept that does not exclude the notion of movement; and Mendès had too strong a belief in reality and in life not to base all political or economic activity on that movement.

It was he who resurrected the old terminology of the nineteenth century, which had opposed the party of "movement" to what he called the party of "limits"; this was how he described the attitude of the traditional conservative right trying to dam up the thrust of popular aspirations—that is, movement. Although he did not exclude the concepts of progress and reaction, required by contemporary jargon, Mendès returned to the term "movement," which, more than the reassuring "progress," implies both the uncertainty and the complexities of the struggle for a new society.

The first contract is one that binds the representative to those he represents. Against Rousseau, Marx, and a substantial number of contemporary observers, Pierre Mendès France strongly defended the concept of representation. A democrat deeply attached to public order, he mistrusted political spontaneity, feared the excessive concentration of power, and believed in the mechanisms of election and mandate. As a deputy for more than twenty years, he was as confident of having been a faithful representative of his constituents of Eure or Isère as he was of the national interest. Since he had seen the Third Republic collapse and the Fourth disintegrate, he suspected all forms of parliamentary fetishism. But he remained nostalgic for institutions that gave the people the opportunity to be heard through the voice of its representatives: denouncing the collapse of wheat prices in 1932, as he denounced the monarchical character of the institutions of the Fifth Republic twenty-five years later, he knew that he had thus carried out his democratic function.

It is hardly necessary to point out that he was not among those who saw an opposition between politics and morality. Not only because the raison d'être of the public man was, in his view, to contribute to the establishment of a more just society, but also because he believed that there was a relationship between means and ends. Like Léon Blum, he believed that means affect ends. And among all the means that a political man may readily learn how to manipulate with the justification of an honorable end, there remained the use of the truth.

When he wrote a book that was a sort of Pantheon to honor his masters in democracy, from Jules Ferry to Jaurès and Blum, he gave it the title *La vérité guidait leurs pas.* And if one were to object that some of these heroes, like De Gaulle, Churchill, or even Herriot, were not always scrupulously careful in this area, he would reply that a political figure is obliged to be "faithful to his truth." A faithfulness which may, he would agree, lead Lenin or Qaddafi rather far from "the" truth.

Pierre Mendès France more readily emphasized the exactitude, or better, the integrity of the information the statesman owes to citizens, information that is the basis of the social contract, that is, of democracy. When a holder of personal power, hereditary sovereign or military *caudillo,* plays with facts and figures according to the requirements of his image, for reasons of state, or for the glory of the empire, that derives from an entirely different conception of power. But what kind of democracy is not based on accurate information and verifiable data?

In considering his relationship to Charles de Gaulle, we must forget neither the ardent loyalty of the war years and the first battles of the Liberation for the pure and true Republic nor the obstinate rejection of the late 1950s. Unlike the nineteenth-century encyclopedia in which the article on Bonaparte ended with this sentence: "Died on 18 Brumaire of the year VIII," and unlike De Gaulle himself, who defined Pétain as "a great man who died in 1925" (the year when he made fortifications the supreme means of national defense), Pierre Mendès France did not consider De Gaulle after May 13, 1958, as a dead man. However much he may have valued the De Gaulle of June 1940 over the De Gaulle of May 1958, he nevertheless maintained relations of courteous opposition with the latter and even praised on occasion particular successes of this government that he considered hardly legitimate.

When his friend Simon Nora asked him which of the statesmen he had served, encountered, or fought against—from Blum to Churchill, from Chou En-lai to De Gaulle, from Poincaré to Eisenhower—had seemed the most impressive to him, he hesitated and said suddenly: "De Gaulle." "Why, or in what way?" "Because of his sovereignty." An ambiguous phrase that says many things in a serene way. It is certainly more ambiguous than what the general said of Mendès: "I respect only those who resist me, but I cannot tolerate them." And he added, with a touch of admiration: "He is a man who cannot be harnessed." De Gaulle did not harness him, but he marked him deeply.

Léon Blum was nevertheless his preferred teacher, a teacher of optimism. It was Blum who said to the austere young man whom he had appointed as junior treasury minister, as they watched the rising flames ignited by the invention of fascism and the 1929 crisis: "My dear Mendès, the worst does not always happen."

The worst did happen. But Léon Blum's hope was not assassinated, nor was that of Pierre Mendès France, the hope for the advent of a more just society in which man, before making peace with his fellow man, would gradually organize a more just distribution of tasks and profits. In the intellectual and political landscape of Mendès France, the "Blum side" of dawn and optimism occupies more ample ground than that of De Gaulle, the side of active pessimism and a bitter vision of the world.

Even though the Chinese model and the thought of Mao had no place in his intellectual horizon, it is tempting to quote, with reference to Mendès France, the precept with which the Chinese president claimed to sum up his *ars politica:* "Tactical pessimism, strategic optimism." In the short run, one must take an implacable measure of obstacles, resistances, and contradictions, at the risk of expanding and sharpening them. There is nothing worse than failing because of lack of awareness of the dangers.

Before jumping over the wall in Clermont-Ferrand, he measured, centimeter by centimeter, the pile of millstones on the other side. Before meeting Chou En-lai or Pham Van Dong, he evaluated without complacency the depth of the abyss into which France was sinking in Indochina. Before flying off to Tunis, he actively investigated the "preponderant" party and Bourguiba's ulterior motives. And before proposing a negotiated solution for the European army, he unflinchingly confronted the party of those devoted to a "Little Europe." The problems were insoluble.

Once short-term pessimism had cleared off the surface, sharpened the angles, and dissipated illusions, it was incumbent on the optimist to confront the danger. It turned out that the level of the street, in Clermont, was higher than that of the guard's path, and thus more useful for the escapee; or that the Soviets and Chinese were more pressed to negotiate than eager to exploit fully their allies' military advantage. The optimist is not always wrong, "the worst is not always certain," as Claudel and Blum had suggested in different ways.

The pessimist judged men. His severity was not the equal of Churchill's, De Gaulle's, or Stalin's, but it was nonetheless harsh. He attributed the failure of the Fourth Republic almost entirely to the men involved. But this Alceste did not resign himself to a flight to the "desert." Having taken full measure of his contemporaries, the optimist thought, wrote, and acted with reference to a future in which those same men would think, write, and act differently.

Strongly attached to parliamentary control over the executive, he was not thereby an enemy of real power. For long frustrated by the mechanisms of parliamentary government, he attempted to consolidate and stabilize the executive's means of action, and he exercised those at his disposal with a kind of greedy energy, so much so that, when he was defeated, he came close to forgetting their customary limits.

Authoritarian by nature or rather because of a combination of a sense of the urgency of action and the superiority of reason (his reason?), he may have been so attentive to the rules and forms of representative democracy only because he mistrusted the impetuosity of his own temperament. To anyone who asked him this question he would reply that that was far from the truth and that his legalism had nothing to do with self-censorship of self-punishment. He tended rather to reproach himself, as a public man, for a certain "lack of ambition" that diverted him from persisting stubbornly, from ignoring a particular failure or humiliation in order to think only of a higher or more lasting mission.

And it is true that he could often be discovered eager to break off, to leave, to resign, in 1944 in Algiers, again in 1945 (when he carried out his plan), and in 1956 yet once more. In 1958, resigning from all his offices after his defeat in the legislative elections in Eure, he demonstrated the nobility of his ideas more than the determination to have them prevail: the mayoralty and the General Council were good springboards for a return to Parliament, which would have been useful to his fellow citizens and to the country. And this is not to mention his reservations when the premier was designated in 1956. There is no doubt that this behavior was highly reputable. But it was a typical example of the lack of ambition which is also a lack of drive and determination—political virtues.

No one believed less than he did that there was a contradiction between democracy and authority. He had suffered too much from the cult of impersonality aggressively celebrated by the Parliament of the Fourth Republic not to believe that authority, *auctoritas,* based on respect for popular legitimacy, was the supreme weapon of democracy. Thus, he was not afraid to pay homage to exceptional men who, with very divergent styles and objectives, had served the Republic. On June 3, 1953, finally aspiring to investiture by the National Assembly in order to govern, he called upon three models, Poincaré, Blum, and De Gaulle, thereby dispensing with any form of sectarianism and emphasizing uniquely service to the state. In Poincaré, with whom he had respectfully fought in his youth, he hailed the sense of reality, financial rigor, and the determination to succeed. But it is in the space marked out by the two names of Léon Blum and Charles de Gaulle that we must seek to locate his conception of the role of the French statesman.

"He had the virtue that is fitting for the Republic," wrote Robert Fossaert, not of Cato or Robespierre, but of PMF. It would be hard to improve on this, on the condition that we include all that a Roman, or English, historian would suggest of active vigor rather than bilious moralism. Virtue is as much the eagerness to undertake as it is the refusal to compromise. It is also the will to act, and it has often been emphasized that Pierre Mendès France's "activism" had a strong voluntarist component.

What made up his originality, and this brings him close to De Gaulle, was that his very acute awareness of reality, of the bitter weight of the world, and of the attractions of evil, confronted an overwhelming thirst to change this reality and the certainty that he would be able to act on it. Why should the ordinary people of Louviers not be represented by a very young lawyer, a Parisian and a Jew, once he was determined to struggle to improve their condition? Why should the bars of the Clermont prison remain forever locked around him? Why was it not possible for him, with a bold gesture, to give to the French the balance between money supply and production required for the reconstruction of the country? Why should he resign himself to inflation, the pursuit of an absurd war, the ravages of alcoholism, and decadence?

It was possible to act. But to what end? Justice is the great word, perhaps unduly vague. But what else could being a Socialist mean? This expectation of justice, in which is expressed, more than optimism, a kind of prophetic vision, can perhaps be seen as Mendès France's share of the Jewish tradition, a tradition that Massignon asserted was above all testimony of the hope for justice, for oneself and even more for others.

Like Léon Blum, perhaps even more than he, Pierre Mendès France was a citizen of a strictly secular universe, haunted by no prophets and no revelations. Although the anguish that possessed and stirred him was a powerful impulse to action, it did not foster any metaphysical meditations. This form of Judaism seems to have been nothing but a historical link, the consciousness of an unbreakable solidarity. The Dreyfus affair, before the Cartel des Gauches, the Popular Front, the Resistance, and decolonization, was one of the immediate data of his moral and political consciousness. But was this not also the case for the sons of Jean Jaurès and Lucien Herr? Let us grant that the components of Jewish consciousness and solidarity are indefinably rich and complex and that compassion plays an even greater role than knowledge, and knowledge a greater role than faith. And let us also grant that the demand for justice is not only contained in a Book, but is the fruit of an unlimited history.

But however a Jew may experience his Jewishness, anti-Semitism troubles and conditions him from many directions. Anti-Semitic attacks against him, as against Blum (an article on Blum by Thorez, published in November 1940, could have appeared in a fascist rag), did not come only from the right. Jean Recanati, a Communist journalist of Jewish origin quoting Pierre Courtade, reports:

> Laurent Casanova said privately after a speech by Mendès France: "France is certainly not that little Jewish rug merchant." I was told that Casanova said 'France' in ringing, almost regal tones, and that, at 'little Jewish rug merchant' his face had become twisted, expressing vulgarity and disgust.
>
> Mendès was a target of the same attacks [as Léon Blum] coming from the same circles, with the one difference that, in 1936, Blum was openly "the Jew Blum" for a significant fraction of his enemies and stigmatized as such, Jewishness implying a presumption, even proof, of lack of patriotism and of treason, while for Mendès any anti-Semitism that survived (and I believe that some did) was usually half suppressed, concealed, as though it were ashamed to express itself in daylight.
>
> Léon Blum was not ignorant of "the fear of creating fear," but all the witnesses agree that he was never troubled by the vileness of the attacks to which his Jewish origins were subject. As head of the Popular Front government, he knew that, Jew or not, aggressive attitudes were inevitable. I am not certain that this was entirely the case for Mendès. . . . De Gaulle . . . who was also called a "merchant" by the ultras . . . shrugged his shoulders, indifferent. Mendès persevered like De Gaulle, but I do not believe that he remained indifferent. Mendès was made less of iron, more of flesh and blood, a flesh more sensitive to wounds.

One of his most loyal and active friends for the last twenty years, Maître Georges Kiejman, offers this observation about the fact that Mendès France was kept from power when the Republican Front won the 1956 elections:

> I have heard my friends lament: "If PMF had led the government in January 1956, everything would have been different. We would have been saved from the Algerian War, 'Molletism,' and the new Gaullism." I'm not so sure. Mendès would have done everything to negotiate and achieve peace. But would he have been allowed to do what De Gaulle, with so much difficulty,

was able to impose on the army and the *pieds-noirs?* From the point of view of those who love him, as I do, from what I would call the "Jewish mother" point of view, perhaps we should not regret his exclusion in January 1956. . . . It would have been terrible.

But however cruelly he may have been affected by certain causal relations established between his cultural origins and the dislocation of the French Empire, whoever approached him during the grave crises that French Judaism has gone through was unfailingly struck by his serenity. From the debacle of 1940 to the Suez campaign, from the Six Day War to the bombing on the rue Copernic, he was always the one who counseled cool-headedness, minimized accusations of anti-Semitism and neonazism, and relied upon the democratic sense of the French people. He remained among those who believed that the Abbé Grégoire, in 1793, had really achieved the liberation of the French Jews.

His patriotism was made of rough cloth, like old-fashioned sheets. Woven at school and in the tests to which he was subjected from the student Socialist movement to the air force and the mayoralty of Louviers, it was consolidated if not stiffened by his confrontations with the "Eurocrats" and negotiations with the superpowers of this pitiless century. Here he is speaking of his country in the preface to a guide book from the mid-1960s. He describes himself rather well in what he asks the visitor to admire in France:

> The incredible quantity of work invested over the course of centuries in this country which is sometimes criticized for giving itself up to a life of ease. . . . There is nothing here that has been granted to man by a gratuitous gift of nature. . . . It is a commonplace to say that nature in France is the most *humanized* in the world and that our civilization is as much contained in its countryside as in its books: what better proof is there of this than the continuity of human labor from the earliest times?

Effort, labor: Mendès was not afraid of using these words from the Ecole Polytechnique. He saw nothing ridiculous in them. And if there is one subject to which this man who was so careful to listen to the young inevitably remained deaf, it was to their challenge to the religion of effort that was his, to the sanctification of work and of the "meritocracy" of which, consciously or not, he was a symbol. Workhorse: the expression is worn out, one might say worn out by him. If he made it his practice to deal with only one question at a time, this was the better to immerse himself in each one, to draw all the substance from a file, all the information from a colleague, all the concessions possible from an opposing negotiator. He gave himself up to work for fifteen hours a day, entirely incapable of distancing himself from "business" as De Gaulle did once the door to the Elysée office was closed.

But when the president of the Republic called on him to attempt to form a government in June 1953, his old friend Herriot muttered that "Auriol should have called on a professional." However devoted he may have been to public affairs and to the study of the problems of the state, however competent he may have been, he remained in fact an amateur, a marginal figure. He was a different kind of man, outside the political elite, the club that Herriot knew so well because he had surveyed it for so long from the high perch of his seat as president of the Assembly. And this is indeed what led to his parliamentary failure and the least admirable part of his popular support. Perennial French antiparliamentarianism thought that this parliamentarian elected for seven legislatures had a "different" air. And one might have heard about him what a passer-by answered a reporter when she was questioned on the day of De Gaulle's death: "I liked him a lot because he wasn't involved in politics."

This uncompromising patriot, paraphrasing Jaurès, would say that a little patriotism distances one from internationalism, but that a lot of patriotism brings the two closer together. However attached he may have been to the French nation and the French state, he was very open to other civilizations, to England in particular, as has often been pointed out. He was even enough of an Anglophile not to be outraged by Churchill's "empty chair" letter. ("What do you expect? They were exasperated, they no longer had any confidence in us.") And he was attached to American civilization as well, which always remained for him, even when he was goaded by Dulles, the civilization of the country of "Roosevelt's revolution."

There was no French public figure who was less anti-German than he. At eighteen, he wrote the most serene essay imaginable for his teachers at the Institut des Sciences Politiques on Prussian nationalism. And thirty years later, he was the first head of a French government to praise Franco–German reconciliation, speaking before a monument to the dead of the Resistance. As for the Soviet Union, although he often fiercely opposed it, he was always careful to qualify, at least from the economic standpoint, his criticisms of the Stalinist Socialist system; but he did not go as far as Georges Boris, who, around 1955, believed that the Soviet Union was about to establish free bread ("Without gruel, no Sparta," he said to Roger Stéphane, a double-edged phrase that also means that white bread weakens the nations).

And it is almost superfluous to recall, because a hundred public pronouncements are there to show it, that Pierre Mendès France considered the emergence of the Third World as the most significant event of the century, and it is no less superfluous to demonstrate that, with the Vietnamese and Tunisians in the past, and more recently with the Palestinians, he acted in conformity with this historic assumption.

We have emphasized his synthesis of passion and reason. The passion to have the right reasons. We have also pointed to the alliance in him of a sense of reality, like that of a scrupulous accountant, and the long-term vision of a voluntarist prophet. It is as though he wanted to be Poincaré in order to act like Blum—to succeed where Blum had failed. For a prophet is not forbidden the knowledge of how to draw up a balance sheet, and it is recommended to those who would change the world that they be more serious than those who are content to watch it turn.

But did he altogether accomplish a synthesis between short-term requirements where he was masterful and the long-term vision that gave him his aura? It is perhaps here that we can find the flaw. Was he all of a piece, both one and the other simultaneously? Was it an alloy, an alliance, or an alternation? In his passion for accomplishment, a kind of voracity to perform, he sometimes got lost in minutiae at the moment when long-term matters were being decided, and he sometimes took off into the very long term at the moment when detail was necessary. Perhaps he was too eager to "prove himself," too personally implicated, as though he always felt he was on trial, or as though he had always felt the imperious challenge of time, the meagerness of the space of 245 days that history granted him, a space that he never recovered, despite the electoral verdict of 1956, and despite the gaping void of 1968. His was a long-range politics that was marked, strangled, by the short term, urgency, a kind of threatening reprieve.

To make reality rational—that seems to have been the statesman's program. But does it express the man himself—the vulnerable Pierre who is so moving, who soon appears beneath the rather harsh surface of Mendès, beneath the soberly brilliant persona of PMF? We will have said very little of that man if we have not pierced the armor of the performer, the superman according to Dulles, the workhorse of 1954, the maker of plans, the parliamentary fighter, the leader who attracted more hatred and more devotion than any other in the past half-century—except for Charles de Gaulle.

Private life is not what interests us here, but rather that flame of passion that illuminated and animated an entire history. We have already said that for no other public figure of our time has emotion so thoroughly guided behavior. From the letter to Françoise Giroud on the tenth anniversary of L'Express, to the moving letter to Marie-Claire Mendès France on the eve of his failure at Grenoble in 1968, we have already pointed to the capacity for initiative and also the fragility of this political warrior who for three decades had passed through all the testing fires.

This feeling, this power of emotion, which gave resonance to the public life of this master of rationalism, established very special relationships around him. It might be said that, much more than a doctrine of action and reality, Mendésism was and remains above all a kind of fraternity. I have never, he said, called for unconditional adhesion on the part of anyone. To be sure. He solicited too many opinions and criticisms to be satisfied with devotion. But although he rejected the sectarian spirit and dependence, he was nevertheless eager for loyalty, and even more, for friendship. If he was more admired than liked, this is not what he would have wished.

It might be said that I have presented a man worthy of admiration, a personality, an eminent servant of the state, a man passionately devoted to the public welfare, and also a sensitive and passionate being. The portrait might even be moving and the figure call forth admiration. But isn't this a narrative of a series of failures? Is it the duty of a statesman to compel respect or to improve the order of things? It is all very well that Mendès existed; it would have been better if Mendésism had won out.

Failure? If it is true, and this is questionable, that politics is properly concerned with lasting victories (the Edict of Nantes lasted for a century, the "order" of 1918 for twenty years, political Gaullism hardly more than ten), it is necessary to agree as to what, in public life, is success or failure. Should we call success only the forward movement of little flags on a map, or the forced stabilization of the currency, or the presence in the premier's office of the same man for more than five years, or the conquest of an absolute majority in the National Assembly? But we refuse to agree that a war interrupted in one place and a conflict prevented in another are of less weight than the winning of a battle.

And should we count for nothing the transformation of consciousness that was accomplished about the relationship between state and citizen? The rehabilitation of public affairs? The reinvention of a certain political virtue? The belief in the power of the community to change its own fate? Mendésism does not exist, said Mendès France. Very well. But perhaps that is precisely what it is. And this too: a sense of reality aiming toward the possible.

To those who spoke of the failure of the Popular Front of 1936, Mendès France objected that the government led by Blum had accomplished at least one very beautiful thing: reconciliation between the people and the state. "For the first time in generations," he argued, "the people of this country stopped experiencing the state as an instrument of oppression in the service of the wealthy, but they saw it as a possible ally, through which the worst, but also the best could come."

And perhaps PMF's brief period in power, and even more his presence for half a century in the political life of the French, accomplished a symmetrical result: demonstrating to the bourgeoisie that it was not, by virtue of a narrow determinism, the oppressive class, that it could be an instrument for the reform of the state and of the system of production, distribution, and exchange called for by the France of the second half of the twentieth century, like the bourgeoisie of the end of the eighteenth century. In 1936, the French people could glimpse the possibility of making an alliance with the state. In 1954—and ten years earlier, and twenty years later—the French middle classes, the intellectuals, the "technostructure," were offered by Mendésism a historic task—the task of the old Third Estate. It was not the fault of Mendès France that they were not more capable of seizing the opportunity.

The history of Pierre Mendès France poses to its fullest extent the problem of the meaning of political power and of its ends. Effectiveness or bearing witness? Immediate tangible gains or accumulation of long-term values? Toward what does the statesman aim? To be or to do? To act or to teach? And there is this question: Does compromise discredit action? Is it not a duty for one who has assumed a noble task, approved by his electors, the accomplishment of which requires the passage of time? If he denies himself, by any means available, the opportunity to continue, or even to emerge, does the statesman really fulfill his mission, his raison d'être, which is to act?

According to François Goguel, speaking at the seminar of the Institut d'Etudes Politiques in April 1958: "In Mendès France, the politician was not of the stature of the statesman." This formulation is certainly appealing to some Mendésists, but not to all. We may question the value of the antithesis between politician and statesman. If the politician in him vanishes, what kind of showing can a statesman make? Should every man who enters the political arena, charged with general responsibilities in the name of the community, arm himself with all the weapons without which his attempt is nothing but a noble pretense at a form of self-justification— the "politics of the just man," as Colette Audry summed up the career of Léon Blum?

But on the other hand, what is a society that is not enlightened, exalted, or inspired, from one decade to the next, by the exercise of a power that claims to be based on reason in order to assure justice without ridiculing morality or trampling on liberty? Nonsense? It happens that in 1954 a certain government gave the French people, for a few months, the feeling that all action was not useless, that every misfortune was not unavoidable, that all politics was not dirty, that all consensus was not inaccessible, and that every state was not cynically manipulated by the forces of money. The errors of this government, the defects of the man who led it, the brevity of its mission, cannot prevent the nostalgia of the French from taking nourishment from those 245 days and what they accomplished: peace restored (for a while) in Asia, cooperation substituted for violence in Tunisia, the Gordian knot cut in Europe, and France restored to its rightful place in the world.

A man who, having greatly admired him, later became a strong opponent of his, said to us not long ago that what would remain of Mendès France was first of all "the restoration of hope to a generation that politics is not always useless." And further, "the rehabilitation of action enlightened by thought."

To recount the life of Pierre Mendès France, French statesman of the twentieth century, is to raise questions about the relationships between men and power. Here is a political man who exercised authority in the state for only a few weeks in 1938 under the aegis of an exceptional man, for a year and a few months from 1943 to 1945 in the entourage of another extraordinary figure, and finally, for eight months, when he assumed all the responsibilities that authority implies. And this man, whose long exile from power might have made rigid, isolated within the armor of a set of theoretical certainties, fulfilled himself in the exercise of those functions, grew in them, and found his truth in them. Those 245 days are, properly speaking, "the season of Mendès," for whom the exercise of power was both a transcendence and a self-revelation.

Action in the service of the community is thus neither degrading nor futile. Politics is thus not corrupting by nature. Power is not in its essence perverse. It is what one makes of it.

AFTERWORD

Pierre Mendès France died on October 18, 1982. One year and five months earlier, the coalition of French parties of the left (Socialists, Communists, and Radicals), supported by a strong movement of discontent without any particular ideological content, had carried François Mitterrand to power. Mitterrand was an old companion in arms of the negotiator of peace in Indochina, and he brought with him a team that included many of Mendès's disciples and colleagues—Claude Cheysson, Jacques Delors, Michel Rocard, and Charles Hernu.

On May 21, 1981, the day of his inauguration, the new president embraced Mendès France and said: "Without you, I would not be here." And the new premier, Pierre Mauroy, said with a smile: "I often have the impression that I am leading a Mendès France government."

But it cannot be said that the relations between Pierre Mendès France and the new government were of the kind hoped for by the friends of both sides. The former premier, as he had during François Mitterrand's earlier campaigns, had actively participated in the contest for the presidency, notably in a major radio broadcast, the "Club de la presse," in May 1981. Many thought, even in the new president's entourage, that Mendès would accept a ministry without portfolio, lending his prestige to the new government, without taking on burdens incompatible with the fragile state of his health. He let it be known, even before the government was formed, that he would refuse any offers.

Many of us hoped that he would be given special missions. Why not send him to explain to the American public, among whom he enjoyed a certain prestige, that the arrival in power of the left in France under the leadership of François Mitterrand was not a seizure of power by the Bolsheviks—even with four Communist ministers in the cabinet? And above all, why should he not be given a permanent mission to use his good offices between Israel and the Arabs, commanding as he did substantial respect from both sides, as he had shown by sponsoring the 1976 conversations between the Eliav-Peled-Avnery group and that of Issam Sertawi? In the name, and with the resources, of the French government, would he not, this time, have been much more effective?

Nothing of the kind was proposed. The few tasks that were offered him seemed to him either honorific, which he loathed, or linked to the past, while he had always been turned toward the future. Thus he lived for many long months on the outskirts of power, a little melancholy, like a friendly ghost. Some ministers visited him—Rocard, Cheysson. He was invited to a working lunch at the Elysée, on the eve of the summer 1982 devaluation of the franc, which he approved, even finding it too cautious. But without any public expression of his disagreements, he considered the management of his Socialist friends to be too lax, too spendthrift, too adventurous.

It is very difficult to determine why the new head of state associated Mendès so little with his enterprise, failing to give himself the support of a man whose health kept him from a position of responsibility, but whose moral and technical authority, in the monetary, economic, and diplomatic realms, had remained incomparable, in France and beyond its borders.

It cannot be denied that Pierre Mendès France and his friends were a bit troubled by this, although they accepted the situation in silence. Mendès's career as a great citizen and eminent servant of the state, marked by the victory of the left that was his last great joy, thus concluded in a nostalgic gloom, with respect both to the distance at which he was kept and to the state of public affairs under the government of the left.

But President Mitterrand, who had saluted him on the day he assumed power in the Elysée, as we have seen, made a point, after Mendès France's death, of solemnly expressing the homage of the nation to the man who, for almost half a century, had embodied, more than any other French citizen, the spirit of the Republic and the demand for justice.

The Death of Pierre Mendès France

Tribute by President François Mitterrand
Cour D'Honneur of the National Assembly, October 27, 1982

In the course of history there are those privileged moments when integrity has a name, discipline a face, conscience a voice, and in the life of a man there is a moment—his death—when everyone, friend and foe alike, hears the echo of the same message and suddenly—yes, for a moment—all are united.

How can I express the emotion which has moved so many men and women since Monday, October 18, 1982? Do we ourselves know all the reasons for our grief?

Before we were able to pay Pierre Mendès France the solemn tribute which brings us together today, the French nation, our people, and many others throughout the world had mourned his death. They had lost one of their own, someone whom they loved, respected, and admired; one of those who, they knew, lead the way in darkness and uncertainty.

Pierre Mendès France wanted the days following his death to be reserved for his family and his close friends and for the official ceremonies to be kept apart. It is not for me to interpret this wish, so consistent with the conduct of a lifetime. However, I do ask myself this question. Did this man of such an extraordinary destiny and such unique breadth adequately measure the contribution he had made to his country and did he doubt the upsurge of gratitude and sorrow his passing would cause?

If he had such a doubt—and we can easily understand it—since he was opposed, slandered, and insulted for so many years—he knew all too well that a person opens himself to that risk as soon as he involves himself in the affairs of the state. No founder of an order, no bearer of a great message has been spared this fate. And he, more than anyone, taught us that to conquer the ravages of fortune and feel secure at great heights, like Léon Blum, one must have great strength of character.

Did the hostility provoked by the torrent of his brilliant ideas and actions nurture in him this momentary question? In the course of the tumult and weaknesses of the Fourth Republic, he brought illumination and recovery, for which he was applauded by the youth of France. In less than eight months, he stopped the bloodbath of the war in Indochina; struck a spectacular and decisive blow, one that was literally revolutionary, for decolonization, with the emancipation of Tunisia; took the most innovative steps for France's national defense; gave extraordinary momentum to the French economy; and finally introduced a style and a method that have left their mark on those who, wherever they are, have to decide France's destiny.

Doubt could also have surfaced—what great mind has not known it—when, as was said of another, "the eagle having made his nest, they tried to force him to rest in it." He might have feared that since the vicissitudes of politics and the divisions on his side had removed him from leadership of the country, his struggles, his capacities, his warnings would be anesthetized by the easy tribute and the careless respect that a society gives to its bad conscience.

Even though everything has been said, often well said, about this Frenchman whose loss grieves us more than we might have expected, little has been recalled, in my view, about the extent to which he has been a presence among us for the past twenty years; with what deep-rooted fidelity and what dogged tenacity he discouraged those who urged him to place himself above the battle. When I confided to him recently that without him nothing would have been possible, I was, of course, thinking of the role which he had played as a leader for my generation and the confidence he showed me in 1953 and 1954 by counting me among his own. But I was thinking especially of the fact that he had never ceased being an inalienable companion of those who strove to make everything possible for France again.

Pierre Mendès France bequeaths us a faith, a method, and an example. His faith—the Republic; his method—truth; his example—the ceaseless struggle for peace and progress.

For the Republic, ungrateful though it may have been, was his passion. It was, for him, the conquest of liberties, the implementation of human rights and civic virtues, the highest form of development of human societies, where the duty of truth, respect for promises, the scruples of the free spirit, the love of the common good are the basis of the government of peoples. His choices and his refusals were inspired by this passion. It sheds light on the commitment of the young lawyer, the young deputy, and the young minister, his struggle in 1936, his participation in the government of the Popular Front, his action as premier. It sheds light on his presence at the side of General de Gaulle in 1945, and also his departure when he was no longer in agreement. It explains the risk he took in promoting the policy of decolonization for which he became the symbol in the face of increasing hatred. The right of peoples to self-determination, to win independence and dignity, was for him an inescapable conquest of democracy—which France had to assume in order to be true to itself. His passion for the Republic explains his intransigent attitude in 1958. It also explains why he was, until the final day and to the very limits of his strength, committed, unwavering in his solidarity, judging certainly, but at the same time understanding that his role in retirement, remained that of a citizen and a servant of his country.

The confidence of the people cannot be bought. It is earned and to do this one must convince. The Republic begins with the determination to convince. Ardent but methodical, this determination imbued Pierre Mendès France, whether he addressed himself to the humblest, the least informed of the electorate, or the greatest of the great in this world; whether he was speaking to his closest friend in the most personal conversation or to the most anonymous, and even most hostile, audience. To be a *Républicain* was, according to him, to believe that every man can be a judge of the common good.

Like all those who inspire, Pierre Mendès France spoke simply. Nothing is stronger than language which gives everyone the right to understand. This is how myths, religions, and philosophies have spread. This has shaped the words for which men have been willing to fight and even die.

He said repeatedly that "the Republic is a contract," and he applied this maxim to everything. The lucid act between free citizens and those who represent them—neither Montesquieu nor Rousseau had put it differently, nor did any other founder of any other republic; Mendès France, despite failures, setbacks, and the mounting wave of barbarism, simply continued to believe it. His concern was not so much to strengthen the government as to respect those who elected it, to reverse the burden of proof by returning to the citizen the task of being in the front line because ultimately he was the one who made the decisions. Following in the footsteps of Gambetta, Jaurès, Léon Blum, albeit differently, he embodies in my view, the fight for the Republic. He held the highest idea of it. He gave it its most beautiful expression. That is why his memory, which brings us together, will long remain with us.

Let us listen to him describe the duty of the elected official toward his electorate, of the political leader toward the citizens, as he wrote in his book, *La vérité guidait leurs pas:*

> He will have to alert them to error, resist becoming involved in special interests, point out the needs of the common good, confront movements born of passion or incomplete or falsified information, if these threaten or compromise the essential goals for which he has been elected. To do this he will have to have character and courage. It is precisely this which gives his political mission its true purpose and dignity.

What looks like a self-portrait to us is seen by the younger generation as being like him. This is why youth and politics are reconciled in him.

In this respect I have always found it remarkable that no form of demogoguery ever entered his speeches to young people. There is no trace in his remarks of the deceptive strategy which consists for some, when they have a youthful audience, in vaunting their old age, believing they are thus putting the future into their hands. Quite the contrary, when Mendès France addressed our youth in December 1955, it was to tell them directly that they had as many responsibilities as rights.

Moreover, youth is the least credulous age. And Mendès France knew it. Tuning in to young people, as he did in May 1968, did not mean for him necessarily going in their direction, but understanding, in order to accompany and guide a world in change. In another message, he was to affirm that it is impossible to be young and to say, "What's the point!" But to others, to politicians, educators, people with responsibilities, he gave this warning: An action is not sound unless its effect and impact on the young are assessed when it is conceived, formulated, and applied.

It is thus that he inspired, brought to life, and nurtured the birth of ideas, reforms, and projects that the government of France is now implementing. We find his ideas coming up in the colloquia at Caen and Grenoble, in studies of the *Cahiers de la République,* in the reports of the small seminars where he showed the best of his character and imagination. This work remains valid for those among us who might be tempted to think and act, having in mind only the immediate or the provisional.

Another area in which Pierre Mendès France showed his visionary quality was the Third World. He quickly went beyond sermons and preaching and never referred to the subject in terms of charity. He simply observed that in this world the poor remained poor and were growing in number; and that the rich, who believed they could remain rich indefinitely, were preparing their own ruin by maintaining their dominion.

The man who had so often proclaimed our, that is Europe and the West's, debt to the United States, a country he loved—just as I do—was the first to denounce the "international monetary order," so-called out of irony or paradox, and the supremacy of the dollar, source of so much trouble and harm, whose first victims are always the poor nations. Once again, the Third World, for him as for us all, was unacceptable. But it was also an affront to human reason, which he valued above all else. "Man cannot build the end of mankind with his own hands," he said time and again in speaking of the arms race and also especially when citing the unbearable irrationality of relations between the West and the Third World. His proposals for the indispensable new monetary system are no secret; they are based on guaranteed prices for raw materials and on development tailored to the identity of each state.

A great many acts of the Mendès France administration are still awaiting the verdict of history.

While the debate, and its conclusion, on the ratification or rather the nonratification of the treaty for a European defense community is now over, it left a long and bitter aftertaste for many sincere democrats, committed Europeans, who were perhaps too impelled by their ideal of imagining Europe differently from what it really was. In a step that was out of character, Pierre Mendès France abstained in the final vote, and with him, his ministers. But he hastened immediately to map out a new path which we are still following and on which we have continued to progress toward Franco-German friendship. It was at the Hôtel Matignon when he was in office that I met a German chancellor for the first time. In these things as in all others he reacted as a patriot of an old and great tradition.

He loved the United States, as I said, even when he spoke up to that country, and refused to call the logic of hegemony "imperialism"—telling our trans-Atlantic allies that this could rebound on them with bitter consequences if they were not careful.

With respect to the Soviet Union he knew that it encompassed a great people, friends of France through a long history. Although he did not accept its internal government, he did not allow this factor to enter into consideration in watching over the necessary balances among the different countries of the world.

But what is called patriotism, ladies and gentlemen, that is, ascribing a fundamental value to one's country, was not an abstract concept or an uncertain ideal for Pierre Mendès France. And he proved it. When war was declared in 1939 he did not ask questions: he joined the fight. His place was at the front. Someone pointed out to him that as a member of parliament he could ask for a special posting and so he went into the air force. As a static war between the Maginot and Siegfried lines was expected and as action was not anticipated for a while, he requested an immediate assignment to the army in the Levant that was supposed to encircle the enemy by way of the Balkans.

Promoted to lieutenant, he hammered away at the High Command for new assignments. The collapse found him back in France. He sought to rejoin his unit in Morocco and embarked on the *Massilia*. Arrested and tried for desertion, he was sentenced May 9, 1941, to seven years in prison. A succession of witnesses, his superior officers, took the stand. They praised him, to a man, and not content merely to clear the defendant of all suspicion, to term the accusation a scandal, they testified that they had rarely seen a French officer so calmly and so stubbornly set on joining battle. While he was in prison he tried to escape many times. Before the last attempt, in which he was successful, he wrote to the then authorities the letter which I now quote:

> It is of course forbidden to take the law into one's own hands but providing one can find and defend one's honor. . . . I cannot allow my dishonor to be affirmed without resorting to the only remaining means of protection I have—the most solemn and the most dramatic: I reclaim the liberty to which I have never ceased to have the right. . . . However, if France were one day to appeal again to its children I should ask permission to serve in the most vulnerable position as I did already in 1939–40.

He succeeded in joining De Gaulle in London after countless difficulties and setbacks. When the leader of the Free French asked him what he wanted to do, Mendès France replied simply: "I am in the air force. I want to resume my service in a fighting unit." And that was what he did.

One would have to be very unobservant to believe that Pierre Mendès France's action was limited to the brief seven months and seventeen days he spent at the head of the government of France from June 1954 to February 1955. One summer, one autumn, and then a few days. But history does not make that kind of reckoning. Léon Blum for one year. Gambetta and Jaurès, for so little, forever, for always.

This man, who was in government so briefly yet so fully, showed a respect for Parliament that was not, we have to admit, reciprocated.

Witnesses remember the uproar that drowned his remarks that February 5, 1955, when he was beaten by a coalition of opposing interests—he had probably refused to count all the votes that he might have had—and against all custom tried to express his feelings and make known the enormity of the task that awaited his successor.

I lived that moment with him and can still hear him cry:

Duty forbids giving up.

All of Mendès France was in this avowal. The pain he felt at seeing himself deprived of the means to pursue the policy he thought was right for the country; the conviction that a just policy would sooner or later be taken up by others after him.

Until today I have never described the scene which a handful of us witnessed. In his office at the Palais Bourbon, Pierre Mendès France, hunched over, head in hands, suddenly looked at us with sorrow etched on his face. In a low voice he murmured: "I did what I could. What will become of the Republic?"

The goals, the method, and this ethic, too, merged for Pierre Mendès France in the very way he conceived his options. For while he was careful to listen to opposing opinions, he belonged, and I quote, "to the camp of those who thirst for humanism and socialism, beliefs which are more and more widely shared and which hold out the greatest promise for the future." And he added: "I am one of those people who are continually motivated by the desire, by the passion to have a part, be it ever so small, in a great undertaking that will never be finished and which is ever more urgent."

As for the supreme importance he attached to social justice with due regard for the laws of the economy—he had that tough capacity to face up to reality—this will remain the law of our society, the society at least that the majority of French people wanted and still want to build.

Over the last few years his political role seemed to fade. He belonged to history, people seemed to think. Generation after generation with mixed loyalties claimed his legacy. And yet his influence continued to be alive, ever-present, enormous, as we see today, an enduring witness to the democratic conscience.

I will take only the example of his recent appeal for a return to peace in the Middle East. He had given the matter a lot of thought over the years and was saddened that the fratricidal war continued. He who was so discreet offered his advice. He wanted peace between these peoples whom he loved. And as a French Jew himself he sensed more than others, better than others, the necessity of history. He had suffered on his own account and been subject to many indignities. He had an awareness of what he was, a Frenchman who was always in the forefront of battles for France and who was loyal, loyal in everything, to that which had made him.

> Life uses men up and casts them off and seems to reserve a privileged fate to but a few.
>
> For those few, old age is not the stage leading to oblivion . . . but rather a transition to their place in history.
>
> Death itself . . . respects those existences whose images grow sharper in the form which the future will remember.
>
> Their example will serve as a model or in any case a precedent because their behavior shaped customs and even institutions; because it will continue to influence public opinion in favor of the causes they served; and because others will carry on the same struggle without ceasing to rely on them.

These are the words of Pierre Mendès France, and he applied them to Zola, Jules Ferry, Jaurès, Blum, Churchill, and De Gaulle. Who would not have liked to write them for Mendès France himself?

Ladies and gentlemen, his message cannot be contained in a few simplified traits.

This austere, determined man was above all a kindhearted man.

People for him were diverse, and their differences had to be taken into account. But all had the same need, that is, to seek their emancipation, and to become or to remain free. How are they to be inspired, how are they to be equipped to become the creators they may be? How is each one's talent to be recognized? To be sure, Pierre Mendès France, like Lincoln and Jaurès, died without completing his task. Unless the task was precisely that! "All is creation," Jaurès said, "all is man's creation, even bread, even wine."

I am searching for the final words to express my feelings at this very moment. Before you and before France I am trying to define what Pierre Mendès France was and I can find no other definition than this:

Pierre Mendès France awakened our consciences.

To his wife I say, "He was your tenderness and your life." To his children, "He was your counselor and closest friend." To his followers, to all his followers I say, "He was your companion and guide. I am one of you."

To all the people of France I say. "He was a part of our honor, he was a part of our history. Time will remember him."

NOTES

PROLOGUE

1. Pierre Mendès France wrote his name without a hyphen. We have done the same.

2. The principal source for this report of the session of June 17–18, 1954, is the *Journal officiel,* June 18, 1954.

3. In *Le Figaro.*

4. See below, p. 238.

5. The European Defense Community involved the "integrated" rearmament of Germany.

6. And even though they were for pursuit of the war in Indochina.

7. Reliable witnesses report that the remark was: "He's only a little timid Jew." Alexander Werth, *La France depuis la guerre* (Paris: Gallimard, 1957, p. 528.

8. *"Shit in silk stockings."*

9. The motion was proposed by Yvon Delbos, former minister of foreign affairs in the Popular Front government.

10. The general did not answer the message directly. But four days later, on June 22, he stated: "Whatever the intentions of its members, the current regime can produce only illusions and inconsequential impulses. I ask the French people to believe that I am not involved, either directly or through intermediaries, in any of these schemes. National recovery is possible. It will begin when an end has been put to the headless, soulless system without grandeur that was rebuilt against my will after our victory in war and which, since then, has dissipated the opportunties of France and the men who might have served her."

Unattributed quotations throughout this book are from conversations with the author, not specifically identified by date.

THE SCHOOL OF THE REPUBLIC

1. ROOTS

1. Where it is written without an accent on the "e."
2. Letter to the author from Professor Saraiva of Lisbon.
3. In my youth in Bordeaux, I heard people say: "*They* didn't kill Christ!"
4. In the context, this means Portuguese Jews.
5. Robert Weill, *Les Marchands portugais "nouveaux chrètiens" juifs de Bordeaux* (Bordeaux: Association Abraham Furtado, 1979), p. 15.
6. Christian converts who had secretly remained attached to the Jewish religion.
7. This was the torture of the *strappado.*
8. Cardozo de Bethancourt, *Revue des études juives,* vol. 25.
9. Theophile Malvezin, *Histoire des juifs à Bordeaux* (Bordeaux: Lefebvre, 1785), p. 163.
10. On this subject, see an article by M. Pluchon in *Etudes haïtiennes,* no. 1.
11. Of which Cahn is a variant.

2. FIRST IN HIS CLASS

1. Who had been rehabilitated and restored to his rank in 1906.
2. And Jean Zay, whose mother was Christian, was an agnostic Protestant.
3. Where André Malraux had been enrolled six years earlier.
4. Was he really fourth? Mendès France told the story that when the chief examiner brought in the examinations, his was on top of the pile, but that an administrative officer pointed out in a low voice that "that character" couldn't be named first in the class. The first two on the list were two officers from the war college. A careful examination of the number 4 on his file reveals that it was written over. The figure 1 can be read underneath.
5. *Le Cadran solaire* (Paris: Laffont, 1980), p. 338.
6. Philippe Chassaing, "L'Enragé des années trente," *Actualité* 2 (April 1970).
7. *Le Cadran solaire,* p. 98.
8. André Coutin, *Huit siècles de violence au quartier Latin* (Paris: Stock, 1969), p. 330.
9. Mendès France became a member of the Paris bar in October 1926.
10. This article has not been located.
11. More precisely, the Bank for International Settlements, whose headquarters is in Basel.

3. A TWENTY-FIVE-YEAR-OLD DEPUTY

1. In the very interesting thesis he defended in 1965, on radicalism in the department of Eure, Gilles Rossignol indicates that Pierre Mendès France made "his political debut" in the region as early as July 1927, when he spoke on "secular education." Mendès France did not remember this episode.

2. Maurice Viollette, leader of the Republican-Socialists, very close to the Radicals.

3. He had joined more than two years earlier.

4. *Le Nouvelliste de l'Eure,* April 17, 1932.

5. The absence of any note in the local press, which loved this kind of story, encourages skepticism.

6. The name refers to the group of young officers around Enver Pacha, who undertook a thoroughgoing reform of the Ottoman Empire beginning in 1908.

7. "Le Mouvement Jeune Turc," *Cahiers de la République,* no. 2 (1956).

8. The movement's organ, *La Flèche,* attracted as diverse and lively an audience in the mid-1930s as *L'Express* did in the 1950s.

9. Even though the leader of this last organization, La Rocque, was not antirepublican.

10. Notably in the film by Claude Santelli and Françoise Verny, *Le Mémoire du peuple.*

11. In traditional French political iconography, white is associated with monarchism, red with radicalism, and blue with defense of the republican form of government. Trans.

12. A collection of candidates' campaign statements.

13. In his thesis on *Le Parti radical dans l'Eure,* Gilles Rossignol asserts that the text published by *La Dépêche de Louviers* was indeed called a "campaign statement" by the newspaper.

4. WITH BLUM

1. One might object that Mendès participated in the Charléty meeting on May 27, 1968. In fact, during a period when illegality reigned, this meeting was authorized by the government, in an enclosed space, where no violence was either committed or advocated. (The author was present at the meeting.)

2. In letters to *L'Express* and *Le Monde* in 1954, Sauvy asserted that the Popular Front had been a national catastrophe. It is true that in 1936 he had been an adviser to Paul Reynaud, an active opponent of Blum.

3. The contemporary phrase was "pump priming."

4. *The General Theory* appeared in 1936. It was translated into French by Jean de Largentaye only ten years later. Boris, and then Mendès, read it in English in early 1937.

5. Alfred Sauvy, *Histoire économique de la France entre les deux guerres,* vol. 3 (Paris: Fayard, 1965), p. 274.

6. *Journal des débats,* March 17, 1938.

7. Who were responsible for aborting the plan.

8. *Histoire économique de la France entre les deux guerres,* pp. 274–277. (August 4, 1789, was the date when the nobility surrendered a number of its privileges. Trans.)

THE WIND OF FREEDOM

5. THE INSULT AND THE PITY

1. Paris: Fayard, 1977.

2. Another useful source, very thorough on this subject, is Jacques Nantet, *Pierre Mendès France* (Paris: Centurion, 1967).

3. *Ibid.,* p. 40.

4. We mention these details because they formed the background to Mendès France's trial in 1941, in which one of the staff officers was a witness.

5. *Liberté, liberté chérie,* pp. 20–21.

6. *Ibid.,* p. 46.

7. *Pierre Mendès France,* p. 49.

8. *Liberté, liberté chérie,* p. 61.

9. Brother of Emmanuel, who was later De Gaulle's minister of the interior and then a progressive deputy, and of Henri, a monarchist militant who was involved in the "execution" of Darlan in Algiers.

10. *Liberté, liberté chérie,* p. 61.

11. *Ibid.,* p. 68.

12. *Ibid.,* p. 70.

13. *Ibid.,* p. 82.

14. *Ibid.,* p. 84.

15. *Ibid.,* p. 87.

16. *Ibid.,* p. 171.

17. *Pierre Mendès France,* p. 73.

18. In the same circumstances, but in good health, it took the author five days, from June 12 to 16, 1940, to make the same trip. I have verified that this was the average time.

19. From Strasbourg.

20. *Liberté, liberté chérie,* p. 197.

21. *Ibid.,* p. 205.

22. Later deported with all of his immediate family, almost none of whom returned.

23. The excellent film by Ophuls, Harris, and Sédouy, *Le Chagrin et la pitié* (The Sorrow and the Pity) has a charming version of this story.

24. *Pierre Mendès France,* p. 87.

25. The letter was obviously left behind to confuse the pursuers.

26. *Liberté, liberté cherie,* pp. 254–255.

27. Mendès France wrote this sentence in 1942, to thumb his nose at the Vichy authorities. In fact, he was not able to contact his wife until February 1942, through the intermediary of the United States Consulate in Greece.

28. Minister of war.

29. Molotov's predecessor as minister of foreign affairs until 1939.

30. *Liberté, liberté chérie,* pp. 400–409.

31. According to Paul Dreyfus, *Histoires extraordinaires de la Résistance* (Paris: Fayard, 1977).

32. Jewish Socialist Party.

6. I GO TO WAR

1. Georges Boris, *Servir la République* (Paris: Julliard, 1963), p. 295.
2. *Ibid.,* preface, p. 14.
3. Comité Français de Libération Nationale, first form of what became the provisional government of Algiers.
4. Pierre Mendès France, *Choisir* (Paris: Stock, 1974), p. 33.
5. A group of three stations supplying power to Paris, its suburbs, and part of Bordeaux.
6. Mendès France's crew.
7. "A reaction," observed Mendès France, "that does not express anti-Semitism, which was foreign to De Gaulle, but the problem that would be posed by my joining a cabinet containing René Mayer, whose presence was criticized by the French of North Africa, who *were* anti-Semitic."
8. He became ambassador to Rome and French representative on the Allied Commission for Italy.
9. The Vichy government, which continued to operate for six months longer.
10. Referring to the United States.
11. England.
12. This resignation was not known, unlike the one that came a year later.
13. The commissioner for social affairs.
14. Viénot was ambassador of the Provisional Government in London.

7. MINISTER OF RIGOR

1. Laval's finance minister.
2. Darlan's finance minister.
3. François Bloch-Lainé, *Profession: fonctionnaire* (Paris: Seuil, 1976), p. 57.
4. From September 1944 to April 1945.
5. At the last moment, there was not enough room in the car for François Bloch-Lainé.
6. Conversation with the author, May 6, 1980.
7. Georgette Elgey, *La République des illusions* (Paris: Fayard, 1965), p. 32.
8. *Ibid.,* p. 33.
9. Vol. 1 (Paris: Armand Colin, 1970), pp. 20–21.
10. Edouard Depreux, *Souvenirs d'un militant* (Paris: Fayard, 1972), pp. 207–209.
11. Conversation with the author on May 6, 1980.
12. *Profession: fonctionnaire,* p. 72.
13. *Ibid.,* p. 73.
14. Another supporter of the principle of control, Jean-Marcel Jeanneny, points out for his part that the great obstacle to its application was the lack of means of communication and transportation.
15. Vol. 3, pp. 118–119.

16. Jean-Raymond Tournoux, *La Tragédie du général* (Paris: Plon, 1967), p. 180.

17. Vol. 3, pp. 426–436.

18. *Ibid.,* p. 122.

19. Cousins of the Mendès France family whose son had been deported. They hoped for his return. He did not come back, nor did his wife, his sister, or his brother-in-law.

20. That is, "no" to the replacement of the 1875 Constitution with a new one, and "no" to the proposed constitution. The Communists voted "yes-no"; the general, the MRP, and the Socialists, "yes-yes."

8. CASSANDRA AND INDOCHINA

1. Roy Jenkins, *Nine Men of Power* (New York: British Book Center, 1970), p. 25.

2. The expression was invented practically simultaneously in 1955 by Alfred Sauvy and Georges Balandier.

3. Alain Gourdon, *Mendès France ou le Rêve français* (Paris: Ramsay, 1977), p. 46.

4. Edouard Depreux, *Souvenirs d'un militant* (Paris: Fayard, 1972), p. 219.

5. Created in 1952.

6. Leclerc died in 1947.

7. Conversation with the author, May 6, 1980.

8. *Mon septennat* (Paris: Gallimard, 1970), p. 391.

9. *Mendès France ou le Rêve français,* p. 54.

10. *Mon septennat,* p. 403.

11. But he was never, as has been claimed, "the lawyer for the Néo-Destour."

12. All the more because its neighbor to the east, rearmed by Moscow, had given the example.

13. Paris: PUF, 1953.

9. IN THE ANTECHAMBER

1. Who was not yet using the name Viansson-Ponté.

2. Mendès France voted for this leader of the right who called for a reform of the Constitution giving the head of government the right to dissolve Parliament.

3. *Mon septennat,* pp. 536–540.

4. In *Mendès ou Pinay,* Alfred Fabre-Luce denounced the role played at the time by the candidate's "little Jewish brain trust."

5. *Souvenirs d'un militant,* p. 405.

6. *Europe-Magazine* (August 1953).

7. *Mon septennat,* pp. 545–546.

8. A word that must be used, although Mendès France execrated it.

9. Hubert Beuve-Méry.

10. In their forefront, several historians place, in addition to General Salan, General Blanc, chief of staff of the army. But in a conversation with the author in

May 1980, René Pleven asserted: "Not at all! General Blanc was saying: 'Dien Bien Phu is Verdun!'"

11. The text of a "secret report" by General Salan, which was in fact the summary of a conversation between this very pessimistic officer and Pierre Viansson-Ponté.

12. Robert Buron, *Carnets politiques: Les Dernières Années de la IVe République* (Paris: Plon, 1968), p. 108.

THE FIRE OF ACTION

10. PMF

1. In his history of the Fourth Republic, Jacques Fauvet writes that René Coty believed so little in the success of Mendès France that he had already made overtures to Edgar Faure.

2. But neither Georges Bidault nor the military leaders (who were perhaps unaware of them) informed Mendès of the nuclear aspects of the negotiations with Washington about "Operation Vulture," at a time when dispatches used "Easter eggs" to refer to atomic bombs and when Dulles proposed their use to Maurice Schumann, in a conversation on a staircase of the Quai d'Orsay.

3. In the vocabulary of the time, the Communists.

4. Still known as the Council of the Republic.

5. In February, he succeeded Mendès as premier.

11. THE GENEVA RICE PADDY

1. In 1979, a very interesting study on the role of China during the Indochinese negotiations was presented as a thesis at the Sorbonne by the excellent Sinologist François Joyaux: *La Chine et le règlement du premier conflit d'Indochine,* (Geneva), 1954. Using the archives of the Foreign Ministry and his knowledge of Chinese history, Joyaux demonstrates in particular that Chou En-lai played a decisive role in the negotiations by forcing important concessions on the Vietnamese Communists. It seems, in fact, that, beginning with his meeting with Ho Chi Minh in June 1954, the head of Chinese diplomacy had made it clear to the Vietnamese leaders that they would lose all or part of their aid from the Socialist camp if they did not make enough concessions to facilitate the agreement.

It is true that Joyaux, quoting a Soviet diplomat, also reveals that the objective of the Soviet Union at Geneva was not to unify Vietnam, even under the authority of Ho Chi Minh, because such a solution would have contributed to "placing Vietnam directly under Chinese domination." Aiming chiefly to illuminate Chinese ideas and practices toward Vietnam, considered by Peking as a satellite for more than a milennium a tributary of the empire, Joyaux comes to the observation that the two great Communist powers in fact agreed in their common desire to use Hanoi as a pawn in their already rivalrous strategies—both so obsessed by the concern to "contain" the regional development of Vietnam that they encouraged the installation of the United States in the southern part of the country.

According to Joyaux, the spokesmen of Hanoi saw this as a demonstration of Chinese Machiavellianism and hegemonism. But they could just as well, if they wished to, recognize it as proof of Soviet imperialism; we shall see later how Molotov behaved toward Pham Van Dong during the final hours of negotiations.

12. SIX DAYS THAT REASSURED THE WORLD

1. Quoted by Pierre Rouanet, *Mendès France au pouvoir* (Paris: Laffont, 1965), pp. 143–144.
2. Later, Bidault declared on several occasions: "He stole my peace!" maintaining that he had never stopped searching for an agreement since the Berlin conference. But he seems never to have understood that he had to pay the price for it.
3. Was this decision, a hope, or a commitment? The lack of precision in the text opened the way for interpretations that were in part responsible for the next conflict.
4. Immediately after the conference, a Foreign Office expert, drawing up an assessment, wrote on this point: "A separation at the thirteenth parallel hewed closer to *reality* than the choice of the seventeenth that we obtained."
5. It is well known that in 1956 the Saigon government, supported by Washington, refused to carry out the election, with the Socialist camp, incidentally, not reacting very vigorously. Two years after such difficult negotiations, this significant aspect of the agreements appeared to have been forgotten by everyone, or almost. And three years later, war resumed.
6. Made up of India, Poland, and Canada.
7. Jean Sainteny, *Face à Ho Chi Minh* (Paris: Seghers, 1970), p. 128.

13. BUILDING CARTHAGE

1. As Waldeck-Rochet reminded him in the Chamber on June 18, 1954.
2. Its most nefarious crime was the assassination, in December 1952, of the union leader Ferhat Hached.
3. Roger Stéphane, *La Tunisie de Bourguiba* (Paris: Plon, 1958), pp. 18–20.
4. Conversation of Roger Stéphane with the author, January 1981.
5. *Le Monde,* July 17, 1954.
6. *Mendès France au pouvoir,* p. 202.
7. Carried off without warning from his palace ten months earlier and deported to Madagascar.
8. (Paris: Stock, 1974), p. 69.
9. The Tunisian debate of August 10.

14. THE "MENDÈS SYSTEM"

1. Françoise Roth and Serge Siritzky, *Le Roman de "L'Express"* (Paris: Atelier Jullian, 1980), p. 49.

15. THE EUROPEAN DEFIANCE COMMUNITY

1. Conversation with the author, November 18, 1980.
2. Conversation with the author, May 30, 1980.
3. Conversation with the author, October 25, 1980.
4. Conversation with the author, September 15, 1980.
5. General secretary of the Foreign Ministry. Trans.
6. Paul-Henri Spaak, *Combats inachevés,* vol. 1 (Paris: Fayard, 1969), pp. 277–279.
7. Koenig, Chaban-Delmas, and Lemaire. Three other Gaullist members of the cabinet, Fouchet, Ulver, and Catroux, held firm.
8. Robert Buron, *Carnets politiques* (Paris: Plon, 1968), pp. 129–130.
9. According to Jacques Fauvet, "The slip was less involuntary than it appeared to many." He had already made and corrected it before the Foreign Affairs Committee.
10. *Combats inachevés,* p. 294. The version of this note published by Rouanet is still more brutal.
11. *Mendès France au pouvoir,* p. 270.
12. *Combats inachevés,* p. 291.
13. In a letter to *Le Figaro,* which had published excerpts from Spaak's memoirs critical of him, Mendès France wrote on February 17, 1959: "The delegation present in Brussels rejected any genuine revision, any adaptation of their previous decisions in order to move closer to us."
14. Conversation with the author of November 1980. For his part, Maurice Duverger sees nothing "unconstitutional" in the neutrality of a government on the question of ratifying a treaty.
15. *La IVe République* (Paris: Fayard, 1965), p. 277.
16. *Combats inachevés,* p. 303. A little further on, Spaak characterizes the step as "premature."

16. THE SUBCONTRACTING OF THE ECONOMY

1. The expression is from François Bloch-Lainé.
2. *Cahiers de formation ouvrière* (December 1954).

17. A ROPE AND SOME KNIVES

1. François Fourquet, *Les Comptes de la puissance* (Paris: Editions Recherches, 1980), p. 216.
2. René Mayer had fallen eighteen months earlier by an absolute majority, followed by Joseph Laniel. The Constitution provided that if the same thing happened within this time period—which expired on November 22, 1954—to a third government, that government could dissolve the Assembly and call new elections.
3. Jean-Raymond Tournoux, *La Tragédie du général* (Paris: Plon, 1967), pp. 178–179.
4. *Mendès France au pouvoir,* p. 350.
5. *Mendès France ou le Rêve français,* p. 179.

6. "Men who have courageously voted for our government are not a part of it."

7. *Souvenirs d'un militant,* pp. 423–424.

8. *Le Monde,* January 18, 1955.

9. *La IVe République* (Paris: Calmann-Lévy, 1968), p. 183.

10. *Mendès France au pouvoir,* p. 280.

11. This was, as we have seen, his father's first name. Strange camouflage. Similarly, Blum, according to his enemies, had chosen that name to conceal his origins.

12. July 3, 1954.

13. Also arrested were Roger Stéphane and Gilles Martinet for having "divulged" confidential information. Stéphane spent several weeks in prison.

14. It was reported that Louis-Gabriel Robinet was all the angrier because Baranès was also *Le Figaro*'s informant.

18. ALGERIA IS FRANCE

1. Franz-Olivier Giesbert, *Mitterrand ou la Tentation de l'histoire* (Paris: Seuil, 1977), p. 120.

2. *Mendès France au pouvoir,* p. 376.

3. But by November 3, the PCF organ began to denounce cases of torture.

4. *Blocs-Notes,* vol. 1 (Paris: Flammarion, 1958), p. 133.

5. A simplification to say the least. New elites would have been found had they been looked for.

6. Which remained troubled by attacks by European counterterrorists.

7. *Mendès France au pouvior,* pp. 448–449.

8. And, according to their informants, soon to be overthrown.

9. The Franco–Tunisian agrements were signed by the Edgar Faure government in June 1955.

19. AMERICA WITHOUT DOLLARS AND EUROPE WITHOUT JOY

1. Which prohibited the installation of new foreign military personnel in South Vietnam.

2. Like James Richards, future chairman of the Foreign Affairs Committee.

20. "TONIGHT OR NEVER!"

1. 314 votes. In that event, the government would not automatically be overthrown and would be able to explain itself before resigning.

2. *Carnets politiques,* p. 146.

3. *De Léon Blum à de Gaulle* (Paris: Fayard, 1971).

THE PASSION TO BE RIGHT

21. RADICALLY YOURS, OR THE VERY YOUNG TURKS

1. Many Mendésist Radicals were troubled by what seemed to them to be a strategy of fellow traveling with the PCF in the Jacobin faction.

2. *Mendès France ou le Rêve français*, p. 186.

3. *The French Radical Party; from Herriot to Mendès France* (Toronto: Oxford University Press, 1961), p. 201.

22. UNDER THE PHRYGIAN CAP

1. *Le Roman de "L'Express,"* p. 96.

2. *Mendès France ou le Rêve français*, p. 190.

3. Conversation with the author, December 20, 1980.

4. Conversation of the author with Gaston Defferre, December 20, 1980.

5. *Souvenirs d'un militant*, p. 440.

6. When I asked him a few years later what would have happened if he had been able to set foot in Algiers, the general answered with a broad smile: "Those people would have killed me, my friend."

7. *Carnets politiques*, p. 186.

8. *L'Information radicale* (June 1956).

9. October 27, 1957.

10. Businessman, head of the Lesieur food oil company, who had been involved with the Giraud faction in the Algiers plot of 1943 and had taken a position in favor of the emancipation of Morocco, where he was living.

23. NO TO DE GAULLE

1. *Le Temps qui reste* (Paris: Stock, 1973), p. 92.

2. Where the Algiers activists had made inroads.

3. Pierre Mendès France, *La Politique et la vérité* (Paris: Julliard, 1958), p. 306.

4. Pierre Viansson-Ponté, *Histoire de la République gaullienne*, vol. 1 (Paris: Fayard, 1970), p. 97.

24. FOR A CONCRETE SOCIALISM

1. *Souvenirs d'un militant,* p. 523.

2. *Mendès France ou le Rêve français*, p. 209.

3. Then premier.

4. *La République moderne* (Paris: Gallimard, 1962), p. 235.

25. THE YOUNGEST ELECTORATE IN FRANCE

1. If a successful candidate to the Assembly was named to a government position, his substitute *(suppléant)* would assume his seat. Trans.

26. CHARLÉTY: A REFORMIST IN THE REVOLUTION

1. The friends of Daniel Cohn-Bendit.
2. Pompidou was in Kabul.
3. *Histoire de la République gaullienne,* vol. 2, p. 464.
4. (Paris: Albin Michel, 1976), pp. 116–117.
5. *Mendès France ou le Rêve français,* p. 242.
6. Conversations with Charles Gombault, Maurice Schumann, and Georges Kiejman.
7. That morning, May 27, when he presented the agreements to the Renault workers, CGT leader Georges Séguy had been booed. Mendès France later thought that if Pompidou had had a free hand with the unions, the Charléty demonstrators would not have been treated as well as they were.
8. Conversation with Charles Hernu, September 1980.
9. *L'Ere des ruptures* (Paris: Grasset, 1979), p. 66.
10. Adrien Dansette, *Mai 68* (Paris: Plon, 1971), p. 313. In his *Journal d'un fédéré,* Claude Estier, reporting this conversation, asserts that Mitterrand criticized Mendès for setting himself up as an antagonist of the PCF, and that it was Mitterrand who mentioned Jacques Monod.
11. Gaston Monnerville, *Vingt-deux ans de présidence* (Paris: Plon, 1980), p. 357.

27. THE SHOCKING BEHAVIOR OF GRENOBLE

1. *Pour préparer l'avenir* (Paris: Denoel, 1968), p. 115.
2. Due to the death of his wife and his own illness.
3. Except for Mitterrand, easily reelected in Nièvre.
4. *Le Figaro littéraire* (April 1969).
5. Unpublished letter of July 4, 1969.

28. THE STONES OF SISYPHUS

1. Letter to Claude Nicolet, January 16, 1970.
2. Conversation with the author, December 1980.
3. Conversation with the author, January 1981.
4. The interview, conducted in November, was not published until December 9.
5. From September to December 1976.
6. November 1977.

INDEX

Abbas, Ferhat, 304, 305, 365
Acheson, Dean, 180
Adenauer, Konrad, 274, 275, 279, 324, 330
Alain (Émile Chartier), 76
Alamichel, 117, 118
Alphand, Hervé, 157
Altschuler, Georges, 214
Alverguat, 389
Amrouche, Jean, 376
Antier, Paul, 11
Arafat, Yasser, 431
Ardant, Gabriel, 49, 151, 157, 158, 191, 259, 262, 338, 438, 441
Argenlieu, Thierry d', 181
Aron, Raymond, 206, 217
Astier de La Vigerie, Emmanuel d', 12, 15, 182
Astier de La Vigerie, François d', 108–11, 116, 119, 123
Astier de La Vigerie, Jean, 145
Audry, Colette, 393, 456
Auriol, Vincent, 54, 83–87, 89, 91, 160–61, 179, 185, 186, 194–95, 197, 199, 211, 453

Backmann, René, 420
Bacon, Paul, 214, 215
Bailly, 119, 120
Bao Dai, 218, 219, 222, 223, 240

Baranès, André, 299, 300–301, 302
Bardoux, Jacques, 11, 324
Barjonet, André, 411
Barrillon, Raymond, 196, 412
Barthélemy, Joseph, 39–40, 41
Bastid, Paul, 107
Bayet, Albert, 66, 90
Baylot, Jean, 297, 298
Bedell-Smith, Walter, 219, 220, 227, 233, 234, 236
Begin, Menahem, 433, 434, 435
Ben Amar, Tahar, 255
Benbahmed, Mostefa, 333
Ben Bella, Ahmed, 382
Ben Gourion, David, 429
Ben Khedda, 363–364
Ben Youssef, Salah, 309, 310
Bergasse, Henri, 251
Bergeret, 116, 118, 119, 122
Bergery, Gaston, 63, 67, 73, 346
Berthelot, François ("Robert"), 134
Berthelot, Philippe, 51–52
Berthoin, Jean, 15
Bertrand, William, 66
Bettencourt, André, 252
Beuve-Méry, Hubert, 16, 191
Beyen, Johan-Willem, 273–74, 275
Bichet, Robert, 335

Bidault, Georges, 7, 12, 96, 156, 178, 182, 199–201, 203–8, 211, 213, 216–18, 239, 263, 266, 270, 277, 283, 296–97
Billières, René, 408
Billoux, François, 7–8, 9
Blanc, 212, 213
Bloch-Lainé, François, 157, 162, 444
Blum, Léon, 10, 47, 62, 72, 73, 74, 80–98, 113, 122–23, 137, 178–80, 196, 256, 283 339, 353, 387, 388, 429, 446–51, 454–56, 461, 462, 467
Blumel, André, 135
Bollaert, Emile, 187
Bonnet, Georges, 50, 53, 55, 56, 63, 66, 69, 85, 98
Bonnet, Henri, 205–6, 316
Borgeaud, Henri, 308, 329
Boris, Georges, 15, 37, 49, 83, 88–91, 92, 94, 96, 137, 139–140, 146, 150–51, 157, 177, 180, 195, 214, 215, 246, 259, 261, 262, 268, 286, 302, 313, 330, 376, 377, 387–88, 392–93, 436, 453
Botherel, Jean, 428
Bourdet, Claude, 244, 307, 308, 331, 365, 389
Bourgès-Maunoury, Maurice, 270, 272, 279, 350, 372
Bourguiba, Habib, 188, 244, 245, 246, 248–249, 255, 308, 309, 310, 448
Bouscat, 111
Bouxom, Fernand, 336
Boyer de La Tour du Moulin, 250, 252, 255
Brebisson, Colonel de, 205, 207
Briand, Aristide, 48, 60
Briquet, Doctor, 59, 60, 74, 77
Broglie, Jean de, 392
Brossolette, Pierre, 139
Bruce, David, 268, 274
Burindes Roziers, Etienne, 389
Buron, Robert, 11, 15, 206, 214, 215, 272, 279, 287, 296, 297, 320, 322, 332, 336, 341
Buu Loc, Prince, 217–18, 219, 240

Cahn, Isidore, 33–34
Caillaux, Joseph, 4, 54, 66, 85, 86, 92, 95, 96, 179, 340, 346, 347, 348, 436
Caillavet, Henri, 317
Cain, Julien, 107
Campinchi, César, 55, 66, 67, 71, 107, 108
Camus, Albert, 311, 355, 364, 445
Casanova, Laurent, 451
Catroux, Diomède, 317
Catroux, Georges, General, 147–48, 179, 180, 305, 361–63
Cayrol, Roland, 396
CED (Communauté Européne de Défense),

8, 188–90, 195, 198, 214, 224, 229, 257, 260, 263, 265–72, 275–79, 291–92, 294, 296, 321, 324, 357
CFDT (Confédération Français Démo-cratique du Travail), 410, 411, 418
CFTC (Confédération Français des Travail-leurs Chrétiens), 264
CGT (Confédération Générale du Travail), 83, 94, 168, 264, 290, 409, 411, 421, 438
Chaban-Delmas, Jacques, 12, 15, 214, 265, 279, 291, 353, 356
Chautemps, Camille, 66, 86, 106, 173
Chauvel, Jean, 213, 216, 220, 221, 222, 224–26, 229, 232
Chauvin, 59, 74, 77, 97
Chéron, 68, 83
Chevallier, Jacques, 317, 362
Cheysson, Claude, 205, 217, 229, 313, 458, 459
Chou En-lai, 204, 208, 217, 220, 221, 224, 228–30, 234, 235, 246, 314, 448
Churchill, Winston, 106, 108, 141, 142, 203, 225, 276, 280, 316, 324, 325, 453, 467
Cicurel, Lily. See Mendès France, Lily
Claudel, Paul, 449
Claudius-Petit, Eugène, 215, 279
Clemenceau, Georges, 10, 93, 142, 325, 346, 347, 348
CNPF (Confédèration Nationale du Pa-tronat Français), 264
Cogny, General, 204
Cohen-Hadina, André, 246
Collins, Lawton, 314, 315
Colonna, Antoine, 251
Combes, Emile, 66, 75
Comert, Pierre, 137, 139
Cot, Pierre, 15, 37, 63, 67, 68, 71, 80, 86, 89, 97, 130, 140, 147, 178, 179, 182, 198, 324, 346
Coty, René, 15, 199, 211–12, 214, 263, 277, 298, 337, 358–62, 364, 378
Courcel, Geoffroy de, 136
Courtade, Pierre, 451
Courtin, René, 158
Cripps, Stafford, 178
CRS (Compagnies Républicaines de Séc-urité), 305, 403
Cusin, Gaston, 86, 89, 94

Daladier, Édouard, 55, 66, 67, 69, 74, 80, 96, 97, 98, 102, 107, 108, 122–23, 173, 293, 294, 346, 347
Daniel, Jean, 311, 355, 375, 414
Darlan, François, 106, 109, 116, 119, 128, 140
Daudet, Léon, 38, 43

David, Jean-Paul, 372
David, Marcel, 295
Déat, Marcel, 80, 94
Debré, Michel, 174, 375, 395
Defferre, Gaston, 146, 214, 295, 353, 357, 358, 360–61, 363, 395, 423, 424, 425
Degache, Colonel, 117, 120, 121, 122, 172
Delbos, Yvon, 66, 68, 80, 107, 108
Delors, Jacques, 458
Delouvrier, Paul, 172
Delteil, 207, 223, 229, 237, 239
Depreux, Édouard, 160, 177, 295, 359, 361, 387–88
Descamps, Eugène, 413
Des Inards, 84
Dides, Jean, 297, 298, 299, 300–301
Diem, Ngô Dinh, 219, 234, 240, 241, 319
Diethelm, André, 148, 156, 194
Donne, Raymond, 239
Dorgères, Henri, 77
Douket, 125, 126
Dreyfus-Schmidt, 178
Dronne, Raymond, 302
Dubedout, Hubert, 397, 418
Duchêne, Louis, 134
Duclos, Jacques, 7, 10, 11, 87, 198, 298, 413, 424
Duhamel, Jacques, 371
Dulles, John Foster, 203, 204, 206, 226–28, 234, 236, 240, 242, 271, 274–75, 279, 297, 314–16, 319, 325, 453, 454
Du Moulin de La Barthète, 115
Duplessis, Maurice, 313
Duval, Alexandre, 59, 60, 62, 69, 77
Duverger, Maurice, 377, 398

Eden, Anthony, 208, 219–20, 232, 233–36, 242, 269–70, 276, 279, 280, 281, 301, 323, 429
Eisenhower, Dwight D., 141, 203, 225, 240, 314, 316, 322, 324
Eliav, (Lyova), 431–32, 433
Ely, 212, 213, 222, 235, 238, 241, 242, 246, 314, 315
Estienne, Marie-Hélène, 420

Fabiani, Jean, 323
Fabre-Luce, Alfred, 412
Faure, Edgar, 55, 116, 117, 188, 189, 190, 211, 215, 216, 233–34, 258, 264, 272, 284–88, 298, 315, 317, 332, 338, 348, 349, 350, 352, 354, 356, 358, 359, 361, 371
Faure, Paul, 47
Fauvet, Jacques, 197, 214, 277, 290, 297, 334
Faÿ, General, 118–19, 181, 212

FEN (Fédération de l'Education Nationale), 411
Ferniot, Jean, 214
Ferry, Jules, 244, 340, 429, 447, 467
FGDS (Fédération de la Gauche Démocrate et Socialiste), 405, 408, 414, 424
Filion, Gerard, 313
Fleurieu, Marie-Claire de, see Mendès France, Marie-Claire
FLN (Front de Libération Nationale), 355, 381, 382, 390, 395
Folin, Jacques de, 229
Fonlupt-Espéraber, Jacques, 114, 115, 116, 119–22, 125, 296
Fossaert, Robert, 443, 450
Fouchet, Christian, 246, 249, 250, 252, 253, 254, 291, 298, 300, 309–310, 329, 404, 409–10
Fouques-Duparc, Henri, 111
Frachon, Benoît, 290
França, Luis de, 19, 20, 23–26
Francis, Ahmed, 304
Frédéric-Dupont, 207, 208, 213

Gaillard, Félix, 350, 376, 382
Gambetta, Jules, 340, 462
Gamelin, General, 93
Gary, Romain, 143, 338
Gaulle, Charles de, 8, 12, 15, 93, 97, 104, 106, 108, 109, 117, 130, 132, 136–39, 141, 143, 144, 146–148, 152–53, 156, 158, 160, 161, 165–69, 172, 173, 177–79, 185, 189, 196, 215, 242, 244, 246, 265, 283, 288, 291–93, 317, 322, 324, 326, 339, 375–85, 389–92, 412–414, 416, 418, 422–26, 429, 443, 447–50, 467
Gazier, Albert, 295
Geismar, Alain, 411
Georges-Étienne, René, 45, 47, 48, 55
Georges-Picot, Léone, 11, 302, 313, 354
Germain-Martin, 54, 71
Giard, Jean, 400
Gide, Charles, 49
Giesbert, Franz-Olivier, 428
Giraud, Alphonse, 147
Giroud, Françoise, 187, 193, 259, 260, 339, 367, 368, 371, 376, 454
Giscard d'Estaing, Valéry, 11, 122, 174, 428
Glaymann, Claude, 399
Goetz, Roger, 157
Goguel, François, 456
Goldmann, Nahoum, 431
Gombault, Charles, 45–46, 69, 136, 137, 139, 316, 409
Gombault, Georges, 90, 137
Gouin, Félix, 177, 178
Gourdon, Alain, 187, 349–50, 354, 405

Gregh, Didier, 147, 157
Gregoire, Abbé, 452
Grenier, Fernand, 147
Grimaud, Maurice, 404, 409–410
Gros, Brigitte, 354
Grumbach, Marcelle, 36, 38, 42, 64, 69
Grumbach, Salomon, 90, 107
Grunebaum-Ballin, Paul, 439
Gruson, Claude, 172, 262, 289, 330, 439
Guindey, Guillaume, 157, 158
Gutt, Camille, 151–52, 162

Harrod, Ray, 438
Ha Van Lau, 205, 207, 223
Hernu, Charles, 406, 407, 458
Herriot, Édouard, 37, 42, 44, 47, 50, 61, 63,
    65, 66, 67, 71, 98, 107, 110, 173, 188, 195,
    199, 244, 278, 293, 323, 339, 346, 347,
    348, 353, 356, 372, 429, 453
Heurgon, Marc, 405
Hirsch, Étienne, 317
Hitler, Adolf, 62, 66, 87, 97, 106, 107, 130,
    153, 367
Ho Chi Minh, 5–6, 185, 190, 199, 201, 202,
    204, 218, 224, 228, 242
Hoppenot, Ambassador, 316, 318
Hughes, Emile, 279
Hussein, King, 434

Ibert, Jacques, 107

Jacquier, Marc, 45, 48, 55
Jacquot, General, 181
Jammy-Schmidt, 66, 107
Jaurès, Jean, 4, 37, 64, 387, 388, 393, 429,
    447, 462, 467
Jeanneney, Jean-Marcel, 107, 417
Jeanneney, Jules, 82, 417–19, 440
Jèze, Gaston, 39, 49
Johnson, Alexis, 220
Johnson, Lyndon B., 203
Joxe, Louis, 404
Juin, Alphonse, 5, 238, 249, 250, 251, 252,
    254
Julien, Charles-André, 74, 244

Kahn, Marcel-Francis, 407
Kapeliouk, Ammon, 432
Kayser, Jacques, 63, 66, 67, 68, 98, 346
Kerillis, Henri de, 96, 103
Keynes, John Maynard, 49, 83, 94, 175–76,
    437, 446
Kiejman, Georges, 404, 406, 407–8, 420,
    451
Koenig, Pierre, 12, 252, 265, 270, 272, 298

Labarthe, André, 139

Labéda, Jean, 60, 78, 86, 97
Labi, 411
La Chambre, Guy, 222, 238–39, 242, 315
Lacharrière, René de, 259
Lacoste, Robert, 160, 295, 363–64, 368,
    374, 375, 387
Lefebvre, Henri, 402
Lagrange, Léo, 80–81, 86, 97
LaGuardia, Fiorello, 153
Lamine, bey Sidi, 188, 252, 253
Lamoureaux, 66
Lamour, Philippe, 43, 44
Laniel, Joseph, 199–201, 206, 207, 211, 212,
    214, 217, 244, 245, 266, 299–300
Lapie, Pierre-Olivier, 341
Largentaye, Jean de, 157, 262
Lattre de Tassigny, 185, 186, 188
Laurent, Augustin, 168, 295
Laurent-Eynac, 54, 103, 119
LAURS (Ligue d'Action Universitaire Ré-
    publicaine et Socialiste), 44–48, 64
Laval, Pierre, 60, 61, 63, 82, 83, 107, 109,
    110, 116, 173
Le Bal, 11
Lebrun, Pierre, 87, 96
Lecaneut, Jean, 13
Leclerc, 115, 117, 180, 181, 184, 185, 239
Le Coq de Kerland, 102, 103, 120
Legatte, Paul, 286
Legendre, Jean, 7, 301–302
Léger, Alexis, 141
Legouez, Modeste, 77, 78
Lejeune, Max, 362, 368, 387
Leloup, Nicolas, 57
Lemberg, Jan, 135
LeMire, Henri, 59
Lepercq, Aimé, 156, 158, 159, 165
Leprêtre, 113, 115, 116–19, 122, 129, 141,
    172
Letourneau, Jean, 190
Le Troquer, André, 8, 14, 107
Lindon, Raymond, 68
Lodge, Henry Cabot, 318
Longchambon, Henri, 317
Lourde, 124, 126, 129
Luchaire, Jean, 71
Lucien, 102–6, 116, 119, 120, 132
Ludwig, Emil, 103
Lussy, Charles, 12, 295

MacArthur, Douglas, Jr., 226
Malraux, André, 331, 445
Mandel, Georges, 98, 107, 108, 115
Mandle, Armand, 59, 61, 71
Mandouze, André, 361
Marchais, Georges, 423
Marchandeau, 66

Marin, Louis, 87
Marquet, Adrien, 62, 94, 107
Martinaud-Déplat, Léon, 66, 68, 254, 293–94, 297, 298, 299, 308, 347, 372
Martinet, Gilles, 389
Marty, André, 15, 414
Masmoudi, Mohammed, 247–48, 249, 255, 376
Massignon, Louis, 450
Massu, Jacques, 376, 414
Mauriac, François, 37, 198, 199, 219, 257, 297, 306, 307, 310, 311, 331, 370, 376, 380, 385, 389, 421
Maurice, Gaston, 48, 55
Mauroy, Pierre, 458
Mayer, Daniel, 160, 177, 278, 323, 387, 398
Mayer, René, 147, 159, 190, 191, 194, 255, 263, 270, 277, 279, 306, 308, 329, 330, 332–33, 347, 350, 372
Meir, Golda, 429
Mendès France, Bernard, 70, 171, 425
Mendès France, Cerf-David, 33, 34, 35, 39, 46, 171
Mendès France, David, 29
Mendès France, Isaac, 29–31
Mendès France, Jules-Isaac, 32–33
Mendès France, Lily, 15, 16, 69, 97, 105, 111, 113, 114, 128, 129–30, 171, 379, 400
Mendès France, Marcelle, 38, 64, 69
Mendès France, Mardochée-Jean, 28
Mendès France, Marie-Claire, born Schreiber-Crémieux, 69, 107, 406, 407, 408, 419, 426, 454
Mendès France, Michel, 70, 97, 171
Mendès France, Moïse, 29, 31, 32
Mendès France, Palmyre, 33, 34, 36, 64, 171
Menthon, François de, 261, 296, 330, 335, 336
Michelet, Edmond, 291
Mitterand, François, 15, 198, 214, 215, 245, 258, 297, 298, 300, 301, 302, 304–8, 329, 333, 336, 353, 354, 357, 381, 382, 395, 406–8, 412–15, 423, 428, 458, 459
Moch, Jules, 86, 94, 160, 168, 177, 189, 190, 277, 317
Mollet, Guy, 11, 194, 198, 215, 263, 271, 277, 279, 295, 353, 355–65, 367, 368, 387, 388, 389, 416, 423–25, 429
Molotov, Viatcheslav, 204, 206, 208, 228, 231–37, 271, 318
Monnerville, Gaston, 67, 68, 215–16, 304, 415
Monnet, Jean, 53, 147, 148, 157, 161, 262, 265, 312
Monod, Jacques, 399, 400, 409, 415
Mons, Jean, 299, 301

Montagne, Rémy, 114, 383, 384, 392, 419
Monteil, André, 114, 215, 296
Monteil, Vincent, 330
Montsabert, 12
Morgenthau, Henry, 152, 176
Morice, André, 255, 346, 349, 372
Moro-Giafferi, Vincent de, 71
Moulin, Jean, 299
MRP (Mouvement Républicain Populaire), 4, 7, 11, 12, 178, 198, 199, 214, 215, 219, 268, 290, 296, 297, 311, 320, 331, 369
MTLD (Movement for the Triumph of Democratic Liberties), 306, 308
Murville, Couve de, 326
Myrdal, Gunnar, 176

Naegelen, Marcel-Edmond, 8
Nasser, Gamal Abdel, 364, 367, 430
Navarre, Henri, 199, 212
Ngo Dinh Diem. See Diem, Ngô Dinh
Nicolet, Claude, 440
Nixon, Richard M., 203
Noguès, 108, 109, 110
Nomy, 212
Nora, Léone. See Georges-Picot, Léone
Nora, Simon, 82, 181, 213–14, 259, 287, 302, 330, 354, 448
Nutting, Anthony, 318

OAS (Organization de l'Armée Secrète), 391
Ornano, 115
Ostoya, Paul, 44
Oualid, William, 49

Palewski, Gaston, 324
Palmade, Maurice, 60
Parodi, Alexandre, 222, 268, 275
Paul-Boncour, 64
PCF (Parti Communiste Français), 8, 9, 196–98, 268, 320, 352–53, 381, 409, 421, 423, 424
Pélabon, André, 298, 299, 305–6
Peled, Matityahou, General, 432, 433
Pennès, 110
Perré, 118, 119, 121, 172
Perrin, Francis, 317
Perroux, François, 437
Pérussel, Yves, 252
Pétain, Philippe, 93, 106, 109, 115, 122, 125, 173, 447
Pflimlin, Pierre, 376, 377
Pham Van Dong, 204, 205, 218, 220–23, 228, 229, 234, 235, 239, 240, 242, 448
Philip, André, 160, 168, 177, 178, 179, 273, 376

Pinay, Antoine, 188, 192, 195, 211, 265–66, 277, 278, 412, 423
Pineau, Christian, 190, 364
Pleven, René, 138, 148, 156, 158–70, 177–78, 182–84, 188–90, 200, 203, 263, 278, 288, 299, 300, 353, 438
Poincaré, Raymond, 4, 49, 50–51, 58, 68, 83, 85, 90, 93, 196, 340, 436, 443, 450, 454
Poinso-Chapuis, 7
Pompidou, Georges, 48, 399–400, 404, 409, 410, 417, 425, 428
Postel-Viray, 157
Prebitsch, Raul, 176, 442
PSA (Autonomous Socialist Party), 387, 388
PSU (Unified Socialist Party), 389, 402, 410, 411, 418, 421, 424

Quesnay, 54
Queuille, Henri, 66, 151, 283, 372

Rabin, Itzchak, 433
Rachet, Lucien, 376
Radford, 203
Rancourt, 142, 143, 144
Recanati, Jean, 451
Régnier, 83
Reynaud, Paul, 83, 84, 87, 96, 97, 98, 105, 115, 141, 190, 194, 278, 338, 369, 436
Riquebourg, Jean-François, 157, 158
Robertson, Walter, 220
Robinet, Louis-Gabriel, 301
Rocard, Michel, 404, 405, 424, 443, 458, 459
Rochat, 114, 115–116, 122, 125
Roche, Emile, 66, 85
Roosevelt, Franklin D., 140, 152, 164, 169, 180, 261, 453
Rouanet, Pierre, 292
Rous, Jean, 244
RPF (Rassemblement du Peuple Français), 179, 185, 198, 298
Rucart, Marc, 66
Rueff, Jacques, 91

Sadat, Anwar El, 433, 434, 435
Sainteny, Jean, 180, 185, 241, 242, 315
Saint-Laurent, Louis, 313
Salan, Raoul, 5, 185, 300, 376–77, 381
Salengro, Roger, 81
Sarraut, Albert, 66, 78, 346
Sary, Sam, 236, 237
Sauvageot, Jacques, 405, 411
Sauvy, Alfred, 82, 93, 95
Savary, Alain, 200, 214, 246–47, 248, 295, 369, 387, 423
Schreiber, 135

Schreiber-Crémieux, Marie Claire. *See* Mendès France, Marie-Claire
Schreiber-Crémieux, Suzanne, 69, 107
Schuman, Robert, 189, 190, 265, 270, 273, 277, 278, 296
Schumann, Maurice, 48, 139, 168, 267, 376, 409
Schwartz, Laurent, 389
Senghor, Léopold, 48
Serre, Philippe, 97, 104
Sertawi, Issam, 432, 433
Servan-Schreiber, Émile, 192
Servan-Schreiber, Jean-Jacques, 187, 192, 193, 195, 198, 214, 259, 316, 353, 354, 357, 358, 376
Servan-Schreiber, Robert, 192
Seynes, Philippe de, 267, 269, 313
SFIO (Section Française de l'Internationale Ouvrière), 8, 11, 198, 215, 268, 294–296, 331, 356, 357, 387, 438
Siegfriend, André, 5
Slim, Mongi, 249, 308, 309, 310
Soustelle, Jacques, 7, 48, 214, 324, 329, 376
Soutou, Jean-Marie, 267, 313
Spaak, Paul-Henri, 270–75
Stamm, Jean, 124
Steeg, Théodore, 60, 66, 68
Stéphane, Roger, 182, 246, 247, 249, 453
Sturmel, Marcel, 84

Ta Quang Buu, 207, 223, 237, 239
Tardieu, André, 51, 60, 61, 63, 65, 72, 82, 83, 85
Tarr, Francis de, 350
Teitgen, Pierre-Henri, 267, 277, 282, 296, 330
Temple, Emmanuel, 317
Tessan, François de, 66, 80
Thorez, Maurice, 8, 81, 87, 160, 352, 451
Tillion, Germaine, 330
Tixier, Adrien, 141, 156, 160, 168
Tixier-Vignancour, Jean-Louis, 300, 302–3, 369
Tomlinson, Tom, 268
Touraine, Alain, 402
Toynbee, Philip, 370
Tran Van Do, 233

UDSR (Democratic Union for the Socialist Republic), 198, 215, 353, 357
UFD (Union of Democratic Forces), 382
UGS (Union de la Gauche Socialiste), 389
UNEF (Union Nationale des Etudiants Français), 405, 409–411

Vallon, Louis, 54, 167, 204
Valois, Georges, 52, 114

Vanier, Jean, 399, 417
Verdier, Robert, 387
Verlhac, Jean, 397–98
Viansson-Ponté, Pierre, 193, 260, 300, 354, 404, 406
Viénot, Pierre, 80, 107, 108, 110, 113, 114, 115
Vinson, Fred, 176
Viollette, Maurice, 60
Voizard, Pierre, 245
Vyshinsky, André, 318

Waldeck-Rochet, 13, 14

Waldeck-Rousseau, René, 263
Weil, 397
Werth, Alexander, 67
Weygand, Maxime, 102, 109
White, Harry, 176
Wiedemanin-Goiran, Fernard, 84
Wiltzer, Alfred, 107, 110, 114
Wormser, Olivier, 157
Wybot, Roger, 298, 299, 301

Zay, Jean, 55, 63, 64, 67, 68, 76, 80, 86, 98, 107, 108, 110, 111, 113, 114, 115, 125
Zola, Emile, 38, 429, 467